International Management

Strategy and Culture in the Emerging World

David Ahlstrom
The Chinese University of Hong Kong

Garry D. Bruton
Texas Christian University

SOUTH-WESTERN
CENGAGE Learning™

Australia • Brazil • Canada • Mexico • Singapore • Spain • United Kingdom • United States

SOUTH-WESTERN
CENGAGE Learning™

International Management: Strategy and Culture in the Emerging World
David Ahlstrom, Garry D. Bruton

Vice President of Editorial, Business: Jack W. Calhoun

Vice President/Editor-in-Chief: Melissa S. Acuña

Sr. Acquisitions Editor: Michele Rhoades

Developmental Editor: Elizabeth Lowry

Marketing Manager: Nathan Anderson

Marketing Coordinator: Suellen Rutkay

Sr. Marketing Communications Manager: Jim Overly

Executive Marketing Manager: Brian Joyner

Content Project Manager: Holly Henjum

Media Editor: Rob Ellington

Frontlist Buyer, Manufacturing: Doug Wilke

Permissions Account Manager/Images: Don Schlotman

Permissions Account Manager/Text: Margaret Chamberlain-Gaston

Production Service/Compositor: Integra Software Services

Sr. Art Director: Tippy McIntosh

Cover and Internal Designer: Mike Stratton, Stratton Design

Cover Image:

    Main Image: Adam Pretty, Getty Images

    Secondary Image: Veer, Inc.

Photo Researcher: PrePress PMG

For product information and technology assistance, contact us at
Cengage Learning Customer & Sales Support, 1-800-354-9706

For permission to use material from this text or product,
submit all requests online at **www.cengage.com/permissions**
Further permissions questions can be emailed
to **permissionrequest@cengage.com**

Library of Congress Control Number: 2008943332
Student Edition ISBN 13: 978-0-324-40631-3
Student Edition ISBN 10: 0-324-40631-2

South-Western Cengage Learning
5191 Natorp Boulevard
Mason, OH 45040
USA

Cengage Learning products are represented in Canada by Nelson Education, Ltd.

For your course and learning solutions, visit **www.cengage.com**

Purchase any of our products at your local college store or at our preferred online store **www.ichapters.com**

Printed in the United States of America
2 3 4 5 13 12 11

This book is dedicated to my wife Serene. Quite a number of cases and stories in this textbook have come from our many trips as part of my research and teaching around Asia. But even during our vacations, I have often had to meet entrepreneurs or visit factories to gather information for this textbook. Serene has been very patient with me as I toured factories in China or visited government officials in various East Asian capitals. I treasure the time spent with her traveling and seeking out real-world examples of international management to bring back to our students and readers.

David Ahlstrom

This book is dedicated to my children: John Louis, Stephanie Rose, and Faith Elizabeth Bruton. The greatest joy in traveling and living outside the United States has been the ability to share those experiences with you. Whether it was singing Christmas carols in the dark in Tibet following a blackout or traveling across Turkey in a bus, each and every experience with you has been the best in my life. Hopefully our adventures will only get better in the future.

Garry D. Bruton

Brief Contents

Contents

Preface

WHY INTERNATIONAL MANAGEMENT

For business the world is becoming increasingly global. A firm's competitors may no longer be in a neighboring city but in a distant country. Products such as marble monuments and headstones could previously be produced in the United States in Vermont or Georgia and be assured of a relatively secure market. Yet today it is cheaper to mine marble in China, produce a monument there, and ship it to the United States than to produce the same product domestically. But it is not just manufacturing that is moving abroad. Services are also frequently conducted abroad. It is well known that services like telephone support centers are now often located in India. But less well recognized is that many professional services also take place abroad including the reading of MRIs, conducting of stock analysis, and preparing basic legal documents. In the future firms will readily pick and choose where they accomplish any given step in their value chains. This change is not just occurring in large firms—even entrepreneurial startups are taking advantage of globalization to cut costs and benefit from talent around the world.

As firms go international, many of the basic management principles taught in North American business schools need to undergo scrutiny to see how they apply overseas. For example, it has been widely taught in business schools that firms should only pursue related diversification. However, outside of North America there is evidence that unrelated diversification may in fact generate better performance results, particularly in those settings where market and legal institutions may not be well developed. Similarly, the dominant form of organization outside the United States is a business group; family controlled business groups play a dominant role in many regions of the world. However, in the United States there is no similar organizational form. Most textbooks ignore these issues because their focus is on North America, with illustrations from the United States. But students must get to know the world and its companies to successfully compete in today's global market.

As firms move internationally the cultural challenges they face increase. It is predicted that in the future the BRIC nations (Brazil, Russia, India, and China) will have a larger combined economy than the G6 nations (United States, United Kingdom, Japan, Germany, France, and Italy). The future economic growth for firms from North America—and where students will need to compete—may well be in the BRIC and other emerging economies. Thus, students also need to understand the cultures and institutions around the world.

WHAT MAKES THIS BOOK DIFFERENT AND VALUE-ADDING?

This book has four key features that makes it different from most other management textbooks and add value for both the instructor and the students:

1. The book is designed to be instructor friendly. Instructors do a better job teaching a class when the textbook they use has been designed to help them in the classroom. This textbook was designed by instructors who teach the course and who have surveyed and spoken to instructors from around the world. As a result it includes the most common topics covered in international management courses. Additionally, supplemental materials in the instructor's manual enhance the instructor's ability to supplement the lectures and exercises.

2. The book is also designed to generate maximum discussion in class. Exercises and discussion boxes are written so that the instructor does not have to look up answers in the instructor's manual but can just discuss the topic at hand using the material in the book, or even right from the instructor's knowledge of the topic in question. We have found from using the text in class that many exercises and discussion boxes can be distributed in class, then referred to directly in a lecture and discussed immediately.

3. There are numerous references in the book to film or television productions that are readily available from Amazon or most university libraries. We have found that showing video segments to accompany relevant portions of the book enlivens lectures and adds significant heuristic value to the course, because students can remember the videos and the lessons they conveyed, especially when properly debriefed in class or used as part of course homework.

4. The book is written to help students learn. The style is clear and direct, and the authors have tried to avoid slang that can frustrate readers from non-English speaking countries. In addition we have tried to link theories and evidence together in a way that tells a story about the thought process behind the research. For example, in the leadership chapter, we don't simply list leadership theories but explain the thinking that went into each extension or new leadership model. Also, all chapters begin with a chapter outline and include brief reviews of key points, as well as key terms.

5. Finally, the book is designed for students and classes from around the world. It will help students from North America by introducing them to major foreign countries and regions important to twenty-first century business such as China, India, and Latin America. Almost all examples in the book are non-North American examples. In addition, rather than always focusing on the problems that Americans have in doing business overseas, we also discuss the problems that non-Americans (for example, Chinese) have when they try to do business outside of their own countries. As a result the book is one of the first to have a non-American-centric view of the world.

TEXTBOOK LAYOUT

Thus, there is a need for a textbook that provides perspectives on management from outside of North America and an understanding of culture in countries that are less well understood, such as China and India.

1. The text brings a perspective to management from outside the United States. To accomplish this, it presents the dominant management thought in North America on given issues and then shows what occurs internationally. The text employs a rich set of non-North American firms and examples from countries around the world.

2. Understanding culture is paramount. We address how cultures in different regions of the world affect the managerial issues discussed in each chapter.

The topics that will be examined in this text include:

Chapter 1 – Introduction
Chapter 2 – Culture and international management

Chapter 3 – Economic/Legal/Political environment
Chapter 4 – Corporate strategy
Chapter 5 – Business and operational strategy
Chapter 6 – Market entry decisions
Chapter 7 – Motivation
Chapter 8 – Leadership
Chapter 9 – Decision making
Chapter 10 – Influence and negotiation
Chapter 11 – Evaluation and control
Chapter 12 – Human resources management
Chapter 13 – Structure of the International Firm
Chapter 14 – Future of International Management

The following diagram shows an example of how chapters are organized.

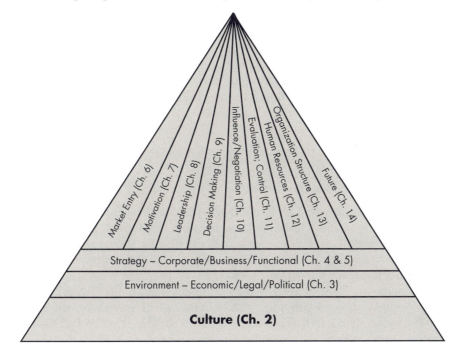

The diagram illustrates how culture provides a major foundation for this text. The book next builds on the understanding of culture to lay out foundation issues concerning analysis of a firm's environment and its strategy. We study these first because in practice a firm utilizes its understanding of environment and strategy to direct implementation issues. We examine implementation issues in Chapters 6–13 of the text. These issues range from motivation and human resources concerns to leadership in an international setting.

UNIQUE FEATURES OF THIS TEXT

This text includes in its chapters a consistent set of unique features. The text seeks to ensure that there is rich set of illustrations to help students understand its core concepts. In addition the text seeks to make the application of these concepts clear to students as they seek to use the ideas in analyzing cases or applying to a business setting. As a result each of the core chapters includes:

1. An opening short case to set the stage for the topic being investigated, and case questions at the end of the chapter.

2. Three short vignettes that provide examples of firms that illustrate the chapter's concepts.
3. A short case that further illustrates how a particular firm dealt with the issues being discussed, with questions at the end of the chapter to help guide the discussion of the case.
4. A concluding vignette that details how to do business in a specific country.
5. Three culture boxes provide specific illustrations of cultural issues connected to the chapter topic.
6. An ethics box that applies the topics to international ethics.
7. Managerial guidelines at the end of the chapter to help students apply the concepts to their own work.
8. Extensive exercises at the end of the chapter that include in-class and out-of-class exercises, as well as discussion questions that are useful for class exercises.

In addition, **Chapter 14, Future of International Management**, focuses on the future of international managers and their organizations. Entrepreneurship and entrepreneurial firms in the world economy, greater concern about the environment, and increasing attention given to the poorest populations and regions of the world are just several of the pertinent issues explored in this chapter.

SUPPORT MATERIALS

A full set of support materials is available for adopting instructors.

- **Instructor's Manual with Test Bank (0-324-42202-4).** Prepared by Ansr_Source, the Instructor's Manual (IM) contains learning objectives, general teaching suggestions, case discussion guide, and chapter outlines. The test bank is also available on the book's Website at www.cengage.com/Management/Ahlstrom.
- **Instructor's Resource CD-ROM (0-324-42197-4).** Prepared by Ansr_Source, the key instructor ancillaries (Instructor's Manual, Test Bank, ExamView, and PowerPoint® slides) are provided on CD-ROM, giving instructors the ultimate tool for customizing lectures and presentations. The PowerPoint slides are designed to be used as a supplement in class lectures.
- **Website.** A host of ancillary materials are available for students and instructors on the text Website (www.cengage.com/Management/Ahlstrom). Students will find a glossary of key terms and definitions, separated by chapter. For faculty, PowerPoint® slides, the instructor's manual, and the test bank are available for each chapter.
- **Global Economic Crisis Resource Center**. The new online web portal features the solutions you want in an easy-to-use teachable format, including:

  - A global issues database
  - A thorough overview and timeline of events leading up to the global economic crisis
  - Links to the latest news and resources
  - Discussion and testing content
  - Text specific content
  - A built-in instructor feedback forum so we can hear your suggestions to make this cutting-edge resource even stronger!

  For more information on how you can access this resource, please visit www.cengage.com.

Acknowledgments

We'd like to thank a number of friends and colleagues who commented on and critiqued certain chapters:

Marc Ahlstrom, *Burlington County College*

Ron Abernathy, *University of North Carolina, Greensboro*

Balbir B. Bhasin, *Sacred Heart University*

Al Rosenbloom, *Dominican University*

Emeric Solymossy, *Western Illinois University*

Peggy Takahaski, *University of San Francisco*

Yohannan T. Abraham, *Southwest Missouri State*

Michael Young, *The Hong Kong Baptist University*

Robert Desman, *Kennesaw State University*

Annette Gunter Crow, *University of Central Oklahoma*

Jim Kennelly, *Skidmore University*

About the Authors

David Ahlstrom

David Ahlstrom is a professor in the Department of Management at The Chinese University of Hong Kong. He has lived in the Asia-Pacific region for nearly 20 years, 14 of which he has spent teaching in Hong Kong in the areas of organizational behavior, international business, and the management of technology and innovation. Before entering academia, Professor Ahlstrom worked in marketing and international sales in the computer industry. He has published over 50 refereed journal and book articles in publications such as *Academy of Management Review*, *Strategic Management Journal*, *Entrepreneurship Theory & Practice*, *Journal of International Business Studies*, and *Asia Pacific Journal of Management*. He is the incoming editor of *Asia Pacific Journal of Management*, the official journal of the Asia Academy of Management.

Professor Ahlstrom is one of only about two dozen trainers certified to teach the Cialdini method of influence. He has trained or consulted with numerous government organizations and Fortune 1000 firms in East Asia and North America, primarily in the areas of influence, negotiation, and workplace decision making.

Garry D. Bruton

Dr. Garry D. Bruton is a professor of entrepreneurship at the Neeley School of Business at Texas Christian University where he holds the Fehmi Zeko Faculty Fellowship. Dr. Bruton was one of the founders of the entrepreneurship program at TCU and he still serves as Academic Director of the Neeley Entrepreneurship Program.

Dr. Bruton's research focuses on entrepreneurship in emerging economies and he has published or has forthcoming over 65 academic articles in leading journals such as the *Academy of Management Journal*, *Strategic Management Journal*, *Journal of Business Venturing*, *Journal of International Business Studies*, and *Entrepreneurship Theory & Practice*. He is the incoming editor of the *Academy of Management Perspectives*, a leading academic journal.

In 2005, Professor Bruton was the first holder of the Hall Chair in Entrepreneurship in Emerging Markets offered by the Fulbright Foundation in Poland. He is currently the President of the Asia Academy of Management which represents all management professors with an interest in Asia research. Professor Bruton lived and worked abroad in Eastern Europe, Russia, and Asia multiple times over the last fifteen years.

1

INTRODUCTION TO INTERNATIONAL MANAGEMENT

Overview

Business is becoming increasingly global. The barriers to trade continue to fall, and the level of trade among countries continues to rise. The result is that a firm's competitors may no longer be in the next state or province but in a country that it hardly knew existed a few years ago. This chapter lays the foundation for the study of international management. The topics covered include:

- Status of internationalization of business today and how we got to this position
- Drivers of internationalization
    - New technology
    - Greater access to information
    - Changes in how people save, spend, and invest
- Why we study international management
    - What you believe you know about doing international business may not be as complete or thorough as you think
    - Changes in major players in international business
    - Rise of business ethics as a critical concern
- The plan for the rest of the book

TOYOTA AND SUCCESSFUL INTERNATIONALIZATION

Today, Toyota is not only viewed as one of the top-quality firms in the world, but it is the world's most profitable auto manufacturer. However, when Toyota began in 1937 as a spin-off from Toyoda Automatic Loom Works, its products were not perceived as high quality. The firm built its quality image with years of hard work. One key element in that success has been the firm's ability to adapt and change as its environment has changed. In the 1990s the firm was, and still is, the dominant firm in the highly fragmented Japanese automobile market. Toyota had international operations but most of its international sales came from the export of cars produced in Japanese plants. Profits were long heavily dependent upon the Japanese market and the captive set of distributorships the firm controlled. However, in the 1990s as the economic bubble in Japan burst, Toyota had to look internationally to increase sales.

Initially, the firm dealt with its declining Japanese sales through greater international sales served by exporting cars from its plants in Japan. The response by the political establishment, particularly in the United States, was fiercely negative. Toyota was criticized for providing no jobs to the U.S. economy, while profiting significantly from their open access to U.S. markets and U.S. distribution—something that U.S. auto firms did not enjoy in Japan.

Prior to the 1990s, the firm had manufacturing facilities around the world; however, these efforts were not extensive. As a response to the political pressures in the United States

that arose at the time, Toyota began to set up manufacturing operations in the United States and other countries. Both Toyota and the U.S. government agreed to the voluntary guideline that 75 percent of Toyotas sold in the United States would also be produced there. Similar goals exist for other major regions of the world. Today, Toyota has a goal to hold 15 percent of the world's auto market and 15 percent of the U.S. auto market. In 2005, the firm had approximately 12 percent of the U.S. market. The firm has established six manufacturing facilities in the United States to meet current demand, with future plans to build two more manufacturing facilities to meet the expected sales growth and the goal of locally producing 75 percent of autos sold in the United States.

As a result of increasing its international focus Toyota, for the first time, will produce more cars outside of Japan than inside. Thus, Toyota has quickly become a truly global company. The difficulty for the firm has been maintaining the quality of the firm's products as it expands. The methods used to ensure this include:

- Reducing the number of people on the board of directors from 60, a common number for Japanese organizations, to less than half. The expected effect is that the board (and the firm) will become more responsive to environmental change and make decisions more quickly.

- Adding five new non-Japanese top executives to ensure that the firm adopts and maintains a global outlook.

- Creating the Toyota Institute to train managers around the world and to ensure that the global managers are using consistent methods.

- Flying groups of workers from Japan to facilities around the world to ensure that the best methods are used in each of Toyota's geographically scattered manufacturing plants.

- Using joint ventures actively to ease market entry in new locations.

- Creating a Global Production Center to ensure state-of-the-art production methods are used around the world.

One result of these efforts is that Toyota has become the most profitable firm in the world, beating out U.S. giant General Electric, which held the top spot for several years. The firm has been able to gain this position with a clear vision of its goal (to become a successful worldwide auto company), how it was to achieve this (focus on the customer needs, quality manufacturing, and a commitment to innovation, even at the lower end of the marketplace), and adapting the company as the environment changed.

The more Toyota has internationalized, the greater its success. Today, it is one of the most internationalized auto firms in the world. Studying the success and methods of such firms offer other businesses the chance to replicate this success.

The car company in front. (2005, January 29). *Economist*, pp. 65–67.

Shirouzu, N. (2005, February 22). Toyota targets U.S. market with bold expansion plan. *Asian Wall Street Journal*, pp. A1-A2.

Globalization
Globalization is a modern term used to describe the changes in societies and the world economy that result from dramatically increased international trade, foreign direct investment, and cultural exchange.

Business today is focused on international competition and opportunities afforded by **globalization**. As recently as 1990, a business person in North America typically viewed their firm's competitors as those firms in a few bordering states or provinces in Canada. These areas were also the business person's principal target markets. Similarly, in Europe, in a country such as France, the competition and market for its goods were primarily located in France. For many small countries in

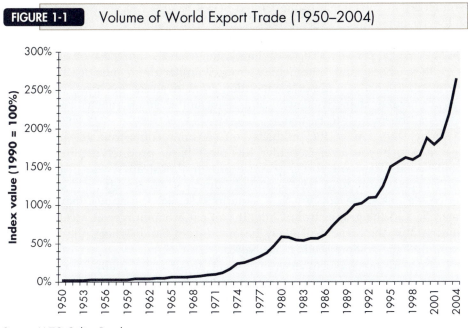

FIGURE 1-1 Volume of World Export Trade (1950–2004)

Source: WTO Online Database

Europe the market and competition may have included a neighboring country but even then the foreign market was relatively close.

Today competition comes from a vast number of countries around the world. In the U.S., a dramatically increasing number of companies, not only large corporations but medium and small firms, obtain a growing percentage of their overall revenue from overseas markets. The same is true throughout Europe, Asia, and the rest of the world. As a result, international management—the process of applying management concepts and techniques in a multinational environment—is rapidly gaining importance. Figure 1-1 demonstrates the continued expansion of world trade.

Thus, international concerns will be a major part of future managers' professional lives. This chapter will establish the rationale and the method for the study of international management. The flow of this chapter is summarized in Figure 1-2. We will first examine the benefits of internationalization for society.

BENEFITS TO CONSUMERS OF INTERNATIONAL TRADE

Domestic markets that are open to foreign trade help not only business but also consumers. Consumers benefit from less-expensive and higher-quality products, particularly when there is international trade. For example, it is

FIGURE 1-2 Chapter 1 Conceptual Flow

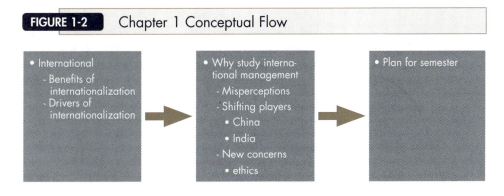

estimated that consumers in the United States have saved approximately $100 billion by obtaining cheaper products from China since 1978.[i] To put this in perspective, it is estimated that the savings from globalization for each U.S. family is $9,000 per year. These savings come from the purchase of such things as clothes, shoes, and automobiles from manufacturers outside the United States. Additionally, without competition from overseas business, companies typically make changes slowly and reluctantly. International competition pushes all businesses to be better.

Today, very few of the products you consume come from the immediate area in which you live. Consider the most basic product required for all people, food. The food you eat can be grown almost anywhere in the world and shipped fresh to a neighborhood supermarket quickly and efficiently. Notice the next time you are in a supermarket that the apples may be from Australia and the grapes from Chile. If you eat a hamburger at McDonalds in Saudi Arabia the bread will likely be made from Saudi wheat, the beef from Spain, and the sesame seeds from North Africa. Similarly, many other products you may not have otherwise thought about are actually imported. For example, historically a high percentage of granite headstones and monuments used in the United States came from northern Georgia or Vermont. Today, however, many are from China. It is actually cheaper to cut, polish, and ship stones from China than to produce them in the United States. This is true for a number of other heavy items, such as furniture that was once considered too expensive to produce overseas due to high shipping costs. Today, shipping, production, and coordination costs and tariffs have decreased so much it is now cheaper to produce products overseas and ship them to consumers in North America and Europe. For example, Stickley, a famous furniture maker based in Syracuse, New York, is a firm best known for making furniture based on designs from the 19th-century U.S. creative movement known as "arts and crafts." Yet a high percentage of Stickley's classic American arts-and-crafts-style furniture is now made in Vietnam and shipped to the U.S.; the labor costs for furniture manufacturing in Vietnam are less than half of the costs in China—$125 per month per worker. The high valued-added design and marketing, however, remain in the United States.

Not only products but also services have become more global. Today it is possible for customers in North America or Europe to undergo an MRI (magnetic resonance imaging, which gives a three-dimensional perspective of a person's internal organs) and have it read by doctors in India. The results are given to the patient, who may not even know that their MRI images have traveled around the world. Other firms incorporate international operations in their production process in some manner even if parts of their operations remain in their home nation. For example, salmon caught in the United States is typically shipped to China, deboned, and shipped back to and sold in the U.S. Thus, firms and consumers today can benefit by obtaining the best and least expensive products and services from anywhere in the world.

While products are flowing into local markets from international locations, local firms are also able to export their own products overseas. The flow of trade is two way—it flows both into and out of any given country. This fact is often overlooked. For example, in North America there is considerable concern over outsourcing of jobs to India and China, though these markets are becoming major customers for North American firms.

Outsourcing occurs when activities, such as computer programming, that were once part of a company's internal operation, are performed by other firms outside of the United States at a lower cost. There are many examples, such as phone operators based in India working for GE Capital. On any given day they might be calling a customer in the U.S. inquiring why a credit card payment is late. These

Outsourcing

Outsourcing (or contracting out) is often defined as the delegation of non-core operations or jobs from internal production to an external entity (such as a subcontractor) that specializes in that operation.

Indian operators assume western names and often try to pick up the accent of the region they represent. Swissair moved its entire accounting division, including its computers, from high-wage Switzerland to low-wage India to take advantage of lower labor costs for secretaries, programmers, and accountants. British Airways World Network Services, based in Mumbai, India, keeps track of the British airline's frequent-flier miles. Selectronic, a telecomputing firm in Delhi, obtains doctors' dictation though a toll-free number in the United States, transcribes the recordings and sends the results back as text to an American health-maintenance organization. America Online recently established an operation comprised of 600 Filipino customer-service representatives in Manila, who answer 10,000 to 12,000 technical and billing enquiries a day, mostly from the U.S., amounting to about 80 percent of AOL's customer email. In 1999, the employees in the Philippines were paid about $5.50 a day—about one third more than minimum wage in that country, and about what an unskilled worker earns in the United States in an hour.[ii] Other companies, such as Adobe have hired large numbers of support representatives in the Philippines, where the English and communication skills are good and people are generally computer literate.

As a result of such actions, the Bureau of Labor Statistics estimated that the number of outsourced jobs in the United States, or jobs taken from Americans and moved to other countries, increased from 6.5 million in 1983 to 10 million in 2000.[iii] However, less reported is the fact that the flow of jobs is not one way— the number of jobs *insourced* to the U.S. increased even more than those outsourced in the same period, growing from 2.5 million to 6.5 million over about the same period.[iv] It is also important to note that the jobs that were insourced are at higher pay levels than those outsourced. Thus, for every $1 of jobs that are outsourced, the insourced jobs generate $1.14.[v] While numerically there are more jobs outsourced than insourced, the insourced jobs produce greater value for society. Interestingly, some firms are also moving some of their previously outsourced jobs back to the U.S. Infosys recently moved nearly 1000 customer-service jobs for a major U.S. client to New Jersey. This was to satisfy the demands of the U.S. firm for more premium service from service agents more familiar with the North American market.

These facts are likely of little consolation to the person losing a job because of outsourcing. International trade, however, is beneficial for the general economy, particularly in the long run. Economics and trade theory would highlight the fact that free trade in this situation is allowing countries to specialize in services that they perform better than other countries in the world.[vi] Thus, in the United States it is more expensive to produce garments, such as t-shirts than to have them produced and imported from China. This in turn allows for the U.S. to spend more time and resources on what it does best, such as developing technology and other intellectual property, including books, music, games, and films; exporting retail services (such as Wal-Mart and Starbucks); and growing wheat, corn, and soybeans for the world's population.[vii] However, it should be recognized that some people, such as Alan Blinder, a Princeton economist and former Federal Reserve Vice Chairman, argue that the pain of outsourcing may become greater in the United States. It has typically been thought that outsourcing applied mostly to low-skilled jobs. Professor Blinder argues in the future as many as 40 million jobs may be lost as increasingly high-skill jobs, such as accounting, financial analysis, and computer programming, which do not have to be done locally, are outsourced to lower-cost environments. These high-skill jobs can occur in any location with the resulting data shipped to any location in the world.[viii]

This chapter lays the foundation for the examination of international management. International management focuses on how individuals manage a global business. This should not be confused with international business. International

Unlike international business, which looks at how entire firms compete on an international level, international management focuses on how individuals manage a global business.

David Young-Wolff/PhotoEdit

business focuses on the macro approach to operating internationally. Thus, international business is less concerned with individual interactions and more on how an entire firm behaves as it competes internationally. There are some topics that are relevant to both international management and international business. However, the focus in our discussion here will ultimately connect back to the individual.

In laying the foundation for our study, we'll first briefly discuss globalization and the three factors that have driven its growth. We'll then review the reasons why we study international management. For example, there are aspects of conducting business around the world with which you may not be familiar. Studying international management as part of your studies helps to prepare you for the global environment in which management occurs. Another reason is the rapidly changing environment in which international management occurs. There are new economic players in the world economy, such as China and India with which you may not be familiar. These new players are rapidly changing the dynamics of international management. The book has a special focus to help introduce competitors from such emerging markets to you. The final reason we study international management is the growing role of ethics in conducting business internationally. As business grows to be more international, the ethical expectations on such businesses are also rapidly changing and these situations can be very different from what a business operating in a single country faces. Thus, students need to be aware of this critical domain. The chapter concludes with the structure in which the book will follow in studying international management.

A GLOBAL WORLD

You will be far more likely than your parents to seek a job far away from your home country. This growing level of internationalism started primarily after the end of World War II in 1945. At that time, the average protective **tariff** of manufactured goods was 40 percent. That is, a 40 percent tax on average was added to a manufactured good when it was shipped to and sold in another country. That 40 percent tax tended to discourage trade between nations. However by 2005, the average tariff had fallen to 4 percent and trade between firms in

Tariffs
Taxes on imported (not exported) goods.

different countries has become the dominant factor in business. For example, consider changes in the Japanese and U.S. tariffs over the past century:

	1913	2004
Japan	30%	3.1%
United States	44%	3.7%

Two Periods in the Globalization Trend

The increasingly global world after World War II can actually be seen in two distinct periods. The period immediately after World War II is often referred to as the period of "Big Unit" capitalism. **Big Unit Capitalism** is characterized by stable economics with large domestic firms, a high degree of central planning—even in many free-market economies, government ownership, and powerful trade unions. Taxes were very high in nearly all countries—U.S. marginal tax rates for upper-income earners were as high as 94 percent during this period. Big Unit Capitalism from the end of World War II until 1971 produced a period of unmatched economic growth. During this time the real wages of production workers in the United States grew a solid 2-1/2 to 3 percent annually and boom and bust cycles became much less severe than in prior economic periods. During this time conveniences once available only to the rich became accessible to nearly everyone. This included not only washing machines and televisions, but automobiles and air travel. One management consultant pointed out that business people during this time period only had to open their mail to take orders (and not go out to hustle and sell) and sales would increase 10 percent per year.[ix] It is only a slight overstatement to say that stability and growth during most of the post-war period came to be expected almost as a birthright by those who lived in the more developed countries of the west. This period of stability promoted an ever-increasing rate of international trade.

The start of the second period of globalization can be traced to 1971. In that year President Richard Nixon announced that the United States would no longer redeem international dollar holdings at the rate of $35 per ounce of gold. This commitment had formed a central foundation of the international financial system set in place around the end of World War II. This financial system was referred to as the **Bretton Woods System** (from the small town in the state of New Hampshire where the agreement was reached). This system established the value of all the major world currencies with respect to each other. The ability to have convertible currencies prevented the practice of economically strong nations paying for their imports in their own currency, which at that time would not have been easily convertible. With payment in a non-convertible currency, the outcome was that the other country typically then had to spend that money to also buy their imports. Bretton Woods also created mechanisms to support countries that ran into balance-of-payments difficulties. Specifically, the agreement led to the creation of two international agencies: 1) the international bank for reconstruction and development to finance rebuilding from the war; this bank is referred to as the World Bank, and 2) the international monetary fund (IMF). The outcome of this agreement was to help tame the wild economic fluctuations that occurred between World War I and World War II. However, the system became confining to member states and their economic flexibility so that by 1971 President Nixon and other world leaders felt it was time to loosen those controls. The result was a more flexible economic environment that further aided international trade. In this new environment, the U.S. rapidly expanded exports and imports by over 800 percent between 1973 and 2002, while Japan saw a 900 percent jump in both items.

Big Unit capitalism
A Big Unit economy will be dominated by Big Business, Big Government, and Big Labor. The Big Unit economy generally produced efficient but rigid, pyramidal organizations and government departments that were full of soft niches that relaxed standards and did not demand (and reward) excellence and accountability in work and educational quality.

Bretton Woods system
The Bretton Woods system was a negotiated monetary order after World War II to govern monetary relations and currency exchange rates among independent states.

STATOIL AND VIEWING INDUSTRY ON A WORLDWIDE BASIS

International management requires that the firm consider its industry in a worldwide context and not focus on a single item such as exchange rate. The oil industry is clearly an example of such a situation. Oil is a limited natural resource that is expensive and difficult to find. As a result most of the world's major firms have determined that their best strategy is to purchase existing oil firms and their assets rather than focusing on finding new sources of oil. This has resulted in an active merger and acquisition market for oil companies that have taken shape in recent years.

An exception to this purchasing of oil assets strategy is Statoil, a Norwegian oil firm. In the new century, this firm devoted substantial resources to finding new oil reserves. This has resulted in new production that has come online with an estimated 1.75 million barrels of oil daily in 2008.

Statoil did not base its strategy on what it saw happening in Norway, or even Europe. Instead, it examined the worldwide demand for oil and what it expected to happen in the industry. The strategy was not without risk because the oil industry is prone to

cyclical behavior. Additionally, due to the costs and time to bring production online, the choices the firm was making had very long term implications. However, the firm correctly looked at factors, such as the growing demand in China and India and the political instability in parts of the Middle East and predicted that the investment in exploration would pay off. They bet correctly and the payoff was substantial.

Cummins, C. (2005, April 29). Statoil puts bet on growth. *Wall Street Journal Europe*, p. M1.

Drivers of Globalization

Three major factors have helped drive the expansion of globalization since the 1971 collapse of Bretton Woods. These were technology changes that impacted how people and organizations communicate; changes in access to information, and changes in how individuals invest and save. These three changes are discussed next.

Multinational enterprise
Large firm that operates in a large number of countries.

Drivers of the Globalization Era: Technology Changes Historically, international trade was the domain of large **multinational enterprises**—large firms that operate in a large number of nations. But changes in computer and communications technology today allow individuals and organizations to communicate easily and with a wider range of individuals than ever thought possible at a very low cost. This change has promoted the growth of international business among a wide range of firms from very small to very large. To illustrate the power of the technology, after the Indian Ocean Tsunami at the end of 2004, churches and charities were able to solicit donations from around the world just by using lists of email and one or two personal computers connected to the internet. Before governments were even able to generate a statement on that terrible disaster, individuals and charities had organized major relief efforts worldwide. This same technological change allows even the smallest firms to have access to suppliers and customers far away from their local regions.

The power of technology is the result of innovations involving computerization, compression technology, and digitization. Digitization is the process by which sounds, video and film, television, photos, documents, and any other form of data are put into simple binary computer codes and then transferred by copper and fiber-optic cables, microwave, and satellite across the street and around the world. The innovations in computers, data storage, and communications have greatly facilitated digitization, which in turn facilitates communication and commerce. For instance, advances in microchip technology have resulted in computing power doubling roughly every 18 months over the past 30 years, while advances in compression technology mean that the amount of data that can be stored on a square inch of disk surface has increased 60 percent every year since 1991.

The outcome of computerization, compression technology, and digitization is that the cost of storing data has fallen from five dollars a megabyte to five cents,

SONY AND INCREASING INTERNATIONALIZATION

Sony is one of the leaders of technology in the world. A strong signal of the growing internationalization of business in the world came when, in 2005, Howard Stringer was appointed as the first non-Japanese CEO in Sony Corporation's history. Stringer had previously been head of the corporation's U.S. operations. One of the key goals of the new CEO is to bring greater cooperation and coordination to the firm, whose far flung international operations were not currently operating effectively as a unit.

There are a variety of examples of the lack of coordination that troubles Sony. For example, in 2004 both the PC division and the Walkman group released hard-drive music players to the market. There was no coordination in the release or any effort to prevent the cannibalization of each product's customers (i.e., taking each other's customers rather than finding new customers). Similarly, in 2004 Sony had started its new Connect product, which supplied online music as a direct competitor to Apple Computer's iTunes Store. The initial Connect product was not successful in large measure due to the lack of coordination between the different units of the firm. The software was produced by the Tokyo-based personal-computer group, which did not work well with the Walkman (also produced in Japan but by the audio team). Both teams, in turn, were not familiar with potential web-surfing customers in the United States, which would have been the dominant market for the product. The end result was the initial failure of the product, and its removal from the market.

Facing this difficult situation, Stringer signaled his strong belief in greater coordination as he emphasized the issue in his initial communication to the firm's employees in March 2005. By April that year the restructuring of the firm had begun with the promotion of figures in the firm who would emphasize coordination. The firm later that year announced the merger of different units, requiring different work groups to talk to each other.

Stringer was an unexpected appointment to CEO. He does not speak Japanese, is not an engineer, and is not known for his marketing expertise. His main claim to fame was that he turned around Sony's movie and music business in the U.S. However, in 2003 the Sony board was slimmed down and greater numbers of independent directors were appointed to make the firm similar to other major international firms. These new board members wanted professional managers who could bring fundamental change to the warring and uncoordinated units. Stringer was an insider in that he was knowledgeable about Sony, but his background represented a fundamental break with much of the past, and he was believed to be able to bring fundamental change in the organization. He was the ideal person to be a change maker at the firm.

A memo from Sony's new chief. (2005, March 8). *Business Week Online.*

Sony restructures management teams. *Surface Mount Technology, 19(4),* 24.

Dvorak, P. (2005, June 29). Sony's new CEO fights discord at rival units to find iPod alternative. *Wall Street Journal,* pp. A1, A8.

Schendler, B. (2005). Inside the shakeup at Sony. *Fortune, 151(7),* 94.

making computing power stronger and more accessible every day. These innovations in telecommunications have steadily decreased the costs of phone calls and data transfers, while steadily increasing the speed, distance, variety, and quantities of information that can be transmitted on a phone line, cable, or radio signal. The lower cost has made phone and other forms of communication available to a wider range of people than could have been imagined before. The number of mobile phone subscribers in the world has surpassed two billion, with the bulk of the new growth now coming from large, emerging economies such as China, India, Eastern Europe, Latin America, and Africa. Thus, today individuals and businesses are able to identify and work with a wider range of firms and people than have ever occurred in history.

Drivers of the Globalization Era: Changes in Access to Information Related to the expansion of technology for communication is the expansion of information. Historically, societies were better connected and had a better flow of information when they had access to navigable rivers or deep-water ports because information could get to them easier.[x] Today information flows so much more easily. The internet and satellite dishes that allow the transmission of television are two of the key changes. These changes have made it difficult for governments and media oligopolies to block or exclude information from the airwaves (or cyberspace). Consider a country such as Iran, which tries to limit access to large amounts of information by its citizens. But today Tehran is filled with satellite dishes, so despite the government's best efforts, its citizens remain well informed.

The change in the amount of information available began with the globalization of television. Throughout much of the Cold War era, television and radio broadcasting were restricted businesses, because the spectrums and technologies available for transmission were limited. Governments either ran most television broadcasting directly or highly regulated it. This began to break down, first in the United States, with the advent of cable television, which could carry many more channels than could be broadcast over the air. Then, in the 1980s, other versions of multi-channel television began to spread around the world, thanks largely to the falling cost of putting satellites into orbit.

Those who visited the Middle East during the Cold War period would recall customs agents going through luggage to make sure there was no contraband, such as pornographic video tapes, prohibited magazines, or politically sensitive material. Traveling to China with a Bible as late as the 1990s could get you detained at customs, with the Bible confiscated by border control. Today, although some borders are still quite strict, customs officials find it much more difficult to check every USB memory stick being carried across the border for information of which they do not approve. However, the flow of information around the world is not perfectly seamless. Many firms such as Google and Yahoo, who supply or are conduits of information, must actively consider how much they wish to cooperate with governments, such as China's, which try to limit their citizens' access to information.

For businesses, this access to information allows firms to assemble technologies, raw materials, and funding for products or services for customers around the world. For example, this flow of information has contributed to Taiwan's advancement from a primarily low-wage manufacturing center of low-cost electronics to one of the world's leading high-technology centers in only 25 years. Today, Taiwan is a leader in areas, such as the development and manufacture of flat screens for televisions and computers. It has done this by moving up the production ladder. In the past, it produced low-cost electronics with everything on location in Taiwan, a small and resource-poor environment. Greater access to

For the most part, technological advances have dramatically enhanced the flow of communication and information.

Diamond Sky Images/Digital Vision/Getty Images

information now allows firms in Taiwan to be interconnected with engineers in Silicon Valley (the second largest ethnic group in the Silicon Valley are Chinese) to generate ideas for new products. Taiwanese firms are also connected with the People's Republic of China to facilitate in the manufacture of the products. Thus, the ability of Taiwanese firms to obtain and send information around the world has allowed the nation to move up the production ladder. (The People's Republic of China [PRC] sees Taiwan as a renegade province, while some Taiwanese are seeking independence from China. This causes significant political problems for politicians. However, this has not limited opportunities, and today Taiwan businesses are some of the largest investors in the PRC.)

This access to information affects even the most remote location today. The flow of information about the need to be able to act on specific problems has led to a new invention from Massachusetts Institute of Technology (MIT) called the "fab lab." This product is a collection of commercially available machines that can be used to make just about anything with features bigger than those of a computer chip. Among other tools, it includes a laser cutter that makes two-dimensional and three-dimensional structures, a device that uses a computer-controlled knife to carve antennas and flexible electrical connections, a miniature milling machine that maneuvers a cutting tool in three dimensions to make circuit boards and other precision parts, a set of software for programming cheap computer chips known as microcontrollers, and a jigsaw (a narrow-bladed cutting device, not a picture puzzle). Together, these can machine objects with precision within one-millionth of a meter. The fab lab's purpose is to give backyard and desktop inventors— particularly those in poor countries who lack a formal education— access to design houses and job shops to produce prototypes. Thus, the fab lab can provide the resources necessary for entrepreneurs in poor countries to implement their ideas to create usable products.

As a result, the fab lab allows those in poor and remote locations the ability to solve their problems. For example, a dairy farmer's income is tied to the cream content of his cows' milk. In Pabal, an Indian village with a population of approximately 5,000, students at the Vigyan Ashram science school use a fab lab to build a sensor that will give Pabal's farmers a precise measure of the milk's fat content. The lab is also being used to produce solar-powered items that will harness the relentless local sunlight. In Norway, Sámi animal herders—who are among Europe's last nomads— are using fab labs to make radio collars and wireless networks to track their animals.

Within the next few years the fab lab will allow individuals and small businesses to customize products to their needs. At $20,000 each—not a trivial amount of money in a poor country, but within range of a village or local government—the fab lab will release an outpouring of entrepreneurial talent. This new production capability, coupled with the flow of information now possible allows one to imagine the great range of options available.

Drivers of the Globalization Era: Changes in How People Save, Spend, and Invest For much of the post-Cold War era, most large-scale domestic and international lending or underwriting was done by big commercial banks, investment banks, and insurance companies. These firms preferred to lend to companies with proven track records and "investment-grade" ratings. This made it difficult for an upstart or new business to get needed cash since the financing for firms often depended more on one's interpersonal business connections than the business idea.

A **disruptive innovation** is an innovation that changes the economics or technological standard of an industry. A disruption in the world of finance came about with the creation of "commercial paper"—a quick way for a firm to raise money through a debt offering. **Commercial paper** are bonds that corporations issue directly to the public in order to raise capital. The creation

Disruptive innovation
A new technological innovation, product, service, or business model that overturns the existing dominant innovation or technological standard in the marketplace.

Commercial paper
Bonds that corporations issue directly to the public in order to raise capital.

of this corporate bond market introduced some pluralism into the world of finance and took away the monopoly of the banks. The "securitization" of home mortgages occurred in the 1970s, when bonds in dominations as small as $1,000 were created. This made it possible for mortgage lenders to begin to serve this small market.

In the 1980s, financier Michael Milken noticed that firms with financial problems, or those with little capital or operating history, were being asked to pay interest rates at 3 to 10 percentage points higher than normal—if they could get any loans at all. However, these companies went bankrupt only slightly more often than the top-rated blue-chip companies, whose bonds offered much lower rates of return. This spurred Milken and others to create high yield or "junk" bonds, which carried higher interests rates with only slightly higher risk. These high-yield bonds offered an alternative opportunity for financing, while the public could invest in growing firms or firms undergoing turnarounds while enjoying higher interest. Firms, such as telecommunications firm MCI, were founded with high yield bonds, and when properly issued, these bonds can be an important financing vehicle.

Other changes to disrupt the old system were also occurring in global finance. For decades, big banks lent large amounts of money to foreign governments, states, and corporations and carried these loans on their books at their original (par) value. In the late 1980s many Latin American nations were unable to pay their debts. U.S. Treasury Secretary Nicholas Brady helped to get Latin American debts to the major commercial banks converted into U.S. government-backed bonds. These Brady bonds, as they came to be called, were then held by banks as assets or sold to the general public as mutual funds and pension funds with higher than normal rates of interest. Once again, individual investors could now own a small part of Mexico's debt along with a small part of Argentina's debt, and a small part of Russia's debt, to receive higher interest rates. The risk is shared and spread out, and the bonds trading on the open market with their prices signaled by the market. With these changes, countries had to manage their fiscal situations carefully, or their bond values would drop, making it harder for that country to raise money or renegotiate the loan. If a country is not careful about its fiscal management, then the U.S. Treasury, not to mention the pension funds and numerous individual investors, would not agree to create (or buy) that country's debt. This introduced fiscal discipline to these nations but also lead to far greater interdependence among nations and investors around the world.

Market for corporate control
The ability to take over a poorly performing firm and turn it around to profitability.

Finally, the **market for corporate control**, or the ability to take over a poorly performing firm and turn it around, is beginning to expand worldwide. For example, historically in Japan and South Korea big banks dominate the finance industry. These banks typically then also were part of the cross holdings by groups of businesses called *kieratsu* in Japan and *cherobols* in Korea. As a result, the market for corporate control in Japan and Korea was weak because the capital for takeovers was not readily available, plus the banks would pump capital into their affiliate firms, even if it offered a very low return on capital. Takeovers were also frowned upon for cultural reasons, and because so many bank boards and corporate boards were connected to each other investors in those Asian countries had little control over their investments.

By the year 2000 things had changed, as Japan opened up its financial-service sector, and British and U.S. investment banks and finance firms, such as GE Capital, entered in large numbers. Foreign competition forced Japanese banks to become more discriminating lenders and this, in turn, forced Japanese companies to become more efficient. This has led to a more rational use of capital in Japan and to more accessible capital for startups and new players. Korea has had similar reforms. In 2006 this change became clear as U.S. investor Carl Icahn began the first hostile take

HYNIX SEMICONDUCTOR OF SOUTH KOREA AND RESTRUCTURING

As noted, one means Korea had used to formulate its economic growth has been to rely on a business form called chaebol. These business groups were typically active in a very wide range of businesses and were also officially favored by the government (the organizational structure of a business group will be discussed more in Chapter 13.). One aspect of the government support was that the firms carried relatively large debts from banks because they were viewed as low risk. This structure served the country well until the value of the nation's money (the won) rapidly dropped in value in 1997. The result was that the large debts held by the chaebols could no longer be serviced because their debts were valued in dollars, which did not drop, and they were generating Korean Won, which now took many more to be equal to a dollar. This created a downward spiral in the economy as many businesses began to fail and created an economic crisis in Korea, popularly referred to as the IMF crisis. This is because the general population blamed the IMF-imposed monetary controls for the crisis.

One troubled firm that emerged from this difficulty was Hynix. The firm was created in 1999 when the government directed that Hyundai Electronics Industries take over LG Semiconductor. This was accomplished by having different chaebols combine their semiconductor units into one entity. The new entity also took on the existing firms' debt. This situation was made more difficult as the semiconductor market went into decline in 2001 with the prices of semiconductors dropping an estimated 80 percent. This resulted in the prediction for the firm's failure.

However, management began an aggressive turnaround effort in 2000. The firm turned much of its debt into equity in 2001; many of the banks that held that debt were owned by the

government and encouraged officially to make the exchange. The existing shareholders' equity was diluted by this debt-for-equity swap but it was better than the firm going into bankruptcy. Additionally, this allowed the firm to limit its debt payments. The firm then also began aggressive cost-cutting measures. These measures included not only laying off employees but selling five business units. Both actions culturally are not widely done in Korea. The crisis situation facing the firm gave it greater cultural flexibility in making such changes.

The operational changes were so significant that within a few years the firm became one of the world's most efficient manufacturers. A key partner in these efficiency moves was the firm's unions. The union movement in Korea is quite strong, and the firm's unions became active players in helping to increase the success of the firm. The active-union movement in Korea is unique in Asia, which has notoriously weak unions and a very unsupportive environment to even seek to organize unions. In many nations, union organizers lives are still threatened for their beliefs.

Another key component were the ethical standards pursued by the firm, which included an aggressive effort to create transparent operations and finances in which individuals clearly can see what the actions were and why they were taken. Historically, Korean firms' transparency was low. The move to international standards on transparency encouraged confidence by suppliers, customers, and investors, which also aided the firm's recovery. Although the firm in 2005 was fined $185 million dollars in the United States for price fixing of dynamic random access memory (DRAM) chips. U.S. computer makers, including Dell and Gateway, claimed

that inflated DRAM pricing was causing lost profits and hindering their effectiveness in the marketplace. The U.S. government then charged a variety of firms including Hynix under antitrust laws and won.

Here are a few key points in the company's history:

2007 Achieved the top-level operating profit margin in the firm's history
Appointed Mr. Jong-Kap Kim as the new chairman and CEO
2006 Posted record high revenues
Established global manufacturing network with complete construction of Hynix-ST Semiconductor Inc. a wholly owned manufacturing subsidiary in China
2005 Emerged from Corporate Restructuring Promotion Act ahead of schedule
Signed System IC Business Transfer Agreement with System Semiconductor
2002 Sold HYDIS, TFT-LCD Business Unit
2001 Spun off Hyundai Syscomm, Hyundai CuriTel, and Hyundai Networks
2000 Spun off Hyundai Image Quest and Hyundai Autonet

Today Hynix is the world's sixth largest semiconductor manufacturer in the world and is argued to have the largest market share for semiconductor chips in the fast-growing China market. The restructuring of the business group was critical to this success. Interestingly, because the economy of Korea has recovered since the 1997 crisis, such reform occurs far less frequently today.

Choe, Sang-hun. (2005, September 2). Hynix has become comeback darling. *International Herald Tribune*, pp. 1, 8.

Lee, J. (2004, April 29). S. Korean Hynix eyeing China venture. *Associated Press*.

over of a Korean firm, Korea Tobacco & Ginseng (KT&G) Corporation. It was reported at the end of 2005, in fact, that 39.7 percent of the stock of Korean listed companies was held by foreigners. Companies in countries like Japan and Korea are increasingly challenged by foreign competition and can no longer depend on their governments or affiliated banks or pensioners to support them despite their single digit returns on equity, as was the norm previously.

The Effects of Globalization

Competition has increased greatly in the past two to three decades with the advent of globalization and the energizing forces of technological changes and major financial innovations. Of course, change and reform are more difficult for some people and firms than for others. To imagine the changes occurring in the world, picture a weekly poker game among a group of six friends.[xi] These six individuals have been playing for a long time and the game has become a social event rather than a competition. To assure that no one loses or wins too much money, a number of formal and informal rules have evolved: raises are limited to 25 cents and three per round; only two or three relatively simple kinds of poker games are allowed, and if one player starts to win too much, he or she usually eases up so as to not keep winning. The sophistication of play is not very high, and there is no pressure to make it better. However, the arrangement is very comfortable for all involved, though not so good for those not invited to the game and permitted only to watch from the outside.

Now imagine that the spectators have built up to the point that those running the poker game permit three newcomers to be added. The newcomers successfully convince the house to adopt their kind of poker. The changes include the dealer's choice of any game, which means that now the raucous Texas Hold 'em that is played at the Poker World Series is a choice instead of just the simple five-card draw that all had enjoyed playing before. Previously the maximum bet was 25 cents, with informal limits on bet raises but now table stakes are allowed. This means you can bet anything you can carry to the table—not just the house's poker chips. Further, the newcomers argue, there should be no limits on raises, and no informal norms to restrict competitive play, such as developing informal alliances.

A few hours later, the results are predictable. The quality and sophistication of play has become higher than usual and the game is more interesting. You can win more money than before if you are careful and good (or lucky), but you can also lose much more. The distance between the biggest winner and the biggest loser is considerably larger than under the rules of the old genteel poker game. Some people will start grumbling about the disparity between the big winner and everyone else. Also, the person who normally won in the past is no longer on top because the skills needed to play only two kinds of poker and the skills needed to play a broader range of the dealer's choice with table stakes are much different. However, players can learn and there are new opportunities to gain more if you begin a winning streak.

This is the situation that now faces business around the world. The friendly competition that existed before has been replaced with hard competition from around the world. Globalization has introduced new competitors into many industries, and all kinds of rules limiting competition have dissolved. Some of these rules were formal: government regulations, labor agreements, and corporate bureaucratic policies. However, many rules limiting competition informal; the "I won't hit you if you won't hit me" variety or the "let's all set our prices at this level" have also been eliminated. The instability of the industry, the speed of change, the problems and opportunities for producers, and the availability of higher-quality or lower-priced goods and/or services to consumers have all been changed. Just as in the hypothetical poker game, both the strategies and career paths needed to win have also changed in some very important ways. What worked well for much of the late 19th and 20th centuries in economic and commercial terms—especially big-unit capitalism and central planning, with bureaucratic management—is less likely to lead to success today, either for firms or countries.

There are those who oppose the increasing levels of global business, just as those who would oppose changes in the poker game. In any city where leaders from around the world come to discuss world trade, you will find the streets filled with protestors that oppose globalization. Such individuals typically are focused on how globalization will impact the poor and their own livelihoods. There are merits to some of these arguments. Many countries have tended to send those most dangerous and environmentally damaging activities to offshore vendors. Thus, because the strict environmental laws in Europe and Canada may raise the costs of doing business a firm can simply move its operations to an emerging economy where the costs are lower and the controls less. For example, ships that are no longer profitable for use are taken to Bangladesh, where there are typically torn apart for their useable metal and other parts. Some of the work is done by young children and the potentially dangerous articles in the ships, such as asbestos insulation, may not be handled in a manner consistent with safety standards typical of most developed countries. It can also be seen that many poor countries are expected to open their borders to international trade, particularly manufactured goods, but there is not a reciprocal effort to open developed economies to the agriculture goods that poor nations produce. For example, the United States, Europe, and Japan still subsidize their farmers and limit agricultural imports. The result is these developed regions expect the Caribbean Islands to allow free access to their markets but limit access of the outside sugar industry to their markets. This result is that citizens of the U.S., for example, paying three times the world average for sugar, but it does protect powerful farm interests in Louisiana, Florida, and Hawaii.

Despite these negatives, the evidence shows that the world's people (including the world's poor) are best served by international trade.[xii] Those who oppose globalization seek to force nations to freeze what they do best at one point in time. Thus, protectionism "freezes the current job situation." This assures those on the bottom of the world's population would have little hope of improving their positions. The greatest opportunity for the poor around the world is free trade. There is no question that technological progress, such as trade, creates losers as well as winners. The Industrial Revolution involved painful economic and social dislocations that societies of the day had to deal with. They proved difficult but manageable problems, and nearly everybody would now agree that the vast gains in human welfare were worth the cost.[1]

WHY STUDY INTERNATIONAL MANAGEMENT?

It is human nature to assume that what we view as normal or traditional will also be what is viewed as normal or traditional in other countries and cultures. Similarly, individuals from different cultures will often develop assumptions about themselves and others that may not have any association with reality. To be successful in international business you should be open to things that may

---

[1]In Chapter 14 we will explore the future impact of globalization and trade in more detail. Recent academic research argues that, while in the past globalization has benefited developed economies, at some point it becomes a curvilinear relationship with the impact becoming more negative. This is because salaries begin to be negatively impacted not only for lower-skill employees but also for professionals. Thus, earlier the wage pressure on manufacturing and other low-skill domains simply pushed more individuals to move up the value-added scale and focus more on professional related skills in mature economies. But as professional activities begin to be outsourced there may be little room on the value-added scale for individuals in mature economies to move. The evidence to date still favors the benefits of international trade. However, at the end of the semester more of the argument about the negatives of such trade will be introduced and you will be asked to determine what you think the future holds.

challenge your assumptions. This does not mean that everything that happens differently in other parts of the world is right or that you need to change to match every situation. We will see as we discuss ethics that there are things that a business person can rightfully say you are not going to change even if a given behavior is accepted by many in that region.

Instead, international management teaches that through education and study you will learn some of the things that differ from what is considered right in your society; differences that you may face when managing an international firm. This knowledge will allow you, as a business person, to begin to think about what you would do in different situations. Preparation through education is the key to success because it prepares you to successfully respond to those different settings rather than simply to react without a rationale. We will see a wide variety of situations to familiarize you with different cultural settings. However, we do this within a strong theoretical framework and practical models of analysis to prepare students to analyze and understand in a wide variety of situations what they may face, even if the setting is not the exactly the same as illustrated in the book. There are two other reasons beyond developing a stronger understanding of other cultures, which also encourage students to study international business—shifting players in international business and increasing importance of business ethics.

Shifting Players in International Business

As students begin their study of international management, they need to recognize that the international business environment is undergoing rapid change. Fifteen years ago large international firms could reliably assume that they needed operations in North America, Japan, the European Community (predecessor to the European Union), and a few other major economies, such as Argentina in South America. The world has changed considerably since that time and these changes have created both greater complexity and more business opportunities.

USSR
The Union of Soviet Socialist Republics, the communist federation of states headed by Russia.

The Soviet Union (**USSR**) has broken up and free-market economics have been adopted, which has opened many new market opportunities. The USSR was formed with Russia at its core, but included numerous other nations that are now independent, including Estonia, Latvia, Lithuania, Georgia, Belarus, Ukraine, Azerbaijan, Tajikistan, Uzbekistan, and Kazakhstan.

European Union
Twenty-seven European countries bound by specific treaty and standard legal and commercial agreements in a large number of areas.

Foreign Direct Investment (FDI)
Investment by foreigners in a nation, typically in plant and equipment.

The European Community has given way to the **European Union** (EU), which now includes 27 European countries. Some of the nations that are now a part of the EU were once part of the USSR. These markets represent new market opportunities for business. During this time China has also opened its economy and is now the largest recipient of **Foreign Direct Investment (FDI)** or investment by foreigners typically in plant and equipment, in the world.

As a result, the world is more complex but also has more business opportunities than it ever has. This section will review some of the major institutions that impact that complex environment. The section will initially review trade agreements and the resulting organizations that impact the growth in trade. These agreements are in some cases multinational and in other cases bilateral agreements between two states. The section will also review the growth of some of the new major players on the world's economic stage. And finally, the section will highlight two organizations that are key supporters of international trade. These institutions grew out of the Bretton Woods Agreements and are important supporters of free trade around the world.

Multinational and Bilateral Agreements One of the major changes in international business is that of the growth of bilateral (between two nations) and multinational agreements and the strength of those agreements. These agreements may involve a great number of nations all over the world or involve nations in a small region. The agreements may also be very broad in nature or very specific. Below is a discussion of a few of the key agreements of which students should be aware.

The European Union. The roots of the European Union (EU) can be traced to the European Coal and Steel Community that began with six members in 1951. Those original six members were Belgium, West Germany, Luxembourg, France, Italy, and the Netherlands (part of the reason why the shock of the defeat of the EU's proposed constitution in 2005 was so great was because two of the original members of the EU–France and the Netherlands–led the defeat.) Today, the EU consists of 27 member nations including: Austria, Belgium, Bulgaria, Cyprus, the Czech Republic, Denmark, Estonia, Finland, France, Germany, Greece, Hungary, Ireland, Italy, Latvia, Lithuania, Luxembourg, Malta, the Netherlands, Poland, Portugal, Romania, Slovakia, Slovenia, Spain, Sweden, and the United Kingdom.

The EU has created a borderless union of 27 countries approximately the size of the United States with an increasingly standardized business environment. Some things, such as tax laws, are determined locally, but many issues, such as product standards and the nature of expected competition, are determined centrally by the EU governmental body. Most nations in the EU now also participate in a single currency referred to as the Euro. The gross domestic product (GDP) of the EU stands at $16.62 trillion, while that of the U.S. is lower at $13.84 trillion; the EU's population is about 490 million, which is 185 million larger than the U.S. population of 304 million.[xiii] This makes the EU the third largest population in the world, following only China at 1.3 billion and India at 1.1 billion.[xiv] Thus, the region is larger but, in per-capita terms, has a lower economic impact than does the United States. As will be discussed in greater detail later in the book, and as can be seen in Figure 1-3, there are other nations

FIGURE 1-3 European Union Countries

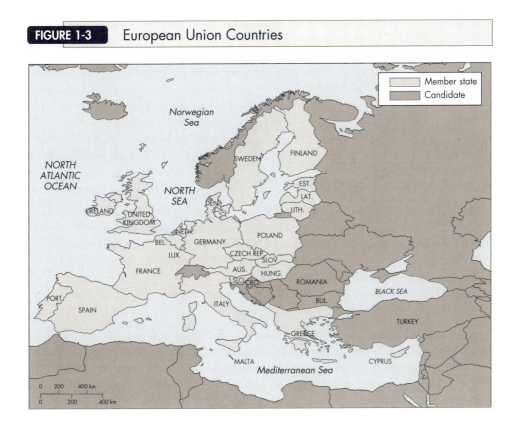

that are also candidates for EU membership, including Turkey, that will significantly expand the size and population of the EU.

The original multinational agreements that led to the formation of the EU tended to be quite specific and limited. However, the broad base of powers now taken on by the central authorities are now being directed by the bureaucracy associated with the EU. The result is that often the EU is setting the standards for the world in areas such as mergers and acquisitions and environmental domains.

World Trade Organization (WTO)
An international organization that oversees a large number of agreements defining the rules of trade between its member states.

WTO. The **World Trade Organization**, or WTO, was established in 1995 and is composed of 148 countries from around the world. The countries that are part of the agreement are committed to the promotion of trade. As signatory to the agreement, the member nations agree to abide by the rules of trade that the group develops. The establishment of rules is an umbrella agreement called the General Agreement on Trade and Tariffs (GATT), which was established in 1948. The WTO provides the ability to evaluate disputes when they arise and reach a solution, which could be difficult under the GATT alone.

Thus, the WTO did not eliminate GATT—their agreements still exist. Instead, the WTO simply created a structure to solve problems that arise under the GATT agreements and encourage the further promotion of trade. One of the key elements of the WTO is that it has the equivalent of a legal system to evaluate the case of both sides and decide who is right. The WTO even has the ability to impose penalties on those nations that do not act in the manner in which the WTO determines they should.

The GATT agreement is not a document that does not change and adapt as the environment changes. Instead it is a document that undergoes regular change as dictated in part by the outcomes of regular meetings on the nature of the agreements. The level of tariffs and barriers to trade continue to fall around the world.

NAFTA
The North American Free Trade Agreement, known usually as NAFTA, links Canada, the United States, and Mexico in a free trade sphere. NAFTA went into effect on January 1, 1994.

NAFTA. NAFTA (the North American Free Trade Agreement), an agreement signed in 1994 between Canada, the United States, and Mexico, has created a largely free-trade zone between these three nations with all tariffs eliminated as of 2003. Since the passage of NAFTA, trade between the three nations has exploded. In ten years it was found that:

- U.S. exports to Canada grew from $87.8 billion to $145.3 billion.
- U.S. exports to Mexico grew from $46.5 billion to $105.4 billion.
- Mexican exports to the United States reached over $138 billion.
- Mexican exports to Canada grew from $2.7 billion to $8.7 billion, an increase of almost 227 percent.
- Canada's exports to its NAFTA partners increased by 104 percent in value.[xv]

This outcome was quite similar in Europe when, in 1985 Spain and Portugal joined the European Economic Community, what the EU was called at that time. At that time, there were many fears about the decline in wages in Europe, as those two Iberian-Peninsula countries each had average per capita incomes of about $3500 per year. Fifteen years later, European wages continued to climb, and per capita incomes in Spain and Portugal had risen to about $15,000 USD per year, comparable with higher-income countries.

Japan-Thailand Trade Agreement. Another area of rapid growth are bilateral agreements between two nations. The Japan-Thailand Trade Agreement went beyond established regional trade agreements and allowed Japan, which has one of the world's most protected markets for rice, in part due to its strong farmer lobby, greater access to rice grown in Thailand. In turn it allowed Thailand greater access to Japanese manufacturing goods. Such bilateral agreements are actively pursued by active trading nations. The United States has bilateral agreements in place with Jordan, Chile, Singapore, Australia, Morocco, El Salvador, Nicaragua, Peru, Bahrain, Guatemala, the Dominican Republic, Oman, Costa Rica, and Honduras, plus pending agreements with Korea, Panama, and Colombia. Bilateral agreements have increasingly replaced new world-wide agreements because such broad agreements have been harder to reach (e.g., the last round of negotiations to lower trade barriers in the world, referred to as the Doha round, have been in negotiation since 2001).

New Economic Players It was noted earlier that 25 years ago it was reasonably fair to assume the major economic players in the world were either in Europe or North America. It is now a much more complex world. This section will review two major players that are new to the world-economic stage. These two countries have approximately 50 percent of the world's population. There are other interesting economic players that we will also discuss throughout this book but the sheer size of these two markets merits particular attention. These two markets, China and India, have experienced rapid economic growth in the past few years as illustrated by Figure 1-4.

China. China is the world's largest country in terms of population with about 1.2 to 1.5 billion. The reason for that population range in China is that as many as 300 million people (the same as the U.S. population) are believed to be undocumented workers in larger cities. China was a doctrinaire communist country until 1978, when Deng Xiaoping became its leader. He made the famously pragmatic statement that he did not care whether the cat was white or black as long as it caught the mouse. This statement meant he did not care whether the system was called capitalism or socialism as long as the people prospered. During the last 30 years China has experienced economic growth averaging about 9 percent annually. In 2007, China's current GDP stood at over $3 trillion, behind only the U.S., the EU, Japan, and Germany, though in purchasing-power parity terms it may be larger than all economies but those of the United States and the EU.[xvi] It is important to remember this is in terms of total GDP; with its population size in per-capita

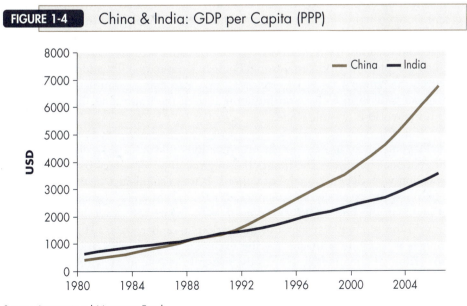

FIGURE 1-4   China & India: GDP per Capita (PPP)

Source: International Monetary Fund

HINDU RELIGION AND ITS IMPACT ON BUSINESS

Despite the fact that Hinduism is the world's oldest religion and the dominant religion in India, it is one of the world's least understood religions, and what non-Hindus do know may not be accurate. For example, many individuals do not understand that Hinduism is a monotheistic religion. Instead, many individuals in the West mistakenly believe that Hindus believe in multiple gods. In fact they believe in one God; however there are different manifestations of that God. To a Hindu, it places limits on God to think that he or she must have one given form. Instead, God as an infinite power has the ability to take many shapes.

Hindus believe that God and souls are eternal. Thus, because souls do not die (only the body that houses the soul dies), once the body dies the soul will be reborn into another entity. The nature of the entity in which the soul is born is dependent on the prior life the individual lived. However, unlike Christianity or Islam, a soul is never condemned to an eternal life of damnation in hell. Instead the soul can improve or change each time it is born. The basis of the actions the person has taken in a life is their karma.

The soul can improve their karma with the actions they take in each life.

For a business person doing business in India, the Hindu religion will have a variety of impacts. For example, many Hindus are vegetarians because killing animals is killing God's creation Another aspect of business that is affected is gift giving. Gifts typically are not opened in the presence of the giver for fear of offending him or her if the gift is not liked; this might create negative karma. (Do not wrap gifts in black or white because these colors are considered unlucky. Instead, use the lucky colors green, red, and yellow.) Hindu society is very hierarchical, made up of a series of castes This same focus on structure results in the leader of the organization being very powerful and typically in charge of all key decisions.

Jain, L. C., Makhija, R., Mookerjee, A., Mysore, V., Raghavan, A., Ramachandran, J., Rao, A., Roy, S., Shah, A., Viswanathan, R., Vora, A., Seshadri, D., & Vikalpa, V. R. (2006). Understanding India from a business perspective: Opportunities and challenges for MNCs. *The Journal for Decision Makers*, 31(3), 95–119.

Hinduism. http://encarta.msn.com/encyclopedia_761555715/hinduism.html.

terms, the country is still relatively poor. However, today China is seen as the greatest market opportunity in the world. This book will cover China and Chinese business in great detail because it is believed by the authors that this nation will ultimately be an economic powerhouse that will rival the United States and the EU.

India. India is the world's largest democracy and it also has the world's second largest population with approximately 1.1 billion people. The nation has undergone an economic revival in recent years and now has a GDP of $3.7 trillion in purchasing-power parity terms. The economy has averaged growth of about 7 percent since economic reform commenced in 1991.[xvii] This growth has helped to reduce poverty there by about 10 percentage points and has helped to produce a sizeable middle class. Two additional assets for India are large numbers of well-educated people, who possess strong English language skills and considerable growth in the nation's software services.[xviii] We cite many examples of economic change and growth in China and India because of the importance of these countries on the world economic stage.

Other Players. There are two other organizations that have a significant impact on international business. The first is the International Monetary Fund (IMF), an organization with over 180 member nations. It was established in 1944 as part of the Bretton Woods Agreements, mentioned earlier, that were negotiated between countries near the end of World War II as a means of providing additional stability to the economic systems of the various member states. The IMF's basic function is to provide a means for the exchange of currencies among different nations. Thus, in a manner similar to the Federal Reserve in the United States for individual banks, the IMF helps national banks exchange funds. The IMF also advises nations on how to establish sound economic policies. The bank can also lend to different nations if their balance of payments is such that they have shortages that threaten the stability of their monetary system. In such lending, the IMF typically imposes standards of behaviors that require the country to conduct certain reforms.

The World Bank, in contrast, is funded by over 100 countries with the stated goal of fighting poverty and improving the living standards of people in the developing world. Thus, the World Bank is a development bank that provides loans, policy advice, technical assistance, and knowledge-sharing services to low- and middle-income countries in an effort to reduce poverty.

Summary: Shifting International Players One of the recent trends in international management has been the growth of multinational and bilateral agreements with the goal of encouraging free trade. The success of such agreements has greatly encouraged and promoted the development of future world trade; each nation now seeks to obtain agreements with other key nations in order to obtain an early advantage in the market. It is expected that trade barriers will continue to fall in the future. Thus, the impact of international management will continue to expand. The world's competitive environment will continue to also expand with new competitors, such as China and India now challenging firms from more mature economies in North America and the EU in many domains.

Ethics Concerns

A critical issue that has always effected international management is business ethics. However, concerns for business ethics is greater today than at any time in history. Typically, things are done differently around the world. Many of these differences will confront the ethics of the business person. However, just because a given behavior or action is acceptable locally does not mean the international business person or the firm need to match the actions of those in the local environment. In arguing that in international management the business person needs to be open to cultural differences does not mean that the business person has to accept the local standard for behavior as correct in all situations. For example, because it's acceptable to discriminate against women or minorities in a given culture does not mean that you, as a business person, or your firm should practice that behavior.

Legal Foundation Chapter 3 will address legal institutions in far greater detail, however, it's important to address here some of the legal aspects that have an impact on business ethics. The absolute minimum level of ethics a business must observe are the legal standards of its nation. It is important for an international business to recognize that the laws of its nation do not necessarily stop at its country's border. Two major pieces of legislation that affect international management in the United States are the Foreign Corrupt Practices Act and the Sarbanes Oxley Act. These laws affect U.S. businesses and foreign businesses that have subsidiaries in the United States. Each of these major acts will be reviewed in turn.

Foreign Corrupt Practices Act. This act grew out of revelations that some U.S. firms had paid bribes to obtain contracts overseas. These bribes were seen as corrupting a capitalist system so that rather than the best product or firm winning a contract, the business that paid the biggest bribe got the job. As a result, it was made illegal to pay bribes to organizations and government officials in foreign countries. Even if others in a foreign country, including those in charge of the nation, believe it is acceptable to make payoffs to government officials or executive managers of major foreign firms to secure business, these

PARMALAT AND ETHICS

It is clearly a violation of ethical standards to file false financials. A number of well-publicized situations in which firms, such as Enron, filed such false financials in North America exist. But these situations are not limited to North America. Parmalat, an Italian firm based in Milan that was publicly listed in 1991 and produces several food products—milk in particular—is a case in point. The financial success allowed the family that controlled Parmalat to buy a small local football (soccer) team on which they spent the money to turn into one of Europe's major teams. After the initial listing, the company also expanded rapidly overseas. Ultimately, the firm would have over 36,000 employees with operations in 30 countries.

The firm's international expansion was funded by its 1991 public listing. However, during this time the firm also took on extensive debt, which included over $8 billion in bonds. The firm was able to obtain the debt in part by hiding over $10 billion in losses over a 10-year period. The firm's deceit was discovered when Parmalat claimed to have an account with over $4 billion at Bank of America that did not exist. It was discovered later that the CEO of the firm had pilfered over $600 million from the firm. The firm filed for bankruptcy protection in 2004 though it still operates today.

Competing internationally is hard. Recall the cases of fraud that have been notable in developed economies, such as the United States and the EU, and then consider what occurs in transitional economies that are moving from communism to market orientation where corruption may be endemic. Thus, fraud is something that consistently must be guarded against. It is interesting to note that the executives who conducted the fraud were convicted but none is expected to spend any time in jail. Instead, they are expected either to do community service or be confined to their homes.

Hamilton, S. (2005, Spring). How going global compromised Parmalat. *European Business Forum*, 65–70.

Edmondson, G., Cohn, L. (2004, January 12). How Parmalat went sour. *Business Week*, pp. 46–48.

Galloni, A. (2005, June 29). In Parmalat case 11 are convicted after plea deals. *Wall Street Journal Europe*, pp. A1, A8.

kinds of payoffs violate the U.S. law. In many emerging economies payments to officials, high and low, are an established means of conducting business.[xix] But this still does not justify such payments. This law applies to U.S. firms even if the payment is not made in the United States but occurs in the foreign country. If a U.S. citizen or firm is involved in this kind of bribe, it is a violation of the law. The law does, however, allow "facilitating payments." Sometimes payments to government officials can remove the bureaucratic barriers to investments that create jobs and certain payments may be legal for U.S. firms and individuals. However, it is critical that a firm's legal department be checked with before undertaking any such "expense."

Sarbanes-Oxley Act. The Sarbanes-Oxley Act was passed in response to perceived business misconduct. The act was considered for a number of years, but the bankruptcy of Enron, and the governance and accounting problems highlighted as a cause for the bankruptcy, led to the ultimate passage of the act. The Sarbanes-Oxley Act's major provisions include:

- CEO and CFO certification of financial reports
- Real-time disclosure of material events
- Requirement of audit-committee independence
- Accelerated reporting of trades by insiders
- Ban on loans to any insiders, including executive officers and directors
- Prohibition on insider trades during pension fund blackout periods
- Required reporting if business has a code of ethics for senior management
- Auditor independence assured by restricting non-audit services and rotation of audit partners
- Enhancement of criminal and civil penalties for violations of securities law
- Enhanced civil sanctions

It is important to note that the costs of the Sarbanes-Oxley Act have been quite high, particularly for small firms. Figure 1-5 shows that today, as a result of the

FIGURE 1-5   Cost of Sarbanes Oxley

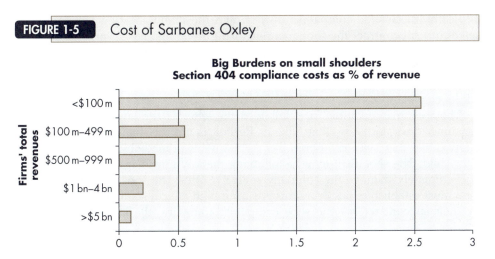

Big Burdens on small shoulders
Section 404 compliance costs as % of revenue

Source: AeA http://www.economist.com/business/displayStory.cfm?story_id=3984019

Sarbanes-Oxley Act, accounting as a percentage of operating expenses for smaller businesses has become quite high in the United States.

Beyond the Legal Foundation of Ethics Business ethics is more than simply enforcing the law. To rely on ethics laws to direct a firm's ethical behavior has proven insufficient. A firm can cause significant harm to its business and its stakeholders by simply relying on the law for its guiding principals. For example, major shoe manufacturers, such as Nike and Reebok, typically have their shoes made in emerging markets, such as Indonesia, China, or Vietnam.

SHERATON IN MEXICO

The danger in relying on legal standards alone is that the answer may not be clear. In Mexico, the Sheraton Hotel was playing host to a visiting group of dignitaries from Cuba. The plan was for them to discuss with a group of American business people how trade could be increased between the two nations, particularly in the oil industry.

Today trade is prohibited between the U.S. and Cuba. This trade limitation became stricter in recent years under former President Bush. Today the trade embargo is so strict that only limited humanitarian goods such as medicine can be shipped to Cuba. The U.S. Treasury Department knew of the meeting between the Cuban dignitaries and American business people at the Sheraton Hotel. As a result, the Treasury Department threatened the Starwood Corporation (the owner of Sheraton) with a violation of the law if they allowed the meeting to go forward. The penalties for violation of the law, include a $1 million fine and up to 10 years in jail for a firm's CEO.

However, the Mexican government also has laws on its books that prohibit firms from participating in illegal boycotts, and the Mexican government considers the boycott of Cuba to be illegal. It should be recognized that many countries have such laws including the United States. At one time Arab nations refused to do business with firms that did business with Israel. There are strict laws that prohibit U.S. firms from participating in such a boycott. The result was that the Sheraton was faced with making choices about conflicting laws. The U.S. government said it would violate U.S. law if it allowed the meeting to occur while the Mexican government said it would violate Mexican law if it did not allow the meeting to go forward. What was the firm to do?

Ultimately, the Sheraton cancelled the meeting and obeyed the U.S. law. As a result the firm was roundly criticized in the Mexican press. Initially the hotel was ordered to close for business permanently by the Mexican government; after extensive lobbying the closure order was changed to a fine of over $20,000. However, simply obeying the law in this setting would not have given Sheraton direction on which was the ethical choice because the laws were in conflict.

Sheraton's Fawlty Torres. (2006). *The Economist*, 378(8468), 34.

ETHICS

Typically, these shoe companies do not own the manufacturing factory themselves but subcontract the shoe manufacturing to others. However, a number of different times these offshore manufacturers have subcontracted to firms with harsh working conditions, often for very young children (children are prized in manufacturing for their small and nimble fingers, which allow them to do things adults cannot).

The shoe manufacturers had followed the letter of the law. But the average consumer does not know that Nike or Reebok is not the manufacturer. All they know is that they see a shoe from that company being made by a very young and poor child. The shoe firm may be following the law but images of such children will ultimately damage the company severely. Thus, the shoe firms have found they must establish ethics programs ensuring high ethical standards are followed by their subcontractors—the shoe companies following the law by itself is not enough.

Often the first step beyond simply following legal standards is the creation of an "ethics code" of do's and don'ts by the international firm. But such codes have proven to be unsatisfactory. The reason is that most codes cannot cover the full range of ethical issues that a firm will face. The result is that individuals will say they felt a given action was consistent with the code of ethics when most individuals in the firm believe it does not. Thus, most firms move beyond either simply following the law or developing a code of do's and don'ts to seeking to have individuals develop a sense of what the firm's view of ethics is.

The means that a firm will seek to have specific training include cases and illustrations demonstrating the nature of the judgments that the firm wishes to have pursued. The firm will also seek both positive and negative illustrations to demonstrate their support for given ethical values. The positive reinforcements are statements that recognize and reward individuals for things consistent with the ethical values of the firm. The negative reinforcements are firing or punishing of individuals who violate these ethical standards. Firms have found that if they do not pursue such demonstrations of support, then ethics become only words that often are not taken seriously. Therefore, most international firms will ensure that there are public demonstrations, both public and private, that illustrate the firm's ethics.

As a result, ethics are something that each firm must establish individually. In developing their ethical standards, things that firms need to keep in mind include the following:

1. Business ethics is, in part, concerned with understanding the firm's stakeholders and their needs and desires. Stakeholders are those individuals and institutions that affect the firm's success. To illustrate, employees, regulators, customers, and suppliers all impact the success of a firm. These individuals and firms have needs and desires that may not align perfectly with the firm's goal of profit maximization. These goals and desires need to be considered by the business. Often when firms have found themselves in ethics-related problem situations, it's because they've allowed their desire for profit maximization to unreasonably override all other factors in the firm. By considering such stakeholders and the impact on their actions, firms are able to make more rational decisions that are less likely to cause ethical problems.

2. External reference points are useful to judge whether behaviors are ethical. International businesses must consider more than what the behavior standards are in a given country. The firm must also determine what the standards are for business in the broader global community. For example, a business unit for a multinational firm that operates in Cambodia may find that it is acceptable behavior for Cambodian businesses to hire workers under the age of 12 or 14 years. In fact, providing the jobs to these young people may be highly valued since it allows the children to provide their families with critical resources.

BRAZIL – CULTURE AND ETHICS

The Brazilian economy is one of the major economic engines in South America with a GDP of approximately $1.5 trillion. Because Brazil was colonized by Portugal, most of its citizens speak Portuguese.

Conducting business in Brazil is largely based on personal relationships. Therefore, having personal connections is critical. If a business person does not already have such relationships, building them is an important long-term process. Punctuality is not of great importance in Brazilian business although the classic advice is for the foreigner to be on time but not to expect the Brazilian to be on time. This is because you are more dependent on seeing them than they are on seeing you. This is particularly the case if you are in the country for a short time. It is important when setting meeting times between other meetings that individuals leave plenty of time because traffic in all major cities is horrible. Private offices are not the norm in the country so there are typically a lot of interruptions to any meeting. The final decision in any negotiation will ultimately be made by the senior manager at the firm.

Corruption is widespread in Brazil. This corruption has a strong negative impact on costs in the country. For example, the cost of handling containerized cargo in the nation's port is twice what it is in the United States or Europe.[2] The corruption occurs with government officials and their political parties. Today, a major corruption scandal rages where the money did not go to individuals but to the President's political party to run his campaign. The term used by Brazilians for someone who helps facilitate payments to these individuals is the *despachante* or middle man. If doing business in Brazil, firms will need to determine how to deal with such requests for payments. Some are bluntly illegal under the Foreign Corrupt Practices Act in the United States. But some could be considered facilitating payments, which are legal. Each firm will need to determine how it will handle each of the different activities.

However, the business unit is part of a worldwide business. The manager needs to think how that action appears globally. The firm needs to help managers develop those external standards and ensure they are fully understood and practiced throughout the firm.

3. Firms need to glorify the stories and examples of those judgments that individuals make that demonstrate the kinds of ethical standards they want to encourage. Ethics is somewhat like art—it is in the eye of the beholder. Thus, for employees to understand what ethical behavior is, they need to be shown which behaviors are appropriate and which are not.

   For example, many firms believe a business should add more to society than just jobs. If this is the case for your firm, then stories that provide examples of where that occurs need to be promoted. For example, ABB is a major Swiss engineering conglomerate. The firm has determined that part of its ethical standards include not only building major transmission facilities but also helping to provide electricity to individuals in locations where they normally would not have access to it. Thus, in Tanzania, the firm helped to build at its own expense, a system to provide electricity to parts of the population who normally would not have received electricity. The firm ensures that employees understand the firm has a commitment to more than making money at any cost.[xx]

4. Dialogue is very important in developing ethical understanding within a firm. Ethical standards within the firm do not develop by themselves. The leadership of the firm must demonstrate and talk about what behaviors they approve of and what ones they do not. Employees must feel free to ask about those issues. This is particularly true in international businesses because new or unknown situations could develop on a regular basis.

Ethical Choices It was noted earlier that firms help employees gain a deeper understanding of the firm's views on ethics. Examples of the issues that firms may choose to discuss, or develop cases to allow for discussion are listed below. It

[2]Business Basics in Brazil. http://www.brazilbrazil.com/basicbiz.html

is important to note that a typical situation is for managers to face settings that pit one "right" value against another "right" value. Consider the dilemma of the following situations where there are two "right" alternatives:[xxi]

- It is right to protect the endangered spotted owl in the old-growth forests of the American Northwest—and right to provide jobs for loggers.
- It is right to provide children with the finest public schools available—and right to prevent the steady upward march of taxes.
- It is right to refrain from meddling in the internal affairs of sovereign countries—and right to help protect the innocent in warring regions where they are subject to significant aggression and genocide.
- It is right to resist importing products made in developing countries to the detriment of the environment—and right to provide jobs, even at low wages, for citizens of those countries.

Tough choices like these do not center upon right versus wrong. They involve two rights. They are genuine dilemmas precisely because each side is firmly rooted in one of our basic, core values. Four such dilemmas are so common to our experience that they stand as common ethical conflicts that all of us are likely to experience:[xxii]

- Truth versus loyalty
- Individual versus community
- Short term versus long term
- Justice versus mercy

Ethics Summary Though many people think of ethics as a simple choice of right versus wrong (usually when they say "right" they mean what fits their definition of right), ethical choices in international management often mean choosing between either two bad choices where you try to do the least harm, or paradoxically as the examples above suggest, between two rights. The latter often proves the tougher challenge. The exercises at the end of this chapter will demonstrate the difficulty in balancing these tough choices. Read them and think about what you would do in those settings.

SUMMARY

This chapter laid the foundation for the study of international management and examined the drivers for the internationalization of business, including technology, information access, and financial changes. The current status of globalization in business was then discussed. The chapter highlighted some factors that challenge students' understanding of international business. Finally, the topics of ethics and the important issues that it plays in international business were addressed.

By studying the theory and models of international business you will be able to understand how to work in different international settings. This book employs numerous rich examples and models of international business in various settings, allowing students to apply these concepts and to become familiar with some situations that may arise within an international business.

The book will initially explore the topic of culture. It is the foundation for most differences found in international business. The list of following chapters is below and is summarized in Figure 1-6:

Chapter 2 – Culture and International Management
Chapter 3 – The Economic, Legal, and Political Environment

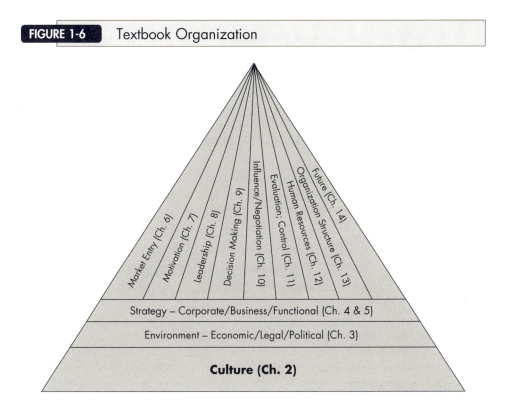

FIGURE 1-6 Textbook Organization

Future (Ch. 14)
Organization Structure (Ch. 13)
Human Resources (Ch. 12)
Evaluation; Control (Ch. 11)
Influence/Negotiation (Ch. 10)
Decision Making (Ch. 9)
Leadership (Ch. 8)
Motivation (Ch. 7)
Market Entry (Ch. 6)

Strategy – Corporate/Business/Functional (Ch. 4 & 5)

Environment – Economic/Legal/Political (Ch. 3)

Culture (Ch. 2)

Chapter 4 – Strategy Fundamentals and Corporate Strategy
Chapter 5 – Business- and Functional-Level Strategy
Chapter 6 – International Market Entry
Chapter 7 – Motivation
Chapter 8 – Leadership
Chapter 9 – Decision Making
Chapter 10 – Influence and Negotiation
Chapter 11 – Evaluation and Control
Chapter 12 – Human Resources Management
Chapter 13 – The Structure of the International Firm
Chapter 14 – The Future of International Management

MANAGERIAL GUIDELINES

Studying international management provides students with a foundation to international business. At the end of each chapter are points that will be useful to the students and business people as they implement the material presented in the chapter in their actual work. There is also a table that presents additional information in a very accessible and applicable format. Finally, at the end of the managerial guidelines in each chapter are additional readings and web pages that can be used for students who wish to gain more information on the topics covered in that chapter.

1. The pace of internationalization has increased in recent years and will likely expand further in the future.
2. There are many cultural differences that can easily be misunderstood if the business person does not expand their understanding of the setting before beginning to conduct business in the environment.

3. The manager can prepare for these cultural differences before conducting business in a given environment. Therefore, it is wise for a business person to seek to expand his or her understanding of different business environments before attempting to conduct business there.
4. Legal standards should always be observed—if not, long term consequences to the business can be severe.
5. Legal standards, however, are not enough. Additionally, the firm needs an active policy detailing their ethical standards and how those standards are to be acted upon.

Table 1-1 will be useful to students and managers as they enter different international markets to ensure that they are not allowing their biases to color their expectations and interpretation of those settings.

TABLE 1-1   Misperceptions and Misunderstandings of Major Countries and World Regions

Countries and Regions	Misperceptions and Misunderstandings
China	China sees itself as a highly developed and cultured country that became only temporarily poor in the last century. Those doing business in China need to acknowledge this belief and act accordingly. If foreign business people publicly call China a developing country, they will likely insult local government officials and business people (though organizational systems should be carefully designed to accommodate China's underdevelopment in key areas, such as the rule of law).
European Union	Those not familiar with Europe may think that all European countries are alike, even lumping the Nordic countries (Sweden, Norway, Denmark, and Finland) and the United Kingdom with Continental Europe. In spite of Europe's nominal unification, citizens of these countries see themselves as being quite distinct from one another and may even be insulted if you fail to recognize those differences.
United States	People not from the United States only know the country from its movies, television programs, and other media. They are often surprised to know that the United States has four major, distinct subcultures that differ considerably from each other and from how Hollywood portrays Americans. Their different views affect everything from how they see the U.S. position in the world to what products they buy.[xxiii]
Japan	Those who are not familiar with East Asian countries may assume that major countries, such as Japan and China are quite similar. Some students even mix up China and Japan, believing that Hong Kong is in Japan and Tokyo is in China. Yet China and Japan are as different as France and Germany and the two countries have some long standing differences dating back to two wars fought in the last 120 years. Japan sees itself as quite distinct from most other East Asian countries. In particular, Japan is a high-trust society that depends heavily on shame to control behavior. This differs from the lower-trust societies of China and East Asia (Taiwan, Hong Kong, and the overseas Chinese communities in East Asia), where more rules and sanctions on behavior are typically utilized.
India	India is a much more heterogeneous country than most outsiders realize. Although predominately Hindu, it has a large and vocal Muslim minority and a fast growing Christian minority among the large poorer sector of society. India has numerous dialectic groups and major differences between the cultures of the north (thought to be more formal and bureaucratic) and south (thought to be more entrepreneurial and less respectful of the rules).
Middle East	It is tempting to see the Middle East as one monolithic, Arab, Islamic culture. There are twenty-five or so states in the Middle East today, yet the briefest look through the histories and sacred texts of the region suggests there were hundreds of other possibilities for modern statehood. There are many would-be countries: Samaritans and Nabaeans, Jephusites and Hadhramis, Sumerians, Sabaeans and Sassanians, Kurds and dozens more. And they are quite distinct in their beliefs, culture, and sometimes even practices of Islam and other customs. Pan-Arab movements occasionally arise but have had little historical success.[xxiv]

Latin America	Like the Middle East, Latin America is comprised of numerous countries. Although most Latin Americans speak Spanish, more citizens of the largest country in the region, Brazil, speak Portuguese and not Spanish. Latin American countries also have very different traditions and differing populations. Argentina, for example, has many more citizens of Italian and German origin than those of Spanish origin. Some countries, such as Bolivia, have a heavy native Indian influence.
Africa	Africa is quite diverse. There are a large number of tribes with their own traditions. In addition, some African countries have been influenced by France and Belgium—so called French Africa. Others have been more influenced by Great Britain or Germany and The Netherlands. The influence is not only in terms of language, but each country left its particular institutions. Those with a strong British influence are more successful, such as South Africa. While ignored economically for many years, South Africa's wealth of resources is creating new economic growth and opportunities in the region. Particularly interesting has been the ability of other emerging economies such as China to invest successfully in Africa in spite of political turmoil.

CULTURE AND DOING BUSINESS IN GERMANY

Germany has the fifth largest economy in the world. The nation of approximately 82 million is technologically advanced and produces some of the world's highest-quality products in electronics, steel, chemicals, machinery, and machine tools. Germany also has a distinct culture that business people must take care to understand when doing business there.

The Germans have a well-deserved reputation for order and punctuality. Thus, in doing business in Germany it is important that punctuality be maintained. Additionally, the rank of the person needs to be acknowledged because titles are important in recognizing the order of things. For example, a person with a doctorate is referred to in German as "Mr. Doctor." A person holding a doctorate and a professor position is referred to as "Professor Doctor." The Germans are also often sticklers for the rules and conditions of a contract. We will see that in many nations contracts are little more than guidelines for behaviors at one point in time. However, this is not the case in Germany.

When eating, the Germans generally hold their forks in their left hand and knives in their right throughout the meal. It is also normal for meals to be served with beer. Thus, even at a McDonald's the most widely consumed drink is beer. Germans tend to be very well versed in international affairs and knowledgeable about the world. They also tend to be direct and honest in their answers.

In the early 1990s, Germany reunited the former communist East Germany with the democratic West. The unified nation continues to pour billions of dollars each year into efforts to help East Germany match the economic progress of the West. However, the economic and political divide between the two regions of the country remains large.

CULTURE

ADDITIONAL RESOURCES

Friedman, T. L. (2000). *The Lexus and the Olive Tree: Understanding Globalization*. New York: Anchor Books.

Friedman, T. L. (2007). The *World Is Flat 3.0: A Brief History of the Twenty-first Century*. New York: Picador.

Bhagwati, J. (2004). *In Defense of Globalization*. New York: Oxford University Press.

EXERCISES

Opening Vignette Discussion Questions

1. Why do you think Toyota has been so successful?
2. How easy do you think it has been for Toyota to adapt to the changes it faces?
3. Do you think it would be easy for an international firm, such as Toyota, to lose its focus on what it is trying to achieve?

DISCUSSION QUESTIONS

1. While the flow of information has increased around the world, firms, such as Google and Yahoo!, still must compromise on what information they will provide to their customers if they are to have access to markets such as China's. Do you think this is an appropriate compromise or not?
2. How has the formation of the EU created new opportunities for member countries? Of what importance are these opportunities to international managers in other geographic regions such as North America or Asia?
3. Many multinational corporations have secured a foothold in China and India, and many more are looking to develop business relations there. Why does this region of the world hold such interest for international management? Identify and describe some reasons for such interest.
4. Do you believe that ethics can be taught? Why or why not?
5. Do you think the Foreign Corrupt Practices Act in the United States or similar laws that exist around the world are good?

IN-CLASS EXERCISES (adopted from Kidder, 1996)

1. Tough organizational choices

Tough organizational choices do not always involve professional codes or criminal laws. Nor do they always involve big, headline-size issues. They often operate in areas that laws and regulations do not reach. That was the case for a corporate executive with a worldwide manufacturing firm, who faced such a choice shortly after becoming manager of one of his company's plants in California. He learned that the producer of a major television series was regularly using the plant's parking lot for filming on the weekend. Top management at his firm's corporate headquarters had given the producer permission to do the filming on the weekend, when the lot was empty, and did not ask for any money. The former plant manager, Mr. Gray, was giving up weekend time with his family without pay in order to be on location and assist the television crew.

So this year, after Mr. Gray retired, the new plant manager decided that he would do the same. The shoot went as planned. At the end of the day, the producer came up to him, thanked him for his help, and asked how the check for five hundred dollars should be made out. Surprised, the manager replied that it should be made out to the corporation. Surprised in turn, the producer responded that the check had always been made out to Mr. Gray and wondered if he should simply make it out to the new plant manager. He learned from the producer that Mr. Gray had asked to be compensated for a full day at the parking lot on the weekend and since the company did not ask for money from the film company, they agreed to pay Mr. Gray.

The company incurred no expenses because of the shoot so it did not ask or expect any payment. The plant manager, however, was giving up an entire weekend day with no additional compensation, except for what the television company was offering him. And it was the asset of his company that made the shoot, and the compensation, possible.

Discussion: To whom should this money have been given (if anyone)? Was this a payment to the corporation or a contribution for the plant manager's personal services? If the latter, was it a payoff to ensure that the same site would be available next year, or a gesture of appreciation for the manager's helpfulness? Furthermore, if he did turn over the check to the corporation, would that lead to questions about what happened to last year's money and cause trouble for

Mr. Gray, who may have rationalized the issue in a different way and felt comfortable accepting the money? What would you do if you were the new plant manager in this case? What would you tell your boss? Or would you just take the check and keep quiet? It is a lot of money, and they seem to want to pay it to you and not the firm.

2.   African plane

You are working for a multinational enterprise in west Africa. Imagine that there has just been an incident between your country and the country in which you are working. A military cargo plane from your country crashed into a large, new building that was just built downtown. Although it was clearly an accident and fortunately only a couple of locals were killed, the populace has become very angry and their government seems to be mobilizing them for major protests. You cannot believe that anyone would blame your company for it, though your firm is one of the main suppliers for that type of plane. You hear loud noises outside of your building and wonder what you should do next. The street outside is filled with people waving signs, and the crowd seems to be moving quickly, headed toward your country's embassy. Busses are already unloading a number of protesters. It is a four-kilometer walk back to your house, and you cannot make it unnoticed on the main streets, but the side streets are known to be unsafe.

Discussion: What do you do about getting out of this situation, or do you just ride it out? What do you do about work? What can you do about protesters and the media who are certain to confront you?

3.   Consider the following vignettes in each of the four ethical dilemma categories and consider what you would do in each setting. Each setting contrasts two ethical rights.

Truth versus Loyalty. As a professional working for a large defense-electronics firm in Ireland, John found himself riding a roller coaster of concern about layoffs. Every few years, it seemed, top management slashed jobs as work slacked off, only to hire again when things started looking up. So when John and his team members noticed that the executives were again meeting behind closed doors, they suspected problems.

John's boss, however, was a good friend—and also talkative. So John did not worry about asking him about the future. John's boss explained the contingency plan at length, mentioning that, if layoffs were needed, John's team member, Jim, would likely lose his job. He also made it plain that John was not to mention this to anyone.

Not long after that conversation, Jim approached John and asked whether he could confirm what the rumors were saying: that he (Jim) would be the target. That request landed John right in the truth-versus-loyalty dilemma. Because John knew the truth, honesty compelled him to answer accurately. However, he had given his word to his boss not to break a confidence, and felt a strong loyalty to that relationship.

Discussion: How would you handle this dilemma?

Individual versus community. In the mid-1980s, the administrator of a residential-care facility in Great Britain received a letter from a nearby university hospital, where his elderly residents typically went for medical care. The letter reminded him that five of his residents had recently had surgery at the hospital. It also informed him that the medical staff suspected that some of the blood used in their transfusions may have been tainted with the HIV virus. While making it clear that the probabilities of infection were low, the letter asked him to call the hospital immediately and arrange further testing for these five patients.

That letter presented him with a difficult question: What should he tell, and to whom should he tell it? Given the public and professional ignorance about AIDS in the 1980s, and with legal regulations offering him little guidance, he felt certain that if he told his staff, their fear would be so great that they would refuse to enter the rooms of those five residents, making it impossible to deliver even basic care to them. Suppose he did not tell the staff and one of them contracted AIDS? Surely he would be responsible.

As it happened, none of the five ultimately tested positive, but that crucial fact was unknown at the time. What was he to do? He knew it was right to honor the individual rights of each of those five residents—the privacy of their medical histories, the expectation of high-quality care at his facility, their dignity as individuals. It was right, in other words, to say nothing.

On the other hand, he knew it was right to protect the community from disease. The staff had not signed on for hazardous duty. Most of them saw themselves as unskilled hourly workers, not members of a life-endangering profession to which they had been called by duty and prepared by intensive training. Never mind that they might all phone in sick the day after the announcement. They deserved protection so they could continue to deliver care, with full regard for safety, to the many other residents who were not among the five exposed to AIDS. So it was right to tell them.

Discussion: What would you do?

Short Term versus long Term. When he graduated from college with a degree in science, Andy had found a solid job in his profession, married, and had two sons. Twelve years later, he moved to another firm that promised steady advancement within its managerial ranks. A devoted family man, he admired his wife's dedication to raising the boys. He also observed that his sons, who were approaching their teen years, benefited greatly from his fatherly friendship and advice, especially as they approached what he and his wife realized could prove to be a difficult period in their upbringing. So he made a commitment to spend plenty of time with them, playing baseball and helping with their schoolwork.

However, he also loved his work, and he was good at it. It quickly became apparent that, to advance rapidly up the managerial ranks, he needed an MBA. An evening and weekend program was offered by a nearby university that would allow him to continue full-time employment. But it would soak up the next few years of his life and throw most of the family activities into his wife's hands.

Andy's dilemma set the short term against the long term. It was right, he felt, to honor his family's short-term needs; to stay close to his sons at a time when his influence was so important. Yet it was right to build for the long-term needs of his family by equipping himself with an education that would make him a better provider in the coming years, when he would presumably need to pay college tuition for his sons.

Discussion: What should Andy do?

Justice versus Mercy. The feature editor of a major daily newspaper in the state of New South Wales (NSW), Australia found himself in charge of a broad array of different departments. Like most newspapers, this one ran features on education, books, science, and the arts—as well as on cars, chess, stars, gardening, and food. The skill of the writer is important as a well-crafted story could seize and hold attention just as well as a breaking front-page sizzler.

A new young woman writer for the food page had just been hired. She had come from one of Australia's finest universities, and had progressed rapidly to the point where, as assistant editor, she wrote regularly. She had submitted a story on fruit recipes that was awaiting publication in the next few days.

The next day the chief food editor—a woman with decades of experience and one of the best in the business anywhere—came into the editor's office. In one hand she held a copy of the story on fruit. In the other hand she held a battered, tan cookbook some 30 years old. She laid each on the editor's desk. In the pages of that cookbook was the young woman's story, printed almost word for word.

Among the cardinal sins of journalism, one stands supreme: never plagiarize someone else's work. Nothing is drummed more insistently into the minds of young journalists. Copying someone else's work defrauds readers, violates intellectual property, and can ruin careers. This was no right-versus-right ethical dilemma. For the young writer, it was a pure and simple case of right-versus-wrong moral temptation—and she had made the wrong choice.

In spite of the apparent clear-cut answer to her wrongdoing, the editor still felt he faced an ethical dilemma. On one hand, he wanted to grab her by her lapels and toss her out of the front door and onto the street, telling her to never come back to the newspaper, or to any paper or magazine anywhere in New South Wales. On the other hand, the editor wanted to quietly ask her what could have possessed her to copy a story and recipe from a published source.

The editor wanted to see justice done in a very clear-cut situation of right and wrong. Yet he also wanted to be understanding and compassionate to a young journalist, who had just made one mistake, which could still be quietly corrected.

Discussion: It was right to enact justice, but mercy is also a virtue. How would you handle this situation? Can you work out a solution that is both merciful and just?

TAKE-HOME EXERCISES

1. On balance, how has globalization performed in the countries that have become most globalized? Select a country that globalization has helped and explain how and why that country was helped. Give examples.
2. Research the pros and cons of globalization. How can firms and governments help to reduce the effect of globalization's cons? If you enter the term "anti-globalization organization" into an online search engine, you will be able to locate many arguments against globalization.
3. How can firms, nongovernment organizations (NGOs), and governments help to reduce the effect of globalization's cons? Are there such efforts under way in the world now that you can identify?
4. Locate a recent accounting or bribery scandal that has occurred in your home country. Read the stories about the situation? What rationale was offered by those who committed the offense? What do you think of their rationale?

SHORT CASE QUESTIONS

Hynix Semiconductor of South Korea and Restructuring (p. 13)

1. Discuss why you think business groups have developed in environments, such as Asia but not in North America? (We will discuss this issue later in the book to a greater degree.)
2. Why do you think South Korea has developed a tradition of strong unions when most of the rest of Asia has not? How will this impact your business dealings in the country?
3. Why do you think the effort to reform business groups has now slowed as the economy has improved, especially when the result for Hynix looks so good?

2

CULTURE AND INTERNATIONAL MANAGEMENT

Overview

One of the key challenges in doing business internationally is the considerable differences in culture around the world. When we talk about culture we are discussing those subtle but profound things that shape differences in values and behavior in societies. Cultural differences can be seen in a wide range of everyday things, such as how close individuals stand when talking (North Americans stand about one arm's length apart when talking, but people in other countries tend to stand much closer together), the nature of communication between individuals (for example, in Russia, China, and Japan there is a great hesitancy to say no directly in response to a request, while in Anglo countries such as Australia and the United States there is no similar hesitancy), and how influential each country's legal system is (in China the legal system has great flexibility in how different laws are interpreted and enforced, while common-law countries, such as the United Kingdom or the United States, rely on a large body of case law and commentary). To understand why management can differ in diverse areas of the world it is vital to understand culture and its consequences. This chapter will examine culture—a topic that provides important foundational material for much of what we will examine later in the book. The topics covered in this chapter include:

- Learning about different cultures that exist around the world.
- Conceptual models for better understanding the world's cultures.
- Understanding the impact of environmental factors on culture.
- Identifying distinctive management styles that exist in different countries.

CULTURAL CONFUSION: AN ACCENTURE MANAGER IN INDIA

A senior information technology manager working for Accenture from the United Kingdom was running a major IT and support operation in India. Accenture is a major consulting firm and the support operation was on behalf of a large consumer electronics firm. The manager was concerned that the Indian IT support employees were not being helpful to the customers calling from the U.S., the United Kingdom, and other Commonwealth countries. He knew about the lack of assistance to those customers because there were many complaints. These problems had reached a crisis point, and the client was asking Accenture to considering canceling the contract.

The manager had carefully instructed his Indian employees on how to help the customers who were calling. The Indian employees he found were easily trained and very attentive. Indian culture was very hierarchical with the group playing a very strong role. As the employees were trained in the various regional accents they expected to hear in the United Kingdom and elsewhere, they learned the material quickly. The employees were even taught how to use similar spoken inflections. The manager was therefore surprised when the customers were still unhappy and giving their customer service very low ratings.

Customers reported that the Indian employees answered their questions too narrowly and literally, and they made little effort to supply extra information that the customer needed but did not know how to ask for. This puzzled the Indian employees who felt they were answering the questions asked—what more could the customers want? The employees also felt that some customer requests were difficult to figure out: customers used slang that the Indian employees did not understand, and they insisted on urgent action that the Indian staff had trouble understanding—how could the customers be in such a rush at midnight to fix a

computer problem? The British site manager decided that he needed to conduct more training, especially something management scientists were calling "empathy training" to help employees better understand the customers and their needs, particularly the urgency to get a computer fixed.

To illustrate the difficulty faced at the firm, one customer was making a second call about the printer on his home network not printing. The Indian employee did a nice job diagnosing the problem in the second call, figuring out that it was a simple communication problem of some kind, perhaps with the mechanical AB switch the customer had set up with his PC to switch between the printer and another device. The employee had become convinced that it was a hardware problem and that the customer had to contact the computer store that sold him the switch and cable. The customer was not happy with that, because in a prior call, the Indian support staff had told him how to set up the printer and advised him to buy the switch in the first place. Now the customer felt that the support center was not being helpful about the resulting problem. He did not believe the switch was broken. He asked to speak to the manager, and since the United Kingdom manager was unavailable at that time, he took the call. After questioning the customer, the manager discovered that the customer had purchased the wrong type of AB switch—the switch purchased was designed to attach two PCs to one printer, rather than attaching two printers to one PC, which is what the customer actually wanted (the two types of switches are generally not substitutable for each other). The customer was understandably irate, and asked, "Why didn't the staff warn me that there are *two types* of AB switches? That is an easy mistake to make if you don't know these devices well!" The support staff had initially been too casual in instructing the customer, and had not reminded the

customer to be careful not to buy the wrong type of switch.

The British manager angrily told his staff later that one simple reminder to the customer in the original call would have avoided this problem, and later, one additional question would have identified the problem, rather than telling the customer that they could not help and to simply contact the vendor the next morning.

Similar problems occurred when customers were instructed to buy a certain type of DVD player but were not warned about possible compatibility problems between regions; nor were customers warned about the differences between different types of PAL (British and South American) television systems. In all these cases, irate customers were understandably upset that their time was wasted, especially when a simple reminder from the support staff could have avoided these unnecessary problems. "How can I get the staff to think just a little outside of their job descriptions to let the customer know what to do and what to watch out for?" the British manager wondered.

The manager, based on his cultural expectations, assumed his employees would take the initiative and go beyond the instructions of the job, putting themselves in the customer's place. He did not reason that many of the Indian employees would be uncomfortable doing this. The cultural impact of strong hierarchical and group orientation provides many benefits, but the negative is that the employees did not want to be accused of not following their supervisor's instructions and answering customer queries to the letter. Moreover, they believed that their bosses were paid to make decisions outside of the prescribed steps, not them. The switch problem was held up by the British manager as an example of how to think beyond the customer's stated problem—not how to set up an A-B switch per se, but how to solve

(Continued)

his networking problem. Customers, the boss explained, are not always able to state their problems clearly, and, it takes asking many questions to find out what a customer's problem really is. Moreover, it is important to take the time to find this out, and put oneself in the customer's shoes.

Once the manager instructed his employees that they should ask questions beyond the basic diagnostic requirements, he even recommended two more specific questions to be sure the employees did not miss anything: "What is your situation now?" and "What are you trying to accomplish

with this hardware/software?" With this help, the employees became less anxious about looking beyond their literal job requirements. This small training step overcame a cultural difference which had the potential to derail the success of the entire business operation.

Culture
Acquired knowledge people use to interpret experience and actions. This knowledge then influences values, attitudes, and behaviors.

Understanding culture is fundamental to understanding many of the differences in business around the world. A firm operating in a single country only has to contend with the culture of that country. As a result, most managers do not find much difficulty in adjusting to regional variations within their own countries.[i] However, as business expands to different countries, the culture in each of those diverse regions must be taken into account; managers and companies that ignore cultural differences do so at their peril. The Daimler Chrysler merger will be discussed later in this text, and this short case will show that cultural differences can lead to significant difficulties in international business.

In broad terms, **culture** is the acquired knowledge people use to interpret experience and actions. This knowledge, in turn, influences the values, attitudes, and behaviors of those people. Culture, thus, is connected to the knowledge, beliefs, customs, and habits acquired by members of a society. The impact of culture on international business depends on in which regions of the world a firm is active. For example, someone from the United States would have little difficulty doing business in Canada, the United Kingdom, or Australia. However, that same person might find a very different cultural environment in countries such as India or China or even Germany. Cultural differences affect a wide range of issues: they can create a great deal of misunderstanding and strife for a manager and damage an organization's reputation in a foreign country for years. For example, early in its economic reform, China asked a number of major multinational enterprises to help modernize its industry. At the time of the request, China's market was not seen as the dynamic, growing market it is today. Thus, many firms declined, expecting to be able to pursue such opportunities later if the market proved to be more attractive. However, the officials that had invited these firms felt a loss of "face" (a cultural characteristic we will examine in detail later but that can be described as respect) when their offer was refused. As a result, when these multinational enterprises later decided that it was time to enter the China market, they were surprised when the Chinese government officials were not supportive. A lack of understanding of the cultural impact of saying no, a rational economic choice at the time, has hampered these firms' ability to enter the China market. What seemed like a rational business choice to the managers violated cultural norms in China, and hindered their later efforts to enter the growing Chinese market.

This chapter focuses on national cultures and how they impact management in different countries. There are many cultures, just as there are many languages, and it is impossible to learn about every one in detail. There are, however, some basic frameworks that help to describe and summarize national cultures that are useful in a wide range of settings. These frameworks can help students and business people to understand the similarities and differences in the national cultures of the world. It is possible to see clusters of cultures in various regions of the world. In addition, there are certain cultural protocols or etiquettes that are relevant to a variety of situations. The understanding of these broad differences will allow you to understand culture's consequences on managing internationally in a multitude of diverse settings.

PIZZA HUT AND THE ROLE OF LOCAL TASTE

An illustration of the difficulties culture can represent to a firm is the dilemma that market strategists at Pizza Hut faced in the mid-1980s. Pizza Hut, which was bought by Pepsi in the late 1970s, was encouraged by Pepsi management to "go international." At that time, Pizza Hut already had a number of overseas operations, mostly in Western European and Latin American countries. In particular, management wanted Pizza Hut to expand to new markets, such as China, where economic reforms had caused a takeoff of annual GDP growth to about 10 percent per year throughout the 1980s. The China experts warned Pizza Hut that Chinese people would not eat pizza because they do not like cheese, or cannot digest it, and tomatoes are not part of Chinese cuisine. "The Chinese consumer will reject your product, so don't bother," one well-known management academic told Pizza Hut during her presentation to their top management. "It is against Chinese culture to eat pizza," she added.

Pizza Hut was not so sure about that. Top management recalled that Kentucky Fried Chicken (KFC) was told something quite similar about the Hong Kong and Mainland China markets, that is, that Chinese cuisine already had so many types of chicken dishes that people would not like the southern U.S.–style fried chicken. In response, KFC modified their recipes slightly while introducing some side items that fit with local tastes (and price points), and KFC was able become the most successful fast food restaurant in China. Most importantly, KFC noticed that the Chinese urban consumer was becoming more mobile, and had disposable income to spend on the one child the government would let families have (China's one-child policy started in 1979).

Pizza Hut cut down on cheese and tomato sauce, and added local toppings such as soy sauce chicken, tuna fish, corn, and crab sticks. They even introduced new pizzas, such as the Thousand Island dressing pizza, which didn't use tomato sauce, and the Homemade Sweet & Creamy Pizza, which look like small apple turnovers, with a topping of sweetened condensed milk. In reporting to top management, the head of global business development reminded management that culture and tradition were not the only forces working on consumers in a given society. Local tastes are important; not only do they change, but so-called nontraditional products can be repackaged to fit local tastes and a country's changing socio-economic environment.

Ahlstrom, D. (2009). But Asians don't do that: The limits of culture as a predictive analytical device. *The Chinese University of Hong Kong, Faculty of Business Working Paper Series*, 2008–2009.

This chapter will initially illustrate the depth of impact culture has on society and then define the concept exactly. This discussion will include the range of impacts culture can have and the common mistakes firms make in dealing with culture. We will then examine different frameworks that can be used to better understand culture in a given situation. Figure 2-1 summarizes the flow of this chapter. There can be subcultures in a country, for example in Spain there are subcultures, such as the Basque and Catalonians. But here we will focus on countries' primary cultures because they will allow us to better contrast cultures around the world.

CULTURE DEFINED

Anthropology is the study of human culture and customs (*anthropos* in Greek means humankind, and *-logy* refers to the study of something). Though people often think of the study and application of "culture" in terms of rainforest tribes, all societies have a culture that is relevant to business and affects the workplace and general commercial environment.

FIGURE 2-1 Chapter 2 Conceptual Flow

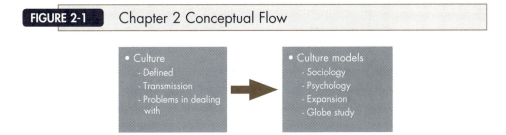

To illustrate the power of culture, consider that Hispanic people from Central America and the Caribbean started moving to the United States and Canada in large numbers after World War II. These new immigrants continued to exhibit cultural patterns in terms of beliefs and behaviors consistent with the Latin American culture. However, their children and grandchildren picked up cultural patterns consistent with North American culture very quickly, including the use of English. As a result, after two or three generations in the United States, the descendants of Hispanic immigrants have largely become indistinguishable from the general population. Spanish is no longer their primary language, the population is only slightly more likely to be Catholic, and children are just as likely to marry someone who is not Hispanic.[ii] Some of the most distinguishable aspects of U.S. culture include its high trust (in a high trust society, people will typically trust someone until that person proves untrustworthy), reliance on an abstract rule of law, the importance of punctuality, and a strong "can-do" spirit. These aspects of the culture, and even regional English usage patterns, are readily accepted by all immigrant groups within two to three generations after arriving.

In broad terms, culture can be defined as the acquired, collective knowledge of a group that they use to interpret experiences. This knowledge in turn translates into values that guide behaviors. Thus, culture includes the knowledge, beliefs, customs, and other capabilities and habits acquired by members of a society. Culture is not genetically-based or encoded but is learned by people and encouraged by societies and governments.[iii] When you talk about culture and its effects, you are primarily talking about learned behaviors of a wide range of people in a given society. Culture is not set in stone, and will change as the society undergoes change and new traditions are introduced and inculcated.[iv] However, such changes are typically slow and occur over a period of time.

HOW CULTURE IS TRANSMITTED

Culture is transmitted through its people in a variety of ways—both formal and informal.[v] Informal transmission happens every day as individuals interact with each other, watch television, or read books. Formal transmission can occur through efforts to socialize an individual, such as in schools and government.[vi] For example, Japan has a strong and distinct culture. In this society parents and grandparents consciously spend considerable effort educating children about Japan and its culture. Young Japanese children are taught at a very young age about the hierarchy in society and how they should behave. This is illustrated by the concept of *giri*, which loosely translates to the right way to behave, though it often refers directly to the rather formalized system of gift giving and exchange relations in Japanese society (when gifts are given, to whom, and how much they should cost). People from western societies are often surprised at the degree to which this formal (though largely unwritten) system of gift giving is refined in Japan. Even those who are visiting Japan for an extended stay for the first time are influenced by *giri* and the extent to which Japanese people give gifts. To violate one's *giri* obligation is to make a major social blunder—much more so than an etiquette misstep in the United States or United Kingdom.[vii] Japan has a group-oriented culture where participation in, and consistency with, the group (whatever that group may be) is extremely important. Part of fulfilling one's *giri* can involve giving the correct gifts at the correct time, making sure they are properly wrapped, and that they are in the right price range. Thus, if a manager is given a gift by an employee, protocol dictates that the manager (a person with a higher status in this situation) should give a gift that is (at least slightly) higher in value than what he or she received. Failing to understand and act appropriately on *giri* is a serious

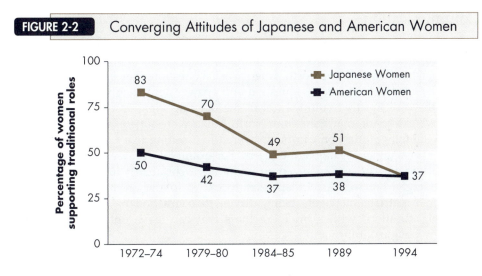

FIGURE 2-2   Converging Attitudes of Japanese and American Women

social offense that carries the stiffest of Japanese penalties: shame and perhaps even exclusion from the group.[viii] In contrast, if one fails to bring a gift or violates some other social norm in North America, such as not saying "Good morning" to coworkers, people may be offended, but it is unlikely to create major problems.

However, even an old, well-established culture like Japan's does change. For example, male and female roles have historically been very clear in Japan, considered to be a society dominated by men and masculine values.[ix] Women were thought to hold (and be accepting of) a subordinate role in Japanese society. However, recent studies show that Japanese women now have very similar attitudes to American women in terms of women's roles. These merging values can be seen in Figure 2-2.

One outcome of this shift in culture is that marriage and birth rates are dropping significantly in Japan. Historically, a Japanese woman worked until she married, then she was expected to quit and become a homemaker. Japanese women's attitude toward work has changed in a manner consistent with the United States and Europe, where many more women want to work professionally and not fully devote themselves to raising children. And with this option of professional advancement and more educational and economic opportunities, many Japanese women have postponed marriage and opted for very small (or no) families.[x]

CULTURE'S IMPACT

The impact of culture on organizations is broad. For example, culture can affect all aspects of the management of a firm including, but not limited to, strategy, hiring, pay/promotion, organization, and evaluation of performance. This wide range of issues is addressed in the following chapters.

To illustrate the extent of the impact of culture, we initially examine cross-cultural communication. The nature of communication in an international firm will be further explored later in the text as will a variety of other issues including negotiations, human-resource management, leadership, decision making, and evaluation and control. In this section we use this examination of part of the communication concerns for an international firm to illustrate that culture can affect organizations in a wide variety of unexpected ways. Following the discussion of communication, we then examine the broad roots of what leads to cultural problems for managers. This will lead to a discussion of the major cultural mistakes that firms often make and how they can avoid them.

Communication

Communication is one of the most critical factors in the success of a business. A wide range of cultural issues affects communication in an international firm. For example, when people from North America ask a question, they expect the listener to understand the intent of the question and answer accordingly. But this is not always the case in other cultures (recall the opening vignette on the Accenture manager). As a result, managers from North America are surprised when they find out how literally a question can be answered in a setting like China, even when there are no significant language barriers. For example, Chinese employees typically work in enterprises organized around a hierarchical structure in which they are encouraged not to think independently but to follow orders precisely. This results in expatriate managers being driven to distraction by their employees answering questions with a brief exactness that can leave out important (and seemingly obvious) information.

Expatriate managers in China have observed that employees in China who have been trained in the more traditional, hierarchical organizations are more likely to answer questions quite literally and fail to think laterally about the intent of the questioner or about the actual problem.[xi] Imagine, for example, that you asked an employee of yours in China if a local bus will stop at a certain train station. It would not be uncommon for that employee to answer literally and simply say "no." Yet you must remember that the employee may be failing to tell you that the bus stops a few minutes' walk away from the station.[xii] The Chinese employee is answering literally that the bus does not stop in the train station's bus bay and may have failed to grasp the intent of your question, which was to find out if the bus stops in the *vicinity* of the train station, not if the bus stops literally in the train station's bus bay. For expatriates in China or other hierarchical countries where answering queries literally and doing exactly (and often only) what is being asked is customary, it is important to keep asking questions to be sure the intent of your question is understood. Imagine how such simple, cross-cultural communication misunderstandings can affect a firm considering that there are a multiplicity of situations that can occur in a business setting on a day to day basis. You can start to understand how frustrating an international assignment can be and how it is important to prepare yourself and train your coworkers and subordinates in handling these and other problems.

Culture has an impact on not only how communication takes place in an organization but also what is actually communicated.[xiii] In the United States and other Anglo countries, such as Australia and the United Kingdom, managers tend to be focused on work-related issues when they are in the workplace. Managers typically do not want to know (and often legally cannot ask) about issues outside the sphere of work such as the worker's children, divorces, illnesses in the family, and personal finances. However, in other cultures, the manager's role is similar to that of a father. In Latin American societies, such as Mexico, the manager is expected to want to know and be willing to help on many personal issues. The same involvement by the manager is true for Chinese organizations, except in Hong Kong, which is more similar to the United States.

The manner in which information is communicated is also impacted by culture. For example, in the U.S. communication in business tends to be direct. If a mistake is made, managers are taught to confront the person directly. Similar approaches are consistent with Northern European culture in general. However, in other societies such a direct confrontation is seen as rude. For example, in East Asia, such a confrontation causes the person who is confronted to lose **face**, or the respect of his peers. The result of such a confrontation is that the person confronted may leave the organization; not necessarily the outcome intended. In such a situation, confronting the person privately so that the person can keep the respect of others is very important. If the person has seniority in the company, it may be

Face
Respect of a person's peers; avoiding embarrassment.

COMMUNICATION: MONOCHRONIC AND POLYCHRONIC

Edward Hall expanded his framework on communication by including the notion of monochronic versus polychronic cultures. Monochronic societies tend to do things in a linear way, valuing punctuality and strict schedules. Most Northern European cultures, including the Anglo-American culture, are considered monochronic; Germany tends to be the archetype for this dimension with a strong emphasis on being on time for any meeting. In Latin America and the Middle East, people tend to be more polychronic: schedules are more fluid, and people tend to do more than one thing at a time.

Business people from a monochronic culture, such as the United Kingdom, can get frustrated when colleagues from polychronic cultures, such as Italy, do not show up on time for a social dinner. In the Italian business person's mind, when he said dinner was around 8:00 pm, he expected you to go there and talk to other friends or colleagues, and perhaps start dinner, and he would arrive when he could. One U.S. business person mentioned that if he wants his Italian or Latin American colleagues to arrive at an 8:00 pm, he will tell them that dinner will start about 7:30 pm, to provide some cushion for the lateness that is common in less than crucial meetings. However, sometimes you just have to wait for people.[xiv]

It's always good to be on time for social gatherings as well as business meetings in different countries, regardless of the type of culture. An individual may be from a polychronic culture, but it does not mean he or she will tolerate someone being late to their meeting. If the person is from a monochronic culture, he or she is likely to not see you if you are late.

CULTURE

necessary to speak to his or her assistant to present the negative information, rather than speaking directly to that senior person.

Communication can be verbal or non-verbal.[xv] Anthropologist Edward Hall highlighted this in his famous book and 1960 article with Mildred Reed Hall, "The Silent Language of Overseas Business."[xvi] The Halls argued that high-context and low-context cultures exist. Low-context cultures include most cultures of the developed west, such as the United States, the United Kingdom, and Europe. High-context cultures include those of East Asia, India, and Africa.

In high-context cultures, the context in which what is spoken plays a major role in communication and the behavior of individuals. The status of the person who is speaking, why the person is speaking (was it initiated by the speaker or was it in response to a question), and the other person's status all impact the nature of how something is to be communicated. In contrast, in low-context cultures, such as the United States, the information is very straightforward, and the context has less impact on how such information is likely to be spoken and interpreted.

Americans and British, for example, generally value direct and clear communication. Most people from Anglo countries would not add honorific terms to their communication, such as calling a customer "honorable customer." In East Asia and other developing regions, such as the Middle East, communication is much higher context and such honorific terms are commonly used. Nonverbal cues are quite important in high-context cultures. For example, in most East Asian cultures, nonverbal signals, such as silence, or indirect answers, such as "That will be very difficult" (usually a polite way of saying "no" in East Asia from Japan to Indonesia) are critical to understanding what is being communicated.

So, in high-context culture:

- communication is less direct
- speech is unhurried and drawn out
- greater emphasis is placed on the context or nonverbal cues and less emphasis is placed on the actual information
- interpretation is looser, which sometimes can be problematic for the listener because answers may be indirect and it takes experience on the part of the listener to interpret what was really said
- face is very important: direct, embarrassing questions or statements are to be avoided, or asked in a very discreet way, sometimes via an intermediary

In low-context culture:

- the primary interest is the information and the context is less important
- the listener wants to get lots of information
- lack of clarity or ambiguity is generally regarded as negative
- interpretation should be unequivocal
- direct and embarrassing questions are often asked; face-saving is not very important

Communication between individuals from low-context and high-context environments can be particularly problematic. Even when individuals are proficient in a foreign language, they tend to retain the speech patterns and local dialects of their home country and culture. In addition, individuals interpret communication on the basis of one's own cultural norms.[xvii]

Problems in Dealing with Culture

Parochialism
Belief that there is no other way of doing things except what is done in one's own culture.

Culture's influence is widespread and can often affect unexpected areas. One problem is **parochialism**, or the belief that the only way to do something is the way it's done in one's own culture. People who believe this are often simply unaware of other ways of doing things. However, such individuals' inability to recognize that they are treating other individuals with less than full respect can cause difficulties in the workplace.

Ethnocentrism
The ethnocentric view of culture holds that an individual or a firm will believe that their own way of doing things is the best, and will not seek to adapt to local cultural practices.

Ethnocentrism is related to parochialism in that it reflects a sense of superiority about a person's or firm's homeland. Ethnocentric people believe that their ways of doing things are the best, no matter what cultures are involved. With parochialism the person may not know that there are other ways of doing things, but with ethnocentrism they know there are other ways but still believe their way is the best. Both parochial and ethnocentric people tend to project their values onto others, and see foreign cultures as odd or of little or no value to them. Another potential problem in dealing with culture is **polycentrism**. Polycentrism is the opposite of ethnocentrism in that people seek to do things the way locals do—"When in Rome, do as the Romans do," as the old saying goes. Although this aphorism reflects a useful approach to doing business in foreign lands, it can sometimes become a problem. For example, if a manager is abroad for a long time, he or she may start to "go native" and no longer accept the views of the home office, choosing to adopt the culture and practices of the local setting. This can result in the local culture having the final say on things such as bribes and the status of women or minorities, which may be values inconsistent with the parent firm or even homeland laws. Polycentrism is a major source of ethical lapses at many firms.[xviii]

Polycentric
The polycentric view of culture holds that multinational enterprises (MNE) should treat each international subsidiary largely as a separate national entity. This means that the subsidiary should do things in a local manner, and MNE subsidiaries may come to differ from each other.

Common Culture Mistakes

International businesses can make many potential cultural mistakes. Even firms that are culturally savvy will occasionally make cultural missteps. For example, Coke is one of the world's most admired and widespread international companies. However, when the firm entered the China market, they chose some Chinese characters for Coca-Cola that when read in Chinese sounded like Coca-Cola. Unfortunately no one at Coca-Cola bothered to check the meaning of these characters, which actually meant "bite the wax tadpole." This was certainly not an attractive name for a beverage that at the time was unfamiliar to the general Chinese population. The firm had to backtrack and choose a new set of Chinese characters for Coca-Cola. The characters they settled on still sound like Coca-Cola, but the name's meaning now gives a good feeling. Firms that need to create product names using Chinese, or other foreign languages, should be certain to get help to avoid unexpected or embarrassing translations.

Protocol
Rules for how individuals in a business setting are to interact with each other.

Protocol is how individuals in a business setting should interact with one another. An example of protocol is understanding proper etiquette when a

McDONALD'S AND ADAPTING IN CHINA

McDonald's has been successful in the Mainland China market, due in no small part to its understanding that a restaurant meal for most people in China is a big treat, particularly for children. McDonald's came to China with the expectation of opening a fast food hamburger restaurant positioned similar to those in the U.S. and their successful franchises in Hong Kong. McDonald's learned early in the strategic planning process, and from its experiences with its first few restaurants, that it faced a very different environment in China. McDonald's in North America and Hong Kong provides a cheap meal, but McDonald's cannot ever be as cheap as the food stalls and other low-cost venues in China. Realizing this, McDonald's moved aggressively to position the restaurant as a fun, mid-range priced restaurant, with high quality. To provide that quality the firm actually has limited wait staff service in some locations.

McDonald's also decided to focus on a particular niche in the market: children. China has a one-child policy that limits an urban family that is not an ethnic minority to a single child. This child is typically given a great deal of attention by the parents and grandparents. As a result, in spite of China's modest per capita income, the combination of two parents and four grandparents can produce a reasonable level of purchasing power for each child. So McDonald's determined to focus on children by doing things like running special parties for children, and having the latest toys for children (McDonalds is one of the major toy retailers in China).

The firm convinced Chinese consumers that a trip to McDonalds is a special occasion, and McDonalds has created a more upscale environment in many of its Chinese restaurants than anywhere else in the world. They have also effectively reinforced this position, keeping it different from its low-priced image in the United States and in China's special administrative region of Hong Kong.

---

prospective client or business partner arrives from overseas. Does he or she expect to be met at the airport? Should you bring him or her to lunch, or arrange a banquet dinner in their honor? To Americans, these may seem like unimportant points, but to a business person from China or other East Asian countries, this is very important and signals your commitment and seriousness about their business.

Even sophisticated firms with in-house experts to advise on avoiding cultural gaffes will still make them, including protocol mistakes. For example, not long after the recent purchase of IBM's personal computer division by the Chinese computer firm Lenovo, one of the top Lenovo executives from China visited the U.S. to meet key officials of IBM. IBM did not send anyone to the airport to meet this senior executive. As a result, the Chinese executive felt slighted and this incident has had an impact on efforts to integrate the two firms. A similar situation occurred when a senior programmer from China, working temporarily in Canada in one of the early China–Canada "worker exchange programs," caused what became a difficult international incident for the Canadian government when she refused to hand over a significant amount of sensitive computer programming she had written for the firm, even threatening to return to China with it. Her reasoning was that she felt slighted by her Canadian host firm from the moment she had arrived in Canada. For example, although an executive from the firm did meet her at the Toronto airport in the morning, the executive who met her simply brought her to breakfast, and then left. She was, in her mind, never given a proper greeting or the expected Chinese-style banquet—standard for important foreign visitors. She felt she was treated like a student intern, not the foreign dignitary that she was (she had 20 years experience in the science and technology field). This and other related "face" issues conspired to create a small crisis in the firm and even an international incident. Not understanding the expected protocol is another potential mistake and, as with communication, minor missteps can create major problems for managers and their organizations.

Culture-based mistakes that firms make can include even simple issues, such as how individuals interact with each other in a society. In many Eastern cultures, it is more common for people of the same gender to hold hands or clasp arms in public than it is for people of the opposite gender to do so. In Hong Kong, foreign visitors may be surprised to see so many teenaged girls holding hands. Yet in Hong Kong and many societies in that region, such hand holding is simply a sign of friendship; while the same behavior in individuals of the opposite gender can be seen as too forward and is usually frowned upon, at least by the older generation. In contrast, in most European and North American countries it would be unusual for two individuals of the same sex to hold hands unless there was a sexual relationship between them.

A telecommunications company was trying to expand its operations in Saudi Arabia. The negotiations had been going very well between one of the top executives of the firm and a prince, who was a major shareholder in the local firm the telecommunications company wanted to partner with. The negotiations went so well, in fact, that when the two of them went for a walk, the prince took the American executive's hand in his. To the Saudi, this was a sign of the strength of their friendship and comfort level. However, for the American it was surprising and a source of discomfort. A mistake would have been the business person reacting either physically or verbally based on his misunderstanding of the prince's intent and cultural norms. It is important to observe the behavior of those in the country that you would like to understand, particularly in terms of protocol and communication.

Avoiding Cultural Problems

Cultural sensitivity
Heightened awareness for the values and frames-of-reference of the host culture.

In the case of the telecommunications executive mentioned in the previous section, while he was surprised when the Saudi prince took his hand during their walk, he was able to react appropriately because his colleagues had prepared him for situations like this. Such training helped raise his cultural sensitivity. **Cultural sensitivity** is a state of heightened awareness for the values and frames of reference of the host culture. Managers must keep an open mind about other cultures, and be aware that they may be able to learn from them.[xix]

ANALYZING CULTURE

Knowing that culture can significantly affect how an organization conducts international business and that a variety of potential mistakes can be made when conducting business is important. The manager needs to understand culture well enough so that he or she is prepared to be successful in international business and avoid cultural gaffes. This section presents a variety of well-known frameworks that are useful for understanding the many dimensions of culture. These frameworks in part have been taken from the fields of sociology and psychology. As a result, we label the first model sociology and the second psychology. The third framework is labeled as expansive because it builds on the psychological framework, making it even more expansive than its original form. The last framework, from the major GLOBE study on culture and leadership, is the most recent. It's based on the psychological model, but is useful in developing clusters of nations that share cultural characteristics. Each framework is useful in different settings and for different people.

Sociology Framework

Kluckhohn and Strodtbeck developed a framework called dimensions of value orientation.[xx] This framework examines six dimensions, four of which are especially helpful to international managers in understanding important values of different cultures. The six dimensions include:

- Time orientation (past, present, or future)
- Space orientation (private, mixed, or public)
- Activity orientation (being, thinking, or doing)
- Relationships among people (group, hierarchical, or individualistic)

- Relations to nature (subjugation, harmony, or mastery)
- Basic human nature (evil, mixed, or good)

The first dimension focuses on time orientation. Cultures place different emphasis on history and tradition. The U.S. is less oriented toward history and tradition, compared with countries in Asia or the Middle East. Americans typically are willing to throw out old ideas and try new things; the society places only limited emphasis on historical events (to illustrate this point, U.S. students should quickly write down who fought the U.S. in the War of 1812 and what major U.S. city was burned during that war).[1] Contrast the United States' lack of historical emphasis with a country such as Saudi Arabia, which sees itself as the historical seat of Islam where tradition is paramount. Saudi Arabia continues to wrestle with change, while ensuring changes are consistent with their culture and their perceived traditions and history of Islam. For example, Saudi Arabia permitted television only when calls to prayer could be televised.

A culture's time orientation can also be an area of concern in terms of punctuality. In the United States or Germany, if someone asks you to be somewhere at a given time, then they expect you to be there at that time. In other regions, such as South America, the start time for a dinner or reception could be anywhere from one to two hours after the appointed time. If you arrive on time you may be there by yourself for a bit. Locals know that the start time for a social event is flexible and won't arrive exactly at the appointed time. This can throw off people from North America or Northern Europe, who believe that 7:00 pm means 7:00 pm and certainly no later than 7:05 pm.

A second key dimension of concern is space orientation. This dimension is concerned with whether space is viewed as a public good. In many parts of the world, usually the more crowded places like Japan or Hong Kong, space is viewed as a public good. Such an orientation is demonstrated in an office environment where most everyone works in a common area with cubical dividers. To someone from Australia or the United States, where space orientation is much more private, such working arrangements could be uncomfortable. If an Australian or a North American is waiting in line, he usually will stand back about a foot behind the person in front of him, and even further back at an ATM. In Japan and China the person will stand much closer. This can be unsettling to Westerners, who do not want strangers standing so close to them. Similarly, in some countries in the Middle East, such as Israel, it is more common for people to stand quite near during a conversation, whereas most individuals from North America would prefer to stand at arm's length. How close people stand to each other is reflective of their judgment about what their personal space is. Judgments on such things can vary widely. In the Middle East, it is considered rude for a person to step back the distance of an arm's length during a conversation. If that happens, the Middle Easterner is likely to close the gap by moving close to the other person again. To most Westerners, this lack of space in a conversation is also unsettling, but it is likely that backing up will be misinterpreted by the Middle Easterner as a sign of rejection or even rudeness.

Activity orientation refers to how proactive individuals are in society. Individuals in many societies are deterministic and believe little can be done to change fate. Consider the political situation in Russia, a culture that is not proactive. Most Russian politicians are viewed by the public at large as ineffective and often corrupt. However, the same public feels that there is little that can be done to change politics and so they assert little effort to do so. In contrast, the Canadian public is focused on "doing." An active effort is taken on by many citizens to influence the actions of the country and to help point businesses in the direction they view as right. The challenge in this is not a lack of action but rather too many conflicting actions.

---

[1]The War of 1812 was fought between the United States and England and the major U.S. city burned was Washington, D.C. In many societies, this justifies long-term resentment and hostility. Yet the United States and England are now two of the closest allies in the world, despite having fought two major wars and having come close to hostilities again during the U.S. Civil War in 1861. Contrast the U.S.'s response to the War of 1812 to the ongoing hostilities in the Balkans in Eastern Europe, conflicts that have been going on for centuries.

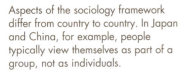

Aspects of the sociology framework differ from country to country. In Japan and China, for example, people typically view themselves as part of a group, not as individuals.

Asia Images Group/AsiaPix/Getty Images

Confucius
Chinese philosopher who lived from 551 to 479 BCE. He was from eastern China and was a well-known and well-traveled teacher and philosopher.

Another dimension to the sociology framework is the relationship among people. People can view themselves principally as part of a group, and identify with that group, or as individuals. As noted before, in Japan the focus is often on the group. For example, the classic Japanese phrase "A nail that sticks out needs to be hammered down" can mean those individuals who "stick out" need to be hammered down to conform to the group. Similarly, most Chinese people have a strong focus on the group and how they fit into the appropriate hierarchy.

To understand why Chinese people see themselves as part of a hierarchy, it is important to understand a little about Confucianism, the philosophy that forms the basis for many aspects of Chinese culture. **Confucius** (551–479 BCE) was born in eastern China and was a well-known teacher and philosopher. He lived at approximately the same time as Socrates, Buddha, and Plato. Confucius argued that a hierarchical ordering of relationships was the key to maintaining a healthy and stable society, that is, people should know their place. If people acted according to their station in life, social harmony, which was the ultimate goal of a society, would prevail. Confucius believed the hierarchy should put husbands above wives, parents over their children, elder siblings over younger siblings, and rulers over citizens. He argued the importance of reverence for age and learning. Today hierarchy is particularly important in China and Korea (two countries where Confucian influence is strong). This generally makes for a stable society, but does not lend itself to the building of a commercial system, though it has been argued that once a commercial system is in place, Confucianism's long-term thinking helps promote its development.[2]

To illustrate the differences in individual- and group-oriented cultures, consider how people from each group select a restaurant. In a group-oriented culture, such as China, individuals prefer to eat at crowded restaurants. In fact, if faced with the choice of eating at two similar restaurants, one with a long line and the other without a line, a Chinese person will most likely choose to eat at the busier restaurant. This contrasts

[2]Confucius argued that a "superior" person (literati) should stay away from the pursuit of wealth, though not necessarily from the wealth itself. Therefore, becoming a civil servant was preferred to becoming a business person and conferred a much higher status in the Confucian hierarchy. Today, entrepreneurship is viewed in different ways throughout East Asia. It's still common for successful entrepreneurs (more so than average citizens) in Hong Kong, Taiwan, China, and Singapore to hide their wealth and downplay their success. A rich entrepreneur in Hong Kong or Singapore, when asked about his or her business, will respond, "We are doing okay," even if they are actually doing very well.

with individual-oriented cultures, such as Canada or the United States, where individuals would more likely focus on finding a new restaurant that others do not know about, that offers something unique and is not so crowded. There is evidence that Americans today are even less likely to view themselves as group oriented or as part of a hierarchy than they were even 25 years ago.[xxi] The lack of understanding led to major problems at the opening of the U.S.–based Disney Corporation's new theme park in Hong Kong. Disney built food facilities that were not consistent with the demand of Chinese consumers, who like to eat meals only at certain times of the day (in Hong Kong, it often seems to visitors that all of the roughly seven million citizens of the territory are trying to get into the restaurants at 1:00 pm, the start of the lunch hour). This contrasts with Americans who do not mind eating lunch at different times. When Hong Kong Disneyland opened, many guests were unhappy that restaurants were not prepared for the crowds of people all insisting on having lunch at 1:00 pm.

The relationship to nature is a dimension in the sociology framework that has become increasingly important to business. The role of environment and how a society views it is critical. While Kluckhohn and Strodtbeck discuss the relationship to nature in three distinct views, it is more realistically a continuum. Few modern societies subjugate themselves to nature. But the level of harmony with or mastery of nature can vary widely. The Nordic countries, such as Finland and Sweden, place a very high priority on a clean environment and working with nature. The end result is low levels of pollution, recycling, and an active promotion of alternative energy sources. Contrast this to China, where the environment has traditionally received a much lower priority than economic development. The result is that more than 25 percent of China's citizens do not have clean water to drink and 16 of the world's 20 most polluted cities are in China.[3]

Kluckhohn and Strodtbeck's dimension of the basic nature of man is one that affects managers as they interact with workers. Does the culture view workers as employees wanting to do a good job or as people who must be closely monitored because they will most likely take advantage of the firm? The view in many cultures, such as that of Bhutan, is that workers want to perform well. Bhutan is a small Himalayan kingdom that believes that the quality of life and the happiness of its citizens are the key to the nation's success. In contrast, Chinese workers are typically treated harshly as they are viewed largely as replaceable and having a strong inclination to take advantage of their employers, given the chance.

Psychological Framework

Another valuable cultural framework was created by organizational psychologist Geert Hofstede.[xxii] His initial data were gathered from two surveys with over 116,000 respondents from over 70 countries around the world—making it the largest organizationally based study ever conducted. The individuals in these studies all worked in the local subsidiaries of IBM and as a result, they formed a narrow but well-matched sample. That is, they were similar in most respects except for their nationality (and national culture). What accounts for systematic and consistent differences between national groups within an otherwise homogenous multinational population is the different nationalities.

Hofstede identified four dimensions along which cultures can be distinguished: power distance, individualism collectivism, uncertainty avoidance, and masculinity femininity (sometimes called production orientation). Later, Hofstede developed a fifth dimension, Confucian dynamism, or long-term orientation, which will be discussed last.

---

[3]China's protection of the environment is likely to improve with economic growth. Some see the effort and performance on behalf of the environment for the 2008 Beijing Olympics as a herald of China's level of commitment to improve the environment.

Power Distance Power distance is the extent to which less-powerful members of institutions and organizations accept the unequal distribution of power and submit to authority. Managers from western countries may assume that employees want responsibility and will take it if given a chance. However, in high power-distance countries, people are more likely to obey the orders of their superiors and often do not value being "empowered"—they may feel uncomfortable with making decisions that they feel should be made by their boss. Because bosses behave one way and employees another in your own country, does not mean that this will be the case in a foreign country.

The effect of this dimension can be measured in a number of ways. For example, organizations in low power-distance countries generally will be decentralized and have flatter organizational structures. These organizations also will have a smaller proportion of supervisory personnel, and the lower strata of the work force will consist of highly qualified people. By contrast, organizations in high power-distance countries will tend to be more centralized and have tall organizational structures.

Americans have a fairly low power distance. They prefer to do things for themselves rather than seek outside help and are generally egalitarian; bosses are often called by their first names and meetings are informal. Foreigners visiting the United States regularly comment that it is difficult to tell the wealthy from the poor in appearance, conversation, and behavior. In Sweden and other Nordic countries in Europe, people are even more egalitarian.

Indeed, in many societies, lower-level employees tend to follow orders as a matter of procedure. In societies with high power distance, however, enterprises are organized with assumptions of hierarchy and obedience; examples include Latin America, South Korea, China, and India. In India, because power distance is

---

VOLVO FORD MERGER: SUCCESSFUL CULTURAL INTEGRATION

Cultural similarities in the Nordic countries and North America can be seen in the 1999 Ford Motor Company acquisition of Volvo's automobile operations.[4] The merger has been far more successful than that of the Daimler Chrysler merger, which is discussed in a later vignette. In fact, the Volvo Ford merger has been cited as one of the two most successful mergers that has occurred in the automobile industry in recent years. Some of its success can be traced to the formation of 19 teams to search for synergies in every possible area of the two firms quickly after the merger. However, the merger has also been aided by the cultural closeness of the two countries involved, Sweden and the United States.

Cultural differences abound between the two nations. The Swedes are more commonly focused on group decision making than are the Americans. This approach is in part due to the fact that the Swedes tend to be more egalitarian than Americans in decision making; what Hofstede refers to as power distance.[5] However, there are more similarities than differences in the two nations. Almost all Swedes speak English very well, so communication problems are minimized. The Swedes, like the Americans, focus on facts and figures to support their decision making. The creative process in decision making is also similar in the two nations, with greater value placed on knowledge and understanding than on the position of the person providing the data. A similar emphasis on the facts and figures to build knowledge and understanding means that individuals in the two nations evaluate problems similarly.

The result of the cultural similarities has been a largely smooth integration between the two firms despite the distance between the two countries. The smooth integration has allowed the full range of strategic and financial goals of the merger to be met.

Executive Planet. Business Etiquette. *Sweden— Let's Make a Deal, Parts 1, 2, and 3* (see the Sweden entry in http://www.executiveplanet.com).

de Geer, H., Borglund, T., & Frostenson, M. (2003). Anglo-Saxification of Swedish business: Working paper within the project 'Scandinavian Heritage'. *Business Ethics: A European Review*, 12(2), 179–189.

Tierney, C. (2004). Ford purchase of Volvo is rare success story: Acquisition pays off with pooled strengths. *The Detroit News*. http://www.fordforums.com/f349/eu-ford-purchase-volvo-rare-success-story-64074/ (accessed September 28, 2008).

Wernle, B. (1999, September 13). Now the real work begins at Volvo. *Automotive News Europe*, Vol. 4, Issue 19.

---

[4]The truck operations went to another firm.
[5]Thus, the cultural differences in egalitarian decision making between the Germans and Swedes would be even greater than anything experienced by the Americans, despite the fact that both Germany and Sweden are in fairly close geographic proximity to each other in Europe.

FIGURE 2-3 Power Distance Index in Several Countries

Country				
Arab World	80	Indonesia	78
Argentina	49	Ireland	28
Australia	36	Israel	13
Brazil	69	Italy	50
Canada	39	Japan	54
Chile	63	Mexico	81
China	80	Poland	68
Denmark	18	South Africa	49
East Africa	64	South Korea	60
El Salvador	66	Spain	57
France	68	Sweden	31
Germany	35	Turkey	66
Greece	60	United Kingdom	35
Hong Kong	68	United States	40
India	77	West Africa	77

high, employees generally expect bosses to make nearly all of the decisions. In Confucianism-based countries, it is believed that correct answers exist and are to be found in books or from authorities, such as bosses, teachers, or sagely wisdom. Organizations in high power-distance countries will have a large proportion of supervisory personnel, and the people at the lower levels of the structure often will have low job qualifications. This latter structure encourages and promotes inequality among people at different levels. Figure 2-3 lists the power-distance societies.

Individualism Collectivism Individualism collectivism is the second dimension of Hofstede's framework. He defines high-individualistic societies as consisting of loosely linked individuals, who view themselves as largely independent of groups that make their own choices—the groups in which they are members, be it a church, a political party, a social organization, or group at work, do not make decisions for them. People in high-individualistic societies, such as those of Australia, Canada, and the United States, are motivated by their own preferences, needs, rights, and contracts and they tend to primarily look after themselves and do things by themselves. They are more likely to adopt new ideas, be inventive, and try new things.[xxiii]

Collectivism is the tendency of people to associate with groups where group members look after each other in exchange for group loyalty. They work together more readily and do not mind subordinating themselves to the goals of the group. Japan scores high on Hofstede's collective index. The roots of this tendency may come from Japan's historical dependency on rice farming. Rice farming under Japan's difficult and colder weather conditions required that a whole village work together to grow rice. Historians have argued that this collective organization of the village has carried over into today's Japanese companies.[xxiv] When Japanese business people introduce themselves, they normally include the name of the company they work for with their names. For example, a manager may say, "Hello, I am Mr. Hamada of Toyota," or "Ms. Saito of Sony." The

FIGURE 2-4   Individualism Collectivism in Several Countries

Country					
Arab World	38	France	71	Mexico	30
Argentina	46	Germany	67	Poland	60
Australia	90	Greece	35	South Africa	65
Brazil	38	Hong Kong	25	South Korea	18
Canada	80	India	48	Spain	51
Chile	23	Indonesia	14	Sweden	71
China	20	Ireland	70	Turkey	37
Denmark	74	Israel	54	United Kingdom	89
East Africa	27	Italy	76	United States	91
El Salvador	19	Japan	46	West Africa	20

identification with the group in Japan is so strong that companies influence even the clothes people wear outside of work and where they spend their leisure time.

The effects of individualism and collectivism can be measured in a number of specific ways. Hofstede found that, in general, wealthy countries tend to have higher individualism scores while poorer countries tend to have higher collectivism scores. The U.S., Canada, Australia, Denmark, and Sweden, among others, have high individualism and high GDPs. Conversely, Indonesia, Pakistan, and a number of South American countries have low individualism (high collectivism) and lower GDPs. Figure 2-4 lists various countries based on individualism.

EGALITARIANISM IN SWEDEN

While power distance in many Asian and Latin American countries is high, in the North American and the Nordic countries of Europe, power distance is low, particularly in staunchly egalitarian Sweden. The Nordic countries have a long history of egalitarianism, possibly because of their location in a challenging northern climate. In many respects, Sweden is a country of relatively small class differences. Many people even consider the very concept of social class outdated, because it has become notoriously hard to define. A Swedish manual laborer may well earn as much as a lower official, and his children can choose to study at the same university as those of the company president. All in all, the principle of equal opportunity has had a strong position in Swedish society, much due to the long predominance of the Social Democratic Party.

The ideal that each and every person has the same value is manifested in the Swedish forms of address. Just as in Anglo-Saxon countries, Swedes use only one form when speaking to a single person: *du* ("you"). This contrasts with the more polite forms of the pronoun present in more hierarchical countries, such as in Latin America, southern Europe and Japan. Irrespective of one's gender, age, or social class, *du* can always be used. Although Swedish contains a more polite form of you, *Ni* (derived from the German *Sie*), which was previously used between strangers and by children addressing adults, it is rarely used today, mostly by older people or when addressing more than one person.

A recent story about the King of Sweden is illustrative of Sweden's egalitarianism. When the King of Sweden went Christmas shopping for his family (an act that would be highly unusual in other monarchies), the salesperson demanded to see his "government issued picture identification (ID)" in order to allow him to use his credit card. The king could not produce any ID, and the (lowly) salesperson was not persuaded by other shoppers' argument of "This is our king. I can recognize him from TV," until the king searched the bottom of his pockets and discovered a coin with his face on it, truly a most authentic piece of government-issued picture identification.

Peng, M. W. (2006). *Global Strategy.* Mason, OH: Thomson/ South-Western.

Uncertainty Avoidance Uncertainty avoidance is the extent to which the members of a culture feel threatened by uncertain or unknown situations or by ambiguity in a situation. Countries organized around high uncertainty avoidance have populations that tend to have a higher need for security and a strong belief in experts and their knowledge; examples include Germany, Japan, and Spain. People in cultures with low uncertainty avoidance are more willing to accept the risks that are associated with the unknown, and accept that life must go on in spite of this uncertainty. Examples include Denmark, the United Kingdom, the United States, and Canada.

Countries with low uncertainty avoidance are associated with willingness by their members to work in situations where they do not know people well, and do not require previously established relationships to conduct business. Although all cultures have a system of reciprocity and obligation, the high uncertainty-avoidance countries usually depend more on personal connections to conduct business than do the lower uncertainty-avoidance countries, which depend more on impersonal contracts.

The effect of uncertainty avoidance can be seen in other ways. Countries with high uncertainty avoidance cultures tend to have a high degree of structure in organizational activities, more written rules, less risk taking by managers, lower labor turnover, and less ambitious employees. Low uncertainty avoidance societies are exactly the opposite: they tend to have less structure in organizational activities, fewer written rules, more risk taking by managers, higher labor turnover, and more ambitious employees. The organization encourages personnel to use their own initiative and assume responsibility for their actions. Figure 2-5 provides an uncertainty avoidance index for several countries.

FIGURE 2-5   Uncertainty Avoidance in Several Countries

Country		Country	
Arab World	68	Indonesia	48
Argentina	86	Ireland	35
Australia	51	Israel	81
Brazil	76	Italy	75
Canada	48	Japan	92
Chile	86	Mexico	82
China	40	Poland	93
Denmark	23	South Africa	49
East Africa	52	South Korea	85
El Salvador	94	Spain	86
France	86	Sweden	29
Germany	65	Turkey	85
Greece	112	United Kingdom	35
Hong Kong	29	United States	46
India	40	West Africa	54

FIGURE 2-6	Masculinity Index in Several Countries

Country	
Arab World	52
Argentina	56
Australia	61
Brazil	49
Canada	52
Chile	28
China	66
Denmark	16
East Africa	41
El Salvador	40

France	43
Germany	66
Greece	57
Hong Kong	57
India	56
Indonesia	46
Ireland	68
Israel	47
Italy	70
Japan	95
Mexico	69

Poland	64
South Africa	63
South Korea	39
Spain	42
Sweden	5
Turkey	45
United Kingdom	66
United States	62
West Africa	46

Masculine Feminine This dimension refers to the distribution of roles between genders and the more dominant role in a given society. A country high on the masculine dimension places more value on success, money, and a more assertive outlook. Femininity or relational orientation is the term used by Hofstede to describe "a situation in which the dominant values in society are nurturing and caring, interpersonal harmony and relationships, with an emphasis on the quality of life." Figure 2-6 summarizes scores for countries using Hofstede's dimensions for masculinity.

Countries with a fairly high masculinity (low femininity) index, such as the Germanic countries and the U.S., place great importance on earnings, recognition, advancement, challenge, and production. Production is placed ahead of relationships and achievement is defined in terms of recognition and wealth. The workplace is often characterized by high job stress, and many managers believe that their employees dislike work and must be kept under control.

Cultures with a very high masculinity index, such as Japan, tend to favor large-scale enterprises, and economic growth is seen as more important than conservation of the environment. The school system is geared toward encouraging high performance. In Japan, young men are expected to have good careers and to stay with one company, and those who fail to do this often view themselves as failures. Fewer women hold higher-level jobs and often society expects them to devote themselves to their children's education, although as noted before, women's attitudes on this matter have changed (Figure 2-2). There is high job stress in the workplace, and worker satisfaction in Japan tends to be low.

Cultures that score lower on masculinity (higher on femininity) tend to favor small-scale enterprises, and they place greater importance on environmental conservation. The school system is designed to teach social adaptation. Some young men and women want careers; others do not. Many women hold high-level jobs, and they do not find it necessary to be assertive. Countries with a low masculinity index (higher femininity), such as Norway and Thailand, tend to place great importance on cooperation, a friendly atmosphere, and employment security. Individuals are encouraged to be group decision makers, and achievement is defined in terms of the social environment. Managers give their employees more credit for being responsible and allow them more freedom, which leads to higher

MANUFACTURING CHINA: MATTEL

The ability for Hofstede's model of culture to provide insight can be seen in a specific problem in Chinese manufacturing. China is one of the major manufacturing centers in the world, and there is much discussion in mature markets that Chinese goods will displace all manufacturing. What is not recognized commonly is that in some industries, almost all manufacturing is in fact done by Western companies and then the products exported to mature markets in North America and Europe. Thus, in high-technology domains close to 90 percent of Chinese exports are actually products manufactured by Western companies to export to their home markets.[xxv]

The other major type of Chinese manufacturers is original equipment suppliers. In this process, these firms take their designs and products to the Chinese manufacturers, who produce the product and charge the Western firm some percentage for doing so. The Chinese firms in this domain typically are in low value-added domains such as clothing and toys. In 2007, Mattel announced a recall of over 20 million toys. These toys were found to have dangerous problems, such as lead in the paint and magnets that could be swallowed.

The recall has its roots in cultural differences. Mattel is a Western company that is used to working in a fairly low power-distance typical in the U.S. and Europe. Thus, the employees are expected to be able to operate without direct supervision and not depend on a rulebook or their supervisors' orders to get things done. But in China, with its high power distance, most employees are more accustomed to being directed by a boss (or by a list of rules). Combine this with the collective orientation, and there is a strong tendency for the employee to do exactly what their employer is telling them to do. Thus, if the senior manager says to use paint with lead because it is cheaper, it is not common for the Chinese employees to question that instruction. However, Mattel, being accustomed to working with suppliers from the United States, assumed that Chinese suppliers would act the same way; Mattel did not believe it was necessary to monitor its Chinese suppliers as closely as it should have if it had understood the cultural differences. The behavior of the Chinese supplier may have also been further affected by the higher masculinity value in China that causes financial rewards to commonly outweigh all other forms of rewards, sometimes to the neglect of other values.

One other cultural difference in Chinese and U.S. firms can also be noted in this case. The Chinese manager tragically committed suicide when the recall occurred. Some may argue this is because of the loss of respect that such problems cause to the reputation of the firm and the manager. It is likely as significant as the fact that the death penalty can be given in cases where the government feels fraud and damage was caused to the national effort of economic development.

ETHICS

employee satisfaction. Typically, less job stress is found in the workplace, and industrial conflict is somewhat uncommon in these societies.

Confucian Dynamism Hofstede and colleagues later added a final fifth dimension, Confucian Dynamism, also known as long-term orientation. They sought to address why many Asian countries had undergone such rapid economic development. This dimension identifies if the culture of a region builds on Confucian teachings. It emphasizes thrift, perseverance, a sense of shame, and following a hierarchy. Hofstede argued that these concerns dominated in Asian countries, such as Taiwan, Hong Kong, and Japan, to a larger degree than in the West. Figure 2-7 shows several countries and their long-term (dynamism) orientation.

Integrating Hofstede's Dimensions

Learning about the cultural values of countries can be useful. However, learning about every culture is a very daunting task. Therefore, it is helpful to cluster together countries with broad similarities in their cultures. Such clustering can be seen if countries are aligned in terms of pairs of dimensions. To illustrate, Figure 2-8 plots 53 countries on the power distance and uncertainty avoidance pair of dimensions. There are 10 clusters of countries that are generated from the 53 individual countries; the countries in the cluster having greater similarity with each other than with the other countries. One cluster is composed of those nations with a common British heritage such as the United Kingdom, Australia, Canada, New Zealand, and the United States in the upper left-hand quadrant, which is characterized by small power

FIGURE 2-7   Dynamism in Several Countries

Country	
Australia	31
Brazil	65
Canada	23
China	118
East Africa	25
Germany	31
Hong Kong	96
India	61
Japan	80
Netherlands	44
New Zealand	30

Norway	20
Pakistan	—
Philippines	19
Singapore	48
South Korea	75
Sweden	33
Taiwan	87
Thailand	56
United Kingdom	25
United States	29
West Africa	16

FIGURE 2-8   Power Distance, Uncertainty Avoidance, and Country Clusters

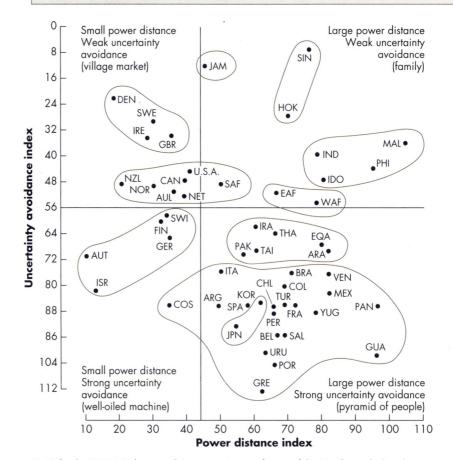

Source: G. Hofstede (1991) *Cultures and Organizations: Software of the Mind.* Maidenhead, UK: McGraw-Hill.

FIGURE 2-9	Uncertainty Avoidance and Masculinity (Career Orientation) Country Clusters

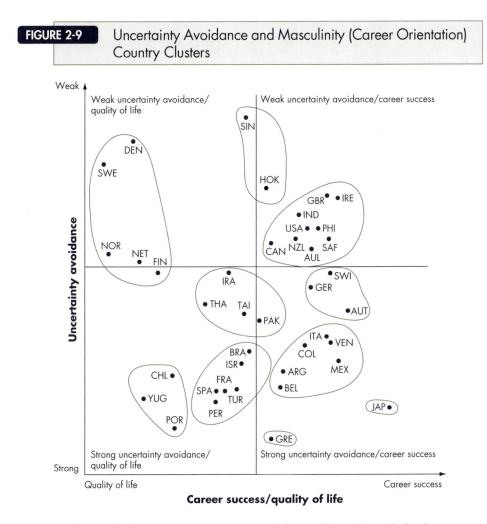

Source: G. Hofstede (1991) *Cultures and Organizations: Software of the Mind.* Maidenhead, UK: McGraw-Hill.

distance and weak uncertainty avoidance. These countries tend to be moderately unconcerned with power distance, and they are able to accept conditions of uncertainty. In contrast, many Latin American and southern European countries are characterized by large power distance and moderate uncertainty avoidance. One exception is Japan, which has a high uncertainty avoidance and a notable lack of interest in entrepreneurship among its people.

Another perspective can be seen in Figure 2-9, which maps the position of 53 countries in terms of the uncertainty avoidance and masculinity femininity, or production orientation combination. The most masculine country is Japan, followed by the Germanic countries (Austria, Switzerland, and Germany) and Latin American countries (Venezuela, Mexico, Argentina). Many countries in the Anglo-American cluster, including Ireland, Australia, the United Kingdom, and the U.S., have moderate degrees of masculinity. So do some of the former colonies of Anglo-American nations, including India, South Africa, and the Philippines. The Northern European cluster (Denmark, Sweden, Norway, and the Netherlands) has low masculinity, indicating that these countries place high value on quality of life, preservation of the environment, and the importance of relationships with people over money.

The clustering of these cultural factors into various two-dimensional graphs helps to show how nations can share similar cultural traits. Business people who are aware of the general cultural orientation of a nation in which they are working can more easily understand how to approach business in that nation.

Expansive Framework

Another helpful culture framework was developed by the Dutch researcher Fons Trompenaars, who expands on Hofstede's work. Trompenaars administered research questionnaires to over 15,000 managers from 28 countries, both developed and lesser-developed. Trompenaars used seven dimensions to differentiate national cultures, building on Hofstede's five dimensions. Trompenaars' seven dimensions include 1) individualism versus collectivism, 2) time orientation, 3) universalism versus particularism, 4) neutral versus affective, 5) specific versus diffuse, 6) achievement versus ascription, and 7) relationship to nature.

Two of Trompenaars' dimensions overlap with Hofstede—individualism versus collectivism and achievement versus ascription (similar to Hofstede's masculine feminine production orientation dimension). Some dimensions are similar to the sociology framework of Kluckhohn and Strodtbeck, including time orientation and relationship to nature. Trompenaars' view of time orientation is a little bit different, however, in that time is thought of as sequential versus synchronic in addition to past, present, and future orientations. In sequential cultures, such as the U.S. and Germany, schedules rule the business; things are usually done sequentially and not out of order, when possible. When a meeting is in progress, it is not considered polite to take phone calls, or do instant messaging, while in a synchronic (polychronic using Edward Hall's terms), such as in the Middle East and Hong Kong, it is quite common for people to take a phone call during a meeting. Though many from sequential cultures, such as Germany's, would consider this impolite, in a synchronic culture where people multitask even in meetings, it is not uncommon for that call to be answered and for the person to stop the meeting.

There are also unique aspects to this framework, such as Trompenaars' universalism versus particularism. (See In-class Exercise #1 at the end of this chapter.) In cultures emphasizing a universalistic orientation (such as the U.S., the United Kingdom, and Germany), people believe that absolute values, such as goodness or truth, are applicable to all situations. Judgments are more likely to be made without regard to the particular situation. In particularistic societies (China and much of Latin America) each situation must be judged separately. One outcome of this is that how people are treated can depend highly on their relationship with one another. Thus your friend might expect to get your business regardless of your needs and the value of his company's product because, after all, you are friends. Judgments in a particularistic society emphasize one's position in a hierarchy and one's loyalty, especially to family and friends.

Another unique cultural dimension from Trompenaars' model is neutral versus affective. Neutral cultures, such as those of Singapore and Japan, tend not to show emotion, particularly in public. In contrast, affective or the more emotional cultures (Brazil, Mexico, and Italy) do not discourage the expression of emotion. The specific versus diffuse dimension focuses on how a culture emphasizes notions of privacy and access to privacy. In specific cultures (for example, the United Kingdom), individuals have large public spaces and relatively small private spaces. Diffuse cultures (such as Southern Europe), on the other hand, make no clear distinction between public and private spaces.

Finally, the specific versus diffuse dimension is loosely related to Hofstede's power distance dimension, although it also has some unique aspects. A specific

DAIMLER CHRYSLER MERGER AND THE IMPACT OF CULTURE CLASH

In 1998, Daimler of Germany and Chrysler of the United States merged. The combination was intended to generate a company that would reach the critical mass necessary to compete on a global basis. The economies of scale in the auto industry are great. It is expected that worldwide the number of firms will decline dramatically over the next 50 years as the industry consolidates, seeking to reach the critical mass necessary to survive.

Contrary to expectations, the value of Daimler's stock declined with the announcement of the deal and would continue to decline until it was worth less than 50 percent of its original value. Daimler would ultimately have to sell Chrysler to private equity investors. Daimler purchased Chrysler for over $36 billion and would ultimately sell it for less than $5 billion. Combining two firms is always very difficult and, in this case, problems arose that could not be overcome.

Particularly problematic in integrating the two firms were their differences in culture. Some of these differences were firm specific. For example, the two firms focused on two different types of products. Daimler sold high-end, highly engineered automobiles. In contrast, Chrysler was a scrappy, cost-conscious company. The Germans were aware of this difference but they were never able to truly value the American brands. This had two results. First, the brands of the two firms were never integrated, which meant that brand management for this newly combined firm became confusing. Additionally, the two firms were never able to fully integrate their supply chains. The Daimler engineers felt using the Chrysler lower cost/lower quality inputs would damage their brand image, and Daimler did not want to share its parts with Chrysler. Chrysler would ultimately get some steering and suspension components, a transmission, and a diesel engine from Daimler. But generally, there was little integration of the two firms, with both Daimler and Chrysler largely keeping their supply chains separate. Compare this to the previously discussed Ford Volvo merger, in which the input parts were fully integrated across the two firms. The separation of Daimler and Chrysler is clearly illustrated by the fact that there were corporate headquarters in both the United States and Germany. A single corporate headquarters was never created.

Another clear difference is the language difference. Almost all young Germans speak English. But Americans seldom learn German, and language-learning ability for individuals over 40 years old tends to be much less than for younger people. The result was that language difficulties would continue to plague the two firms working together. However, more critical to the failure were the differences in national cultures of Germans and Americans. German culture tends to be very hierarchical, while Americans, as noted earlier, are very egalitarian and prefer flat organizations. One impact of this was that the Germans felt Americans were too unstructured, while the Americans found the Germans too rigid. To illustrate, Germans typically take a problem, analyze it, discuss the potential solutions, pick one, and then move on. Americans use a much more interactive process. They not only have active discussions with large numbers of people, but they revisit issues as new information or insights become available. At Daimler Chrysler, the Germans felt that once the decision had been made, they would not revisit a problem. The Germans also felt very uncomfortable with the active give and take of the Americans. The Americans saw such interactions as healthy, but to the Germans, they were confrontational and very uncomfortable. The result often was that the Americans would think a consensus had been reached when in fact the Germans just did not want to argue.

The means to analyze many of the problems at Daimler were also different. The Americans felt comfortable stopping at their bosses' or anyone else's office and discussing the issue at hand. They considered this creative. Germans, however, had a structured approach in which lower-level employees generated extensive analysis of the problem and then passed that analysis up the hierarchy until a decision was made. This approach resulted in the Germans having much larger staffs than the Americans.

This does not mean that Daimler did not realize they had a problem and try to address it. For example, to encourage communication among the various parties, the firm forced both firms to use IBM Lotus Suite, which allowed instant messaging among the parties, but this did not address the underlying differences. The outcome of these differences was that the synergy initially expected between Chrysler and Daimler was never been realized.

Corcoran, G. (2007, May 14). Was Chrysler buy a 'deal from Hell'? Mr. Bruner weighs in. Wall Street Journal Online. http://blogs.wsj.com/deals/2007/05/14/was-daimlers-buy-of-chrysler-a-deal-from-hell-robert-bruner-weighs-in/

Edmonson, G. & Welch, D. (2005, August 15). Dark days at Daimler. BusinessWeek, pp. 31–38.

Ostle, D. (1999, November 22). The culture clash at Daimler Chrysler was worse than expected. Automotive News Europe, Vol. 4, Issue 24.

Woods, L. (2007, May 18). How Daimler, Chrysler merger failed. Pressbox. http://www.pressbox.co.uk/detailed/Business/How_Daimler_Chrysler_Merger_Failed_122434.html

culture might be more likely to assign decision responsibility to a boss, thus giving specific responsibility for outcomes, whether positive or negative. A more diffuse society will be more accepting of the diffuse assigning of responsibility.

The GLOBE Study

The GLOBE study is a recent, large scale research effort that involved over 150 researchers from 61 different countries. This research sought to examine the interrelationships between societal culture, organizational culture, and organizational leadership. The research team initially identified nine different cultural items. While Trompenaars built on Hofstede's work, the GLOBE study built not only on Hofstede's work but also on the work of Trompenaars, and Kluckhohn and Strodtbeck.

The first six items in the GLOBE study were based on Hofstede's earlier works. However, the GLOBE study made variations in some of Hofstede's variables. The uncertainty avoidance and power distance were largely the same as Hofstede's earlier work. However, the individual group orientation variable was split into two parts—societal collectivism and in-group collectivism.

- Societal collectivism is the degree to which organizational and societal practices encourage the collective distribution of resources and collective action.
- In-group collectivism is the degree to which individuals express pride, loyalty, and cohesiveness in their organization or family.

Similarly, the masculinity variable of Hofstede was split into two variables, referred to as gender egalitarianism and assertiveness.

- Gender egalitarianism refers to the degree to which an organization or society minimizes gender role differences and gender discrimination.
- Assertiveness is the degree to which individuals are confrontational.

The seventh cultural item is future orientation. It is drawn from Trompenaars and concerns the importance placed in the society on the delaying of gratification and the importance of planning. The eighth cultural dimension is humane orientation, and it is drawn from the work of Kluckhohn and Strodtbeck and concerns the degree to which individuals are rewarded for being fair, caring, and kind to others. The last dimension of the framework is performance orientation. This is the one element that is not based on the other culture frameworks, though it bears some resemblance to Hofstede's masculine feminine dimension. This dimension is most closely related, however, to David McClelland's need for achievement (discussed later in Chapter 7, Motivation). Performance orientation is concerned about the extent to which achievement is a motivator.

One contribution of the GLOBE study is that it has allowed the clustering of countries and cultures to be more specific than was possible with Hofstede's initial work. The result has been the recognition of a number of country clusters that share a similar cultural orientation. Using such clusters allows individuals to quickly gain insight into what the culture of a nation would be, based on its cluster. The following countries are seen as belonging to the same clusters:

- Latin Europe: Spain, Portugal, Italy, French Switzerland, France, and Israel
- Eastern Europe: Albany, Georgia, Greece, Hungary, Kazakhstan, Poland, Russia, and Slovenia
- Germanic Europe: Austria, Germany, the Netherlands, and Switzerland
- Anglo: Australia, Canada, the United Kingdom, Ireland, New Zealand, South Africa (white sample), and the United States
- Southern Asia: India, Indonesia, Iran, Malaysia, the Philippines, and Thailand
- Arabic: Egypt, Morocco, Turkey, Kuwait, and Qatar

The GLOBE study will be revisited again in Chapter 8, Leadership.

Culture Framework Integration

Each cultural framework has some overlap with each other, but they all also have characteristics that make them unique. It cannot be said that one framework is right and another is wrong. Instead, each framework takes a complex domain (culture) and breaks it down in a manner in which people can readily understand it. Once a business person, for example, begins to build a foundation of understanding their actions, she or he can be more directed and logical, and less likely to violate cultural norms.

If a business person is going to work in a new environment or if a firm is moving into a new market, then rather than relying on a single model of culture, typically multiple frameworks of culture should be employed, because the frameworks are not mutually exclusive. Thus, a business person or a business can gain different insights by using the various frameworks to identify elements that the frameworks see differently and those where there is agreement. The goal is to gain insights to help prepare the business person and firm to make directed and logical choices. However, it is important to note that each framework is merely a tool, and tools are only as useful as the skills of the person using them. Thus, frameworks should be employed as guidelines to help the manager, not as laws written in stone.

SUMMARY

Culture is fundamental to differences in business around the world. Managers can make numerous pitfalls associated with culture. However, managers who analyze culture in the different societies in which they operate are more likely to be successful. Four major frameworks can be used to help one understand cultural settings. These frameworks (Kluckhohn and Strodtbeck, Hofstede, Trompenaars, and GLOBE) each approach the domain of culture slightly differently, but they all have the potential to help a business person clearly understand the environment in which they are operating.

The related concept of values is also important to the international operation of a business. Values concern individual predispositions, while culture is concerned with entire societies. Both can and do change as society changes. Upcoming chapters will demonstrate how culture and values shape a wide range of managerial issues, including the strategy of the firm, human resource management, communication, decision making, leadership, and evaluation and control in the firm.

MANAGERIAL GUIDELINES

A number of managerial guidelines should be used to direct the actions of managers, based on culture and its role in the organization.

1. It is important to recognize that culture is pervasive in business. Businesses that operate in different countries must evaluate their actions in light of cultural differences.
2. Managers must evaluate the cultural differences that exist between themselves and others as they begin to conduct business across national borders.
3. The greater the cultural difference, the more crucial it is for the manager to understand that key cultural dimensions can influence how their communication and actions are perceived.
4. Sensitivity training is useful for preparing managers to address the cultural differences that can exist as they conduct business across national borders.
5. Do not project your own culture and value system onto others. Projection means that you assume other people think the way you do. In any cross-

cultural interaction, this is not a good assumption to make. This does not mean that you should abandon your own values when working in another culture. But do not assume that others share your values and preferences, and will act the way you would.

6. Managers, on the whole, must be prepared to overcome the bias of believing their culture or way of doing business is best. Business people should not violate their personal ethical standards or those of the company. For example, while it may be acceptable in some societies to discriminate against women or minorities, if you are from an advanced economy in Europe or North America, such behaviors are not typically acceptable either personally or legally. Local business partners may practice discrimination and encourage you to do the same, but being culturally accepting does not mean that you have to allow or participate in such actions that violate your or the company's ethics.

7. Communication is affected by culture; so not only what you say but how you say it is important. In many nonwestern countries, hierarchy is important, as is age; managers must be sensitive to protocol associated with age, status, and seniority.

8. Almost all business people understand that you may not know all the intricacies of their culture. As a result, it is typically acceptable to ask them what is appropriate in a given situation. The fact that you are trying to adapt to their culture and understand their language will be appreciated.

9. One way to learn about a culture is to carefully observe how the locals behave, particularly the leaders of a society (such as bosses, professionals, and politicians). How do they meet and great people? How do they ask people to do things and thank them for help? How do they relate to their peers, subordinates, and authority? When do they give gifts and what do they give? Table 2-1 summarizes some of the issues on which a manager should focus as she or he considers culture in different settings.

TABLE 2-1   Cultural Etiquette around the World

Etiquette	Specifics	Example
Greetings	How do people greet and address one another? What role do business cards play?	In Japan and China, business cards are very important. Give and receive them with two hands and read them when you receive them, and put them away carefully (never into a back pocket!). Bring large numbers of cards on any foreign business trip or try to create one if you do not have one, even if you are a student. Keep some in your travel bag so you do not forget to have some on hand. It is very embarrassing to travel to a meeting around East Asia having forgotten your business cards.
Degree of Formality	Do people in the firms I am visiting dress and interact formally or informally?	The U.S., Canada, Australia, and New Zealand are less formal than most countries. Though khaki pants are okay in these countries, they may be too informal for most business settings elsewhere. Usually, darker clothes and suits are necessary for most business settings worldwide. Work on a manufacturing or shop

floor would be an exception. Bring more formal clothing just in case. In Singapore, Indonesia, Malaysia, the Philippines, and in other parts of Southeast Asia, ties are not commonly worn in business settings, although quality business attire is. Be sure to inquire about this with your host organization. Never, ever wear flip-flops or sandals in a business setting in foreign countries unless you are 100 percent certain such informality is acceptable.

Personal Inquiries	What kinds of questions are acceptable?	Be careful when asking questions about someone's spouse and family unless you are sure this topic is okay (in Islamic countries one should not ask about family). While most people from Western countries usually do not mind family questions, they do not like personal questions about their health, appearance, how much they earn, what they are eating for lunch, why they like cold drinks and not hot drinks, their marital status, and other personal details. Consider these topics *off limits* until you know that person well enough to ask such personal questions.
Gift Giving	Do business people exchange gifts? What gifts are appropriate? Are there taboos associated with gift giving?	Japan has a widely recognized system of gift giving often known as *giri*. *Giri* guides people in when to give gifts, to whom, and at what value. Ask people who know, or consult a book, such as *Kiss, Bow or Shake Hands* (Morrison, T. & Conaway, W.A., 2006) for information on this and other protocols worldwide. Gift giving is less formalized in China and other parts of East Asia, but is still important.
Touching	What are the attitudes toward body contact?	For most countries, shaking hands is okay, even in countries where the practice is not common, such as Japan. When meeting a businesswoman from a nonwestern country (for example, in India, East Asia, the Middle East, and Africa), it is usually best to wait until she extends her hand first to shake hands.
Eye Contact	Is direct eye contact polite? Is it expected?	Indian people will typically make direct eye contact and even stare at total strangers. This is not considered impolite in India, though in many countries it is considered rude and some people might consider it aggressive act, so staring is best avoided. In contrast, many East Asians will avoid direct eye contact, making some Westerns think they are not listening. Do not make that assumption. As always, check the norms of the country to which you are traveling.
Physical Distance	How close do people stand next to each other?	In some countries, such as the Middle East, businessmen (though not women) will stand or sit near to the person with whom they are talking, and at a proximity that most Westerners would feel uncomfortable with. North Americans, for example, will normally stand at arm's length, or even sometimes side by side when talking. If someone is standing too near, resist the inclination to back up, as the person will just close the distance again, and may feel that you are being rude.

TABLE 2-1   (Continued)

Etiquette	Specifics	Example
Emotions	Is it rude, embarrassing, or usual to display emotions?	Most U.S. business people avoid showing emotions, except for small talk and jokes. In Germany and Austria, it is generally considered a bit frivolous to start off a meeting with a joke. Most countries in East Asia have less small talk and jokes at business meetings, and lighten up at lunches and dinners instead. Southern Europeans and Latin Americans, on average, will normally express more emotion at meetings. Latin American business people, for example, may start describing you as "my good friend" even though you have just been introduced to them a few minutes earlier.
Silence	Is silence awkward? Expected? Insulting? Respectful?	Many less-expressive cultures do not mind some silence at a meeting. Do not feel that you need to fill in the silence with comments or questions. Feel free to take some healthy pauses in conversations to think or write something down.
Speaking Style	How do you address people? Is it proper to use first (given) names?	In Asia, you normally would not address people by their given names unless you know them or are a colleague at the same level or above in the organization. At meetings, the one running the meeting may be addressed more formally, such as "Mr. Chairman" or "Mr. Supervisor" though as always, watch for the norms within the organization. In Australia, the U.S., and Canada, first names are regularly used. Even a professor will commonly be called by his or her first name in Australia by students.
Eating	What are the proper manners for dining? Are certain foods taboo?	Most cultures are proud of their cuisines and special drinks. Make an effort to enjoy the food and drink with your host. Definitely do not criticize the food in the host country. Try not to be too picky about the food—this is a good way to insult your host and harm your chances of doing business in that country. On the other hand, do not assume that just because people do not want to go out for lunch, dinner, drinks, and so forth that they do not like you. While some cultures encourage a lot of after work socializing, such as in Japan or Latin America, others, such as in North America, do not.
Body Language	Are certain gestures or forms of body language rude?	If you are going to a new country for the first time to do business, buy a book such as *Kiss, Bow or Shake Hands* or check international business Web sites, such as www.executive planet.com, so you can learn which gestures or body language to avoid. For example, most East Asians would consider you impolite if you slumped low in your chair with your feet up, or clasped your hands behind your head and leaned way back in your chair when speaking or listening. They would wonder if you are paying attention to them. In Thailand and the Middle East, it is considered quite rude to show the bottom of your foot or shoe.

CULTURE AND DOING BUSINESS IN INDIA

India is the second most populous nation in the world with over a billion citizens. India encompasses over 3,250,000 square km in land mass, making it physically the seventh largest country in the world. There are 24 languages spoken in India by its one billion citizens. As a result, the language of business is often English because it is a common language spoken by all well-educated Indian people. In fact, it is estimated that for 90 million people in India, English is one of their three major spoken languages.

Business in India tends to be organized around family business groups. Business groups are a concept that will be discussed in greater detail later in the book, however, it is sufficient to say now that these are highly diversified entities in which a given family controls the business. As a result, it typically is helpful to have introductions to various firms with which you wish to do business. There are communities from different parts of India, with their own distinct dialects, that have a disproportionate impact on business in India. The most important communities include Marwari, Gujarati and Chettiar. People from these communities have controlling interests in some of the largest Indian business houses and commonly prefer to do business with individuals also originally from these regions. Another significant group in Bombay is a religious group known as the Zoroastrians. The small group practicing this religion has generated some of the most significant business groups in India. The religion has a three-fold path "*Good*

thoughts, good words, good deeds." As an outcome of this belief, they actively conduct many good works in India.

The negotiation process in India typically is a slow moving process because Indians prefer to build relationships before conducting business—an important part of their culture. The approach to time also tends to be quite lax. It is important to make appointments in advance and, for foreigners, it is important to be on time, even though their Indian host may not always be on time. Hierarchy also tends to be quite important in the culture, so paying appropriate respect to individuals, such as standing when senior members of the firm enter a room, is important. This same focus on hierarchy will typically result in final negotiations always needing the approval of the senior management of a firm. There is a cultural tendency not to say "no" directly because it may be seen as rude. As a result, phrases such as "we will need to consider this issue further" or "it may be difficult" may in fact mean no.

Other cultural difference need to be heeded as well. For example, pointing with your finger is considered rude; Indians prefer to point with the chin. Displays of public affection are not appreciated, so greetings that include hugs or kisses should not occur. While moderate aggressiveness is often revered in the Western workplace as a sign of confidence and ingenuity, in the Indian context it is seen as a sign of disrespect.

ADDITIONAL RESOURCES

Axtell, R. E. (1998). *Gestures: The Do's and Taboos of Body Language Around the World.* New York: John Wiley & Sons.

Baker, C. & Willis, P. (2004). *Cultural Studies: Theory and Practice* (2nd ed.). Thousand Oaks, CA: Sage Publications.

Martin, J. & Chaney, L. (2006). *Global Business Etiquette: A Guide to International Communication and Customs.* Westport, CT: Praeger Publishers.

Morrison, T. & Conaway, W.A. (2006). *Kiss, Bow, or Shake Hands (The Bestselling Guide to Doing Business in More Than 60 Countries).* Avon, MA: Adams Media.

EXERCISES

Opening Vignette Discussion Questions

1. How could the problems that arose in the opening vignette have been avoided?
2. If you were in charge of sensitivity training for Accenture, what do you think should be included in the training prior to sending someone to India?
3. Based on the vignette, discuss what the cultural characteristics of India, using the Hofstede model to describe these characteristics.

DISCUSSION QUESTIONS

1. Compare and contrast the differences and similarities in the various culture frameworks discussed in the chapter.
2. Is cultural convergence occurring in the world? That is, do you think that the various world cultures are coming closer together, or are they getting more different and prone to conflict? Why or why not?
3. If you were going to conduct cultural-sensitivity training for someone coming to your country, what do you think they would need to know to successfully navigate the culture?
4. What would be a common list of issues you should be taught about, if you were about to be sent to China to conduct business?

IN-CLASS EXERCISES

1. You are a manager responsible for marketing promotion in a widely dispersed multinational enterprise based in Canada. Some marketing people under you who are based around the world have gone to Mexico for a key meeting (you stay behind in Canada). After the meeting has gone on in Mexico City for a few days, you get a call from the Mexican marketing executive in charge of running the meeting and producing the worldwide promotion campaign proposal. She is quite upset with one of the colleagues from Taiwan. She tells you that they worked for several days planning a new company promotional campaign along with several colleagues from different countries in Latin America, Russia, Japan, and Taiwan, all of whom arrived in Mexico City right before the meeting started. The job proved quite challenging and took a few days to complete. She feels that the group is doing a nice job and should be rewarded. At the end of the first day, she said that she wanted to treat everyone to a nice dinner at a local five-star hotel, paying out of her own (not the group's) budget. However, the group member from Taiwan announced that he was quite tired and was not able to join the group for dinner or drinks after work. The Mexican executive said she was surprised and disappointed by his attitude. After all, she said, "... this is a chance for the working group, which may have to interact regularly in the future, to get to know each other. In fact, not only did the Taiwanese colleague say he did want not go to dinner that night, it turned out that he didn't want to go to dinner on any of the other nights either, saying it had been a very long trip from Asia, he wanted to go to bed early, and he didn't drink anyway." He even turned down a chance to go to a festival that was an annual custom in Mexico City.

   The Mexican executive was so upset about the Taiwanese colleague's refusal to join the group for their first dinner of the conference that she called you very late at night at home to tell you what happened. "The meeting is going well and our advertising plan looks fine. It is our colleague from Taiwan—how can he behave like this?" the Mexican executive asked. "This is really rude of him!" She guessed that it must be that he didn't like the group and maybe didn't like Mexican food. She suggested that you should send someone else from the Greater China group in the future, because this guy is hurting the camaraderie and morale of the group, which is serious when it comes to a creative effort, such as marketing and promotion. "These social events are important to company morale—we always do things this way in Latin America, and it works well," she tells you.

   You decide to contact the Taiwanese colleague by email to find out why he seems to be making the Mexican marketing executive so upset and is apparently hurting the morale of the group. The Taiwanese colleague emails back, saying that his Mexican host is overbearing and not listening to him when he says he is tired and needs to go back to the hotel and rest. "It's like talking to a brick wall," he tells you. "I just do not feel like going out to dinner—it was a long trip, I am not feeling that well, and besides, we are already working all day. I need to go back to the hotel and rest. I wouldn't mind seeing the city a little, but we are working all day—it's too much. If this were a sales situation it would be different, but working for nine hours on a tough plan is enough, I need to go to the gym early in the morning before we meet and then rest at night. I have told her this, and she just ignores me, saying I must not like her and our group. That's nonsense. Tell her to back off a little and give me some personal space."

As the marketing manager back at the home office, how would you handle this problem and smooth things out in your group? You do not want to lose the Taiwanese colleague—he understands the Greater China market well, which is central to your growth plans. The Mexican marketing executive is also valuable—she is a loyal employee and quite effective in her position in Mexico and all around Latin America. How can you fix this problem so they can work together? Just telling both of them to "listen better" is not adequate; you have to be more specific in your recommendations. Can you think of anything about culture and people's personal preferences that is likely to be influencing both of your subordinates' behavior and how to fix this problem?

2. You have been assigned to help prepare a key employee, Raymond, a chemical engineer from Mainland China, who will be moving to a rural region in North America to work in the fast-growing tar sands oil-extraction industry. That region has almost no Chinese people living there. Raymond will relocate his whole family and is expected to stay for three years; they will be one of the only Chinese families in the town. Raymond is a talented chemical engineer in his late thirties who is important to the firm's success in the North American market in the fast growing new oil-extraction industry.

Raymond has not spent any time in the West or much time working with people from outside of China. His wife is an accountant and they have two kids, a 14-year-old daughter and a 15-year-old son. Raymond speaks English pretty well. His family does not speak English well, but they understand some and should be able to get by okay.

Break into groups for the following activities. Complete Exercise A before reading Exercise B.

Exercise A: Your group should prepare a list to help with Raymond's training before he leaves. The list should tell him about what to expect—both at work and after work in his new North American community. Tell him about some of the cultural issues he may run into with his coworkers and customers in the chemical business, and how he should handle them. You also want to give some advice about living in such a place (say semi-rural [non-urban] United States or Canada).

Exercise B: After about two weeks on the job, Raymond calls you at company headquarters. He is upset about his new home, and his family is unhappy, and they don't want to stay. In particular, he has two questions for you:

i. No one came to greet him and his family at the airport upon their arrival in the U.S., so he had to find his own way to the company, which was a long ride from the airport through very unfamiliar roads in the countryside. Later, Raymond's managers invited him to a nice breakfast at a hotel overlooking the Rocky Mountains. They apologized for being very busy and having to catch a flight right after that. Raymond called you to talk about this behavior. "I feel insulted by my new colleagues," Raymond said. "Imagine only being invited to a breakfast meeting on my first visit here. And having to find my own way to the company! The company told me that I am a key employee here to do a big job, and yet no one greeted me at the airport. In China, this would never happen. A new employee and his family are treated to a nice banquet. That is how we always treat important visitors in China." I wonder why they did not do the same for us?"

    Raymond is obviously angry about his initial treatment. As a manager in charge of these personnel moves you are worried, because first impressions tend to influence later experience. How can you explain this situation to him better? Are the Canadians just being rude?

ii.   In his first week in the new town, Raymond's daughter went out to the local shopping mall with two new classmates. While walking around, her friends suddenly stepped into a food shop and bought some snacks to eat. They came out with the food and drink but did not buy anything for Raymond's daughter. She came home upset and wanted to know, "Why are the foreigners so unfriendly?" Raymond did not understand this either. "People should not buy something to eat only for themselves without offering anything to their friend," he told you. "What is wrong with these Canadians?" He wants to know what he should tell his daughter. What do you do as Raymond's boss? Would you tell Raymond to stop complaining about such trivial matters and just get his work done? Or is there anything else you could recommend?

3.   Compare your answers given in Exercise A with those in Exercise B (both i and ii). Did you prepare Raymond for the problems that came up in Exercise B? Knowing about these problems, how could you have better prepared Raymond, as asked in Exercise A?

TAKE-HOME EXERCISES

1.   Go to the Web site http://www.executiveplanet.com and select two different nations. Contrast the impact of culture on negotiations in those nations. Report your findings to the class.
2.   Form a team and summarize what you believe the primary cultural aspects of your home country to be. Report your findings to the class.
3.   In your view, how do foreign nationals misunderstand your country? Make a list of the most important of these. Are they cultural in nature? Historical? Political? Other? What types of training could a firm pursue to overcome these misunderstandings?
4.   In 2005, a number of Chinese firms sought to buy U.S. firms. This includes the China National Offshore Oil Corporation purchase of Chevron, the Lenovo purchase of IBM's laptop business, and Haier's purchase of Maytag. Research one of these proposed acquisitions. Which ones were completed? What would be the cultural implications of each of the proposed acquisitions? In other words, would some of the mergers be expected to be more difficult because the nature of the integration that would be required, or the business involved?

SHORT CASE QUESTIONS

Daimer Chrysler Merger and the Impact of Culture Clash (p. 57)

1.   What are some of the major differences you see in doing business in Germany if you are an American?
2.   Renault Motors is a French firm that owns Nissan Automobile of Japan. Why do you think this merger worked when the Daimler Chrysler merger did not?
3.   Think of ways that the Daimler Chrysler merger could have been encouraged to succeed.

3

THE ECONOMIC, LEGAL, AND POLITICAL ENVIRONMENT

Overview

Differences in culture seen in Chapter 2 can produce variations in the economic, legal, and political environment of a firm. Each of these macro factors in turn influences the actions of the international manager by determining what the firm should and is able to do. This chapter examines the economic, legal, and political environmental issues and their impact on international management. The specific topics that will be examined include:

- Market versus other types of economies
- Diamond of national competitiveness
- Civil versus common law
- Shari'a or Islamic law
- Political risk

TEXACO CHEVRON AND ECUADOR

In April 2005, the president of Ecuador abolished its Supreme Court and announced a state of emergency. In response, many Ecuadorian citizens filled the streets and ultimately forced the president to seek political asylum in Brazil. Lucio Guierrez, was the fifth president in Ecuador in the last nine years. Three of the presidents were removed from office by the nation's congress or by coup. The other two were vice presidents who filled in until the next election. As of 2008 the president of the country is Rafael Vicente Correa Delgado, an individual whose campaign was supposedly funded in large part by a rebel group from Colombia that has a strong relationship with drug exports.

Ecuador has experienced a solid economic growth in recent years. However, that economic growth was not well dispersed. The lower segments of the population, which often are of South American Indian ancestry, have hardly participated in the economic growth. A key resource for Ecuador has been oil. Texaco Chevron (now Chevron) was one of the original investors in Ecuador and helped to develop this key resource.

However, Chevron ultimately faced a multi-million dollar law suit in U.S. courts, not Ecuadorian courts, filed by Ecuadorian native Indians. These individuals charged that Chevron had polluted the environment. As part of the drilling process the firm created large sludge pits that held the waste from the oil drilling process. There are an estimated 600 pits that now hold an estimated 20 million gallons of waste. This waste, if it were to leak into the rivers and ground water, would ultimately contaminate much of the region's drinking water. The Indians charged that the same safety standards used in the United States were not followed in Ecuador by Chevron. The company countered that those standards in the United States were not in place until after they had stopped drilling in Ecuador, much of the drilling actually dating from almost 25 years ago.

The Indian plaintiffs drew part of their legal standing from the Ecuadorian constitution and other international documents that recognized the right of indigenous people to be consulted about the development of their homelands. Chevron pointed to the fact that it signed an agreement with the Ecuadorian government in 1995 in which it agreed to pay $40 million to help clean up environmental problems and was indemnified (released) from future claims. However, in 2005 Ecuador's attorney general said he did not believe that the indemnification was legal because the controller general's signature was not on the agreement. Chevron pointed out that the controller general only effected public funds and the money they had given to correct the problems had no public funds involved.

Chevron exited Ecuador in 1992. Almost 15 years later, issues created by individuals no longer in the firm are still affecting Chevron. Ecuador is largely a broken state without an effective government; the nation has changed its president every two years, typically by force, and is largely without executive control. Agreements that were made by Chevron years ago have now been called into question. The U.S. courts ruled after 10 years that the court case was more appropriately to be judged in Ecuador, not the United States.

The case had been filed originally in the U.S. due to the stronger rule of law and more generous liability that could be forced on the company. What will occur with the legal case now is not clear. Rather than put the former supreme court justices back in place after Guierrez fled the country, the congress has decided to fill the court with all new appointees. Thus, much of what had been done had to restart. In 2008 the case continues to drag on.

As critical as the lawsuit is to the firm, the public relations issue is equally as important. Typically, at each shareholders meeting, Indians in native dress show up and receive extensive publicity about their cause as they charge the firm with endangering the lives of children. Thus, Chevron's reputation and its profitability are clearly affected by the international political and legal processes it faces around the world.

A coup by Congress and the street. (2005, May 2). *Economist,* p. 51.

Balch, O. (2005). Indigenous opposition prevents oil exploration in Ecuadorian Amazon. *Ethical Corporation.* May 2. http://ethical corp.com/content.asp?ContentID=3658.

Grumbel, A. (2005, April 27). Amazon pollution: Victims of "Toxico." *UK Independent Environment.*

Chapter 2 highlighted culture as a major defining difference in international management. Culture in turn leads to a number of systematic differences that affect how firms compete in international markets. These differences are broadly referred to as environmental domains because they are in the environment of a business and shape its actions in pervasive ways. Specifically, Chapter 3 examines three environmental domains particularly important to international firms: economic, legal, and political. A student who may be planning to manage an international business needs to understand these three environmental domains in whatever region of the world in which it will operate. This chapter will walk the student through an analysis of the three domains.

FIGURE 3-1	Chapter 3 Conceptual Flow

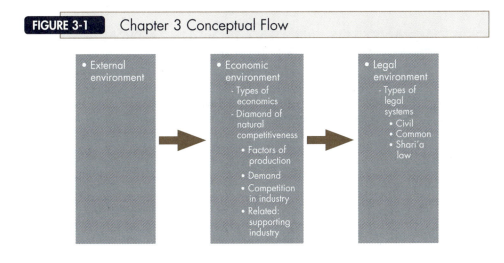

As we begin this chapter, it is important to note that while the movement toward market-based systems is a worldwide trend, there are other significant types of economic systems that merit discussion. Thus, in examining the economic environment, we shall also briefly examine other systems, such as socialism. Then the economic models that exist for the analysis of country competitiveness and forces of globalization affecting firms and individuals are presented. Next, the foundations for much of the world's legal environment center on two basic types of legal systems, common law and civil law; both systems will be examined. The chapter also considers another important system of law—Shari'a or Islamic law. Finally, the political environment for international business, specifically political risk and how it affects international management, is also examined. Figure 3-1 summarizes this flow through the chapter.

ECONOMIC ENVIRONMENT

Today, it is the conviction of many (including the authors of this text) that market-driven economic systems produce the best results for the widest number of a country's citizens and will continue their gradual spread around the world.[i] A **market-based economic system** is based on the negotiated establishment of prices between buyers and sellers of goods and labor. A **price** of something in this system is the exchange ratio between what sellers are willing to sell a good or service for and what buyers are willing to pay for it. Prices are usually expressed in terms of the amount of money needed to acquire an item or service, though they can exist in barter systems with the price given in terms of goods. Thus, if demand for a good is high but its supply is low, the product's higher price will reflect that demand. In market economies, individual entrepreneurs have the freedom to create companies to meet demands for goods or services. In such a system the means of production are held by individuals and shareholders, not governments, spurred by the opportunity to make a living and earn some profit. Market-driven economic systems, albeit with varying levels of government intervention, have a long track record of excellent economic and employment growth.[ii]

A market system is encouraged by free trade between nations. One way nations can increase international trade is by lowering the tariffs they place on products from other nations. There has been a steady march to reduce tariffs. The mean level of tariffs around the world had fallen to 10.4 percent in 2002; it was 26.1 percent 20 years earlier. The tariff on manufactured goods fell even lower to about

Market-based economic system
Relies on individuals in the society to determine the price of any good.

Price
The exchange ratio for goods and services between what the seller is willing to sell the good for and what the buyer is willing to pay.

DEUTSCHE BORSE AG AND THE INTERNATIONALIZATION OF PERFORMANCE EXPECTATIONS

A key part of the economic environment of a firm is the level of economic liberalization in an economy. Worldwide, the movement to freer markets can be seen in a wide variety of ways. Deutsche Borse AG is the stock exchange operator in Germany. Investors in Germany (the world's fourth-largest economy following the U.S., Japan, and China) have been passive with executives' tenure based on deciding when to leave; German investors did not force involuntary departures. However, investors of the firm were quite critical of the failed effort by Deutsche Borse to take over the London Stock Exchange. As a result, Mr. Werner Seifert was forced to resign as head of the exchange by his 21-member board.

Mr. Seifert's tenure had been successful in many ways. He had grown a small regional stock market, which he took over in 1993, to become one of the world's largest electronic stock exchanges. The stock exchange developed active markets in derivatives as well as clearing and settling trades, and became became publicly traded in 2001. Deutsche Borse attempted to take over the London Exchange in 2005. The attempted takeover failed and Mr. Seifert was blamed for the failure. The investors, as a result, became dissatisfied and forced his removal. This change in the CEO of one of the leading firms in Germany is interpreted by many as a watershed event in which similar actions are likely to become the norm in a country which historically was more concerned with good relations than performance.

Taylor, E. & Reilly, D. (2005, May 10). Shareholder revolt topples Deutsche Borse bosses. *Wall Street Journal Europe*, pp. A1, A6.

4 percent in 2002. Countries like India and China, which once severely restricted free markets, have increasingly embraced them, and have experienced rapid economic growth. This has resulted not only in more foreign products entering their markets, but in both countries becoming major exporters and recipients of foreign direct investment. This increased flow of trade has resulted in steadily increasing living standards for people in these countries. Tariffs are expected to fall further with the implementation of WTO regulations, increasing the availability and choice of goods and services worldwide.

No economic system is completely free of flaws. People in many EU countries and others around the world criticize the movement to a market-based economic system because they say it undermines the quality of life and the health of the society. For example, in 2005 a new constitution was proposed for the EU. Each European country approached the approval of the constitution differently—in France approval went to a vote of the people. The citizens of France voted against the constitution despite the support of the constitution by almost all major French political figures. France was one of the founding members of the EU and the commission that wrote the constitution was chaired by former French President Valérie Giscard d'Estaing. One of the major factors cited for France's eventual "no" vote on the constitution it originally spearheaded is that the citizens of France viewed the document as being too pro-market in its outlook. For example, it was cited by the opposition that the constitution used the term "competition" 47 times and the word "market" 78 times, but the phrases "social progress" and "employment" were not used at all. It is interesting to note that in a 22-country survey published in 2006, France was the only country that disagreed with the statement that the best system is "the free-market economy." In that poll, only 36 percent of French respondents agreed, compared with 65 percent in Germany, 66 percent in Britain, 71 percent in the United States, and 74 percent in China.[iii]

There has also been a backlash in certain Latin American and Middle Eastern countries against the move toward freer market-based systems. Reflecting populist movements common in a number of countries, Costa Rica elected its first socialist government in 2005, and Venezuela enacted new laws restrictive of private property. There were also socialist politicians elected as president in nations as diverse as Bolivia, Brazil, Chile, Ecuador, Honduras, Nicaragua, and Peru, though not all were anti-free market.

Despite the steps in these various countries to mitigate aspects of market-based systems, the overall trend toward freer markets likely will continue as the world moves to greater levels of foreign trade and globalization.[iv] The market-based economies backed by systems of free trade have consistently demonstrated the ability to produce the most prosperity, competitive firms, and products at the best prices. Those countries with efficient market systems are also the countries with the highest per capita income and the highest levels of economic growth.[v] As a result, market systems have gradually been displacing less efficient economic systems as more and more people learn about and experience market systems.[vi] The successes in India, China, Southeast Asia and elsewhere in introducing marketing reforms have also led to the biggest declines in poverty in world history. The Institute for International Economics recently reported that world poverty fell from 44 percent of the global population in 1980 to 13 percent in 2000, its fastest decline in history. Though much work remains, this result indicates that the United Nation's main Millennium Development Goal of reducing world poverty below 15 percent has been achieved.[vii]

The economic system that is considered to be the opposite of a market system is a socialist command economy or socialism. **Socialism** takes several forms; in its purest form, the state owns all assets. The belief is that if assets are held by all, then all individuals will benefit and be equal. A socialist *economic* system should not be confused with a communist *political* system. **Communism** is a political system that also relies on dictatorship to govern its populace. It uses a socialist command economy to establish a classless society based on the common ownership of property and the means of production, but socialism and communism are not identical.[viii] To illustrate, Israel was founded as a socialist country. The settlement of that nation was pioneered by an economic unit called a *kibbutz*. The kibbutz was principally an agricultural entity; although they also often had small manufacturing operations. The kibbutz, as an entity, held the title to the property and assets of people in the kibbutz. All individuals in the kibbutz were paid the same, and workers were asked to do what the kibbutz needed although it was not necessarily what the workers wanted to do. In some *kibbutzim*, children even lived in a common house and not with their parents. Today, the kibbutz movement is a historical footnote. Although the Israeli government still owns large parts of the economy, there has been an increasing emphasis on private enterprise in recent years, particularly in high technology, where Israeli companies have been quite successful. During its entire modern history, Israel has had an active and vibrant democracy. Thus, while Israel had a socialist economic foundation, politically it is a vibrant democracy; such systems are called social democracies. In contrast, Cuba and North Korea also have socialist economic systems but with a communist political system. These countries have repressive political systems and very poor economies. Figure 3-2 highlights the political orientation of the various states of the world.

Socialism can be practiced with the means of production being owned by the government. An alternative form of socialism used in the Nordic countries of Europe allows private property, but the tax and social-service system seeks to impose more equal economic outcomes on individuals. Even in simple things, such as a speeding ticket, the fine is based on the income of the individual, not a set price. For example, in 2004, Jussi Salonoja was fined $210,000 in Finland for going 20 kph over the speed limit.[ix] His family is a very wealthy sausage manufacturer and his fine was based on his income, not the violation. It should be recognized that the Nordic countries of Europe (Norway, Denmark, Finland, and Sweden) with their small, homogeneous populations have been successful with their social-democratic economic models. For example, Norway is ranked as the most desirable country in the world to live in because of its high standard of living and economic health; the per capita GDP is higher in Norway than in the U.S. Similarly, Sweden has some of the strongest economic growth in the industrialized world. An outcome of a social democratic system is that the countries in this region also have the lowest differences between the incomes of men and women and the

Socialism
An economic policy that can take several forms, in which in its purest form, the state owns all assets of the society. The belief is that if the assets are held by all then all individuals will benefit.

Communism
A political system that relies on a dictatorship to govern and establish a classless society based on the common ownership of property and the means of production.

FIGURE 3-2   World Political Systems

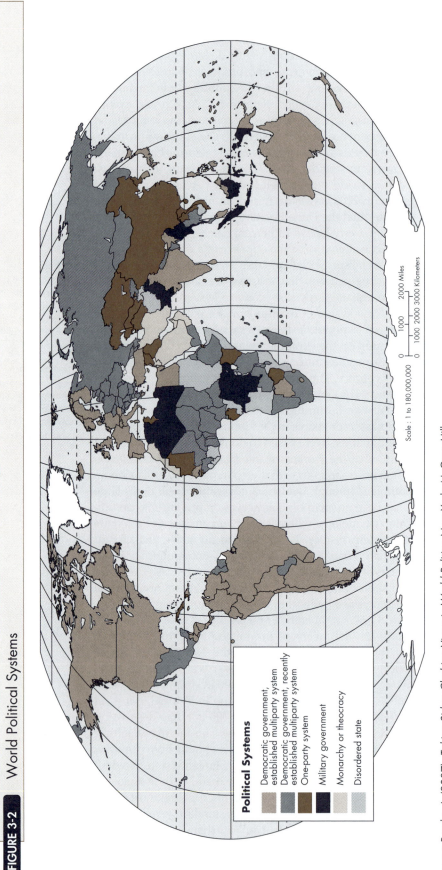

Political Systems

Democratic government, established multiparty system

Democratic government, recently established multiparty system

One-party system

Military government

Monarchy or theocracy

Disordered state

Scale : 1 to 180,000,000

0   1000   2000 Miles
0   1000   2000   3000 Kilometers

Source: Rourke, J. (2007). *Taking Sides: Clashing Views in World Politics.* New York: McGraw-Hill.

longest life expectancies in the world. This model has also produced a number of globally competitive firms, such as Electrolux and Nokia. In Sweden, privately owned firms account for about 90 percent of industrial output, of which the engineering sector accounts for 50 percent of output and exports.

Today, there are a wide range of different mixtures of socialism and market-driven orientations in various countries. For example, China refers to its system as socialism with market characteristics; large segments of the economy are open to foreign investment and profit making, while other parts are still owned by the government.[x] Russia claims it has moved to a market-based system from its former socialist system. However, when the Soviet Union collapsed and Russia emerged as an independent country, the former assets of the state were privatized and the individuals who ended up with the established businesses, particularly in the natural resources sector of the economy (minerals, oil, natural gas) were closely connected to the government. Many of these so-called oligarchs became fabulously rich. Today the market system in Russia is more accurately referred to as oligarch capitalism because only a few well-connected individuals control many of Russia's primary production assets.[xi]

An annual ranking of the free-market orientation of the world's countries is produced by the well-regarded Fraser Institute in Canada, called the Economic Freedom Rating. The 21 countries with the most market-oriented economies and the 21 with the least market-oriented economies are listed in Figure 3-3. It is interesting to note that Hong Kong has continued to be ranked as the freest market in the world for a number of years in this system.

In the United States, there has arisen the common belief that democracy and free-market economics go hand in hand. It is the belief that it is difficult to have one without the other. This is referred to widely as the Washington Consensus. Thus, the U.S., and Europe to a slightly lesser degree, connects the development aid provided to poor nations with the requirement that those nations promote both democracy and free markets. In contrast, Russia and China typically argue that democracy is not required for a successful free-market economy. They argue that a government can generate significant economic growth without generating many democratic reforms. This model is widely referred to as the Beijing Consensus, although the Chinese do not refer to it this way themselves. Particularly among countries lacking traditions of democracy, such as those in Africa, this model has increasing appeal. Based on this philosophy, China grants aid and conducts extensive trade and FDI with countries, such as Sudan, which most Western governments consider to be rogue nations and refuse to trade with. In particular, many have questioned why trade has continued with Sudan in light of their campaign of genocide in the Darfur region. Governments disagree about whether to engage or isolate countries, such as Sudan or North Korea, as well as about the correct approach to fostering economic development.

Thus, in analyzing international business in a given setting it is initially important that the manager first gain an understanding of the economic freedom in that nation. The manager will also want to gain an overall view of the economic environment, including its level of economic development, the wealth of the nation, whether that wealth is evenly spread in society or not, and the nation's economic growth rate. After that the firm should seek to gain more detailed insight into the industry of interest in that nation relative to the rest of the world.

Economic Analysis Tools

The foundation for the recognition of the value of economic perspective to business can in part be traced to Adam Smith. This Scottish philosopher and economist is best known for *laissez-faire* economics. That is, the belief that the freedom to determine prices and competition without the interference of the government or the guilds would result in the best economic outcome. The result of his writings

FIGURE 3-3	Market Freedom Rankings

Ranking	Country	Ranking	Country
1	Hong Kong	103	Benin
2	Singapore	104	Chad
3	New Zealand	105	Romania
3	Switzerland	106	Syria
3	United Kingdom	107	Columbia
3	United States	108	Niger
7	Australia	109	Rwanda
7	Canada	110	Ukraine
9	Ireland	111	Sierra Leone
9	Luxemburg	112	Gabon
11	Estonia	113	Togo
11	Finland	114	Russia
11	Netherlands	115	Burundi
14	Denmark	116	Rep of Congo
14	Iceland	117	Guinea-Bissau
16	Austria	118	Algeria
16	United Arab Emirates	119	Venezuela
18	Belgium	120	Central African Republic
18	Botswana	121	Democratic Rep. Congo
18	Kuwait	122	Zimbabwe
18	Oman	123	Myanmar

Source: Fraser Institute, Canada

was that in the late 1700s, the United Kingdom became an increasingly free economy and spread that philosophy to Western Europe and its colonies, particularly the newly formed United States of America.[xii]

Building on the work of Adam Smith some years later, the economist David Ricardo systematically studied country competitiveness. In his theory of comparative advantage, Ricardo explained why it can be beneficial for two countries to trade, even though one of them may be able to produce all goods necessary. A country will reap gains from specializing in products that it is best at producing and then trading those products to other countries. Even if one country somehow were the lowest-cost producer of all goods, it would still benefit from specializing in a limited number of goods and then trading. In today's terms then, a country such as China may be able to produce many different goods cheaply. However, it is in China's national interest to focus on the products that it is best at producing, rather than trying to produce everything so as to maximize its comparative advantage. This, in part, explains why China dominates global sock production (75 percent of sock production occurs in China). Other countries in turn can similarly focus on what they do best. For example, the United States is very strong in high technology and would do better to emphasize this strength. This **theory of comparative advantage** forms the basis of modern trade theory. The refinement of the theory of comparative advantage is the Heckscher-Ohlin theorem, which states that a country has a comparative advantage in the production of a product if the country is relatively well endowed with inputs that are used intensively in producing the product.[xiii]

Today, research in the area of how nations prosper is known as **developmental economics**. This research has identified a range of factors that encourage economic development and the competitive advantage of nations. For example, the weather is seen as a major factor in the economic potential of a country: regular and well-dispersed rainfall benefits agriculture and allows a society to store food and spend time on other productive activities. Other factors that help or impede economic development include geography, particularly navigable rivers and ports,[xiv] the presence of disease vectors,[xv] what people eat,[xvi] the understanding and application of science,[xvii] and an environment that fosters creativity and entrepreneurship.[xviii]

While a wide range of issues have been examined, three principal perspectives have received the greatest attention in developmental economics.[xix] The first of these is referred to as neoclassical theory and is based on the work of Nobel Prize-winning economist Robert Solow.[xx] This view argues that economic growth comes from the investment in physical and human capital. The second view was popularized by Harvard economist Jeffrey Sachs and is referred to as geographic and location theory.[xxi] It argues that climate conditions and access to major markets is the root of most economic growth. Thus, if a region has a climate that is too tropical (hot) it decreases the energy of employees and makes it hard to store goods, and as a result the region will not prosper. Similarly, if a region is not close enough to major markets, making transportation costs too high, it will not prosper.

The last major view of developmental economics is the institutional approach, which emphasizes the socio-political-cultural factors that affect decision making and actions in subtle but profound ways.[xxii] Institutions create checks and balances, facilitate political cooperation, and reduce political uncertainties. Institutions can be formal structures, such as the law, or a system of contracts and property protection. The institutions can also be informal as was noted in Chapter 2. Culture is often thought of as an informal institution that impacts how economic transactions are managed[xxiii] and how business is conducted in different countries.[xxiv] Researchers and policy makers have realized the importance of institutions, such as a consistent and practical rule of law, or widely held commercial conventions about paying bills on time or delivering the promised product and other norms.[xxv] In this view, a society gains from the smooth management of markets that facilitate the efforts of firms to conduct their business.[xxvi]

The authors believe that the first and third theories (neo-classical and institutional) have the greatest impact on international management. The second stream of thought (geographic and location theory) sees developmental economics as out of the hands of the managers. This is because climate and geography are not items that managers can affect. In contrast, the first and third streams of research are based on a view that management actions are critical.

A model that incorporates the neoclassical stream of thought in developmental economics extensively and to lesser degree the institutional stream of research was developed by Harvard Business School professor Michael Porter. This model is particularly useful for analyzing a region's competitive posture in a given industry segment, and is referred to as the "diamond" of national competitiveness.

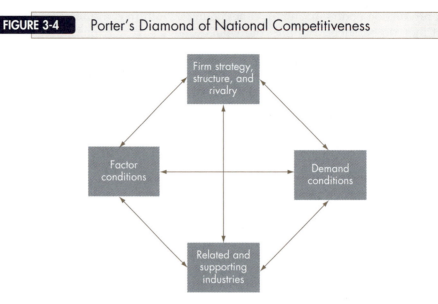

FIGURE 3-4   Porter's Diamond of National Competitiveness

The Diamond Model of National Competitiveness

The Diamond of national competitiveness focuses on why certain countries (or regions within them) are especially competitive in certain industries and are able to generate wealth. This model is designed for industrialized nations and emphasizes how they develop a competitive advantage. The emphasis is on creativity, and the human capital necessary to carry on the innovative processes a view consistent with neo-classical economics. It is important to note this model is designed for mature economies, so it applies best to countries and industries with a strong technology focus. Before applying the model, a manager must analyze the country's level of economic development and reliance on technology. The four factors of the Diamond are factors of production, demand, related and supporting industries, and rivalry.[xxvii] Each of these four elements is examined in turn. Figure 3-4 illustrates Porter's Diamond model.

Factors of Production   Factors of production represent those natural endowments that a nation possesses, such as land, labor, and capital. Traditionally, an abundance of land and mineral resources, and an abundance of labor and capital, were seen as the reasons that nations did well in international business. This view of production factors originated with the concept of comparative advantage that the Swedish team Heckscher–Ohlin put forth at the turn of the century.[xxviii] But this view of how a nation economically succeeds was challenged by Porter.

Porter drew his arguments from analyzing a country, such as the United States, with less than 5 percent of the world's population, but producing an estimated 20 percent of the world's gross domestic product (GDP). The U.S. does have significant endowment of natural resources. For example, the percentage of arable land (land that is useable for agriculture—i.e., not desert or mountains) is 25 percent in the U.S. In contrast, the estimate of such land in China is 12–15 percent. But while such natural resources may have been of immense value at one time in the economic development of the nation, Porter argues that these assets are less responsible for economic success today in industrialized nations, such as the United States.

To illustrate, Japan has neither extensive land, nor natural resources; it is situated on a small, rocky island. Yet Japan is the leading manufacturer of autos, machine tools, and consumer electronics. Japan also lacks cheap labor. In fact, Japan's labor is more expensive than comparable labor in the United States and other developed countries.[xxix] In spite of these apparent disadvantages, Japan has one of the largest and most successful economies in the world. Central to the Japanese success is specialized labor with strong intellectual capital and knowledge. Thus, rather than focusing strictly on natural resources or wages, a country's major concern should be productivity and creativity. The classic example is the consumer electronics industry. In the U.S. and Japan, a similar concern over employee wages arose in the 1970s in the consumer electronics industry. The response of U.S. firms was to ship production overseas, seeking cheaper wages. This resulted in lower production costs, but the firms found it difficult to control quality, and they lost their incentive to create new products. In contrast, Japanese firms designed ways to cut labor costs by mechanizing the process and creating circuit boards that could be slipped into consumer electronics with a minimum of human contact. Japanese firms also continued to push forward on more advanced products. The outcome was that Japanese consumer electronic products of the 1980s and 1990s were of better quality and were produced more efficiently. Today, U.S. firms have exited from analog consumer electronics industries, such as televisions and display screens, video recorders, tape players, and camcorders, where they were once the dominant producers; Japanese firms dominate those industries even though they are facing tough new competition from South Korean and Chinese manufacturers, and from U.S. firms that have now entered from the digital consumer electronics industry, such as Apple.

In classifying Porter's Diamond model of national competitiveness as a neoclassical model, it should be recognized that Porter was not necessarily talking about increasing the human capital of all workers. Instead, the focus is on generating cutting-edge research and development and creative breakthroughs. The government's role is seen as helping to fund research and development, and funding universities to help generate the next generation of creative ideas.

Demand Traditionally, it was also thought that a country had to be big to be economically successful. This was one rationale for the Japanese incursion into China and Southeast Asia that led to the Pacific War in World War II. The Japanese leadership thought they would expand the territory under their control, creating a continental economy by taking over coastal China and Southeast Asia, and thus increase the demand for their country's products. This would in turn support growth, allowing their firms to expand internationally and dominate given industries. However, if this were really a requirement, then countries that are relatively small, such as those in Scandinavia or the Netherlands, could never be successful because they have such small domestic markets. Yet, the Nordic countries are strong international competitors in a number of industries, from furniture to mobile phones.[1]

As a result, Porter argues that the concern should not be the size of demand but the quality of the demand for those products in the nation. For example, **white goods** include washing machines, dryers, and refrigerators. In Germany, the climate is cold and wet, and environmental standards are strict. This requires that clothes washers be very advanced—that is to be energy efficient, with very high spin rates (to dry the clothes more quickly). Consumers are quite demanding in Germany due to the climate and the concern for the environment. As a result, German white-goods firms, such as Bosch, are among the most competitive in the world in this industry.

Similarly, Italians are among the most sophisticated consumers of fashion in the world, and this is reflected, among other areas, in shoes. Many Italian shoe firms are the most profitable and famous brands in the world, in spite of the fact that they are relatively small family-owned firms, such as Ferragamo and Ballin. Thus, the quality of demand can result from different forces in a society, but the result is still a strong focus on quality. This focus results in domestic firms that

White goods
Goods such as washer, dryers, and refrigerators.

---

[1]We use the term Nordic countries for Denmark, Finland, Norway, and Sweden rather than Scandinavian countries. The Finns are not a Scandinavian people. The other three nations' languages are very similar to each other, while the Finns speak a language that is related to Hungarian.

have high standards and innovate rapidly to anticipate future trends and regulations, which results in the ability to be very competitive worldwide.[xxx]

In conducting an analysis of demand, the demographics of the consumer, such as average age, racial characteristics, religion, and income, should be considered. These factors help explain the nature of the demand for that given product and the future outlook for that demand. For example, the most rapidly aging populations in the world are in Asia. In Korea and Japan there is a trend toward small families and as a result the population is aging. This results in a rapid growth in product demand in entertainment and services to older people, including travel packages for retirees.[xxxi] This aging of the population also has major implications for the competitiveness of those countries' firms, if they can not find qualified people to staff businesses.

Related and Supporting Industries It is difficult for a firm or a group of firms to be world-class producers if they do not have industries that are not also world-class producers to supply inputs or use their products. The reason is that businesses need to know about new inputs and needs of the market before their competitors. If a business does not have world-class suppliers, too often it learns of shifts in the nature of inputs when competitors already are using those inputs. A world-class customer will also come to a firm and tell them of new products and new processes they need. Without such insights, the firm can only find out about such things from competitors.

Retailing is an industry in which U.S. firms do very well around the world. To illustrate related and supporting industries, consider the world's largest retailer, Wal-Mart. It sells consumer goods from the leading firms around the world. Its suppliers maintain large staffs on location in Bentonville, Arkansas, the location of Wal-Mart's headquarters, in order to work with Wal-Mart's buyers on what new products or product modifications are needed by global consumers. This working relationship results in manufacturers who supply Wal-Mart constantly being pushed to produce better products, and at a lower cost for Wal-Mart and other similar retailers. The flow of information is not simply from Wal-Mart; these firms also bring to Wal-Mart new ideas and new products, which in turn push Wal-Mart to better serve its customers. Thus, the suppliers and Wal-Mart are constantly pushing each other to be better. Today, Wal-Mart's major growth comes from its international markets, including Mexico and China.

A similar example can be found in French retailer Carrefour, the world's second largest retailer. Carrefour has similar relationships with European suppliers and, like Wal-Mart, is a major global competitor. In many countries, the greatest competition is between international firms, such as Carrefour or Wal-Mart, with local firms often seeking protected niches so they do not have to compete against these very efficient international competitors. It is interesting to note that the global consumer-goods industry is dominated by European and U.S. firms. Similarly, European and U.S. retailers are also among the world's toughest competitors in consumer goods. In contrast, there are limited areas of consumer goods that are dominated by Asian or Latin American firms. Retailers from these regions are not major international powers as international retailers and have been excluded, until very recently, from these markets.

Industry Strategy and Structure The last component of the Diamond is industry strategy and structure. Broadly, this element refers to the nature of the competition in an industry. Porter, and many economists, argue that it is necessary for firms to face tough competitors somewhere, hopefully in their home market. This is because if a firm has little or no competition, there will be little incentive to innovate. This was always the flaw in the failed "national champion" model of industry, utilized in the past by developing countries, such as Indonesia and India. The governments of countries that supported the national champion model

---

THE NEWSPAPER INDUSTRY: WORLDWIDE ENVIRONMENT IS CHANGING

As noted earlier, many times a firm's financial performance is determined by broad industry trends and structure. The newspaper industry in most industrialized nations is in a slow but deliberate decline. Newspaper circulation fell between 1995 and 2003 by 5 percent in the U.S., 3 percent in Europe, and 2 percent in Japan. Rupert Murdoch, one of the world's richest men, made his fortune initially in newspapers and magazines as the head of the News Corporation. He told the American Society of Newspaper Editors in April of 2005, "I believe too many of us editors and reporters are out of touch with our readers."

The reason for his indictment was that today young people are more frequently getting their news from the Internet. A CNN/USA Today poll found that 44 percent of online youth aged 18–29 often read weblogs (blogs). There are now worldwide networks where individuals post stories themselves. The power of such networks can be seen in recent events in Ukraine, where the initial stories about the government corruption in the political process that eventually led to a change in the Ukrainian government in 2005 came from blogs, not the established media.

However, blogs are only part of the trend. There are collaborative Web pages where individuals can discuss issues. There are also Web sites, such as Google, where the news of the day can be pulled from around the world. Thus, the newspaper industry will most likely continue losing readership. The difficulty for newspapers is how to deal with such changes in an effective manner because the change is cultural, technological, and disruptive to their business model, not due to the poor operation of the newspapers.

Yesterday's papers. (2005, April 23). *Economist*, pp. 59–60.

---

thought it was best to have one "national champion" firm in an industry, that is to have one firm that supplied virtually the whole country with a product, say shoes, to build scale and save costs on marketing (after all, why spend so much on advertising and promotion if you are a monopoly?), and then use those monopoly profits to sell shoes globally. The flaw in this thinking is that if one firm can supply the whole of India or Indonesia with shoes at a guaranteed profit, there is little incentive to innovate and upgrade product lines. Why improve if one can produce shoes for two dollars and sell them for three dollars in a protected market, ad infinitum? It turns out that the shoes will sell in Indonesia, but it is highly unlikely that they will become globally competitive. India utilized historically a similar protected market system, and now is saddled with numerous brands that are known only in India and are wholly uncompetitive in overseas markets.

Firms need both tough customers and competitors to push them. New Zealand is a country that historically had a protected market. This country of four million feared it would be swallowed up by major international firms if it allowed full and free competition. However, in 1984, in the face of sluggish economic growth, the left-of-center Labour party, following other British Commonwealth countries, deregulated industry, privatized state owned firms, cut industry subsidies, and pushed through a major switch from an income to a consumption tax. Even the local postal service was opened up to competition. Initially, this resulted in some pain to both consumers and workers, but ultimately the economy grew to be one of the strongest in the world, with growth in individuals' income and their businesses becoming some of the world's most efficient.[xxxii]

This experience contrasts with the former socialist systems in the USSR and China where if one did not like the local service there were no other options. (The USSR was the Union of Soviet Socialist Republics, the communist federation of "republics" headed by Russia. The USSR broke up in 1991 as each of the separate republics moved away from communism and most asserted their independence from Russia for the first time in decades.) In the USSR and China, consumers had no options for where to go for products because all the stores were the same. The result was that clerks often ignored customers, and merchandise typically was behind counters where the customers were not allowed to inspect it. Instead a product was handed to consumers once they purchased it. To purchase a good, the person would need to pay at one place and then take their receipt to the clerk who would hand them the product.

Even if an economy is generally competitive, a firm needs competitors that push it to improve. For example, Poland has undergone a rapid economic transformation since it left the heavy influence of the Soviet Union and the Communist Party. However, Poland's national airline, LOT, is still government controlled and heavily subsidized. The common advice given to customers is to approach LOT's service desk holding the ticket between the hands in a "prayer position" because it may only be through divine intervention that the staff will help you. Indian nationals will tell you that India's national carrier, Air India, was very much the same until competition shook up India's air-travel market.

Summary of the Diamond   There are several factors that should become clear as the Diamond model is considered. One is that competition is not bad for countries and industries. A major flaw in the socialist system is the idea that it is best to have one big firm, or national champion. Officials in the USSR argued that the capitalist system of multiple firms competing with different product offerings was terribly inefficient, and that it was better to have one firm working to create the one best product in its category and not waste time with multiple organizations, multiple research and development departments, marketing, too much administration, and so forth. Numerous economists and management scholars have countered that although command economies can be temporarily efficient, they tend to curtail innovation and significantly hinder additional economic development. Perhaps the capitalist system is less efficient in the short run, but robust competition and innovation is produced in the long run.[xxxiii] Why go through the sweat, difficulty, and risk of innovation if a firm can sit in its protected market, getting richer all the time, until it falls so far behind technologically that its government can no longer keep competitive products out of the market, and then the game will be over? Few people know that the USSR was the first mover in calculators around 1970. The USSR insisted on having one organization produce the "people's calculator," which was initially superior to what Americans and Japanese firms were producing at that time. The Soviets even exported the calculator to Soviet bloc countries (those nations aligned with the USSR, such as Bulgaria and Romania) with some initial success. Yet there was little incentive to innovate and the Soviet calculator and its successors quickly fell behind competitive products around the world. In spite of having some first-mover advantages in calculators and certain micro-computing products, Russian firms are generally uncompetitive on the global market for these products today.

Other Country-Level Economic Concerns in Emerging and Transitioning Economies

Other economic variables are important as you analyze a nation. As stated in the previous sections, the focus of the Diamond model is on mature economies. But in analyzing nations, you'll find that many may not be mature economies. In particular many firms from mature economies are today entering emerging economies in order to access the expanding markets in those nations. Coca-Cola is the world's most widely recognized brand and one of the world's largest corporations. Today the firm's major sales growth is in emerging markets, not in mature markets like Europe or the United States.

When we think of emerging economies, we are talking about rapidly growing economies that typically employ market-based economic methods to grow. There

---

IKEA IN THE UNITED STATES

While the Diamond model is useful for understanding large macro settings, it should not be forgotten that firms ultimately have to make individual choices that affect their success. The Swedish firm Ikea is a major global furniture retailer that has been very successful taking well engineered but affordable furniture to a wide variety of markets around the world. Ikea was founded in 1943 and now has 215 stores in 33 countries. The privately held firm has estimated annual worldwide sales of over $15 billion. The chain has been in the United States for 20 years but has only 25 U.S. stores.

Ikea initially stumbled when it came to the U.S. It sold European-size beds and bedding products that didn't fit well with other accessories. Beds in the United States are typically much larger than in Europe; consistent with the fact that homes are larger in the U.S. The firm also stocked home products that were based on the metric system, so items like measuring cups were the wrong size. The firm also appeared at a time when the U.S. economy was in recession. The combination of a poor economy and poor understanding of the market resulted in a disappointing beginning for Ikea.

Ikea has since repositioned itself by adjusting to the market, with the U.S. contributing the second highest amount of revenue to the firm behind Germany. The firm was also aided by the fact that they were an early mover in the appearance of national furniture firms. Historically, the furniture industry had been very fragmented with only local competitors. In the 1980s, national furniture-retailing firms began to develop in the industry, and Ikea was a participant in that movement. Ikea also aggressively pursued modular furniture so people could customize their furniture more easily. This fit with the increased sophistication of markets for home furnishings.

This trend was not only in the United States but also in markets such as Singapore, Malaysia, and Hong Kong.

Ikea's efforts to better understand the market continues. There is a growing Hispanic market for the firm. They realized by visiting the homes of such customers that their furniture would be used in a setting where there is more family entertaining and a need to be able to move furniture and reshape it. There was also a greater value placed on leather furniture. Finally, there was a greater need for the ability to place family photographs around the home. Ikea created several novel and substitution products for existing offerings in the marketplace. The firm has made numerous adjustments to its markets and is doing well in most of its foreign markets today.

Koncius, J. (2005, September 15). Ikea's U.S. director keeps eye on demographics to push line. *Asian Wall Street Journal*, p. M8.

---

is an important subset of emergent economies called transitional economies, which are moving from former central planning to a free market. Particularly, we think of transitional economies as those in the former USSR, Eastern Europe, and China. These economies present unique opportunities for firms from mature economies but they have a unique economic setting for managers.

Transition economies continue to deal with the remnants of the old central planning, statist system. There typically are very large and complex bureaucracies associated with the government in these countries. The government regulators often still reflect the old socialist mindset more than a free market approach to regulation, although there are some exceptions, such as Estonia. The economy is still also often littered with largely inefficient state-owned enterprises. Though some state enterprises, such as China's national energy companies, function fairly well, most state enterprises often employ too many people and require various levels of government support.

To further illustrate, a few more details of the world's largest transition economy, China, can be helpful. The 1.3 billion people in China offer tremendous economic potential to firms. But the majority of the economy is still owned by various government entities. Even many large firms, such as Lenovo, are principally owned by a given government entity; in the case of Lenovo the largest shareholder with over a third of the firm's stock is a government entity. Almost all publicly listed companies from China are government controlled firms and continue to be even after they are listed. The government controls what firms are listed and they feel that the government firms are the ones that are in need of capital for restructuring. Therefore, they list those firms, although the dominant shareholder is almost always the government.

In analyzing economic variables in transitional economies, the role of the government is far more significant than in mature markets. Even firms from

Europe, which have familiarity with relatively high levels of government involvement, are surprised at the level of government involvement in China. The ability to deal with these government entities is critical because of the selective use and enforcement of regulation. A good working relationship with a wide variety of government entities ensures that the selective enforcement of the laws or rules does not occur for the Western firm.

It is important to note in discussing China that it is large and there are multiple levels of government that are critical. Thus, the nation is less like a unified market (like the United States) than an early predecessor to the European Common Market. There are some common government entities across the larger area, but each region still largely controls its own economic regulation. Thus, just because a product is produced in Shanghai and the central government likes it, this does not mean that it can be sold in another province. Each province largely controls its own marketplace.

It is important to note that, unlike the analysis of Porter's Diamond model, in emerging or transition economies, natural resources can be critical. To illustrate the importance of natural resources to developing nations, consider the rapid economic advancement of the Gulf States of Kuwait, Oman, the United Arab Emirates, Qatar, and Bahrain since their independence in the 1960s and 1970s. At the time of their independence, their economic development was similar to that of Africa. However, since their independence, the growth in the value of oil has allowed these nations' GDP to explode. Today, the windfalls from oil have allowed these nations to develop a well-educated work force with economic development based only partly on oil, as other industries have been developed.

However, beyond that, managers doing business internationally will want to investigate other key aspects of a country, such as average level of education. It was noted that many transition economies have high levels of education, but that is not always the case. Vietnam has a literacy rate of 97 percent, but in neighboring Laos it is only 43 percent with over 57 percent of the nation's children today receiving no formal education. For a firm looking to expand and open a new factory, the level of education can have tremendous impact on the cost of finding qualified workers and the cost of training those workers.

Firms will also want to examine things such as transportation. China is well recognized today as a manufacturing hub in which firms locate in order to manufacturer goods for export. But almost all of this manufacturing activity occurs along the coast of China. In part this is because the transportation system in China remains very primitive. It can take much longer for goods to make their way across China to the coast than to ship the goods by freighter from China to Los Angeles. A related concern with transportation is the level of technology available in the nation. There are many emergent economies where electricity is not consistently available, and neither are hard wired telephones. Even wireless telephones do not operate in many areas of Africa. Therefore, managers need to determine the level of technology that can be supported in a given country. For many Western firms with their heavy reliance on just-in-time inventory and computers, such limitations can be severe enough to require very creative solutions.

The health status of the nation should also be examined. Life expectancy in Africa is actually declining and is now approximately 47 years. This is less than two thirds of what it is in developed economies, such as Europe or North America. The high prevalence of AIDS—over 13 percent of the population—will likely decrease life expectancy further. (Figure 3-5 illustrates the decline in life expectancy in Africa.) Other issues are more prevalent in emerging markets, such as corruption (discussed in part in Chapter 1, and in the section of this chapter titled Legal Environment), which a firm should also examine and evaluate.

AIDS in Africa: Life Expectancy
Changes in life expectancy in several African countries. Botswana has been particularly badly hit, while public education projects campaigns have had a positive effect in Uganda.

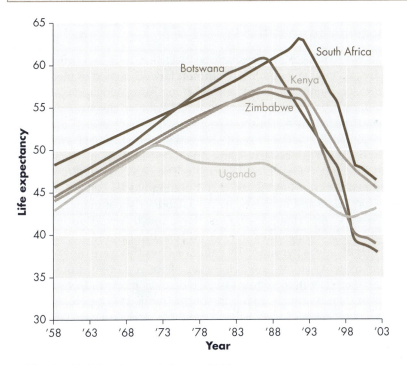

Source: World Bank, *World Development Indicators,* 2004

LEGAL ENVIRONMENT

A firm seeking to understand a market will then also wish to understand not only its economic environment but also its legal environment. Too often business people see the legal system as an enemy when it should be viewed as a valuable facilitator. One of the great advances of the world came as individuals began to write down the law and have established means to do simple things like sell property among themselves. Consider countries such as Angola or Somalia where there is no legal system to speak of; it is virtually impossible to conduct business there. During the Angolan civil war, international oil firms had to pay their employees partly in cases of beer, because institutions had broken down to the point where it was a barter society. Thus, local employees had money deposited in an international account offshore, but for them to pay for food they needed cases of beer to trade for needed items. It was noted above that there are many unique characteristics of emergent economies. One of the key characteristics is the status of the rule of law and whether it exists. If there is not a rule of law, then the risk to the business is much higher. The firm cannot depend on the enforcement of contracts, protection of its products from being copied, taking the profit they make out of the country (called **repatriation of profits**), or even preventing the entire firm from simply being taken away from the rightful owners.

The legal and regulatory environment not only is important to establish how business will operate, it can in fact provide a competitive advantage to a business. For example, in domains such as environmental regulation the new regulation can enable local firms to anticipate world demand and gain a first-mover advantage in

Repatriation of profits
The ability of a firm to take the profits it makes in a country out of that country.

different technologies that will soon be required worldwide. For example, European regulators require paper manufacturers to produce chlorine-free paper. Historically most of the world has used chlorine in the production of paper, but not using chlorine results in a savings of 88 percent in the freshwater used. As the world moves to chlorine-free paper production, it is the European firms that are able to sell the expertise and equipment around the world.

Legal Systems around the World

Common law

Legal systems primarily built on legal precedent established by judges as they resolve individual cases; those case opinions have the force of law and strongly influence future decisions. Common law originated in medieval England and is used in the United Kingdom, the British Commonwealth, and in Britain's former colonies, such as the United States, Singapore, Hong Kong, and India.

Civil law

Originated in Ancient Rome and is used on the European continent and to a lesser extent, in China today. This approach to the law uses statutes and comprehensive codes as the primary building blocks, relying heavily on legal scholars to formulate and interpret the laws.

Most of the world's legal systems can be classified into two broad categories—common law and civil law systems. **Common law** originated in medieval England and spread to its colonies, such as the U.S., Hong Kong, Singapore, Australia, New Zealand, India, and several African colonies. Common law systems are primarily built on legal precedent established by judges as they resolve individual cases; those case opinions have the force of law and strongly influence future decisions, particularly by lower courts. **Civil law** originated in Ancient Rome and has two major branches today: French and German. The civil law tradition uses statutes and comprehensive codes as the primary building blocks, relying heavily on legal scholars to formulate and interpret the laws. Under the common law system, legal precedent is very important, and judges have much leeway to interpret a law's intent and provide commentary that will be used in future legal rulings. What is not prohibited by law is permitted by common law. There are differences in French and German systems of civil law. However, there is more commonality between the two than there is with common law. Civil law is more widely spread throughout the world than is common law. In contrast with a common law system, civil law judges have less leeway and rule according to strict codes. Unless something is permitted under civil law's written legal code, it is generally prohibited.

To illustrate, studies have shown that different legal systems consider the investors in different societies. Studies have shown that common law countries have greater protection of investors than do civil law countries.[xxxiv] The areas examined included voting rights attached to shares, protection of shareholder voting mechanisms against the abuse of management, and remedial rights of minority shareholders. The German system of civil law was next in protecting these rights, and last were the French-based civil law systems around the world.

It is important to note that there are other systems that fall neither in the common law tradition nor in the civil law tradition. For example, China has had a completely different system of law. Chinese civilization (timed from the emergence of the pictograph writing system of Chinese characters) is over 3000 years old. It was the Chinese who actually invented the concept of the functional bureaucracy during the Qin dynasty in 221 BC. However, the advanced development of a society that covered a very large territory resulted in a legal system in which only very few broad directions were given and local authorities had broad ability to interpret the law. Until the establishment of the Chinese Republic in the early 1900s, fewer than 500 written laws existed for all of China.[xxxv] As a result, local officials in China were given the authority to interpret and enforce those laws—something they still do today, in spite of the central government's desire to curtail their power.[xxxvi]

This broad approach to the legal system continued after the Communist takeover of China in 1949 when nearly all of the old laws were thrown out. The law then became basically what the Communist Party said it was, and this often came from the interpretation of Chairman Mao Zedong's speeches and writings. For example, if Mao said that 10 percent of all people were (illegal) counter-revolutionaries, then 10 percent of the people would be charged as counter-revolutionaries and punished, irrespective of any offense. Prison commandants and city officials were charged with filling these "quotas" every year.[xxxvii] Moreover, there were virtually no commercial laws concerning property, employment, responsibility of individuals and organizations, product

LAW, REGULATION, AND ENTREPRENEURS

The law has a significant impact on entrepreneurs as they begin to establish their businesses. For example, in the Philippines, Pablo Planas invented a device called the Khaos Super Gas Saver over 30 years ago. The product is designed to aid in fuel efficiency by regulating the mixture of oxygen and fuel. The device will result in more efficient burning of fuel and less air pollution because less carbon dioxide is produced. The device costs approximately U.S.$100, but with older or less-fuel-efficient vehicles used in most emergent markets, it has the potential to provide significant benefit.

It took Mr. Planas 30 years to get the product in production. The normal process to start a business in the Philippines entails the filing of 11 different documents and the completion of other procedures typically requiring about 50 days. The cost is about 20 percent of the per capita income of an individual in the Philippines. Contrast this to the low cost, two-day process in Canada. Once the person has the approvals for the business in the Philippines they must have the capital to fund the business themselves. Banks are discouraged from lending to entrepreneurs unless they have assets to secure the loans completely—a no-risk loan. As a result Mr. Planas tried for 30 years to get his business going. At 67 years old he finally found an investor who invested less than $60,000 to help start the

business. The firm now produces 500 units a day, employs over 135 people, and is looking at starting a second factory. The World Bank reports that the experience of the Philippines is not that unusual. The nations that may need entrepreneurship and new businesses the most are often the ones that have the greatest barriers to their creation. As famed Peruvian economist Hernando de Soto has lucidly shown, entrepreneurs in the lesser developed countries are constrained by numerous regulations, not the least of which is the time and expense to just register the business and start (legal) operations. In early research for his well-known book *The Mystery of Capital,* De Soto found that in Peru, permission to set up a small business and acquire the appropriate licenses took an average of 289 days and cost 31 times the average Peruvian's monthly salary. Experiences in other lesser-developed countries were similar; in Mozambique it will take 145 days to simply get all the licenses needed to start a business. By contrast, in Hong Kong, one of the more entrepreneurial locations in the world, it takes just two days.

Soto, H.D. (2000). *The Mystery of Capital: Why Capitalism Triumphs in the West and Fails Everywhere Else.* New York: Basic Books.

Hookway, J. (2005, May 9). A paradox for poor nations. *The Wall Street Journal,* p. A20.

safety, and so forth. Today there is an increasing body of written law in China that follows a civil law system.

In China, legal precedent is only used for guidance and does not take on legal status as in common law systems. However, the tradition still exists of local government officials (not judges) having broad ability to interpret what a given law means. This has made doing business in China difficult, even for the locals who know the system. If someone wanted to take a company's used shampoo bottles from the trash, wash them, and put his or her own cheap shampoo in them and sell them as an original branded shampoo, virtually nothing could stop him or her from doing so. Today, the legal system in China still results in an environment where copying of products is so bad that business people there joke that in China, "R&D means read and duplicate." While China is quickly attempting to build a legal system, the government's effort to devolve from strong central control to more local control has slowed the development of a legal environment. This localization of the law and its interpretation is frequently a cause of great frustration for Western business people. The movement to have a more consistent legal environment is strong, but will take a number of years to complete.

Other legal systems that merit discussion are the theocratic systems, of which Islamic or Shari'a law is the most important. **Shari'a law or jurisprudence** is inspired by the Koran, the Sunna, the **Hadiths**, and the work of Muslim scholars over the two first centuries of Islam, as well as some older Arabic law systems that predate Islam. The resulting systems of jurisprudence derived from Shari'a can be viewed as quite harsh by most Western standards, where issues of personal behavior are concerned. For example, for stealing, the right hand can be cut off. The penalty for female adultery in some Islamic countries is death by stoning. Strict forms of Islamic law are practiced in countries such as Sudan, Saudi Arabia, Pakistan, Afghanistan, Iran, and others.

Shari'a law
The law system inspired by the Koran, the Sunna, the Hadiths, older Arabic law systems, parallel traditions, and the work of Muslim scholars over the two first centuries of Islam.

Hadiths
Several volumes compiled well after the Koran. A major source of Islamic law and moral teachings.

ISLAM AND BUSINESS

The name Islam comes from an Arabic root word meaning "peace" and "submission." The religion is one of the monotheistic faiths, along with Judaism and Christianity, that draws its roots from a common root: Abraham. Islam was founded by the Prophet Muhammad who was born in A.D. 570 at Mecca, in Saudi Arabia. There are over one billion Muslims in the world today. Although usually associated with the Arabs of the Middle East, only 10–15 percent of Muslims are, in fact, Arab. Part of the reason only estimates can be given is that Muslims do not formally belong to a given mosque, and mosques do not maintain membership roles. Instead, Muslims are individuals who define themselves as Muslims and follow its principles.

There are five basic beliefs, or pillars, that are the foundation for the Muslim religion. The first pillar is the profession of faith or, the *shahadah*. *Shahadah* centers on the fact that Muslims believe God is the central factor in their lives. The second pillar is ritual worship, or *salah*. Muslims are required to pray formally five times a day— at dawn, midday, afternoon, evening and night. The prayers are to be said facing the Saudi Arabian city of Mecca,

Muhammad's birthplace and the holiest city of Islam. The entire body says the prayers, not just the voice. Thus, those praying bend with hands on knees, kneel with hands on thighs and finally bow their heads to touch the floor. Each motion is accompanied by verses from the Koran.

The third pillar is fasting, or *sawm*, during a month in the Muslim calendar called Ramadan. During Ramadan, Muslims are to refrain from eating, drinking, smoking and having sex from dawn to sunset. Typically during Ramadan, Muslims have breakfast before dawn and do not eat again until after sunset. The fourth pillar is almsgiving, called *zakah* in Arabic. Muslims pay a specified amount of money, typically 2.5 percent of one's accumulated wealth each year, to assist the poor and sick. The fifth pillar is the *hajj*, or pilgrimage to Mecca. Islam requires that every believer make at least one visit to Mecca in a lifetime if physically and financially able to do so.

The population of Muslims continues to expand around the world. Today, Muslims are in every nation. However, unlike some religions in the world, the conduct of business and the religious faith for Muslims cannot be separated. Thus, it is likely Islam's impact will continue to grow in the world.

Muslims around the world have different sects, which affects how they view Shari'a law and other doctrines. Two major sects within Islam are Shia (Shi'ite) and Sunni. The Shia dominate in Iran and Iraq and constitute an important minority in Afghanistan, Kuwait, Lebanon, and Pakistan. The Sunni constitute the majority of Muslims worldwide. Shia Muslims believe that the son-in-law and cousin of Muhammad was the prophet's rightful successor. Ali ruled as the fourth Caliph (leader) after Muhammad, but was assassinated in 661. Today Shia Muslims continue to see their spiritual leaders as chosen by God, such that they have greater authority than do leaders in the Sunni movement. As a result, a Shia Imam has come to be imbued with pope-like authority and infallibility, and Shia religious hierarchy is similar in structure and religious influence to that of the Roman Catholic Church.

In contrast, Sunni Islam more closely resembles the host of independent churches of Anglo-American Protestantism. They are called "Sunni" because they accept the "sunnas"—the oral traditions and interpretations of the Koran. Sunni Muslims see their religious leaders as scholars, jurists, and prayer leaders, who may offer non-binding opinions on religious law. Shia and Sunnis also interpret some elements of the Koran and Hadiths differently, which affects their interpretation of Islamic law. Although the differences to most outside observers are not seen as major, they can be a source of significant debate and conflict within Islamic countries.

It is important to realize that Muslims will often (but not always) be guided by Shari'a-based law even if they do not live in a country that is governed by that law. For example, Shari'a-based law dictates that interest cannot be charged on loans. Thus, banks cannot directly pay interest on deposits or charge interest on money that is loaned from the bank to others and still be consistent with Shari'a-based law.

Following Shari'a law, mortgages to buy homes could not exist because they involve interest payments. However, there are Muslim-oriented banks and mortgage companies throughout the world that provide an equivalent service. Also, some large organizations, such as the HSBC banking group, have units that follow Shari'a law, in which two means are used for mortgages. In both, they do not charge interest but accomplish the same purpose and typically at the same profit. One method is called the *ijara method;* here the financial institution is considered to be the buyer of the property, and the customer pays rent to the financial institution. Thus, the consumer reimburses the purchase price by installments for a given number of years, with some specific service fee calculated into each monthly payment. Once the purchase money has been repaid, the property is transferred to the occupier.

Another method is called the *murabaha method.* Here the financial institution buys a property at the price agreed upon between the occupier and the original vendor and then immediately resells it to the occupier at a higher price. The amount of that higher price is paid back in installments over a period of years to the financial institution. Thus, in both cases the Muslim legal requirement that interest not be charged or paid is met, but the effect is the same as an interest-bearing mortgage—individuals buy their homes over time and the bank is paid extra for this risk. In the future, as the wealth and influence of the Muslim faith spreads, there will be an increase in the need for businesses that allow followers to operate in international business while helping them meet the requirements of their faith.

International Law

International managers need to follow international law. International law concerns those laws, typically arranged by treaty, that affect multiple countries. Typically, international law is more opaque and complex than domestic laws and regulations, as multiple jurisdictions and legal traditions may be involved. Understanding and conforming to key laws, regulations, and unwritten commercial conventions present a major problem for multinational firms. There are several principles governing international law and commercial practice.

International Jurisdiction International law provides for three types of jurisdictional principles. First is the nationality principle, which holds that every country has jurisdiction over its own citizens no matter where they are located. Therefore, a U.S. manager who violates U.S. law, such as the U.S. Foreign Corrupt Practices Act (the act, reviewed in Chapter 1, deals with bribery) can be arrested and found guilty in the United States even if the manager committed that act in a foreign country. Second is the territoriality principle. This principle, which dates back to the European Renaissance traders, holds that a country has jurisdiction within its own territory. Therefore, a Chinese firm that sells appropriated intellectual product in the United States can be sued under U.S. law—something that happened recently in the Cisco-Huawei suit, in which networking firm Cisco successfully sued the Chinese firm Huawei for copying its technology. Third is the protective principle that gives a country jurisdiction over behavior that adversely affects its national security, even if that conduct occurred out of the country. Therefore, the actions of a terrorist training camp that has targeted U.S. installations, enterprises, and citizens abroad is subject to the application and enforcement of U.S. laws, even though the terrorists' camp may be located in a remote African countryside.

Sovereignty and Sovereign Immunity This principle is consistent with the realist view of international relations. It holds that governments have the right to rule themselves as they see fit to secure their national sovereignty, integrity of borders, and laws. This effectively means that one country's court system cannot be used to resolve injustices or impose penalties on another organization or individual unless the host country agrees. Thus U.K. laws require equality in the workplace for all employees, but U.K. citizens who take a job in Hong Kong cannot sue their Singapore-based employer for age discrimination under the provisions of U.K. law for equal opportunity. Similarly, while a class action suit against companies in

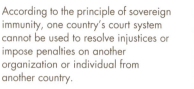

According to the principle of sovereign immunity, one country's court system cannot be used to resolve injustices or impose penalties on another organization or individual from another country.

EyePress/ AP Photo

the United States is a common occurrence, lawyers have found it impossible to bring class action suits for discrimination against companies in Asia.

Doctrine of Comity *Comity* is from the Latin *comitas,* which is also the source of the English word *courteous.* In international relations, comity represents a state of mutual harmony, friendship, and respect among countries. Specifically, comity states that there should be mutual respect for the laws, institutions, and governments in other countries in the matter of jurisdiction over their own citizens. It is the principle that countries will extend courtesies to other countries to enforce their judgments and recognize the validity and effect of their executive, legislative, and judicial acts when necessary, such as enforcing a lawsuit against a firm or arresting a fugitive from another country.

Act of State Doctrine The act of state doctrine holds that all acts of other governments are considered to be valid by a country's courts, even if such acts are inappropriate in that country. For example, foreign governments have the right to limit what a foreign retailer like Wal-Mart does, even if those legal limits violate U.S. law.

Treatment of Aliens Countries have the legal right to refuse admission of foreign citizens and to impose arbitrary and sudden restrictions on their right of travel, where they can stay, and in what activities they can participate. China, for example, has placed limits on what cities and towns foreign nationals can travel to. Foreigners that violate these laws will be detained and even arrested. After the 9-11 attacks, the United States placed restrictions on foreigners primarily from certain Middle East and West Asian countries traveling on certain types of short-term visas in order to prevent them from overstaying their visas. This could mean restricting them to the city limits of the town in which they were staying, for example. Although critics condemned the United States, the actions were within the limits of international law and precedent.

Forum for Hearing and Settling Disputes This is a principle of U.S. justice as it applies to international law. U.S. courts can dismiss cases brought before them by foreigners; however, they are bound to examine key issues of the case. Commonly such cases may be reverted back to a foreign jurisdiction for judgment and enforcement. U.S. courts may decline to be involved after that. As noted earlier, U.S. courts sent the Chevron case back to the Ecuadorian courts to settle (see the opening vignette, Texaco Chevron and Ecuador).

International Institutions In recent decades, numerous supranational institutions intended to govern international relations have arisen. These supranational institutions, such as the United Nations, the IMF, and the WTO, provide guidance for countries in their international relations and negotiations with other countries, though they are profoundly dependent on the consent of member states to obey international law and regulations imposed by international institutions. There is no suprastatutory authority that can enforce international law without the consent (and sometimes collaboration) of member states. For example, contrary to popular belief, United Nations resolutions are not binding under international law and do not constitute an "international statute or enforceable judicial ruling."[xxxviii]

International Business and Protecting Intellectual Property

There are a few legal issues concerning international business that merit particular discussion. One such issue is the protection of intellectual property rights. The United States is a technology-intensive nation where intellectual property is routinely and aggressively defended. However, this is not always the case worldwide. For example, it is estimated that over 90 percent of the software in Chinese government offices is illegal. Illegal copies of movies are often available in foreign countries, such as Russia, before the movie has officially opened.

There are several key types of concerns in intellectual property. The first is a **copyright** or the right to have exclusive right to control reproduction or adaptation of creative works, such as books, movies, music, paintings, photographs, and software. Typically, the copyright holder has the exclusive right to control the product for between 10 and 30 years, depending on jurisdiction. A **patent** is granted to a new, useful, and non-obvious invention. It gives the patent holder a right to prevent others from copying the invention without a license for 20 years from the filing date of a patent application. A **trademark** is a distinctive sign that is used to distinguish the products or services of different businesses.

To date there is no harmonization of the laws governing intellectual property. Some nations have made agreements with other nations to mutually recognize the intellectual property filings, but others do not. The result is that firms may have to file their copyright, patent, or trademark in a many different countries. This has been a particularly difficult issue in China, which was closed to the outside world for so many years that many major firms did not bother filing their copyright, patent, or trademark there. But once these major firms sought to enter the market, they would find that a local firm had already filed the documents for that copyright, patent, or trademark and claimed it as their own. The international firm would then have to enter the local legal system and seek to ensure that their rights were observed. This can be expensive and difficult. Even today, many firms find that they must seek to aggressively enforce their intellectual property in other countries. For example, in China there are well-known and widely visible firms, such as Starbucks where the name is in Chinese characters and not English. The Starbucks you know uses its name spelled out in English throughout the world. The setting in the firm that has the Starbucks name in Chinese characters looks somewhat like the Seattle based company's store, but was not as clean and the products not as good as those in the authentic Starbucks. Starbucks has fought to prohibit this clear violation of its intellectual property with some success.

Copyright
The exclusive right to control reproduction or adaptation of creative works, such as books, movies, music, paintings, photographs, and software. Typically, the copyright holder has the exclusive right to control the product for between 10 and 30 years, depending on jurisdiction.

Patent
Granted to a new, useful, and non-obvious invention. It gives the patent holder a right to prevent others from copying the invention without a license for 20 years from the filing date of a patent application.

Trademark
A distinctive symbol used to distinguish the products or services of different businesses.

POLITICAL ENVIRONMENT

Nationalize
When a government decides a good or factory will be owned by the national government.

Expropriation
When a government seizes the ownership of a private asset or assets.

Finally, a firm seeking to understand an international market will want to understand the political setting in a given nation, particularly the political risk, which can have an immediate and dramatic impact on a firm. For example, in the 1950s and 1960s many governments in the Middle East, and in parts of Africa and Latin America, acted to **nationalize**, or take over business assets owned by a foreign firm or even by local private owners. When a firm is nationalized its property is **expropriated**, or seized, and the government effectively says that it is theirs. In the case of the Middle East, the nationalized assets included oil producing facilities. The Suez Canal was even nationalized, provoking the Suez Crisis of 1956. Many of the leading oil companies today, such as Saudi Aramco and Kuwait Petroleum Corporation, are government corporations. In the case of the oil companies that owned the assets at that time, they were typically paid for the assets that the government took, although their negotiation ability in this setting was limited. However, sometimes there is no payment at all for the assets, as occurred following the Cuban revolution.

Today, the political environment can be turbulent for a business and still be critical to its success. Bolivia is a very poor country in South America and much of the population is indigenous Indians who have not participated in that country's economic progress. Bolivia has major concentrations of natural gas in its western highlands. There are contracts that exist to export that gas to countries such as the United States. The Bolivian courts threw out those contracts despite extensive spending by many oil and gas companies preparing to export the gas. The result is that the gas contracts signed, and money spent to date, might simply be ignored. The political turmoil is not only in the legal domain. Bolivia is also the third largest producer of cocaine in the world. The political turmoil is such that the coca growers actually have a political party that at the time of the writing of this book is the third largest party in the nation, and the president of the nation actually belongs to that party. Bolivia can therefore be seen as having a very volatile political environment, which is impacting business.

GLOBAL POVERTY

ETHICS

Global poverty is a critical issue that faces businesses and business people today. The level of poverty at a time of world economic growth has fueled widespread criticism of globalization. For example, 0.13 percent of the world's population controls 25 percent of the world's assets, while 20 percent of the world's population consumes 86 percent of the world's goods.[xxxix] One outcome of this high level of poverty is that every day an estimated 27,000 children die of preventable diseases.

The world's greatest economic gaps between rich and poor exist in Latin America.[xl] Typically, oligarchic families control the vast majority of the economies of many nations in Latin America. For example, it is estimated that 2 percent of the population in Guatemala owns over 75 percent of the agricultural land. The result is that over 55 percent of the population lives in poverty.

Businesses must recognize and address this issue even though it is argued by some that businesses have no obligation to do so. In fact, some will argue that it is inappropriate for businesses to address poverty issues because it wastes the shareholders' resources. However, beyond the moral imperative to address such poverty, there is also the need for international firms to recognize they compete in nations as guests of the nation's citizens. They need to provide benefits to the nation. If not, they may face severe penalties, such as expropriation of assets. A firm is also creating the future consumers of its own products. A nation, such as Guatemala, with 56 percent poverty results in limited demand for many consumer goods. Increasing the income and consuming power of the nation will create further demand for that product.

While it can be clearly seen in this example that the gap between rich and poor is a major concern, it should be recognized that many people outside the United States see similar gaps between rich and poor in the U.S. The income gap between rich and poor in the United States is the highest in the industrialized world; the income of the top 1 percent is greater than that of the bottom 40 percent. Interestingly, the gap between rich and poor in China recently surpassed that of the U.S. European countries may not want to imitate these 2 nations' models of economic development, in spite of their significant economic growth in recent decades.

There are a variety of strategies to control political risk. First among these is obtaining insurance. Firms can buy political-risk insurance, which will cover lost assets if they are nationalized or lost by some other means from political risk. Another means to control political risk is for a firm to diversify its investments so that it does not place all of them in a single highly volatile environment. Similarly, it was noted earlier that a firm may choose to enter a nation in a joint venture. One of the key motivators in highly risky environments is to help control the political risk. The environment may be highly turbulent, such as in Venezuela, for most American firms but if the proper partner is selected that risk can be at least partly controlled. Similarly, working closely with high-profile groups external to a nation, such as the World Bank, can help to limit the political risk. The individual nation may feel little loss in nationalizing a single firm's assets, but if the firm at risk is acting in response to requests from a group such as the World Bank, the government may not be willing to irritate the powerful stakeholder. Similarly, firms can limit their political risk by acting in a socially responsible manner in which their value to society is well established. In such cases nations have a harder time justifying to their people that nationalizing the firm is in their best interest.

Many governments choose to **privatize** their ownership in businesses they control. When a government privatizes a business, the state-owned enterprise is sold to private individuals or groups. Following the fall of communism in Eastern Europe, large numbers of government-owned businesses were sold to private investors. Some firms are referred to as privatized even though the government still largely controls the business. For example, in China today, all listed firms are still controlled by the government to some degree. A listed firm, or one called privatized, does not mean the same thing in this environment as in a mature market. The public listing is seen primarily as a means to provide funds to the firm, not to shift ownership to private individuals.

Privatize
When government-owned businesses are sold to private individuals or groups.

The analysis of business and the role of government in China can get even more complex. Some firms, called "**red hats**," are private firms but they seek to look like government-owned firms so that they can receive favorable treatment by regulators. Other firms are government owned but the government allows professional managers to run them. Thus, there are firms that look like private firms but actually are state-owned enterprises, and there are also businesses that appear to be government owned but are actually private firms. Different levels of government also own businesses. Businesses owned by the central government often are in what is referred to as pillar industries or the core industries, such as steel and defense. Almost all of these businesses lose money. Some businesses are owned by provincial governments. **Township and village enterprises** are unique types of Chinese businesses that grew out of worker brigades and were organized by Chairman Mao, the chairman of the Communist Party at the founding of the People's Republic of China. As China moved more to a market economy it founded businesses typically without the heavy regulation of the businesses of the central government or provincial government. As a result they tended to be more flexible and their control was better because it was local. The absence of extensive regulation has allowed this type of government business to be quite successful and therefore the backbone of the nation's economic growth. Many township and village enterprises are still losing money, and some of China's most successful domestic businesses are losing money as well, such as Haier, which is recognized in Europe and the United States for its attempt to take over Maytag.

Red hats
Businesses that the government owns, but which they allow professional managers run.

Township and village enterprises
Unique types of businesses in China that grew out of worker brigades organized by Chairman Mao, the chairman of the Communist Party at the founding of the People's Republic of China.

In China, each level of government will be most receptive to helping the businesses under its jurisdiction. Thus, there is often conflict between the different levels of government and regulations generated that may conflict with each other. Frequently a Western business will believe that obtaining support from the central

REMINBI PEG AND ITS IMPACT ON WORLD TRADE

One of the controversial economic issues in trade today is what is referred to as the Reminbi (RMB) peg. The currency of the People's Republic of China (China) is called the RMB or the yuan. The value of the RMB was historically pegged to the U.S. dollar. The peg has been set at different levels over time, including three, five, and most recently, about eight to the dollar. It was this value no matter what the value of the dollar. That is, if you had a U.S. dollar, you knew that it was worth 8.28 RMB. However, as of late 2005 China pegged their currency to a wider variety of currencies including the euro and the Japanese yen.

The U.S. dollar, since the start of the new millennium, has been in decline relative to other currencies. Thus, an American selling something in Europe in 2000 may have been able to sell its product for $100 in the U.S., but would have to sell that product for 110 euros in Europe to get the same money back. By 2008 that same $100 product in the U.S. would sell for approximately 65 euros. This has driven U.S. exports down as U.S. products have become much cheaper to customers in Europe. (Recognize that for a tourist from the U.S. who takes his or her dollars to Europe, the effect is just the opposite—foreign travel has become much more expensive.) However, relative to China, the $100 product in 2000 held approximately the same value until 2005. If a U.S. product sold for $100 in the U.S., it would have to sell for 828 RMB in both 2000 and 2005.

The difficulty from the U.S. government's perspective is that most countries' currencies are allowed to float against each other. Thus, countries with strong economic policies have currencies that increase in strength, but these countries sell less and other nations in turn seek to strengthen their own industries. It is a natural balancing among international traders. However, it is estimated that if the Chinese currency were allowed to freely float, its worth would be up to 40 percent higher and might move back to about five RMB for one U.S. dollar. The impact of a stronger RMB would make Chinese goods more expensive outside of China. Many government officials around the world think that as a result, the explosion of Chinese exports might slow down. Thus, in the U.S., there are laws now proposed to require the Chinese to allow the free float of their currency or penalties will be imposed on their exports to the U.S.

In 2008, the U.S. dollar was worth 6.87 RMB—a 17 percent decline in the value of the RMB relative to the U.S. dollar. The result has been to make the U.S. products cheaper in China and Chinese goods more costly in the U.S. However, the **trade deficit** with China has not changed dramatically in the U.S. In the future, it is likely that China will allow the currency to freely float. While allowing the currency of China to be more realistically valued is good for international trade, it will not affect the U.S. trade deficit significantly. The U.S. has one of the lowest savings rates and highest levels of deficit spending in the industrialized world. These factors have a far greater effect on the U.S. trade deficit than does the RMB's value. The debate on whether the solution to the U.S. trade deficit is to be found through higher taxes or lower spending is not the goal here. However, it is clear that the excessive levels of deficit spending are not sustainable. The U.S. national debt has also doubled since the start of the new millennium, and will have a significant impact on U.S. economic policy and international relations with its trading partners in the coming years.

Students should realize that while a low value of the U.S. dollar may sound like a cure-all for the international trade difficulties of a nation, it is a short term and costly solution. The value of a nation's currency decreases when other nations do not believe the government's economic program is sufficient. A nation's currency valuation can be conceptualized similar to a stock's value. A stock represents what the public considers the value of the company. The currency exchange rate is the evaluation of the world as to the value a nation can produce and its economic management skills. Thus, it is not a vote of confidence in the international market when a country's currency continues to fall.[xli]

Trade deficit
A negative balance of trade when a country is importing more than it exports.

government in Beijing is all that needs to be done to be successful. Then the firm attempts to conduct business in a distant province, only to discover that the officials with the real power over the firm are in the province capital and not in Beijing. An international business may also find itself in competition with a local enterprise in which the regulators have direct financial interest. Thus, China is a great example of the need to understand the political environment of where a firm intends to do business.

National Risk and Corruption

Some services specialize in generating reports on specific countries and their political standing. The elements of national risk include economic and/or financial risk, such as changes in the terms of trade, and rapid increases in production costs

FIGURE 3-6   Corruption Rankings

- Least corrupt
  - Finland
  - New Zealand
  - Denmark
  - Singapore
  - Sweden
  - Switzerland
  - Norway
  - The Netherlands
  - Canada
  - Australia

- Most corrupt
  - Congo
  - Guinea
  - Afghanistan
  - Sudan
  - Chad
  - Uzbekistan
  - Haiti
  - Iraq
  - Somalia
  - Myanmar

Source: http://www.worldaudit.org/corruption.htm

and energy prices. It also includes political risk that considers factors, such as wars, conflicts internal and external, territorial disputes: social factors, such as civil unrest; and religious conflicts. There is a wide range of firms that provide such services. These include Moody's, Standard & Poor's, Economist Intelligence Unit, and Political Risk Services. These services have become particularly active since the 1997 Asian financial crisis, during which many international firms were caught unaware and as a result suffered significant financial losses.

Other services rank countries' level of corruption too. Many countries have major problems with corruption. For example, in China, the fire department may not come to put out a fire if requisite fees have not been paid to different entities and officials. Many of these fees have nothing to do with fire protection and instead may be things like tree planting fees. The ultimate recipient of such fees is typically believed to be an official who pockets the fees. As a result of such issues many Taiwanese firms in China have joined together to provide their own fire departments. In other nations, such as Nigeria, corruption is so prevalent that all manners of documents and filings can only be obtained with major payments to those who are in charge of the regulation.

Transparency International is one of the agencies that ranks countries by their level of corruption.[xlii] Figure 3-6 lists the most- and least-corrupt nations in the world.[2] Students from the U.S. should note that their nation is not in the top 10 for the perception of corruption in the world, a fact that probably challenges their preconceived idea of themselves.

SUMMARY

This chapter has examined economic, legal, and political environments and how they affect international management. These three concerns affect culture and, in turn, shape international management in significant ways. The pursuit of business internationally cannot ignore the economic, legal, or political environments of the nations in which they compete. If they do, they run the risk of failure because these three critical domains have the potential to override all of the firm's good efforts in strategy and operations. The next two chapters will examine strategy concerns. Following that will be seven chapters that concern operations. Table 3-1 applies the material from this chapter.

---

[2]The ranking is discussed in terms of transparency—more corrupt nations being less transparent and less corrupt nations being most transparent.

TABLE 3-1   Steps in the Evaluation of a Country's Environment

Evaluation by Manager	Factor and Implication
1. Whether economy is mature or emerging	In a mature economy, many items, such as transportation, education of the population, and general health of the population can be assumed to be within an acceptable range. There are different levels of emergent economies, however, the items that typically must be explored include • status of transportation • education level of the population • health status of the population • rule of law in the nation
2. The macro economic environment for the nation and the firm	The issues will include: • wealth of society • attitude toward free enterprise • economic growth rate • distribution of wealth in the society
3. In-depth analysis of the industry of interest—initially looking at how the industry in that nation stacks up in the world	The Diamond of National Competitiveness is a valuable tool for this analysis. In using the results of this analysis, the firm will typically gain insight into the local demand. It will include an analysis of the consumers in that nation, including their religion, income, and demographics (i.e., average age and ethnic identity)
4. The industry and its profitability in a given country	Profitability of the industry can be located in any number of standard industry sources. More discussion follows in Chapter 5.
5. The legal nature of the nation	• Whether the rule of law is present. • Whether the nation relies on civil law or common law The level of protection for businesses is typically greater under common law.
6. The political stability of the nation	The greatest risk is political expropriation and nationalization. However, the political process in any nation is critical to a business and must be understood.

MANAGERIAL GUIDELINES

The international manager should remember as they conduct business that:

1. Business does not exist in isolation. The general economy of a country in which a business operates, and the nature of the industries in which that firm operates, will affect that business' success.
2. Michael Porter's Diamond of Competitive Advantage is an excellent model to understand country competitiveness. But it needs to be understood that the insight from the model is only as good as the person who employs and interprets the resulting information.
3. Competition makes a firm stronger and is not to be avoided. Ultimately, competing internationally requires tough competitors. If a firm avoids competition it will ultimately become less competitive and eventually be unable to compete internationally. Thus, avoiding competition hurts the firm, its employees, and its home country in the long run.

4. Legal systems are connected to the culture of a given country. The legal systems of countries vary widely, and it is critical that the manager understands the legal environment in which the firm is operating.

5. There are business opportunities that exist for business people from the legal system. The legal system may require environmental controls that may lead to new products that can be sold to others. There are also opportunities to generate products that meet legal requirements for various groups, such as for Muslims under Shari'a law.

6. Political risk and corruption are realities that the business person must understand and monitor. The best product may not be sufficient for success if the government is highly unstable or corruption is extensive.

7. Even if the environment is quite corrupt, a firm must remember that the actions of firms from mature markets are limited by laws, such as the Foreign Corrupt Practices Act. Simply because others in an environment pay bribes does not mean that the firm or its employees can or should. See Table 3-2.

TABLE 3-2 Country Competitiveness

Country	Question about Competitiveness	Reality
Japan	After seeing Japanese firms come to dominate major industries, many people argued that it was only a matter of time before Japanese firms would dominate most major industries.	Japan's top companies, such as Toyota, Honda, Hitachi, Sony, and many other well-known firms, are highly competitive around the world. But Japan is not competitive in all industries; Japanese firms are not globally competitive in many information technology industries, micro computing, or many household products like detergents. Porter's Diamond Model helps to explain why Japanese firms would have trouble in certain industries—in the case of IT industry factor inputs including research and development and related and supporting industries are weaker than in countries such as the U.S. and the U.K.
China	Since China has the lowest cost of any major economy, won't Chinese firms simply take over all industries?	This is the same fallacious argument that was made about Japan in the 1980s (though it was odd that anyone could have thought Japan would be able to maintain a low-cost position). Indigenous Chinese firms have been slow to compete globally because of a host of strategic problems within its businesses and other challenges with government interference. Moreover, David Riccardo's theory of comparative advantage states that even if a country were able to outcompete all other countries in every industry (something that Porter tells us is impossible), they would still choose to specialize in the industries they were best at, and use those goods to trade with other countries. Thus, China may be best at light manufacturing and would benefit from trading with the U.S. in digital products (software and new consumer electronics applications), in which the U.S. is particularly strong.

TABLE 3-2 (Continued)

Country	Question about Competitiveness	Reality
Europe	How is Europe doing competitively?	Europe is a big place so it is hard to generalize. The U.K. has been effectively encouraging its IT and media industries and has created an excellent regulatory climate for banking and finance. France and Germany have many strong companies, but their macro-economic environment and strict labor laws are discouraging to new business (and thus industry) formation. Italy and Spain have been able to specialize in industries, such as fashion and tourism, but also have high costs. Eastern Europe is experiencing very solid growth in recent years.
East Asia (Ex-Japan)	Are other East Asian economies following in the path of Japan?	This was thought to be true in the 1980s, perhaps up through the Asian Financial Crisis of 1997–98. Most of these economies, from South Korea to Singapore, got hit with a healthy dose of reality in that much of their growth had been attributed to the injection of more capital investment into what had been a largely capital-free environment (few factories and other machinery, phone lines, trucks, etc.). At some point, the returns from additional capital will start to decline and the economy's growth will level off, even going into decline if good investments in intellectual capital and new business creation cannot be found. These economies have toiled hard to make the transition to higher value-added products and services and will probably take different paths (Korea in heavy manufacturing, Taiwan in light manufacturing, Singapore in medicine and education, and so forth). As developmental economists remind us, no country can take growth for granted.
Africa	Will African firms become more competitive?	Certain African countries have been experiencing some competitive success. Nigeria, in spite of its ongoing political problems, has benefited greatly from the price increases in oil and other commodities. South Africa and several other English-speaking African countries have experienced solid growth in recent years. The global footprint of African firms is still quite low, and these countries have yet to experience the high growth that is possible with initial heavy investments in capital.
India	Will India be the next China?	Most large Indian firms are not yet globally competitive. India will likely continue to be strong in the IT outsourcing industry, and related and supporting industries are now growing out of this. India has much potential: even its tourism sector is functioning at only a tiny percentage of where it could be (given adequate investment in infrastructure).

CULTURE AND DOING BUSINESS IN CHILE

Chile is one of South America's strongest economies. It has one of the strongest traditions of free trade in the southern hemisphere. Chile's economy in 2004 grew by over 5 percent annually. The per capita GDP was approximately $11,000. The nation itself is 4,000 miles long and only about 100 miles wide. The northern part of the country is the driest place on earth with parts of the Atacama Desert never having had rainfall in recorded history. The southern part of Chile resembles Sweden or Norway, with glaciers and fjords.

Chile has a strong sense of history, so in conducting business in Chile recognizing things such as the continuing dispute with Argentina over the control of areas in Antarctica (Chilean Antarctic Territory) is important. This area is believed to hold oil and will likely increase in importance in the future. Another historical dispute is with Bolivia, over land ceded in the 1880s to Chile (the Atacama Corridor).

The business environment in Chile shares some commonality with other cultures in the region. For example, relationships in conducting business in Chile are very important. Therefore, if one does not have a relationship with the business person with whom one wishes to conduct business, it is wise to seek an introduction from a third party. Chileans in conversation also sit closer to each other than is common in North America. There are also unique differences that distinguish Chile from other nations in South America. In Chile contracts are followed closely. The nation's history has helped to develop an importance on adhering to the rule of law. Chile was a democracy for 45 years until 1973 when the U.S. government helped to overthrow the elected president, Salvador Allende, who was a Marxist. Chile became a military dictatorship from 1973–90 with many abuses of human rights. In 1990, Chile returned to democracy and the rule of law. The overthrow of democracy and the abuses of human rights under a military dictatorship increased the importance of the rule of law in Chile. Consistent with this focus on law in the nation, corruption is much lower in Chile than in many other Latin American countries.

CULTURE

ADDITIONAL RESOURCES

Friedman, T.L. (2000). *The Lexus and the Olive Tree.* New York: Farrar, Straus and Giroux.

Landes, D. S. (1998). *The Wealth and Poverty of Nations: Why Some Are So Rich and Some So Poor.* New York: W.W. Norton.

Olson, M. (2000). *Prosperity: Outgrowing Communist and Capitalist.* New York: Basic Books.

Soto, H.D. (2000). *The Mystery of Capital: Why Capitalism Triumphs in the West and Fails Everywhere Else.* New York: Basic Books.

EXERCISES

Opening Vignette Discussion Questions

1. How does a firm protect itself against political risk in a situation like Texaco Chevron, who is being sued for activities conducted a relatively long time ago?
2. Why do you think the Ecuadorians used the U.S. court system rather than their own? What do you think of this?

DISCUSSION QUESTIONS

1. It is currently against the law for businesses in the United States to sell oil equipment to Iran. However, many firms still do so through their European or Caribbean subsidiaries. What do you think of this type of activity? Should governments enforce their political goals through limitations on business?
2. Do you see increasing standardization of the environment for business as the power of the WTO, EU, and others increases?
3. What issues do you see that legally could impact international firms in the future that are not currently major topics of concern?
4. Is it a market opportunity or a limitation when dealing with a nation that has a large Muslim population that follows Shari'a law even though it isn't the law of the land?

IN-CLASS EXERCISES

1. After being largely ignored for long periods of time, Islam has become a potent force influencing today's world. Discuss the current role of Islam. Identify some of the unique characteristics you understand about Islam and what questions you have about the religion. After discussing these issues, what are the challenges that foreign firms face in doing business in a majority Muslim country?

2. What evidence is there to support the view that a common business culture is spreading throughout the world? Consider factors such as economic and political systems, globalization, the improvement of computers and communications, international institutions, and education.

3. At first glance, the Diamond model only seems to be useful to describe a country's national competitive environment for local firms. Is there any way a firm can use the Diamond model to improve its competitiveness? Give two example of how this might be done.

4. Assume that you are assisting the vice president in charge of Colgate's toothpaste division. You are researching an aggressive push into the mainland China market, just a few years after mainland China's reforms started in 1978. In researching this for your boss, you learned that many mainland Chinese people do not use toothpaste; rather, they use locally made tooth powder. Many more in the countryside use nothing. Local distributors add that more and more urban mainland consumers are using toothpaste, but prefer fruity flavors, such as banana, made by the state-owned enterprise. You are told that Colgate has no plans to create such flavors, but they want you to investigate the Chinese market for the purposes of distributing and manufacturing. The average consumer for toothpaste in mainland China is a young urban resident who is open to new products. What would you recommend to your boss about how to proceed with evaluating the environment in China for selling Colgate toothpaste there? Are there any initial observations you will make that can help to guide your strategy later?

TAKE-HOME EXERCISES

1. Research the international oil industry. Focus on what are referred to as the major oil companies. Give an assessment of the general environment facing these firms. Is it favorable? How is it changing? How should a major firm such as Exxon respond to the political changes and new environmental demands on its main businesses?

2. Research the country of Brazil. Pick an industry that is globally competitive. Conduct a diamond of national competitiveness analysis of that industry.

3. If you wanted to conduct business in a country like Somalia, what are the legal and political issues you might face? Briefly research the country and develop the outlines for an international company that moves there.

4. Read about Shari'a law and identify a new potential business that might serve the needs of this religious community.

SHORT CASE QUESTIONS

Reminbi Peg and Its Impact on World Trade (p. 92)

1. In approximate terms, what do you think will be the exchange rate between the U.S. dollar and the Chinese RMB?

2. What would be the best strategy for a large multinational when faced with vast swings in the value of the U.S. dollar?

3. Why do politicians talk so positively about the dollar's decreasing value?

4. What is the long-term outlook for the U.S. dollar?

4

STRATEGY FUNDAMENTALS AND CORPORATE STRATEGY

Overview

Once a firm understands the key elements of the external environment (covered in Chapter 3), it must set its strategy, or the broad direction it plans to take in the foreseeable future. Deciding the direction of the business allows a firm to ensure its various activities are consistently targeted in a coherent direction. Businesses, like people, must select certain activities in which they can excel, lest they be pulled in numerous directions and not perform well in any of them. Developing a clear and coherent strategy is particularly important for an international business since its operations may be in a wide variety of countries, which can pull the firm in a number of different directions. An international business with a coherent and consistent strategy will ultimately perform better than one without. This chapter will establish the fundamentals of strategy and specifics of corporate strategy for international firms. The specific topics covered in the chapter include:

- The definitions of strategy
- The strategy process
- The different levels of strategy
- Corporate-level strategy
    - mergers and acquisitions
    - alliances

AHLSTROM CORPORATION

Ahlstrom is a Finnish company that was founded in 1851. The firm has evolved from its original focus on timber mills to become one of the world's leaders in fiber-based materials. These include nonwovens and specialty papers used in a large variety of everyday products, such as filters, wipes, flooring, labels, and tapes. Typically, the consumer would not know Ahlstrom's products but they will know other firms' names that include Ahlstrom's products as inputs. Some of the major product areas that utilize Ahlstrom's as input include:

- automobile door panels
- baby and sanitary wipes
- coffee filters
- disposable cleaning cloths
- double-sided tape
- engine filters
- exhibition banners
- flooring
- hygiene products
- labels for beverages, food, and cosmetics
- pet-food containers
- roofing
- sandpaper
- self-adhesive bandages
- surgical gowns
- tea bags
- wall coverings

Ahlstrom had sales of about 1.6 billion euros in 2005 with 6,585 employees; 25 percent of the employees were in France, 17 percent in Finland, 13 percent in the United States, and 12 percent in Germany. The other employees live and work in 16 other countries. The firm is organized into three different divisions.

Ahlstrom's direction is set by its mission "to be the global source for fiber-based materials."[1] In turn, it identifies four cornerstones upon which it builds its strategy. These cornerstones are: long-term customer relationships; teamwork to develop new applications from their knowledge base; focus on the expansion of high-value-added and growth segments; and a strong focus on financial and competitive targets. The result of combining these different elements is that the firm is clear on its direction. Ahlstrom is a global firm focused on producing fiber-based materials. Ahlstrom focuses on the upper, more expensive end of the market, where the company can create new products and add value. The firm is also very clear that they have strong financial- and performance-based evaluation.

In pursuing this strategy, Ahlstrom has engaged in an active merger and acquisition program. For example, in 2004 the firm bought Green Bay Nonwovens, a U.S.-based manufacturer that made inputs to the wipes market with specialty spun-lace and resin-bond technologies. This acquisition allowed Ahlstrom to enter this product market for the first time. Since Ahlstrom bought an existing firm, it acquired the existing technology and customer base of that firm. Thus, Ahlstrom was able to enter this market immediately.

In 2002 the firm bought Papelera del Besós, a Spanish filtration media and specialty paper supplier. The acquisition helped expand Ahlstrom's activities in filtration. However, just as important, the acquisition allowed Ahlstrom to expand into Spain in a significant way. Prior to the acquisition the firm only had two sales offices in the nation, and Ahlstrom felt it needed a greater presence in Spain.

The firm has not always followed its mission statement as closely as it does now. In the past Ahlstrom made some acquisitions and investments that were not related to the firm's focus on fiber-based materials. As a result, in 2001, it made several divestitures of different businesses. For example, it sold its American subsidiary, Ahlstrom Development Corporation, that year. The firm also spun off Ahlström Capital Oy as a private investment company and Ahlström Osakeyhtiö to manage the historical Noormarkku manor in Finland, as well as other assets with heritage value. Ahlstrom Development held equity interests in several power plants, but sold the interests to Golden Power Acquisition, a subsidiary of El Paso Corporation in Houston, Texas. This was all done to better focus the Ahlstrom Corporation on its core businesses in fiber-based materials.

The firm works to carry the strategy through in various functions. For example, the mission statement and strategy indicate that Ahlstrom wishes to focus on high-value-added segments of the market that allow it to use its knowledge base. As a result, the firm organizes 26 different research teams to study various product areas and how to expand the creative products in the given area.

Ahlstrom has been able to do as well as it has because of its clear focus on its goal. The firm has taken steps to expand internationally through mergers and acquisitions. These mergers and acquisitions have taken the firm into new nations and new product areas. However, those new areas have all fit with Ahlstrom's overall direction. In fact, when the firm finds it has expanded into an area that does not fit, it sells those assets. Ahlstrom tries to ensure that all its actions are consistent and support that strategy.

Strategy
A coordinated set of actions that fulfills the firm's objectives, purposes, and goals.

From its understanding of the external environment (economic, legal, and political), which was examined in Chapter 3, a firm establishes its international strategy. **Strategy** is a coordinated set of actions that allows the firm to meet its objectives and goals and therefore is the basis for the firm's international behavior. Frequently,

[1]Ahlstrom uses the term vision and not mission, but the meaning is essentially the same.

FIGURE 4-1 Chapter 4 Conceptual Flow

individuals confuse a firm's strategy with strategic planning, but the two are not the same. Strategic planning is the process by which a firm decides its direction over the next several years. The typical outcome of such planning is a formal statement containing the firm's strategy for a given time period. However, strategy is more than the document that results from such planning efforts.

Strategy is an effort by which an organization defines the nature of the products and/ or services it provides, and the markets in which the firm competes. A strategy also helps define the type of organization the firm intends to be, and the nature of the contribution it intends to make to its various constituents. From the strategy, the firm will establish policies that ensure its efforts are consistently targeted in the desired direction. These decisions are not random choices but, instead, are built on an understanding of the firm's external environment and an understanding of the firm's internal assets. The process we will use in this chapter to examine these issues is summarized in Figure 4-1.

STRATEGY FUNDAMENTALS

The first section of this chapter will address the building blocks of a firm's strategy. The initial discussion will focus on a firm's resources and capabilities. Then the strategy process will be examined.

Resources and Capabilities

Firms need a variety of resources and capabilities to operate in today's competitive markets.[i] **Resources** are the tangible and intangible assets that firms possess, essentially that which can be bought and sold, hired and fired, valued and depreciated. Tangible assets are those things, such as a plant and equipment, that a firm possesses. The intangible assets are items like the reputation of the firm, relationships with customers, and the culture of the firm. Typically, intangible assets are the harder resources to develop but are more likely to differ from those of other competitors.

Capabilities are functional skills and routines that a firm develops, and are the foundation on which a firm implements its strategy. Many firms are similar to their competitors in most areas. For example, airlines, such as Australia's Qantas and Hong Kong's Cathay Pacific, are similar in most aspects. However, to be successful, both of these firms, and all others, need unique resources and capabilities that help to distinguish them from the competition.

At least some of the firm's resources and capabilities should involve what are referred to as **key success factors**. That is, the resources and capabilities must involve things that are important to customers, which helps determine a business' success in that industry. Using the airline example again, an airline can have the capability of designing the best uniform for its employees. However, such a

Resources
Tangible and intangible assets that firms possess.

Capabilities
Functional skills that a firm develops and which are the foundation on which a firm builds its strategy.

Key success factors
Things that are important to customers and help determine a business' success in a given industry.

capability is not linked to a key success factor—few customers will choose an airline because of its nice uniforms. Instead, some of the common resources and capabilities that are connected to key success factors in the airline industry include an information system that allows the airline to better match demand and flight frequency, the organizational routines to turn planes around faster, and the ability to work well with their employees and unions to generate maximum efficiency.

Typically, one or two special capabilities will be the most critical to the firm's success. These particularly important capabilities are called **core competencies**. The best global competitors normally possess at least one core competency, and they know how to utilize it to their advantage. For example, Sony is said to have a core competency in miniaturization, Canon in micromotors and imaging technologies, and Disney in developing new characters and stories along with the animations that bring them to life.[ii]

Notice that a core competency like miniaturization differs from a basic functional capability such as marketing ability. Core competencies are rarer and typically cut across functional boundaries; that is, you cannot find a department of miniaturization at Sony. Because Sony's miniaturization skill cuts across functional department lines, the firm has to integrate different functional areas to create the core competency. Thus, it would be incorrect to say a firm has a core competency in marketing; instead, it would be more accurate to describe a firm with good marketing as having a strong capability. It is difficult to copy a core competency because there is no established method or textbook on issues of establishing a successful miniaturization program— much of the knowledge is tacit and resides with Sony's people and in its organizational routines. Sony, with its core competency of miniaturization, has successfully made products smaller, which has allowed the firm to move consistently from the manufacturing of radios, to the Walkman, to now producing the iPod-type digital Walkman.

Leading firms around the world often can illustrate a similar core competency in at least one domain. For example, Japanese automaker Honda has a core competency in engine building. Such a core competency involves more than just a functional area, such as design engineering. While engineering is a clear part of the competency, it also includes the ability to assemble the engines, and source the parts that are needed to build the engines. This helps Honda to build a variety of end products that have engines as the core product, such as automobiles, motorcycles, outboard motors, and snowmobiles.

Core competencies are not only present in high technology and manufacturing firms, but also in service firms. For example, Disney's core competencies include its ability to develop new characters and stories, and then apply those characters to different settings—a process that Disney refers to as "imagineering." To illustrate, the firm developed the movie *Haunted Mansion* based on a ride in its amusement park, Disneyland. The highly successful *Pirates of the Caribbean* series of films was also loosely designed around the popular Disney ride of the same name. From its films, Disney also integrated some of the key elements into a variety of stage shows, including its Disney on Ice.[iii] Similarly, the firm developed the character Buzz Lightyear for its movie *Toy Story*, then created toys and cartoons based on the character, and also integrated the character into the various stage shows.

A firm's resources and capabilities are used to build the firm's core competencies which, in turn, are the building blocks for the firm's strategy and its competitive advantage. A **competitive advantage** results from something that the firm does better than any of its competitors. The goal of the firm is not to simply do something better than its competitors for a single day or month; instead the goal is for the business to be able to sustain the competitive advantage over a significant period of time. The ability to have a competitive advantage over a period of time is called a **sustainable competitive advantage**.

To illustrate, Cemex is a Mexico-based firm that was established in 1906 as a local cement provider. Today the firm is one of the world's leading cement manufacturers with facilities in North and South America, Europe, Asia, and Africa. Cemex has developed a strong capability to utilize technology to modernize an

Core competence
A key skill the firm possesses that is rare and crosses functional or departmental boundaries. Thus a core competence will often combine capabilities from multiple departments.

Competitive advantage
Something that a firm does better than any of its nearest competitors, which allows the firm to have an advantage with customers over those competitors.

Sustainable competitive advantage
The ability to have a competitive advantage over a period of time.

Any number of resources and capabilities can become the building blocks for a firm's competitive advantage, something the firm does better than any of its competitors.

industry that historically had not changed for decades. This technology has not only allowed the firm to develop better methods in order to produce cement at a consistently high quality, a key demand for its key customers in large construction projects, but also allows the firm to cut delivery times. The average standard in the industry is to have a four-hour window for cement delivery. Cemex, in contrast, guarantees its deliveries at a specific time. It is able to do this through advanced production methods, scheduling software, and delivery technology that allows the firm to synchronize its deliveries to a level not employed in the rest of the industry.

Cemex's ability to consistently deliver a high-quality product on time has built considerable customer loyalty. In large construction products, lost time equals lost productivity and money for builders. The craftsmen are paid whether or not they are working on the building, so the ability to accurately predict and deliver what is needed, when it is needed, is critical to the construction company's own success. As a result, Cemex has developed a defendable competitive advantage based on a key resource—its relationship with the customers. This competitive advantage, in turn, is linked to its core competency in the utilization of technology.

The ability to perform an activity better than any of the firm's competitors will lead to a sustainable competitive advantage only if the activity is something that customers value and that other firms cannot easily duplicate. Thus, a competitive advantage must not only be something a firm does better than its competitors, but it must be something that affects the customers' purchasing decisions. From a competitive advantage, the firm is able to build value for the shareholders or owners of the firm.

Strategy Process

Managers responsible for the strategy process should pursue regular strategic reviews. These reviews will help the business better understand itself and its environment, including the issues discussed in Chapter 3. This understanding will help the firm not only develop the right strategy now, but also make adjustments when needed. Strategy needs to be a living concept that changes and evolves as the world changes. For an international firm, changes in the environment are more active than for a firm that only competes in a single market.

For example, the performance of McDonald's in the United States has been lackluster in recent years, but the firm is making extensive profits internationally, particularly in Asia. In fact, McDonald's sees Asian countries, such as China and India, as significant growth markets. However, in Asia different skills, capabilities, and even market position are needed as compared to a mature market. In part, this is because there are different food preferences, different eating habits, and higher expectations from a restaurant in the United States in terms of what locals believe the food quality, service, cleanliness, and atmosphere should be. In India, McDonald's has created a menu that matches the needs of the country with hamburgers not made of beef (eating beef conflicts with the Hindu religion). Instead, the firm serves vegetarian-, chicken-, and mutton-based foods consistent with the local religious dictates. The restaurant chain also has specialized curry-based foods that match local tastes. McDonald's has implemented new training methods to ensure that the restaurant is kept clean to the expected standards. In many countries, educating employees on simple things, such as why and how to clean the washroom, takes considerable effort, and a firm also has to educate and enforce rules about unsold food needing to be thrown away after a certain amount of time. Imagine how difficult this is in a country where hunger and deprivation are still commonplace. However, if this rule is not followed, quality cannot be maintained. Additionally, the restaurant cannot allow the food to be given away; if they did, there would be an incentive for employees to cook more than could be used. Thus, the rule is that unsold food must be thrown away after a given period of time.

Although many think of McDonald's as having a simple product and standardized service, the India example demonstrates that their restaurants have significant local customization, particularly in the menus. Their strategic process is very complex; not only the United States, but also Europe, Asia, Latin America, and Africa must be considered, each with its own unique tastes and needs. This is a much more complex strategic planning process than for a fast food firm like Hong Kong's Café de Coral, a restaurant chain that, until recently, was focused on a single region whose menu concentrated purely on Cantonese cuisine that matches local tastes. (It is interesting to note that Café de Coral has recently bought a small fast food firm in the United States and is experiencing the new challenges of global expansion, branding, and the development of international strategy.)[iv] Thus, an international firm needs to develop a strategic process that ensures such richness and complexities are considered.

The strategic process in a firm can be divided into three different activities. While the components are presented here in discrete units, in an ongoing business they are all part of a continuous process that occurs simultaneously. The three components of the strategy process include:

1. Planning
2. Implementation
3. Evaluation and control

The strategic process is summarized in Figure 4-2 and each component is examined in detail next.

| FIGURE 4-2 | Planning Process |

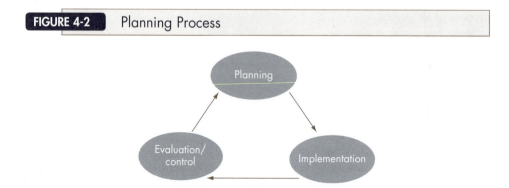

STARBUCKS IN JAPAN

Starbucks has a strong image around the world. All Starbucks stores, regardless of geographic location, have large, overstuffed chairs, small bistro-type tables, and high-quality, high-priced coffee. However, while Starbucks is a successful international firm, it also illustrates the critical need to gather information and fully understand a local market. Japan is Starbucks' largest international market with over 500 stores today. Until 2005 the firm had only been competing in Japan with classic coffee shops that the firm operates itself. Starbucks had not ventured into the $10 billion market for coffee in cans, bottles, and vending machines that exists in Japan; most coffee in Japan is consumed in this manner, not in coffee shops or restaurants. The coffee in these settings is typically stronger and not as sweet as U.S. coffee.

As Starbucks gained greater knowledge and experience in the Japanese market, it decided to enter the market for ready-to-drink coffee. In 2005 Starbucks began to sell chilled coffee in cups in 10,000 convenience stores around the country. This was the first time that Starbucks entered the ready-to-drink market outside of the United States. It designed the chilled coffee to meet the specific needs of the Japanese market, with two drinks offered (latte and espresso), both of which were less sweet than similar drinks in the U.S.

Thus, it was only after learning more about the market and gathering a more complete set of data that Starbucks recognized that the relevant industry on which to focus was the national market of Japan. Starbucks learned that it needed to include prepackaged coffee products in its product line and reformulate its products, and it has become quite successful in Japan.

Woods, G. P. (2005, September 27). Starbucks bets drinks will jolt Japan sales. *Asian Wall Street Journal*, p. A7.

Planning Planning is the systematic gathering of information from which the firm then sets its mission, performance objectives, and ultimately its strategy. The steps in the planning process include:

1. Data gathering
2. Mission generation
3. Objective setting
4. Strategy establishment

Data Gathering. During the strategic planning stage, the firm gathers extensive information on the external environment and its internal capabilities. This information gathering process is critical because it helps establish the foundation on which the firm bases its plans.

A key part of the strategy process is the analysis of the external environment. Much of this analysis is conducted when the firm reviews the key issues detailed in the external analysis discussed in Chapter 3. The issues examined should include, but are not limited to, an analysis of economic trends, government policy in the nations where the firm is active, industry status, resources available in the industry, worldwide competitors in each nation in which the firm is active, and the general environment that affects the firm's success.

The information gathered should also include an understanding of the firm's internal capabilities. The internal analysis focuses on the classification of the capabilities and core competencies of the firm. The difficulty for the firm here is to accurately appraise what is done better (strengths) and worse (weaknesses) than others and why. This review should be performed interactively with the firm identifying not only what internally is judged to be better, but what key customers and others see as the firm's core competence. Self-appraisal is not always accurate, so it is important that the firm get the views of customers and other outsiders. The physical assets of the firm should also be inventoried in the evaluation of the internal strengths. Thus, the information-gathering should begin very broadly with the external environment in which the firm competes, and become more specific, ultimately examining the physical assets of the firm.

Mission
A simple statement of the basic purpose or reason for the business to exist and its activities.

Mission. From the information gathered, the firm sets its mission.[2] The **mission** of a firm is a simple statement of the basic purpose or reason for its existence. The mission identifies what is unique about the firm and the scope of activities it wants to pursue. Limiting the firm's activities helps to ensure that the firm stays focused on what it principally sees as its reason for being. The firm will include its "reason for existence" in its mission statement, which should be posted throughout the organization to help it remember its fundamental direction. For an international business, it is especially easy for a unit in a country that's far from the corporate headquarters to lose focus on the firm's ultimate goal. The mission statement helps every business unit and person, no matter where they are in the world, to know what the business is about.

Sometimes a mission statement is very simple. For example, a mission statement of pharmaceutical firm Abbott Laboratories is to be a "leader in cost-effective medicine," which helped to effectively direct the firm toward developing a variety of simple medical treatments and tests. However, more typically, mission statements are longer, with approximately 30 to 60 words. For example, the Mexican cement firm Cemex's mission statement is

> To serve the global building needs of our customers and build value for our stakeholders by becoming the world's most efficient and profitable building-solutions company.

Cemex's mission statement clearly states the industry in which the firm wishes to compete: building solutions. This focus will keep the firm from diversifying into food products, coal mining, or other ventures that may look profitable but are not connected to construction. The mission statement also states that the focus of the firm's efforts is to build relationships with customers (previously noted as a competitive advantage in this industry) with the strong use of efficient technology. Thus, this short statement will help the firm stay clearly focused and not lose sight of why it exists.

Objective Setting. Once the broad mission of a firm is set, the firm builds on that mission to establish measurable objectives and performance targets that will help it fulfill its mission. These measurable objectives and performance targets state in specific terms what is to be accomplished in a given time period. The time period over which objectives and performance are targeted may be as long as five years. However, even if the objectives and targets extend that far into the future, the firm will likely also establish short- and mid-range objectives and targets. These short- and mid-range objectives and targets can be visualized as small steps that ensure the longer-range objectives and targets are met.

Such short-term goals are helpful for international firms because they help firms manage their widely varied markets. Cemex is expected to establish quarterly and annual sales objectives for each market in which it is now active. These are short-term goals with the long-term goals stating where the firm wishes to be in three to five years in that market. The firm also establishes long-term goals for new markets into which it wishes to expand over the next three to five years in order to achieve its targeted total corporate sales goals. As noted in Chapter 3, the environment in each of these different markets can change rapidly. The firm must be willing to change its short- and long-term objectives as conditions change.

---

[2]Some firms also include value statements or vision statements prior to the mission statement. These statements tend to be narrower than a mission statement and are used to build the mission statement. Many firms will have only a mission statement. Here we start with the broadest type of statement—a mission statement—since it is the most clearly defined, and all types of businesses usually have this type of statement.

Establish Strategy. Based on the business's goals and objectives the business can now establish a strategy that helps to ensure that the actions the firm takes will lead to the accomplishment of the objectives and targets.

There are three different levels of strategy that a firm must develop. Each of these different levels of strategy should build upon one another. The first level of firm strategy is referred to as corporate-level strategy. This level of strategy is concerned with determining what mix of industries the firm should compete in and the level of diversification that will lead to high performance. The second level of strategy is called business-level strategy, and indicates how the firm will compete in each of its chosen product markets or businesses. The third level of strategy is the functional level, which is concerned with implementation in the different functional areas, such as marketing, finance, and operations. Strategic management is a cascading process in which the firm's strategy becomes more specific as it moves down through the organization. Each of the specific levels of strategy will be discussed in more detail.[3]

As noted, the corporate strategy determines the particular industries in which the corporation will choose to compete. Thus, the **corporate-level strategy** determines how diversified the firm will become, and in which industries, as part of the corporate strategy. One aspect of a diversification strategy that is unique to international business is that the firm must determine how diversified to be not only in terms of product but also geographic region. Thus, a firm may choose to diversify only regionally or it may choose to diversify to broader geographic areas around the world. As might be expected, firms most often start with regional diversification and then typically move to diversify to a broader geographic area.

The **business-level strategy** of the firm is concerned with how the firm will compete in each product-market or industry once they have been chosen. As a result, if a firm competes in multiple industries or product markets, each of these may have its own business-level strategy. A wide-range of business strategies has been proposed. However, in the broadest terms, business strategy can be perceived as being either a low-cost position in the market, typically where the business sells a product or service at or near the lowest price possible, or the business can sell a differentiated product that has special features that allow the firm to charge a premium price.

Functional-level strategies are the strategies of the different departments, such as accounting, engineering, and marketing, that act in support of the given business strategy. For example, if the firm is employing a low-cost strategy, then the engineering department will put much effort into innovations on the production process to minimize costs. In a low-cost strategy, money normally will not be invested in cutting-edge products that have a narrow market. The different levels of strategy are summarized in Figure 4-3. Corporate-level strategy is discussed in greater detail at the end of this chapter. Chapter 5 examines the business level and functional strategies in more detail. However, before examining these topics, the other two steps in the strategic process—implementation, and evaluation and control—are discussed in more detail.

Implementation Once the strategic plan has been developed, the firm must then implement the plan. Activities in a firm are not isolated; actions in one area have implications for employees in other areas of the business. The result is that implementation of the strategy requires that the firm conduct all of its activities in a manner that is consistent with the mission and chosen strategy. Chapters 6 through 13 will cover in detail the aspects of the international business that concern strategic implementation and how they affect each other. The implementation issues covered

Corporate strategy
Establishes how diversified the firm is to become and in what domains that diversification will occur.

Business strategy
How the firm will compete in a specific product-market.

Functional strategies
Strategies of the different departments, such as accounting, engineering, and marketing, that act in support of the given business strategy.

---

[3]Some texts will examine business-level strategy prior to corporate-level strategy. However, this approach ignores the cascading effect of strategy. An organization in practice first picks what industries in which to compete and then how to compete in those industries. Thus, we begin with corporate strategy here.

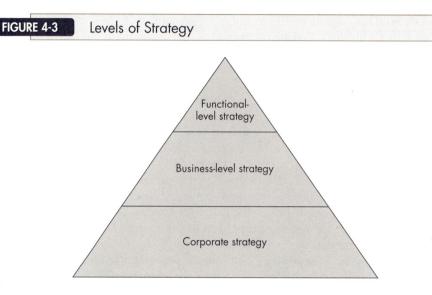

FIGURE 4-3   Levels of Strategy

in detail in this book include market entry (Chapter 6), motivation (Chapter 7), leadership (Chapter 8), decision making (Chapter 9), influence and negotiation (Chapter 10), evaluation and control (Chapter 11), human resource management (Chapter 12), and organizational structure (Chapter 13). A critical issue stressed in each of these chapters is that culture is an underlying foundation that impacts each aspect of the firm.

A useful tool to conceptualize how all the aspects of the firm's implementation of its strategy fit together is called value-chain analysis.[v] A **value-chain analysis** breaks the firm's activities into primary activities and support activities. Primary activities are the major categories of activities that must take place in a firm to actually produce its products and services. These commonly include the inbound logistics of inputs, the operations or actual transformation of the inputs into a product (the production process), the shipping of the product or outbound logistics, the marketing of the product, and servicing of the product. On the other hand, support activities back up all of primary activities.

Each of the primary and support activities is affected as a firm expands internationally. To illustrate the impact, consider a single support activity: human resources. From this support function the firm will select, train, and design rewards for employees in a manner consistent with the chosen strategy. The human resource management function will vary in each country. An international business will need different human resource policies in each country in which it operates, including compensation systems; it will need to ensure that individuals with all of the appropriate skills do the required tasks; and it will need a means to connect all of these issues to both the support and the primary activities of the firm. These different activities all involve multiple concerns for the firm. For example, ensuring the firm has the right people for the tasks involves not only recruitment, but also training and retention. Thus, an international firm's value chain is quite complex when fully developed. But the value chain is a valuable tool to see how the different parts of the firm are needed to support each other. Figure 4-4 summarizes the parts of a value chain.

Each of the various activities must be consistent with the firm's strategy. How the firm manages its value chain is discussed in greater detail in Chapter 5.

Evaluation and Control After the strategy is formulated and implemented, the firm must evaluate the outcomes of those efforts. After the strategy is implemented the firm must ensure that the goals and objectives are being met and if they are not, then

Value chain analysis
Breaks the firm's activities into primary activities and support activities.

Value Chain

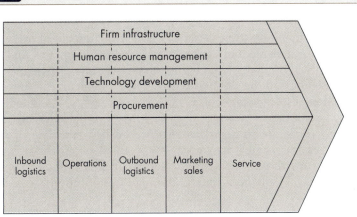

adjustments must be made. This is referred to as evaluation (comparison of actual outcomes with expected outcomes) and control (adjustments as needed). The concept of evaluation and control is examined in detail in Chapter 11. However, suffice it to say that the firm must determine why it is not meeting its goals and objectives and either change its activities or change its goals. Determining if goals have been met, if not why not, and how the firm needs to change in the future to better meet those goals increases in complexity as the international complexion of the firm changes. Clearly identifying the cause of a failure becomes more difficult as the environment becomes more complex due to the various settings facing the international firm.

BAMA PIE: STRATEGY DEVELOPMENT PROCESS

A good example of strategy development is Bama Pie, started in 1927 in Tulsa, Oklahoma. The firm produces pies and other related food products, including the crust used in Pizza Hut pizzas and the biscuits and fruit pies for McDonald's. In fact, Bama Pie is the international supplier of McDonald's pies worldwide. As part of this development, the firm created corn and red bean pies that are standard fare in McDonald's in other parts of the world. In 2004 Bama Pie was the Baldrige Award recipient as one of the four firms in the United States with the best quality program. It remains a low-cost provider, but has been able to do this while being a leader in the quality movement nationally.

Bama Pie's strategic-planning process is not a single activity but an ongoing process that allows real-time response to changes in the environment. The firm uses a series of formal strategic-planning meetings in which teams describe, through visual maps, the previous outcomes, measures, and value-creation processes for the firm. This occurs at the firm's different facilities around the world. These teams then develop long-term goals in their relevant areas, including those that concern overseas markets. These goals are then formalized by the strategic-planning team and expressed throughout the organization so that employees understand their roles in achieving firm success. More specifically, the strategic action plans, including timelines and milestones, are generated for each area, and these items are expressed to each employee. The strategic-planning team ensures that all groups' strategic plans are consistent with the firm's corporate mission and goals.

This interactive but simple process has helped to propel a firm once on the verge of failure into a leadership position in the global food-processing industry. The change from near failure took extensive commitment by the workers. But a strategic process in which they participated educated them both to the problem and the solutions that were necessary. Thus, in a manner consistent with Deming's quality control recommendations (discussed later in this text), Bama Pie established a process in which it gathers extensive data in its production process, changes one aspect of that process, collects new data, brings that data back to the strategic teams, and then identifies another change to make. The involvement of the individuals in the process allows the firm to continue to make extensive changes in a very timely manner. Today, Bama Pie is a national symbol of quality and a model for other firms seeking to achieve world-class status.

Summary of Bama's 2004 Application for the Malcolm Baldrige National Quality Award.

DIVERSIFICATION AND CORPORATE-LEVEL STRATEGY

It was noted that there are three parts to the firm's strategic process—planning, implementation, and evaluation and control. In planning, the data gathering would include much of the material highlighted in Chapter 3. The mission setting and objective setting will be unique to each firm. However, the first step in the strategy selection is to develop a firm's corporate strategy. As noted, corporate-level strategy determines in which industries or product-markets a firm will compete. Thus, corporate strategy has also been called "portfolio management" because it is concerned with managing the portfolio of businesses held by the company. There are three means to effect that diversification—1) mergers and acquisitions (M&A), 2) alliances, and 3) internal diversification.

Mergers and Acquisitions

The principal means by which a firm changes its portfolio of businesses is through mergers and acquisitions. The terms mergers and acquisitions are commonly used interchangeably. However, they represent different types of business expansion. An **acquisition** refers to the outright purchase of a firm or some part of that firm. The result of an acquisition is that the acquiring firm typically remains the dominant force in the newly combined business, with managers from the acquiring firm often filling critical management roles in the newly expanded business. In contrast, a **merger** occurs when two firms combine as relative equals. As a practical matter, it is often difficult to differentiate mergers from acquisitions. As a result, the terms are often used together: merger/acquisition.

Merger and acquisition represents a major economic force in the world economy. The M&A trend started in the 1980s in the United States and now has spread to a number of countries in Europe and East Asia. The value of takeover activities in the United States stayed in the range of two to three percent of GDP during the 100 years before the 1980s. By the late 1980s, M&A activity stood at approximately six percent of U.S. GDP, and by the late 1990s, during a flurry of activity, M&A activity reached 15 percent of GDP.[vi]

M&As are now spread worldwide; between 2001 and 2004 there was an estimated $6 trillion of M&A activity worldwide. About 60 percent of this activity occurred outside the United States.[vii] The level of M&A activity outside the U.S. since 2004 has grown significantly. The level of cross-border M&A activity in 2005 reached an estimated U.S. $900 billion of activity, 50 percent more than the year before.[viii]

On the whole, mergers and acquisitions have a poor record of performance. Consistently, over the past decade, approximately 60 percent of mergers/acquisitions have failed or significantly underperformed expectations three years after the deal.[ix] The perception of the difficulty in achieving success in a merger or acquisition is the reason the stock of an acquiring firm typically falls when a merger or acquisition is announced, though stockholders of the target firm are usually paid a premium for their shares.[x]

Reasons for Mergers and Acquisitions

Despite the mediocre results of most mergers and acquisitions, record numbers of firms continue to pursue M&As, because M&As can allow a firm to accomplish a variety of strategic goals, including:

- Entering a new market quickly
- Avoiding costs and risks of new product development
- Acquiring an established brand name

Acquisition
The outright purchase of a firm or some part of that firm.

Merger
Occurs when two firms combine as relative equals.

- Completing a product portfolio
- Gaining market share
- Acquiring new knowledge and capabilities

Rapid Market Entry Acquisition of a new business allows the acquiring firm to gain immediate access to the customers, distribution channels, and/or the geographic area served by the acquired firm. If there are barriers to entry in a given market, a firm can circumvent such restrictions by acquiring one of the existing competitors. Typical barriers to entry include high levels of customer loyalty, distribution channels where wholesalers are unwilling to take on new firms, government hostility toward outside firms that market their product in a country but do not produce it there, or a geographic area where the best retail locations are already taken. In 1990, General Electric (GE) bought Tungsram, a state-owned light bulb maker under the old Socialist regime in Hungary. This allowed GE to secure a brand name familiar to Europeans, purchase an organization with factories in place, and obtain an established distribution network around the former Soviet bloc countries. GE accomplished all of this quickly with the acquisition, and has since been able to secure a strong regional position much quicker than if the firm had tried to accomplish them internally.

Avoid Costs of New Product Development The expense of developing a new product can be quite high. It is common for large sums of money to be invested and no viable product to be developed. A merger/acquisition can be used to minimize a firm's costs of undertaking its own research and development (R&D) in certain product areas. Instead, the business purchases another firm that has already conducted the R&D to develop the product. This can be particularly important if a firm feels it is behind in entering a given market. For example, in 2005, Chinese personal computer manufacturer Lenovo bought IBM's PC division for about $5 billion. This was done to build Lenovo's name outside of China and to learn IBM's microcomputing technology.

Acquire an Established Brand Name A firm can also acquire an established brand name to give it instant recognition in a new market. This can be particularly important for firms entering a new foreign market. For example, most people outside of the United Kingdom have not heard of Reckitt Benckiser. However, it is likely they have heard of the brands that the firm controls, such as French's Mustard, Calgon, Mop & Glo, and Lysol. The firm's strong brands have made Reckitt Benckiser one of Europe's premier consumer-products firms, with particular competency in cleaning products. The firm has annual revenues approaching $4 billion, and excellent growth potential.

Reckitt Benckiser is widely touted as a takeover target for any consumer-products firm seeking to compete in Europe that does not already have strong, well-established brands in that market. Reckitt has outperformed the industry worldwide for five years in a row, and most importantly, sustained its excellent track record for innovation: new products account for about 40 percent of annual revenue.[xi] Thus, if a major consumer-products company wants to move into Europe, Reckitt would be an excellent vehicle in which to do so.

Complete a Product Portfolio Firms can also pursue an M&A to allow the firm to offer a full portfolio of products. The total package of products that complement each other is typically referred to as a **product platform**. For example, Skoda Auto (pronounced "shkoda") is a venerable Eastern European car company, founded in the late 1800s in the old Austro-Hungarian Empire, now the Czech Republic. Skoda was acquired in 1991 by Volkswagen and is now a profitable division of the German car maker. By acquiring Skoda, Volkswagen obtained a brand capable

Product platform
A package of products that complement each other

of growing Volkswagen's total sales with a strong distribution network and brand in Eastern Europe, a domain where Volkswagen had no significant operations. Skoda was also a strategic purchase, as Volkswagen wanted to fill the lower part of its corporation's product offering; Skoda is now the low-cost option in the Volkswagen platform.

This strategic approach has been successful, both financially and strategically, for Volkswagen. In fact, Skoda's results since the acquisition by Volkswagen have significantly exceeded expectations. In 2004, the company's pretax profits doubled to $209 million on sales of $6.65 billion. Since 1991, production has increased from 170,000 cars with old Soviet bloc style technology to 451,000 cars with the new improved technology Volkswagen could provide. The quality of the Skoda cars is such that they now compete successfully in Germany, a market with high demand for quality that is also very competitive.[xii]

Market Power When a firm has enough market share to shape a market's actions it is said to have market power. Obtaining market power can be a strategic motivation for a merger or acquisition. When a firm has market power, its position in the market becomes dominant such that other smaller firms follow their pricing lead. Thus, if the firm with market power lowers prices, other smaller firms are forced to do the same. The market power of a firm can also force all key suppliers to do business with the dominant firm.

To illustrate, Mittal Steel is the world's largest steel firm and is based in Rotterdam in the Netherlands. Initially from India, Mittal Steel is largely controlled by Lakshmi Mittal with facilities in the United States, Romania, Mexico, and Kazakhstan.[4] The firm's strategy turns on importing new efficient management methods into previously inefficient mills that it acquires. For example, in 1992 Mittal gained control of a two-million-ton plant in Mexico for $220 million. This plant, Sibalsa, was losing $1 million a day before the takeover, but Mittal was able to increase employee output fivefold and soon it was accounting for 63 percent of Mittal Steel's profits, becoming the "crown" of the firm. As the world's largest steel firm, Mittal Steel is able to negotiate with suppliers to gain cost advantages others cannot obtain. Mittal also is able to help shape the steel industry and the prices that are paid for the product around the world because it sells such a high percentage of the industry's output.

Knowledge Acquisition Finally, a firm may pursue a merger or acquisition to gain knowledge about a particular domain. The most valuable asset of a firm is knowledge. If a firm does not have a viable understanding of a domain, it can purchase a firm with employees that possess that knowledge. Thus, a major retailer such as Wal-Mart often acquires an ongoing firm as they move into a new market. For example, in Central America, Wal-Mart's 2005 acquisition of controlling interest in the Central American Retail Holding Company helped Wal-Mart acquire valuable knowledge about this important market. This purchase gave Wal-Mart 363 supermarkets and other stores in the following five countries: Guatemala (120), El Salvador (57), Honduras (32), Nicaragua (30) and Costa Rica (124). Today, Wal-Mart is the largest retailer in Central America, the rapid expansion caused, in part, by the knowledge it acquired in the acquistion. The firm's stores carry the name *Piaz, Hiper Piaz,* and *Dispensa Familia.* However, one risk of a strategic effort is that if the staff of the acquired firm controls the knowledge of the organization, those individuals may leave during or after the acquisition. This threat is particularly severe in high technology-related domains, which are so dependent on the knowledge of the individuals in the firm.

---

[4]Despite starting in India, today the firm has no Indian operations.

When moving into a new and unfamiliar market, a firm will often acquire or merge with an existing firm in that market in order to gain the knowledge possessed by the existing firm's employees.

Another M&A Motivator

The reasons above are the positive reasons that motivate M&As. However, there is evidence that there is another motivation for mergers and acquisitions that may predominate, even if managers do not recognize it—managers' salaries will increase as the size of the organization grows. As a result, it is widely argued that one of the principal motivations for mergers and acquisitions is the fact that it will either enhance the reputation of the manager or increase his or her financial return.[xiii] The underlying theory for this belief is called **agency theory**.

Agency theory can explain why managers may be motivated to pursue such mergers and acquisitions. Historically, agency theory comes from the recognition that those who own firms and those who manage them are now separated, and agents may act in their own best interest rather than that of the firm. Self-interest motivations promote growth of organizations through mergers and acquisitions because managers can obtain higher salaries with larger or more complex organizations.[xiv] See Table 4-1 for **the factors motivating a firm entering into an M&A or alliance**.

Agency theory
The recognition that those who own firms and manage them are now separated. Thus, the agents may act in their own interest rather than those of the shareholders.

Types of Mergers and Acquisitions

Mergers and acquisitions can be analyzed along two key dimensions:

* Related versus unrelated diversification
* Horizontal versus vertical integration

Related/Unrelated Diversification Determining if a merger or acquisition is related concerns whether the skills or abilities of the acquiring and acquired firms are similar. If the firms in the merger or acquisition rely on similar skills to conduct the critical activities of the firms, then it is related diversification. In the case of firms that have dissimilar skills or abilities, it is an unrelated or conglomerate diversification. Skills or abilities allow acquiring firms to better understand the activities and needs of each firm. Such an understanding also allows smoother integration and maximizes synergies. Skills and abilities are particularly important in international settings because there are variations around the world in different industries. For example, how consumer goods are used, produced, and distributed varies from country to country. Therefore, the concern that

Greg Baker/AP Photo

TABLE 4-1   Factors Motivating a Firm Entering into an M&A or Alliance

	Merger and Acquisition	Alliance
Environmental Risk: i.e., political turbulence, economic instability (high inflation)	M&As are more likely in less turbulent environments. In high-risk environments, firms are less likely to want to commit resources necessary for an M&A.	In settings with high environmental risk, firms will tentatively seek out alliances because there is less financial commitment. This is especially true if the firm is not familiar with the environment. Once the firm learns the environment it may be more willing to pursue M&A.
Firm Size	Larger firms are more likely to pursue an M&A because they are more likely to have the resources and expertise.	Smaller firms are more willing to pursue an alliance because it limits their financial exposure.
Legal and Regulatory Setting	Some countries' regulations and enforcement of laws are such that firms are allowed access to a country's market only if the firm employs local people and produces the product locally. Thus, pursuing an M&A may be the only option to operate in the market.	Alliances are more likely to be pursued in high-risk settings where the legal and regulatory environment is very unstable.
Managerial	Managers like to run larger organizations. Evidence shows that they have a higher compensation in larger firms also.	Alliances are a good way to test a new market and to see if two firms can share technology and other assets effectively. Managers like alliances in entering developing countries if the systematic country risk is high.

arises is whether there are differences in the core skills required in each firm to be successful. If there are differences, then we would not call the diversification related.

This does not mean that the firms must have similar skills in all aspects of the two businesses to be related diversification. However, they should be similar in those areas deemed most critical to the businesses. Thus, firms may appear to come from two very distinct industries, but if both firms rely on similar skills, such as marketing, and if both firms employ those skills in a similar manner, the merger or acquisition can be considered related. To illustrate, the merger of the international pharmaceutical firms Ciba and Sandoz to create Novartis was a related and successful merger. Both firms relied on similar technical and marketing skills.

In contrast, some seemingly related acquisitions prove to be only weakly related to the existing business and therefore more difficult and expensive for the acquiring firm to integrate. In 2000, London-based Cable & Wireless plc. (C&W) decided to sell their Hong Kong division—Hong Kong's largest telecommunications provider, Cable & Wireless HKT Ltd. (also known as Hong Kong Telecom)—to Pacific Century Cyberworks (PCCW). At the time, PCCW was an Internet-based business with extensive property interests in Hong Kong. PCCW argued that the telecommunications basis for its Internet business was compatible to the skills necessary to run a large phone company that was the principal supplier of fixed-line and wireless service in Hong Kong. PCCW's executive chairman, Mr. Richard Li (Li Tzar-kai), the son of Hong Kong's powerful and well-known tycoon Mr. Li Ka-shing, is very influential in Hong Kong. (Note that in most Chinese names the family name is first, not last as in the West.)

The PCCW acquisition of the C&W unit was one of the biggest corporate mergers in Asia's history. Four top international banks underwrote the U.S. $12 billion loan that PCCW needed for the takeover, making it the biggest loan ever in Asia at that time. The four banks had also put together another thirty enthusiastic banks to syndicate the loan. While a rational argument about the common skill sets between PCCW and C&W can be generated, critics at the time of the acquisition

FIGURE 4-5 PCCW Stock Price

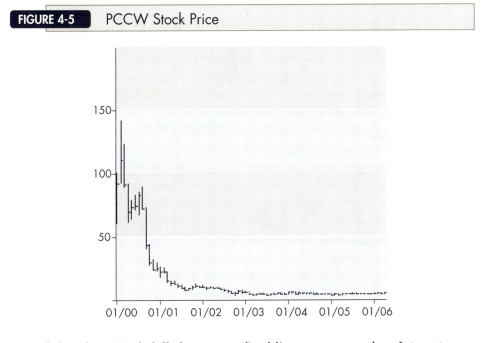

argued that the critical skills between a fixed-line operator and an Internet company are fundamentally different. The results of the merger would appear to also support this view. PCCW's share price declined ultimately by about 85 percent after peaking in early 2000. In hindsight, PCCW did not have the skills necessary to run a huge telecommunications company; their major asset seemed to be Richard Li's (and his father's) connections.[xv] Figure 4-5 highlights the stock performance of PCCW in recent years. (The length of the lines in the chart show the range of prices, while the cross line shows the average price.)

In general, firms that pursue related M&As perform better than those that pursue unrelated M&As.[xvi] In cases where there are similar skills or products acquired, it is easier to understand how to integrate the two businesses (or how to integrate a purchased product line if it is only a partial acquisition). It is also easier to understand how to manage the acquired firm or to place new management in the acquired firm if incumbent managers leave the business.

Horizontal / Vertical Integration Mergers and acquisitions can also be classified as either horizontal or vertical. **Horizontal** M&As involve acquired and acquiring firms that are at the same stage of the production process in the same industry. The focus in this case, in contrast to relatedness, is not on the similarity of the skills and abilities possessed by the firm but on the industry in which the two firms operate. In a horizontal merger or acquisition the products supplied by the merged firms are similar, but in a **vertical** M&A one firm is a supplier to the other. For example, U.S.-based Unigen Pharmaceuticals has aggressively taken over worldwide suppliers of the delicate plants needed for their pharmaceutical and nutritional products. Through this backward integration, Unigen is able to better control quality from the farm to the consumer, while ensuring steady supplies. Unigen cultivates plants and controls their cultivation in South Korea, Mexico, Russia, the United States, and Hainan Island in China.

In the future, the firm expects to forward integrate by creating new distribution outlets for its products. Hainan Island produces aloe vera for Unigen, and this island is also targeted as a future site for a resort and spa for customers and partners of the Unigen family of companies. Thus Unigen, using their suppliers' farms as a base, will also forward integrate into the growing market of health spas that use their products.[xvii]

Horizontal merger and acquisition
Occurs when the acquired and acquiring firms are in the same industry.

Vertical integration
When a firm expands its business into areas that are at different points along its production path for a given product.

HUTCHISON WHAMPOA: UNRELATED DIVERSIFICATION / BUSINESS GROUPS

Outside mature markets, such as those of the United States and Europe, a common type of organizational form is the **business group**. The business group is a set of firms that are technically separate, but are connected to each other through common ownership or cross-holdings of stock. Some of the most widely-recognized types of business groups are the *keiretsu* in Japan and the *cherobol* in Korea, although such business groups also dominate in Latin America and play a prominent role in Europe. The firms within most business groups are typically in unrelated industries and thus are said to be highly diversified. In mature markets, a *related* diversification strategy typically works better than unrelated or conglomerate diversification. However, in less developed markets where legal contracts may be difficult to enforce and capital and labor markets inefficient, evidence suggests that business groups with unrelated diversification perform better than firms pursuing related diversification. This is because the members of the group can be assured that the other members of the group will meet any contractual obligations, and the business group can self-fund their needs rather than having to go to a public equity market, which may not exist in some markets.

To illustrate business groups and their diversification, consider Hutchison Whampoa of Hong Kong, the conglomerate built up by well-known Hong Kong billionaire Li Ka-Shing. Mr. Li bought control of the then-troubled conglomerate Hutchison Whampoa from the U.K.-based banking powerhouse Hongkong & Shanghai Banking Corp, now HSBC. Mr. Li's Hutchison business group has now reached annual sales of nearly $20 billion per year. The firm competes in diverse activities that include five major areas—the operation of ports and activities associated with containerized cargo; telecommunications, including a major wireless phone company and heavy investment in 3G technology; property and hotel development and management; major retailers; and a major Canadian energy company. The business group, which includes sister firm and important property developer Cheung Kong, has over 180,000 employees in 42 countries and is highly profitable.

Even within these five major areas, there is major diversification. For example, the port management firm manages five of the world's seven most active ports in the world, from Panama to Hong Kong. The retail firms in Asia include drug stores, Watson's PARKnSHOP supermarket, TASTE food galleria, Fortress electrical appliances store, Watson's Wine Cellar, and Nuance-Watson duty free operator. In Europe, ASW's retail network comprises health and beauty chains DC, Drogas, Kruidvat, Rossmann, Savers, Superdrug, Trekpleister, Spektr and Watson's, as well as luxury perfumeries and cosmetics retail brands Marionnaud, ICI PARIS XL, and The Perfume Shop. A.S. Watson is the world's largest health and beauty retailer. The energy firms include not only oil-tar firms in Canada but also electricity suppliers in Hong Kong. Thus, the business group includes both wide geographic and product diversification.

Business groups that are as unrelated as this are highly unusual in mature markets, but in developing markets, such as Asia and Latin America, groups like this and others with similar levels of diversification will be the dominant form of business. In the United States, Hutchison would be encouraged to divest some of its less-related holdings or even spin off completely the Cheung Kong property-management and development side of the business so it could be more accurately valued by Wall Street. In Hong Kong, though, few analysts or investment banks would make such a suggestion to Hutchison management. In spite of well-publicized problems with its 3G investment, Hutchison has effectively managed most of its assets and has some big winners among its "unrelated" firms, such as Canada-based Husky Energy, which has achieved solid growth amidst the boom in Canadian oil and natural gas exploration. In addition, Husky Energy is co-chaired by Mr. Li's close associate Canning Fok and his eldest son Victor, so Mr. Li will probably keep his and Hutchison's stakes in Husky for years to come. If oil prices remain high, it is quite likely that Husky Energy will continue its solid growth and could grow to be a major part of the parent firm.

Hutchison Whampoa Website: http://www.hutchison-whampoa.com
Husky Energy Inc.—Fact Sheet—Hoover's Online. Website: http://www.hoovers.com/husky-energy/–ID__56221–/free-co-fact sheet.xhtml.

Several advantages can accrue to vertical integration, from better quality control of supplies to the quality of distribution to customers. Supplies can be obtained readily, which is particularly important for difficult or uncertain suppliers or unique inputs. Some economies of scale may accrue if suppliers are holding up the production process; for example, airlines are investigating purchasing and refining their own oil to cut the cost of jet fuel and to serve as a competitor to the energy firms they feel are taking advantage of them. Vertical integration can also reduce opportunism and market uncertainty, a major concern in emerging product markets. Therefore, it is more common for firms to forward integrate in turbulent product markets than in mature ones.

The Challenges of M&As

As noted previously, the majority of mergers and acquisitions are not considered to be successful. There are a variety of issues that lead to the failure of mergers or acquisitions. However, for international firms, often the primary problem is poor implementation. Typically, the implementation problems revolve around:

- Cultural differences in the firms involved
- Insufficient planning for the necessary degree of integration of the two firms
- Moving too slowly to combine the firms
- Not identifying key individuals to retain in the newly combined firm
- Not integrating the two firms' operational systems

It is important to plan a merger or acquisition carefully. A merger or acquisition requires that the firms involved work together to some degree. If there is absolutely no interaction, then this is a financial investment that approximates a mutual fund. The greatest implementation barrier to international firms working together in an M&A is the cultural differences of the firms involved. To illustrate, Britain's Vodafone and Germany's Mannesmann merged in 2000. However, the firms in the two countries typically operated very differently. The German firm had very hierarchical decision-making with responsibilities in the firm well defined and not easily changed, consistent with German culture. In contrast, the British firm prided itself on being an egalitarian environment in which communication should occur in the most efficient method possible without regard to an individual's position in the firm, and the organization structure should be flexible. Efforts to combine firms from the two cultures proved difficult. Vodafone did well financially following the merger but these results were seen as being achieved despite the merger, not because of it.[xviii] Too often, firms do not consider cultural differences, which was the case with this merger.

Combining a number of business functions after the M&A must be planned for. For instance, two firms may have different compensation and reward systems. To illustrate, in cross-border M&As, European managers often have lower compensation than their American counterparts. This is partly because of the extra level of benefits that Europeans enjoy in their countries, including relatively less-expensive medical care and, in some countries, free university schooling for their children. If a European firm is acquired by an American firm, the differing levels of compensation need to be addressed by the acquiring firm to avoid feelings of inequity among the European managers.

A firm whose acquisition program is recognized as one of the best in the world is Cisco Systems. The firm was founded in 1984, and between 1989 and 1999 it had a compounded growth rate in sales revenue of 89 percent per year. Though Cisco's growth slowed after the technology stock crash of 2000, it was able to recover and continue its growth strategy. This growth has come not only from smartly increasing demand for its networking products, but also from numerous small-firm acquisitions. Cisco had a clear strategy to gain competitive advantage through such acquisitions of small firms around the world with new and often potentially disruptive technology. Continued success depends on those acquired firms being integrated into the parent firm. As a result, Cisco has a well established system that it follows for the acquisition of technology and technology-focused firms. This system includes:

- Strong due diligence on the firm prior to acquisition to identify all potential issues and problems and critical differences in the acquired firm
- One-third of the top management from an acquired firm retained to fill slots in the new unit
- A buddy system to match up key employees of the acquired firm with key employees in Cisco

- Customization of each integration effort to match the unique needs of the firm
- Conversion of existing systems, such as computers to Cisco systems, to take advantage of economies of scale
- 90 days to complete the integration of the acquired firm into Cisco

Thus, the firm has been successful by following a consistent and clear process that begins with a strong planning effort and a committed implementation program.

The cost of poorly planned M&As can be high, as can be seen with Quaker and Snapple. In the acquisition of Snapple by Quaker, poor planning resulted in the inability to integrate the distribution of Snapple Ice Teas with Quaker's Gatorade sports drink. Both were food product companies, but they had different cultures. Quaker expected to benefit from the synergy of putting two powerful brands together under one corporate parent, using one distribution channel and coordinated marketing. This proved to be difficult as the distributors for the two products did not want to work together. In addition, Snapple was typically packaged and sold differently from Gatorade, and to a much different customer segment. Snapple consumers were older and drank Snapple as a soda-substitute beverage with meals, whereas Gatorade was used more as a thirst quenching water substitute during and after playing sports or exercising. There was little synergy in those brands, making cross-advertising and -selling difficult. In addition, it did not help that Quaker bid up the price of Snapple and bought at a huge premium during the booming U.S. stock market of the 1990s. After millions of dollars in losses, retail stores increasingly unhappy with the unwieldy shape and weight of Snapple's bottles, Quaker's unresponsive culture, and battles between distributors, Quaker finally divested Snapple, losing a billion dollars in the process. [xix] Right after Snapple was sold, the CEO of Quaker resigned. Quaker was then acquired by PepsiCo in December 2000 for $13.4 billion, all in stock. [xx] This price was much lower than the expected price just a few years earlier, prior to the Snapple problems. [5]

A firm can not only affect its portfolio of companies by acquiring businesses, it can also divest units or businesses as part of its corporate strategy. To illustrate, IBM has decided to get out of the notebook computer business. IBM initially formed an alliance with Legend Computer in China to learn about the China market, but the relationships built during this process helped IBM conduct the necessary negotiations when it decided to exit the laptop market. The result was that IBM sold the business to Legend Computer (now called Lenovo) in 2004, exiting it with a good price for the PC division and the ability to continue to work with Lenovo on other joint projects in China. Leaving the laptop market allows IBM to focus on other key aspects of its business and gives Lenovo more of a global presence and a measure of relief from being too dependent on the tight margins in China's PC industry.

Strategic Alliances

Strategic alliance
A partnership of two or more corporations or business units to achieve strategically significant objectives that are mutually beneficial.

A **strategic alliance** is another option in a firm's corporate strategy and is defined as a partnership of two or more corporations or business units to achieve strategically significant objectives that are mutually beneficial. This usually means that the firms will partner to produce and sell a given product or service. The exact nature of the partnership can vary widely, ranging from simple marketing agreements to creating

---

[5]Note that this is an example that involves U.S.-only firms. Almost all examples in this text are international in nature. Unlike most textbooks, which rely heavily on U.S.-based examples, this textbook has avoided them. A U.S.-based example is used here because there is so much written about the Quaker-Snapple acquisition that if a student or instructor wishes to do more research they can find a ready supply of information with books, cases, and numerous stories written about the failed acquisition.

ADITYA BIRLA GROUP AND THE SUNLIFE GROUP OF CANADA ALLIANCE

The alliance of the Aditya Birla Group and Sunlife Group of Canada is a good example of why firms create alliances. The Aditya Birla Group is one of the largest conglomerates in India and one of the world's largest aluminum and insulator manufacturers. The firm's sales are approximately $6 billion a year. In the mid 1990s, Aditya Birla formed a series of joint ventures with Sunlife of Canada. Sunlife has sales of over $16 billion a year and is a leading financial firm in Canada. The two companies established three joint ventures that offered mutual funds, wealth management services, and life insurance. The joint venture was to bring Aditya Birla Group's knowledge of India together with Sunlife's knowledge of financial markets.

The result has been successful for both firms. For example, the alliance exceeded the $1 billion mark in United States variable annuity gross sales for the first five months of 2007, representing an increase of 66 percent over the comparable period in 2006. Both Aditya and Sunlife have extensive international operations, and have sought to ensure that the cultural issues of the two firms are not barriers to the success of the joint venture. In part, this comes from the large international exposure of both firms. Aditya has operations in 26 countries while Sunlife has operations in 12. Thus, both firms come to the venture with broad international exposure. This includes not only the corporate officers but also the local managers assigned to the venture by both parties.

Aditya Birla and Sunlife Group also have sought to ensure there are no cultural conflicts through specialized training and the employment of consultants who have aided the managers in the joint venture. These individuals have sought to ensure that the communication and interaction between all parties are productive and not culturally misunderstood.

CULTURE

a formal joint venture organization with its own organization structure, offices, corporate name, and products. The costs and level of commitment of each type of partnership can, in turn, vary widely, although the cost and level of commitment of each type of alliance is less than in a merger or acquisition. One aspect of an alliance that mergers and acquisitions do not have is monitoring costs. These are costs that arise as each firm monitors the partnership to assure that all of its goals are accomplished in a manner expected and that there are no negative consequences from the partnership. Choosing the type of alliance depends on which one creates more benefits than costs for the firm. Additionally, other factors, such as the learning that occurs in such alliances, need to be considered.

Reasons for Alliances

A wide variety of reasons for alliances has been proposed. Kogut brought consistency to these various reasons and argued that the reasons could be summarized into three broad categories:[xxi]

- Organizational learning
- Cost savings
- Strategic behavior

Organizational learning in alliances occurs as firms attempt to gain knowledge about products, processes, or markets from their alliance partners. This type of alliance will allow the firm to gain a better understanding of a given domain without having to commit extensive resources to the effort. The amount of learning through any alliance is dependent on three factors: 1) the intent to learn; 2) the receptivity to new information, and 3) the transparency of the partnering firm. The form of the alliance will vary according to the type of learning desired. (Different forms of alliances are discussed later in this section of the chapter.)

Learning about a market through a joint venture is a particularly powerful motivator when a firm seeks to enter a developing market. For example, when Wal-Mart entered China it partnered with local firms in the new cities it entered to learn about their challenging environment and distribution system.

CULTURE MISTAKES: WHY YOU MAY WANT AN ALLIANCE

When major firms compete in a foreign market without the benefit of a knowledgeable partner, they often make mistakes, sometimes major ones. For example, in 2004, Pepsi had to remove an advertisement from Indian television. The ad showed a young, happy child serving Pepsi to two well-known cricket players, and was aired during a well-known tournament in India. The firm was sued and the advertisement killed because it was viewed as glorifying child labor.[6]

There are also problems with translation. For example, at one time, Coors Beer had a slogan of "Turn it loose." When that phrase was translated into Spanish, it was understood to mean "Suffer from diarrhea." In the United States, the Milk Producers Association had a huge success with their advertisement campaign, "Got milk?" But the translation of the phrase in Mexico was, "Are you lactating?" Parker Pen marketed a ballpoint pen in Mexico with an advertisement that supposedly said "It won't leak in your pocket and embarrass you." However, the Spanish word *embarazar* was incorrectly used for the word embarrass. As a result, in Spanish, the ad actually read, "It won't leak in your pocket and make you pregnant." In Taiwan, Pepsi's slogan "Come alive with the Pepsi Generation" translated as "Pepsi will bring your ancestors back from the dead."

There can also be difficulties with images. For example, in 1997, Nike employed a "flaming air" logo for its Nike Air sneakers. However, Muslims thought it looked similar to the Arabic rendering of God's name, "Allah." As a result, Nike had to remove over 38,000 pairs of sneakers from the market.[7]

The nature of China is that the culture and political power can vary widely from one major city to another. Thus, joint ventures in such situations allow learning about the local "system," such as legal standards, consumer characteristics, labor markets, and building relationships with the government and local distributors.[xxii]

There are transaction costs associated with an alliance, such as the legal documents required to form the alliance, building any independent facilities needed by the alliance, and monitoring the alliance. However, there are also costs that can be reduced or eliminated because most costs are shared. For international firms from mature markets, cost savings often occur through lower labor costs and can be particularly significant. For example, it is estimated that IT costs can be cut up to 70 percent when programming is done in India. Similar savings levels have been found in a wide range of other activities from back-office operations, service work, telephone support centers, and even the reading of X-rays.

Alliances may be pursued for strategic reasons as well. A competitor may have entered a given market or geographic region, or a firm may wish to match its competitor's actions. However, if this firm does not wish to commit the level of resources necessary to purchase another firm or to internally develop operations to match the competitor, then an alliance is an option. Particularly if the firm is not sure that the competitor has made the correct decision, or if the firm has a lack of resources, a strategic alliance is advisable. This strategic choice is less expensive since two firms will share the costs of the activity. Additionally, the long-term commitment is lower because the alliance can be abandoned if necessary.

Most often, when individuals think of alliances they think of joint ventures, or formal agreements between two or more firms in which a new, separate entity is created. However, joint ventures are just one type of alliance. Alliances can be differentiated along several dimensions; however, the most important dimension is the formality of the alliance.

[6]"Pepsi ad depicts child labour?" *BS Corporate Bureau in New Delhi* | October 09, 2004 http://in.rediff.com/money/2004/oct/09pepsi.htm
[7]The examples cited here are taken from "Translations That Embarrass Marketing Departments" http://www.i18nguy.com/translations.html

FIGURE 4-6	Alliance Types

Formal			**Informal**
Equity joint venture	Subcontract	Licensing	Understanding between parties

Types of Alliances: Formal versus Informal

The formality of the alliance is critical because it sometimes determines the costs and risks involved with the alliance. Formality of an alliance can be conceptualized as a continuum with joint ventures anchoring the more formal end, and informal alliances where no formal documentation exists anchoring the other. We begin our discussion with the more formal alliances and move to those that are less formal. (Figure 4-6 summarizes the range of alliances available.)

In an equity joint venture two or more firms both put some resources into a new, separate entity. The level of equity can vary from very small amounts to large multimillion-dollar investments. A joint venture commonly has detailed agreements covering what each party is to provide in the joint venture, what each can expect from the joint venture, and how each is to operate within the joint venture.

An example of a successful joint venture is Placer Dome Turquoise Ridge, Inc. The joint venture was formed by the Canadian mining company Placer Dome and the U.S. firm Newmont Mining. The joint venture was owned 75 percent by Placer Dome and 25 percent by Newmont Mining. It operated the Nevada gold mine that had previously been run solely by Newmont Mining. The new joint venture brought in the expertise of Placer Dome to run the mine, and as a result it had lower operating costs than those of the U.S. company. The joint venture expects to mine 30,000 ounces of gold a year, or $90 million worth of gold at current market prices.

Often equity alliances do not last a long period of time, but there are also examples of long-term, successful, equity joint ventures. One of the best known and largest strategic alliances is the long-running joint venture in Asia-Pacific called Caltex. This entity is a joint venture between the energy firms Texaco and Standard Oil of California. Caltex has operated around the Pacific Rim since 1926, and is a well recognized brand for energy products, retailing, and charity in some of Asia's poorest regions.

Alliances that are intermediate in their formality are agreements that have clear documentation but less interaction between the parties, and less agreement between each party in the alliance is required. Examples of intermediate alliances include consortia and licensing agreements. **Consortia** are characterized by several organizations joining together to share expertise and funding for developing, gathering, and distributing new knowledge. For example, Dr. Woo Suk Hwang of Korea in late 2005 led the formation of a consortia of 10 research teams around the world to study stem cells. The consortia had teams in the United States, Korea, and England. It had the leading scholars on stem cells in the world working together, seeking to develop new insights into how stem cells can be used to solve a wide range of disease and disorders, from paralysis from spinal cord injuries to Alzheimer's. (Interestingly, Dr. Hwang later was forced to resign due to evidence that he faked some of his data. The consortia is a loose organizational form, so the various parties in the original consortia were not substantively harmed by this embarrassing situation.)

In a **licensing arrangement**, one firm agrees to pay another firm for the right to either manufacture or sell a product. The firm selling the right to this product typically loses the ability to control various aspects of the product, such as how the licensee produces or sells it. There will be a contract between the parties, but the contract in the licensing agreement commonly specifies only the item to be sold and its cost.

Consortia
Where several organizations join together to share expertise and funding for developing, gathering, and distributing new knowledge.

Licensing arrangement
One firm agrees to pay another firm for the right to either manufacture or sell a product.

ALLIANCE OF MERCK AND THE GATES FOUNDATION IN AFRICA

ETHICS

Alliances can involve more than two firms. Pharmaceutical firms face a difficult ethical situation in very poor countries and regions, such as Africa. These firms sell products such as AIDS medications that can have a positive impact on the lives of many people. Yet even if those drugs were sold at cost, no one who survives on a $1 or $2 a day would be able to afford them. It has been noted earlier that Africa is being decimated by HIV/AIDS. The fact that so many individuals were dying of AIDS and they could not obtain medicine that would extend their lives led Nelson Mandela to claim that large pharmaceutical firms were exploiting the disease. There was a massive outpouring of protest and condemnation in addition to Mr. Mandela's statements about the pharmaceutical firms in the early 2000s. As a result of this highly negative profile, pharmaceutical firms began committing to serve the poor and ensure that they received life-saving drugs.

The country suffering the worst of the AIDS crisis is Botswana in southern Africa. It is estimated that the infection rate of AIDS in the country may be as high as 36% of all adults. In 2000 a new alliance was formed to address this problem, the African Comprehensive HIV/AIDS Partnerships (ACHAP). This alliance was made up of the government of Botswana, Merck & Co., Inc./The Merck Company

Foundation, and the Bill and Melinda Gates Foundation. The alliance was formed out of a need for all parties to address the problem. The approval and support of the government was needed if the effort to deliver the drugs was to proceed smoothly throughout the country. Merck had committed to provide the medicine to the population, but it had no skills in the delivery of the drugs themselves to the very poor. This required that public health experts be hired and an infrastructure be developed in order to support the existing clinics treating those with AIDS and to develop clinics where none previously existed. To do this, the Gates Foundation experts were needed. The Gates Foundation was founded by Bill Gates of the Microsoft Corporation and is the world's largest charitable foundation with assets estimated at over $34 billion and billions more committed from famed investor Warren Buffet and others. Mr. Gates has recently stepped down from Microsoft to devote himself to the foundation and its charitable activities.

The outcome of this alliance has been very successful. It is now estimated that half of those who can benefit from antiretroviral (ARV) therapy for AIDS are now receiving these lifesaving drugs. The alliance is continuing its effective work in combating this deadly disease.

Another type of alliance that is intermediate in its formality is subcontracting. The activities subcontracted may or may not be high-value-adding activities to the business, but the activities outsourced are not what the firm's competitive advantage is built upon. For example, today firms like Hong Kong's PCCW subcontract their computer networks and related support to other firms like IBM. The firms also combine computing and telecommunication resources to provide similar telecommunication and network management services to major customers.

Informal alliances have the least written about them in academic literature because they are the least documented. In such an alliance, two firms agree to support each other's activities in some manner. The agreements are strictly informal with few, if any, legal protections to enforce the agreements.

The Challenges of Alliances

The major challenges facing strategic alliances can be summarized as:

- Finding the proper partner
- Ensuring that there is a shared vision
- Getting the timing right
- Communicating effectively and efficiently
- Protecting intellectual property
- Measuring real costs and profits from the alliance

Before a firm can identify the proper partner or understand the costs of what it is attempting to do, it needs to have a realistic set of goals for the alliance, and an understanding of what the partner firm will bring to the alliance. Once these issues have been dealt with, the firm can develop an understanding of the costs and the best potential partner. Once an alliance is entered into, the firm must be proactive

KVANT AND IBM: A FAILED ALLIANCE

The Kvant and IBM alliance shows how difficult it can be for an alliance to succeed. The economic liberalization in Russia in the early 1990s led to widespread speculation that the nation was beginning an economic transformation that would produce tremendous economic growth. IBM had been active in Russia since the 1970s, but had no manufacturing facilities there. The firm wanted to participate in the potential economic growth in Russia, but rather than rushing in and opening a factory, IBM decided to form a strategic alliance with one of the leading computer manufacturers in the former Soviet Union. Kvant had recently become a private firm but had a strong history of technological success in the Soviet Union.

The two firms formed an alliance in 1993 to assemble laptop computers. The alliance production varied according to the number of orders, but ranged up to 4,000 a month. Product quality was consistent with the worldwide standards of IBM, which are quite high. Although the alliance experienced some initial success, it was cancelled in 1996, despite the relatively heavy investment by IBM in training and equipment, because IBM learned how difficult it was to deal with certain Russian institutions and practices. For example, the Russian government had initially promised there would be tariff-free importation of computer parts, but the government never followed through on that promise. The tax on imported parts remained, and that was added to the 20 percent value-added tax (or VAT) on the finished product. The government, in the early stages, allowed certain charitable organizations to import goods tariff-free and did not charge them taxes. The net effect to the PC's price was such that a group of Russian Afghan War veterans could go to Europe and buy IBM laptops, bring them back into Russia and still enjoy a 30 percent cost advantage over the IBM laptop the joint venture had assembled locally. Furthermore, the Moscow city government had also committed to buy large numbers of the IBM product and to provide other support to the joint venture, but ultimately failed to do so.

IBM's experience demonstrates that even two willing parties to an alliance may find that there are factors in the external environment that negatively affect the ability of the alliance to succeed. A firm must have an institutional strategy to cope with the elements in the institutional environment, such as the government, other powerful organizations, and individuals that can cause difficulty for a new entrant. IBM failed to cultivate connections with different levels of government in Russia that are necessary to navigate the sometimes treacherous local environment.

Bruton, G., & Samiee, S. (1998). Anatomy of a failed high technology strategic alliance. *Organizational Dynamics*, 27(1), 51–64.

in managing its relationship with the partner firm. Understanding each other's needs and ensuring they are met takes time and effort by both parties. There will be ambiguities but an active effort must be made, typically built on effective and efficient communication among the parties.

Occasionally, alliance partners may have seemed to share the same goal(s) for the alliance, but in fact, there is no shared vision. In those cases, the firm must act quickly to build a shared vision or it should leave the alliance. Without common goals, building a successful alliance is difficult. Finally, the firm must ensure that, while it partners with another firm in an alliance, it does not eliminate its own competitive advantages. Often international firms enter an alliance to learn about the other firm's technology or customers. That firm can then leave the alliance and become a competitor once it has gained the knowledge it wants. This is a problem that many Western firms worry about in working with alliance partners in rapidly growing economies, such as those of China and India. The weak legal protections in these environments can result in the shared information providing a competitive advantage to a firm that later becomes a competitor. In many ways, the ability to avoid such situations relates to the need to identify the proper partner and to share a common vision with that partner. A firm must also understand the true costs and profits accruing from the alliance. Without such information, sound judgment on the effectiveness of the alliance is not possible.

SUMMARY

This chapter has laid the foundation for understanding an international firm's strategy. The firm's strategy should be based on an ongoing process built around planning, implementation, and evaluation and control. The planning process should include the development of the firm's mission, goals and objectives, and strategy. The mission, goals and objectives, and strategy need to develop at each level of the firm's structure (corporate, business, and functional). Corporate strategy concerns the portfolio of businesses that the corporation chooses to operate in. The principle means that a firm has to affect its portfolio through mergers and acquisitions or alliances. Mergers and acquisitions can be classified as either related or unrelated, or vertical/horizontal. Alliances are differentiated by their degree of formality in the alliance.

MANAGERIAL GUIDELINES

1. Misunderstanding a firm's culture can reduce the likelihood of a successful merger with that firm and other corporate strategy actions. Taking the time to understand the cultures of the firm you would like to acquire can reduce conflict and smooth the integration process.
2. The firm needs to clearly establish its mission and strategy. As the firm expands internationally, it is easy to lose focus on where it wishes to go as it is pulled in various directions. The preparation of a clear mission statement and strategy will prevent this loss of focus.
3. A focus on the skills necessary to operate a firm in an M&A or alliance is one of the key concerns in evaluating the prospect of conducting such activities. If a firm does not already have the skills necessary in the M&A or alliance, it will have only limited ability to analyze or address problems.
4. Planning is a critical step as a firm enters into an M&A or alliance. Due diligence is the research on the nature of the situation the firm will face in the M&A or the alliance. The firm should conduct planning based on that due diligence. The fast pace of events after the M&A or alliance begins will require advance planning in order to manage various situations that arise. If a firm doesn't plan properly, problems will arise that could have been prevented through better planning.
5. People are a key resource and at the same time, represent a potential stumbling block to success in a merger, acquisition, or a strategic alliance. Often, managers focus on a financial analysis that shows likely synergies and cost savings and ignore the fact that most mergers and acquisitions perform poorly and many fail to produce any value at all. The principal reason for that failure is related to incompatible firm systems and cultures that prevent the different people in the firms from working together effectively. See Table 4-2.

TABLE 4-2 Corporate Strategy around the World

Country or Region	Corporate Strategy
East Asia	The market for corporate control (buying and selling of firms or major divisions of firms) was traditionally nonexistent in Asia. Originally, it was argued that Asian firms in Japan or Taiwan, for example, were somehow "different," and firm owners were so loyal to their communities and employees that they would never sell their firms to outsiders; others argued that Japan would never have corporate raiders, and so on. In recent years, however, the market for corporate control in East Asia has heated up considerably, helped partly by studies in economics and management that have shown the importance of an active market for corporate control for firm governance, innovation, and shareholder value. This has also been encouraged by governments that realize equity markets and the banking and finance industries can be further developed by allowing a more fluid corporate control setting.

North America	U.S. and Canadian firms have been perhaps the fastest to abandon conglomerate or unrelated diversification strategies. This started to occur after work in finance and management in the 1970s showed that conglomerates consistently underperformed more focused firms. The trend toward divestment and focus was perhaps strengthened by the active market for corporate control and the availability of private equity and active investment bank participation in that market.
Europe	Conglomerate strategies are also now falling out of favor in Europe, as the case on the Ahlstrom Corporation of Finland illustrates.
India	Conglomerates are still quite important in India. Major conglomerates include Reliance—a diversified group of manufacturing companies that is active in polymers, chemicals, fiber intermediates, petroleum, textiles, and procurement—and Tata, also in numerous businesses from tea (for which they are perhaps best known) to automobiles. It has been argued that conglomerates are still quite useful in India and other emerging economies as firms must develop their own labor markets and be active in insuring and financing their operations. This becomes less important in more developed markets where financing is more available, the rule of law is stronger, and labor markets are very active.

CULTURE AND DOING BUSINESS IN SOUTH KOREA

South Korea in the 1960s had a level of economic development that was similar to that of many of the poorer nations in Africa and just above its North Korean rival. Today, South Korea has left North Korea far behind as it has built a strong economy with a per capita GDP of approximately $25,000, comparable to many European economies and more than ten times that of its Communist rival to the north. The transformation came about through a close partnership between government and big business. Today, the Korean government is increasingly seeking to open the market to greater competition.

Korean men frequently greet each other with a slight bow, which is a sign of respect. The importance of respect is also seen in the use of formal titles when addressing individuals. Respect for the status of the person with whom you are conducting business is important, with the senior person in the group given special deference. Personal relationships are important and critical to conducting business as well. If you do not have a prior relationship with the person, an introduction is helpful.

Harmony and structure are culturally important. Therefore, showing anger or other strong emotions in meetings is generally inappropriate. In a Korean firm, decisions are made by group consultation, although the top manager will usually have the final say. Therefore, the time required to reach decisions may seem longer than is typical in the western world. The importance of harmony and structure results in senior managers having greater power and influence than they may have in the West. This emphasis also results in great respect being given to those who are older and have high levels of education.

When meeting a Korean business person, his or her business card should be accepted with two hands and handled with great respect. The card is considered to be an extension of the person, so do not write on it or place it in a back pocket. At a meal, when someone pours a drink for you, it is polite for you to take the bottle or teapot from that person, and fill that person's cup as well. This is different than in China, where it is polite to refill everyone's cup at the table yourself, before refilling your own.

https://www.cia.gov/library/publications/the-world-factbook/geos/ks.html (website accessed December 9, 2009)

CULTURE

ADDITIONAL RESOURCES

Sirower, M. (1997). *The Synergy Trap*. New York: Free Press.
Gatignon, H., & Kimberly, J. R. (2004). *The INSEAD-Wharton Alliance on Globalizing: Strategies for Building Successful Global Businesses*. Cambridge: Cambridge University Press.

EXERCISES

Opening Vignette Discussion Questions

1. Do you think the Ahlstrom corporation would have as clear a strategy and follow it so closely if the firm were in a commodity area?

2. Do you think that Ahlstrom is encouraged to pursue its strategy so closely because it is based in a small country like Finland?

DISCUSSION QUESTIONS

1. Why would a firm that has a well-defined strategy perform better than a firm without one?
2. Differentiate corporate- and business-level strategies.
3. Differentiate strategic planning and a strategic process in a firm.
4. What is the strategic mission of your school? If you do not know it, should the school have made it known to its students in the same way a firm makes its mission statement known to its workers?
5. How could an international merger or acquisition differ from a domestic-only merger or acquisition?

IN-CLASS EXERCISES

1. You are a young financial professional at your company, a medium-sized (US$200 million in annual sales) information technology (IT) firm on the U.S. West Coast in the Silicon Valley. Your boss, the vice president of finance, must make a recommendation to the CEO about a possible acquisition of a small IT firm with some innovative technology that may be able to bring some new users into the wireless email market that is located in Europe. She has asked you to help prepare an internal report on the merits of this acquisition.

   About one month later, you finish your report on the financial status of the firm and its accounts based on solid due diligence and an effective analysis of the firm's accounting data and those of its competitors. The auditors are satisfied with your results, and you hand in the report to your boss. She studies the report and tells you it looks fine, but she wants more. She asks you to go back to your report and add more information about whether your company should actually buy this smaller IT firm. Needless to say, you are puzzled; you performed the due diligence well, ran the numbers according to your training and studies in finance, and correctly found that the acquisition candidate's finances are solid, as are their sales and profits. Their asking price is reasonable. What else could your boss want? She hasn't really told you and she doesn't have the time to explain herself fully—she just told you to "figure it out."

   List and describe *three more topics*, apart from the financials, that you could address in your report to help your boss with her recommendations to the CEO. Describe what those topics should be and why such information may be helpful regarding the merits of the acquisition. Give examples to illustrate where possible.
2. Write a mission statement for your career. How are you trying to implement that mission? Be prepared to present your mission statement to the class.
3. Churchill China plc is a major global manufacturer and distributor of ceramic tableware. The English firm can date its founding back to 1795. Churchill China has developed the following mission statement: "To be a leading provider to the tabletop market and deliver value through excellence in design, quality, and customer service." Break into groups and analyze this mission statement. Do you believe that it is a good mission statement? How can it be improved?
4. Assume you are representing a U.S. firm in the pharmaceutical industry. You are assigned to develop an alliance with a Japanese pharmaceutical firm to co-produce a heart medicine. This medicine is one that your firm developed, but

you want the alliance to result in the manufacturing of the product in Japan. What are the issues you want to discuss with the Japanese firm as you begin your negotiations? What are the concerns you have as you proceed in these negotiations?

5. You assist a top manager in a major European luxury garment and accessories firm that subscribes to a fairly strict corporate code of conduct. Your firm is thinking of acquiring a supplier in Indonesia to make the highest line of shirts your firm offers, in order to better control supply and quality—these shirts have to be top-drawer variety and must be completed on time for demanding retailers. Your company performed its due diligence carefully: you flew to Indonesia with your firm's auditors to ensure the supplier's operation and finances are solid and, with the help of a major accounting firm, determined that the supplier is in good financial shape with modern factories and an experienced workforce. The employee dormitories are old and not particularly clean or well-lit, but in good enough shape so that they can be renovated. You are confident that you can start this project some time in the next 12 months. A few weeks after your firm purchases that Indonesian supplier, you are sent to Indonesia to take stock of the renovations that are needed and to see what else the factory will require. You leave on rather short notice, so there is no time to prepare anything—you figure you can come up to speed once there.

One colleague of yours who transferred to Indonesia from your home office meets you at the Jakarta airport in a huff. "A documentary filmmaker from the United States, with his publicity people in tow, is here to record the 'filthy conditions' in the dormitories," he tells you. "He says he will name me, our boss, and you by name as co-conspirators who are plotting to keep workers living in squalid conditions to make more profits for luxury-goods fat cats. Can you believe that?" Suddenly, the filmmaker appears in the airport arrival area with his camera and microphone and asks if you want to comment on the squalor that you are presiding over in Indonesia. "I've seen cluttered dorm rooms before," says the filmmaker, "but this is ridiculous." You protest that renovations are planned. "Sure, sure," the filmmaker replies. "Didn't your fat-cat luxury company earn about $200 million in profit last year? Why can't you spend some money on the workers?" At this point, you are tempted to tell the filmmaker what he can do with his microphone, but you think better of it. "We are here to work on some renovations," you repeat loudly. "Besides, what did you expect to see here? Ivy League College dorms complete with broadband and air conditioning?"

Was it a good idea to respond to the documentary filmmaker in that way? How might that look on film, especially in the hands of a wily film editor? How can a company respond when confronted with sudden press inquiries about its divisions and suppliers? What kind of preparation might have helped you better manage this situation?

TAKE-HOME EXERCISES

1. Find a Latin American company on the Internet (with an English language Web site). Read about the description of the firm and then write a mission statement for that firm based on the principles of effective missions. (Do not copy its current mission statement, but think up an ideal mission statement for that firm.)

2. Research a Fortune 500 firm that is pursuing some form of diversification. Identify whether that diversification is related or unrelated and give your reasons for saying so.

3. Pick a recent merger or acquisition in which at least one of the parties involved was a European firm. Was the merger or acquisition vertical or horizontal in nature? Explain your answer.

4. The opening case was about the success of Toyota. Research the major recent strategic actions of General Motors (5–10 major strategic actions over the last three or four years). Comparing these actions to Toyota's, why do you think Toyota's performance is ascending while General Motors is in decline?

5. Explain what merger and acquisition professionals mean by "synergy." Why is synergy difficult to achieve? Provide an example of a merger or acquisition in which one of the parties was from outside your home country. In describing the merger and acquisition, was synergy discussed? If so, describe where they believed that synergy would be found. Do you think they will be able to achieve that synergy?

SHORT CASE QUESTIONS

Hutchison Whampoa: Unrelated Diversification/Business Groups (p. 116)

1. If you had to predict, will business groups continue to exist in Continental Europe, or do you think that diversification patterns will come to reflect those in the United States and the United Kingdom?

2. What cultural reasons do you think exist for the development of business groups in Asia? Think specifically of the role of family and inheritance.

3. Hutchison Whampoa comprises both high-technology 3G wireless firms and mature industries, such as retail grocery stores. How do you think this firm makes key decisions?

5

BUSINESS- AND FUNCTIONAL-LEVEL STRATEGY

Overview

Once a firm determines its corporate-level strategy (where it will compete), it must decide on its business-level strategy (in which domains it will compete). An international firm must decide not only what business-level strategy it wants in one market but also whether it wants to have the same business-level strategy for each country in which it competes or whether to give its managers in other countries the responsibility for creating their own business strategies. This chapter discusses how firms balance the choices about business-level strategies. The special case of entrepreneurial firms and business-level strategy is also examined. The chapter then covers functional strategies for specific domains, such as marketing, finance, and accounting, which are developed from the business-level strategy. A part of the functional-level strategy that will be examined is quality management. The major topics covered in the chapter include:

- Porter's Five Forces model to understand competition within an industry
- Business-level strategies—low cost versus differentiation and broad versus narrow
- Global versus multi-domestic strategies
- Functional strategies
- Quality management

HSBC

The Hong Kong-Shanghai Banking Corporation (HSBC) is one of the world's leading banking organizations. The firm's history is one of survival. HSBC was one of the leading banks in China (and in Asia) prior to the communist revolution in that country. Following the revolution, the firm had to struggle with the loss of many of its assets, and it had look for other regions to operate in because it had lost its major market—China. The result was a major international expansion effort that continues today. The bank is now based in London, with operations in 77 countries and territories in most major countries around the world.

HSBC organizes itself into five major geographic regions with five main lines of business in each region (personal commercial services, commercial banking, corporate investment banking, private banking, and other activities). The firm follows a modified global strategy, that is, it allows some variation in its actions to conform to the differing banking laws in each nation. However, it is critical for an international bank to have consistent standards. For example, simply because it is more difficult to obtain information to validate a loan application from a commercial client in China does not mean that the bank can accept lower standards of information without having commensurate higher interest rates. Risk management for a worldwide bank requires reasonable standards to be met across the board. In situations where these standards cannot be met, the risk is perceived as a higher expectation of higher rates of return. At some level, a deal may be discarded if standards cannot be met. Therefore, the firm has uniform risk standards that must be met around the world.

HSBC has developed an evaluation and control system that is consistent with the modified global strategy used by that firm. HSBC holds its country managers responsible for the quality of the portfolio in their particular country. The bank allows many loans to be approved without receiving permission from London headquarters, but as the size of the loan increases, so does the need to have others outside the nation, or region, approve it. Having these checks and balances ensures that each country's operation functions according to corporate goals and does not take too many risks.

One critical functional area for a global financial institution, such as HSBC, is the internal audit. The accounting function in a business with great geographic dispersion ensures that the organization operates as intended. For example, a few years ago Barings Bank—one the largest and oldest financial institutions in Great Britain with over 200 years of history—was driven into bankruptcy due to the activities of a rogue trader in Singapore. That single trader conducted a large and enormously risky trading scheme that was not caught by the parent company for several years; by that time it was too late. ING bought what was left of Barings and kept the name, which had considerable brand equity. Thus, internal auditing and control are critical to firms with widely dispersed global operations.

The Asia Pacific area for HSBC includes Singapore, Australia and New Zealand, Malaysia, the Middle East, Indonesia, South Korea, Thailand, Japan, mainland China, India, and Taiwan. It is common for many businesses to include the Middle East with their Asian businesses despite the great religious and cultural differences in the two regions. This is because the region is not large enough to support its own regional-office structure, and the size of the market and location make Asia the natural domain for it to be combined with. For HSBC, Singapore and the Middle East represent the largest areas of activity in the Asia-Pacific region, but mainland China is considered to have the greatest growth potential.

HSBC typically charges a premium for its products. However, the high quality of the services it offers resulted in a wide variety of awards. In 2004 alone, for example, awards included:

- Best Bank and Best Bond House in Hong Kong—*FinanceAsia* Country Awards
- India-Best Foreign Bank—*FinanceAsia* Country Awards
- Indonesia-Best Foreign Bank—*FinanceAsia* Country Awards
- Best Bank in Hong Kong—*Euromoney* Awards for Excellence
- Best Regional Cash Management—*Euromoney* Awards for Excellence
- Best Bank at Risk Management—*Euromoney* Awards for Excellence
- Most Admired Corporate Brand—Most Admired Brands Poll
- Best Trade Finance in Asia—*Asset Magazine*
- Best Domestic Bank in Hong Kong—*Asiamoney*
- Best Domestic Bond House in Hong Kong—*Asiamoney*
- Best Foreign Exchange Bank—*Global Finance Magazine*
- Best Managed Company in Asia—*Asiamoney*

Thus, HSBC charges a premium, but it offers a high-quality product that is worth the price. HSBC has built a successful organization through the effective integration of strategy, structure, and operations, and has done so while operating in a large number of countries and diverse markets.

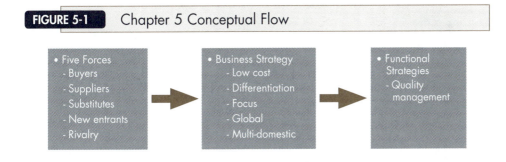

FIGURE 5-1   Chapter 5 Conceptual Flow

- Five Forces
  - Buyers
  - Suppliers
  - Substitutes
  - New entrants
  - Rivalry

- Business Strategy
  - Low cost
  - Differentiation
  - Focus
  - Global
  - Multi-domestic

- Functional Strategies
  - Quality management

Chapter 4 established the means by which management decides what businesses (industries) in which they want to compete. However, once a firm enters a particular product-market, such as the hotel industry, that firm must develop a strategy for that particular business. The **business-level strategy** is how a firm will compete in that product-market.[1] From this understanding of the business-level strategy, the firm will then develop its functional-level strategies for each business domain, such as marketing, finance, and operations. This chapter will analyze how firms develop strategies based on their environment. It then discusses business-level strategies and how they lead to functional-level strategies. Figure 5-1 summarizes the chapter discussion.

Business-level strategy
How a specific business will operate in order to succeed in that specific marketplace.

PORTER'S FIVE FORCES MODEL

Before developing the firm's business-level strategy, the business must understand what forces determine the profits in an industry. One tool to make such analysis is called Porter's Five Forces model. This model is based on **industrial organization (IO) economics**. This specialty within the economics discipline argues that all firms in a particular industry face forces within their industry that significantly affect profitability. If a firm understands these forces, then it can develop a business-level strategy that allows the business to either take advantage of or protect itself from these forces, which in turn allows the firm to be consistently profitable. The model focuses on how five forces in an industry (buyers, suppliers, new entrants, substitutes, and rivalry) impact each other, not how they impact an individual firm. A sixth force, complementors, is now widely used with this model and will also be discussed here. We shall explore the world auto industry to illustrate the concepts as we go through the model. Figure 5-2 summarizes the model.

The forces in the Five Forces model are analyzed from the perspective of how they are able to limit industry profits. For example, in some industries such as the pharmaceutical industry, firms are able to consistently earn higher profits than those in other industries. Some of the forces that constrain profitability in less attractive industries are stronger than in the pharmaceutical industry. If all five forces are weak, then it is likely that the industry will be an attractive one with firms that are quite profitable. For there to be above-average profits, at least some of the five forces must be low so that the firms in that industry can take advantage of them. If all of the five forces are high it is almost certain that the industry is low-profit. Once the forces are understood, a firm can develop a strategy that utilizes them to their advantage. Even though an industry's five forces may all produce an unfavorable environment, it is still possible for individual firms in that industry to earn above-average profits. For example, Southwest Airlines has a very steady record of profits and growth in spite of the low profitability of the U.S. airline

---

[1]Here we discuss the concept of product-market to refer to a specific industry sector because the authors feel it is a clearer term than industry.

FIGURE 5-2   Porter's Five Forces Model

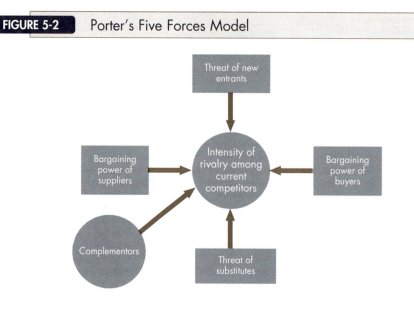

industry. Southwest Airlines developed a focused low-cost strategy, which has allowed it to maximize traffic in the markets it serves and carefully plan its capacity.

In reviewing the model in Figure 5-2, it is important to note that the industry analyzed is in the center of the model. The buyers discussed are those who buy from that industry, and the suppliers are the suppliers to that industry. As we discuss "industry," we mean the industry in the center of the model. When considering the power of a force, a variety of things can or cannot generate power for that force. The strength of a force is evaluated with respect to both quantitative and qualitative factors, such as the concentration of buyers or their ease of switching products. Each force will be described in turn.

Bargaining Power of Buyers

Individuals or firms who actually purchase the output of the industry are the buyers. These can include consumers, distributors such as retail stores, and industrial buyers. Identifying the buyers in the model can sometimes be confusing. The concern focuses on who actually makes the purchasing decision. For example, for a manufacturer of jeans, the main purchasers are the distributor and retailer, though the retail customer is also a "buyer" for the jeans. Thus, the analysis of the buyer can be complex and students need to be careful that they include the relevant buyers in their analysis.

In North America, auto dealerships are individually owned, and some of them are very large customers for the auto industry. Dealership owners are thus an important buyer of auto manufacturers' output, as is the average auto customer. However, there are also many auto dealers owned by the auto manufacturer. In Japan, automobile firms such as Toyota, Honda, and Daihatsu own their own dealer networks. The fierce competition in Japan has encouraged more forward integration, as auto manufacturers look to control distribution and repair of their products and to get closer to their customers, as well as locking out the competition; in North America, dealers carry multiple auto brands, but this is much less common in Japan. The characteristics that determine if the power of the buyers is high include:

- Concentration of buyers—if buyers are more concentrated (a small number of buyers purchasing about half or more of the industry's output), then buyer power is high.
- Ability to switch among different suppliers in the industry—if a buyer can switch from supplier A to supplier B easily, then the buyer's power is high.
- Impact of goods from the industry on buyers' output—if it is critical to the quality of what is produced, then the industry has power.

Bargaining Power of Suppliers

Suppliers are those firms or individuals that provide input into the creation of the industry's output. The concern in the Five Forces model is to examine the direct inputs into the product manufactured by the industry under investigation. The inputs can include widely recognized items, such as raw materials, fixed assets, and financial support. One frequently overlooked input is labor. Continuing the example of auto manufacturing, labor is typically well organized and strong in many countries. In South Korea, foreign firms making auto parts often have a representative in the Korean government dedicated to helping them with labor problems, because the unions are so strong. The strength of the labor movement in South Korea was so great that it was actually cited as the cause of the closure of the GM-Daewoo joint venture in the 1990s (General Motors was invited back after the Asian financial crisis in 1997–98 by Daewoo and the Korean government, and they have a new joint venture with more favorable conditions for GM). The concern with labor is not whether the employees are good workers or important to the process, but instead, are they powerful enough to demand a premium for their services? In this example, Korean labor is an important supplier that at times was able to bid away many of the profits of an entire industry. The factors that make suppliers powerful include:

- Demand for supplier's products—more demand drives the price of supplies up in a market-based system.
- Whether quality and performance of inputs are differentiated—greater uniqueness of an input allows a higher price to be charged and decreases the ability of client firms in the industry to switch easily between suppliers.
- Ability of the industry to vertically integrate—a credible threat of backward integration (that is, owning your own supply) will weaken the power of suppliers. Suppliers that are expensive and powerful tend to bid away the profits of the industry.

New Entrants

If an industry is experiencing high returns, then other firms will wish to enter that industry. These potential new rivals believe that they may be able to make similar or better returns. As will be discussed in Chapter 6, these new entrants can actually have lower costs because they may not have to educate potential customers about the product, and may be able to learn from the mistakes of those already in the industry.

Ease of entry into an industry also comes from its industry structure. For example, in the automobile industry, the equipment necessary to produce cars at acceptable quality and cost is very costly, even for governments, so there is a strong barrier to a new car company entering the market with a product offering that competes directly with existing products in the market. These barriers are so high that there have been no major new entrants to the auto industry since the late 1950s, with the exception of some specialty cars, such as the short-lived DeLorean, which was produced in Ireland. (The DeLorean was seen in the popular *Back to the*

SPAIN AND SHORT-TERM EMPLOYMENT

In Porter's model, unions are a supplier. That is because the unions are organized. One strategy firms have developed to limit the power of unions is to hire workers only on a temporary basis. Today, the hiring of such temporary workers is on the rise in many countries, especially in Europe.

Typically in Europe there are strong government and union controls on how firms must approach their human-resource strategy. The result is that European culture generally focuses on worker protection and lifestyle concerns to a much greater degree than in other places, such as Asia or the United States. This has generated an approach to employment in which it is typically difficult to reduce or increase employee numbers. For example, in Germany and France, employers must notify employees of layoff plans anywhere from two weeks to seven months in advance. If there is at least one union or workers' council involved, then the government must oversee the process. In France, in some cases the government must even approve the layoffs. A company will have to negotiate with the workers' representatives over the terms of severance. If more than 20 people are laid off, the company and the workers' representatives must negotiate a plan to help the workers find new jobs. These plans can run hundreds of pages long, take months to negotiate, and involve expensive payments to the workers.

Spain illustrates a new trend in Europe—the growth of temporary workers. In fact, one-third of Spain's workforce is made up of temporary workers. These employees typically make low wages, have none of the protection generally given to workers in Europe, and are not unionized. However, employing such workers allows firms to cut costs significantly. This can be critical to the success of new entrepreneurial businesses that have limited cash.

However, the experience of Spain, with so many workers now in low-paying temporary jobs, has heightened the debate in Europe as to the right approach to the regulation of worker layoffs. Countries like Germany are criticized for their inflexible protections for workers. However, those who support such protections offer the growth of temporary workers as proof that a deregulated market is also not good for the nation. This debate will likely continue with culture and the perceived role of government and the purpose of work having as much influence as economics. In 2006 France attempted to allow greater flexibility in the hiring and firing of workers under the age of 25, partly in response to high unemployment among this group, but the resulting riots forced the government to back down. The issue promises to continue to be a concern, not only in Spain and France, but across Europe.

Johnson, K. & Carreyrou, J. (2005, September 30). Amid Europe's gloom, Spain finds a miracle with short term jobs. *Asian Wall Street Journal*, pp. A1, A10.

Future series of films.) The investment to get into the microprocessor and chipset business to compete with Intel and AMD is similarly high; at least $10 billion is required just to build a chip foundry and acquire the equipment, personnel, and distribution needed to get started in the business (and that does not include other expenses, such as branding, selling, and working with the allied industries that need to work with the chip foundry). Thus, the structural characteristics of an industry frequently affect access to that industry. These structural characteristics include:

- In many industries it is more efficient to build or make products in large volumes, and a firm may have to enter at an unfeasibly large size to obtain the necessary **economies of scale**.
- The relationship between size and capital costs; the more money it takes to get into the industry, the less likely firms will enter it.
- If an industry has many differentiated products, or different products than customers are familiar with and loyal to, entry is discouraged.
- In many industries, such as retail, competition is so strong that firms are hesitant to give shelf space to a new, untested product. This limitation on the access to distribution channels limits entry into the industry.
- Patents and proprietary knowledge also limit entry because firms must spend much time and effort building the knowledge and resources needed.

Additionally, the reaction of the existing firms in an industry can affect the ability of others to enter. If an industry is known for vicious competition, then that will limit new entrants. Many consumer-goods domains have such a reputation. These domains typically have many commodity goods, or goods with little differentiation. Thus, a new entrant must understand that if it enters the market, the existing firms may cut prices or try to disrupt its market entry.

Substitute Products

Products that perform a similar function but are not considered to be in the same product category are referred to as **substitute products**. This differs somewhat from the economist's definition; for an economist, any product that can be substituted and used in place of the focal product is called a substitute. Thus, for an economist, Pepsi is a substitute for Coca-Cola, and so is orange juice. But in business, orange juice is a substitute for Coke, but Pepsi is not—rather Pepsi is a competitive product. To use another example, a substitute for an auto is a motorcycle. A bicycle could also be a substitute product for a car. For instance, many delivery people switched from cars to bicycles in New York City in the 1990s as traffic and parking became increasingly difficult and expensive. In congested city centers, many Domino's Pizza delivery people use bicycles or motorbikes for deliveries as they are cheaper and more convenient. To illustrate this note, let's examine the differences in traffic make-up in the Philippines and France. Cars are too expensive for most people in the Philippines, so they are much more likely to travel by motorbike or bicycle. The effect of substitute transportation is the creation of a ceiling for the pricing and profitability of the focal industry (e.g., autos). If the gap in the price-quality tradeoff becomes too big, buyers will begin to explore other options to satisfy the need. Thus, substitutes form a ceiling on the price that can be charged for a given product. The factors that impact the power of substitutes include:

- Ability of customers to compare quality, performance, and price – if customers cannot compare, they will be hesitant to switch.
- Ability of a product to bring good-enough performance criteria to the customer. Some customers will switch to a lower quality substitute product when that substitute has become good enough for many customers.
- **Switching costs**, or the cost of switching from the industry's product to a substitute—high switching costs lower power.

Motorcycles and bicycles are considered substitute products for cars, often chosen for their affordability and convenience.

Piotr Powietrzynski/Photographer's Choice/Getty Images

Rivalry

Rivalry among firms in an industry under examination is the last of Porter's Five Forces. The tougher the rivalry, the more likely firms are to cut prices, which lowers profitability in the industry. Rivalry is typically the force that has the greatest impact in the Five Forces model.

A variety of factors affect rivalry, but one of the key factors is differentiation. If firms in an industry can differentiate themselves from each other, rivalry is lowered and profits increase. It is for this reason that commodity products typically are high-rivalry, low-profit industries. As shoppers go to a supermarket to buy fruits and vegetables, they are bombarded by specialized products, such as Black Angus beef. A producer tries to create differentiation for a product that is considered to be a standard commodity and that usually has to compete on price. Continuing our example of the auto manufacturing industry, rivals in the industry are those firms that also manufacture automobiles. In this example, trucks and vans are typically included in the industry, but not motorcycles. The factors that affect rivalry include:

- Number of competitors—more rivals increase the number of firms trying to attract the same number of customers.
- Growing demand for the product—if demand is growing, then there is lower rivalry because it is easier to get new customers, and less need to fight for customers through price wars or heavy promotion spending.
- Increasing payoff from successful strategic moves—an industry may be low profit, but the hope is that one firm will be the survivor, so there is a willingness to compete very aggressively.
- Exiting an industry costs more than staying—this encourages firms to stay in an industry and compete even if profits are low. **Exit barriers** keep firms in an industry and thus can exert downward pressure on profits. Such exit barriers can also be emotional ties to a given industry, which result in someone not wanting to leave the industry despite it having a poor profitability future. Another exit barrier is specialized assets that allow a firm to do just one thing, which increases rivalry as the firm cannot leave that industry. For example, what can a firm do with tire-making equipment apart from making tires?

Illustration of Porter's Five Forces Model

In the example of the auto manufacturing used above, a review of the Five Forces model demonstrates that a variety of forces have an impact on a firm's ability to make a profit. Suppliers of most inputs to the car, such as auto parts, are typically plentiful and not organized, so they are not a threat to profits. The only major exception is organized labor, which is very strong around the world; even in Asian nations, such as Korea and Japan, autoworkers are heavily unionized and thus are powerful suppliers. Buyers include auto dealerships, fleet buyers (such as rental car companies and police forces), and individual customers. Buyers are not organized. Consumers, because of their ability to switch cars, can negotiate lower prices. The rivalry among auto companies also enhances a customer's ability to get a good bargain. New entrants into the industry are not a threat because of the cost and size of the required operation. Substitutes are not much of a concern in most markets. There is public transportation, motorbikes, and bicycles, but most individuals around the world still prefer to own a car if they can. Finally, the rivalry in the auto industry is fierce. Over-capacity exists worldwide; firms have to run at such large economies of scale to be efficient that there is usually too much production capacity and an oversupply of cars. The cars produced are specific to that year, which also creates pressure to cut the price of year-end models to sell down inventory. As a result, auto manufacturing carries very modest profits in much of the world. See Figure 5-3 for a list of forces and their analyses.

| FIGURE 5-3 | The Five Forces Model and the Automobile Industry |

Force	Strength of force	Comment and trends
Buyers	Moderate to high	Although cars are well differentiated, customers have low switching costs. The big-fleet buyers (rental cars, cities, police departments) have a lot of bargaining power, and auto firms earn very little profit from these sales.
Suppliers	Low to moderate	Most auto inputs are commodity products or easily obtainable parts ordered from specialty suppliers, on an original equipment manufacturers (OEM) basis. Labor can be a powerful force for some firms, such as General Motors and the Korean auto firms in particular.
Substitute products	Low	If one lives in a city, it is mass transit. Alternatively, it can be a bicycle or walking.
Potential entrants	Low	Economies of scale make it very difficult to produce cars profitably without major investments in capital, labor, and distribution. New technologies in drive and power systems are being introduced primarily by the automakers themselves.
Rivalry	High	Because of high capital costs and worldwide overcapacity, firms compete fiercely for new (and each other's) customers.

Contrast auto manufacturing with the world's most profitable industry: pharmaceuticals. Suppliers (i.e., chemical firms and machinery) are typically plentiful and not organized or differentiated. Buyers are doctors and hospitals, and they are not price sensitive, because the doctors' focus is on medical properties of the drugs, not their cost. New entrants into the industry are not a threat due to the cost and time required to have a drug approved for use and the lack of adequate substitutes, although generic drugs have had a significant impact on prices of medications in certain areas. Other than recent entrants into the niche area of biotechnology, the last major pharmaceutical firm entered the North American market in the 1950s. New technology in biotechnology and genetics may facilitate new entrants that come in with a new technology standard and approach, but even here the time to get a drug approved in the world is typically measured in years, which limits even this type of new entrant.

Finally, rivalry in the pharmaceutical industry remains limited. Timeframes for most new drug development are so long that firms know clearly what their competitors are doing, and they actively avoid challenging each other directly. Most pharmaceutical firms focus their drug development in specialized areas, such as chronic heart and kidney disease, and do not offer a full range of drugs, so product differentiation is very high. The result is that the drug industry has been one of the most profitable industries in the world for many years, but the industry is under increasing price pressures today as insurance companies and governments are increasingly asserting their power as major purchasers of drugs. Additionally, generic drugs bring a low-cost rival to the big-name pharmaceutical brands and create pressure on the industry to lower prices.

Complementors

A sixth force later added to Porter's original model is **complementors**, which are products that sell well with another product, or that complement a product to make it easier to buy or use.[i] Thus, computer software and hardware, because both are required to run computers, are considered complementors. The more personal computers sold, the more need for operating systems, software, and computer semiconductor chips. These four computer-related industries have a benefit in encouraging the industry and each others' growth.

To illustrate how an individual firm can use a knowledge of complementors, Microsoft has built one of the most profitable firms in history on encouraging numerous complementors. Microsoft develops platforms for personal computers (DOS and later Windows). Its policy initially was to make extensive information about the systems available to other software and hardware developers. As a result, software developers employed Microsoft's operating system as they developed new software packages. Developers then conformed to the conventions and requirements of Windows and DOS, aided by Microsoft's developer tools. This led to an explosion of software that employed Microsoft's operating platforms. Microsoft and other software makers encourage the sales of both of their products. The vast majority of software runs under Microsoft operating systems, because software makers continue to develop their products around a system with good developer tools and a large base of users. This in turn encouraged hardware makers to produce products compatible with MSDOS and Windows systems. Thus, the three—Microsoft operating systems, software developers, and hardware makers—complement each other and encourage the sale of each others' products.

Key complementors in the auto industry are energy companies and their distributors (that is the gas or petrol stations). Energy firms' ability to drive down the cost of oil some 90 percent in the first decades of the twentieth century, through scale economies and better exploration and production technologies, led to new applications for oil and natural gas, including efficient internal combustion engines and power turbines—key growth drivers of twentieth-century industrialization and rapid economic growth.[ii] Their ability to distribute petroleum products to automobile customers nearly anywhere further enhanced the value of the automobile, driving sales and encouraging the development of the interstate highway system in the U.S.—another complementor of the auto industry. Every new gas station or mile of new road increased the value of an auto and fueled car sales. New complementors, including a distribution system for fuels such as hydrogen, will constitute a key force encouraging alternative fuel vehicles in the twenty-first century.

Firms do not have to be passive recipients of their competitive environments. Once managers have completed their analysis of the five forces and complementors, they can use that information to understand how to compete more effectively. Thus, a firm should develop its strategy based on its understanding of the forces in its industry.

BUSINESS-LEVEL STRATEGIES

Once a firm determines in which industries it will compete and the nature of the forces in those industries, it must determine what strategy to use in its individual businesses. The strategy process is not a random process, but one that systematically builds one step at a time. Figure 5-4 illustrates how the different levels of strategy fit together.

Strategy professionals, consultants, and researchers have proposed a wide range of classifications for business-level strategies. However, in simplest terms, business-level strategy can be viewed using a two-by-two matrix similar to the one shown in Figure 5-5, which describes four generic business-level strategies.[iii]

The generic-strategies matrix is useful for analyzing firms that are competing in the same product-market in a relevant geographic domain, for example, the hotel business in the United Kingdom. Defining the product-market in an international setting is more difficult than in a single country. The relevant geographic area is based on a judgment about the nature of the competition from firms in the same product-market. For example, product-market for airline companies that fly intercontinental is worldwide because major airlines are able to fly to all parts of the globe and compete for customers traveling between international locations.[2]

---

[2]Domestic markets for airline companies are quite restricted, for example, only U.S. carriers can fly between two U.S. cities, such as Los Angeles and Chicago. Thus, the product-market for international flights and domestic flights would typically be analyzed separately.

FIGURE 5-4   Level of Strategy

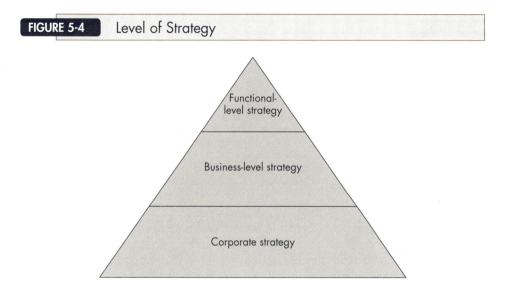

However, health-care companies, such as hospitals, compete against others only in a given location; thus, hospitals in Singapore compete only against other hospitals in the Singapore area.[3] Most people do not typically travel far for health care and legal issues related to providing health care vary widely as you move around the world.

Using the generic-strategies matrix, it is also important to note that what constitutes low-cost and differentiation positions can vary around the world. To illustrate, in the United States, Pizza Hut is considered to be a fairly low-cost restaurant. However, in emerging economies, such as Poland and Brazil, Pizza Hut is seen as a differentiated restaurant with higher service and costs than many local firms. Pizza Hut does not operate its business very differently in different parts of the world, but in Poland, the cost relative to local chains and independent businesses is substantially

FIGURE 5-5   The Generic Strategies

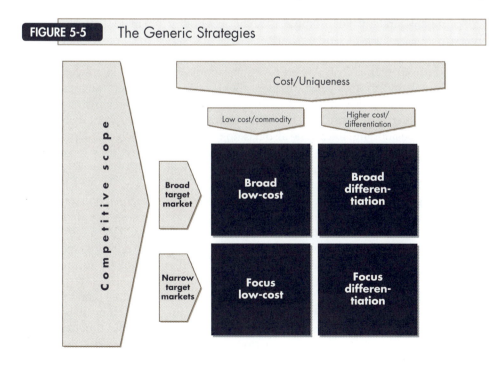

[3]This is starting to change as hospitals try to attract patients from foreign countries, particularly for cosmetic surgeries and other elective treatments.

| FIGURE 5-6 | Pizza Hut in Poland and the United States |

Poland

- Per capita income: $12,700
- Low penetration by international restaurant chains
- Model of customer service remains limited in many restaurants; in particular, service is very slow and not exacting
- Transportation to restaurants is relatively difficult—explosion of autos but roads still mostly Soviet era; good public transport in some cities

United States

- Per capita income: $42,000
- High penetration by international restaurant chains
- High level of service expected in almost all restaurants, even in most fast food restaurants
- Easy transportation by automobile to restaurants for most consumers

higher, and people's perception is that Pizza Hut is a more upscale chain. The same is true of McDonald's in China and Thailand, where it is viewed as a relatively nice restaurant with comfortable furnishings that could even be appropriate for a first date or other special events. The variations in what constitute low cost and differentiation makes geographic and industry boundaries important. (Figure 5-6 highlights some of these differences for Pizza Hut in the United States and Poland.)

Cost and Uniqueness

Low-cost strategy
Where a business seeks to sell a product at or near the lowest possible price in the firm's chosen market segment.

A **low-cost strategy** occurs when a business sells a product at or near the lowest price in the firm's chosen market segment or segments. This strategy sometimes involves a commodity product that is difficult to differentiate, such as many agricultural products—how much extra would you pay for a particular brand of milk? Low-cost strategies can be used not only for products but also for services. For example, a firm using low-cost strategy in the airline business is Ireland's Ryanair. The airline flies to a limited number of European nations, such as the United Kingdom, Ireland, Italy, Germany, Sweden, and France. Ryanair, headquartered in Dublin, Ireland, has a clear strategic position as a low-cost airline, with the various aspects of firm functions supporting this strategy. For example, Ryanair does not fly into major airports, which are expensive because of landing-rights charges and other costs of operating in a major city. Thus, while Ryanair advertises that it flies to Milan, Italy, in fact it actually flies to nearby Bergamo Orio Al Serio Airport, about 25 miles (40 kilometers) from Milan. Ryanair mostly flies short, frequent flights with a maximum range of about 500 miles (800 kilometers) in order to further control costs by reducing aircraft type and other maintenance, spare part, and service arrangements. Consistent with a low-cost strategic positioning, the airline also has no first class seats, which maintains the simplicity of the operation, speeds the boarding process, and reduces turnaround time of the airplanes. Ryanair cuts costs in every way possible, and in turn, charges its customers some of the lowest prices in its markets.

Differentiation strategy
Seeks to provide some aspect of a product or service that differs from that of competitors, such as higher quality, to increase the likelihood of customers paying a premium for the product.

At the right side of the generic-strategies matrix is the differentiation strategy. A **differentiation strategy** provides some aspect of the product or service that differs from that of the firm's competitors, such that customers will pay a premium for the product. Thus, an airline like Germany's Lufthansa will generally not try to match the low fares of low-cost airlines like Ryanair. Rather, Lufthansa will try to provide a higher level of service in terms of scheduling, coverage of major cities, reservation service, quality of first and business class, and even more comfortable economy-class seats. To maintain this level of service, though, Lufthansa must also charge higher fares.

Therefore, the two major categories of strategies are low cost and differentiation. Although the generic-strategy matrix seems to indicate otherwise, in practice, there is no strict dividing line between the low-cost and differentiation categories. Typically, one of the generic-strategy positions will be the dominant focus of a given firm and that firm will compete most closely with other firms pursuing a similar generic strategy.

CAFÉ DE CORAL: DIFFERENTIATION IN HONG KONG FAST FOOD

One criticism commonly leveled at East Asian firms is that they only copy their competitors. For example, some argue that East Asian technology firms copy products from Western firms and just adapt them for the Asian market, typically pursuing low-cost commodity strategies with little or no differentiation when they copy those products. This image is not totally accurate. Many firms in Asia have developed strong differentiation and quality in their products. It is also recognized by many firms in Asia that

their long-term success depends on an increasing focus on differentiation and creating unique products.

In Hong Kong, the fast food industry is mature and saturated. Fairwood and Café de Coral are two Chinese-style fast food restaurants in Hong Kong that have a long history. Locals complained often that the two firms were indistinguishable from each other, splitting the market in almost an oligopolistic fashion. However, Café de Coral has increasingly moved to differentiate itself from Fairwood. Specifically, the firm

improved the decor of its restaurants and upgraded the menu. Café de Coral has also announced an overseas expansion that will try to take the concept of authentic, lower-priced Chinese food globally.

Time will tell if Café de Coral's new positioning will work, but its financial performance has been quite solid over the past several years, and its initial expansions outside of Hong Kong into neighboring Guangdong province and other large cities in mainland China have been successful so far.

Competitive Scope

The second dimension of the generic-strategy matrix is **competitive scope**, meaning the breadth of the market that a firm will target, the range of customers and distributors sold to, and the geographic region the firm will cover. For convenience, competitive scope is typically divided into a dichotomous variable—broad or narrow. As with the low-cost, differentiation dimension, the dividing line is not always clear. The key to understanding competitive scope is if a firm tries to serve a broad range of customers with a broad range of needs, or targets a particular distributor, customer group, or geographic region.

Bang & Olufsen is a Danish company that focuses on high-end, home-entertainment systems—a very narrow scope. The firm produces a narrow range of products that are technologically some of the finest in the world. To illustrate, a Bang & Olufsen television set may cost $19,000; a set of stereo speakers $8,000. The firm focuses strongly on innovation, incorporating the latest and best technology into its systems. Bang & Olufsen continues to manufacture its products only in Denmark, a high-wage country, believing that if it outsourced its manufacturing, it would not be able to provide the hands-on supervision consistent with its differentiation strategy. The immediate location also allows the firm to fulfill special orders quickly in a way that could not occur with worldwide sourcing.

In contrast, an example of a broad-based approach is the Toyota Corporation. Toyota is active in all major vehicle markets around the world. It also produces a range of automobiles from the low-end Echo to the mid-range Camry (the best-selling car in the U.S.) to the high-end Lexus. Thus, the firm does not narrow its product offering in any significant way and is following a broad-based strategy in its industry.

Competitive scope
The breadth of products a firm will offer, such as the range of customers and/or distributors sold to, and the geographic region the firm will cover.

Connecting Low Cost/Differentiation and Competitive Scope

Firms pursuing a broad scope can normally be characterized as having either a "broad-low cost" or "broad-differentiation" strategy. One firm that pursues a broad low-cost strategic position in Europe is Ibis (www.ibishotel.com). This chain of hotels is a major supplier of hotel rooms across Europe, but competes in a wide variety of other regions of the world also. Ibis typically is perceived as one of the lowest-cost chains across Europe, drawing a wide range of clients, including business, holiday, and group travelers. While Ibis offers clean rooms, they are relatively small and sparse. Ibis is part of the Accor Group, which also owns the mid-range brands Novotel and Mercure and the Sofitel chain, the company's upscale brand. Accor also owns the low-end Red Roof Inn, quite familiar to people from North America. Thus, the corporate-level strategy of the firm is based on the hotel business with all of its diversification efforts related to that industry, i.e., related diversification. In the portfolio of businesses that are a part of Accor's corporate strategy, Ibis is the firm's major low-cost provider; the corporation refers to it as its "economy" brand. Ibis ensures this position by the nature of the amenities offered, the size and quality of the rooms, and the location of the hotels. Thus, Ibis is called a broad-based low-cost competitor.

In contrast is the Oberoi Group, which is headquartered in India and pursues a broad-based differentiation strategy. India has the world's second largest population. While its economy has grown dramatically in recent years—over six percent per year since 1994—India remains poor, with 25 percent of the population living below the international poverty line of about $1 per day and an average per capita GDP of only $3,100. However, India is also home to some of the world's finest hotels. The Oberoi Group has 30 hotels and 5 resorts, most of which are in India, although the corporation has hotels in six other countries. These hotels and resorts are perceived as one of the most expensive non-boutique accommodations to be found in each location in which it competes, catering to both business and holiday travelers. Oberoi Group's hotels and resorts are known for having well-furnished rooms, gym facilities, and some of the finest restaurants in their localities. They are also located in cities with major airports, so easy access to their accommodations is available. The hotel group provides a premium product and charges accordingly, and is described as providing a broad-based differentiated product.

Firms may also choose to pursue either a low-cost or differentiation strategy, employing a more narrow scope, sometimes also known as a "focus strategy." These firms focus on a narrow segment of the market, a segment they believe they can serve better than their more broadly based competitors that are trying to serve a wide range of customers. With a focused strategy, a firm will try to serve a particular type of customer, a particular distribution channel, and a geographic region, often with only one product. As with broad positioning, narrow positioning can be adopted with either the low-cost or the differentiation strategy.

To illustrate, in the retail industry, one of the leading firms in the Middle East is Alshaya, which sells a wide range of products that are international franchise brands of the highest standards. Thus, Alshaya concentrates on offering high-quality, higher-priced goods. However, the firm has made the decision to focus on the countries in the Gulf Cooperation Council, located around the Arabian Peninsula. For example, Alshaya has 201 stores in Saudi Arabia, 155 stores in Kuwait, 124 stores in the United Arab Emirates, 44 stores in Qatar, 27 stores in Bahrain, and 11 stores in Oman. This geographic focus allows the firm to meet the somewhat unique needs of consumers in the Middle East. Alshaya understands these special needs much better than any other firm with worldwide operations because it is not distracted by seeking widely divergent markets. Part of what Alshaya recognizes about the region better than foreign retailers are the means to serve the special needs of those who adhere to Islam. Thus, this would be called a narrow- or focus-differentiation strategy.

A retailer with a focus low-cost strategy is the British firm McArthurGlen. The company operates 13 designer outlet shopping malls in Europe. McArthurGlen has chosen to focus on European locations. Over one-half of the malls are in the United Kingdom, with the remaining malls in four other European countries. In their outlet malls all stores must offer goods at a heavy discount. Many of these goods are name brands but over-productions, seconds, and end-of-season items. Thus, they have a narrow, low-cost focus.

Often there are a variety of focus differentiators in a market, but each focuses on a somewhat different customer base. This allows various competitors to each have a differentiated strategy, and allows them to meet the needs of that particular type of customer more effectively. However, low-cost competitors are competing on cost, and typically a limited number of models can be successful in the low-cost segment. But each of the business-level strategies offers the potential for a firm to be successful or to fail.[iv]

Changing Business Strategy

Firms can change their business-level strategy, but doing this is difficult and should be engaged only with full consideration of the difficulties that can arise.[v] To illustrate, Volkswagen (VW) in the 1970s and 1980s was associated in North America with the VW bug and VW van. Historically, these products were low-cost products with a strong image of economy. Volkswagen's product mix changed over time. The change in Europe was gradual, and it was much easier as VW produced a range of cars from the lower to the higher end. However, in North America and Mexico, the firm continued to emphasize its low-cost strategy for a longer period of time. In the 1980s, VW sought to shift quickly to the luxury car models in North America and Mexico that had long been successful in Europe. For example, VW started selling several new higher-end models in the United States, such as the Jetta. However, the VW brand was still associated with inexpensive, economy cars by consumers in North America and Mexico who did not want to pay the premium prices associated with VW's newer products. North American consumers thought, "why spend a lot of money for a VW when I can buy a nice Toyota or Ford for the same price?" The result was that the initial effort to shift strategy in North America and Mexico was not successful. VW then had to try again with an enormous amount of marketing to change the consumer image of VW as a cheap car manufacturer. This was such a big problem for VW that for a while they almost completely withdrew from the North American market. VW started to come back by focusing its marketing on younger consumers, who had no established image of VW.[vi]

Business-level strategy is often easier to change when a firm faces a difficult competitive setting. The difficulties facing a firm encourage individuals in that firm to support the change. Often a change of strategy will be opposed by employees unless they are convinced it is necessary, and the potential of business failure provides the evidence of the need for change. For example, the successful strategy change by the Swiss firm ETA occurred as the firm faced financial challenges in the 1970s. The Swiss watch industry had moved from dominating the world watch industry to being almost driven out of most market segments as digital watches became the standard. ETA created the Swatch brand in this environment to compete as a low-end, good-quality, plastic-molded watch. But ETA soon realized that it could not out-compete the numerous Japanese firms, the U.S. firm Timex, and a number of small Hong Kong watch firms. Therefore, ETA decided to move Swatch up-market to a differentiation position by adding a fashion component to the brand. Swatch watches were rolled out in new collections twice per year, just like in the high-fashion industry.[vii] Through effective advertising, customers were encouraged to own multiple watches of different colors, much like clothes and fashion accessories. This was much different from traditional habits, in which customers would only own one watch and not buy another one until the first watch stopped working. Swatch changed the industry: the watch was now viewed as a fashion item, with customers wearing different watches depending on the occasion. This change required not only alterations in customer perceptions, but also dramatic internal organizational changes. These internal changes were difficult, but the threat of the firm's failure encouraged employee support.

SAMSUNG: CHANGING STRATEGY

In the late 1990s it would have been difficult to imagine Samsung as a leader in the electronics industry. The Korean firm was known mostly for producing lower-cost goods copied from others, such as microwaves and TVs, and sold through discount retailers. However, by 2003 the firm was an acknowledged leader in electronics. In 2003 alone the firm introduced 100 new products to the U.S. market. These products had won numerous design awards and the firm was quickly developing an image as a differentiated producer.

The transformation began in the early 1990s when Samsung Chairman Kun Hee Lee sought to reposition the firm as a producer of branded, differentiated goods. To achieve this he developed an in-house design team that partnered with some of the leading product designers in each field in which the firm produced products. Samsung also began to send its managers out internationally to learn about the markets where it wanted to compete. Finally, Samsung created design centers around the world for the first time so that Samsung's products would have worldwide applicability, rather than simply hoping Korean products would be relevant in other parts of the world. Samsung Chairman Lee also constructed a $10 million educational facility to educate his managers. Courses for the workers in the educational center were in English because Chairman Lee believed that workers needed to have an international perspective. A key success factor in all of these activities has been the strong leadership of Chairman Lee and a clear strategy of becoming an international competitor. These efforts are still too new to be able to fully see their outcomes. However, at this stage it appears that Samsung is laying the groundwork to be able to fully participate as a global competitor.

Samsung targets the high-end to up margins and profits. http://www.expresscomputeronline.com/20021104/cover.shtml

Samsung's lessons in design. http://www.cdf.org/issue_journal/samsungs_lessons_in_design.html

Business-Level Strategic Risks

Risks are associated with each of the different strategies. For the low-cost strategy, there is the danger that others may figure out how to offer the same product at a lower cost. This is the difficulty that faces many firms in developed markets: sudden competition from firms in low-cost emerging markets. Certain firms and industries may have been the low-cost competitors at one time, but they are ultimately displaced by even lower-cost competitors from other locations. For example, at one time Japanese steelmakers were the lowest cost in the world and were among the strongest. However, today low-cost Japanese steel firms have been displaced by even lower-cost Chinese and Indian steelmakers, which, in certain product segments, are now the lowest-cost and most-efficient producers in the world.

Another risk to the low-cost strategy is that individuals no longer care as much about price but instead are willing and able to pay more for a higher-quality product. This occurs often as markets mature. One example is the tough competition between international fast-food companies, such as the Spanish firm Telepizza, which is moving into many emerging markets. International fast-food firms typically move into a market as its economy improves. Although the food is typically more expensive than local options, a percentage of the local population will shift to the international fast-food company as an upscale alternative. Telepizza has been very successful moving into emerging markets and taking advantage of these changes.

If maintaining a low-cost position in the market is difficult, firms may seek a more differentiated position that will enable them to charge a premium price for their product. Yet differentiation is no guarantee of long-term success, particularly in fast-moving markets. Unless a firm is vigilant, its differentiation will be matched or surpassed by competitors that predict the next technological change or shift in market preferences. A low-cost competitor can figure out an inexpensive way of adding new features to a product, causing customers to move away from the original differentiator. For example, for decades Encyclopedia Britannica was the dominant differentiated brand for encyclopedias for homes, libraries, and schools because of the excellent scholarship that went into its entries, as well as the encyclopedia's top quality graphics, paper, and binding. (Encyclopedia Britannica was founded in eighteenth century Scotland, before moving to the United States in the twentieth century.) There were cheap alternatives produced by other firms, but they did not challenge Britannica's dominance as the broad-differentiator in the encyclopedia market. In the 1980s, however, Microsoft licensed one of the competitive encyclopedias perceived as a low-end product, Funk & Wagnall's, and placed it on the new CD-ROM under the Encarta brand. Encarta was priced cheaply, at about $30 for an encyclopedia CD, compared to nearly $1000 for a set of Britannica encyclopedia books. Sometimes Encarta was even included free with new PCs. Characteristic of a low-cost product, Encarta was of considerably lower quality; its entries were fewer and shorter than those of Britannica, and the pictures and graphics were typically of lower quality, perhaps causing Britannica executives to downplay Encarta's competitive threat—surely people would recognize the real quality of their product! However, the significant price difference encouraged people to overlook the less-favorable characteristics; Encarta was just good enough for many customers who simply wanted their children to have access to an encyclopedia, even though it was not the best.

Microsoft's Encarta did introduce some product criteria that Encyclopedia Britannica could not match. The increasing power and graphic ability of personal computers by the late 1980s allowed the Encarta encyclopedia to regularly add new features that the book-based competitors could not match, such as sound, 3D graphics and oversized charts. In addition to sound, Encarta would later incorporate short video clips and internet links.

Britannica executives were slow to respond to Encarta's threat, seeing it only in terms of its obvious features—a cheap encyclopedia with so-so writing and mediocre graphics, little different from a computer game. Although Encarta was an inferior encyclopedia, customers valued it for its convenience, added features, and lower price. This solved Microsoft's problem, which was how to provide the right tools for children to learn, while delivering them via a desirable and powerful new medium, the personal computer. Encarta proved to be a major threat and eroded Britannica's market share steadily during the 1990s. As a result of the shift in what the customers valued, Britannica sales dropped precipitously and the firm was sold in 1996 for less than half of its book value.[viii]

Another risk to differentiation strategies is that the differentiation may no longer be valued to the same degree by consumers who are no longer willing to pay the premium associated with the product. For example, British Leyland was a United Kingdom company selling the Land Rover, Jaguar, MG, Mini, and Triumph brands. British Leyland was heavily focused on the United Kingdom market. Consumers in this market ultimately shifted in significant numbers to cheaper foreign imports. As a result of this shift in demand, the firm's sales dropped dramatically, and the business was nationalized in 1977 as it was on the verge of closing. The government has since sold the various brands to other firms, mostly foreign investors that heavily market the car brands internationally as part of their broad portfolio of brands.

There are risks in pursuing a focus-based strategy as well. A focuser may be attacked by a more broadly positioned firm that is able to serve a range of market segments effectively. In the personal computer field, the focused firms selling desktop PCs mostly to their home markets, such as NEC in Japan, Acorn in the United Kingdom, and Great Wall in China, were decisively beaten by U.S. firms, such as Hewlett-Packard (HP) and Dell, which were able to provide a wider range of microcomputer products and worldwide support to customers. The desktop personal-computing market has moved toward broadly positioned firms that can offer more customized products (i.e., Dell), or can provide a wide range of system solutions (i.e., Lenovo and HP).

SWISSAIR: STUCK IN THE MIDDLE

Historically, Swissair was one of the flagship international businesses in Switzerland, and the airline was known for excellent quality throughout Europe. Swissair, however, filed for bankruptcy in early 2001. It had sought to be a global player but never was able to reach the critical mass needed to be successful. In large part these problems were rooted in the fact that the airline never developed a clear strategy. The firm, in the late 1980s, sought to form an alliance with high-quality airlines in Europe (AUA, KML, and SAS), all of which followed a differentiation strategy. The alliance failed, however, because it was never clear who was to lead the alliance. Swissair then sought to expand into small regional airlines. For example, in 1995 the firm bought 49.9 percent of Belgian Sabena Airlines, and later pursued a major investment in the Polish Airline LOT. Swissair also bought a 70 percent share in a low-cost regional airline named Crossair. These regional airlines had significant problems, however, and Swissair did not have expertise in restructuring airlines—it was not even able to reorganize its own cost structure.

In reviewing the airline's actions, Swissair appeared to lack a clear strategy—it was attempting to use both the low-cost strategy and the differentiation strategy at the same time by investing in various airlines.

Swissair itself was a major European carrier offering a differentiated service, but then the firm had sought to invest in bankrupt and troubled airlines throughout Europe that were operating with low-cost strategies. As a result, Swissair's image became blurred. Was it a high-quality airline or a regional airline? Was it offering a differentiated product or a low-cost product?

The outcome of this confused strategy was, as stated earlier, bankruptcy. At the time of the filing Swissair grounded its fleet, stranding thousands of customers throughout the world. The Swiss are known as stoic people, but in response to the grounding, citizens demonstrated in the streets, in one of the largest demonstrations by the Swiss in recent memory, with 10,000 participants.

The only comparable corporate situation in Switzerland occurred in the 1970s when the Swiss watch industry collapsed. However, that industry has been aided by an innovative new watch enterprise, Swatch, which created a major new position for the Swiss in the watch industry: the differentiated fashion watch. However, no new product category has yet been created for the Swiss airline industry. In the wake of the collapse of Swissair, Swiss International Airlines was created from Crossair. Swiss International Airlines is currently positioning itself as a premium airline

through a differentiation strategy, and aims to set new benchmarks in customer service and product quality. Swiss International Airlines operates a broad range of short- and long-haul aircraft.

Swissair's inability to identify a strong direction and make decisions when faced with a crisis is reflected in more than just the firm's bankruptcy. In 1998, 229 people died in the crash of a Swissair flight from Europe to the United States. The pilots smelled smoke and requested that they be diverted to a nearby airport for an emergency landing. The pilots then, in accordance with the rules when faced with smoke of unknown origin, shut off the power supply to the cabin. But in this case, following the rules to the letter caused the circulation fans to shut down, which caused the fire to spread back into the cockpit. Ultimately, the fire destroyed the various control systems, and caused the plane to crash. This lack of creative decision making is often cited as an example of when following the rules can be the wrong decision. This decision making will be covered in more detail later in the book.

Bonsu, H. (2001). A nation in shock: Swissair crisis. *BBC News.* http://news.bbc.co.uk/1/hi/programmes/crossing_continents/1677085.stm

Garstka, M. (2002, April 4). When global strategies go wrong. *Wall Street Journal Online.* www.wsj.com.

Stuck in the middle
Where a firm has neither a clear low-cost nor a clear differentiation strategy or is unwilling to commit itself to a broad or sufficiently narrow market segment.

Many firms succeed by not pursuing a pure low-cost or pure-differentiation strategy.[ix] Rather than focusing on being the lowest priced in the market or having a differentiated product, some firms try to have a product or product mix that is the best value in its category. One early major empirical study on the profit impact of market share (PIMS) suggested that firms with a high market share (i.e., broad positioning) would be the most profitable, but later research demonstrated this to be untrue. Both broad and focused positioning can be profitable. The least profitable firms are those without a clear vision of where they compete.[x] This corresponds to what Michael Porter has called being **stuck in the middle**. That is, if a firm has neither a clear low-cost nor a clear differentiation strategy, or an otherwise distinctive niche, customers will not know what to expect from the firm, and its performance will be suboptimal.

Business-Level Strategies: Global versus Multi-domestic

International firms must also decide if they will pursue the chosen business-level strategy in the same manner in all countries in which they compete. If a firm chooses to compete in the same manner in all countries, it is called a **global strategy**. In contrast, a firm that allows each market to adapt to the local conditions and pursue the strategy they choose best in that local market is using a **multi-domestic strategy**.[xi] We shall define these strategies briefly here but will expand on them further in Chapter 6 as we discuss market-entry strategies.

Global Strategy With a global strategy, a business has operations in multiple countries with the same business-level strategy in each country. In this situation a local manager is not given much flexibility to address the specific needs of the local market. Instead, there is a uniform decision by the corporation about how to address given problems or about how to present the product through marketing. The benefits of such a strategy are that it:

- helps to ensure the maintenance of a quality image of the firm and its products
- ensures obtaining the maximum benefits from economies of scale

To illustrate these benefits, consider international firms, such as Nestle, Bayer, or Johnson & Johnson. Individuals buy such firms' products anywhere in the world because of the firm's good reputation. Each of those firms has a quality image. Thus, whether it is a medicine, consumer product, or an industrial product, customers know that the product is characterized by quality and reliability. These corporations help to ensure that quality image is maintained by pursuing a global strategy. If they were to allow each business unit in each country to adapt to the local conditions, they would run the risk of destroying that quality image. An individual manager could inadvertently hurt the firm's image by making changes to a product. For example, a manager in an emerging market, such as Russia, might choose to use a cheaper input so he or she could lower the price of the product. However, if that input lowered product quality or caused harm to consumers, it could destroy the brand worldwide. This risk grows as the firm grows and competes in more and more markets. It may have numerous products in each of those markets, which makes monitoring managers' actions in each country difficult. Therefore, the firm protects one of its most valuable assets, its brand and quality image, by ensuring that managers only pursue certain types of actions.

Pharmaceutical firm Roche, which is headquartered in Switzerland, is active in over 170 countries with a wide range of products that now have a high degree of standardization. The medications themselves cannot be changed to reflect local situations because, by its nature, medicine is a specific set of chemicals mixed to exact specifications and approved by government agencies. The remaining option for localizing would be marketing efforts, including product packaging. The reason for Roche's employment of a global strategy can be illustrated by the fact that if Roche were to allow packaging to be changed by all of its country managers, the firm would have to monitor up to 170 different packaging schemes. Any new versions of the product would result in Roche needing the same number of new packaging schemes. Specific language or images used in some countries may in fact express something that would cause trouble for the firm in other markets. For example, it is common in Taiwan to have scantily clothed women on billboards for things as mundane as home loans. Images like this might work in Taiwan, but would be considered inappropriate in the more culturally conservative countries in the Middle East, and could lead to protests or demonstrations by those who find them demeaning to women or generally inappropriate.

Global strategy also assists a firm in achieving economies of scale. Economies of scale occur when a firm enjoys declining unit costs as production increases over a relevant range of time. One of the greatest benefits to a large global firm comes when it

Global strategy
When a firm chooses to compete in the same manner in all countries.

Multi-domestic strategy
A parent company allows each market to adapt to local conditions and pursue the strategy they believe to be best in that local market.

can obtain scale economies in its various activities. This ability to obtain economies of scale is an outcome of the firm's ability to buy in bulk, using centralized purchasing. In addition, there are economies of production that may accrue to a globalized firm serving many markets with the same product line. Such economies of scale are in fact one of the key advantages of large organizations over smaller ones that typically cannot match the larger firms' cost savings gained from those economies.

Multi-domestic Strategy A multi-domestic approach to business strategy may also confer some benefits. These include:

- greater ability to match the needs of each market
- greater ability to hire locals to do key advertising and related activities

Markets can have significant differences in their characteristics. For example, Thales S.A., a French aerospace and defense contractor, is a top local player in British, Dutch, Australian, South African, South Korea, and Singapore defense markets. Typically, players in the defense industry manufacture their product in a single country, and then export its products to other countries. Thales has, in contrast, pursued strategic alliances and purchases that have established the firm in a wide variety of markets. The defense industry is highly political in each country, and while Thales has some common manufacturing approaches, it has also sought to maintain the local character of each of its international operations. Thales has been successful with its multi-domestic strategy because it focuses on expanding into countries with high skill levels and strong defense budgets. The overall effect has been to create one of the most profitable defense companies in Europe.

A multi-domestic positioning strategy is common with many consumer products firms, particularly those in food and beverage, which must customize their products to local tastes. While a medicine will be formulated and packaged the same regardless of where it is sold and consumed, the mix of food products that a restaurant firm like McDonald's brings to its restaurants can differ by country. McDonald's sells beef hamburgers in the United States, while in India, lamb and mutton are used in hamburgers, and beef is not on the menu. Similarly, in Asia, the firm still uses wheat-flour hamburger buns, but it also makes available sandwiches with buns made from rice. A consumer may order a hot cherry pie at a McDonald's in the U.S., but in East Asia a consumer is more likely to order a red bean pie for dessert. (Red beans are a traditional dessert in Asia and are much sweeter than the beans consumers might eat in the U.S., and Chinese people often have red bean soup for dessert.) In northern Europe, McDonald's serves beer and french fries topped with mayonnaise, while in the U.S., soft drinks are on the menu and the fries will be accompanied by ketchup. Thus, customization by region is allowed around the world by McDonald's.

Choosing a Global or Multi-domestic Strategy

The question of whether a global or multi-domestic strategy is best is not easily answered. The answer depends on the nature of the firm making the choices. If the firm has built its success on a strong image it will probably wish to follow a global strategy so that it can maintain that image. In contrast, firms that deal with a product that can have widely divergent consumer demands, like food, will typically pursue a multi-domestic strategy.

The choice of which strategy to pursue involves trade-offs. As a firm expands internationally, it often finds that a global strategy is useful as it makes its initial expansion overseas. Use of a global strategy allows strong control over the expansion and ensures that the expansion will occur in the desired manner. However, over time, a firm may find that strong control limits its ability to gain greater market share. The ability to gain a foothold in a new market may be achieved by pursuing the same model used in the firm's home market. Expanding to become a significant competitor

WAL-MART IN EMERGING ECONOMIES

Wal-Mart, the world's largest retailer, is also one of the more widely criticized companies in the United States. Though Wal-Mart brings lower prices to a community, it also pays extremely low benefits and wages and does not always offer healthcare benefits. Many Wal-Mart employees must get healthcare coverage through public assistance. The company has been cited as discriminating against women and minorities in promotions. The result is Wal-Mart has become a target of boycotts by groups, such as WakeupWalMart.com.

However, internationally the firm is seen very differently. In many emerging economies, Wal-Mart is known for bringing reasonably priced goods to people who previously did not have access to them, as it did in rural areas of the U.S. In many areas in Mexico, prior to Wal-Mart's entry, retailers tended to offer poor-quality goods, with high prices and mediocre service. Local retailers were typically part of highly diversified, wealthy family businesses that cooperated with each other in limiting competition and fixing prices. However, Wal-Mart has refused to collude in such price fixing and has as a result introduced competition to the market. Today, goods typically are the same price in many remote areas of Mexico as they are in Mexico City because of the competition that Wal-Mart has introduced. Similarly, Wal-Mart has raised the level of service provided to customers. When competition was low there was little need to offer customers good service or product guarantees, but with the introduction of competition, customer satisfaction has become an essential part of retailing in Mexico.

Wal-Mart has also created significant economic opportunities for many individuals. The established retailers often paid very poor wages and did not promote individuals based on performance. Wal-Mart introduced a true meritocracy where those who performed best are promoted. Employees can also participate in stock ownership programs, something that large family-owned businesses almost never offer. Wal-Mart has a fine reputation in Mexico and in many emerging economies such as China for excellent employee relations. As a result, Wal-Mart has become a highly preferred employer for new university graduates in those countries.

Thus, while Wal-Mart may not always be highly respected by some in its U.S. market, in emerging international markets it is widely seen as having brought a revolution to retailing, particularly in countries with very few retail chains. The difficulty in making ethical choices and evaluations internationally is that there are a number of different effects to account for, such as Wal-Mart's influence on upgrading the retail climate in general for all Mexican customers, regardless of whether they actually shop at Wal-Mart. Wal-Mart may appear controversial to some, but it has also brought much to the citizens of the countries it serves.[4]

Lyons, J. (2007, March 5). In Mexico, Wal-Mart is defying its critics. *Wall Street Journal*, p. A14.

Vedder, R. & Cox, W. (2007). *The Wal-Mart Revolution: How Big Box Stores Benefit Consumers, Workers, and the Economy.* Washington: AEI Press.

ETHICS

requires greater adaptation to the demands of the local market. If a firm has put strong controls in place that limit the ability to adapt to the local situation, it may not be able to expand once it is established in that market.

One way that firms solve this issue is by allowing some degree of variation in each given market. In this setting, corporate headquarters does not allow each country to have completely different operations. Instead, headquarters allows the local firms to pursue a multi-domestic strategy, but the choices in each nation are constrained within given parameters. This strategy is referred to as a transnational strategy, which seeks to combine elements of both multi-domestic and global strategies. Typically, a firm pursuing a **transnational strategy** will determine how much flexibility is to be allowed in a given nation (i.e., the degree in which the strategy allows a multi-domestic approach). Often the degree of variation allowed changes as the firm becomes more established in a given market. To illustrate how such flexible parameters can work, Pizza Hut (part of Yum Corporation) allows some variation in pizza toppings in each market. For example, in Hong Kong they serve a topping of cuttlefish (like squid) and place less cheese on the pizzas, because cheese is not a traditional part of Asian diets. (Recall the boxed vignette in Chapter 2, Pizza Hut and the Role of Local Taste, that discussed the role of local tastes and product adaptations.) Pizza Hut also allows small variations in the crusts they offer in different regions of the world. However, the firm

Transnational strategy
Strategy that combines aspects of multi-domestic and global strategy.

---

[4]It is interesting to note that while Wal-Mart is rather successful in emerging economies, it has had problems in some of the more developed countries, such as Germany, where it recently had to sell all of its 85 stores to European retailer Metro.

places limits on the number of options available, and a local Pizza Hut must choose from these options so that the corporation can maintain its economies of scale.

FUNCTIONAL STRATEGIES

runctional strategies
Those strategies that direct what occurs in individual functional areas, such as marketing, finance, and accounting.

Strategic tactics
Strategic actions that help to implement a strategy, such as a new promotion program that would implement a focus on differentiation business strategy.

Functional strategies are those strategies that direct what occurs in the individual functional areas. Actions in these domains are where strategic tactics are undertaken. **Strategic tactics** refer to actions that help to implement a strategy, such as a new promotion program that implements a focused differentiation business strategy. The successful use of strategy tactics is critical to the ultimate success of the business.

Functional strategies should flow from the business-level strategy. To illustrate, if a firm chooses a low-cost business-level strategy, then the marketing functional strategy chosen should be developed in a consistent manner. For example, it may be exciting for the marketing department to develop a worldwide marketing strategy that has print advertisements in the leading magazines and newspapers of the world, and television advertisements that feature leading stars of television and movies from every country in which the product is sold. But that marketing approach would not assist the firm in implementing its chosen broad low-cost business strategy, because it would not be consistent with the business-level strategy. A firm using a focused, low-cost strategy probably would not spend a great deal of money building a brand name through high-priced media—it would spend its resources in the support of its primary distribution channel, such as small retail shops. Several major functional strategies will be briefly reviewed in turn.

Marketing

The marketing function covers a wide range of activities in an international firm, including designing the firm's marketing program that encompasses the "4Ps"—product, pricing, promotion, and place (distribution). The nature of this program will depend on the chosen business-level strategy and other factors, such as whether a business will sell to other businesses (B to B) or to consumers (B to C). Marketing programs to other businesses typically are affected less by the culture of a given society than are those marketing to consumers. That does not mean that there is not a cultural impact, but most of the information in marketing to businesses is very systematic and focuses on what the given product does and its benefits. In contrast, marketing to consumers is heavily influenced by local culture, and elements of the marketing plan for consumers will often be driven by locals.

To illustrate the importance of a functional marketing strategy, consider Procter & Gamble's experience in Russia. The average Russian consumer has only a $100 a month after taxes to spend, which might not appear to be a viable market for a large consumer products company. However, that amount has been rising by approximately 20 percent per year since the late 1990s.

Procter & Gamble's marketing group helped the firm to understand the potential of the Russian market. They also helped the firm understand how to market products in an area where the income is relatively low but rising. For example, the marketing group found through their research that Procter & Gamble focuses on the American brand image because of its association with quality. Therefore, it chose to keep its English labeling on products because of the quality image of the American product. Procter & Gamble's marketing also helped the firm to target its pricing of products in Russia. The marketing group helped the firm in other ways as well. One of Procter & Gamble's products is Tide laundry detergent, which typically sells for $6 in the United States. That same product is now produced in Russia, and the lower production costs allow it to be priced at about $1 in Russia. This lower price makes the detergent affordable by the local population.

DO RETAIL BRANDS TRAVEL?

One part of a functional marketing strategy is concern for brand. A recent survey of 40 retail clothing and grocery store brands in France, Germany, and the United Kingdom (the stores included hypermarkets, supermarkets, and discounters; the clothing brands, both specialist and department stores) by the global business-consulting firm McKinsey demonstrated the power of a multi-domestic strategy in consumer-products businesses. This study shows the importance of tailoring products and services to national tastes. In the clothing and grocery segments, customers in France emphasize service and quality; in Germany, price and value are more important, while in the United Kingdom, affinity (the social associations of stores) was most important (see Figure 5-7). This can be further shown in Germany, where the discount food market accounts for about one-third of all grocery sales, compared with a little less than 10 percent in the United Kingdom and France. German culture is often thought of as pragmatic and thrifty, while the United Kingdom is more hierarchical, with status and title being important. French consumers generally value a higher level of service and often show some disdain for self-service products and lower-cost firms.

Understanding what customers value about a firm's product or service in each geographic market can have significant financial benefits. Customers in the McKinsey survey spent twice as much money at their favorite shops in each product category as they spent at competing stores. As retailers, such as Tesco and Zara, move into new countries, even within Europe, they may have to define themselves not once but many times over. Retailers that depend on a single formula to deliver service can find themselves in a weak position in some markets. Reliance on a single formula is widely cited as the root of the problem for firms such as Eddie Bauer and Marks & Spencer as they expand into different international markets. Figure 5-7 summarizes some of the McKinsey report's findings.

Child, P. N., Heywood, S. & Kliger, M. (2002). Do retail brands travel? *McKinsey Quarterly*, Number 1, 11–13.

FIGURE 5-7   What Do Retail Consumers in Different European Countries Value Most?

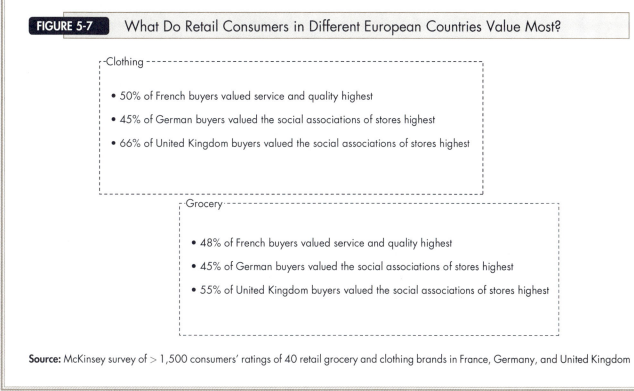

-Clothing-

- 50% of French buyers valued service and quality highest
- 45% of German buyers valued the social associations of stores highest
- 66% of United Kingdom buyers valued the social associations of stores highest

-Grocery-

- 48% of French buyers valued service and quality highest
- 45% of German buyers valued the social associations of stores highest
- 55% of United Kingdom buyers valued the social associations of stores highest

Source: McKinsey survey of > 1,500 consumers' ratings of 40 retail grocery and clothing brands in France, Germany, and United Kingdom

Another issue in presenting Procter & Gamble's products that was identified by the marketing group is that years of communist propaganda in the old Soviet Union had resulted in the population ignoring much product information. Procter & Gamble changed to market their products more directly, based more strictly on the products' benefits, rather than the nuanced advertisements customary in the U.S. In part, these actions have resulted in Procter & Gamble's Russian sales now being estimated at over $500 million, with a growth rate of 50 percent per year for the past several years.[xii]

Accounting

Accounting is not only concerned with maintaining information about the financial status of the firm, but also with providing data on how the firm is meeting its strategic objectives. Chapter 11 will discuss in far greater detail the role of accounting in the internal analysis of a firm and its critical role in a firm's evaluation and control. Evaluation and control concerns the ability of a firm to evaluate its current performance against where it planned to be, according to its goals. Clearly accounting can provide important performance measures on whether a firm is meeting concerns like profitability or inventory turnover. However, it will be seen in Chapter 11 that accounting can also be valuable in helping a firm understand how efficient and effective it is being in different aspects of its business.

A few key issues should be mentioned here, however, that affect the international operation of a functional strategy, such as accounting. One is that there aren't uniform methods of reporting accounting information around the world. The European Union has ruled that the 7,000-plus companies listed in its member countries should use International Financial Reporting Standards (IFRS) rather than GAAP (Generally Accepted Accounting Principals), which is used in the United States. The result is that there will be differences in areas such as financial instruments, business combinations, pensions, deferred tax, segment reporting, and leasing. Figure 5-8 contrasts the differences in IFRS and GAAP in the United States. Discussions are now in progress to reconcile the differences and merge these two accounting standards into a single standard.

To illustrate the impact of the European Union's change in rules, consider telecommunications firms, which will need to recognize revenue differently than they have in the past. Pharmaceutical companies will account for drugs under development differently. Firms in financial services will likely find that the mark-to-market or 'fair value' provisions will result in greater earnings volatility. The accounting department within a corporation having units in different countries will need, therefore, to not only consolidate financial information that is in different currencies but also consolidate information that may have been generated using different rules. However, whatever business-level strategy the firm pursues, it clearly needs to know what it is spending around the world and what the impact of those expenditures are. The information generated will also play a critical role in the allocation of costs to units in different nations. **Transfer pricing** refers to the pricing of goods and services within a multi-divisional organization. Goods from one division that are sold to another must be priced, even if no money actually changes hands within the company. The determination of the transfer prices will be governed by the accounting method used and the accounting and tax regulations, and in turn will affect division of the total profit among the parts of the company.[xiii] The role of transfer pricing and taxes can play a particularly significant role for international business. The taxes a firm pays in each nation can vary significantly. A firm must pay taxes on business activity in each nation. So if a low-tax entity can charge a high transfer price on a product shipped to a high-tax environment, then the company can reduce its overall taxes. Thus, where the business operations occur and the transfer price charged on components shipped from each nation is critical to an international business.

Transfer pricing
Pricing of goods and services within a multi-divisional organization that are supplied to other divisions or foreign subsidiaries.

Finance

The functional finance strategy of a firm concerns principally the means in which the firm funds its chosen activities. Financing for those activities must be present before they can be carried out, and the financing should be consistent with the strategy chosen. Thus, if a firm has chosen a low-cost business strategy, that means that the cost of funds has to be kept low. This is true to some extent with any

FIGURE 5-8	Comparison of Accounting Functional Rules

Subject	IFRS	U.S. GAAP
Components of financial statements	Two years' balance sheets, income statements, cash flow statements, changes in equity, and accounting policies and notes	Similar to IFRS, except three years required for public companies for all statements except balance sheet.
Balance sheet	Does not prescribe to a particular format; an entity uses a liquidity presentation of assets and liabilities, instead of a current/non-current presentation, only when a liquidity presentation provides more relevant and reliable information. Certain items must be presented on the face of the balance sheet.	Entities may present either a classified or non-classified balance sheet. Items on the face of the balance sheet are generally presented in decreasing order of liquidity; public companies must follow SEC guidelines regarding minimum-disclosure requirements.
Income statement	Does not prescribe to a standard format, although expenditures must be presented in one of two formats (function or nature). Certain items must be presented on the face of the income statement.	Presented as either a single-step or multiple-step format. Expenditure must be presented by function.
Exceptional items	Does not use the term, but requires separate disclosure of items that are of such size, incidence or nature that require separate disclosure to explain the performance of the entity.	Similar to IFRS, but individually significant items should be presented on the face of the income statement.
Extraordinary items	Prohibited.	Defined as being both infrequent and unusual, and are rare. Negative goodwill is presented as an extraordinary item.
Statement of recognized gains and losses, other comprehensive income	Separate the statement of recognized gains and losses either in the notes or highlight them separately in primary statement of changes in shareholders' equity.	Disclose total comprehensive income and accumulated other comprehensive income, either as a separate primary statement or combined with income statement, or with statement of changes in stockholders' equity.
Statement of changes in shareholders' equity	Statement showing capital transactions with owners, the movement in accumulated profit and a reconciliation of all other components of equity. The statement must be presented as a primary statement.	Similar to IFRS, SEC rules allow such information to be included in the notes.
Cash flow statement– format and method	Standard headings, but limited flexibility of contents. Use direct or indirect method.	Similar headings to IFRS, but more specific guidance for items included in each category. Use direct or indirect method.
Cash flow statement– definition of cash and cash equivalents	Cash includes overdrafts and cash equivalents with short-term maturities (less than three months).	Cash excludes overdrafts but includes cash equivalents with short-term maturities.

Source: Price Waterhouse Coopers http://www.pwc.com/Extweb/pwcpublications.nsf/docid/9D5D8BE60E1E00C880256ECA0046246B/$file/PwC_IFRS_SD2005.pdf

company, but firms selling a more differentiated product may be able to raise higher-cost funds, say, from a short-term credit line, whereas the low-cost firm would prefer not to do that, instead meeting financing needs through current cash flow or longer-term, lower-cost financing.

A finance strategy should not only provide financing, but should also help a firm identify those key areas that can be done more efficiently or cheaply. The finance department of Germany's Mucos Pharma GmbH helped the firm identify the ability to do clinical trials for a new head and neck cancer drug in India. The firm worked with SIRO Clinpharm of India to find 650 out of 750 volunteers for the trial. The Indian firm visited five hospitals in India over 18 months to find the necessary volunteers. To find the remaining 100 volunteers in Europe, Mucos Pharma spent nearly twice as much time and recruited patients from 22 hospitals. The financial group's advice about conducting the drug trials in India saved Mucos Pharma considerable financial resources and time.

A business may choose to buy an existing firm or to fund the entry internally. The methods used can have a significant impact on a firm. For example, Teledyne CEO Henry Singleton was able to enter a number of technology businesses around the world by using Teledyne's shares to fund the acquisitions, grow firm revenue, and provide opportunities for additional stock sales and stock splits. Thus, his financial strategy played a significant role in Teledyne's ability to expand significantly over a number of years.

Operations/Production

A firm's operational and production process should also be consistent with the chosen business strategy. A firm pursuing a differentiation strategy will be able to run a production line that can produce many variations and customize the output if necessary. A differentiated firm worries about costs, but this is less central than generating the highest-quality product, with variations customized for different distributors.

A low-cost firm, on the other hand, will try to avoid numerous production variations and seek to minimize customization, as both of these add cost to the product that they may not be able to pass along to customers. For example, VTech, the Hong Kong-based maker of cordless telephones and educational toys, makes just a few variations of its popular cordless telephone. Large firms for which it performs the manufacturing regularly put pressure on VTech to produce more product variations, but VTech tries to keep these variations to a minimum to keep costs down, which is consistent with its lower-cost positioning.

Turnkey operation
One part of the company is responsible for setting up the plant and equipment while another operates the plant.

Often, when setting up an operation or production in a foreign country, a firm will use a turnkey operation. In a **turnkey operation** one part of the company is responsible for setting up the plant and equipment. This will include not only establishing the infrastructure but also conducting the training. This unit then puts the plant into operation. A different unit of the company will then be responsible for running the firm over the long term. The ability for large firms to have such segmented operations in which individuals develop the expertise in establishing operations, while others develop the expertise in running such units, is why many large firms are so successful in pursuing international operations.

Research and Development

Research and development (R&D) is a critical concern for business. Concerns such as how to ensure the flow of information throughout an organization and how to ensure that the research is creative and not bureaucratic are central in developing a strategy for this functional area. As can be imagined, these concerns become more critical in the international firm. The R&D process is based in creativity, but creativity is heavily influenced by culture. For example, it was discussed earlier that many cultures are hierarchical, in that individuals look to those above them for approval and decisions. In such settings, independent action is often not looked on approvingly. But creativity is not hierarchical. There is a strong element of individuals discovering things that other people did not think were possible. Thus, international firms must generate their R&D strategy carefully.

One of the major trends in R&D strategy in international business today is the location of the R&D facilities in domains such as China and India, in order to take advantage of the very bright employees that can be hired there at relatively low cost. One major concern with such strategies is that there must be strong control of the information produced. As noted earlier, in many such emerging economies, respect for intellectual property is weak. It does an international firm little good to develop a new product if product information and design is leaked and copied before the firm can even bring it to market.

Supply Chain Management

You will recall from Chapter 4 the concept of a value chain. A value chain analyzes the inputs, both internal and external, of what a firm produces, and breaks down a firm's actions into primary and support activities. The value chain is useful for analyzing different functional elements so that a firm can integrate its functional activity with others. Value chain management argues that the different functional areas should seek to optimize their input into the total activities of a firm and its business-level strategy.

The concept of supply chain is related to the value chain, but it focuses mostly on inputs to a firm and where that firm ships its output. Thus, supply chain management recognizes that inputs and how outputs are delivered are critical, and a firm's ability to integrate these activities has a large impact on firm profitability.[xiv] But the focus is less on internal aspects of a firm and more on how the firm manages and works with its suppliers. For example, Hewlett-Packard has over 400 suppliers worldwide as it purchases more than $53 billion worth of inputs. Working with such a complex supply chain can be difficult. It is critical to Hewlett-Packard's financial well-being that those inputs be managed so that supplies are always available in the quantities and at the quality needed; inventory must also be managed to avoid excess storage costs

The aspects in which HP works with these suppliers are quite broad. It was noted before that a firm can be negatively affected if a supplier does something wrong and the firm receives the blame. The manufacturing of many technology-related products can create difficult pollution problems. A technology industry supplier may be tempted to simply dump polluted materials into a river, which would be very injurious to the environment and people living in the area. Alternatively, that supplier might use young workers (typically 16-18 years old) in toxic settings requiring excessive overtime or working without protective gear. In such instances, the media and politicians would not necessarily criticize the supplier, who might not have a name that most individuals would recognize. Instead, that supplier's customers would be criticized—perhaps big firms with well-recognized names and deep pockets to pay for any damages. As result, a firm like HP must be diligent in investigating and working with suppliers on a wide range of issues in addition to quality and production schedules. Figure 5-9 summarizes HP's recent examination of these issues for suppliers that HP considers to be high risk for potential violations of HP's supplier guidelines.

Quality Management

Another major functional concern for international firms is the firm's quality. Many firms establish a quality-control department. Typically, however, quality is considered to be a functional concern and it is not limited to a single department in the same way that marketing is. In large measure, this broader approach to quality is due to one of the founders of the quality movement, Dr. W. Edwards Deming.[xv] Dr. Deming held a Ph.D. in statistics with a specialty in manufacturing process control. Following World War II he was hired to conduct the census in Japan. The Japanese had been a world-class producer of military hardware prior to the war, but their consumer goods were considered rather shoddy. (It is hard to believe today that "Made in Japan" was synonymous with cheap goods in the post-WWII years.) Because the new postwar Japanese constitution prohibited the manufacture of military hardware, Japanese firms needed to develop world-class consumer goods to survive. Dr. Deming convinced the *keiretsu* in Japan, the vertically and horizontally integrated business groups that dominate the Japanese economy, to adopt his system of quality control. The highly integrated nature of business in Japan led to the widespread adoption of Deming's concepts of quality in Japan.

Keiretsu
Vertically and horizontally integrated business groups that dominate the Japanese economy.

FIGURE 5-9	HP Value Chain Evaluation for 2005

EICC code provisions	Nonconformances		Comments
	Major	**Minor**	
Labor management system			
Management system elements	1–10%	21–40%	Some suppliers lack basic management-system elements (e.g., policy statements, management commitment, internal risk assessments, ongoing training for workers beyond new employee orientations, effective corrective action process, communications) for proactively managing risks and ensuring continual improvement in human resources.
Health and safety			
Machine safeguarding	1–10%	21–40%	Nonconformances generally relate to enforcement and monitoring of ongoing use of machine safeguards.
Industrial hygiene	1–10%	41–100%	HP continues to work with suppliers to evaluate and control workplace exposure to controlled materials and to use personal protective equipment (PPE) appropriately.
Occupational safety	11–20%	21–40%	Nonconformances relate to the need for appropriate PPE and enforcement of the use of PPE.
Emergency preparedness	21–40%	21–40%	HP continues to work with suppliers on emergency and fire-response procedures, evacuation drills, and equipment.
Occupational injury and illness	1–10%	21–40%	Risk assessment, reporting, tracking, and corrective action processes should be improved in some cases.
Physically demanding work	1–10%	41–100%	HP continues to work with suppliers on use of ergonomics programs.
Dormitory and canteen	11–20%	21–40%	Nonconformances generally relate to hygienic conditions and personal space in dormitories and canteens.
General			
EICC awareness	11–20%	41–100%	In 2005, HP increased outreach and education through Supplier Forums to help suppliers better understand and incorporate EICC requirements into their operations.
Supplier management program	21–40%	41–100%	HP continues to work with suppliers to develop management processes for suppliers to monitor their own suppliers (including labor contractors) for SER.
Labor			
Freely chosen employment	1–10%	1–10%	Processes are generally in place to ensure that employment is freely chosen.
Child-labor avoidance	11–20%	11–20%	Workers below the age of 16 are extremely rare. Nonconformances generally relate to young workers between the ages of 16 and 18 working at night or conducting hazardous work.
Nondiscrimination	21–40%	21–40%	HP continues to work with suppliers to make its expectations clear in this area.
Humane treatment	1–10%	11–20%	Nonconformances generally relate to unclear communications to workers about disciplinary processes and wage deductions.
Wages and benefits	11–20%	1–10%	Nonconformances generally relate to use of deductions, varying accounting procedures, lack of worker understanding of pay calculations, and payment of flat hourly rates or wages despite overtime.
Working hours	41–100%	1–10%	HP continues to work with suppliers on processes for controlling excessive overtime and providing rest days.
Freedom of association	0%	1–10%	Means for communications between management and workers are generally in place.

Environmental

Product-content restrictions			See "Eliminating materials of concern" in Materials innovation section
Hazardous substances	21–40%	21–40%	HP continues to work with suppliers regarding on-site hazardous-materials labeling, handling and storage, and monitoring of vendor processes for off-site disposal of hazardous wastes.
Wastewater and solid waste	1–10%	11–20%	Nonconformances generally relate to monitoring of water and solid-waste treatment processes.
Air emissions	1–10%	1–10%	Exhaust systems for capturing fumes are widely used; air emissions monitoring is widely conducted.
Environmental permits and reporting	1–10%	1–10%	Permits generally available for inspection.
Pollution prevention and resource reduction	1–10%	11–20%	In some cases, reduction goals and performance metrics are not in place or reviewed to ensure that they are met.

EHS management system

Management-system elements	1–10%	21–40%	While ISO 14001 and/or OHSAS 18000 certifications are in place, some suppliers do not perform comprehensive risk assessments.

Ethics

Business integrity	1–10%	11–20%	Nonconformances generally relate to lack of formal ethics policies or standards of business conduct by suppliers and lack of worker-ethics training and awareness of requirements.
Disclosure of information	0%	1–10%	Processes and contracts are generally in place.
No improper advantage	1–10%	1–10%	Suppliers generally have policies ensuring that bribes are not accepted by management.
Fair business, advertising & competition	1–10%	11–20%	In some cases, ethics policies do not include fair business and competition statements.
Protection of identity (whistleblower)	1–10%	11–20%	In some cases, suppliers lack processes for workers and external stakeholders to report confidential ethical concerns.
Community engagement	0%	1–10%	Suppliers generally participate in community activities and provide donations.
Intellectual property	1–10%	1–10%	Processes and contracts are generally in place.

Source: (http://www.hp.com/hpinfo/globalcitizenship/gcreport/supplychain/performance.html)

It was not until the 1980s that product quality became a high-profile issue in the United States. At that time it was feared that because of the quality and cost advantage of their goods, Japanese firms would come to dominate most industries of the world. U.S. and European firms were losing competitive advantage in market after market as a number of highly visible industries such as automobiles and consumer electronics were increasingly being dominated by Japanese manufacturers.[xvi] After studying Japanese organizations, U.S. researchers and business leaders discovered that one key to the Japanese success was the quality of their products and the lean manufacturing system it enabled—systems developed in part by Dr. Deming who had tried unsuccessfully to convince U.S. firms to adopt the same system. The result of this recognition of why Japan firms were successful was the quick and widespread adoption of quality efforts in the United States and other developed countries. Today, the importance of building quality into a product from the beginning rather than simply trying to catch defective products at the end is widely accepted, and there are many different proponents of quality with many different approaches. Most firms have developed their own unique quality program that matches their setting. However, a review of Dr. Deming's fourteen points shows that many of those points are present in today's quality programs. Figure 5-10 summarizes Deming's 14 points.

FIGURE 5-10   Deming's Fourteen Points

1. Create constancy of purpose (have a long term view).
2. Adopt a new philosophy (senior management has to be committed to the program).
3. Cease dependence on inspection. (The goal in quality production efforts are to limit variance between any two items produced. If a firm does it right the first time there will be no need to inspect each product since there will be limited variance in the products.)
4. Move toward a single supplier. (A strategic supplier results in less variance in inputs, which limits variance in outputs.)
5. Improve constantly. (Quality is not a goal that stops; instead it is a continuous process of always trying to improve the product.)
6. Institute leadership. (The problems that arise are not due to the workers, but instead to the system in which they work. The key is to change the system, not the workers who operate it.)
7. Institute training. (Individuals only do what you want if you show them consistently what you want them to do. Do not assume they know. Thus, continuing education is critical.)
8. Drive out fear. (Change will not occur among employees if they fear the loss of their job. Encourage change by limiting fear. Without fear, employees will try new things and identify things that need to be changed.)
9. Break down barriers between departments. (The internal customer for what you do must be understood so their needs can be met. A high-quality product will be provided to the external customer only if a high quality product is provided to the internal customer first.)
10. Eliminate slogans. (The goal is to change the system that individuals work in. A slogan to do better will have no impact if the system is the same.)
11. Eliminate management by objective. (To focus exclusively on numbers misses the strategic changes and actions that are needed. Long-term focus requires more.)
12. Remove barriers to pride of ownership. (Employees need to understand how their work impacts the final output of the firm.)
13. Institute education. (Training and education of the quality process is important.)
14. The transformation is everyone's job.

Source: Deming, W. Edwards, *Out of the Crisis*, pp. 23–24: "Fourteen Points," © 2000 Massachusetts Institute of Technology, by permission of The MIT Press.

SUMMARY

This chapter has examined business-level and functional strategies. Business-level strategies should be consistent with the chosen corporate-level strategy, and functional strategies, also called strategy tactics, will flow from the business-level strategy of a firm. It is important that a business not have different levels of strategy acting independently of each other. Instead, a firm's strategies are designed to build consistently on each other. The two broad categories of business-level strategy are low cost and differentiation. Once a firm decides on one of these, it must also determine the competitive scope for that strategy—broad or narrow. The firm must then determine how much variation it will allow in the strategy as it is implemented around the world. The

MOTOROLA AND SIX SIGMA QUALITY

In 1988 Motorola Corporation became one of the first companies to receive the Malcolm Baldrige Quality Award. The heart of Motorola's quality effort is its Six Sigma program, which ensures that there are no more than 3.4 defects per million products produced. The path to developing this program has been a difficult one for the firm. The impetus for the program occurred in the 1980s, when a Japanese firm took over one of Motorola's television production plants in the U.S. The Japanese were able to take the plant, make a variety of changes, and produce televisions with less than 5 percent of the defects that Motorola had been producing.

To achieve Six Sigma, Motorola invests a great deal in employee education with approximately 40 percent of all employee training focused strictly on quality issues. The firm also benchmarks all of its activities against the best in every discipline to ensure that it is performing as well as it can. In doing such benchmarking, Motorola does not limit itself to firms strictly in electronics. For example, if you want to learn about customer service you may benchmark against a firm such as FedEx, which is known around the world for excellent service. Motorola seeks to build its quality programs from the bottom

up, focusing on the workers in the process. This involves not only education but also placing workers in teams to help analyze problems and solutions to most issues that arise in the firm. Motorola also rewards employees when these team efforts generate savings. Overall, the effect of the Six Sigma program has been to make Motorola one of the world's top-quality firms.

Pyzdek, T. (1999). *The Complete Guide to Six Sigma* (Chapter 1). Hamilton, OH: Quality Publishing. http://www.quality America.com/knowledgecente/articles/Six Sig_pg1-3. html.

firm then builds its functional strategies based on business-level strategies. Primary functional strategies, such as marketing, finance, accounting, and production, are essential to the effective implementation of a firm's strategy. The value chain is a helpful tool for assessing a firm's activities and their fit with firm strategy. There are two basic concerns that overlap between different functional areas, value chain management and quality management. While these two concerns occur within specific functional areas, they will affect multiple functional areas when they are implemented.

MANAGERIAL GUIDELINES

As managers consider the business level and functional strategy, they should follow these guiding principles:

1. A firm must have a clear understanding of where it wants to go and how it will get there if it is to be successful. Without such an understanding, a firm will waste effort in the pursuit of many conflicting activities.
2. There are many different strategies a firm can pursue to be successful. A firm needs to identify which is the right strategy, given its capabilities and industry.
3. Defining a firm's industry should include focus on the nature of the competition in that industry and relevant competitors. Almost all products are sold around the world today, but that does not mean that every analysis should be a worldwide analysis. Such broad definitions do not help a manager design useful strategic actions.
4. Functional-level strategies of a business must be consistent with the business-level strategies. Designing sub-strategies that are not consistent with a firm's mission and position in the market can waste valuable resources.
5. Quality is a key strategic resource that cannot be ignored as a firm develops its strategic posture.

The following points help the student or practitioner determine which strategy—multi-domestic, global, or transnational—is appropriate for their firm.

Multi-domestic Strategy

- Strategy, resources, and operating decisions are decentralized to strategic business units (SBU) in each country.
- Business units in each country are independent of each other; assumes that markets differ by country or regions.
- Decision-making authority is pushed down to the local level, and each business unit is allowed to customize product and market offerings to specific needs.
- The corporation as a whole foregoes the benefits that could be derived from centralization and coordination of diverse activities.
- Multi-domestic strategy is used by firms that need to tailor to local markets: retailers, consumer goods, services (legal, accounting).
- **Advantage:** Products and services are tailored to local markets.
- **Drawback:** Costs tend to be higher than other international strategies because of customization and duplicated facilities.

Global Strategy

- A global strategy involves a high degree of concentration of resources and capabilities in the central office and centralization of authority in order to exploit potential scale and learning economies.
- Decisions regarding business-level strategies are centralized in the home office.

- Products are standardized across national markets; customization at the local level is thus necessarily low.
- Strategic business units (SBUs) are assumed to be interdependent.
- Economies of scale are emphasized.
- A global strategy is used by firms that can produce standardized products in one or a few centralized locations, such as technology products (chips, consumer electronics).
- **Advantage:** Scale economies and lower production costs than other international strategies.
- **Drawback:** Lack of customization may hurt a firm against more focused competitors.

Transnational Strategy

- A transnational strategy seeks to combine elements of global and multidomestic strategies.
- A transnational strategy seeks to achieve both global efficiency and local responsiveness.
- Decisions regarding business-level strategies are centralized in the home office—strategic business units (SBUs) are also interdependent.
- Organizational learning is emphasized by capitalizing on knowledge flows (which take the form of decisions and value-added information) and communication between different divisions of the organization.
- Knowledge is developed jointly and shared worldwide.
- The MNE's assets and capabilities are dispersed according to the most beneficial location for a specific activity. Simultaneously, overseas operations are interdependent.
- A transnational strategy is used by firms needing global sourcing and logistics (e.g., Benetton, Citicorp).
- Global intelligence and information resources (e.g., Andersen Consulting, McKinsey Consulting) are often involved.
- **Advantage:** Scale economies less important than organizational learning. Firm hopes to lower production costs than in other international strategies.
- **Drawback:** Costs may be higher than the global firm. Cannot out-focus other competitors.

CULTURE AND DOING BUSINESS IN MEXICO

CULTURE

Mexico has a population of 110 million people and an annual per capita income of about $9600, one-fourth of the U.S. However, the economic viability of Mexico is highly segmented with greatest economic growth in the northern part of the country, near the United States. An estimated 40 percent of Mexico's citizens live below the poverty line, with poverty being particularly high in the southern part of the country. This poverty is in part what has driven the simmering Zapatista revolution in southern Mexico. Mexico has 12 international trade agreements that cover trade with 40 different countries. The result is that 90 percent of its trade is conducted without the impact of tariffs.

As a heavily Catholic country, Mexico places a strong emphasis on family. Consistent with this culture is the importance of nurturing business relationships. It is also important that personal introductions be made if one does not know an individual before a meeting. The person making the introduction is essentially validating you as an acceptable potential business associate.

Mexican society tends to be reasonably formal in doing business, and formal titles are the norm. Thus, a physician will always be called Doctor, while a person with a doctorate would be called Professor. The reliance on titles even applies to other professions, with formal titles being given with surnames for an engineer (Ingeniero), an architect (Arquitecto), or lawyer (Abogado). Mexicans will typically also have two surnames—one for the father and one for the mother.

ADDITIONAL RESOURCES

Barney, J. (1996). *Gaining and Sustaining Competitive Advantage*. Indianapolis, IN: Addison-Wesley Publishing Co.

Christensen, C. M., & Raynor, M. E. (2003). *The Innovator's Solution: Creating and Sustaining Successful Growth*. Boston, MA: Harvard Business School Press.

Peng, M. W. (2000). *Business Strategies in Transition Economies*. Thousand Oaks, CA: Sage Publications.

Porter, M. E. (1998). *Competitive Advantage: Creating and Sustaining Superior Performance*. New York: Free Press.

Zook, C., & Allen, J. (2001). *Profit from the Core: Growth Strategy in an Era of Turbulence*. Boston, MA: Harvard Business School Press.

EXERCISES

Opening Vignette Discussion Questions

1. Why would a differentiated product that charges a premium be more successful in the banking industry than a clothing-store chain?
2. Do you think that a quality image is more important in a region of the world where corruption and transparency are greater problems?
3. Do global banks, such as Citibank and HSBC, have an across-the-board advantage over small, local banks? Or are local banks able to differentiate themselves and their services from those of global banks?

DISCUSSION QUESTIONS

1. How should a firm's business and functional-level strategies fit together?
2. What is the difference between a global and a multi-domestic strategy? Provide an example of each.
3. Do you believe that Dr. Deming's Fourteen Points would be practical in today's business environment?
4. If you were in a large food-processing firm, such as Campbell Soup, would you pursue a global or multi-domestic strategy? Why?

IN-CLASS EXERCISES

1. Separate into teams. Each team should think of how the different functional strategies at a firm with a low-cost strategy, such as Wal-Mart or Southwest Airlines, might be implemented.
2. Create a generic business-level strategy matrix for the hotel industry in your country. Try to give at least one example per generic strategy (e.g., focus-differentiation, broad-low cost, etc.) of a hotel pursuing that strategy.
3. McDonald's is positioned as a low-cost fast food restaurant in Hong Kong, but is perceived as a more differentiated, higher quality restaurant in mainland China. Discuss why McDonald's is perceived differently in mainland China. How do you think McDonald's could implement that different positioning and benefit from it?
4. Why do you think European consumers value different aspects of the retail experience differently? What does this mean to the average clothing retailer in setting up business in the United Kingdom, Germany, and France, for example?

TAKE-HOME EXERCISES

1. Identify a corporation from outside your home country. Research that firm and give its corporate strategy, the business-level strategy for one of its units in a given country, and a functional strategy within that unit.

2. Southwest Airlines in the United States pioneered the same strategy as Ryanair, which was discussed in this chapter. Research Southwest Airlines and contrast it to the strategic actions of Ryanair. Identify specific ways Ryanair is similar to and different from Southwest Airlines.

3. Develop a chart that contrasts low-cost airlines, such as Ryanair, with differentiated carriers, such as Lufthansa.

4. Many U.S. consumers want their meals in a hurry, but with more service and higher-quality food than in traditional fast food restaurants. The result has been the rise of fast-casual restaurant chains, such as Daphne's Greek Cafe, Boston Market, and Panera Bread. The intent of fast-casual restaurants is to deliver a quality home-cooked meal, such as a roast chicken, or fresh salad and bread, in a comfortable setting, and quickly. Many consider the concept of fast casual to be a major restaurant niche that will be as important as fast food, and perhaps even surpass it in the coming years. How are fast-casual restaurants positioned in the generic strategies matrix compared with the major fast-food restaurants? Do you think this concept of fast casual can be brought to countries outside of the United States and Canada where few such restaurants exist today? Be specific in your answer about what country you are thinking of and why the concept would or would not work in that country.

SHORT CASE QUESTIONS

Swissair: Stuck in the Middle (p. 146)

1. What are the factors in a firm's culture that may keep it from clearly choosing a strategy (stuck in the middle) and also allow structured decision making similar to that which led to the crash of Swiss Flight 111?

2. Can you identify any firms in your home country that are stuck in the middle today? Would you classify airlines that seek to be both low cost and differentiation as being stuck in the middle?

3. What would be the means to avoid being stuck in the middle?

6

INTERNATIONAL MARKET ENTRY

Overview

Up to this point, this book has examined issues that are foundational for international managers—understanding the culture of a region or country in which they are doing business, understanding that country's external environment (economic, political, and legal), and developing the strategy for the firm accordingly. Now we begin to examine how the firm implements that strategy in an international setting. The first implementation concern for a firm is how to enter a foreign market. Some of the relevant approaches, such as mergers or joint ventures, were discussed in Chapter 4 when diversification was addressed. However, there are other ways to enter an international market, including import/export, licensing, greenfield ventures, and franchising, which are examined in detail in this chapter. We will explore in depth how firms use each of these methods to balance the tradeoff between risk and control. We will also begin the discussion of implementation of market entry issues such as planning, timing, and integration. The topics covered in this chapter include:

Motivations for internationalization

Methods to internationalize

Typical pattern of internationalization

Transnational firms

Born global firms

Implementing international market entry

JEEP'S JOINT VENTURE IN CHINA

Beijing Jeep is one of the oldest joint ventures between a U.S. and Chinese company, and was formed in 1984 between American Motors and Beijing Autoworks. The only way a foreign firm could enter China at that time was through a joint venture. Today a firm can enter China without a partner in most industries, but often an alliance with strong local partners that have a good relationship with a key branch of the Chinese government can still be beneficial.

At the time, the formation of the Beijing Jeep joint venture was a giant step for an American company. The Japanese auto makers were aggressively attacking the U.S. automotive market, and it was argued that the movement to China would open new avenues for sales of American cars and reduce costs. The joint venture was originally funded through $8 million in cash from AMC (Jeep's parent at the time; today Jeep is owned by Chrysler) and another $8 million in technology, which provided AMC a 32 percent ownership stake in the joint venture. Beijing Automotive Works put up another $35 million in cash and assets for a 68 percent ownership stake in the firm.

Negotiating the deal was only the start of the process for the joint venture. It quickly became clear that actually producing vehicles was going to be far more difficult than originally expected. The first issue on the table to be determined after the venture started was which vehicle to produce. The Chinese wanted a new style of jeep for the military that soldiers could jump in and out of very easily, while Jeep wanted to produce jeeps consistent with their existing product lines to avoid the cost of a new design. Negotiations resulted in

the firms settling on assembly kits for the Jeep Cherokee. Thus, both parties ended up with a product different than they originally envisioned.

The next difficulty was how to arrange hard capital to pay for the importation of the kits, because the export of hard currency was prohibited by the Chinese government. It took special secret agreements with the government to eventually free up hard currency to purchase the kits from the U.S. The joint venture was considered to be a model of what the Chinese government hoped other international firms could do in China. Therefore, the government was supportive of the joint venture at the highest levels and actively sought to ensure its success, but this did not prevent much interference from various lower-level governmental departments, which regularly interfered with Beijing Jeep's operations. The Chinese plant's modernization also took more extensive resources than initially expected. Again the Beijing government sought ways to aid the joint venture. One way was requiring local government-related entities, which are very common in China, to order Jeeps when they needed vehicles. As a result there was a continuing flow of orders for the Jeep Cherokees that were produced.

The central government's strong support resulted in the joint venture eventually becoming successful after much difficulty. As a result of the government support, it was estimated that between 1984 and 1995, the joint venture produced over $50 million in profits. In 1994, for example, an estimated 34,000 vehicles were sold. However, in 1995, the Beijing government declared that it would no longer favor the Jeep over other vehicles. There were now other car manufacturers in

China that objected to the official support given to Beijing Jeep. As a result, sales of the Jeep Cherokee declined steadily, with estimated sales of only 5,000 units in 2000.

The Beijing Jeep joint venture had grown overly dependent on its relationship with the government, and when government support was withdrawn, the firm could no longer sustain its prior sales. The government in China plays a central role in business, and can determine a firm's success or failure. That does not mean, though, that a firm can neglect issues such as customer satisfaction, product design, and development of adequate distribution channels. Beijing Jeep had not focused on those issues when the official government support dried up, and they suffered as a result.

Chrysler has now responded to the problem. They are focusing on developing better products and developing better distribution channels. In 2004, they introduced a new Jeep product designed specifically for China. This has resulted in the firm recovering some of its market share. But the joint venture must be aggressive. There are presently 16 international joint ventures in China manufacturing cars and many of the local firms produce cars of similar quality. Thus, today China has one of the most competitive car markets in the world. In a turn on history, Chrysler now is studying the potential of using cars developed and produced in China to ship to North American and European markets—which was part of the joint venture's original intent over a quarter century ago.

Mann, J. (1997). *Beijing Jeep: A Case Study of Western Business in China*. New York: Perseus Distribution.

Young, M. & Tan, J. "Beijing Jeep and the WTO." Richard Ivey School of Business Case.

The earlier chapters established the foundations of international management. Now we will look at implementation concerns as a firm internationalizes. A key part of that implementation is entering a foreign market. Firms are motivated to expand internationally for a variety of reasons. For example, a firm may enter a market due to its growth potential. To illustrate, in North America fast food restaurants, such as Kentucky Fried Chicken (KFC) and McDonald's, are growing slowly. Yet in China, they are experiencing fast growth, with new restaurants opening up every week to

FIGURE 6-1 Chapter 6 Conceptual Flow

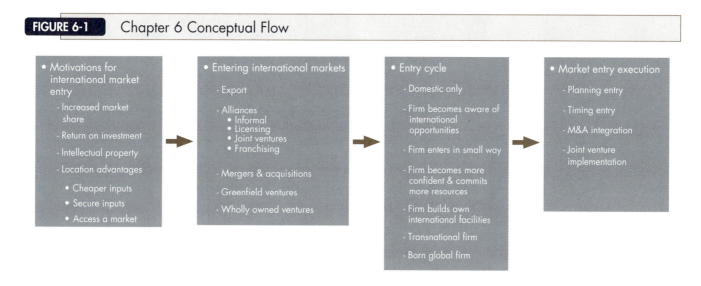

serve the exploding demand for convenience. Alternatively, firms may expand internationally into markets that are more competitive than their home market for the purpose of learning to meet tough standards. For example, Chery Automobile Co. is China's eighth-largest auto maker. Chery sold 90,000 vehicles in 2004, including 8,000 in exports to Iran and Malaysia.[i] Chery has currently aligned itself with a distributor that is building a network necessary to sell its new $19,000 convertible and other similarly lower-end models in the U.S. The firm feels that its low-priced cars will be attractive to market segments in the U.S. even though the U.S. automobile market is not growing. Thus, it may be easier for the firm to earn profit in the U.S. than in China.

Reasons for entering a foreign market will be addressed first in this chapter. A firm can mitigate the risks it faces by way of the method chosen to enter the market. This chapter will then explore the various tradeoffs with different methods of entering an international market. Some of these methods were examined in Chapter 4 (mergers and acquisitions, and joint ventures). We'll review those methods and introduce others that managers can use in their internationalization efforts. The chapter then discusses the typical cycle of expansion, and the implementation issues that are of concern when a firm does enter foreign markets. Figure 6-1 summarizes the material flow of this chapter.

CULTURE AND SPEECH

To illustrate the difficulties in carrying out a successful market entry, consider that many cultures have speech rituals that carry meaning in addition to the words spoken. Such differences can affect efforts to expand internationally and a firm's interactions with others. For example, in North America, most people greet each other by saying, "How are you?" It is simply a greeting; people are not looking for a health report. In fact, if you answer with a long list of problems, the other person will feel uncomfortable. Many people from Taiwan may ask, "Where are you going?" To a North American this seems intrusive: "Why is he asking me this?" The proper answer is simply, "Over there." It is a conversation ritual and does not mean the Taiwanese person actually wants to know your daily travel plans.[ii]

Many people from Hong Kong and mainland China will ask, "Have you eaten yet?" (asked in both Chinese and English). To most westerners, this is an odd question and often elicits a strange expression—to a Westerner, it sounds like the Chinese person is asking the listener to lunch. Once again, this is only a communications ritual, much like "How are you?" Possibly, it has its origins in the time when food was scarce in China—indeed, to look for work in Chinese is literally "to look for something to eat." In the Middle East, one traditional greeting, other than "Peace be with you" is "Are you sweating yet?" Its origins are easy to understand—if you were sweating, that means you have had water to drink, a special concern in the Middle East's desert climate. Thus, as a firm enters a new international market, its employees will want to find out what the typical greetings are and how, in fact, people are expected to respond to them.

CULTURE

MOTIVATIONS FOR INTERNATIONAL MARKET ENTRY

There are significant challenges facing firms that want to move into an international market. When SAP entered the U.S. market, for example, it determined that to be competitive it had to offer stock options to top management, an action it had not contemplated before. For software companies in the U.S., this was the norm and to attract talent, SAP knew it would have to adapt. This was a shock to the German firm's culture. Historically, wages in most German firms also fall in a narrower range between the average worker's salary and top management's compensation (including stock options), compared with U.S. firms. However, ultimately SAP was successful with its move into North America. It decided that for SAP to properly compete in the "war for talent" in the challenging North American information technology industry, it had to offer stock options.[iii]

Most European firms entering the United States are not nearly as successful as SAP. An estimated three-quarters of European firms' efforts to enter the U.S. market through mergers and acquisitions have been unsuccessful.[iv] If this is the case, why do firms continue to pursue international expansion efforts? European firms are encouraged to enter the United States by the same factors that encourage all firms to expand internationally, including:

- seeking increased market share
- obtaining economics of scale
- improving return on investment (ROI)
- intellectual property concerns
- looking for favorable locations

Increased Market Share

Firms can gain market share by expanding internationally. The impact of increased market share can affect a firm in several ways, including offering new sales when the firm's existing market is saturated. In the above example, SAP was at one time principally focused on the continental European market. Although SAP had some sales in the U.S. market, it had not developed a network to support or create large sales in this country. However, SAP realized that the European market was saturated and offered limited growth. The U.S. market offered the greatest potential; it was a large and expanding market with the most advanced information technology sector. There were competitors in the market, but SAP felt it could compete.

The example above of China's Chery automobile is also an instance of a temporarily saturated market with much overcapacity—this time in China. The U.S. auto market is competitive, but Chery feels it may offer some excellent opportunities, particularly at the low price point for which it can deliver its small cars. Thus, firms can see new sales opportunities even when it appears the market they are moving into is competitive.

Economies of Scale Alternatively, a firm may determine that additional sales are needed to allow efficient use of the firm's existing production capability, the additional sales coming from international sales. The Japanese auto industry suffered a decline in the domestic market in the early 1970s, which left most Japanese firms with over-capacity in their domestic production facilities. The Japanese firms realized they needed international sales to be able to operate those plants at the most efficient scale. As a result, they moved aggressively into the U.S. auto market.

But in other industries a single market may not be large enough to support the capital outlay needed to conduct an activity, so a firm must consider international entry to obtain the necessary economies of scale. For example, consider Airbus.

Developing, building, and testing new aircraft is expensive. Airbus was initially created as a French–German consortium in 1970. Later it was joined by CASA of Spain and British Aerospace to create a truly European firm. The markets in each country of the firms that combined to create Airbus were not large enough to justify the capital outlay to design and build advanced aircraft. Instead, the European firms combined to serve all of Europe, and eventually determined that the European market was not large enough. Today, Airbus must look to worldwide markets to sell its planes and secure commitments from airlines for new planes that are still being designed. The capital outlay required for large commercial passenger aircraft is so large that there are effectively only two strong competitors worldwide in this industry—Boeing and Airbus.[1]

ROI

Firms may also choose to enter international markets because the potential for profit is greater in that market. In perfectly efficient markets, there are no above-par profits. In mature markets, such as Europe and the U.S., there is great competition and typically the closest approximation to the perfect competition that economists discuss. Thus, for many firms, it is difficult to generate excess profits.

However, as firms expand internationally, the number of unfilled markets and the potential for greater profit increase. Consider our earlier example of KFC, which is part of Yum! Brands, a spin-off from Pepsico that includes Pizza Hut, Taco Bell, and KFC. The firm initially was called Tricon for the three (thus "tri") brands it represented. The company is now called Yum! and includes a variety of other restaurant concepts, such as Long John Silver's and A&W Restaurants (the beverage A&W Root Beer is owned by another corporation). Yum!'s market in the U.S. was mature; it had steady profits, but not much potential for growth. International markets, specifically in Asia, offered the firm great potential growth and profits. Though you only occasionally see an A&W restaurant in the U.S., they are more common in some Asian markets. The demand is also high for KFC. The reason for KFC's success is not only good management, but also that chicken is a principal source of protein in the region. Thus, by entering China, KFC has been able to increase its ROI. In fact, the international operations of Yum! will soon represent the greatest percentage of the firm's revenues and, ultimately, its profits.

Intellectual Property

Weak patent protection in some countries encourages firms to expand overseas rapidly in order to preempt imitators or secure patent protection in those major, foreign markets. If a firm is not active in those markets, its product can be copied more easily. The copies, in fact, may be of poor quality and can harm the firm's brand. Countries such as Russia, China, and India have very weak protection of intellectual property. For example, it is estimated that almost all computers in Russian businesses and government are running illegally copied software. Illegal copies of many movies appear for sale on the streets of Moscow even before the film has opened in theaters within the country. Street copies are made from the original movies before they are shipped to a Russian theater or from an original version in another country, where the movie has already opened. Thus the illegal copies on Russian streets were not only inexpensive, but were of good quality.

The film and entertainment industry has recognized this problem. Now major studios place a small identification code on every original motion picture copy that

---

[1]This may change as new competitors loom on the horizon. Canadian firm Bombardier and Brazilian firm Embraer are gaining market share at the low end of commercial jet travel with 100-seat planes. If they are able to move up-market with lower-cost jets, they will pose a threat to Boeing and Airbus.

INTERNATIONAL RETAILERS AND INDIA

The motives to enter a market can be illustrated by the Indian economy, which has been booming with over 7.5 percent growth for the last three years. It is predicted that for the next decade, at least, the economy will continue to grow at 6 percent or better. In this expanding economy, consumers have shown a tendency to spend more than those in other emerging economies. For example, in India, consumption as a percentage of the GDP is over 60 percent compared to 40 percent in China. At this time the market is also very fragmented and relatively poorly served. For example, only 4 percent of the 15 million retailers in India have retail space of over 500 square feet. Thus, the national retailing market of over $250 billion is served by very small stores with a very limited selection of stock and relatively high prices.

The result is that the Indian retailing environment appears very appealing to international retailers, such as Wal-Mart, Tesco of Britain, and Carrefour of France. However, these firms' ability to enter the market was prohibited until 2006, when the Indian government said that international firms could enter through a joint venture in which they could hold 51 percent ownership. However, a retailer could handle only a single brand. Thus, a shoe store could only sell Nike shoes, or a grocery store could only sell its own brand—obviously excluding most major retailers from competing in the Indian market.

This liberalization was strongly opposed by India's Communist party, which is supported by India's large number of small retailers. The party has opposed any effort to liberalize the retail sector. However, international firms such as Wal-Mart continue to lobby the government for greater liberalization. The big international retailers see significant opportunities in India, similar to what was found in Mexico and China. Wal-Mart's goal is to be able to enter and compete in India freely. To do so, Wal-Mart is willing to operate through a joint venture. Wal-Mart has also committed to significantly increasing their local purchases and offering employees managerial training and ownership opportunities, much as they have done in Mexico, China, and other emerging economies.

Coming to market. (2006, April 15). *The Economist*, pp. 65–67.

is sent to theaters. As a result, if it is copied, the studios can trace and prosecute those responsible for not safeguarding the movie. However, the movie industry has also dealt with the reality that a movie that is sold in the United States for $20 is not affordable in countries such as Russia and China, where annual per capita incomes are well under $10,000. Thus, film and TV studios and their distributors employ discriminatory pricing so that movies are sold at different prices in different markets. These firms might prefer not to be in a market such as Russia, but they realize they must or their product will be there illegally. The creation of region-specific DVD players is a partial solution. DVDs and DVD/CD players have technology to make it difficult for cheaply sold movies from Russia or other markets to be played on a DVD player in North America or Europe.

Location Advantages

Firms can also choose to expand internationally to obtain location advantages with that international market. Location benefits are typically of three types:

- lower costs are obtained for inputs such as labor
- vital inputs to their product are secured, such as in the oil industry
- a specific market is accessed

Cheaper Inputs To illustrate why a firm may enter an international market, recall from Chapter 4 the discussion of the value chain. A firm may internationalize as part of an effort to manage its value chain effectively, particularly with respect to minimizing costs. For example, consider that up to a 70 percent cost savings can be gained by having software programming done in a lower-cost location, such as India or Russia, where quality engineering talent is abundant. In manufacturing, the labor cost in some lesser-developed countries is not measured in dollars per hour, but in dollars per day. Thus, there can be significant cost savings in moving production to a lesser-developed country.

When considering the potential to obtain low-cost inputs, managers must recognize that while items like labor costs may be lower, other costs may be higher. China is a good example of this conundrum. It is not necessarily cheaper to produce all items in China than in Europe or other developed regions of the world. Although hourly labor costs are approximately U.S. 80 cents in China, worker productivity is significantly lower. The costs of parts and other inputs are also often higher, monitoring and quality-control costs are higher, and transportation of raw materials and finished product adds further to the cost. For this reason, a firm must carefully consider what product it is manufacturing, where it is producing the product, what shipping costs are from the place of production to the point of the sale, and what other benefits and costs it faces by manufacturing in a foreign location. Thus, the decision is more complex than simply assessing the cost of labor or some other input is cheaper in a given location.

Secure Inputs Firms frequently enter an international market to secure inputs or raw materials. An international firm, such as the French tire firm Michelin, could not produce tires without raw materials that come from outside France. Global energy companies, such as Shell from the United Kingdom and Holland and Exxon-Mobil from the United States, have to be active in foreign markets to obtain their major inputs (petroleum, natural gas, and other chemicals). Neither Shell's nor Exxon-Mobil's home market can supply a significant part of inputs that are needed by the firm. Thus, firms may expand internationally to secure access to crucial inputs.

Access a Market Firms may enter a foreign country to gain access to that market. Many firms enter China not only because of the low cost of labor, but also to gain access to its growing market. Firms recognize that China has the world's largest population along with the fastest-growing economy. They acknowledge that they will need to be in that market as it matures. The companies enter today, not as much for immediate profit, but to build a presence in China over time so that they can take advantage of its future growth.

The United States attracts consistently one of the highest, if not the highest, amount of foreign direct investment (FDI) in the world. (In 2006, FDI into the U.S. was $177 billion, the U.K. $169.8 billion, China $71 billion, France $88.4 billion, Singapore $31.9 billion, Russia $28.4 billion, and India $9.5 billion.)[v] Part of the reason firms invest so heavily in the United States, which has some of the world's highest labor costs, is that they want easier access to the world's largest market for many different types of goods. Thus, these firms are expanding into the U.S. not to achieve cost advantages, but to gain access to consumers.

The desire for market access can be driven by a belief that the best manner in which to serve a market is to be located there. However, such location choices can also be made to overcome trade barriers erected to imports. As noted in Chapter 1, trade barriers in the form of tariffs have dropped significantly in recent years. In fact, there are now efforts to create tariff and code **harmonization** internationally so that they have the same standards for products and how they are treated in regard to tariffs. However, significant levels of tariffs still exist in some countries, which discourages imports. For example, India had tariffs of over 150 percent as recently as 1990, which made it difficult for firms to import even a personal computer—a process that was both expensive and time consuming. And it was nearly impossible for individuals in India to buy a PC. After India largely turned its back on socialism and started economic reforms in 1991, tariffs have gradually fallen, and were 24 percent in 2000.[vi] However, India still has the third highest level of tariffs for major countries worldwide and significant restrictions remain in some sectors. In fact, Indian information technology executives like to remind observers that one of the main reasons the Indian IT sector was able to develop so quickly was that government officials and politicians did not understand it and were not

Harmonization
Efforts between nations to have the same code of standards for products and how they are treated in regards to tariffs.

able to interfere.[vii] Therefore, firms often choose to open facilities in India so they do not have to pay to import goods into the country. A nation may also have non-tariff barriers. For example, Japan and Korea have both been accused of excessive requirements for an imported product to be approved for sale there. These requirements include excessive product testing and proof of the product's ability to do what it claims. Therefore, firms may choose to expand into those countries through acquisition as a means to overcome such **non-tariff trade barriers**.

Another means used occasionally to overcome trade barriers that merits mention is **indirect imports**. Although these are slowly going away, many countries still have import barriers that limit the quantity of a product from a particular country. A prime example of this is in the garment industry. It was common for developed economies, such as those in the EU or the U.S., to limit garment imports from China, Hong Kong, and other textile-producing economies. The more developed economies wanted to protect their domestic producers from low-cost competitors from developing economies that might come to dominate the industry and put domestic producers out of business. The old trade treaty on quotas, the Multifiber Agreement, was so strict that it was almost impossible to mail even a single shirt from Hong Kong to the U.S. as a gift for a relative—even a hand-me-down shirt. So while many garments might be sewn predominantly in China, they would be shipped to Vietnam, the Philippines or smaller places, such as the Maldives in the Indian Ocean, for production completion. The garment would have a label saying that it was produced in Vietnam, the Philippines, or the Maldives, and would be counted in import quotas as an import from that particular country, not from China, even though most of the value added occurred in China. The effect of indirect imports was to raise the cost of garments. A new agreement on Textiles and Clothing was signed in 1995, which dismantled the Multifiber Agreement with all protections finally expiring in 2005. The expected result was that in garment sectors such as socks, China would dominate world production, as a great many of the world's socks are produced around Shanghai in the Yangtze River delta. The rapid increase in Chinese-made garments entering western countries soon motivated politicians in the EU and the United States to seek bilateral agreements limiting Chinese garment imports, despite possible violation of WTO rules. Ultimately separate agreements were reached to delay free trade in garments several more years. The effect was to encourage the continuation of such indirect imports. However, in the future as free trade continues to expand, the effect of indirect imports should decline.[2]

ENTERING INTERNATIONAL MARKETS

Just as there are many reasons firms would like to go international, there are also a number of ways in which firms can enter an international market. In this section we see four major means of internationalization, and some of these means then have different underlying methods. The first is **export**, or shipping a good from a home market to markets outside the home country. Exporting is still the dominant type of international activity for many firms because it requires the least investment overseas. The next way to enter an international market is through an alliance with a firm in that country. We looked at one of the major types of alliances—joint ventures—earlier. Other types of alliances that we will look at in depth here are informal alliances and franchises. A firm may also enter an international market by purchasing a firm in that country. Finally, a firm may want to have a stand-alone operation in a country that it builds itself. This is called a

Non-tariff trade barriers
A barrier to free trade that takes a form other than a tariff, for instance quotas or inspection requirements for imported products such as VCRs, automobiles and dairy products.

Indirect import
Goods may have most of the value added in one country but due to trade barriers the product is shipped to another country where final production on the good occurs, with the good then being listed as an export from that country.

Export
The shipping of a good from the home market to markets outside the home country.

[2]A specialized type of indirect import is used by some firms to circumvent government rules. For example, laws prohibit trade between the U.S. and Cuba, and the U.S. and Iran. Some firms circumvent these rules by selling to entities in other countries that re-export to Cuba or Iran. We do not focus on this type of indirect export because it is relatively rare and ethically questionable.

greenfield investment. These different methods can be visualized as having different levels of commitment and cost to the internationalization effort. The method with the least commitment and cost is exporting to a given nation. Alliances typically involve more risk and costs but less than a merger or acquisition. The risk with a merger or acquisition is greater, and the cost typically associated with a greenfield venture is greatest, although whether risk is higher is not always clear. Thus, a firm has to balance the cost of each type of entry with the goals it hopes to accomplish. This section will introduce the methods and discuss how firms balance those costs and risks with the needs of the firm. Each of the internationalization methods will now be examined in greater detail. (See Chapter 4 for more details about mergers and acquisitions and some types of alliances.)

Export

The most immediate way to internationalize a firm is to directly export goods to a market outside your home country. Typically, this occurs when a firm or person contracts with a firm that is currently focused on its home market; the foreign firm then pays to ship the given good to its home country. This is the most typical form of internationalization because it requires the least commitment of resources.

Typically, exporting begins when there are direct sales and the firm is directly contacted by customers. However, this is not a very efficient means to build a large international effort, so such direct sales are usually not a major source of revenues for a business. But as a firm gains international experience, it will often move from waiting for contacts from international customers to hiring an international representative (rep) or dealer. A manufacturer's rep will often handle several firms' products that typically do not compete with each other, such as a variety of IT gear. A dealership is similar, though typically the relationship between the two firms will be closer than with the manufacturer's rep, and a dealership could be an exclusive one, only selling the one firm's products. In either case, the business does not have to establish an international sales force of its own because the rep or dealer will handle promotion and sales in their local country. Many products and services are delivered in this way. For example, the well-known Hong Kong restaurant firm Maxim's is the local dealer for Starbucks and

Exporting goods to a market outside a firm's home country is the most typical form of internationalization since it requires the least commitment of resources.

has an exclusive right to open Starbucks coffee shops in Hong Kong. Starbucks has different licensee dealers in Singapore and Taiwan. Many Japanese electronics firms work entirely through dealers in Hong Kong for the sales and service of their products. Ultimately, a firm may choose to export its product, which is produced in its home country, but will sell directly through its own sales force or even open sales offices in international locations.

Alliances

A firm may wish to commit further to internationalization and, as a result, will seek to have operations in foreign markets. The next strategic step typically is to move from purely exporting to pursuing an alliance with a firm in the desired markets.[viii] In an alliance, a firm moves into a market in association with other firms. In general, the parties involved have less control than if they were to own the firm outright but they also have less risk, because now the two firms share the risk. This pattern of tradeoff between control and risk is one constant in internationalization: when a firm has more control, it assumes more of the risk. There are a number of different types of alliances, and each will be reviewed briefly.

Informal Alliances The least formal method by which to enter an international market is an informal alliance. This typically does not even have a signed document, but is simply a statement by one firm to another along the lines of, "If you help me sell my product in your market, I will help you sell yours in my market." In this situation, there is little investment, and the least control by a firm. Thus, informal alliances would not involve equity investments by either party.

With such informality, nonequity alliances can be difficult to document because there is little written evidence associated with them. For example, in Southeast Asia, the dominant economic power is people who are colloquially called "Overseas Chinese." These individuals are ethnic Chinese whose families emigrated from China at different times over the past few hundred years.[ix] The largest migration occurred in the 1600s when China's Manchu rulers moved the population in its southern coastal provinces approximately 15 miles back from the coast so they could better control trade. The result was that many people, mostly fisherman and traders from China's southeast coastal regions, simply left to find better opportunities in Formosa (Taiwan) and Southeast Asia.[x]

The Overseas Chinese have come to dominate the economies of Southeast Asia.[xi] For example, in Indonesia the Overseas Chinese make up only about 3 percent of the population, but they control large numbers of the publicly traded firms and many productive assets, and they are very influential in government.[3] In large measure, the Overseas Chinese communities were successful because of informal alliances, developed as individuals speaking the same Chinese dialect stayed in contact throughout the Pacific Rim. China has a common written language, but there are 7 major and 200 minor dialects in the country that pronounce the written language differently. Thus, someone speaking the southern Cantonese dialect cannot be understood by a listener who only speaks the Shanghai dialect, although they can communicate by writing or by speaking Mandarin—China's national language. Communication can also be difficult since Chinese pictographs are more difficult and take much more time to learn than alphabetic language systems. While it is fairly easy to represent all the sounds of Chinese using the Latin alphabet, it is rather difficult to faithfully reproduce the many sounds of English or most other languages by using Chinese characters to "spell out" or transliterate the word.[xii]

---

[3]There are disputes about the percentage of publicly owned firms controlled by Overseas Chinese in Indonesia and in other parts of Southeast Asia, but most agree that they exercise a significant influence over business in Indonesia, vastly greater than their small population would normally confer.

The ensuing difficulties in communication were a factor in leading different dialect groups to cluster in different cities around the Pacific Rim: the Hokkien people in Singapore, the Cantonese in Penang (in Malaysia), the Hakka in Taiwan and Singapore, the Teochew in Bangkok (Thailand), and the Zhang Shan people in Hawaii. They also led to each dialect group specializing in a particular trade. In Singapore, for example, the Hokkien people dominated the grocery stores, the Cantonese and Hakkas (traditionally a more nomadic people in China) were in the medicine retailing, the Teochews and Foochows were in fishing, pawnshops, and lunch restaurants, respectively, while Shanghainese dominated tailoring and garments. To some extent these patterns still prevail today.[xiii]

Such informal alliances fostered within dialect groups facilitated global business, going back to the eighteenth and nineteenth centuries. Among individuals with the same dialect, a merchant could deposit gold with a jewelry shop in the Philippines, carry a certificate of gold deposit overseas, and receive that same amount of gold (less a small fee) in Singapore from another gold and jewelry merchant, most likely someone from that same dialect group. This informal network, based on trust and internal sanctions and controls, developed an early banking system that strongly aided the development of commerce among the Overseas Chinese.[xiv]

Today, informal alliances such as those of the Overseas Chinese are less important than in the past, though many of the old professional patterns prevail.[xv] However, in many emerging markets, such informal alliances can still be critical assets in trying to penetrate environments where the rule of law is still developing. Such alliances allow a firm, as it begins to enter a market, to have connections with individuals that will advise the firm and support its efforts. Thus, while the level of risk and commitment of resources by either party is typically low in such informal alliances, these arrangements can be very powerful assets in some settings.

Licensing A more formal type of alliance that still has limited financial commitments by a firm entering an international market is a **licensing arrangement**. In such an agreement, a company outside a particular country agrees to pay a firm within the country for the right to either manufacture or sell its product. The firm selling the right to this product typically loses the right to control various aspects of the product when manufactured or sold by the licensee. Thus, there is an alliance between two firms when there is licensing, but it tends to be much less coordinated than in a joint venture or franchise. For example, there is commonly an agreement between the parties, but the contract only specifies what is to be sold and for what price. As a result, a firm that licenses its goods typically takes on limited risk itself. Instead, most of the risk is borne by the organization obtaining the license. However, the firm has limited control over what happens and the return, in this situation, is typically lower than if the firm had done more than given another party the right to sell its product.

Licensing can have strategic value to a firm as it seeks to enter a market. For example, in the videocassette recorder (VCR) battle between Sony with its Betamax technology and JVC with its VHS technology, licensing played a major role in deciding which technology eventually won the battle of technology standards. Betamax was introduced nearly 18 months before VHS, and Sony was then a larger and stronger company than JVC. Most analysts agreed that Sony's Betamax technology was better than JVC's on most criteria except the recording time, which was longer on JVC's VHS. JVC, however, actively licensed its VHS technology to firms around the world, such as Philips, Hitachi, and Telefunken, to promote VHS and speed its expansion. In contrast, Sony did not license its Betamax technology because it wanted to maintain complete control over the standard and the revenues to be earned from its technology. Therefore, despite the fact that it was not the first to market and probably did not have the better technology, JVC with its VHS video standard proved to be the winner, in large part due to its aggressive and early international licensing alliances.[xvi]

Licensing agreement
A firm agrees to pay a firm for the right to either manufacture or sell a product. The firm selling the right to this product typically loses the right to control various aspects of the product when manufactured or sold by the licensee.

Joint Venture Joint ventures were briefly reviewed in Chapter 4, but because they are one of the major means for international market entry, they are revisited here in more detail. Recall that joint ventures are formal agreements between two or more firms where a new separate entity is created for the purpose of producing or distributing goods and services. In joint ventures, two or more firms contribute equity to form a new third organization. The level of equity can vary from small amounts to multimillion-dollar investments. Thus, the level of commitment and risk to these formal, equity alliances is considerably higher than in informal alliances developed for exporting or licensing purposes.[xvii]

The nature of the joint venture agreement established between parties is critical to how the joint venture is managed and how long it can survive. A joint venture commonly has detailed agreements covering what each party is to provide, what each can expect, and how each is to operate within the joint venture. Most agreements will have a finite time during which the joint venture will exist as a going concern. After that time, each firm can decide whether to continue the venture. However, there are typically clauses in the agreement that allow one firm or the other to leave the joint venture if it is unhappy with the outcome. The analogy of a family is helpful. A couple marries and then may have kids—a joint venture. A joint venture between two firms can have some of the same growing pains as do children, and present the parent firms with difficulties similar to raising children. Childrearing pressures may even cause some parents to end their marriage. The same can be true in joint ventures. Therefore, managing the joint venture is more than simply following a contract. It takes active management for the relationship to survive.

To overcome some of the difficulties in managing a joint venture, both parties must be clear as to what they wish to accomplish and why. An agreement on how the venture is managed and what each is to provide and obtain is part of this process. A joint venture agreement is typically quite long, and the common advice is that considerable discussion needs to occur between the parties prior to establishing the agreement. Agreements are only for as long as the parties believe in the joint venture. This belief is developed through mutual understanding and commitment. Just as individuals need to get to know each other prior to marriage, firms need to undergo a similar process before establishing a joint venture in order to determine their compatibility. (Figure 6-2 summarizes the biology analogy of a joint venture.)

This discussion of a joint venture has been approached as if a long life is the desired goal for a joint venture because that is the most common desire. However, in some cases, firms enter into a joint venture not seeking a long-term relationship. Instead they wish to learn a specific process, technology, or market from their partner and do not see the joint venture as long term. This is a legitimate and strategic approach to an alliance. Such a joint venture can still be successful for both parties as long as they both approach it in this manner. However, too often one party wishes to learn from the other over the short-term, but the other party wishes a long-term relationship. As a result, the short-term party ends up happy when the relationship ends, but the other party rates the joint venture as a failure.

FIGURE 6-2   Joint Venture

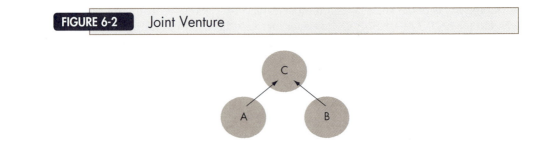

BP JOINT VENTURE IN RUSSIA

Joint ventures are not without significant risk. One key element in picking a joint-venture partner is that you need a firm that understands the local market and the local power structure. In many emerging markets, the government is a critical factor in the ultimate success of a business. Russia is one emerging economy where relationships with the government are critical. Unfortunately, changes in the political environment can result in your joint-venture partner being ideal at one stage but a liability at another.

British Petroleum (BP) is a worldwide energy producer. BP entered into a joint venture with Russian firm TNK in 2003. Three Russian billionaires controlled this local Russian firm. The joint venture looked ideally suited to help BP navigate the turbulent economic waters of Russia when the deal was signed. However, a number of Russian billionaires around this time also began to have political ambitions and actively supported political parties opposed to President Putin. As a result, the government became more aggressive on tax issues with the businesses associated with those individuals.

The most notable of these aggressive tax prosecutions is the famous Yukos case where billionaire Arkady Dvorkovich was arrested, charged with tax evasion, and his oil firm, Yukos (at the time of his arrest one of the 15 largest oil firms in the world), sold at auction to pay delinquent taxes.

In 2004, the BP-TNK joint venture was charged with not paying 4 billion rubles in taxes, or approximately $120 million. In 2005, the joint venture was hit with another tax bill for $770 million for unpaid taxes. In 2005 it appeared as if the billionaire joint venture partners of BP were not helping it navigate the turbulent waters of Russia, but instead had fallen out of political favor to the point where they were attracting problems for the joint venture.

However, by 2008 the billionaires had become closer allies to President Putin. The result was not to lower the government's pressure on the BP-TNK joint venture. Instead, the billionaires began to argue that the joint venture was being managed too much to benefit BP. They were then joined in their

arguments by the nation's largest gas producer, Gazprom. This firm, while technically private, is closely associated with the Russian government. The BP-TNK joint venture by 2008 was the largest oil producer in Russia. If it were to become associated with Gazprom, the government would then have both the largest gas and oil producers.

Thus, allies initially brought to the joint venture by BP did not at first provide much protection from the government since they were not allied with it. But once the Russian partners did become allied with the government, they then joined with those in the government to seek to limit, if not expel, BP from the venture. This helps to illustrate the critical role of partner selection in joint ventures.

White, G. L., & Chazan, G. (2005, April 12). Russian heaps new claim for taxes on BP venture. *Wall Street Journal Europe*, pp. A1, A12.
Kishkovsky, S. (2008, May 30). Standoff grows over Russia-BP venture. *International Herald Tribune*. http://www.iht.com/articles/2008/05/30/business/ruble.php?page=1 (accessed October 5, 2008).

Sometimes, in such cases, the party with a short-term focus becomes a competitor to the party with a long-term focus. Situations where either party is surprised can be avoided if both parties actively conduct strong due diligence and learn about each other before forming the joint venture.

Franchising Franchising is a type of formal equity alliance that was not reviewed in Chapter 4 extensively so we will examine it in more detail here. A franchise agreement is a contract established between a parent (franchisor) and an individual who actually buys an individual business unit (franchisee) to sell a given product or conduct business under its trademark. An estimated 40 percent of U.S. retail business is conducted through franchisors, and the success of franchising in the U.S. has resulted in a rapid expansion of the concept around the world.

A franchisor typically provides the franchisee with extensive direction on how to operate the business. Effectively, a franchisor is selling a formula on how to operate the business. This will include items, such as how products are to be prepared, how services should be provided, how the firm hires its employees, and how the business is to be physically arranged. In addition, a franchisor will normally develop accounting and finance applications for the franchisee to use, and assist in marketing and promotion. The result of these efforts is that a franchised small business is more likely to be successful than a small business that is trying to do all of those activities on its own, learning from its mistakes as it goes forward.

However, a franchise contract also commonly sets standards for behavior by the franchisee that, if not followed, can result in the loss of the franchise. The franchisor

Franchising
A type of alliance where a contract is established between the parent (franchisor) and the individual who actually buys the business unit (franchisee) to sell a given product or conduct business under its trademark.

SONY BMG MUSIC: TROUBLES BETWEEN PARTNERS IN A JOINT VENTURE

Problems arising in a joint venture can destroy a venture that has great potential. The second largest music company in the world is Sony BMG Music. The company is a joint venture between the Japanese firm Sony and the German firm Bertelsmann. Ownership of the joint venture is divided evenly between the two multinationals. Each firm also appoints half of the board. The CEO, however, is determined by Sony. Details regarding this situation were negotiated in the joint-venture agreement.

In 2005, Bertelsmann indicated publicly they wanted the CEO of the joint venture, American Andrew Lack, replaced. However, the CEO of Sony was just as publicly committed to keeping Lack as CEO. Sony's CEO and Lack had been co-workers together at Viacom. The chief operating officer at the time of the formation of the joint venture was someone in whom Bertelsmann had great confidence, but that individual announced he was leaving the firm. This left Bertelsmann seeking to convince Sony to replace the CEO, with the campaign to replace the CEO largely being run through the public media.

Each firm thought it had negotiated an excellent and detailed agreement for the joint venture. It is highly unlikely that either expected to be conducting a public discussion of the CEO of the joint venture a few years after its development. However, legal agreements cannot cover every potential contingency.

Kafka, P. (2005, October 10). Sony's Stringer defends music boss lack. Forbes.com. http://www.forbes.com/2005/10/10/sony-bmg-lack-cx_pak_1010autofacescan10_print.html.

Duhigg, C. (2005, October 11). Sony CEO backs Sony BMG chief. Latimes.com. http://www.latimes.com/business/la-fi-lack11oct11,1,5086457.story?coll=la-headlines-business&ctrack=1&cset=true.

wants to ensure that the product's quality is consistent across all of the units. Thus, a McDonald's restaurant is largely the same anywhere in the world. The franchisor will also require the franchisee to pay not only an initial fee to buy the franchise, but also a continuing royalty. In addition, most inputs used by the franchisee must be bought from the franchisor. The continuing royalty and sale of inputs is actually how the franchisor makes its money, so the goal of the franchisor is to help make the franchisee successful so that there is a continuing stream of revenue. For McDonald's, for example, the corporation makes money every time it sells items such as hamburger wrappers, salt packets, and ketchup packets to franchisees.

Here, franchises are classified as alliances because each side of the venture is dependent upon the other. A franchisor makes its money principally when the franchisee is successful and continually purchases the franchisor's goods. Thus, from our McDonald's example, the franchisor wants its franchisees to sell large numbers of burgers so it can sell the supplies for those burgers. A franchisee is dependent on the franchisor to develop a good support package to the small business. This support should not end once the franchise is purchased. Typically, a franchisee is also dependent on the franchisor for marketing, which is critical to success.

There are two types of businesses that franchise internationally. The first is a firm that already franchises in a mature economy such as the U.S. Yum! Brands (the parent of Kentucky Fried Chicken, Pizza Hut, Taco Bell, A&W, and Long John Silver's) franchises in the U.S. and has numerous franchises in other countries as well. Many times, such franchising is conducted in a manner similar to the franchising activities in the mature economy. Thus, a firm such as Dunkin' Donuts' entry into Poland is likely to follow the same model as in the United States.

Not all franchisors apply the same model when approaching franchising internationally. In the U.S. franchisees are typically individuals who own one to five stores in a given area. The classic nature of franchising is that it provides excellent entrepreneurial opportunities in mature markets, such as the U.S. In other parts of the world a firm such as Yum! Brands often seeks out well-established individuals in the community to franchise its product. For example, in Thailand, KFC restaurants are franchised principally to a single entrepreneur. This individual is part of a wealthy family that is also one of the major food processors in the country, specifically chicken processors. This approach to franchising helps to limit Yum! Brands' risk because the franchisee in this case is well connected politically and very sophisticated in his or her business understanding, although the model differs significantly from that of the U.S.

Another type of firm that franchises internationally is one that prefers to franchise regionally and will not open many franchises in a mature markets. This limits its international exposure, while allowing it to gain experience in smaller, less-lucrative, less-visible markets. Singapore, for example, has a number of smaller, regional franchisors that are well known in Southeast Asia and some other smaller markets, but that have a very limited presence in North America or Europe. Thus, firms, such as the restaurant Fish and Co., or Starbucks competitor Coffee Bean and Tea Leaf, have carefully employed this expansion strategy as they have moved abroad.

On a general note, it is worth noting that franchising is a great entrepreneurial opportunity that students should investigate if they desire to start a business. Consider the franchisors who were fortunate enough to buy the initial franchise rights to several McDonald's in medium-sized markets and thus were able to get those franchises relatively cheaply. Today these individuals are very wealthy and the value of their franchises has increased dramatically. Today there are many opportunities internationally in similar medium-sized markets for franchises. For example, the higher-end fast food chain Carl's Jr. wants to open hundreds of restaurants in East Asia over the next decade, which will present significant opportunities for franchising in that region. It is interesting to note that when McDonald's was initially expanding, it had a policy of providing matching funds to individuals who worked for a franchise store for a period of time, and it would gradually sell that person rights to own a franchise. As a result, in the U.S. and Canada, many franchisees are individuals who started out flipping burgers and earning minimum wage; the same is increasingly true in Asia. Today, many of these individuals are multimillionaires because of the opportunity McDonald's gave them to buy one or multiple franchises and become successful small business owners.

Franchising is also useful if individuals wish to enter a market where they need greater support. Today in the U.S. many hotel and motel franchisees are Indian nationals from the western Indian state of Gujarat. The ability to buy a franchise aided these individuals as they sought to establish businesses in a country in which they were unfamiliar with all of the cultural and business intricacies necessary to be successful. They were also able to bring family members to the U.S. to work in their new properties, often saving money in labor costs and supervision.

Mergers and Acquisitions

One of the most common means by which to enter a new market is through mergers and acquisitions. Mergers and acquisitions were discussed in Chapter 4. Recall that a merger is a transaction involving two or more corporations in which only one permanent corporation survives. An acquisition, on the other hand, is the purchase of a company that is completely absorbed as a subsidiary or division of the acquiring firm. Mergers and acquisitions are not mere linkages between firms—they create permanent changes to the structure of the firms involved.

The control an acquiring firm obtains in a merger and acquisition is far greater than in an alliance because there are no partners that must be consulted. However, the fact that the firm is acquiring an ongoing entity results in pre-established structures, policies, procedures, and culture also being obtained. Thus, an acquisition can act as a **turnkey** operation—that is, the firm can enter the market immediately with a ready-made operation. However, if the firm wishes to change its structures, policies, culture, products, etc., it will take time and considerable effort. Government regulations may not allow large numbers of employees to be laid off, so changes in the firm can be difficult to obtain, particularly changes in its culture. As has been noted before, culture in a business can be particularly hard to change. For example, if an existing firm has had difficult relationships with workers and their union, those ill feelings will not disappear with the

Turnkey
When a firm can enter the market immediately with a ready-made application that allows the firm to start doing business immediately.

merger or acquisition. In fact they often get worse. Thus, a firm has great control, but is limited by the pre-existing nature of the acquired firm. In summary, recall from Chapter 4 that most mergers or acquisitions are not successful even when both of the merging firms are from the same country. An international merger or acquisition adds another complication that must be overcome by the merging parties—consider the Daimler-Chrysler merger that was wrought with problems for years before ultimately failing.

Greenfield Ventures

A firm that builds a wholly owned subsidiary from the ground up is building a **greenfield venture**. This type of venture is the most difficult to pursue, but gives a firm the greatest control because it is able to design every detail of the business. In a greenfield venture a firm inherits nothing that it does not want; contrast this to a merger and acquisition where an acquiring firm inherits the acquired firm's structure, culture, policies, and procedures. The fact that a firm develops the project from the ground up means that it builds its own culture and structure.

It is difficult to build a greenfield venture because a firm must do everything on its own. Typically, the cost of such development is quite high and the venture also has greater risk since it must enter a country and build its brand and various stakeholder relationships. But there are times when it can be useful. For example, if a firm were to enter a transition economy like Poland or Bulgaria it might use a Greenfield venture since the business will likely need to buy a former state enterprise that is being privatized. This existing firm may have a brand with value, but the factory itself is most likely old and outdated. In addition, employees have a culture nurtured in a socialist environment that might be difficult to change. If there is a union like Solidarity in the facility at the time of purchase, employees cannot be laid off without the union's involvement through negotiation. By contrast, it would typically be easier to create and grow a business in a transition economy through a greenfield manner. A prime example of a firm that has done this quite successfully is the French firm Carrefour, the second largest retailer in the world. Carrefour entered the Polish market by establishing a new wholly-owned venture, and now is the second largest grocery chain in Poland. (Carrefour has since bought 27 supermarkets in 2001 and 13 hypermarkets in 2005, but its initial entry into Poland was as a greenfield venture. It built a knowledge base and organizational systems in the country before pursing mergers and acquisitions.)

The keys to success for a greenfield venture are patience and adequate support by a corporation. The firm will have no one else to call on for support, and the building process will take time. Thus, a firm must have the resources and the commitment necessary to build a business over the long term. This approach will allow a firm to have strong control over a venture and to establish the new business to precise specification.

Wholly Owned Subsidiary

In addition to understanding the different means to enter a market, a concept that also needs to be understood is the organizational outcome of some of these efforts. Organizationally when a firm moves into a new international market through a merger or acquisition or a greenfield venture, it can make the resulting entity part of the existing firm. Alternatively, a firm may wish to create a wholly owned subsidiary. A **wholly owned subsidiary** is an organizational form that focuses strictly on the country in which the organization has entered.

Where to Enter A firm may be clear about which benefits it wishes to achieve but it still may have a wide variety of nations to choose from. As a result, the firm may look to other economic concerns in making its decision. These include:

Li Wa/Shutterstock

- Transportation costs: Transportation requires the presence of an infrastructure so that a firm can ship products produced from an international facility. Thus, whether roads or shipping are readily available can affect not only cost but timeliness of the delivery of the good. A related issue therefore is the location of major customers that the international facility will service.
- Tax and government incentives: Taxes can play a critical role in the profitability of a firm. Governments often offer firms not only hard assets, such as land, but also concessions, such as tax reductions, if a firm locates in that nation. Governments do this because attracting a new firm will create job opportunities for their citizens. As noted in the discussion of transfer pricing in Chapter 5, the tax rate can in fact be a major factor in choosing where to locate a facility. A good example Microsoft, which has located its major European operations in Ireland. The Irish tax rate is 12 percent on profits versus the European average of 25 percent. The European Union assures equal access to all of Europe so Microsoft's Irish location assures a much higher profitability for the firm. Microsoft is not unique in using Ireland in this manner; other technology-intensive firms, such as Intel and Johnson & Johnson's Janssen Pharmaceuticals unit, have also located there, in part due to the tax incentives.
- Labor quality: Labor quality around the world can vary widely. Simply because someone is called an electrical engineer does not mean that he or she has the skills that a typical graduate in North America or Europe may have. At the same time, in some settings, labor is both much cheaper and as well trained as in the United States or Europe. Therefore, in selecting a location, a firm must understand the true qualifications of a country's workforce and whether the labor supply will be sufficient. To illustrate, there has been an explosion of auto manufacturing in Slovenia. The workers are very well trained and motivated, and there was a tremendous cost savings for firms moving there. However, there are now far too many firms chasing too few well-trained workers in Slovenia. The result is a labor shortage of workers with the necessary skills and rising wage costs for those workers that can be hired.

Organizational Learning Firms may want to locate in a country or region from which they can learn from excellent suppliers or demanding customers. Fish and Co., the Singapore franchisor of "seafood in a pan" restaurants around Asia, plans to open a

DOING BUSINESS IN MYANMAR

ETHICS

Firms must decide if they are willing to enter and do business in a nation even if the nation is not considered a good member of the world community. Myanmar was formerly known as Burma. That country's elected leaders were overthrown in 1962 by a group of generals who wanted to form a distinctive Burmese path to socialism. Since that time, Burma has been ruled by a repressive military dictatorship, and the generals in charge have enriched themselves while brutally suppressing any effort by the people to return to democracy. There are widespread accusations of the use of slave labor and suppression of minorities. Democracy demonstrations in the late 1980s were suppressed with thousands killed. In 2007, the poverty and repressive totalitarian leadership contributed to another round of large protests demanding the loosening of political and economic controls. The Myanmar government responded by killing a large number of protesters and even brazenly shooting a Japanese journalist—a killing that was witnessed by tens of millions on international television and over the Internet.

Opposition to the military dictatorship is led by Aung San Suu Kyi. Her father was one of the founders of modern Burma, so her status and high profile has allowed her to avoid the most repressive actions of the government, but Suu Kyi has been under house arrest for much of the past two decades. In 1991, she was awarded the Nobel Peace Prize for her efforts to peacefully return Myanmar to democracy.

Today, there are widespread prohibitions against U.S. firms conducting business in Myanmar. The result has been that almost all U.S. firms have now withdrawn from the country. But European companies are only limited from investing in a few state-owned enterprises. Myanmar has many valuable natural resources. Firms from Mainland China are actively investing in Myanmar because China's government has few prohibitions and, in fact, encourages its firms to locate there.

The difficulty for a European firm is that there appear to be many business opportunities there. Additionally, although the laws do not prohibit investment in Myanmar, some regulations discourage full activity there. However, Myanmar's government is clearly a repressive one whose human rights abuses are notorious and numerous. The difficulty for a firm therefore becomes how to balance these non-quantifiable concerns as it considers entering a market. As firms increasingly expand to emerging markets, such concerns become more widespread and paramount to determine.

single restaurant in New York's Times Square. While it is a bit unconventional for a franchisor to open just a single restaurant in a country—franchisors typically benefit from promotion and scale of economies that accrue from regional concentration—Fish and Co. seeks to learn from the large and dynamic casual dining market in the U.S. The founder, Mr. Ricky Chew, has stated that he recognizes the U.S. as the leader in casual dining, particularly in terms of a restaurant's abilities to deliver quality service from entry-level employees along with a good quality of food and environment. He also points out that U.S. consumers are very discerning about mid-range priced casual dining and will handsomely reward a quality restaurant chain—or effectively demolish the reputation of a firm that fails to provide value or gives poor service. Chew wants to learn from the toughest customers and compete with the best competitors in casual dining, such as Panera Bread, Red Lobster, Olive Garden, and many other specialty restaurants.

Overall, the selection of a country in which to locate is a balancing of a firm's various concerns. The difficulty is ensuring the firm makes a thorough and complete analysis of the tradeoffs involved and matches them with the firm's goals. The firm, in conducting such an analysis, must recognize that its bargaining power to obtain any benefits from the government, such as training of employees or tax abatements, are at peak levels when the firm is thinking of locating there. Once a firm makes a major investment in capital assets, its ability to leave is reduced, as is its negotiation ability.

INTERNATIONAL ENTRY CYCLE

We discussed previously that a risk–reward relationship is present in internationalization, just as it is in all other business activities. As risk goes up so does the potential reward. Early research in international management argued that most firms go through a progression of steps as they move to become international. A firm starts as a domestic firm and slowly builds up to being a truly international competitor. (This is an idealized model, as a number of firms go international quite early based on the demands of its industry to seek the needed labor and clients.) At each step, as a firm gains more confidence about its ability to operate successfully in different international markets, it takes on more risk and accordingly has the opportunity for more reward. Next, we will cover the typical steps in the internationalization process.

Firm Starts Only in a Domestic Market

Most firms based in large continental markets, such as the United States or Brazil, will focus on the domestic market and not pursue any international sales. Even large multinational firms, such as Cisco, began with a focus on selling their products in the domestic U.S. market. Focusing on only the domestic market is less common in areas like Europe. The European Union has resulted in most individuals thinking of themselves as European and less as citizens of a given country. Thus, firms in Europe frequently start with a broader vision of who they are and where they need to compete. The manner in which Europeans define where they compete is also affected by the fact that nations in Europe are geographically close to each other. For example, it is less than an hour's train ride from Bratislava, the capital of Slovakia, to Vienna, the capital of Austria. Thus, conceptualizing a business in Europe is often not done with a given national market in mind.

Firm Becomes Aware of International Opportunities

During this stage, sales will arise internationally without a firm's active effort. The firm does not seek out sales, but if the product is good, individuals from other nations will approach the firm and ask to buy it. For example, the first Volkswagen cars came to the United States with returning military families in the 1950s. As other individuals became familiar with the cars, they actively sought out Volkswagens. Thus, an international demand developed for the car initially. The risks to an internationalizing firm at this stage are low—the payment check may not clear from a foreign party, or the product may be lost in shipping. However, consistent with the low risk, the returns are not high. The return on a given product that is sold internationally at this stage may be high but the quantity typically remains quite low.

Firm Enters a Market in a Small Way

As demand increases, a firm begins to try to serve that demand. The first means is typically through licensing. Risk at this stage remains low because the firm has limited liability if things go wrong. A party in an international market pays a licensing fee and has total control of the product. The danger for the firm licensing the product is that it may be used or sold in some manner that is not consistent with the firm's strategic posture. However, the licensing firm gets money from the license and has limited liability if the person or firm buying the license fails. Thus, the risk is increased for the firm, but the amount of revenue typically also increases. For example, the 7-Eleven brand of convenience stores is a common brand in Japan and many other countries and offers an interesting illustration of licensing. A Japanese firm bought the license for 7-Eleven's nameplate relatively cheaply. Today 7-Eleven operates more than 10,000 stores in Japan and Hawaii, and has approximately 7,000 other stores in other areas outside of North America. In an interesting twist, today the 7-Eleven Corporation in the United States, which originally provided the license to the Japanese firm, is now majority held by Seven & I Holdings Co., a wholly owned subsidiary of Japan-based retailer Ito-Yokado Co., Ltd.

Firm Builds International Confidence and Commits More Resources

Typically, as sales increase, a firm will next try to export goods through an alliance, such as a joint venture. In this setting, a firm has greater initial investment and the joint venture cannot be abandoned without incurring some costs. There are also costs to arrange and fund a venture. However, a joint venture affords a firm more opportunity for export. The firm, for the first time, has individuals on the ground in an international location that understand the market. This should lead to sales and profit increases for the firm. In the prior stage of licensing, the fee earned is the same if the party who buys the license sells a lot or a little. But now the firm expanding internationally will directly benefit from increased sales in a joint venture. Thus, the firm is making a greater commitment to the international market and taking on greater risk, but should also be reaping greater value.

A firm, after having had success exporting through a joint venture, may choose to build manufacturing facilities through another joint venture. This will involve greater investment than a marketing joint venture but there is a benefit to the firm from increasing sales, since the firm now has the ability to take better advantage of the local demand faster and will be closer to those consumers.

Wal-Mart today is the largest retailer in the world. It is also one of the largest international retailers in China. It is estimated that by 2010 the firm will have 150,000 employees in its stores and warehouses in China alone. Wal-Mart has pursued much of this expansion in China through joint ventures, though this may change with the recent relaxing of China's retail regulations allowing foreign retailers to own their own stores.

Firm Builds Own International Facilities

Once a firm has had success in an international market from an international joint venture, it may try to develop its own network of distributors and market its goods itself. However, it is likely that the firm will ultimately face increasing levels of competition. In all market economies, even inefficient ones, such as those in transition economies, success draws other firms seeking to do the same thing. (Recall the earlier discussion of sustainable competitive advantage in Chapter 4.) As a result of this competition, the firm often seeks to open production facilities and other operations in these markets in order to serve those markets. This market presence will also typically allow the firm to cut costs because, at a minimum, there are no shipping costs. However, if labor costs are considerably lower in that given market, this may also allow absolute costs to be cut.

Initially, a firm will staff its business with individuals from the home country, but often it will quickly put in place individuals from that country in an effort to save costs. As a firm builds more operations in foreign markets and staffs them at senior levels with locals, it moves closer to becoming truly international. The costs and risks likely will increase as the firm's international commitment rises but so will the rewards. It is for this reason in mature markets of the west that the greater the international diversification of a business, the greater its profitability. For example, Samsung builds its own facilities around the world and employs a wholly owned subsidiary model as it expands across the world today. Samsung Electronics India is a wholly owned subsidiary of Samsung Electronics.

Firm Becomes Transnational

Many businesses develop international aspects but few businesses move to become a special category of international business that management professors Bartlett and Ghoshal called a **transnational firm** in their 1989 book titled *Managing*

Transnational firm
In this type of firm the business assets are highly specialized, but interdependent with the other assets of the firm. The contribution of each nation is integrated with the worldwide network of businesses to provide to the whole the benefits of that nation. Knowledge developed in any unit is shared worldwide within the business.

across Borders: The Transnational Solution. This type of firm has a high degree of internationalization and all the various assets of the business are interdependent. In this setting, each nation's contribution is integrated with the worldwide network of businesses to provide a rich set of benefits to the firm. Knowledge developed in any unit is shared worldwide within the business. Thus, a firm is not just internationalized, but coordination among the various units across borders has reached a far higher level than most businesses ever achieve.

One distinguishing characteristic of a transnational firms is its large size and the large number of countries in which it is active. To achieve the integration that typifies a transnational firm, a business must draw on resources from many countries and units. General Electric typifies a transnational firm, with revenues that are more than the national incomes of all firms in sub-Saharan Africa combined, except for South Africa. The top 300 largest transnational firms control over 25 percent of the world's productive assets. Transnational corporations, as a group, control an estimated 90 percent of the world's patents. Thus, transnational corporations are a major force in the world economy. To illustrate how diverse such firms can be, examine Figure 6-3, which lists the various products of the Swiss firm Nestlé and the markets in which it is active.

Because of their size and influence, many countries and individuals look to transnational corporations for high levels of corporate social responsibility. For example, CFCs are pollutants associated with damage to the ozone layer. CFCs were commonly used in air conditioning coolant units. The Treaty of Montreal called for the elimination of these pollutants and they are now largely unavailable. Prior to that treaty, E.I. DuPont de Nemours and Co. produced an estimated 25 percent of the world's CFC pollutants. As a result, DuPont was an active target and participant concerning CFC elimination. After DuPont developed a substitute for CFCs, it was willing to support the treaty, which was enacted. The 20 largest pesticide corporations control 94 percent of that world market. As a result, these 20 firms are a regular target by activists concerned with pesticides.

Overview of Classic Internationalization Model

A firm takes small steps in moving into an international market. It learns more at each stage about that market and how to compete in the market. As it learns more, the firm begins to assume more and more risk and do more of the activities itself. Figure 6-4 summarizes the typical steps in the internationalization process.

A Born Global Business

Some firms start out doing business internationally and do not follow the pattern outlined above. Often these are technology-focused firms, where global demand for the firm's products is so small that if it relies on any single national market, there is insufficient demand for the firm to survive. Thus, these firms have to enter the global marketplace. This specialized set of entrepreneurial firms are called **born global** because these entrepreneurial firms are global from day one.

Such a firm does not build an understanding of international markets over time. Instead it establishes the firm with different activities occurring in different countries. For example, in the computer hardware industry, a global firm may choose to have its production facilities in China, its research and design operation in the U.S., and its marketing in Europe. The firm does this from the first day of its operation. The growth of born global businesses has increased in recent years. The ability to communicate instantly has tremendously aided in this process, as has the establishment of services such as overnight shipping. For many technological domains, the life cycle of businesses and market demand is such that the firms need to instantly

Born global
Entrepreneurial firms that are global from their inception.

FIGURE 6-3   Various Nestlé Brands

Country	Category	Products or services
Australia	Appliances/ Electronics	Coffee-capsule machines
Belgium	Food	Chocolate bars, coffee, cereal, chocolate, candy, ice cream, toppings
Belgium	Equipment	Coffee makers
Spain	Food	Water, baby food, chocolate bars, coffee, cereal, chocolate, ice cream, pasta, prepared dishes, salsa, soup, yogurt
Spain	Miscellaneous	Pet food
Spain	Equipment	Coffee-capsule machines
United States	Appliances/ Electronics	Coffee-capsule machines
United States	Groceries	Baby food, cereal, chocolate bars, chocolate, coffee, cooked food, ice cream, pasta, sauce, soup, water, yogurt
United States	Miscellaneous	Pet food
France	Food	Chocolate bars, coffee, coffee grain, cereal, delicatessen, chocolate, candy, mineral water, melted cheese, ice cream, cooked ham, milk, sauce, prepared dishes, fruit, sausage, popsicles, yogurt
France	Various	Pet food
France	Equipment	Coffee-capsule machines
Italy	Food	Vinegar, water, juice and soda, toast, cocoa and chocolate, coffee, caramel, cereal, ice cream, baby food, snacks, pasta, frozen dinners, salsa, vegetables, yogurt
Italy	Various	Pet food
Italy	Appliances/ Electronics	Coffee-capsule machines
United Kingdom	Appliances/ Electronics	Coffee-capsule machines
United Kingdom	Groceries	Baby food, cereal, chocolate bars, chocolate, coffee, cooked food, ice cream, pasta, sauce, soup, water, yogurt
United Kingdom	Miscellaneous	Pet food
Switzerland	Food	Chocolate bars, coffee, cereal, chocolate, candy, ice cream, sauce
Switzerland	Equipment	Coffee-capsule machines

Source: Transnational.org (http://www.transnationale.org/fiche/-160548548.htm)

reach all potential customers. These customers may be small in number, but will pay a premium to obtain the product quickly to be on the cutting edge of the change.

MARKET ENTRY EXECUTION

A firm, as it selects in which manner it wants to enter the market, will need to operationalize those plans. A variety of issues affect operationalization. Many of these concerns are discussed in more detail later, but they deserve some mention here. These concerns include planning for the entry, timing the entry, integration

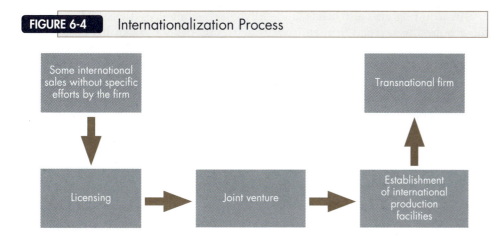

FIGURE 6-4 Internationalization Process

of merger and acquisition firms, and special issues for the implementation of joint ventures. Each of these concerns is discussed in detail in the following few sections. There would be a high degree of overlap in all types of entry-mode implementation if each were discussed specifically.

Planning Entry

Planning plays a critical role in the success of any market-entry attempt. The planning process will be more successful if it involves greater numbers of individuals throughout an organization. These individuals should not only address what is needed to make the market entry successful, but how the market entry will be conducted and why the market entry is necessary. A bias of the strategic management perspective employed in this book is the belief that involving more individuals in conceptualizing and thinking about problems and situations that face the firm generates more insight into the problem.

This process will also generate organizational commitment by managers in the acquiring firm. Success in market entry is often the result of the process pursued, rather than whether the strategy was correct. If incumbent managers in an acquiring firm do not believe that the market entry is a good strategy, they may withhold support and not be fully committed to it. This does not mean the managers will be actively trying to sabotage the market-entry effort. Instead, if they are not fully educated about and committed to the process, individuals can act in subtle, unconscious ways that detract from a venture's success and that ultimately can lead to its failure. Therefore, planning for a market entry can help educate managers as to why the venture is critical, how it will affect their given unit, and develop ways that the organization can ensure the venture's success.

Accurate planning also helps from the perspective of those in the acquiring firm. Before an acquisition, the acquiring firm needs to consider how things such as the compensation system, retirement plan, and health care will be handled. To illustrate, it is difficult for a firm to maintain multiple retirement systems with different salary percentages going into the retirement system. But changing the retirement system can have a big impact on the long-term plans of individual employees. Similarly, it is stressful for an acquired firm's employees to wonder what might happen after the merger or acquisition goes through. If a firm cannot relieve the stress among employees quickly on these issues, such hostility and opposition to the acquisition may build up among employees of the acquired firm that the poisoned environment will prevent its ultimate success. Planning can help overcome such problems.

An acquiring firm also needs to identify which employees it wishes to retain in the acquired or merged firm and what their authority will be in the new entity. One of the key resources in a business is its employees. However, the best employees in almost any situation have multiple job opportunities. If an acquiring firm cannot quickly relieve these employees' concerns, they may seek other employment rather than face the risk of losing their jobs. Thus, the international firm can find that it has lost some of its key people if a plan to reassure those key employees was not put in place.

Often, in a merger or acquisition, there are layoffs and restructuring in the firm that is taken over. As noted before, in many nations these layoffs require the permission of the government. A firm should analyze what restructuring is required and obtain government approvals before sealing the deal. Often a government is willing to approve such restructurings if a firm is on the verge of closing (or if the government is privatizing its firms). However, once an international firm invests its money, it has less negotiating power and less ability to obtain quick approval from the government.

The planning process ultimately creates parameters that are the bases for judging the progress and success of a merger or acquisition. Careful planning can help to eliminate many potential problems that can arise in a merger or acquisition on both sides of the venture. Here we have discussed the benefits of planning in terms of mergers or acquisitions. However, these same benefits apply to all types of market entry. The tendency of many managers is to focus on finalizing the deal. However, thorough planning before, during, and after finalizing the deal in all types of market entry is what produces success for the firm. The American Motors (AMC) and Beijing Jeep joint venture example (see the vignette at the beginning of this chapter) is instructive regarding a firm failing to plan carefully for a market entry, particularly into a complex market such as China's. There were several problems with American Motors' planning for that venture. First, the venture was rushed as they wanted to announce it quickly. This gave American Motors' stock a very healthy boost at that time, but the two joint venture partners failed to agree on a number of key terms up front, hoping that they would somehow be worked out over time.[xviii]

For example, AMC wanted to use China as a low-cost production base to export around the East Asian region, as well as capturing market share in China's emerging auto market, while its partner, Beijing Auto Works, sought to learn AMC's Jeep technology and produce a new Jeep for China's People's Liberation Army (PLA). A number of human resource issues were also left unresolved by the initial planning and JV agreement. For example, the division of powers for Beijing Jeep was not well specified, and the costs and living arrangements for the North American expatriates were not well planned or understood. When AMC accountants back at headquarters in Wisconsin could not figure out why clothing cleaning bills were so high, the expatriate staff explained that they were sending clothes for hotel dry cleaning. The accountants countered that surely somewhere in Beijing there must be a Laundromat, but in actuality, there were almost no laundromats in Beijing in 1983, nor probably anywhere else in the country at that time.[xix] Beijing Auto Works also insisted that its management get the same salaries as the AMC managers, but the money would not be paid directly, because it was being diverted to a special fund for distribution by the Chinese partner as they saw fit. AMC did not plan for other issues, such as import and export permits, hard currency shortages, and problems with local government officials and Communist party cadres, who interfered regularly with company operations. As noted earlier, the venture was saved only through intervention at the highest levels of the Chinese government. Firms hoping to enter emerging economies today have learned much about the planning and preparation required and about problems with supplies, labor markets and government officials, although spectacular

NEGOTIATIONS AND MEETINGS IN DIFFERENT SETTINGS

The AMC Jeep example highlights the importance of reaching an understanding with your partners and not leaving too many key issues unresolved. But reaching such an understanding can be difficult in many situations because business meetings may not operate in the same manner as could be expected in North America.

Business people from North America may be surprised to find that meetings in Latin America or the Middle East can be interrupted a number of times by local managers taking phone calls, or people coming and going. The individual's view in these settings is that their time and attention are not limited to the individuals in the meeting with them. It could be said that the individuals are interrupted because they are so busy. This same attitude will affect individuals shopping for a major purchase. A salesperson will be visiting with the customer when suddenly another customer will walk up and start talking to the same salesperson, interrupting and stopping, for the time being, the first customer's discussions with the sales clerk. The interruption does not mean the meeting or sales effort is over, but is seen as simply a temporary interruption.

One means to overcoming this difficulty in the Middle East is to meet the person you want to talk to in one of the many high-quality hotel lobbies. The lobby will have numerous large comfortable chairs and sofas on which to sit. You should also be able to order tea and light appetizers. This setting can gain the person's full attention (perhaps apart from their mobile phone interruptions). You also have a more relaxed environment for your discussions. Note that in ordering drinks, it is best to order tea or soft drinks, as observant Muslims do not drink alcohol, nor is it readily available in many Middle Eastern countries.

CULTURE

oversights continue to be made by firms from developed economies that have failed to study and learn from these case histories.[xx]

Timing of Entry

A key part of planning an entry is considering the position of competitors. There are benefits to entering a market earlier rather than later. The first firm into an area is typically referred to as a **first mover**. Alternatively, sometimes they are referred to as pioneers. This term applies whether a firm is the first into a new geographic area or country, or has a new product that is the first in a domestic market.

A first mover is able to develop an understanding of a market before any other firm. It is also able to connect with distributors, suppliers, and customers and develop relationships that may be difficult to replicate. For example, almost all the leading Internet firms today were the first significant firms in the domain. Amazon was one of the first and is the dominant Internet book retailer. If you go to a search engine like Google and plug in "books," you will find thousands of firms that sell books online. How has Amazon been able to maintain its position? The fact that Amazon was the first major online bookseller allowed it to be established in customers' minds as synonymous with Internet book sales. The very fact that there are so many other firms that sell books actually helps Amazon, because the greater the clutter, the easier it is for customers to simply go with the firm they know, Amazon.

Those that come after a first mover are called **second movers** or fast followers. Typically those that quickly follow a first mover and those that enter the market at a much later date are differentiated. There are times when moving quickly into a market after the first mover, called a fast second, is the preferable position.[xxi] A first mover may need to educate consumers about the product extensively, and this cost may make it impossible for the firm to move and take advantage when the market begins to develop.

For example, consider containerized cargo, which is loading and offloading a whole "truck container" rather than individual boxes to and from trucks and trains. This is the method used by almost all shipping companies today. Cargo is packaged at a factory into containers that can be pulled by the semi trucks that are on the highways of most countries. Large cranes at a dock then load these containers onto a ship. Then the containers are unloaded by cranes at the port of arrival and transported by truck to their destinations. Prior to the development of this

First mover
The first firm into an area, whether a product or national market. Sometimes multiple firms can enter a product market within the same year and are usually considered multiple first movers.

Second movers
Those that follow the first movers into a market.

Shrinkage
Loss of goods due to stealing or
breakage, often in a retail store.

method, loading and unloading goods onto a ship was performed by human labor, and was expensive, dirty work. Losses of goods at shipping docks were extensive and organized crime was notoriously active in these areas because criminals had access to so many goods with ample opportunity to steal them. The advent of containerized cargo significantly limited the amount of **shrinkage** (the loss of goods due to stealing or breakage) and made the process literally 20 times more efficient than it was in the 1960s, significantly driving down the cost of shipping and facilitating global trade.[xxii] Today, large cranes loading containers on and off ships are standard. The ships they load, in fact, often look more like floating platforms rather than our traditional image of a cargo ship.

While containerized cargo was a great innovation, the firm that was the first mover and pioneered the concept went bankrupt and was never able to take full advantage of the development of the industry that it helped to create. The firm spent all its efforts educating individuals about the potential and helping to set up the system that exists today. It was the fast seconds that took advantage of the industry as it developed.

Late entrants
Firms that enter a market after others
are clearly there.

Some firms enter a market after others are established. These firms are called followers or **late entrants**. Typically this is not a profitable place to be in an industry. However, if customers have low low brand loyalty and primarily are driven by price, a late entrant can have a desirable position. A late entrant can take advantage of the technological progress that has already occurred and manufacture a product in the most efficient manner, since it builds its production and distribution on prior learning from other competitors. To illustrate, in many emerging economies the average income is still quite low. Many Western firms have gone into these markets quickly as first movers and established effective product markets based typically on charging a premium price for their goods. A late entrant, however, is able to come in, learn from the first movers, and sell goods at lower prices. This is true in a variety of industries, such as computers, in which firms such as Dell historically were not active in emergent markets but have lately begun to expand aggressively in some of those markets. Figure 6-5 summarizes the benefits and risks of different timing strategies for international market entry.

FIGURE 6-5 Different Market-Entry Strategies

Entry strategy	Description	Benefits	Risks
First movers, pioneers	Those firms that are first into the industry or nation.	Those industries and nations that have high customer loyalty. The ability to build relationships with suppliers and customers can be highly valuable and result in a defendable competitive advantage.	Those industries or nations with low customer loyalty. The customers will shift to lower-priced competitors quickly once they enter the market. Thus, your costs of establishing the market are hard to recover. Costs of education about the product can be so high that a firm does not have the cash to actually be able to then reap the benefits of customer demand when it arises.
Early followers	Those firms that follow on the heels of the first mover.	An early follower can benefit from the education of the market done by the first mover. Additionally, an early follower can learn from the mistakes of the first mover and avoid the cost associated with those mistakes.	If customer loyalty is very high, critical relationships may be established and a barrier to entry into the market already established.
Late entrants	Those firms that enter the market—whether it be a nation or product market—after it has become established.	A late follower has a low risk due to market uncertainty.	Competition is based on cost and it may be difficult to be profitable.

THE BEER INDUSTRY IN CHINA

The entry cycle must consider the goals of firms at different stages of an internationalization effort. It was noted that firms often start with limited actions in a given foreign country and then, as they learn about that country, they invest more and more in it. The Chinese beer market demonstrates the risks of not pursuing such a step-by-step learning process in a foreign market. The beer industry around the world is very mature with rather slow growth. However, in China it is growing steadily. Between 2005 and 2006, beer consumption was up an estimated 15 percent in China. Yet Chinese people drink, on a per capita basis, less than 20 percent of the beer that Americans do annually, and even less than Europeans, arguing for even more opportunity in the China market. The potential market growth is even greater if you consider that beer consumption along the coast is twice as high as it is in central and western China. In addition, consumption in urban areas is four times the average consumption in rural areas. Thus, as the Chinese society grows richer and there is greater dispersion of income, it is likely that beer consumption could expand significantly, particularly in the poor (but growing) western regions of the country.

Today, the beer industry is highly fragmented in China. Unlike mature markets, where consolidation has resulted typically in a few major companies in each country, China's beer market has over 800 breweries, with the top 25 brewers having less than 50 percent of the market. Contrast this with South Korea, where the top three firms control 99% of the market. But China is a patchwork of local breweries where local brands dominate. This highly fragmented market has attracted many international brewers into China.

In the early 1990s, many major beer brands sought to enter the China market and build a national presence. The result was that by 2000, major brands active in China included Anheuser-Busch, Heineken, SAB, Carlsberg Interbrew, San Miguel, Kirin, Lion Nathan, and Foster's. Each believed that its economies of scale and superior technology would allow it to dominate the market quickly. The only firm that turned out to be highly successful was Anheuser-Busch, which for $1/2 billion and 10 years of effort was able to build Budweiser as China's high-end beer, a much different position than it has the U.S., where it is a mid-market beer. Others largely failed because China's distribution system is so arcane. Individuals from small stores or restaurants come to the factory on a bicycle wanting to buy a case or two. There are no mass distribution channels that work well with mass production. In addition, individuals are loyal to their local brands. Anheuser-Busch overcame these problems by moving early into major cities and selling aggressively in hotels and higher end restaurants, while avoiding the smaller stores. This was quite consistent with its high end positioning strategy—A-B does not want Budweiser's brand diluted by selling outside of higher end stores, hotels, and restaurants.

Today, firms producing beer have reversed their strategy of building national brands and are instead putting together portfolios of local brands. In some situations, brewers will own the local firm and in others they simply partner with the firm. For example, SABMiller is the world's second-largest brewer. It started out as South African Brewing but now is listed on the London Stock Exchange and owns brands such as Miller and the Czech-made Pilsner Urquell. Today, SABMiller has relationships with 30 local breweries in China. These relationships all vary as to the extent of ownership and the impact SABMiller has on operations. In some situations, SABMiller controls the firm outright through its ownership and others are joint ventures.

Inbev, the large Belgium brewer, has pursued a similar strategy. It is now the third-largest brewer in China, with a portfolio of brands that give it 9 percent of the market. These activities include joint ventures with Zhujiang Brewery (the largest in south China), effective control of KK Brewery in Ningbo, and half ownership of Lion Group.

Thus, on the whole, when brewers initially tried to enter China with large operations that mimicked their operations in the more developed economies, they failed. Instead, when they began to enter the market in small steps, viewing the market as a series of smaller markets and strategic positions where greater flexibility was required, they became successful.

Kahn, G., Bilefsky, D., & Lawton, C. 2004. "Another round: Burned once brewers return to China." *Wall Street Journal.* March 10: A1.

Ewing, J. & Webler, J. 2004. "The beer wars come to a head." *Business Week.* May 25, issue 3884: 68.

Xinhua's China Economic Information Service. 2005. "China's beer output up 15 percent in 2004." March 30.

It is important to note that, as in the case of differentiation and low-cost business-level strategies, it is possible to have successful first movers and late entrants in the same industry and in the same international market. These are not mutually exclusive concepts for success. Instead, firms must identify the appropriate market entry strategy for the firm and its products.

Integration M&A

An entry issue specific to a merger and acquisition is integration of the two firms. A firm must act quickly to blend the two organizations. It was noted before that planning is critical. In planning for an M&A, a firm must perform extensive due diligence on the business being acquired. It needs to have the plan in hand about what individuals, systems, and activities are to be blended and how. A timeline for accomplishing this activity needs to be established. Manulife of Canada, one of the most successful acquirers in the financial sector in Asia, has clear timelines and understandings of how each step is to be accomplished before entering negotiations with another firm. Because of such detailed planning, Manulife believes that it can then take the time to ensure that qualitative things, such as organizational culture, which cannot be necessarily planned and arranged, are focused on. If a firm has not done its planning, it will have to spend time after the merger to focus on things like which retirement system to keep. Through planning, those items can be worked out beforehand and issues such as culture can be focused on after the merger. Key points in implementing a merger or acquisition can be summarized as:

- defining clear objectives
- establishing an implementation team
- establishing lines of authority for the implementation
- identifying key employees and teams to ensure they are part of the transition and remain with the firm
- planning for information system integration
- developing a plan for blending the cultures

Joint Ventures Implementation

There are also a few unique differences in the implementation of joint ventures that should be mentioned. Most of these differences center on the fact that the two parties are joining together of their own free will and that within the confines of their agreement, the parties can also leave that arrangement. Therefore, typical implementation concerns include:

- ensuring that the parties to the joint venture have shared goals for the joint venture
- making sure there are no ambiguities in the relationship—the time to talk about those issues are before the agreement is signed, not afterwards
- making sure each firm's strategic position is such that the firm can fulfill its commitment to the joint venture—if a partner firm comes under strategic stress, it may focus less on the joint venture and withdraw its support for the venture
- ensuring intellectual property is protected because a partner today may be a competitor tomorrow

SUMMARY

International market entry is a major decision for firms. A variety of motivations can encourage a firm to move into an international market, including increasing market share; obtaining greater return on investment; protecting intellectual property; obtaining location advantages; or securing access to labor, raw materials, and markets. Any one or multiples of these motivations may be present for a firm. A firm then must determine how it wishes to move internationally—through a greenfield venture, merger or acquisition, joint venture, franchise, license, consortium, outsourcing, or some informal alliance. Each of these has benefits and drawbacks. In a manner consistent with most things in a capitalist society, as the risk of a firm increases so does the reward. Thus, firms will typically start out with a low-risk method of entering a market, such as licensing, and as the firm grows more confident, it may move on to greenfield ventures as the highest-risk, highest-reward type of venture.

A firm must also determine if it wishes to be a first mover, follower, or late entrant. Again, each has it benefits and risks, with an earlier entrant having the highest risk/reward potential. Last, a firm needs to choose how deeply it wishes to move into international activities, whether it is a multinational, global, international, or transnational firm.

All of these choices have their own risks and benefits. However, what is clear from this chapter is that there are a wide variety of choices for a firm. The key in each of these situations is for the firm to make those choices based on its strategic goals and core competencies. Ultimately it must find the right mix for that firm.

MANAGERIAL GUIDELINES

As noted before, many types of market-entry strategies, such as merger and acquisitions, are more likely to fail than they are to succeed. In pursuing market entry, managers are more likely to be successful when they consider the following:

1. Planning is critical to the success of the market entry. The plan becomes a road map a firm should follow in the market entry process. The plan needs to be developed in an interactive manner with a wide range of parties in the organization. This plan will need to be adapted as the setting changes, but it will help the firm not only think of a wide variety of dimensions of the market entry, but also to build organizational support for the market entry.
2. The form of market entry chosen by a firm should match the firm's tolerance for risk, control, and cost. The different choices of entry represent trade-offs among these three items. A firm should find the right balance for its needs and abilities.
3. Firms will choose market-entry methods that require greater costs and carry greater risks as they develop confidence about competing internationally. Firms should not expect to become transnational overnight.
4. Good preparation is essential for market entry, particularly via joint venture. However, proper preparation is doubly important for entering emerging markets where the rule of law and commercial traditions are not in place.

Many firms are entering emerging economies such as China, Russia, and India. There are clear risks and benefits to entering such markets and Table 6-1 summarizes many of those risks and benefits relative to mature markets. In entering such environments, a firm will wish to balance its level of commitment against the risks and expected level of return.

TABLE 6-1 Managerial Guidelines for Market Entry in Mature versus Emerging Economies

Considerations	Mature Economy	Emerging Economy
Amount of government control	Can be high but rules are typically clear	Can vary widely but rules are typically not clear
Restrictions on foreign investment	Typically none	Can be high and the rules can change rapidly
Availability of lower-cost labor, key inputs, or growing local markets	Growing markets will typically be in high technology domains; other product markets are mature with limited ability to obtain low-cost labor or key inputs.	Demand is typically in domains other than high technology. Market growth in these domains can be very high as individuals obtain basic products for the first time. The cost of inputs and labor is typically much lower than in mature markets.

TABLE 6-1 (Continued)

Considerations	Mature Economy	Emerging Economy
Choosing specific locales		
• Access to markets	Cost structures in most firms are such that costs are closely monitored. Additionally, large firms with high economies of scale dominate in many domains. The result is that gaining access to markets can be restricted. Government is typically less of an impediment for most products.	Distribution of products tends to be far more fragmented and less rationalized. There are far more points of contact that need to be maintained and serviced, which can make the costs high. The role of government can be quite high and can limit access to markets.
• Availability of transportation and electricity	Transportation is readily available with trucking, railroads, and air carriers. Electricity is typically readily available at competitive rates.	Transportation can be very difficult with poorly developed highway systems and railways that are typically poorly maintained. Electricity is often in short supply.
• Ease of access by international employees	Travel and communication are typically only limited by differences in time zones.	Travel and communication are often difficult. Often employees will consider being posted in the nation to be a hardship and even travel to the nation is often resisted.
Production Consideration	Increasingly, firms are moving to a global production framework in which parts of products are produced in different countries and then assembled in another. Mature economies, communication, and transportation support this model. Quality can be as good as in any other location in an emergent market.	Production is typically centered in the given country with as much as possible of a product produced there because of difficulties in shipping and integration with production in other countries. Quality can be as good as any other location in a mature market.
Customers	Consumers typically have high levels of consumption and low levels of savings.	Consumers typically have low levels of consumption and high levels of savings. However, increasingly firms recognize that due to large numbers of consumers being underserved, entering the pyramid at the bottom with lower-cost products can be very profitable.

CULTURE AND DOING BUSINESS IN POLAND

Poland is the second-largest country in Central Europe, after Germany, with a population of about 38 million. Prior to 1990, Poland was a satellite of the Soviet Union, with a communist government and socialist economic system. Since 1990, Poland has developed a vibrant democratic system of government and a free-market economy. Poland joined NATO in 1999 and the European Union in 2004.

The country that exists today was largely reconstructed after World War II. The victorious Allied powers determined that the war had partly been caused by having ethnic minorities in different countries. One of Hitler's excuses for invading Poland, the act that touched off WWII in Europe, was to protect the German minority in the country and return the largely German city of Danzig (Gdansk) to German control. Thus, after the war, the Allies designed Poland to contain all the Poles and few minorities. This involved shifting large amounts of land and many people between countries, with

the result that Poland is now 97 percent ethnically Polish. Poland is also largely Catholic—the Polish identity is closely connected to Catholicism. Thus, in doing business in Poland, there is a need to be sensitive to the importance of Catholicism there (Pope John Paul II was from Poland and students still gather outside the window in which he last appeared in Krakow, and say prayers and sing songs at the hour in which he passed away.)

Polish business culture is conservative with individuals being well dressed when they do business. The use of formal titles is also the norm, as it is in most of Northern and Central Europe. The impact of this conservatism is that relationships are very important in business. Individuals need to develop strong relationships in order to conduct business. One side effect of Poland's communist past is that the government bureaucracy is very strong. Thus, building good relationships with regulators and government officials is advisable for most businesses.

ADDITIONAL RESOURCES

Carey, D., Aiello, R. J., Watkins, M. D., Eccles, R. G., & Rappaport, A. (2001). *Harvard Business Review on Mergers and Acquisitions*. Boston: Harvard Business School Press.

Galpin, T., & Herndon, M. (1999). *The Complete Guide to Mergers and Acquisitions: Process Tools to Support M&A Integration at Every Level*. San Francisco: Jossey-Bass.

Lees, S. (2003). *Global Acquisitions: Strategic Integration and the Human Factor*. New York: Palgrave-MacMillan.

Sherman, A. J., & Hart, M. A. (2007). *Mergers & Acquisitions from A to Z*. New York: AMACOM/American Management Association.

Travis, T. (2007). *Doing Business Anywhere: The Essential Guide to Going Global*. New York: John Wiley.

Yan, A., & Luo, Y. (2001). *International Joint Ventures: Theory and Practice*. Armonk, NY: ME Sharpe.

EXERCISES

Opening Vignette Discussion Questions

1. Why did Chrysler (Jeep's current owner) pay relatively so little attention to the joint venture initially?
2. The joint venture initially relied heavily on its relationships with the government, and it seemed to bring benefits to the firm. Was it wrong to focus on such relationships or should the firm have approached these relationships differently?
3. Based on your understanding of China today, do you think government relationships are as critical as they were initially for Chrysler?
4. What are some of the implementation issues that Chrysler could have focused on early to avoid the problems that arose?

DISCUSSION QUESTIONS

1. What do you think of the pressures brought on transnational firms for issues like pollution? Is it is ethical for political groups to target only those firms or is it done because targeting these firms is politically expedient? Are the concepts of political expedience and ethical business practice mutually exclusive?
2. Over 75 percent of FDI from transnational corporations goes to Asia (particularly China) but only approximately 1 percent of FDI goes to Africa. Is it appropriate to compel transnational corporations to spread their investment more evenly to areas such as Africa?
3. Why do you think born global firms are a recent phenomenon? Will such firms become the standard in international startups?
4. Is there a first mover advantage in most retail businesses?

IN-CLASS EXERCISES

1. Separate into teams. Half the teams are to envision themselves as technology companies from a mature western economy such as the United Kingdom. They need to negotiate a joint-venture agreement with a Chinese firm to manufacture goods in China. The other teams are to perceive themselves as the Chinese manufacturer.

   a. Identify the issues that are of concern to each side of the negotiation.
   b. Match up a "Western team" and a "Chinese team." Attempt to come to agreement on three major issues that each team has agreed are critical.

2. Separate into teams. Assume that half of the teams are representatives of a transnational corporation such as Wal-Mart. The other half of the teams are NGOs.

   The NGOs are concerned about the treatment of workers in plants that supply soccer balls (footballs outside the United States). They have found most of the balls are produced by children as young as 5 years old and typically less than 14 years old. Children's dexterity is much better than adults, so they can produce the stitching needed to make a better ball. The children are paid approximately $1 a day. Wal-Mart says that it simply buys the ball from a wholesaler and is not responsible to do more than provide low-cost goods because the children are not the firm's employees. The NGO believes Wal-Mart should do more for the children. Prepare arguments for your side and then meet with a team from the other side of the issue. See if there are compromise situations.

3. From the material you covered in Chapter 2 on culture, write down how the management of joint ventures in China, Russia, Poland, and Venezuela might differ. How should a corporation establish common standards for the corporation but allow for such differences to be addressed? Be prepared to present your answers to the class.

4. It was noted that first movers often have a competitive advantage when it concerns Internet businesses. Assume you are an entrepreneur in Latin America and wish to start a new Internet book-selling business. How would you be able to differentiate your business and be successful? Write down three ways. Be prepared to present your ideas to the class.

TAKE-HOME EXERCISES

1. Pick a country outside of your own. Identify a franchise available in that country that you potentially would like to own in your country. Does this franchise have many differences from a franchise you know in your home country?

2. Research a firm that you believe is a transnational firm. How many products and countries is it involved in? Has it had a major difficulty in one of those countries that appeared in news reports that would appear to be a culture clash between the culture in that country and the dominant national culture of the firm?

3. Research a firm that has recently announced a joint venture in India or China. What is the nature of the firm's partner in the joint venture? Why do you think this firm was chosen as a joint venture partner?

4. Research an international merger or acquisition that has been criticized as ultimately not being successful. (If you go to a search engine and put in terms like international merger acquisition failure you will get lots of potential firms to look at.) Why do you think the merger or acquisition failed? Is there any way to have prevented the problems?

SHORT CASE QUESTIONS

The Beer Industry (p. 189)

1. What are the implications for other businesses of the concentration of the wealth in China in coastal urban areas?
2. What will be the implications for businesses such as SAB as the China market matures?
3. Why do you think that international brands such as Foster's Beer were not more successful in their market entry?

7

MOTIVATION

Overview

Prior chapters addressed the overall elements of a firm, such as its industry and the culture in which it is was located. But now it is time to start to examine how a firm manages people in different settings. Important among these issues is motivation, which encourages people to reach high levels of work performance. Motivation is problematic in international settings because how people are motivated can vary by region of the world. For example, recall from Chapter 2 that culture affects basic issues, such as whether individuals place more emphasis on financial rewards or their lifestyle. This fundamental difference will in turn affect what motivates individuals.

This chapter will review the major theories of motivation, their implementation, and effect. These theories were primarily developed in North America and are reviewed from that setting. We then explore how motivation changes as we apply those ideas in a international setting. The theories will be separated based on whether they principally see motivation as something internal to the individual (content theories) or as part of process (process theories). This chapter examines:

- content (need) theories of motivation:

  Maslow's hierarchy of needs
  Alderfer's ERG
  Herzberg's extrinsic and intrinsic motivators
  McClelland's theory of learned needs

- process theories of motivation

  expectancy
  equity
  goal setting

VIRGIN ATLANTIC, RICHARD BRANSON, AND WHAT WORKERS WANT

Richard Branson did not graduate from a university. Yet today he is one of the richest people in the United Kingdom, and his business interests include over 250 different companies. Best known are his music retailer, Virgin Music; his telecommunications firm, Virgin Mobile; his insurance, financial planning, and credit card retailers, Virgin Money; and the second largest airline in the United Kingdom, Virgin Atlantic.

In each of these firms, Sir Branson (who was knighted by Queen Elizabeth II for his business accomplishments) has often overcome critics who said he could not be successful. A key part of the success is Branson himself; he is the quintessential entrepreneur and will do whatever is necessary to make each of his efforts successful. For example, Branson donned a wedding dress to promote the start of the bridal retailer Virgin Brides. However, another key success factor is his employees and their motivation in working for the companies.

Branson has always seen people as critical to his success. He stated:

Convention dictates that a company should look after shareholders first, its customers next and worry last about its employees. Virgin does the opposite. For us, employees matter most. It just seems common sense that if you start with a happy, well motivated work force you're much more likely to have happy customers. In due course the resulting profits will make your shareholders happy.[1]

One of the key ways that Branson has tried to motivate employees at his firms is to provide them with ample flexibility and make the work both challenging and interesting. Once he empowers employees, he also gives them room to fail. For example, an executive once made a bad choice and lost the firm a large amount of money. When the employee came to Branson's office he expected to be fired. Instead, Branson fired at the employee with a water pistol, then told him to get back to work. That day the executive, and the entire firm, learned to take risks and learn from them, because a failure did not necessarily mean termination.

Often it is assumed that employees are only motivated by money. However, this has not proven to be the case for Branson. His workers want interesting and challenging situations where they can make a visible contribution, an environment that Branson has tried to create for them. A body of research in the West supports the view that money is not a primary motivator for many employees. These studies from a variety of work settings, ranging from heavy manufacturing to computer engineering, consistently find that employees rank appreciation of work and being involved in work as the most important motivating factor.

It should be noted that in these surveys, when asked what they thought workers wanted, supervisors consistently ranked extrinsic motivators, such as salary and working conditions, among the highest motivators, and intrinsic motivators as lowest. Interestingly, in the same surveys, employees also indicated they thought coworkers were most interested in salary.

This situation reflects an extrinsic bias that can be traced to an attribution error. An **attribution error** occurs when people try to make sense out of events in their lives and make assumptions about the issues involved. For example, when asked to assess themselves on driving skill, nearly everyone says they are an above average driver. No one considers himself or herself a below average driver.[i] Thus, perhaps managers assume everyone is interested in money because they themselves are interested in money.

Managers need to be careful that they do not make a fundamental attribution error in assuming that all their employees only want more money. Richard Branson has found a way for his organizations to motivate people. It should be noted that, while Branson puts a premium on creating situations that empower managers, he also says often that he is in the business of creating millionaires. Thus, Branson does not hesitate to motivate individuals who are successful when they perform. Managers cannot assume that the method of motivation they have in their own countries, or motivation methods people like Branson have used, will work in other settings. It is doubtful that Branson's system will work in an African, Malaysian, or Kuwaiti firm because those countries have a different cultural setting. The system Branson created is unique to those entrepreneurial ventures and the cultures in which Branson operates those businesses. There are many ways to motivate employees and colleagues. Firms need to find those that offer the best opportunity for the firm in that setting.

Previous chapters looked at outside factors that affect a business internationally. We now begin to look internally at issues a firm must deal with as it manages in an international setting. The most difficult tasks in international management concern people. One of the key areas firms must focus on as they internationalize is motivating a wide range of people in different settings to do their work well. In

Attribution error
Occurs when people try to determine cause and effect in their lives and make incorrect assumptions about what actions led to particular situations.

[1]Broad, M. (2003, February 18). Richard Branson. *Personnel Today.*

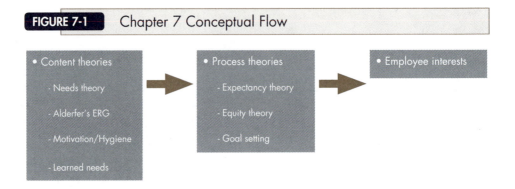

FIGURE 7-1   Chapter 7 Conceptual Flow

- Content theories
  - Needs theory
  - Alderfer's ERG
  - Motivation/Hygiene
  - Learned needs

- Process theories
  - Expectancy theory
  - Equity theory
  - Goal setting

- Employee interests

large measure, this difficulty comes from the fact that what motivates people in one region of the world may be much different in another region. For example, in many parts of Africa it is not uncommon for wages to be partly determined by the size of the employee's family, because motivation comes less from the level of the wage than the approval of the family, tribe, or village. Contrast this with North America, where salary is the primary motivator for performance and no one would even consider the size of someone's family to determine pay. An international firm with operations in both North America and Africa may find that transplanting its focus on pay as a motivator from North America to Africa may actually work to reduce motivation, because it may place the person receiving the monetary reward in conflict with his or her reference group at the company. Thus, culture is important in discussing motivation in international settings because employees in various cultural settings have different values that affect their needs and how they might be motivated. This chapter lays out the component parts of motivation and how motivation can differ in various international settings. Figure 7-1 summarizes the flow of the material we will examine in this chapter.

MOTIVATION COMPOSITION

Motivation
The driving force behind an individual's actions that energizes and directs goal-oriented behavior.

Motivation is an internal state or condition that *activates* a person's behavior and gives it direction toward accomplishing a task. Motivation energizes and directs goal-oriented behavior as well as the intensity and direction of behavior. Motivation is based on emotion, particularly on the search for positive emotional experiences and the avoidance of negative ones. Motivation is important because it determines an individual's effort toward performing a task. Thus, if an individual is motivated he or she will extend high levels of effort toward achieving the organization's goals. A person's level of effort will in turn be affected by the organization's capacity to satisfy that individual's needs and life interests, plus the person's ability to achieve the desired outcome.[2] Motivation can be represented by this conceptual expression:

$$\text{Motivation} = \text{Ability} \times \text{Values} \times \text{Life Interests and Goals}^{ii}$$

In Chapter 2 we discussed Hofstede's well-known model of cultural values, including power distance, uncertainty avoidance, masculinity, individualism, and long-term orientation. An individual's cultural values will affect what motivates

[2]Life interests (sometimes called job interests) represent work activities that one might prefer to do, such as working with numbers or doing influencing and selling. This topic is discussed later in the chapter.

that individual. For example, employees who are more individualistic may be motivated by a need to have jobs that allow them to express themselves or that provide them with some personal space. Employees higher on the collective scale would be more motivated by jobs that permit social interaction and working in teams. You will recall that Hofstede also discussed the masculine feminine dimension of culture. Cultures that had high masculine or production-orientation scores placed more emphasis on money and title, while those with a feminine or relational orientation were motivated more by lifestyle concerns, such as free time, holidays, and company social activities.

Thus, what motivates employees cannot be assumed without first asking questions.[iii] To illustrate some difficulties a firm may face, consider the hotel industry. Hotel employees in China are strongly motivated by bosses' public recognition of a job well done. In contrast, hotel staff in Australia stated they were motivated by a flexible work week. They did not mind working long hours sometimes, but they preferred options to work three days per week, so they could be off the other four days. In a collective-focused society, such as China's, peer pressure and peer recognition exercise strong influence on people, particularly in a work setting. In contrast, Australians typically value a work–life balance. That Chinese employees could be motivated by something as simple as recognition and praise in front of their coworkers came as a complete surprise to their Western managers, as well as the fact that the staff may become upset if supervisors fail to provide such public praise. Similarly, employees in parts of Asia may expect employee housing, which can be scarce and very expensive.[iv] Firms in Latin America have also reported that housing can be a useful motivator.[v]

One outcome of globalization and increasing cultural diversity in the workplace is that identifiying what motivates employees has become increasingly important. However, just as there are a number of motivators, there are also numerous different ways to classify and understand motivations. This chapter will look at a wide variety of these different perspectives on motivation. To do this we break the different views on motivation into categories. First, we look at the "content" theories of motivation. This perspective focuses on employees' needs, and there are four specific theories in this perspective. Next we will examine the process perspective of motivation. This perspective accepts the importance of needs yet focuses on the dynamics of motivation by which needs are examined and fulfilled; three specific theories will be examined. For each of these seven theories we initially look at the basic understanding of the theory that was primarily developed and tested in North America. We then examine the theories' implications and applications in international settings. Next, we address how an international firm can use these diverse theories in developing their own systems to motivate employees.

CONTENT (NEED) THEORIES OF MOTIVATION

Most motivation theories recognize that motivation begins with people's needs. **Needs** are things or conditions people have that can trigger behaviors to satisfy those needs. Unfulfilled needs create a tension that makes people want to find ways to satisfy those needs. The stronger a need is and the greater the person's awareness of it, the more motivated that person is to try to satisfy that particular need. This section examines four content theories of motivation that help global managers understand employee needs and how to better motivate their employees (and themselves). Figure 7-2 summarizes these theories and maps their component parts.

Needs
Represent things or conditions that people would like to have.

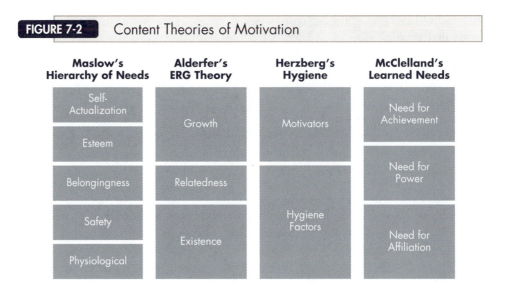

FIGURE 7-2   Content Theories of Motivation

Maslow's Hierarchy of Needs	Alderfer's ERG Theory	Herzberg's Hygiene	McClelland's Learned Needs
Self-Actualization	Growth	Motivators	Need for Achievement
Esteem			
Belongingness	Relatedness		Need for Power
Safety	Existence	Hygiene Factors	Need for Affiliation
Physiological			

Needs Theory

One of the best-known content theories of motivation is Maslow's hierarchy of needs. Outlined by psychologist Abraham Maslow in the 1950s, this theory condenses the innumerable human needs into a hierarchy of five basic needs. (Figure 7-3 summarizes Maslow's model.) At the bottom of the hierarchy are the physiological needs, which include the need to satisfy basic requirements for food, fresh air, clean water, and shelter. In an organizational setting, such a basic need could be represented by salary—employees have a need for a minimum level of basic salary, apart from the opportunity to earn more later. Next comes the safety need—the need for a secure and stable environment and the absence of illness and threats. In a work setting, this roughly corresponds to employee needs for good working conditions and job security. Maslow's third need level is belongingness. Belongingness includes the need for social interaction with other people and affection. In an organizational setting, this could include a job that provides some opportunities for teamwork and social activities. The next highest need is self esteem. Self-esteem can be attained both through personal achievement and via recognition from others. Some jobs provide esteem opportunities as a natural part of the job, such as those in the performing arts or the media, while other jobs have to create such opportunities, such as through employee recognition programs and awards. At the top of the hierarchy is self-actualization, which represents the need for self-fulfillment—a sense that a key goal has been accomplished. Many tasks have clear, built-in milestones that can help to fulfill this need, such as working toward a bachelors or masters degree, while other tasks must have intermediate objectives and final goals created for which employees can aim.

Maslow argued that a person's behavior is motivated primarily by the lowest unsatisfied need at that moment in time. Physiological needs are initially the most important and people are motivated to satisfy them first. Once these most basic needs are filled, the safety need emerges as the strongest motivator. As safety needs are satisfied, the belongingness need becomes most important. In international settings this theory has led firms to focus on the nature of the local economic setting as the principal indicator of an appropriate employee motivator. Thus, in a poor state like Bangladesh, money might be the principal motivator for most people. Only when a person satisfies a lower-level need does the next higher need, such as job security, become a primary motivator. In the economically advanced

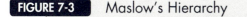

| FIGURE 7-3 | Maslow's Hierarchy |

Self Actualization – self-fulfillment
↑
Self Esteem – recognition
↑
Belongingness – social interaction
↑
Safety – stable environment
↑
Physiological Needs – food, shelter

countries of Europe, higher-level needs such as self-esteem and self-actualization would be expected to be more common, because food, housing, and employment are easily attained. This progression up the needs hierarchy is known as the satisfaction–progression process. Maslow's theory predicts that even if a person is unable to satisfy a higher need, he or she will be motivated by the possibility of fulfilling it until it is satisfied.

Maslow's hierarchy of needs is one of the best-known motivation theories. The model was helpful when initially proposed because it helped firms recognize that employees from different countries may be motivated by different needs. However, today the model is criticized for failing to explain the specifics of employee needs and neglecting job interests. For example, researchers have found that individual needs do not follow the same progression up the scale from lower to higher in the different parts of the world.[vi] Gratification of one need level does not necessarily lead to increased motivation coming from the need to satisfy the next item in the hierarchy, as proposed by Maslow. Moreover, not all people exhibit all five needs to the same extent. For example, some people may have very little in the way of social needs. They might like to work alone and prefer not going out to numerous company functions and lunches, and, in fact, may be annoyed (and thus demotivated) by repeated requests by colleagues or the company to attend social events or to socialize after work. This is usually quite acceptable in North American work settings where firms generally do not stress the social aspect of work. However, many South American cultures place great importance on social aspects and, as a result, employees are more likely to be motivated by a system that gives rewards based on social needs, such as having company dinners or weekend retreats. Most Japanese firms also expect employees to attend social functions and go out together after work to restaurants and bars, making it a little uncomfortable for employees who do not want to socialize so regularly. High social needs may also be important in motivating employees in Northern European countries, such as Denmark, Norway, and Sweden, that stress quality of life over masculine production orientation.[vii] This does not mean that all people in South America or Northern Europe emphasize such needs in the same way, but it is the way the society and its organizations tend to be ordered.

Maslow's model is helpful because it reminds managers who may be inclined to emphasize money as the sole motivator that there are different employee needs and that people are not motivated by the same things at the same time, with culture being a key factor in generating these different needs. A performance package based on bonuses and/or salary increases that is useful in the United States may not be the road to higher motivation and performance for some of its employees. This, in turn, suggests that managers in international firms should strive to find out what their employees really want and how to account for those needs in a motivation-and-reward system.

LINCOLN ELECTRIC IN MEXICO

Employees in countries outside of North America may have different needs than those of employees within North America. U.S. manufacturer Lincoln Electric is well known for its effective motivation-and-reward system based on **piecework**. With piecework, a worker is paid a fixed rate for each unit produced or action performed. Piecework can be very effective for manufacturing and is widely used in China and in high-production operations in East Asia. It is normally combined with a (low) base salary, similar to a salesperson's low base pay and commissions. In many of the world's more developed economies, piecework is staunchly resisted by workers and their unions. Yet Lincoln Electric has maintained a very disciplined and effective piecework system since its founding in the nineteenth century—a system that has been copied, at least in part, by many firms worldwide.

Lincoln Electric was founded in 1895 to make electric motors. The firm today is known as the world's leading manufacturer of welding equipment. Lincoln Electric has a long history of human resources innovation. The firm introduced its piecework system nearly a century ago, in which employees are paid largely for the number of welding devices and other units they can produce—a system that has worked well and continues through today. However, at the same time, the firm also introduced employee advisory committees. Each department in the firm created groups of employees to advise the firm, and these employees meet every two weeks. The creation of such labor groups was a radical innovation at the time. The firm later introduced other radical innovations, such as life insurance for employees, stock ownership plans for employees, annual bonuses based on output for the year, and a strong no-layoff commitment.

All of these human resources innovations continue today. However, today additional incentives are included for minimizing defects and teamwork, but Lincoln Electric employees are largely on their own in figuring out how to produce as much as possible. For example, Lincoln Electric allows individual employees leeway in organizing their workspaces and scheduling their work hours, and the annual bonus for each employee can average over $24,000 per year.

Although Lincoln Electric has been very successful in the United States, it has had trouble implementing this system overseas. As the former CEO, Don Hastings, observed a few years ago in the *Harvard Business Review*:

"[Lincoln's] incentive system is transferable to some countries—especially in countries settled by immigrants, where hard work and upward mobility are ingrained parts of the culture. But in many other places, it won't easily take root. It is especially difficult to install it in a factory that has different work practices and traditions. For example, even though German factory workers are highly skilled, and in general, solid workers, they do not work nearly as hard or as long as the people in our Cleveland factory. In Germany, the average workweek is 35 hours. In contrast, the average factory workweek in Lincoln's U.S. plants is between 43 and 58 hours, and the company can ask people to work longer hours on short notice—a flexibility that is essential for the system to work.

The lack of flexibility was one reason why our [motivation and reward system] approach would not work in Europe."

The Lincoln Electric employee system worked very well with the culture of the U.S. But in Mexico the cultural factors, such as lower individualism and less commitment to production, did not fit well with Lincoln Electric's piece-rate pay system. In addition, the plant in Mexico was unionized and there was a predisposition against workers earning different amounts.

To successfully implement the system in Mexico, Lincoln Electric decided to introduce it gradually. Lincoln Electric allowed a few select workers to opt into the system, and as they began to do well, other workers requested to be allowed into the piecework system. Although cultural values were important in suggesting what motivation system would work, Lincoln Electric was able to overcome any possible hindrances. It effectively used a system of social learning to gradually influence all the workers to understand how the system benefited them. And benefit them it did. After about two years, all 175 workers in the plant had opted into the incentive system. Workers make more money than before and Lincoln Electric has its productive system in place. Culture is important in determining what companies can do, but sometimes it is possible to get something done in spite of local culture and traditions, though a system may have to be implemented carefully, as Lincoln Electric did in Mexico.

Hastings, D. (1999). Lincoln Electric's harsh lessons from international expansion. *Harvard Business Review* 77(3), 162–178.

Piecework
A type of work in which a worker is paid a fixed "piece rate" for each unit produced or action performed.

Alderfer's ERG Theory

The ERG theory was developed by psychologist Clayton Alderfer to overcome problems associated with Maslow's hierarchy of needs theory.[viii] The ERG theory groups human needs into three broad categories: existence, relatedness, and growth (notice that the theory's name is based on the first letter of each need). Existence needs include a person's physiological and physically related safety needs, such as the need for food, shelter, and safe working conditions. Relatedness needs include a person's need to interact with other people, receive public recognition, and feel secure around people (i.e., interpersonal safety). Growth needs consist of a person's self-esteem through personal achievement as well as the concept of self-actualization presented in Maslow's model. Alderfer's existence needs correspond to Maslow's physiological and safety needs; relatedness needs correspond to Maslow's belongingness needs; and growth needs correspond to Maslow's esteem and self-actualization needs.

The ERG theory argues that, different from Maslow, an employee's behavior is motivated simultaneously by more than one need level. A person might try to satisfy the growth needs of meeting a tough goal even though that person's relatedness needs are not fully satisfied. Unlike Maslow's model, the ERG theory includes a frustration–regression process whereby those who are unable to satisfy a higher need become frustrated and regress back to the next lower need level. For example, if existence and relatedness needs have been satisfied, but growth need fulfillment cannot be achieved, an individual will become frustrated and relatedness needs will again emerge as the dominant need and source of motivation.

The ERG theory explains the dynamics of human needs in organizations reasonably well because human needs cluster more neatly around the three categories proposed by Alderfer than the five categories in Maslow's hierarchy. The combined processes of satisfaction–progression and frustration–regression also provide a more accurate explanation of why employees need change over time. Internationally, the model also suggests how cultures with different values may be motivated by different needs. For example, some people from a collectivist society would be motivated by the need to be part of the group. People in such a society would prefer to work in firms that have social events and in which employees work in teams. Employees from a more collectivist society would also prefer that the firm provide lunches and tea breaks in which all employees can participate. Indeed, in many Asian countries it is common for all offices to close from about 1:00 pm to 2:00 pm so all employees can go to lunch together. This is also true in several European countries, as anyone knows who has tried to find open businesses or government offices during lunchtime. In some countries lunch breaks can go on for two to three hours. Employees from such countries may become demotivated by working alone and not having social opportunities at work. But collectivism is not the only cultural value that affects motivation. There are, in fact, a variety of cultural issues that have an impact on motivation. For example, in countries higher on Hofstede's dimension of uncertainty avoidance, security may be a more motivating factor than Maslow's highest need of self-actualization growth and thus be a more important need.[ix] Alderfer's model allows for greater flexibility than Maslow's because it also recognizes that people have different needs though they do not move up in a rigid hierarchy as Maslow suggested originally.

Thus, internationally, ERG theory allowed for more complex models of compensation to be developed, which resulted in the recognition that a mixture of needs must be addressed. For example, it suggests that firms in a poor nation, such as Bangladesh, focus on both wages and the need for relatedness as motivators. Maslow's hierarchy of needs and ERG theory are helpful in reminding managers of the various needs of their employees, but these models failed to address a number of specific work-related needs, such as the often-voiced need to be involved with company decisions and other nonmaterial or intrinsic needs.[x] Subsequent authors sought to address intrinsic needs' impact on motivation in particular.

Motivation–Hygiene Theory

Management scholar Frederick Herzberg found the basic need theories unsatisfying, and sought to examine extrinsic (external) as well as intrinsic (internal, task-related) **motivators**. In Herzberg's formulation, intrinsic motivators include 1) achievement, 2) recognition for achievement, 3) the work itself, 4) responsibility, and 5) growth or advancement. These are all intrinsic in that they are related to the task and the psychological state of the individual. Extrinsic factors include: 1) company policy and administration, 2) supervision, 3) interpersonal relationships, 4) working conditions, 5) salary, 6) status, and 7) security.[xi] Herzberg argued that intrinsic factors tend to be motivators. The more extrinsic, hygiene factors can serve to de-motivate, but not motivate. This model is useful because it breaks the concept of motivation into factors that motivate to take action, and factors that create dissatisfaction and might cause people to avoid doing certain things, but will not motivate them.[3] Thus, motivation is not just putting things in place to encourage behavior, it also is concerned with removing things that could discourage desired behaviors.

To clarify Herzberg's approach to motivation, consider why people may be motivated to travel to a certain city for a holiday. The city-state of Singapore has one of the highest per-capita incomes in the world. Singapore has tight controls over many aspects of life; for example, you cannot buy chewing gum without a doctor's prescription (to prevent people from dropping it on the street), there is little litter because of strict policing with high penalties if you are caught, and you can be fined if you do not flush a public toilet after use. Singapore is therefore well known for being very clean and orderly, but it was not always that way. People find many Asian cities to be cluttered and disorderly, and previously, Singapore was no exception. However, one of the first things that the ruling People's Action Party sought to do when Singapore gained its independence from Malaysia in the mid-1960s was to make Singapore much cleaner and more orderly than any other Asian city. The government believed that if Singapore remained dirty, international business people would be less likely to do business there or travel there for a holiday. As a result of this conscious effort, in the late 1970s Singapore became the cleanest city in Asia and one of the model cities for the world. Thus, the leadership was able to fix a hygiene factor by eliminating those things that would discourage people from traveling to the city.

While a *bad* hygiene factor may prevent (de-motivate) you from visiting a city, an absence of such factors is not enough to encourage (motivate) people to travel to a city for a holiday. Singapore has since recognized this and knows it has to produce specific reasons to motivate people to come there, as opposed to just removing reasons not to. Singapore has developed an amusement park on Sentosa Island, just off of its coast, and is bringing in gambling casinos and other attractions. Recognizing the interaction of both items—reasons to *do* things and taking away reasons to *not do* things—led Herzberg to argue it was necessary to have both motivators and hygiene factors (also called "dissatisfiers") to be successful.

However, while managers need to address both (intrinsic) motivators and (extrinsic) hygiene factors, they will likely address these needs separately. Improving hygiene factors works to minimize job dissatisfaction and employee turnover but does not increase motivation. This separation of issues helps international firms that must address the needs of worldwide organizations. A hygiene factor such as working conditions expected in different settings can vary widely. For example, a furniture factory setting that dissatisfies employees in a rich European country, such as Norway, may gain a dramatically different response in Vietnam.

---

[3]Herzberg's data and research design have been questioned by organizational scholars in recent years, particularly in terms of the narrow sample used (engineers). Nevertheless, it is conceptually useful to discuss needs in terms of motivators and hygiene factors, that is, motivation versus dissatisfaction (demotivation).

Motivators
In Herzberg's motivation-hygiene theory, these are positive influencers, such as job involvement, that are intrinsic to a job and that can push employees to higher levels of performance.

Firms must recognize these differences and improve hygiene factors that potentially cause dissatisfaction in each setting.

When using the motivator-hygiene model, firms also cannot assume that intrinsic items, such as employee growth opportunities and interesting work, will have the same motivational effect internationally. For example, workers in some countries, such as Japan and Greece, are motivated more by job security than growth opportunities or interesting work.[xii] Though Herzberg's work has been criticized because of his methods, particularly using a sample of professionals, his theory does add to our understanding of the needs theories by being more specific about needs and arguing that fulfilling some needs will not necessarily motivate employees to perform better. Employees who are frustrated may say, "The company is just throwing money at the problem by offering me a raise and covering over the real issue," when in reality the firm needs to fix the situation, possibly by giving the employee more interesting work. Thus, extrinsic needs, such as working conditions and (sometimes) additional money, can actually de-motivate. Perhaps once people feel they are getting a reasonable salary, they would prefer improvements in an intrinsic need (such as more interesting work) rather than getting more money for a job they dislike. Recognition of these issues by international firms encouraged them to tailor their motivational systems to a much higher degree than had occurred previously.

Learned-Needs Theory

Harvard psychologist David McClelland studied school children from a very young age and followed them for many years. He found that some factors that motivate individuals are learned from childhood. Particularly, he identified three learned needs that shape their motivation: need for achievement, need for affiliation, and something not emphasized in the other major need theories—the need for power.[xiii] Each of these learned needs will be discussed in turn, with their implications for international business discussed at the end of the section.

Need for Achievement (nAch) One widely studied learned need is the need for achievement, or "nAch." People with a high nAch want to accomplish reasonably challenging goals through their own efforts. They prefer working alone rather than in teams and choose tasks with a moderate degree of difficulty—challenging but achievable. People with a high nAch typically prefer positive feedback and recognition for their successes. That positive feedback could be public recognition from the firm and peers, or it could be recognition from the boss.

McClelland argued that the need for achievement explained why some societies are able to produce more than others.[xiv] Successful entrepreneurs tend to have a high nAch, possibly because they establish challenging goals for themselves and are motivated by testing out different approaches to their goals and then meeting them. To the high nAch person, achieving by completing a task is more important than the financial reward. Corporate and team leaders should have a somewhat lower nAch because they must delegate work and build support through involvement, and thus are likely to have a higher need for power or "nPow." Morgan McCall of the Harvard Business School similarly studied individuals with high needs for achievement; he termed them corporate "high fliers."[xv] McCall found that many were not good team players, as they were motivated more by their own achievements, not the team's. These individuals did perform well in large companies where they were given considerable independence, as though they were running their own businesses. However, you may not want such an entrepreneur in a setting where significant administrative experience is needed. The understanding of nAch shapes which managers may work best in different settings. New markets such as China or Russia, when those

DOES NEED FOR ACHIEVEMENT VARY BY COUNTRY?

CULTURE

Because need for achievement (nAch) is thought to be a learned need, it may differ across cultures and countries. The United States, possibly drawing on the Protestant work ethic and a long tradition of immigration, has long been thought to inculcate high levels of nAch. Studies examined literature, such as the McDuffy Reader series, that was used to teach children in the U.S. in the 1800s and have found consistently high levels of nAch in the pages of those books. Recent studies have similarly measured higher-than-average levels of nAch in the U.S. Another study reported that nAch, as inferred from literature read primarily by preteens in the U.S., was positively related to the number of patents recorded in the U.S. between 1800 and 1950. Bradburn and Berlew similarly analyzed achievement motives in British school readers and showed a strong correlation of achievement themes with Britain's industrial growth.[xvi] Drawing on popular literature in Europe from the Middle Ages, researchers linked increases in apparent nAch to economic growth. Children's literature in China also showed a similar emphasis on encouraging achievement. The evidence is compelling: societies that encourage and reward high achievement have more entrepreneurship and higher sustained economic growth.[xvii] In contrast, societies that do not expect excellence, fail to encourage achievement, and reward idleness while failing to penalize destructive behavior, find that people tend to give them exactly what they are implicitly asking for.[xviii] Management scholars and psychologists from Maslow onward would agree this is not particularly surprising—organizations and societies do tend to get what they encourage and reward. There are still many employers, though, who continue to reward a less desired performance outcome while hoping that improved performance will somehow still occur. Research suggests that this type of hope for improvement is likely to be in vain.[xix] A central lesson in motivation is that you most often get the behavior that you reward.

countries were initially opening to investment and there were few organizational supports, would have been best served by an individual with high nAch and an entrepreneurial bent. However, as markets mature and firms grow, it may be better to put someone with administrative (and international) experience in charge. For example, if a manager has to operate a factory with large numbers of employees and deal with established relationships, a high nAch person may not be the right fit. A high need for affiliation or nAff manager may be needed in such a setting. The skills and interests behind factory management today are much different than what was needed earlier, so an individual with lower nAch fits better now.[xx]

McClelland found need achievement to be relatively common across cultures, although some societies did a better job in training its members to strive for achievement that others.[xxi] For example, in India, researchers found that entrepreneurs trained in the need for achievement performed better than those who were not trained.[xxii] Managers in New Zealand and in the United States showed similar results.[xxiii]

Need for Affiliation (nAff) Need for affiliation, or "nAff," refers to a desire for approval from others, and as a result, it means conforming to their wishes and expectations, and avoiding conflict. People with a strong nAff want to form positive relationships with others; this is much like Maslow's belongingness need and Alderfer's relatedness need. They try to build a favorable image of themselves and take steps to get others to like them. Moreover, high-nAff employees actively support others and try to smooth out conflicts that occur in meetings and other social settings. As with nAch, a key difference is that need for affiliation is learned rather than instinctive.

High-nAff employees tend to be more effective than those with a low nAff in coordinating roles, such as helping diverse departments work on joint projects. Because they are motivated more by relationships and gaining success through the group, they are typically more effective in sales positions in which the main task is cultivating long-term relationships with prospective customers. Generally, employees with high nAff prefer working with others rather than alone, tend to have better attendance records, and tend to be better at mediating conflicts.

Although people with a high nAff are more effective in many jobs requiring social interaction, they tend to be less effective at allocating scarce resources and

Michael Deleon/istockphoto.com

People with a strong nAff (need for affiliation) want to form positive relationships with others, which means they are often effective at selling and negotiating.

making other decisions that may require conflict or confrontation. For example, research has found that executives with a high nAff tend to be indecisive and are perceived as less fair in the distribution of resources. People in these decision-making positions must have a relatively low need for affiliation so that their choices and actions are not biased by a personal need for approval, but a manager may be able to use a person with high nAff by giving him or her the special role of challenging key ideas and new business plans for his or her department, sort of a devil's advocate role. Whereas the high nAff individual may not want to do this on his or her own accord, if given the official sanction, that person may be more likely to take on the task.

There is evidence that culture can encourage greater nAff values in given locations. For example, East Asian societies emphasize harmony. The Chinese have a saying that "harmony is the most valuable." The Japanese have a similar saying, as do the Koreans. This reflects the societal organization and influence of these cultures that encourage people to affiliate and create large social and work groups. The drive for group cohesiveness may override an individual's other learned needs.

The need for nAff can be seen in the way people in Chinese organizations might expect most everyone to go to lunch together. If you do not want to go to lunch with the group at 1:00 pm every day, then some people may wonder why you are upsetting the harmony of the group and its cohesiveness by not joining them. In such settings, it is commonly believed that workers who prefer not to eat with the group do not like their coworkers and are too individually minded. This can obviously be a source of frustration for someone with a low nAff, especially from a culture like that of the United States or Australia, which does not insist that people always do things together in large groups. Such an individual might wonder why his or her coworkers must always have lunch together or hang out together during non-work hours.

International firms relocating managers to a society with a high nAff must prepare that employee to understand that "work time" does not necessarily stop at the end of the day. If after-work drinks and dinner are part of the work ritual, then colleagues will expect the employee to participate. Those high-nAff colleagues will expect that the expatriate have the same nAff as they do, that is, they will project their high nAff onto others (though having read this textbook, the student should again remember that not everyone will have the same values and to avoid projection). Conversely, firms from societies that value large group activities should also realize that people from individualistic cultures may be uncomfortable in large groups and with the personal questions common in those settings. For many international firms from the West, integrating nAff individuals into their motivation-and-reward systems has been difficult. Increasingly, these firms are building sensitivity training for new expat and local managers into their culture to provide an understanding of nAff. However, efforts to deal with the issue beyond such sensitivity training have been limited.

Need for Power (nPow) Need for power, or "nPow," refers to a desire to exercise authority over people and resources. People with a high nPow are thus motivated by the opportunity to be in a position of authority. They frequently rely on persuasive communication (see Chapter 12), make more suggestions in meetings, and tend to publicly evaluate situations more frequently. Some people have a high need for personalized power. They enjoy power for its own sake and use it to advance their career and other personal interests. Power is a symbol of status and a tool to fulfill personal needs, rather than a delicate instrument to serve stakeholders. Others may have a high need for socialized power. These individuals want power as a means to help others, such as improving society or increasing organizational effectiveness.

Corporate and political leaders have a high nPow. However, McClelland argued that effective leaders should have a high need for socialized rather than personalized power. These leaders have a high degree of altruism and social responsibility and are concerned about the consequences of their actions on others. In other words, leaders must exercise their power within the framework of moral and ethical standards. The ethical guidance of their need for power results in trust and respect from employees, as well as a commitment to the manager's vision. Managers may be able to motivate someone with a high need for power by placing them in authority over some resources, such as giving a custodian responsibility for multiple floors and providing him or her some resources to get the jobs done efficiently.

Applying Learned-Needs Theory McClelland argued that achievement, affiliation, and power needs are learned rather than instinctive, and are thus inculcated by cultures and societies. Accordingly, he argued for developing training programs that strengthen these learned needs. McClelland developed an achievement-motivation program in which trainees practice writing achievement-oriented stories and engaging in achievement-oriented behaviors in business games. Trainees also complete a detailed achievement plan for the next two years and form a reference group with other trainees to maintain their new-found achievement motive style.

These programs have had some success. For example, need-achievement course participants in India subsequently started more new businesses, had greater community involvement, invested more in expanding their existing businesses, and employed twice as many people as non-participants. Similar achievement courses for North American small business owners have also reported increases in the profitability of the participants' businesses.[xxiv]

Integrating the Different Content (Needs) Related Theories One of the main points in content theories of motivation is that different people have various needs at different times. Consequently, corporate leaders should not be surprised if distributing the same reward results in different levels of need fulfillment. Rewards that motivate one person may have less effect on someone with different needs. A firm based in a South American culture with a high relational orientation may base its reward system heavily on social activities that the firm provides (e.g., employee luncheons, awards dinners, weekend activities, company retreats). If that firm were to come to a more individualistic society in North America and try to provide a similar motivation-and-reward system, the more individualistic employees in that culture would probably not be motivated by such rewards, and might actually try to avoid them. One American employee working for an Argentinean multinational organization commented, "They expect me to work all day, and then hang out with them [the Argentinean coworkers] at night also? If they want to give us some incentives to work hard, they should just give me a gift certificate for the restaurant—I'll go myself when I feel like going, or perhaps with a colleague but not with the whole department, That's just a pain." Thus, international firms need to offer a choice of rewards in different settings. Research on motivation and culture suggests that emerging economies more often have low individualism, higher uncertainty avoidance, high power distance, and a relatively low emphasis on production-orientation.[xxv] The needs of the extended family are also emphasized over individual needs in many East Asian countries, particularly in the more traditional companies. Activities, commerce, and worship center on the family and maintaining its integrity and prosperity. Businesses are often seen as a family asset and outsiders are not permitted much access to a key aspect of the family's prosperity. Under these circumstances, firms with an individualistic bent will be seen as troublesome for the family. Organizations in emerging markets are more likely to give group rewards and generally do not encourage risk taking.[xxvi] Firms may find it difficult to import a reward system relying heavily on individualism and low uncertainty avoidance to societies that value collectivism and risk avoidance.

Content theories of motivation also warn us against relying too heavily on financial rewards as a source of employee motivation. While money does motivate employees to some extent, there are other powerful sources of motivation, such as challenging assignments and interesting work, learning opportunities, some control over one's workspace and schedule, and praise from colleagues and supervisors. Such needs can be easily met by companies that understand money is not the only motivator, and that pay attention to more intrinsic forms of motivation— needs that do not cost a firm anything to meet, apart from more vigilant and mindful management.[xxvii]

PROCESS THEORIES OF MOTIVATION

Content theories explain the different needs people have in different situations, whereas process theories describe the processes through which need deficiencies are translated into behavior. Three of the most popular process-motivation theories are expectancy theory, equity theory, and goal setting. Figure 7-4 summarizes the process theories and their component parts.

Expectancy Theory

Expectancy theory is a process-motivation theory based on the idea that work effort is directed toward behaviors that people believe will lead to desired outcomes.[xxviii] Figure 7-5 summarizes the relationships in expectancy theory. As can be seen, an individual's effort level depends on three factors: effort-to-performance ($E \rightarrow P$) expectancy, performance-to-outcome ($P \rightarrow O$) expectancy, and outcome valences (V). Employee motivation is influenced by all three components of the expectancy theory model. If any component weakens, motivation weakens. Each component of the model will be examined in turn.

SEMCO: CREATIVE MOTIVATION IN BRAZIL

Once the various needs theories are understood, firms can use this knowledge to build an effective compensation system. For example, in some international settings, employees respond to pay for performance coupled with empowerment when properly implemented. Semco is a well-known Brazilian manufacturer. Its units include:

- the industrial machinery unit, now manufacturing mixing equipment
- Sembobac, a partnership with Baltimore Air Cooler, making cooling equipment
- Cushman and Wakefield SEMCO, a partnership with Rockefeller property company Cushman and Wakefield, managing properties in Brazil and Latin America
- Semco Johnson Controls, a partnership with Johnson Controls, managing large scale facilities such as airports and hospitals
- ERM, a partnership between Semco and Environmental Resources Management, one of the world's leading environmental consultants
- Semco Ventures, offering high-technology and Internet services

- SemcoHR, a human resources management firm
- Semco-RGIS, an inventory control firm

Semco has used profit sharing effectively to help build employee empowerment and engagement such that employees are interested in furthering their employer's interest. Brazilian employees have a fairly low individualism score and, as in most Latin American countries, are considered to be collectivist. This suggests that allowing a group of employees to earn a bonus and collaborate on its distribution will be effective if the nature of the job is such that work can be shared. Commented Semco president Ricardo Semler:

"Profit sharing won't motivate employees if they see it as just another management gimmick, if the company makes it difficult for them to see how their own work is related to profits and to understand how those profits are divided ... Twice a year, we calculate 23 percent of after-tax profit on each division income statement and give a check to three employees who've been elected by the workers

in their division. These three invest the money until the unit can meet and decide—by simple majority vote—what they want to do with it. In most units, that's turned out to be an equal distribution ... The guy who sweeps the floor gets just as much as the division partner.

One division chose to use the money as a fund to lend out for housing construction ... Some of [the division employees] have already received loans and have begun to build themselves houses ... Semco's experience has convinced me that profit sharing has an excellent chance of working when it crowns a broad program of employee participation, when the profit-sharing criteria are so clear and simple that the least-gifted employee can understand them, and perhaps most important, when employees have monthly access to the company vital statistics—costs, overhead, sales, payroll, taxes, profits."

Semlar, R. (1989, September–October). Managing without managers. *Harvard Business Review*, pp. 2–10.

E→P Expectancy The effort-to-performance (E→P) expectancy is an individual's perception that his or her effort will result in a particular level of performance. Expectancy is defined as a probability, and therefore ranges from 0.0 to 1.0. In some situations, employees may believe that they can unquestionably accomplish the task (a probability of 1.0). In other situations, they expect that even their highest level of effort will not result in the desired performance level (a probability of 0.0). For instance, unless you are an expert skier, you probably aren't motivated to try some of the black diamond ski runs at New Zealand's Mt. Hutt. The reason is a very low E→P expectancy. Even your best efforts will not get you down the hill feet first! In most cases, the E→P expectancy falls somewhere between these two extremes.

P→O Expectancy The performance-to-outcome (P→O) expectancy is the perceived probability that a specific behavior or performance level will lead to specific outcomes. This probability is developed from previous experience or social learning derived from watching others. For example, students learn from experience that missing classes either ruins their chance of a good grade or may have no effect at all. In extreme cases, employees may believe that accomplishing a particular task (performance) will definitely result in a particular outcome (a probability of

---

FIGURE 7-4   Process Theories of Motivation

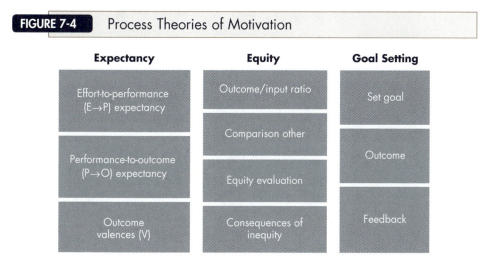

Expectancy	Equity	Goal Setting
Effort-to-performance (E→P) expectancy	Outcome/input ratio	Set goal
Performance-to-outcome (P→O) expectancy	Comparison other	Outcome
	Equity evaluation	
Outcome valences (V)	Consequences of inequity	Feedback

1.0), or they may believe that this outcome will have no effect on successful performance (a probability of 0.0). More often, the P→O expectancy falls somewhere between these two extremes.

One important issue in P→O expectancies is determining which outcomes are most important to us. We certainly don't evaluate the P→O expectancy for every possible outcome. There are too many of them. Instead, we only think about outcomes of interest to us at the time. One day, your motivation to complete a task may be fuelled mainly by the likelihood of getting off work early to meet friends. Other times, your motivation to complete the same task may be based more on the P→O expectancy of a promotion or pay increase. The point is that your motivation depends on the probability that a behavior or job performance level will result in the outcome that you anticipate.

Outcome Valences   The third element in expectancy theory is the valence of each outcome considered. **Valence** refers to one's anticipated satisfaction or dissatisfaction with an outcome. The number may range from −100 to +100 to reflect the overall value placed on the outcome: a maximum positive valence of +100 would be highly desired, while the lowest valence of −100 would be something that a person would work hard to avoid and a valence of 0 would mean no motivation at all. If you have a strong relatedness (social) need, for example, then you would value group activities and other events that help to fulfill that need. Outcomes that move you further away from fulfilling your social need, such as working from

Valence
The anticipated satisfaction or dissatisfaction that an individual feels about an outcome.

FIGURE 7-5   Expectancy Theory of Motivation

In order for workers to be motivated to perform desired behaviors at a high level . . .

Expectancy must be high. Workers must perceive that if they try hard, they can perform at a high level.

Instrumentality must be high. Workers must perceive that if they perform at a high level, they will receive certain outcomes.

Valence must be high. Workers must desire the outcomes they will receive if they perform at a high level.

Effort ⟶ Performance ⟶ Outcomes

home, will have a strong negative valence and you would work to avoid that undesirable outcome.

Notice that some outcomes directly fulfill personal needs, whereas other outcomes indirectly fulfill those needs. You might be motivated to achieve the highest sales in your company in a particular month because "it feels great." This is the direct outcome of growth-need fulfillment. At the same time, you might want to be the top salesperson because you will be mentioned in the company magazine, thereby indirectly fulfilling your social needs.

Expectancy Theory in Practice One of the appealing characteristics of expectancy theory is that it provides clear guidelines for increasing employee motivation by altering your E→P expectancies, P→O expectancies, and outcome valences. Because E→P expectancies are based on self-esteem and previous experience, employees should be given the necessary tools and competencies, clear role perceptions, and favorable situational factors to reach the desired levels of performance. This involves properly matching employees to jobs based on their abilities and their job interests, clearly communicating the tasks required for the job, and providing sufficient resources for them to accomplish those tasks.[xxix]

Even when employees have the capacity and resources to perform the work, they may have low E→P expectancies because of low self confidence. Counseling and coaching may help employees to develop confidence about the skills and knowledge they already have to perform the job. Similarly, E→P expectancies are learned, so positive feedback typically strengthens employee self confidence. Behavior modification and behavioral modeling also tend to increase E→P expectancies in many situations.

The most obvious ways to improve P→O expectancies are to measure employee performance accurately and distribute more valued rewards to those with higher job performance. Many organizations have difficulty putting this straightforward idea into practice. Some executives are reluctant to withhold bonuses for poor performance because they do not want to experience conflict with employees. Other firms fail to measure employee performance very well.

P→O expectancies are perceptions, so employees should believe that higher performance will result in higher rewards. Having a performance-based reward system is important, but this fact must be communicated. When rewards are distributed, employees should understand how their rewards have been based on past (recent) performance. More generally, companies need to regularly communicate the existence of a performance-based reward system through examples, anecdotes, and public recognition of employee performance.

Increasing outcome valences are affected by those things that are valued by employees. This brings us back to what we learned from the content theories of motivation—namely, that companies must pay attention to the needs and reward preferences of individual employees. Companies should develop more individualized reward systems so that employees who perform well are offered a choice of extrinsic rewards, including bonuses, additional vacation time, or opportunities to travel to conferences and training sessions. It is important not to neglect intrinsic motivators, such as career path and control over resources to accomplish a job, as possible reward outcomes that may be valued by the employee.

Expectancy theory also emphasizes the need to discover performance outcomes that have negative valences, thereby reducing the effectiveness of existing reward systems. For example, peer pressure may cause some employees to perform their jobs at the minimum standard even though formal rewards and the job itself otherwise motivates them to perform at higher levels.

Andrea Matone/Alamy Limited

For most employees, rewards such as bonuses, additional vacation time, and opportunities for career advancement are as important as a paycheck. Without a clear reward system, motivation and morale can suffer.

Expectancy Theory Internationally Expectancy theory offers one of the best models available for predicting work effort and motivation in different cultures. All three components of the model have received much support in past research, and there is particularly good evidence that P→O expectancies influence employee motivation. As suggested by the discussion above, in different countries employees may be motivated by much different outcome rewards. For example, in the United States, employees are more likely to have an individualistic orientation. Most Americans will have no expectations that the company should "take care of them." Thus, the outcomes are typically focused on monetary rewards. Asian firms that try to reward North American employees partly through company social activities such as lunches and dinner banquets as they would in Asia may be surprised to find that such "social rewards" are not motivating at all to many North Americans, who, on average, do not value group activities as highly as an Asian staff.

In more collectivist cultures, especially those with higher risk avoidance, employees may believe that being taken care of is an obligation of the company, and will be motivated by the offer of additional job security, perhaps in exchange for loyalty or accepting a lower salary. This used to be true in China until the economic reforms of the 1980s and 1990s dismantled the old "iron rice bowl" system that Chairman Mao and his followers promulgated after the end of the Chinese Civil War in 1949. (The **Iron Rice Bowl** was a concept that the state, through the state-owned enterprises, would meet all of the workers' needs, including food, schooling for children, healthcare, and even recreation and holiday facilities for workers.) Thus, historically Chinese workers were to give their firms (and the state) absolute loyalty in return for having their basic needs met.[4]

Similarly, Brazilians expect that an outcome of their performance will even include being helped with personal financial problems. The personnel departments of larger Brazilian firms typically provide a range of financial assistance to employees. To many Americans this may sound acceptable until they recognize that the firm will also ask a number of personal questions, including ones about home and life plans, which would seem highly intrusive to most North Americans.

Iron Rice Bowl
In China, the idea of the iron rice bowl is that the state meets all workers' needs. This means not only food, but schools for kids, hospitals, and even vacation locations for workers. These benefits were typically organized around the large state enterprises they served.

[4]This system was gradually dismantled starting with China's reforms in the late 1970s.

Brazilians accept that these questions are part of the firm's effort to make sure that employees are getting their health care and retirement plans in order.[xxx]

Equity Theory

Equity theory explains how people develop perceptions of fairness in the distribution and exchange of resources.[xxxi] As a process theory of motivation, it explains what employees are motivated to do when they feel inequitably treated. This theory is widely accepted in the media and popular culture, but research on equity theory is more cautious about its applicability. There are four main elements of equity theory: outcome/input ratio, comparison other, equity evaluation, and consequences of inequity. Each will briefly be examined in turn.

Outcome/Input Ratio The outcome/input ratio is the value of the outcomes received divided by the value of inputs provided in an exchange relationship. Inputs include skills, effort, experience, amount of time worked, performance results, and other employee contributions to the organization. Outcomes are things that employees receive from an organization in exchange for inputs, such as pay, promotions, recognition or an office with a window. Employees receive many outcomes, so it isn't always easy to determine the overall values.

For example, a major European retailer opened a number of stores in China in the 1990s, and brought a large back-office operation there in 2000 to function as a regional Asia headquarters. At that time, they brought a number of expatriate staff from Europe and paid them salaries typical for Europe, plus additional hardship pay for relocating to China. The retailer also had a number of local Chinese managers who worked in the back office in positions comparable to the Europeans. Although they received comfortable pay by Chinese standards, substantial pay inequity existed between the Chinese managers and the Europeans. Although the firm ordered individuals not to talk about salary, this instruction was ignored, and the European salaries and benefits became known. When the large wage discrepancy between employees doing essentially the same work was discovered, the Chinese managers became quite dissatisfied. This puzzled the European management, because they knew that the Chinese managers' pay was at the top of the local pay scale for employees with comparable experience and skills. Why would they expect the same money, the Europeans asked? The heart of the difficulty can be seen in equity theory—workers performing basically the same activity but receiving much lower wages.

Both inputs and outcomes are weighted by their importance to the individual. These weights vary from one person to the next. To some people, seniority is a valuable input that deserves more outcomes from the organization. Others consider job effort and performance the most important contributions in the exchange relationship, and give seniority relatively little weight. Equity theory recognizes that people value outcomes differently because they have different needs and interests. For example, it accepts that some employees want time off with pay whereas others consider this a relatively insignificant reward for job performance.

As with expectancy theory, equity theory has been criticized for being too calculative and too material-achievement focused, and as such, being mostly relevant to Anglo-American settings. For example, in some cultures, equity in outcome is seen as more important than equality in the equity outcome/input ratio. That is, in many societies some feel that employees of about the same age and experience should be paid about the same, even if there are better performers in the group. If a high-performing employee were to stand out by virtue of a higher salary, then that individual would feel embarrassed. Multinational firms have found this to be common in Japan, though it has reportedly been changing with the younger generation now entering the workforce. Historically, Japanese employees valued salaries that were relatively equal, and did not feel comfortable or particularly motivated by being paid more, even if they were productive enough to justify the higher pay. Harmony or "fitting in" with colleagues was more valued than extra pay or promotion.[xxxii] In the outer resort islands of Hawaii, typically thought of as a more relaxed culture, hotel human resources executives have reported that if they pay out bonuses and extra money for working longer hours, the employees will respond by working less, not more. The employees feel that they only need to work to earn a certain amount of money for the week and after that, they can take it easy and take the rest of the week off. Thus, even in a country like the United States there are exceptions to equity theory reliance on the output/input ratio.

Comparison Other Equity theory states that we compare our situations with a "comparison other," but the theory does not identify the comparison other. It may be another person or group of people, or even yourself in the past. It may be someone in the same job, another job, or another organization. Most of the time, we tend to compare ourselves with others who are nearby, in similar positions, and with similar backgrounds. A luxury hotel chain in East Asia needed extra hotel workers for the extended Christmas–New Year–Chinese New Year holiday season, so they brought housekeepers from a sister hotel in Vietnam to its resorts in Thailand for short-term assignments. The hotel chain provided room and board along with the wage that was standard in Vietnam, and employees received more money than they would have otherwise. However, the Vietnamese hotel workers stopped comparing themselves to hotel workers back in Vietnam, and instead compared their compensation with the Thai hotel employees in the Thai resort who were getting paid about twice as much. The result was a difficult situation in which the guest workers were very unhappy about what they thought was inequitable pay. Management was confused because they thought they were paying a nice premium to bring the Vietnamese employees over to Thailand for the holiday season. Finally, the hotel workers tried to organize a union and management consented to increase their pay by about 25 percent. The Vietnamese employees still felt underpaid compared to the locals, but they felt more motivated than before.

People in more senior positions, CEOs for example, compare themselves more with counterparts in other organizations because they may not have a direct comparison within the company. Some research suggests that employees frequently collect information on several referents to form a "generalized" comparison other. For the most part, however, the comparison other varies from one person to the next and is not easily identifiable. As the world continues to globalize the comparisons are increasingly becoming more standardized for many professionals. Those professionals who feel that an organization does not match their comparison other may now not only change employers but even change the country in which they are employed.

Equity Evaluation We form an equity evaluation after determining our own outcome/input ratio and comparing this with the comparison other's ratio. Consider the European retailer situation again. The Chinese managers felt pay inequity because they believed the European managers were receiving higher outcomes (pay) for inputs that they believed were about the same. The over-reward inequity and under-reward inequity is illustrated in Figure 7-6.

In the equity condition, the Chinese managers would believe their outcome/input ratio to be similar to the European managers. In this particular case, expatriate managers are providing the same inputs as the local Chinese managers, so they may even feel motivated to improve their performance. Or, they may just feel that they are more experienced, thus more productive and effective in their jobs.

MOTIVATION IN RUSSIAN MANUFACTURERS

While expectancy theory is popular in the individualistically minded U.S. (with low uncertainty avoidance) international application can present challenges. Americans have a "calculative involvement" in their organizations, which employees can readily understand. This helps to explain the popularity in the U.S. of expectancy theories of motivation, which see employees as generally having a high need for achievement (nAch) and being motivated by consciously expected and well-calculated outcomes. In contrast, as in many developing countries, Russia is high on Hofstede's collectivism dimension and uncertainty avoidance.

Thus, security and social belonging will be highly valued needs in Russian society, particularly given the upheavals of recent years.

An examination of Russian manufacturing managers found that employees may respond positively to motivational approaches emphasizing group benefits that reinforce the importance of team contributions. Empowerment should be done sincerely, and must be backed up by actions that reinforce mutual trust. Employees should also have access to information about the business and its performance. Information about the employees' own departments or other sub-units is particularly

necessary, as this is the level of performance that they can affect.

Thus, in a country such as Russia, motivational approaches focused on the individual are not likely to be eliminated. However, to be successful, such motivation efforts should be tied to development and mastery of work-related skills. As with many developing countries, excellent educational opportunities that will be prized by the employees include overseas training.

Elenkov, D.S. (1998, Summer). Can American management concepts work in Russia? A cross-cultural comparative study. *California Management Review*, 40(4), 133–156.

The Chinese managers would feel inequity and ask for redress, or they would threaten to leave the field (quit) during the Chinese New Year season in January or February.

The equity theory model recognizes that an individual makes more complex equity evaluations when he or she and the comparison other have different outcomes and inputs. By comparing outcome/input ratios, the model states that equity occurs when the amount of inputs and outcomes are proportional. They do not necessarily have the same amount. For instance, we feel equitably treated when we work harder than the comparison other and receive proportionally higher rewards as a result.

FIGURE 7-6 Over-reward versus Under-reward Inequity

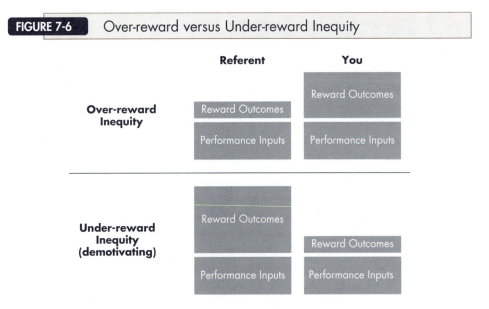

Consequences of Inequity The outcome of the evaluation that inequity exists is that employees will be motivated to take some action. This was seen in the prior example when the Chinese managers tried to reduce the perceived inequity by putting pressure on the European retail firm to increase their pay. There are five possible categories of actions that can be taken to reduce feelings of inequity.

Changing Inputs. Under-rewarded workers tend to reduce their effort and performance if these outcomes don't affect their salary and compensation. Overpaid workers sometimes increase their inputs by working harder and producing more. This effort to increase inputs is similar to the efficiency–wage hypothesis from Nobel Laureate Kenneth Arrow, who theorized that people who knew they were getting paid more than the going market rate would work harder to try to justify that additional pay.[xxxiii]

Changing Outcomes. Employees who feel they are in an under-rewarded situation might ask for more money to resolve the inequity. If they do not receive the pay raise they may take actions that change the perceived outcomes. For example, these employees may call in sick frequently, steal supplies, or misappropriate company money or facilities. Each of these outcomes provides more benefits to the employees. Outcomes change can also come from some action that hurts or harms a firm; such actions provide a psychological benefit to the employee. This situation is seen in the information technology industry when software engineers insert malicious lines of code into applications, or even bring codes home with them and withhold them from the company if they are unhappy. Numerous computer security incidents in Singapore, for example, were traced to employees who felt they were under compensated by their employers.[xxxiv]

Changing Perceptions. In an inequity situation that the employee cannot (or prefers not to) change, he or she may feel it necessary to distort inputs and outcomes to restore perceived equity. This is most common in an overpayment situation. Employees who believe they are overpaid may try to convince others that they are worth the money. They do this by emphasizing perceived inputs such as seniority, training, knowledge, teamwork, contribution, and so forth. In more extreme cases, they may try to take credit for their colleagues' or subordinates' work to boost their perceived contribution. In more hierarchical organizations, this problem of supervisors improperly taking credit for employee actions is something that managers must watch for carefully. It is important for managers not to isolate themselves and to stay in touch with employees throughout the reporting hierarchy.

Leaving the Field. Some people try to reduce inequity by getting away from the inequitable situation. Equity theory thus explains some instances of employee turnover and job transfer. For example, employee turnover in many large retail operations in Europe can be quite high, sometimes over 200 percent, and inequity is often credited by the individuals who leave.

Changing the Referent. If an employee who is feeling inequity cannot seem to alter the outcome/input ratio, he or she might justify the inequity by replacing the referent with someone having a more comparable outcome/input ratio. As was mentioned earlier, people sometimes rely on a generalized referent, so changing the referent to protect one's sense of self esteem is easy and common in the absence of other avenues to right the inequity. This outcome is particularly attractive to international firms. This approach can be used by firms as they help employees to establish what potential referents are obtaining. For example, the rapid economic growth of China has been generated in part through employees' willingness to work for 80 cents per hour, but that same, economic growth has now begun to push wages higher, particularly in South China. The government's control of information and media often results in widespread misperceptions of what wages and benefits other workers are receiving. To overcome misinformation, many firms in South China today are increasingly open about what they are paying and how their pay compares to other firms and industry averages. Firms are seeking to establish a more accurate referent point and comparison for the employee salaries.

Ethics and Equity Workplace inequity extends beyond employee motivation to the organization's ethical conduct. It particularly relates to the rule of distributive justice mentioned in Chapter 1. **Distributive justice** asserts that inequality is all right if employees have fair access to resources and opportunity in the firm so that any inequality is the result of effort. Thus, inequalities are ultimately in the best interest of the firm and its employees; talented workers are rewarded commensurate with their work and ability to improve the lot of the firm's stakeholders. Employees in difficult or more risky jobs could be expected to be paid more under distributive justice.

Applying the distributive justice rule is challenging because it is difficult to determine how far "the least well off" benefit is from those who receive higher rewards. Consider what former General Electric CEO Jack Welsh earned. GE rewarded Welsh with a $9 million annual pension, not to mention a number of other perks including a $15 million apartment. He was also given the use of a GE corporate jet and other company resources. Many critics felt Welsh's employment contract was overly lavish when it finally was made public during his divorce proceedings in 2002. (Welsh agreed to give up some of his benefits after they were made public.)

If Welsh had not stepped in as CEO, it is quite likely that GE would not have done as well as it did. The world of business also learned a lot from GE about restructuring and selecting and training top management. Welch is credited with boosting GE's market capitalization from $13.9 billion in 1981 to an estimated $490 billion by 2001—an increase of $476.1 billion. He and many other CEOs have argued that with market cap increases in the tens or hundreds of billions of dollars, giving a CEO a few hundred-million dollars is no big deal. However, it is important to remember that Jack Welsh did not do it all on his own; there are 300,000 employees at GE and decades of history that played a role in creating GE's market capitalization. GE has had a string of fine leaders over the twentieth century dating back to inventor Thomas Edison himself. Thus, the issue of whether Welsh's pension and other perks are unethical or otherwise problematic likely depends on a person's view of distributive justice.

Perceptions of equity change not only with the country and culture, but also with the times. As the world increasingly is open to more market opportunities, equity comparisons that account more fully for someone's productive input (and not just their salary) may become more accepted.[xxxv]

International Perspectives and Equity We've stressed how managers must be wary of projecting their views and values onto others. It cannot be assumed that everyone shares the same interpretation of equity or that people will get upset if someone is earning more money. Individuals vary in their equity sensitivity—that is, our outcome/input preferences and reaction to various outcome/input ratios. A simple test to determine your own equity sensitivity is at the end of this chapter (see In-class Exercises #1).

At one end of the equity sensitivity scale are the "Entitleds." The Entitleds feel comfortable in situations in which they receive proportionately more than others. Entitleds know how much everyone else is making, or want to find out. They are highly sensitive to anything they perceive as inequitable, and will regularly talk

Distributive justice
Asserts that inequality is acceptable if employees have fair access to resources and opportunities such that they recognize any inequality to be the result of their own effort and not because of favoritism by management.

MOTIVATION IN CHINA

At nine o'clock in the morning, a leadership and motivation workshop begins as Shanghai executives from one of mainland China's biggest computer firms start wrestling with a list of progressive management theories. Ten minutes later, a harried senior executive shuffles in. "Stop everything," someone shouts. The 60 participants are ordered to stand up and hold a minute's silence to focus their collective corporate thoughts on the error of the colleague that came in late. The offender—who is in China's top one per cent of earners—bows his head and walks to a corner of the room for his 10-minute dose of shame, while his colleagues go back to discussing the managerial benefits of lateral thinking over parallel thinking.

Such humiliation is common in Chinese companies for errors in performance. For example, other companies will make employees stand for five minutes, holding their mobile phone aloft if the offending article has rung during a meeting. It is humiliating—but humiliation is a particularly effective motivator in China, human resource managers say, and has long precedent in Chinese commercial culture over the past two centuries, although it runs counter to a lot of modern thinking both in China and the West.[xxxvi]

Many individuals not familiar with modern China will point to writers like Confucius to argue that managers in China practice a polite managerial method that focuses on saving face. However, modern China draws more on criticism and self-criticism as developed by Mao Zedong than from Confucius' teachings. Chinese society has transformed radically in recent years, but many managerial behaviors still relate to actions, such as the criticism sessions, organized by the Communists during Mao's reign.

For example, many Chinese universities still post notices on bulletin boards about students who are in breach of campus rules. Some universities will make violators address student gatherings to publicly denounce their own behavior and spell out their reformed ways. Dunce caps are foisted on underachievers in some primary schools, while in others, teachers make the children vote each week for the worst student in class. Staffs from restaurants, beauty salons, and department stores, among other enterprises, are typically made to line up every day outside the premises for a military-style drill. Model employees are commended and those who are thought to have let the team down are loudly chastised.

Recently, outside one of the many high-priced restaurants in Beijing, a young waitress trembled as her manager screamed at her for spilling something the previous evening. The young lady, who probably earns about 20 Yuan (U.S.$2.30) per day was near tears as her 40-odd colleagues and dozens of people waiting at a bus stop looked on. "She won't be spilling anything today," one onlooker said, nodding in approval.

While the leaders of many mainland (Chinese) companies dislike this approach, many others still use public humiliation because it is often perceived as having a more immediate impact than subtle methods of motivating staff. A human resources manager with a leading mainland domestic appliance firm said the firm had dabbled with the idea of introducing more sophisticated motivating techniques, but decided it was more effective to use its own version of the carrot-and-stick approach. "We don't dangle anything," she said. "We hit them with both the stick and the carrot."

Goff, P. (2003, April 21). Ritual humiliation. *South China Morning Post* (Hong Kong), p. 11.

about people who did not do anything for them, or organizations that mistreat them. Entitleds might accept having the same outcome/input ratio as others, but would prefer to receive more than others performing the same work. Or they may try very hard to work less while still getting paid—in fact they may spend all their time working less, or scheming to work less while maintaining their income. Those who have read the Pulitzer Prize–winning novel *The Good Earth* by Pearl S. Buck about village life in China in the early part of the twentieth century will recognize the Entitled character of the lazy uncle.[xxxvii] He spent most of his time pretending to work or saying that he was going off to work but seldom did, and somehow he ended up well off at the end of the story. For most of the book, the lazy uncle was the happiest character in the novel. Entitleds often talk about what other people get in terms of salary and benefits and whether they are worth it. They often feel that they are unappreciated and underpaid and are willing to share their feelings. Entitleds judge others on what they do for them.

At the other end of the scale are the "Benevolents." Benevolents are tolerant of situations in which they are under-rewarded. They might still prefer equal outcome/input ratios, but do not mind if others receive more than they do for the same inputs as long as they feel fairly treated. They usually like to see an equal workload, but are more accepting of unequal compensation. Benevolents rarely talk about what others are earning and about who "owes them." This group will be concerned about Entitleds who are not doing their fair share of work and seem to be getting a free ride, but they are not demotivated by inequity situations.

Somewhat in the middle is the third group—the "Equity Sensitives." Equity Sensitives want their outcome/input ratio to be equal to the outcome/input ratio of the referent other, and even small differences can create emotional tension and demotivation for them. Like Entitleds, they get upset and demotivated if they discover the comparison person is earning more money than they do. But unlike Entitleds, Equity Sensitives generally do not scheme to get out of work and get by with minimal input.

A company's motivation and reward system needs to account for such differences in people by checking the system, not just for pay equity but for a reasonable balance of workload and other inputs, as well as outcomes. Managers in particular need to identify Entitleds and let them know they are appreciated and that steps are being taken to reward them properly.

Are Entitleds, Equity Sensitives, and Benevolents equally spread around the world? Because equity sensitivity may be based partly on personality, it is possible that different equity-sensitivity behavior is as well distributed around the world as different personality types. However, these differences in distribution are likely due to differences in cultural values. For example, workers in China demonstrate a Benevolent equity orientation when they compare their salaries to what they earned before rather than to what others earn. This may be because of the strong collectivist and high power distance cultural values present in China.[xxxviii] Although there is a test instrument to assess where employees stand on this equity scale, you can easily determine this by listening to people talk about salaries and compensation, or their acceptance of workload, agreeableness toward taking on new tasks, or volunteering for work. Equity sensitivity usually is very evident, and managers need to pay attention to this and emphasize fairness for Equity Sensitives and growth opportunities for Benevolents who may want to work hard in order to learn.

Equity theory has received support in research and practice. Organizational behavior researchers have applied the equity theory model to explain why professional baseball players change teams, why employees steal from their employer, and why people become hostile at work. One of the clearest lessons from equity theory is that we need to continually treat people fairly in the distribution of organizational rewards. Recent research has shown that companies maintaining a reasonably equitable pay environment such that the top paid employee (such as the CEO) does not earn more than 50 times the lowest paid full-time employee outperform companies with more inequitable compensation.[xxxix]

Maintaining feelings of equity is not an easy task. For example, two large surveys, one in Australia and the other in the U.S., reported that about half of all employees feel underpaid. This was true even for over a third of those earning more than $100,000 annually. Major league baseball players in the U.S. reported feeling underpaid and unwanted even when earning millions of dollars per year.[xl] Why do so many people feel this inequity? One reason, as we discussed above, is that people have different levels of equity sensitivity, so they may react differently to the same situation. Some people (Benevolents) are generally content to compare themselves with themselves, so if they are doing better this year than last year, they will generally be motivated—at least inequity perceptions will not be a problem for them in this case. Others (Entitleds) are regularly talking about what everyone else earns, and how this or that company exploits its employees and customers. Employees also have differing opinions about which inputs should be rewarded; should age and seniority be rewarded, employee needs, competencies and skills, or pure performance output? Which outcomes are more valuable than others is another factor to consider in developing a motivation-reward system.

ESTONIAN PAY DISCRIMINATION

Estonia is a small Baltic nation that was formerly part of the Soviet Union. It is located across the Gulf of Finland from Finland. Estonia has done very well since its transition from communism. The Estonian and Finnish languages are very close to each other, and there was an easy and relatively quick movement of Finns into Estonia seeking low-cost highly trained individuals. Estonia has a strong technological foundation and is the home of the founders of Skype, which allows phone calls over the Internet. Estonia has also been blessed with good elected officials who have avoided the corruption that has typified so many transitional economies as they move from communism. The Estonian leaders have also been very innovative, with the nation being one of the first in the world to employ a flat tax where all people pay the same percentage on their income.

Estonia is unique in that approximately 40 percent of its population is ethnically Russian and not Estonian. Since Estonia achieved independence from the Soviet Union, there have been some difficulties in the treatment of the ethnic Russian minority. In general, Estonians feel great hostility to Russia and believe their country was forcefully incorporated into the repressive Soviet Union. As a result, after gaining statehood, Estonia quickly established the need to speak fluent Estonian as a requirement for citizenship, and a large number of individuals whose families lived in Estonia for many years are now officially stateless. This has made travel particularly hard. The official and only language used in schools is Estonian, and discrimination and the overall hostility to Russians has led to several instances of rioting by ethnic Russians.

Research shows that, while at the time of independence there was no discrimination in pay, ethnic Russians, even if they are fluent in Estonian, now receive substantially less pay than ethnic Estonians. The difficulty for international firms who move to Estonia is how to respond to this discrimination. Local Estonians expect to make more than ethnic Russians, so issues of expectancy and equity come into play. But if the firm supports such discrimination, is it acting ethically?

Kroncke, C., & Smith, K. (1999). The wage effects of ethnicity in Estonia. *Economics of Transition* 7(1), 179–199.

ETHICS

It will be difficult to please all types of employees, but firms have to try to regularly check systems for equity, and then tell their employees that they are doing this. Overall, trying to maintain feelings of equity in the workplace will probably always be challenging, but firms must be proactive about it.

Goal Setting

Another major process theory of motivation is the theory of goal setting. Edwin Locke, Gary Latham, and colleagues have done a great deal of work over the years on the importance of goal setting for motivation and performance. Organizations have discovered that goals can yield very effective results and prevent issues of demoralization. Vague statements such as "Do your best" or "Our work is really an art and not a science so we cannot have goals" have been shown by goal-setting research to be unhelpful—goals can be applied for most endeavors, including sports and education and even less-structured activities like research and development.[xli] Goals are identified by setting customer satisfaction objectives or improvements on other key measures, such as a reduction in crime rates for a police force or on-time performance and improved fuel usage for a city bus company.[xlii] Research has shown that organizations that set goals can enjoy higher performance from their employees. Goals are the immediate or ultimate objectives that employees are trying to accomplish from their work effort. Goal setting is the process of motivating employees and clarifying their role perceptions by establishing performance objectives. Goal setting potentially improves employee performance in two ways: first by adding to the intensity and persistence of effort, and then by giving employees clearer roles so that their effort can be directed toward behavior that will improve task performance.

Goal Setting in Practice Internationally Goals must have a measurable outcome and a time or date to determine if that goal has been reached. Failing to set a goal means that the considerable motivational potential of the goal setting will be lost.

Vague statements such as "Do your best" are not really goals and are worthless in motivational and performance terms. Instead, behavioral scholars have identified six conditions to maximize task effort and performance: specific goals, relevant goals, challenging goals, goal commitment, participation in goal formation (sometimes), and goal feedback. Additionally and perhaps most importantly, goals must be made *public*. That means for your goal to increase your motivation and ultimately your performance, you must be specific about the goal and the date by which you will accomplish it, and you must tell someone about it. Secretly set goals have little or no motivational or performance value. Employees put more effort into a task when they work toward specific goals rather than amorphous targets. Specific goals have measurable levels of change over a specific time, such as, "Reduce the defect rate by five percent over the next six months." Specific goals communicate more precise performance expectations, so employees can direct their effort more efficiently and reliably.

Many companies apply goal setting through a formal process known as management by objectives (MBO). There are a few variations of MBO programs, but they generally identify organizational objectives and goals. These goals then move down through the organization with each level determining what is necessary to achieve the larger goal. So, if a firm has decided to expand revenue by 10 percent, there must be a wide range of changes in behavior by various departments, from marketing to production. For the actual sales force, expanding revenue by 10 percent means that they will need to expand the number of cold calls, which are calls made to potential customers without a prior appointment. So one of the goals for the sales force may be to make 20 percent more cold calls this quarter. This goal will be discussed with each employee and at the end of the quarter, the employee's performance will be judged based on that goal. Although MBO has been criticized for creating too much paperwork, it has been effective and is widely applied in business—both domestic-only and international—and is consistent with the empirical evidence on goal setting.

Employees report higher levels of motivation and usually perform better when they have set difficult but achievable goals. Challenging goals also fulfill a person's self-actualization and other intrinsic needs associated with self-efficacy and achievement satisfaction. When employees set their own goals, rather than having the company set goals for them, goals tend to be set somewhat higher. Self-set goals also have the effect of increasing employees' acceptance of the goal. Yet there are limits to difficult goals, if the goals become so difficult that employees no longer have the ability or tools to reach them. Consistent also with the predictions of expectancy theory, effort and measurable performance on the task falls significantly, as shown in Figure 7-7. The optimal range of goal difficulty is one in which the employee perceives a goal to be difficult, but achievable, and the believes that a strategy can be crafted to achieve that goal. Leaders in the organization have a key role to play in showing a path by which employees have some control over their work and can both achieve a goal and benefit from its achievement.

Goals must also be relevant to an individual's job and within his or her control. Telling an employee to work harder without a clear and achievable goal, relevant feedback, and a path to that goal will not motivate him or her and is likely to be confusing. Employees also should be involved in the goal-setting process. Participation in goal formation tends to increase commitment because employees take ownership of the goals, compared to those that are merely assigned by supervisors. In fact, today's employees increasingly expect to be involved in goal setting and other decisions that affect them. Participation may also improve goal quality, because employees have valuable information and knowledge that may not be known to those who initially formulated the goal. Thus, participation ensures that employees buy into the goals and have the competencies and resources necessary to accomplish them. Some managers believe that such participation is not expected

FIGURE 7-7   Effect of Goal Difficulty on Performance

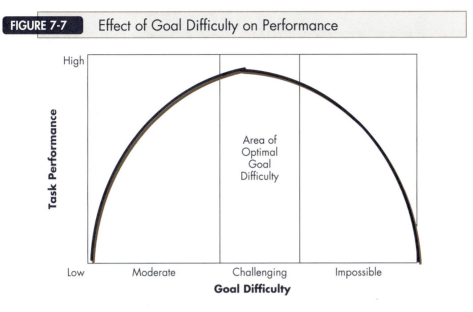

in their region of the world, and managers from China to Latin America report that generating such participation takes time to develop. However, employees ultimately want to participate in goal setting.

Feedback is another necessary condition for effective goal setting. In particular, experts emphasize that effective goal setting requires measurable feedback that matches the specific metrics of the goal. As discussed in Chapter 2, feedback is a powerful source of learning. In terms of goal setting, feedback lets us know whether we have achieved the goal or are properly directing our efforts toward it. Feedback is also a vital ingredient in motivation because employees need confirmation of their actions and goals and affirmation that they are doing a good job, as well as some censure if something needs to improve in their actions and performance.

Limitations   Goal setting has a few limitations. One problem is that when goals are tied to monetary incentives, many employees may try to "game the system" by selecting easy goals, or negotiating performance goals that are already near completion. Employees with high self-efficacy, self-esteem, and need for achievement tend to set challenging goals whether or not they are financially rewarded for their results, while individuals who are lower on those scales are less likely to set high goals for themselves. Employers must balance these considerations in setting up a reward-and-evaluation system. Similarly, management needs to implement checks and balances on employee goals and behavior. For instance, if there are performance goals for production workers with no controls on the quality of what they produce, some employees may rush so they can produce more and be rewarded accordingly. But this will lead to higher levels of defects and product nonconformance, more material wastage, and an increased need for quality control checking and product reworking with all the incumbent costs. So quality control and teamwork goals need to be implemented along with production goals to minimize quality problems.

Another limitation is that goal setting cannot be applied to every performance dimension of every task. We can usually find some measurable goals, but many other dimensions of job performance are difficult to measure and have complex and long-term outcomes. The result is that goal setting potentially focuses employees on a narrow subset of short-term performance indicators. The saying "What gets measured, gets done" usually proves accurate. Thus, organizations must be

NORTH AMERICAN RETAILER: DISCOVERING THE POWER OF SHAME

Goal setting in North America can be a straightforward process and very successful. But as firms move internationally they may need to consider a richer set of motivations than commonly used in North America to be successful. One North American firm, one of the world's largest retailers, opened its first store in China in the late 1980s. Although it was a global firm, it was slow to enter the rapidly growing Chinese market for fear that it would have difficulty understanding the market. A year after entering the market, the firm found that the customers were not that hard to understand. The problem lay with understanding the local workforce and the rules they should impose on it. For example, the retailer was used to trusting employees and giving them a second chance if they were caught stealing. If an employee was caught a second time, only then would the retailer fire the employee and refer the matter to the local police. But the firm was warned by their local managers that this approach would not work in China, where retailers must be stricter and have zero tolerance for stealing. Local managers also suggested firing the employees and allowing shame to do the rest, but the retailer chose to stick to its global policy.

Not long after the retailer opened one of its first stores in China, the store's general manager discovered that a local employee had stolen several small electronics goods. The general manager decided to follow the firm's procedures and give the employee his warning, in spite of protests from the local manager, who argued that the employee should be fired at once. Afterward, the general manager asked that the employee be watched carefully. A few weeks later, the general manager learned that the same employee had once again stolen several more items. He decided to follow procedure, fired the employee, and referred the case to the local police. The police arrested the employee and held him without trial for several weeks. Later, the general manager learned that the employee had received a twelve-year jail sentence, which seemed harsh for petty theft. After that and several other theft incidents, the retailer tightened its security and procedures considerably, and changed to a policy of immediately discharging any employee caught stealing anything, even office supplies. It also changed its global policy by deciding not to notify police about a theft unless it was particularly serious. "Firing an employee and making the reason public is punishment enough; potentially wayward employees get the message quickly, and we have not had any major incidents in quite a while," the general manager said. "Anyway, the threat of several years' imprisonment is always there, though we'd rather not resort to that."

careful in setting goals and measuring employee output. Apart from such concerns, goal setting brings a wealth of well-tested evidence and tools to managers. It is widely supported by research and is generally successful in practice. Goal setting involves measurement of the task, an agreed outcome, and a goal for improving performance.

EMPLOYEE INTERESTS

Recall from the earlier discussion that performance is closely related to motivation, which itself is based on ability, values, and life interests. Life interests indicate whether an employee is likely to be interested in doing the job. Thus, motivation also concerns an employee and what they as individuals like to do. Timothy Butler and James Waldroop at Harvard University identify eight life interests (also called "job interests") that motivate when they fit with an employee's particular bent to do certain tasks.[xliii] For example, some people may like managing others (similar to McClelland's high nAff people). They would do better and be self-motivated (intrinsically motivated) to work on tasks associated with people management, but might not fare well in a job that required them to stare at a computer monitor for eight hours a day, even if they were good at it. Others may enjoy working with numbers or working with technology and would be intrinsically motivated to do that job. Butler and Waldroop give a list of job interests in Figure 7-8, and tasks and vocations that might fit people based on these interests are shown in Figure 7-9. Butler and Waldroop have developed a job-interest inventory that can be viewed at www.careerdiscovery.com, where people can discover their job

---

FIGURE 7-8 The Big 8 "Life Interests"

1. **Application of Technology** – People with these interests are curious about finding better ways to use technology to solve business problems.

2. **Quantitative Analysis** – Good at running the numbers; they see math as the best, and sometimes the only, way to figure out business solutions. Also see math as fun when others consider it very hard work.

3. **Theory Development and Conceptual Thinking** – People with this interest can be excited by building business models that explain competition within a given industry or by analyzing the competitive position of a business within a particular market.

4. **Creative Production** – Some people always enjoy the beginning of projects the most, when there are many unknowns and they can make something out of nothing. These individuals are frequently seen as imaginative, out-of-the-box thinkers. They seem most engaged when they are brainstorming or inventing unconventional solutions.

5. **Counseling and Mentoring** – Some people really enjoy teaching. In business, this is coaching or mentoring. These individuals are driven by the life interest of counseling and mentoring—guiding employees, peers, and clients to better performance.

6. **Managing People and Relationships** – Counseling and mentoring is a bit different from managing. Individuals with the managing life interest enjoy dealing with people on a day-to-day basis, but they focus much more on outcomes than do people in the counseling-and-mentoring category.

7. **Enterprise Control** – Such individuals seem happiest when running projects or teams; they enjoy "owning" a transaction such as a trade or a sale. These individuals also tend to ask for as much responsibility as possible in any work situation.

8. **Influence through Language and Ideas** – People in this category sometimes feel drawn to careers in public relations or advertising where they can write or communicate regularly. Sales, consulting and political/policy or even education careers are also common.

---

interests, what tasks may be most interesting to them, and why their current job may not be motivating them, irrespective of the money it pays. Bosses may find they can *add a task* to a job (such as creative production or influence through language and ideas—that is, a sales or corporate communications function) that fits with an employee's job interests. That new task will motivate the employee to work simply because of his or her interest in the task, even if there is no extra money for doing it. Of course the company must be careful not to overload hard-working employees and should try to take away tasks that those employees do not value.

For example, if you are an accountant, but have an interest in influencing through language and ideas, you may be interested in speaking publicly about the company and its work. That might mean helping in corporate communications, or sales and customer support. It may also mean traveling to university campuses to speak to classes, teaching a seminar, or participating in campus recruiting. Butler and Waldroop's work suggests that employee motivation largely depends on their being interested in their jobs. What employees want is something that firms, no matter in what nation they are operating, must determine.

SUMMARY

One of the main implications of content motivation theories is that different people have different needs at different times. That implies that to motivate employees (or anyone else, for that matter) we need to learn what their needs are. Some employees, particularly younger employees, are motivated by more money. Yet others may be reasonably satisfied with their current salaries and would like more interesting work or an opportunity to influence decisions in their organization.[xliv] Need theories remind us not to rely too heavily on financial rewards as a source of employee motivation. Although some scholars argue that content motivation theories are culture-bound, the evidence so far suggests otherwise. Process theories provide a unique perspective of employee motivation. Each looks at different variables in the workplace and the minds of employees. As a new generation of employees enters the workplace and as globalization creates a

| FIGURE 7-9 | Twelve Pairs of Life Interests & Possible Job Matches |

1. **Enterprise Control and Managing People:**
   CEOs, presidents, division managers, and general managers who enjoy both strategy and the operational aspects of the position – the CEO who enjoys playing the COO role as well.

2. **Enterprise Control and Quantitative Analysis:**
   Investment bankers, other financial professionals who enjoy deal making, partners in Big Six firms, top-level executives in commercial and investment banks, investment managers.

3. **Application of Technology and Quantitative Analysis:**
   Individual contributors who have a strong interest in engineering analysis (systems analysts, tech consultants, process consultants); production and operations managers.

4. **Creative Production and Influence through Language and Ideas:**
   Advertising executives, brand managers, corporate trainers, salespeople, public relations specialists; people in the fashion, entertainment, and media industries.

5. **Counseling and Mentoring and Managing People:**
   Human-resources managers, managers who enjoy coaching and developing the people reporting to them, managers in nonprofit organizations with an altruistic mission.

6. **Enterprise Control and Influence through Language and Ideas:**
   Executives (CEOs, presidents, general managers) whose leadership style relies on persuasion and consensus building; marketing managers, salespeople.

7. **Application of Technology and Enterprise Control:**
   Managers and senior executives in high technology, telecommunications, biotech, information systems (internally or consulting), and other engineering-related fields.

8. **Theory Development and Quantitative Analysis:**
   Economic-model builders, quantitative analysts, "knowledge base" consultants, market forecasters, business professors.

9. **Creative Production and Enterprise Control:**
   Solo entrepreneurs, senior executives in industries where the product or service is of a creative nature (fashion, entertainment, advertising, media).

10. **Creative Production and Managing People:**
    Entrepreneurs who partner with a professional manager, short-term project managers, new-product developers, advertising "creatives"; individual contributors in fashion, entertainment, and media.

11. **Quantitative Analysis with Managing People and Relationships:**
    These individual like finance, yet they also enjoy managing people toward goals. Often enjoy corporate finance over investment banking and sometimes venture capital, although less than the Quantitative-Theory life interest combination.

12. **Application of Technology with Managing People and Relationships:**
    This is the engineer, computer scientist, or other technically oriented individual who enjoys leading a team, particularly long-running efforts as opposed to temporary project management.

Source: Adapted from Butler, T., & Waldroop, J. (1996). *Discovering Your Career In Business*. New York: Basic Books.

more diverse workforce, companies need to examine their motivational practices and check their systems for equity. Pulling these various theories together, an international firm can help to tailor its specific motivation system for a worldwide organization. Meeting employee needs, setting useful goals, and providing employees with work they find interesting and rewarding can all help to create a very motivated workforce, and many of these actions do not require any additional investment. Firms have the tools to motivate employees if care is taken to understand what workers want (see Take-Home Exercise #2).

MANAGERIAL GUIDELINES

1. Recognize employees' individual needs and job interests. Remember that most people, managers included, have an *extrinsic bias* when evaluating others' needs and values while failing to recognize their intrinsic motivators, such as job involvement and autonomy.

2. Give goals and clear feedback to employees.
3. Allow employees to participate in decisions that affect them by letting them set their own goals and exercise ownership over their jobs by giving them tasks they want to do, and provide stock purchase options where possible.
4. Link rewards and performance (*expectancy*).
5. Check the system for equity. Some people are more sensitive to equity problems than others, so managers need to be sure these people feel they are treated equally. Some employees want to see a clear path to promotion; others are motivated by the opportunity to do new things. Each person can be highly motivated if management pays attention to different needs.
6. Improve communication. Most employees like ongoing communication with management and even higher-level employees must keep their bosses informed.
7. Set worthwhile goals. Employees respond well to goals, as well as to job feedback. Public goals and objectives (and small rewards for meeting them) motivate.
8. Facilitate interesting work. Much research on employee satisfaction and performance in recent years has emphasized that employees want interesting work they can understand.
9. Communicate the firm's mission. Excellent leaders motivate by communicating the mission clearly and telling employees the truth about challenges facing the organization.
10. Find out life interests of each employee. Try to put people in jobs or give them tasks that match their life interests.[xxxiv]
11. On an ongoing basis, look carefully at the extrinsic motivators you have at your disposal and use your knowledge of your team's values and interests.
12. Motivation can differ with culture and situation.
13. Poorly delivered criticism can be demotivating and significantly harm performance.
14. Link firm mission with motivation system.
15. The motivation or reward system needs to fit the job type.

Table 7-1 is useful to students and practitioners as they seek to analyze how motivation may vary in different areas of the world.

TABLE 7-1   Motivation around the World

Topic	Evidence
Motivation and money	Money is definitely a useful motivator. Most people want to make pretty good money, and some people are really motivated to make a lot of money. But if someone's monetary needs are fairly fulfilled, giving him or her the opportunity to earn more money may not work well, and may even hurt that person's motivation ("This company just likes to throw money at problems instead of addressing the real issues I have."). It is important to consider the employee's interests.
Regions where money may be more important than the average place in motivating	Money is important everywhere. But people in a high-masculine or production orientation culture may be more motivated by money than those who are not. For example, it is a good bet that people in Hong Kong will be motivated by the opportunity to earn more money. They'll work overtime or take on extra work. But people in a slower-moving place, such as Hawaii, may be more likely to figure out how much money they need and leave it at that. On average, they would be less likely to be motivated to accept extra work just to make a few more dollars.

TABLE 7-1   (Continued)

Topic	Evidence
Misunderstanding employee needs and demotivation	Correctly understanding employee needs is crucial to motivation. Managers will find that motivating people is difficult if they offer things that employees do not want. For example, not all people are motivated by fulfilling social needs, because they simply do not think it is necessary to meet social needs through work. When a company expends efforts on social activities for its employees, it should be sure that employees actually want and value this; if they do not, it will be a complete waste of money. Managers who value social activities themselves (possibly because they are from cultures with a high feminine or relational-value score) may be surprised that employees from other countries (that may have a higher masculine or production orientation score) don't share their enthusiasm for social activities. Managers shouldn't be surprised if employees do not want to participate in company activities.
Motivation across cultures	Sometimes managers find that employees will work hard without more money or any other extrinsic motivators, based on the theory of job interests (or life interests).[xl] A manager may discover that an employee will be willing to take on extra or new tasks simply because he or she enjoys them.
Going against culture	Companies must introduce motivation systems into a foreign location carefully. A slow introduction that allows employees to opt in at their own pace might be a good approach. If successful, the motivation system can then be made available to more employees. Offering employees a choice of gifts in a reward system is generally welcomed.

CULTURE AND DOING BUSINESS IN SOUTH AFRICA

South Africa is the richest nation in Africa. Its 44 million citizens have a per capita GDP of $11,000, and its stock market is one of the 10 largest in the world. South Africa is an ethnically diverse country. Widely diverse African tribes lived in the region when Dutch settlers began extensively settling it in 1652. The British seized the Cape of Good Hope area in 1806 and as a result, many of the Dutch settlers (called the Boers) went further north to establish their own republics. The Boers were finally defeated in the Boer War (1899–1902). The resulting Union of South Africa operated under a policy of apartheid, the separate development of the races. The 1990s brought an end to apartheid politically and ushered in black-majority rule.

Today South Africa has a wide diversity in its ethnic makeup. However, the country is best seen as a country with distinct ethnic groups rather than an integrated ethnic society, such as the U.S. or the United Kingdom. As a result, doing business in South Africa will vary depending on which ethnic group you are conducting business with. Individuals of British heritage tend to be quite reserved, while, those of a Boer background are quite blunt and forward. The native African business people typically have a background in the revolution movement that sought to overthrow the white-only rule. They often have far greater international experience than South African whites, because they were often forced into exile during the revolution. However, their international experience was often with the former communist nations of China and Russia that were supportive of the South Africans' effort to overturn white-only rule when most Western governments were not.

Networks of business people are particularly important in South Africa, although each of the three ethnic groups—the British, the Boers, and the native African business people—will have their own networks. Good educational backgrounds are valued by all the different parties.

ADDITIONAL RESOURCES

Butler, T. (2007). *Getting Unstuck: How Dead Ends Become New Paths*. Boston: Harvard Business School Press.

Wilson, T.B. (2002). *Innovative Reward Systems for the Changing Workplace* (2nd ed.). New York: McGraw-Hill.

Waldroop, J., & Butler, T. (1997). *Discovering Your Career in Business*. New York: Perseus Books Group.

EXERCISES

Opening Vignette Discussion Questions

1. What motivates you? When did you feel most motivated to do something voluntarily? Think about previous jobs or tasks, or a sport or hobby—what was the need that was pushing you to work as hard as you did?
2. Apart from rewards (or punishments), can you think of other things that have motivated you to work hard?

DISCUSSION QUESTIONS

1. Think about your motivation in this class. Which motivation theory best explains it?
2. Motivation is a function of your ability and tools to achieve a certain task, your goals, needs, and interest in the task. Think of a situation in which you were highly motivated. Assess that situation in terms of those four key items. Were all four working well for you?
3. Have you ever been in a situation in which your goals and needs were fulfilled by a job, and you had the right ability and tools but little interest in the work? Describe that situation and how you fixed it.
4. Many people believe that equity theory (inequitable situations) explains a lot of human action. That is, if people make less money than others, they get so upset that they will take tough union action, riot, or even revolt. Recent evidence suggests that equity may not be as important to everyone as was once thought. How upset would you be if you discovered that your friend and coworker, doing essentially the same work, was making more money than you? Suppose that your friend worked for another company. Would you have the same feeling?
5. Why do you think expectancy theory may be most useful in explaining the behavior of major league baseball players? How about highly paid surgeons?
6. In some Latin American countries, employees believe that pay levels should be partly determined by family needs. Their unions insist that those with more children should be paid more, particularly from multinational firms. Discuss this idea in the context of the equity theory model. Do you agree? What if you were an international manager of an MNC suddenly confronted with this demand by several workers—what would you do?

IN-CLASS EXERCISES

1. Equity sensitivity exercise

Measuring Your Equity Sensitivity

This self-assessment is designed to help you to estimate your level of equity sensitivity. Read each of the statements and circle the response that you believe best reflects your position. Then use the scoring key below to calculate your results. This exercise assesses your equity sensitivity. Complete the questionnaire without discussion or help from others.

	Strongly Agree	Agree	Neutral	Disagree	Strongly Disagree
1. I prefer to do as little as possible at work while getting as much as I can from my employer.	1	2	3	4	5
2. I am most satisfied at work when I have to do as little as possible.	1	2	3	4	5
3. When I am at my job, I think of ways to get out of work.	1	2	3	4	5
4. If I could get away with it, I would try to work just a little bit slower than the boss expects.	1	2	3	4	5
5. It is really satisfying to me when I can get something for nothing at work.	1	2	3	4	5
6. It is the smart employee who gets as much as he or she can while giving as little as possible in return.	1	2	3	4	5
7. Employees who are more concerned about what they can get from their employer rather than what they can give to their employer are the wise ones.	1	2	3	4	5
8. When I have completed my task for the day, I help out other employees who have yet to complete their tasks.	1	2	3	4	5
9. Even if I received low wages and poor benefits from my employer, I would still try to do my best at my job.	1	2	3	4	5
10. If I had to work hard all day at my job, I would probably quit.	1	2	3	4	5
11. I feel obligated to do more than I am paid to do at work.	1	2	3	4	5
12. At work, my greatest concern is whether or not I am doing the best job I can.	1	2	3	4	5
13. A job that requires me to be busy during the day is better than a job that allows me a lot time for loafing.	1	2	3	4	5
14. At work, I feel uneasy when there is little for me to do.	1	2	3	4	5
15. I would become very dissatisfied with my job if I had little or no work to do.	1	2	3	4	5
16. All other things being equal, it is better to have a job with a lot of duties and responsibilities than one with few duties and responsibilities.	1	2	3	4	5

Source: Sauley, K.S., & Bedeian, A.G. (2000). Equity sensitivity: Construction of a measure and examination of its psychometric properties. *Journal of Management* 26(5), 885–910.

Scoring Key for Equity Sensitivity

To score this equity scale, called the Equity Preference Questionnaire (EPQ), complete the three steps below.

Write your circled numbers for the items indicated below (statement numbers are in parentheses) and calculate Subtotal A.

_____ + _____ + _____ + _____ + _____ + _____ + _____ + _____ = _____
(1)   (2)   (3)   (4)   (5)   (6)   (7)   (10)   *Subtotal A*

The remaining items in the EPQ need to be reverse-scored. To calculate a reverse score, subtract the direct score from 6. For example, if you circled 4 in one of these items, the reverse score would be 2 (i.e., $6 - 4 = 2$). If you circled 1, the reverse score would be 5 (i.e., $6 - 1 = 5$). Calculate the reverse score for each of the items indicated below (statement numbers are in parentheses) and write them in the space provided. Then calculate Subtotal B by adding up these reverse scores.

_____ + _____ + _____ + _____ + _____ + _____ + _____ + _____ = _____
(8)   (9)   (11)   (12)   (13)   (14)   (15)   (16)   *Subtotal B*

Calculate your total score by summing Subtotal A and Subtotal B.

_____ + _____ = _____
(Subtotal A)   (Subtotal B)   *Total*

2. Professional athletes worldwide have seen significant salary increases since the 1970s. Such salary increases could have the dual effect of creating perceptions of inequity in those who have older contracts signed years before and who have thus fallen behind the increasing salary curve, and creating strong motivation in those individuals to improve performance so as to enhance their bargaining positions as they approach the end of their contracts. Indeed, one formal study of major league baseball in the United States showed that prospective free agents (players whose contracts have expired and are free to sign new contracts with any team in the off-season) typically earn less-than-average salaries. And after signing new contracts, they typically move well ahead of the average (Zimbalist, 1992).

Thus the rapid increase of salaries has often rendered a player's contract uncompetitive only a few years after it was signed. Differences of hundreds of thousands or even millions of dollars annually among coworkers and peers performing similar tasks in nearly identical organizations are highly unusual. Equity theory would predict that players might feel demotivated under those conditions.

In addition to the equity implications raised by salary differentials, high-guaranteed multiyear contracts signed by a large majority of free agents also raises motivational issues that are addressed by expectancy theory. Upon signing a new contract, will players feel the need to raise their performances to justify their large salaries, consistent with equity predictions? Or will players' motivation levels be reduced by contracts that are guaranteed regardless of how well they play, reflecting the predictions of expectancy theory?

TAKE-HOME EXERCISES

1. Assume that 20 Chinese managers are coming to your firm's new regional headquarters. According to the market, they should be paid about $12,000 per year, which is not a lot by U.S. and European standards, but is a pretty good wage in terms of standard of living (purchasing-power parity) in China. But the Chinese

managers are asking to be paid the same as your European managers—about eight times more than the planned salary. This would increase your overhead considerably, and cause your now profitable China operation to lose money. What should you do about this? Should you just pay (after all, it is not your money, right?) and hope that the local managers will become more productive as a result? Should you convince them that they should not be given such a substantial raise? How would you do that? Or would you just fire everyone and try to recruit and train new local managers, which can be a slow and costly process? New hires might try to demand the same higher salaries as well. Describe your action and its pros and cons.

2. Many managers believe that most employees want higher salaries, followed by good working conditions. What do you think? Is this true for you? Take the "What Workers Want" survey below to find out. Remember to answer as if you are the manager in the first column (what you think your employees might want) then as an employee in the second column (what you want). Be ready to discuss your answers in class.

What Workers Want Questionnaire (rank from 1 to 10; 1 is highest)*

Needs	As a manager, what do you think your employees might want?	As an employee, what do you want?
Interesting work		
Full appreciation of work done		
Feeling of being involved		
Job security		
Very good wages		
Promotion and growth in the organization		
Very good working conditions		
Personal loyalty to employees		
Tactful discipline (when needed)		
Sympathetic help with personal problems		

*Adopted from Kovach, K.A. (1987, September–October). What motivates employees? Workers and supervisors give different answers. *Business Horizons*, pp. 58–65.

3. Think of a time when you were really motivated in performing a certain task (such as a sport or a hobby). You felt that you really wanted to wake up early to get at that task. Describe reasons why you felt so motivated. Do you feel this way about your current school work or job? Why or why not?

SHORT CASE QUESTIONS

Lincoln Electric in Mexico (p. 202)

1. How do you think Lincoln Electric would have to adjust its system if they opened a plant in China?
2. Would the result of Lincoln Electric's efforts have been different if it had tried to introduce its system in a desperately poor domain, such as the Sudan, rather than in a relatively wealthy nation, such as Mexico?
3. Why do you think more firms have not tried to copy a system like Lincoln Electric's?

8

LEADERSHIP

Overview

Leadership is the act of one person guiding others toward the attainment of common goals or objectives. How individuals lead and how people respond to that leadership can vary across cultures. For example, people from egalitarian Northern Europe tend to respond positively to leaders who empower them to take responsibility for their jobs. In a high power-distance country such as India, however, leaders are expected to make decisions with less consultation with lower levels; employees there believe decision making is part of a manager's role in the workplace.

Managers of multinational enterprises can face difficulty if they mindlessly transfer the leadership style that has worked for them in their home countries to a foreign setting. What works for a leader in one culture may not work at all in another culture. Instead, the culture and institutional environment of that country must be accounted for in the leadership style employed.

This chapter will establish the foundations for international managers to lead in different cultures. The topics that will be covered in this chapter include:

- Primary leadership theories and how culture affects them in different settings.

- How culture and the institutional setting of a multinational enterprise may necessitate changes in leadership style.

- An examination of different traits, competencies, and behaviors that leaders require when working with different cultures and strategic situations.

NORTH AMERICAN FOOD AND BEVERAGE MANUFACTURER'S LEARNING EXPERIENCE IN CHINA

It has long been a goal of breakfast cereal makers to introduce the Chinese consumer to breakfast cereal. Historically, such food has not been part of the Chinese diet, but with over 1.5 billion consumers the market potential is clear. With changing demographics of two working parents with more consumable income, higher availability of milk and milk-like beverages, and increasing urbanization of the Chinese market, cereal makers believe they may have a good opportunity to enter the Chinese market in a significant way. This pattern of changing social conditions is very similar to what occurred decades ago in North America that led to the increased popularity of easily prepared breakfast cereals.

U.S. and European cereal makers had long tested the market through exports and limited foreign direct investment, selling their products mostly to hotels and to stores where foreigners shopped. One leading U.S. firm invested in manufacturing facilities to prepare for what it hoped would be a big increase in demand as China continued its growth and urbanization. In the process, expatriate managers sought to learn all they could about leadership in China.

The desire to learn about Chinese leadership prompted the company to invest in training in which managers studied the works of Sun Tzu, reading books such as the *Art of War*. Managers also studied the *I Ching*, or "Book of changes"—a classic Chinese book that has been a source of wisdom and inspiration for thousand of years. This training taught managers about the inherent cooperative culture in greater China and about ways to be a successful manager or leader in China. The professors and consultants running the training argued that in China, striving for social needs without regard for immediate personal gain is symbiotic with the philosophy of the *I Ching*, which emphasizes that the greatest welfare is achieved though the joint efforts of individuals creating better social and physical environments. The implication for leadership was that the collective must be emphasized over the individual. Greater value is placed on the ability to lead groups to cooperative output than on giving individual attention and recognition.

However, the training was an idealized version of leadership in China and was not very useful to managers. One of the U.S. expatriate managers commented during the training:

> Given all the training on the idealized Chinese cultural and traditional values, I assumed I could craft a leadership and motivation strategy based on what I understood as Chinese culture. I sought to reward local employees, but only through group incentives. I was told that individual incentives would demoralize the group; it would disturb the group's *wa* or harmony. But for over a year, I had an unmotivated workforce, people were late for work, turnover was high, sick leave was up, and I was rated by the employees as an uninspiring leader—yes, charisma is valued in China unlike what the culture books said. Finally, I heard that other foreign firms in China were using a different system—basically the organization's leader was giving individual employees recognition in front of their peers. It was a remarkably simple system that gave recognition to the line employees and administrative workers. This was completely in contrast with what the consultants who trained us, and the professors whose work I read, stated. But I decided to try it—we changed the reward system to include some individual rewards, recognition from the firm's top management on a quarterly basis, and an award from the firm for high performers. We measured both individual performance and teamwork, and decided to risk some *wa* by recognizing employees— individually—at a quarterly company dinner, and at an annual awards banquet, modeled after the popular awards dinners done at the American firm Southwest Airlines. The consultants warned us not to make the changes, they said it flew in the face of China's harmony and collectivism and went against everything in the anthropology books about China. But we did it anyway. And the results have been quite good—top management's ratings from the employees have gone up, our turnover has gone down, and employee satisfaction with the compensation system is higher than my previous overseas assignments. Chinese employees do like individual rewards and public recognition, they told me that they had had enough of their hard work going unrecognized as under the old system with their boss or some lazy colleagues taking credit for their work. Now is their time to make money and be recognized for what they can do—individually.

Leadership requires the recognition that environments do change and even in cases where leaders think they are being culturally appropriate, they may not be. Thus, a leader is one who determines what needs to be accomplished in a given situation, aligns the goals of the organization with the needs and wants of the employees, and provides the necessary tools for the employees to meet those goals.

Ahlstrom, D. (2009). But Asians don't do that. *The Chinese University of Hong Kong Working Paper Series*.

Leadership is critical to the success of a business—both domestic and international. However, studying leadership in different cultures presents the challenge of first determining what is meant by the term "effective leadership." For example, the founder of the People's Republic of China, Mao Zedong, won a civil war against difficult odds, united a torn country, motivated a level of social change in one of the oldest cultures in the world, and eventually inspired such devotion that millions hung on his every word. However, he also pursued disastrous economic policies that led to the starvation of millions of his citizens, as well as starting and encouraging China's Cultural Revolution, which killed and maimed perhaps millions more. Mao was undeniably a charismatic leader, but was he an effective leader? It is possible to answer yes and no to that question. Charismatic leaders are skillful at inspiring action and change. But what change and at what cost? Thus, the concept of an "effective leader" clearly requires greater definition and qualification.[i]

Once we understand what effective leadership is, then we can examine how leadership changes in different countries and cultures. Well-known leadership scholar Gary Yukl has observed that much of the research on leadership during the decades following World War II was undertaken and published in Western Europe, the United States, and Canada.[ii] However, as argued throughout this text, many assumptions underlying U.S. management practice are somewhat different than in other countries and cultures.[iii] For example, market processes, the stress on the individual over the group, and an emphasis on management and leadership problems rather than on subordinates or followership challenges are aspects of U.S. management style. Another well-known leadership researcher, Robert House, adds that the major theories of leadership, along with most empirical evidence, are from North America and tend to emphasize individualism over collectivism, stress assumptions of rationality, highlight follower responsibilities, and take for granted the centrality of work and democratic values by leaders and followers.[iv]

We know from research in cross-cultural psychology and anthropology that many nations do not have the same cultural values as people in North America.[v] Thus, international business people must acquire a broader understanding of leadership than what is commonly found in the United States. An effective manager operating internationally needs to act in a manner appropriate for the setting in which he or she is located. A manager who fails to take into account the local setting may be seen as inadequate, unfair, or unjust by employees and ultimately be unsuccessful. This chapter will examine these complex issues of leadership around the world. Figure 8-1 summarizes the flow of material in this chapter.

FIGURE 8-1 Chapter 8 Conceptual Flow

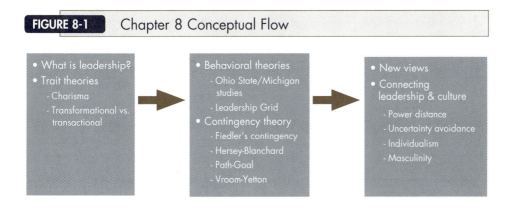

WHAT IS LEADERSHIP?

Leaders

Individuals who significantly affect the thoughts and behaviors of others, often through persuasion and influence.

Leaders are individuals who significantly affect the thoughts and behaviors of others, often through persuasion and influence. (These two related topics are examined more closely in Chapter 10.) Leadership in international and diverse settings therefore involves the ability to inspire the thinking, attitudes, and actions of a variety of individuals and cultures.[vi] Leadership is a relatively new concern for business. For example, while famed steel entrepreneur Andrew Carnegie is considered to have been an exemplary leader and philanthropist, no one in his day sought to offer courses or seminars based on his leadership style. (Contrast this with the books and seminars on Donald Trump or Richard Branson today.) This does not mean that the leadership concept is a new one. The symbols for "leader" existed in the ancient pictographic languages of Egypt and China.[vii] The Chinese philosopher Sun Tzu raised the issue of leadership as early as 400 BCE (see the Sun Tzu and Leadership Culture Box). While the study of leadership may be recent, the concept is one of humankind's oldest.

Leadership is different from management. Management consists of planning, organizing, leading, and controlling a group or organization; managing resources and scheduling is a major part of managing. Leadership, however, is about influencing, motivating, and assisting followers to desired levels of performance. It must also be recognized that simply inspiring individuals is not the sole characteristic of a leader. Leaders must also deliver positive outcomes. Individuals may disagree on whether an outcome is positive, but the results must be viewed as positive by at least some in the organization, or its broader stakeholders, in order for a person to be considered a leader.

In our prior example, it can be argued that Chairman Mao was a leader: he shepherded his followers through World War II and China's postwar revolution to create the People's Republic of China. China was poorly managed during the reign of its last emperor and after his fall in the early twentieth century, the country was ruled by warlords with little concern for the populace. Mao unified China and mobilized its citizens behind several ambitious goals to restore China's infrastructure, environment, and economy after decades of war. However, Mao's policies and his desire to hold onto power would subsequently lead to the disastrous Great Leap Forward of the late 1950s, which created the largest famine in world history,

---

CULTURE

SUN TZU AND LEADERSHIP

Sun Tzu is credited with writing a book titled *The Art of War* in China sometime between 400 and 320 BCE. There is no direct historical evidence that one man named Sun Tzu existed, and it is possible *The Art of War* may have been compiled by a group of philosophers. Nevertheless, the book is the oldest known work on military strategy and diplomacy. Today, *The Art of War* still shapes the strategy not only of the military but also of business around East Asia, which can be seen in negotiation strategies of parties in this region. For example, one of Sun Tzu's quotes is, "The best victory is when the opponent surrenders of its own accord before there are any actual hostilities . . . It is best to win without fighting."

The effect of this quotation can be seen in negotiating strategies in which Chinese parties will seek to delay decisions until just before the deadlines demanded by Western firms working with them. The Chinese hope the result of the delay will be that the Western firm concedes certain items. The Chinese parties will also seek to ensure that the opposing side has no options other than what they offer. Their goal is not to have a disruptive negotiation but instead, to ensure that the negotiation is successful from their perspective without any battles.

Sun Tzu also addressed leadership. He argued forcefully that a defeat of an army was not the responsibility of the soldiers, but instead of the general (the leader). He went on to argue that a general should lead by example and not by coersion. A successful leader is one who takes advantage of opportunities as they are presented. These characteristics match what a modern business student would think is essential to a leader, although students should remember that leadership styles need to change with the situation and the maturity of the followers.

and also the equally devastating Cultural Revolution just a few years later. Therefore, it is very difficult to argue that Mao was a successful leader given the catastrophic events that he set into motion.[viii]

LEADERSHIP THEORIES

Leadership theories can broadly be divided into four categories: trait theories, behavioral theories, contingency theories, and implicit theories of leadership. Each of these four categories will be examined in turn. As noted earlier, much of our understanding of leadership theories is based on research from North America. Therefore, the initial understanding of the theory will be presented and will be followed by the theory's implications for an international business as culture is considered. A richer discussion of how a student can integrate these various theories and the concepts of culture to help direct their managerial actions will follow.

Trait Theories of Leadership

Trait theory argues that there are underlying traits or characteristics of people that lead to either superior leader or follower performance, the right stuff as it were. These traits include a leader's knowledge, natural and learned abilities, values, and personality traits. From ancient times through World War II, most people automatically assumed that leaders were born, not made, and that leadership came naturally. As a result of this belief, schools sought ways in which leaders could be identified, particularly from a young age. Researchers looked for ways to differentiate leaders from non-leaders by their characteristics or traits, and initially focused on physical traits, such as height and physical appearance. However, it was quickly found that leaders come in all shapes and sizes, and all races and genders.

Researchers then turned to common personality traits, including charisma (discussed in greater length below), confidence, vision for the organization or team, decisiveness, and internal locus of control. **Internal locus of control** refers to whether people feel that they can control things themselves or whether outside forces control their future. Figure 8-2 lists some of the personality traits most commonly associated with leadership.

Today, research on personality traits has taken the path of studying competencies—mixtures of traits and learned skills. One trait that has received a great deal of attention and that deserves particular attention is charisma.

Charisma Charisma is the ability to inspire or influence others. This line of research developed primarily in the United States prior to World War II. However, the analysis of charisma fell out of favor after the war because of the strong

Trait theory
Argues that people have underlying traits or characteristics that lead to either superior leader or follower performance.

Internal locus of control
Whether people feel that they can control things themselves or whether forces outside them control their future.

FIGURE 8-2 Personality Traits Commonly Associated with Good Leadership

1. **Charisma** "Natural" gifted leader.

2. **Dominance** An individual's need to exert influence and control over others; helps a leader channel followers' efforts and abilities toward achieving group and organizational goals.

3. **Self-confidence** Helps a leader influence followers and persist in the face of obstacles or difficulties.

4. **Energy/activity levels** When high, help a leader deal with the many demands he or she faces on a day-to-day basis.

5. **Tolerance for stress** Helps a leader deal with the uncertainty inherent in any leadership role.

6. **Internal locus of control** Helps the leader take responsibility for an endeavor's success and not blame outside factors for failure.

7. **Integrity and honesty** Ensure that a leader behaves ethically and is worthy of followers' trust and confidence.

8. **Emotional intelligence** Ensures that a leader is not overly self-centered, has a steady disposition, and can accept criticism.

negatives associated with charismatic political leaders such as Adolf Hitler, Benito Mussolini, and Joseph Stalin. (The first two individuals were the charismatic leaders of the main Fascist movements in Europe, while the third was the powerful and ruthless leader of the Soviet Union.) It is interesting to note that in Germany today, individuals who are considered charismatic still do not do well as politicians. Instead, Germans favor soft-spoken politicians because of this negative association with charisma, and many German politicians have a style that many other countries would consider low key.

The benefits of charisma, along with its drawbacks, have been well documented.[ix] In recent years, however, charismatic leadership that combines learned skills with the ability to transform an organization, in addition to internal traits, has been the focus of research. This type of charisma is referred to as **transformational leadership** and has been shown to have positive effects on organizational climate and performance.[x]

Transformational leadership
A combination of learned skills and the ability to transform an organization in new, substantive ways.

Transformational leaders establish a vision and the key objectives that must be reached to move an organization forward. The charisma of a leader is necessary to generate awareness of a given problem, raise the interest of the followers to address that problem, and encourage their acceptance of the organization or team's purposes and mission. Charismatic leadership also can inspire followers to put the success of an organization and colleagues ahead of their own.[xi] Effective transformational leaders articulate a realistic vision of the future that can be shared, stimulate subordinates intellectually, and attend to the differences among subordinates.[xii] By defining the need for change, creating new visions, and mobilizing commitment to these visions, charismatic leaders can ultimately transform organizations. Follower transformation can be achieved by raising the awareness of the importance and value of desired outcomes and getting followers to transcend their own self-interests and focus on the needs of their colleagues and the organization, which is called employee engagement.[xiii]

Empirical Findings on Charisma The empirical results from decades of study on charismatic leadership show that leaders described as charismatic, visionary, or transformational often have a positive effect on their followers and organizations as a whole. This positive effect is both in terms of organizational performance and on follower satisfaction, organizational and team commitment, and organizational identification.[xiv] Charisma may also increase followers' perceptions of leaders' ability and effectiveness.[xv]

These positive results have been demonstrated in various organizational settings, including small groups, major units of complex organizations, corporations, and in studies on innovation, the military, and even the U.S. presidency.[xvi] Evidence supporting the value of transformational leadership has emerged from all around the world to which we now turn.[xvii]

International Perspective on Charisma The term *leader* evokes a positive image in the United States, but for people in many other parts of the world it evokes quite a negative image.[xviii] For some Europeans, for example, leadership is an unintended and undesirable consequence of democracy.[xix] British, Americans, and Canadians value charisma in their leaders and identify such business and political leaders as Lee Iacocca, former CEO of Chrysler Corporation, World War II British Prime Minister Winston Churchill, and former U.S. President Bill Clinton as effective, charismatic leaders.[xx] But as noted above, Germans do not value charisma in their contemporary business or government leaders. Many German people associate charisma with the blind obedience commanded by Hitler, and the resulting destruction of World War II.

Leadership scholar Bernard Bass notes that charismatic leaders are more likely to appear in societies with traditions of support for them and expectations about their emergence.[xxi] This implies that charismatic leadership might more easily surface in the Anglo-American societies where a preference for charisma exists. Yet there is also evidence that transformational leadership exists in various forms around the world, though perhaps less so in places such as Germany and Russia where people have experienced charisma's negative side in their leaders and are wary of it.[xxii]

Peter Dorfman compared leadership in Western and Asian countries.[xxiii] He and his colleagues showed that charismatic leaders' behaviors are widely accepted in both Asia and the West. The GLOBE study of leadership around the world also concurred. (This study was discussed in detail in Chapter 2.) The GLOBE study found that attributes of charismatic/transformational leadership, including foresight, encouraging, communicative, trustworthy, dynamic, positive, confidence builder, and motivational are universally endorsed as contributing to outstanding leadership. However, certain charismatic attributes were also identified as being culturally contingent. For example, attributes such as enthusiastic, risk taking, and ambitious were identified as characteristics of a leader in the West. In contrast, attributes such as self-effacing, self-sacrificial, sensitive, and compassionate were identified as leadership qualities in East Asian cultures. Charisma and many of its attributes are valued around the world, although different cultures have different ideas of what charisma is.

Transformational versus Transactional Leadership It was highlighted above that one type of leadership associated with charisma is transformational leadership. Transformational/charismatic leadership is traditionally contrasted with transactional leadership; the two concepts are seen as opposite approaches to leadership, though it is possible for a leader to manifest both charismatic and transactional qualities, depending on the situation.[xxiv] Political scientist James MacGregor Burns first introduced the concept of transactional leadership in his treatment of political leadership.[xxv] Researchers in social psychology have now adapted these concepts to the study of business leaders. For example, Bernard Bass defines a transactional leader as one who recognizes follower needs—recall how important identifying needs is to motivation—and tries to see that the organization satisfies those needs if employee performance warrants it.[xxvi] Thus, transactional leaders also use extrinsic motivators very effectively. For example, such a leader exchanges (promises) rewards for appropriate levels of effort, and responds to employees' self interests as long as they are getting the job done. Transactional leadership also seeks to acquire more followers through the exchange process.

Some have argued that transactional leadership is the best approach in dealing with followers in emerging economies where people are poorer and likely to be motivated by what Maslow would refer to as lower-order, material needs, such as money and housing. Research on the importance of social exchange and connections for conducting business in emerging economies, such as China and India, supports this view of the importance of transactional leadership.

In contrast to transactional leadership, transformational leadership occurs when a leader transforms his or her followers in ways that result in followers trusting the leader, performing behaviors that contribute to the achievement of organizational goals, and being motivated to perform at a high level. Transformational leaders increase followers' awareness of the importance of their tasks and of performing well. They not only make subordinates aware of their needs for personal growth, development, and accomplishment, but they also give subordinates a feeling of engagement with the organization by motivating them to work for the good of the organization in addition to their own personal gain. Figure 8-3 summarizes the characteristics of transformational leadership. While transactional leadership may work best in a more difficult environment where followers require

| FIGURE 8-3 | Attributes Associated with Transformational Leadership |

1. Motive arouser
2. Foresight
3. Encouraging
4. Communicative
5. Trustworthy
6. Dynamic
7. Positive
8. Confidence builder
9. Motivational

Source: House, R.J., Hanges, P.J., Javidan, M., Dorfman, P.W., & Gupta, V. (Eds.) (2004). *Culture, Leadership, and Organizations: The GLOBE Study of 62 Societies.* Thousand Oaks, CA: Sage Publications.

the organization to "show us the money" (such as in lesser developed countries), in cultures that value empowerment and understanding the higher goals of the company, transformational, Steven Jobs-type leadership can work very well.

Behavioral Theories of Leadership

Behavioral theories

Leadership theories that argue that specific, learned behaviors can differentiate leaders from non-leaders (or successful leaders from unsuccessful leaders), and are behaviors that can be learned.

The next category of leadership theories is the behavioral theories. **Behavioral theories** of leadership argue that specific, learned behaviors can differentiate leaders from non-leaders (or successful leaders from unsuccessful leaders), and these behaviors can be learned. Unlike the trait theories of leadership, which imply that leaders need to be identified and perhaps nurtured, behavioral theories assume that effective leadership behaviors can be identified and taught to prospective leaders. The initial studies were done at Ohio State and the University of Michigan and established the domain of behavioral leadership. Building on these initial studies, researchers developed the Leadership Grid, which further extended the concepts of behavioral leadership.

Ohio State/Michigan Studies The behavioral perspective of leadership identifies two dimensions of leader behavior: task orientation and people orientation. Task-oriented behaviors include assigning employees to specific tasks, clarifying their work duties and procedures, ensuring that they follow company rules, and pushing them to reach their performance capacity. People-oriented behaviors include showing mutual trust and respect for subordinates, seeking to meet employee needs as a way to build relationships and loyalty to the company, and looking out for employee well-being to reduce turnover. This perspective has been used to argue that the most effective leaders exhibit high levels of both types of behaviors, irrespective of a given situation.

The foundational studies in this area are competing studies done at Ohio State University and the University of Michigan in the 1950s and 1960s. The Ohio State leadership studies argued that leadership behavior had two dimensions: initiating structure (task behavior) and consideration (people oriented behavior). The Michigan study used slightly different terms, production oriented and employee oriented, but the concepts used in both sets of studies are similar. Here we will use the terms task behavior and people-oriented behavior because they are widely used. Both studies argued that leadership behavior could be taught, and stressed the importance of a leader being high on both the task and people dimensions.

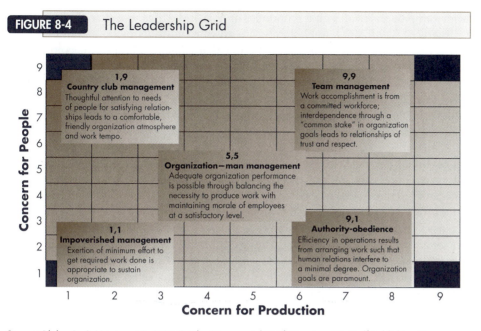

FIGURE 8-4 The Leadership Grid

Source: Blake, R. & Mouton, J.S. (1964). *The Managerial Grid*. Houston, TX: Gulf Publishing Company.

Leadership Grid A similar behavioral leadership theory that followed was the Leadership Grid, with categories based on a 9 by 9 matrix. This grid identifies various types of leadership behavior based on two independent dimensions of concern for production and concern for people. As in the Ohio State and Michigan studies, effective leaders must show high concern for both production and for people, and work to encourage employees to reach their highest levels of achievement. The ratings for leaders on both dimensions ranged from one to nine, with nine being the highest on both dimensions. Leaders were named according to their ratings on the Leadership Grid; for example the ideal leader was seen to be a "9,9" leader—someone who is highest on both concern for production and concern for people (see Figure 8-4).

In this view, the ideal 9,9 leader is seen as being flexible with the ability to get a great deal of effort from followers who maximize their effort for him or her; all of this while the leader works hard to meet the workers' needs. The 9,9 leaders are thought to be responsive to change and innovative. The opposite of a 9,9 leader is a 1,1 leader, who is considered to have impoverished leadership and management abilities. This type of leader exerts minimum effort and gets minimal output from workers, and has little concern for workers' needs. In this environment, managers will often find ways to minimize work, and will punish those who try to do extra for "creating more work for others."

The Leadership Grid identifies several other leadership styles. Familiar to most is the 9,1 or the Authority–Obedience leadership style. This leadership style stresses efficiency in operations and certain, specified results, and it offers no room for creativity. In this setting, working conditions are arranged so human actions are constrained and cannot interfere with the mechanistic output of the work system. A military boot camp is a classic example. A drill instructor is a 9,1 leader, with full attention given to drills and building unquestioning discipline in the troops. In these leaders' view, there is no room for individualism, creativity, or personal concern for the employees (soldiers), beyond what the system has built into it. Managers in more traditional organizations in developing countries are thought to fit this leadership profile, which is more likely to work best with difficult situations in which strict discipline is required and followers are not yet experienced enough to make decisions about their work. The 9,1 leadership approach is thought to be essential in training factory employees in emerging economies of Asia and Africa. But even these employees, many of whom are barely literate, are given room to innovate within their jobs after a year or two on the job. Once employees are able to demonstrate competence with their assigned tasks, supervisors have found that they are able to suggest improvements to individual tasks and maybe to the production process as a whole. This allows the leader to give more freedom to the employees and to "back off" from the strict 9,1 production orientation, giving more concern to the employees and their opinions and growth.

International Perspectives on Behavioral Theories There is evidence that different cultures will find different positions on the Leadership Grid to be most effective. For example, high power-distance cultures may be more open to the 9,1 form of leadership and less likely to question the orders and authority of a leader. In many Asian settings, such as China, this type of leadership is common. This style also characterizes Turkey and several other Middle Eastern countries.[xxvii] It is interesting to note that in many Korean firms, employees start their day with company songs and group exercises in a manner similar to the military, and, in Japan, leaders are often expected to be quite strict with employees, pushing them very hard for the good of the organization.[xxviii]

LEADERSHIP AT PHILIPS AND CHRYSLER

To illustrate different leadership styles, consider electronics manufacturing powerhouse Philips—one of the most well-known companies in Europe. Based in the Netherlands, its former CEO is Jan Timmer—an impressive figure both physically and mentally. Timmer is typically portrayed in the media as being charismatic and, while in office, he masterminded the turnaround of Philips, for which he was praised and admired. However, within months of stepping down, Timmer faced severe criticism, both in the company and the media.[xxix] As is common with many charismatic leaders, it was thought he had put his reputation ahead of the organization's well-being.

When a charismatic leader is primarily focused on his or her own reputation or advancement, the long-term impact on a firm can be negative. People thought that many of the strategic actions Timmer took were to benefit his own career and reputation, and not to help advance the growth and development of the firm, its shareholders, and employees. Timmer did engineer a fairly effective turnaround that helped Philips dig itself out of a big financial hole. Philips did well for a while, but as is the case with many charismatic leaders, Timmer seemed to lose interest and failed to train a top management team to take over

once he left the firm. Philips is still a leader in different segments of the electronics industry, but has not regained its leadership position in the industry.

This also seems to be the situation with Lee Iacocca, the charismatic former leader of Chrysler. Starting in 1979, Iacocca initiated the turnaround of the U.S. automaker, one of the greatest turnarounds in American business history. Chrysler's financial fortunes were greatly improved, its cars improved a great deal through the 1980s, and its strategic situation improved considerably. Throughout the 1980s, Iacocca appeared in a series of commercials for Chrysler's Dodge and Plymouth cars, using the ad campaign "The pride is back" to signal Chrysler's return as a contender in the field. But again, as with many charismatic leaders, Iacocca seemed to tire of the continuing effort needed to build a great firm. Starting in 1982, Iacocca headed the Statue of Liberty-Ellis Island Foundation, which was created to raise funds for the renovation and preservation of the Statue of Liberty. He took over the Italian sports car firm Maserati and U.S. automaker American Motors, and added Gulf Stream jets to Chrysler's increasingly diversified portfolio. Although Chrysler became a stronger car company during his tenure, by the

time Iacocca left in 1992, it was only marginally above where it had been in the late 1970s financially and in terms of rank in the U.S. auto market, and had no foreign presence.

It is common for organizations under charismatic leaders to do well while that leader mobilizes change, extracts hard work and commitment, and inspires financial markets and customers. But it is all too common for a leader to eventually do what's best for him or her personally and not the organization, leaving that organization in pretty much the same state as it was in when he or she took over.[xxx] Such a leader may fail to train and coach followers, fail to build a top management team, and rely too much on his or her own "genius" to get things done.[xxxi] Thus, the proper leadership role will vary not only in terms of local culture, but also by the nature of the situation that the firm faces and the needs for the business at that given time. Charismatic leaders can be particularly effective during a turnaround or other stressful situation, but if that leader cannot put the organization's needs first at all times, the organization and its stakeholders will eventually suffer. As *Good to Great* author Jim Collins puts it, "If you are president of Harvard [University] and it [your work] is all about you, then you shouldn't be president of Harvard."[xxxii]

Some cultures are particularly associated with a certain type of leadership. For example, the leadership style 5,5 is commonly referred to as "organization man management." Adequate organization performance is possible through balancing the necessity to produce while maintaining morale at a satisfactory level. Japanese leadership in average domestic firms is often associated with this style of leadership in which organization man loyalty is prized and promotion is still often based on seniority. Excepting the elite firms, productivity in most Japanese domestic firms is not especially high, and though employees work long hours, they do not have to work particularly hard; productivity in many Japanese service firms, for example, is rather low.[xxxiii]

Contingency Theory

The theories described in the preceding sections are limited to defining types of managers in absolute terms. According to the Leadership Grid, leaders fall into categories based on a 9 by 9 matrix. Behavioral theories imply that the 9,9 leader—the one high on both concern for production and concern for people—has the ideal leadership style. Recent evidence, however, suggests that leaders must adjust their management style to best handle different situations and to meet employee needs.[xxxiv] Sometimes leaders may generally be considered a 9,9, but at times must behave as a 9,1 (coercive, military style). For example, if a firm is in decline there may not be enough time to gather input from all employees to find ways to improve business; instead, decisions must be made and orders followed.[xxxv] In addition, not every culture values leaders who are overly concerned with employee interests. For the average person in more individualist societies, such as the U.S. and Australia, employees may see a manager with a rating of 9,9 as someone who is too personal and who prefers to "pass the buck" when making decisions. They also may not want their manager to be concerned with their personal lives. Indian workers, on the other hand, may find the Anglo-American participatory leadership style uncomfortable as employees tend to feel that a manager is paid to make decisions, and should not be concerned about the opinions of their staff. Students from East Asia and other more hierarchical cultures similarly report that they feel uncomfortable being asked too many questions or for input, because the professor (boss) should be telling them what to do.[1]

Many students may remember a time when a boss, teacher, or colleague asked questions that were too personal. You may have wanted to, or in fact did, tell that person to back off and give you more space and freedom with your work. Leaders need to be sensitive to individuals who may not want (or need) a 9,9 supervisor hovering over them; more individualistic cultures value that personal space. Recent stories about Chinese firms with branches or offices in North America have confirmed that more traditional Chinese bosses are seen as intrusive by North American workers. Those bosses ask specific and personal questions and micromanage employees, phoning them at night or on weekends about work, and even scold them for having turned off their mobile phones. Leaders must use different styles at different times in different settings. The adaptation models of leadership help individuals to understand how a leader may adjust behavior to better fit a particular situation and employees' maturity levels. The theories based on this model, recognizing the need for adaptation, are called **contingency theories**.

Contingency theory
Theory in which the type of leadership needed is based on the situation being faced.

---

[1]This is quite similar to students in the more traditional, hierarchical cultures in East Asia or Africa, who feel a teacher or trainer should have the answers. They tend to get frustrated with teachers or trainers who constantly ask them what they think. "Why doesn't the trainer simply give us the answers? We don't want to hear what these other students think, just what the teacher thinks," students commonly say.

Fiedler's Contingency Theory Leadership scholar Fred Fiedler developed the first contingency model in response to the realization about the impracticality of requiring leaders to behave the same way in all situations at all times. Fiedler argued that there are two fundamental types of leadership: task orientation and relationship orientation. (Notice the similarity to the Ohio State, Michigan, and Leadership Grid models.) Relationship-oriented leaders want to be liked by their subordinates and to get along with them. They are also referred to as high-LPC leaders because they tend to describe their LPC (Least Preferred Coworker) in relatively positive terms. Leaders who are task-oriented want their subordinates to perform at a high level and accomplish all of their assigned tasks. These leaders are also referred to as low-LPC leaders because they tend to describe their LPC in relatively negative terms.

The best leadership style is determined by three conditions or contingencies. The first contingency is the leader-member relationship, which includes the degree of confidence that followers have in their leader, the loyalty given to the leader, and the leader's appeal. The second contingency is task structure, which is the degree to which employees' tasks are routine, in contrast to varied tasks. The third contingency is the power inherent in the leadership position. This variable includes rewards and sanctions available to the position, the leader's formal authority (based on ranking in the managerial hierarchy), and the support that the leader receives from supervisors and the overall organization.

Looking at which leadership style works best in different situations, Fiedler argued that high-LPC leaders (relationship-oriented leaders) are most effective in situations that are moderately favorable for leading. That is, when a situation is not too ambiguous, people basically know what to do, but there is some degree of flexibility for leaders and followers. In contrast, low-LPC leaders (task-oriented leaders) are most effective in situations that are very favorable or very unfavorable for leading, such as unfavorable, mechanistic, or military (extreme leadership) environments.[xxxvi] Low-LPC does not imply that leaders should have no concern for employees, but that they cannot worry too much about being liked by employees; instead, the key is to command employee respect and be sure that workers carry out their duties.

The contingency theory argues that an effective leader's behavior is determined by both his or her personal characteristics and by the three types of situations in which leaders find themselves. This sheds light on why some leaders are effective and others, who may be equally qualified and respected, are ineffective in the same situation. It also helps to illustrate why a leader may be effective in one situation but not in another.

International Perspective on Contingency Theory Leaders from different cultures vary in the assumptions they make about how to lead. In the United States for example, many leaders assume that people's basic physiological needs for safety and security have been met and therefore only opportunities to satisfy higher-order needs will motivate them. They believe that denying these opportunities leads to alienation, lower productivity, and, ultimately, high levels of turnover. As a result, most U.S. leaders believe that the majority of the people who work for them want to develop interpersonal relationships characterized by trust and open communication and they assume that people produce more when a workplace is more democratic and open.

Fiedler's contingency theory of leadership reminds us that it is inappropriate to think there is a single best leadership style. At certain times leaders may need to be more autocratic and at other times less directive. An employee's behavior will affect the type of leadership style needed in a given situation. Fiedler's work encourages managers to consider not only the culture in which they are working but also the nature of the work environment in which the firm is located. Fiedler's work also brings out the important point that managers cannot focus solely on culture. The nature of the employees and the tasks to be accomplished also have a significant impact on the type of leadership that is required.

The nature of the task to be accomplished raises another significant issue that managers should consider as they determine an appropriate leadership style. As leaders move up within an organization, the nature of the needed leadership changes. The leadership behavior of a lower-level manager is commonly more directive and task oriented, and typically the manager's focus is simply on getting the job done. Senior and executive managers, however, are more focused on relationships.

Hersey–Blanchard Situational Leadership From Fiedler's foundation another contingency model was developed by Paul Hersey and Ken Blanchard (a co-author of the well-known book, *The One Minute Manager*). They argued that contingency was the appropriate approach because it allows flexibility in types of leadership as required in different settings.[xxxvii] Specifically, they argued that effective leaders must also vary their style of leadership based on the employees' level of maturity. Hersey and Blanchard identified a three-dimensional approach for assessing leadership effectiveness. An employee's maturity is determined by job maturity (job experience) and psychological maturity (employee self-confidence and ability to accept responsibility).

There are four levels of employee maturity. The least-mature employees must be given much more direction and discipline, while mature employees are more confident and can be given more independence. Training, personal motivation, maturity, and teamwork can substitute for leader discipline and direction. The effectiveness of a leader depends on how his or her style interrelates with employee maturity. Leadership should meet the needs of all employees, from telling employees what to do and how to do it at the lowest level of maturity; to selling ideas to employees at the next level of maturity; to participating with employees at the next level; and finally to delegating to employees at the highest level of maturity.

The willingness and ability (readiness) of an employee to do a particular task is an important situational factor. It's important to remember that employees become more mature with time and leaders must be able to adjust their leadership style appropriately. The degree to which a leader is able to vary his or her style to the level of an employee in a given situation can be crucial to the success of a team or organization (see Leadership under Changing Circumstances).

International Perspective on the Hersey–Blanchard Theory This approach to leadership has important implications for international business. Managers who move from a low power-distance country to a higher power-distance country will find that they must alter their style to fit that new environment. Many managers in the United States believe that people who work for them want to develop inter-personal relationships characterized by trust, communication, and empowerment. They may mistakenly assume that all employees want a democratic workplace and want to be involved in factory-floor decisions. That often is not the case. Employees in high power-distance countries may expect bosses to act in a more directive and formal way and keep their distance, although employees will often welcome a mentoring, teaching approach as they become more mature, consistent with the Hersey–Blanchard theory.

Path–Goal Theory The contingency model that developed next is the Path–Goal theory. The Path–Goal theory proposes that the most successful leaders are those who increase subordinate motivation by charting out and clarifying the paths to high performance.[xxxviii] This contingency model is based on the Expectancy Theory

LEADERSHIP UNDER CHANGING CIRCUMSTANCES

Many students will be familiar with the award-winning ten-part HBO film series *Band of Brothers*, produced by Steven Spielberg and Tom Hanks and based on historian Stephen Ambrose's book of the same title. *Band of Brothers* tells the story of a group of American soldiers' preparation and combat during World War II. The series followed one company of U.S. Army paratroopers from the famed 101st Airborne Division—Easy Company of the 506 Regiment—from their training in boot camp through the end of the war. In the first episode of the series, the recruits of Easy Company meet their new Commander, Lieutenant Herbert Sobel. Lieutenant Sobel trained his men mercilessly—a textbook 9,1 leader. His only concern was for the success of Easy Company (and thus his reputation and promotion) based on group performance measures set down by the Army. Sobel's superiors were confident that if the training measures were correct, everything else must also be going well. Easy Company's performance in physical drills and other competitions quickly earned Sobel a promotion to captain and the accolades of his regimental commander, Colonel Sink. But all was not well. As Easy Company graduated from basic training camp and began to prepare for combat in Europe—improving from raw recruits to more mature soldiers—Captain Sobel still continued to treat them like immature recruits.

That is, he treated them like the unwilling and unable followers at the starting point of the Hersey–Blanchard model, and continued using an ordering style that was abusive to his men. This abusive style had worked well during the initial training—Easy Company outdistanced the other eight companies in the 506th regiment—but as the soldiers prepared in England for the European invasion, Captain Sobel's overly strict treatment and his petty punishments and intimidations caused the men to rebel against his authority.

After several isolated incidents of near insubordination, followed by punishment, the non-commissioned officers (corporals and sergeants) in Easy Company all got together to write letters to Sobel's superior, Colonel Sink. Triggered by a trivial charge against the Easy Company executive officer (and highly respected leader), Lieutenant Richard Winters, and risking a firing squad for mutiny, the noncoms informed Colonel Sink that they did not want to serve under Captain Sobel in the upcoming invasion of Nazi-occupied Europe.[2] Colonel Sink angrily informed them that they could be shot for insubordination during wartime, but he finally took account of the sergeants' concerns about Sobel. Easy Company needed a leader who could adjust to the new, ambiguous (non-training) combat situation with the now mature and well-trained soldiers. Sink removed Captain Sobel from command of Easy Company and gave him command of an airborne training school. A more able combat commander took charge, who generally understood what Easy Company could do and led by example. Captain Sobel's tough discipline had given Easy Company the training to become a fine company, but his style was not appropriate in a leadership role when going into combat with more experienced soldiers. It took the inspired leadership of Lieutenant Richard Winters and others to help Easy Company finally realize its abilities and become one of the most celebrated units in U.S. military history.

Businesses face similar situations—there are times in which a firm needs authoritarian or even coercive leadership to obtain certain goals within a given time period. For example, the turnaround of the Australian firm Brambles after a poor merger took considerably quick decision-making. However, once the turnaround was complete, that same type of leadership wasn't required. In cases like this, firms form groups of CEOs and other leaders to conduct turnarounds. These individuals typically leave the firm after it returns to profit, because the skills they possess are not needed to run the business on a daily basis.

Ambrose, S.E. (1992). *Band of Brothers: E Company, 506th Regiment, 101st Airborne from Normandy to Hitler's Eagle's Nest.* New York: Simon & Schuster.

of Motivation (see Chapter 7, Motivation). The manager's job is viewed as coaching or guiding employees to choose the best paths (in terms of tasks and objectives) for reaching their goals. This is evaluated by the accompanying achievement of organizational goals and individual objectives. As can be seen by the theory's name, goal setting is central. As discussed in Chapter 7, goals are motivational and should be used by a leader to help direct and motivate followers. Further, the Path–Goal theory argues that leaders will have to engage in different types of leadership behavior depending on the nature and demands of a particular situation. It is the leader's job to assist employees in attaining goals and to provide direction and support.

---

[2]That is how it was portrayed in HBO's miniseries, though noncoms did not actually send the letters to Col. Sink. They planned to do so, but the company executive officer found out about their plan and talked them out of it. Sink got word of the mini-revolt anyway and decided to remove Cpt. Sobel from command of Easy Company, sending him to command a paratroop training school.

As a result, managers can have four different leadership styles. These styles include achievement-oriented (challenging goals are set and high performance encouraged), participative (decision making based on group consultation with information shared in the group), supportive (good relations with the group and sensitivity to subordinate needs), and directive (specific advice is given to the group and ground rules established). The effective leader uses each of these four styles as required in different settings.

International Perspective on the Path–Goal Theory Like the other contingency models of leadership, Path–Goal theory specifies different leadership styles for different situations. In **achievement-oriented** leadership, the leader sets challenging goals for employees, expects them to perform at their highest level, and shows confidence in their ability to meet this expectation. This style is appropriate when the employee is not challenged, tends to be mature, and knows his or her job inside and out. With a directive leadership style, the manager lets employees know what is expected of them and tells them how to perform their tasks. This style is appropriate when the follower has an ambiguous job or may not be ready to work independently. Though the leader must assess each setting and employee separately, this approach may generally work best in emerging economies where employees need to be told the exact steps to complete a job, and perhaps just as important, need a list of things not to do. Participative leadership involves managers consulting with employees and asking for their suggestions before making a decision, sometimes called the democratic style of leadership. This style is appropriate when an employee is using improper procedures or is making poor decisions, and should be helped to uncover these problems. In addition, and as will be discussed in the next section, this participative style is most appropriate when employee buy-in is needed for making a difficult decision. In supportive leadership, the manager is friendly, approachable, and shows concern for the employee's well-being. This style is appropriate when the followers lack self-confidence or have just gone through a difficult time at work.

Determining the appropriate leadership style to use involves knowing how employees see themselves in a given situation: are they in control of their success or is it controlled by external factors? For example, in India's newly industrializing regions, employees are characterized by not being in control of their success, perhaps for religious or cultural reasons. They are used to hierarchy and expect managers to take control of a situation. In contrast, employees who believe they have at least some personal control over their destiny will be happier with participative approaches. This will be elaborated on further in the section on Daniel Goleman's work on emotional intelligence and situational leadership below.

Vroom–Yetton Theory The last contingency leadership model was developed by Victor Vroom and Phillip Yetton. This model focuses on how leaders make business decisions. Specifically, this theory argues that the required type of leadership is contingent on these issues:

- whether decision quality is important and followers possess useful information
- whether a manager considers decision quality important while employees do not
- whether decision quality is important when a problem is unstructured and the manager lacks information and/or skill to make the decision alone
- whether decision acceptance is important and employees are unlikely to accept an autocratic decision
- whether decision acceptance is important but employees are likely to disagree with one another
- whether decision quality is not important but decision acceptance is critical

DANISH JOINT VENTURE IN THAILAND

The impact of different perceptions of control can be seen in a joint venture between a Danish manufacturer of building products and a partner firm in Thailand. The Danish expatriate managers had some difficulty managing the Thai workforce at the beginning of the joint venture. Thailand is high on Hofstede's power distance and uncertainty avoidance. Their relatively high power-distance score indicates a high level of inequality of power and wealth within the society, and a distance between bosses and subordinates. The high uncertainty-avoidance index indicates Thailand's low level of tolerance for uncertainty. To minimize uncertainty, Thai society generally has strict rules, laws, policies, and regulations. The ultimate goal of this population is to control everything in order to eliminate or avoid the unexpected.

Denmark and other Nordic countries are essentially the opposite of Thailand, very low on power distance and uncertainty avoidance. Scandinavian leaders typically believe that most people want to be empowered to make work-related decisions. Like

most people of this profile, they tend to project those beliefs onto their subordinates—even those in a foreign country. They develop a system characterized by trust and open communication, and assume that employees are most productive when the workplace is democratic and employees are empowered to make team-based decisions, much like employees in their native countries.

Early on the Thai employees were charged with recreating a team-oriented manufacturing system. This system had worked well in Scandinavia at Volvo and other major manufacturing firms in Denmark. The Danes believed that the Thai employees would understand the local environment better than the expatriates and should have input not just on the joint venture management but on the production system. Yet the first several months were unproductive, while the local employees waited for more instruction from the Danish managers. The result was not innovative changes that fit the local environment as the Danish expatriate managers had hoped, but stagnation.

After three months, the Danish managers changed their approach to a more structured, standard assembly line system. They created very specific jobs for each employee and did not look for employee input on innovative changes that could be made. After some time, the employees learned their jobs and became accustomed to the more democratic (though temporarily coercive) Scandinavian system. After 18 months had passed, the joint venture's production had risen to forecast levels and employees had started to suggest local improvements to production and product. The leadership, which had started out as too egalitarian and unstructured, had moved to a more structured system, and was now gradually loosening up and encouraging innovation. Thus, the leadership style of the managers had to change and evolve as employees evolved and learned more about what was expected and why. The patience of the Danish managers eventually paid off.

Hofstede, G. & Hofstede, G.J. (2005). *Cultures and Organizations: Software of the Mind.* New York: McGraw-Hill.

As a result of these seven contingencies the leader then makes decisions in one of five different ways:

- Autocratic 1—Problem is solved using information already available
- Autocratic 2—Additional information is obtained from group before leader makes decision
- Consultative 1—Leader discusses problem with subordinates individually before making a decision
- Consultative 2—Problem is discussed with the group before decision is made
- Group 2—Group makes decision about upon problem, with leader simply acting as chair

The Vroom–Yetton Model is typically applied using a decision tree. The seven contingencies highlighted above are asked as questions which then, depending on the answer, inform the manager about the required or appropriate style of management for that setting.

International Perspective on the Vroom–Yetton Theory Contingency models can be seen as growing more complex over time. As with many North American–developed theories, the Vroom–Yetton Model assumes participation is good, and this model has proven to be useful in more universalistic societies such as the Scandinavian countries that have a predilection to low hierarchy and power distance. It may be less useful in societies that are higher in power distance, and are more formal,

UNIVERSALISM VERSUS PARTICULARISM: WHEN IN ROME DO AS THE ROMANS?

Culture researcher Fons Trompenaars emphasizes his universalism versus particularism orientation as being a key differentiating dimension of cultures and countries (see In-class Exercise #1 in Chapter 2). In universalistic societies such as those of the United States, United Kingdom, and Germany, people believe in a universal definition of goodness or truth—one that is applicable to all situations. Judgments are likely to be made with little regard to a particular situation. In contrast, people in more particularistic societies, such as China, Russia, and some Latin American countries, take the notion of situational forces more seriously. Judgments take into account contingencies that affect most circumstances, in particular, one's position in a hierarchy and loyalty concerns, especially to family and friends.

When expatriates from universalistic societies work in particularistic societies, they can find themselves in conflict with other members of the local management team. That team may argue that giving special prices and kickbacks to key customers is necessary to facilitate business because of that customer's relation to the firm. Expatriate managers are likely to have problems with this sort of "business as usual" attitude, and may argue that loyalty to longtime customers or suppliers is not as important as offering a fair price and treating all firms in the same manner. A firm's code of conduct and the laws in its home country are important here because expatriate managers need to follow their firm's code and are subject to the laws of their firm's home country, as noted in Chapter 3. Yet a more particularistic society might argue that specific situations allow certain behavior that many in western countries would find unethical. This is becoming a bigger issue as firms from particularistic, developing countries do more and more business in countries such as Sudan, and argue that they have no right or responsibility to say anything about the turmoil and violence going on in those countries.[xxxix]

Trompenaars, F. (1993). *Riding the Waves of Culture*. London: Nicholas Brealey Publishing.

CULTURE

hierarchical, and particularistic. Culture affects values, and decisions are made based on how a decision-maker values an outcome. As we saw in Chapter 2, some cultures, often in the West, hold more universalistic values: universal definitions of goodness, truth, and fairness and the need to always abide by them. Other cultures, often in Asia and Latin America, are more likely to take into account contingencies and circumstances, in particular, one's position in a hierarchy and loyalty concerns (i.e., families and friends). Outsiders are not accorded the same courtesies.

New Views on International Leadership

The theories above were developed in North America. Each has implications for international management, but none directly provides insights as to what should occur internationally. As a result, practitioners have integrated these theories and developed practical means for managers to lead internationally. For example, recent research from the consulting firm the Hay Group studied over three thousand executives worldwide.[xl] The Hay Group has identified a number of different leadership styles, each springing from different components of emotional intelligence. Typically, a leader would call on each of these different styles of leadership in different settings. Daniel Goleman and colleagues built on the Hay Group's extensive empirical research classifications to examine their impact on organizations, and developed more fully the concepts behind each type of situational leadership behavior. The six different leadership styles they specified are coercive, authoritative, affiliative, democratic, pacesetting, and coaching. We will next discuss these concepts and what they mean in international terms. (See Figure 8-5.)

Coercive A coercive leader is typically quite strict, leading by intimidation, bullying tactics, and through direct orders to employees. Although these methods may be helpful in situations requiring a disciplinary style, as we saw in the Fiedler model, they may be disruptive in those settings where creativity and a variety of ideas are required. It is not difficult to understand why Goleman found this style of leadership to be the least effective in most situations. An extreme top-down decision

FIGURE 8-5	Goleman's Situational Leadership Styles

Leadership styles	Method	Phrase	Situation where useful and problematic
Coercive	Demands immediate compliance	"Do what I tell you"	Situation is highly structured and stressful; followers not mature or experienced, requiring strict, mechanistic leadership. Works poorly for an experienced or professional workforce that know their jobs well.
Authoritative / Charismatic	Mobilizes people toward a vision	"Come with me"	To motivate people during difficult circumstances, sell a vision, undertake a turnaround. More of a short-term solution, a telling, charismatic leadership can be hard on followers that might start to value more democratic leadership.
Affiliative	Creates harmony and builds emotional bonds	"People come first"	Build harmony in workforce, increase employee satisfaction and engagement, build loyalty, and reduce turnover. Works well with other leadership styles such as democratic and coaching.
Democratic	Forges consensus through participation	"What do you think?"	To build buy-in or consensus, or to get input from valuable employees—needed for long-term planning and major change. Decision making tends to be slow; does not work well in higher power-distance cultures that expect leaders to make decisions and tell people what to do.
Pacesetting	Sets high standards for performance	"Watch and do as I do, now"	To get quick results from a highly motivated and competent team, like project management, R&D, creative endeavors. Can be tough on a workforce that is being pushed too hard. Pacesetting leaders have a tendency to want to do things themselves rather than delegate. Employee development might suffer.
Coaching	Develops people for the future	"Try this" and "I'll help you"	To help an employee improve performance or develop long-term strengths. Often improves organizational climate significantly. Coaching style takes a lot of time but can be very valuable for employee development and engagement.

Adopted from Goleman, D. (2000). Leadership that gets results. *Harvard Business Review*, March-April, 78–90.

making style stunts innovation: people are afraid to give suggestions or make mistakes. This does not mean, though, that it is always ineffective. In settings in which employees do not want to be accountable for their performance and refuse to respect authority, it can be effective. Firms that operate successfully using this type of leadership are characterized as having rapid decision making and the ability to change course quickly. The coercive style of management does not work well in industries that require innovation and leading-edge development.[xli]

Given the often negative impact of a coercive style on an organization's climate, it should be used with caution and only in special circumstances, but there are times it can be useful. Using a coercive style can break failed businesses of bad habits and shock people into new ways of working. The coercive style is appropriate during an emergency, such as when a company is on the verge of failing; in the face of a disaster such as a fire, a bomb threat, or hurricane; or with problem employees when all else has failed. However, if a leader fails to change his or her style as the situation changes, the long-term impact on the organizational climate can be quite negative. Employee morale is likely to decline if the coercive style remains in place for longer than absolutely necessary. Higher power-distance cultures are more accepting of a coercive leadership style as they are more likely to believe that leaders should act in this way (which does not mean that they necessarily like it).

Authoritative Authoritative leadership is similar to the coercive style, in that it is used to change people's minds in unfavorable situations. Any similarities stop there, however. One of the main differences between the two is that the authoritative leadership style is characterized by enthusiasm and vision rather than criticism and negative tactics—hence it has also been called the charismatic style of leadership.[xlii] This style is called authoritative because leaders tend to impose their vision on the company or team in an assertive manner.

Research has shown that the authoritative style can be one of the most effective approaches to leadership. Authoritative (or charismatic) leaders are visionary and motivating, which gives employees a strong sense of task identity and significance—they know what they are doing and why there are doing it.[xliii] Unlike the coercive leader, the authoritative leader's standards for success are clear and employees are given room to innovate and are not punished for making honest mistakes. Because of its positive impact, authoritative leadership works well in organizational settings such as when a business is adrift. An authoritative leader charts a new course and sells employees on a fresh, long-term vision.

Authoritative leadership also typically works well in high power-distance situations with strong group relationships. For example, Carlos Ghosn, a Brazilian-Lebanese employee of Renault, was sent to turn around the Japanese company Nissan—a company in which Renault has major investments. In three years, Ghosn improved Nissan's performance from $22.9 billion in losses to $7 billion in profits. He was able to do this by ignoring the firm's historic suppliers. Those that came from the *keiretsu* or business group of which Nissan had long been a part. Ghosn instead awarded contracts based on cost and quality considerations rather than on longstanding relationships and traditions. He focused Nissan on building fewer, better products on a narrower range of platforms to increase efficiency, and promoted employees based on talent and performance, not age or seniority (the typical Japanese method). Ghosn also looked for talented people outside of Japan. He consulted his employees for solutions to various issues, but was also able to make decisions on his own when appropriate. Today Ghosn is recognized as one of the top ten business leaders in the world after leading Nissan through an expected and almost unprecedented turnaround.

The authoritative style may be problematic in lower power-distance countries when a leader is trying to lead a team of experts or peers with more experience who may see the leader as overbearing or just out of touch.[xliv] This may also be true in many knowledge industries where employees know their jobs well and do not need enthusiastic cheerleading to get their jobs done. However, authoritarian leadership can be very effective in situations in which quick, dramatic action is required to lead a declining company back to success.

AUTHORITATIVE LEADERSHIP AND RESTRUCTURING

In authoritative leadership, managers and other leaders must be able to make decisions quickly and encourage workers to follow them based on their vision. When a firm restructures, it must make hard choices on what businesses to keep and what businesses to shut down. However, such decisions are not easy and involve sensitive ethical choices for the manager, particularly when a firm is making high profits and chooses to lay workers off in a restructuring effort. But, at the same time, such restructuring can be essential to the long-term health of the firm.

Unilever is the world's third-biggest food and consumer-goods company. The Anglo-Dutch firm's 400-plus brands include Dove soap, Knorr soups, and Sunsilk shampoo. In 2007 it announced a reduction in workforce by 20,000 in Europe—about 10 percent of its worldwide workforce. The goal was to save over $2 billion a year in reduced personnel costs. However, the announcement came as the firm also announced high profits and its surpassing the original profit estimates made to stock analysts.

Patrick Cescau is CEO of Unilever. He is well known for his strong commitment to the betterment of society. In particular, Cescau argues for social innovation in which new products and services are developed to not only meet consumers' need and desire for tasty food or clean clothes, but also for their wider aspirations as citizens. It was clear to Cescau that embarking on the firm's single highest number of layoffs at a time of high profits would be controversial. To successfully complete the layoffs, he relied on authoritative methods. Cescau knew that many people, both inside and outside the firm, would not understand the need for layoffs, but he was confident that it was necessary for Unilever's long-term success. Continued success does not mean, however, that the ethical issues surrounding layoffs like this no longer need to be considered or discussed—they do.

Unilever to cut 20K jobs in Europe. (2007, August 3). *New York Post.* http://www.nypost.com/seven/08032007/business/unilever_set_to_cut_20k_jobs_in_europe_business_.htm.

ETHICS

Affiliative While a coercive leader demands that people do what he or she says and an authoritative leader urges, an affiliative leader believes that people come first. This leadership style revolves around people—its proponents value individuals and their emotions more than tasks and goals. An affiliative leader strives to keep employees happy and to create harmony among them. He or she manages by building strong emotional bonds among employees. This style places a premium on communication and flexibility within an organization.

The affiliative leader is quick to offer positive feedback. Such feedback has special potency in the workplace because it is all too rare—outside of an annual review, most people usually get no feedback on day-to-day efforts or receive only negative feedback. This lack of feedback typically makes the affiliative leader's positive words all the more motivating. Finally, affiliative leaders are masters at building a sense of belonging. They are natural relationship builders.

Affiliative leadership is more likely to be successful where there are lower levels of power distance and more focus on individuality. One of prime example is SAS, the world's largest privately held software company that makes software for analyzing and managing large databases.[xlv] Jim Goodnight was a professor at North Carolina State University when he and several colleagues founded the firm in 1976. SAS today is still largely run a little like a university with the business's culture focused on positive encouragement. SAS believes happy employees will make happy customers. The firm also offers its employees on-site health clubs, day care and medical facilities, hefty cash bonuses, and profit sharing, which helps to build high levels of employee satisfaction and engagement and reduces turnover and absenteeism. As a result, SAS employees are known for being highly committed to the firm. As successful as affirmative leadership has been for SAS, companies that are in decline or in other less-than-optimal situations are less able to benefit from it.

Democratic Style This style is very consultative and is most often associated with the Japanese style of leadership and decision making. It permits a management team and employees to discuss plans and goals and reach decisions collectively, allowing for people to buy into the decision. The democratic style is slow, but when implemented it usually moves along rapidly with few objections. This contrasts with the coercive style, where decisions are handed down by a coercive or authoritarian leader with expectations that the orders will be implemented without question. By letting employees have a say in decisions that affect their goals and how they do their work, a democratic leader increases flexibility and responsibility and keeps employee morale high by listening to employees' concerns. Finally, because they have a say in setting their own goals and the standards for evaluating success, people operating in a democratic system tend to be very realistic about what can and cannot be accomplished.

However, the democratic style has its drawbacks. One of its more frustrating consequences can be endless meetings in which ideas are mulled over, consensus is sought over other goals, and employees are asked about every detail, including how to word trivial memos, announcements, and even meeting minutes. And in the end, the meeting's result can just be an agreement to meet again the following week. Some democratic leaders can use the style to put off making crucial decisions, hoping that meetings will eventually yield a blinding insight, or somehow help them to avoid responsibility. If the democratic style is taken to the extreme, an organization can seem leaderless. Nissan, prior to the appointment of Carlos Ghosn, experienced the risks of this style firsthand. Nissan had been on a downward spiral and appeared unable to address its problems. The business continued much as it had always done, employing a democratic leadership style, while it got into deeper trouble. No one wanted to make any big decisions until Ghosn came along and changed the firm's leadership and decision-making style.

Firms in which democratic leadership works best normally would be associated with very low power distance and a strong emphasis on individuality. Such leadership is typified by Scandinavian firms. For example, the company headquarters of Enator, a Swedish computer consulting company, has an architectural style that typifies management's leadership approach. Management's goal was to optimize their office space to suit the "idea workers" that the firm employs. For example, the building allows people to change their workspace inside the building easily. Also, nameplates and numbers are not on the office doors, so finding someone requires human contact. Enator's goal was to have maximum interaction among diverse people in order to help encourage the generation of new ideas. Democratic leadership also works best in situations that require most people in a department (or firm) to buy into a decision and support it as if it were their own. This may occur when a firm has to make a difficult decision about layoffs or shutting down a product line. Getting people's input about what to do and being transparent about the decision will generally have a positive impact on the organization's climate and the decision outcome.[xlvi]

Pacesetting A pacesetting leader is obsessive about doing things better and faster, and asks much the same of his or her employees. If employees do not deliver, they are out. In this sort of firm, performance can be high for a time, but employee turnover is also high. The difficulty for pacesetting leaders is that often employees feel overwhelmed by managerial demands for excellence, and morale drops. Guidelines for working may be clear in the leader's head, but often he or she does not state them clearly. The pacesetter sees their role as selecting the right people, and training has a much lower priority. In the minds of some pacesetting leaders training should not even be needed if the right people were hired in the first place. Steve Jobs in his first run at Apple was the archetypical pacesetter: a remarkably creative and hard worker, but domineering and terrorizing if employees did not meet his high standards. Apple finally rebelled against Jobs' impossible demands, but not before it was almost torn apart by dissension. Jobs lost the board's support and he resigned in 1985.[xlvii] However, Jobs learned a great deal from his experiences at Apple and came back to the firm about a decade later with a toned-down pacesetting style to lead the company in a very successful turnaround and entry into consumer electronics and retailing.

Cultures that are very high in masculinity often produce more pacesetting leaders, and these do not work well with higher quality-of-life cultures (feminine culture in Hofstede's terms). A pacesetting approach works best when all employees are self-motivated, highly competent, and need little direction or coordination. For example, it can work for R&D groups or legal teams. Japanese culture scores extremely high on the masculinity dimension and are typically thought of as having self-motivated employees who will work long hours with only general directions from management. Thus, pacesetting works well for them.

Coaching This style is more like a counselor than a traditional boss. Coaching leaders help employees identify their unique strengths and weaknesses and tie them to their personal and career aspirations. They encourage employees to establish long-term development goals and help conceptualize a plan for attaining them. They make agreements with employees about their roles and responsibilities in enacting development plans, and they give plentiful instruction and feedback. Coaching leaders excel at delegating. They give employees challenging assignments, even if that means the employees may not be able to accomplish the assignments without help, in order to help the employees grow into their jobs.

Research suggests that of the six styles, the coaching style is used least often but should be used much more. It fits with most cultures and produces a positive

Although coaching focuses primarily on personal development, not on increasing productivity at work-related tasks, it can improve business performance.

Monty Rakusen/Digital Vision/Getty Images

organizational climate.[xlviii] Admittedly, there is a paradox in coaching's positive effect on business performance because coaching focuses primarily on personal development, not on increasing productivity at work-related tasks. Even so, coaching can improve business performance. When an employee knows the boss is using a coaching style and cares about the employee's improvement, that employee feels free to experiment and is not afraid of making mistakes. After all, the employee is sure to get quick and constructive feedback and will be able to learn and become more satisfied and productive.

The coaching style works well in many business situations, but it is perhaps most effective when people on the receiving end of the coaching are supportive of its use. For instance, coaching works particularly well when employees are already aware of their weaknesses and wish to improve their performance. Coaching also works well when employees realize how cultivating new abilities can help them advance. In short, it works best with employees who want to be coached.

Implicit Leadership Another relatively recent development in leadership theory is **implicit leadership**. This theory recognizes that the process by which persons are perceived as leaders follows the same basic social-cognitive processes occurring in other contexts. From this background it is known that people generally find it difficult to cope with large amounts of information they receive from their environment and, as a result, develop cognitive structures—shortcuts to analyze information. These shortcuts include creating categories, schemas, scripts, and implicit theories. A type of script familiar to students is a "date." When a friend tells you that he or she is going out on a date, you immediately understand what that means. No one within the same culture needs the term "date" explained to them—that script is quite familiar. Such cognitive shortcuts are convenient and help people organize and process information more efficiently.

An implicit theory of leadership is similar in that people have certain ideas about the characteristics of leaders and the nature of leadership, and they develop idiosyncratic theories of leadership. As such, an individual's implicit theory of

Implicit leadership
Recognizes the process by which persons are perceived as leaders and follows the same basic social-cognitive processes that occur in other contexts of perceptions of persons.

leadership refers to beliefs held about leaders' characteristics and behavior.[xlix] Leadership can also be based on the idea of a leader's characteristics and what a leader should be.[l] Jeffrey Garten in his book *The Mind of the CEO* described a meeting with the former CEO of AT&T, Michael Armstrong, in complimentary terms, stating that Armstrong showed confidence, enthusiasm, and energy. Garten, showing a common United States and Western Europe implicit view of leadership, based his analysis of Armstrong on traits he thought were appropriate for leaders, stating that if Hollywood were looking to cast someone as a CEO, it would choose Armstrong.[li]

Employees decide about leadership through their ideas about what leader characteristics should be. This suggests that different cultures will vary in their conceptions of effective leadership's most important characteristics. Thus, different leadership prototypes emerge from different cultures.[lii] In some cultures, an individual might need to take strong decisive action in order to be seen as a leader, whereas in other cultures, consultation and a democratic approach may be more generally accepted. In a culture that endorses a more coercive style of leadership, concern expressed by a leader might be interpreted as weak, whereas in cultures endorsing a more affiliative style, such concern proves essential for effective leadership. Recent studies in Europe, for example, have found, as in the United States, those persons perceived as excellent managers and leaders are expected to be high on inspirational leadership. In Eastern Europe, which was long influenced by the technocratic, totalitarian requirements of the Soviet Union, inspirational leadership is not perceived as a characteristic of successful leaders. Instead, excellent leaders in Eastern Europe are those who are thought to be administratively competent. As is expected from the longtime Soviet influence, supervisors in Eastern European firms are often chosen based on their technical skills, while middle managers are often chosen on the basis of political skills and perceived ability to work with senior managers.[liii] Thus implicit leadership theories affect not only how people view leaders, but also how managers are selected. It is easy to see how conflicts arise over differing implicit theories, even for Western European firms based in Eastern Europe.

CONNECTING LEADERSHIP AND CULTURE

The preceding sections presented the major theories and the current trends in leadership. The discussion made clear the possible impacts of different national settings for each of the theories discussed. Despite each theory's differences, you should by now see some commonalities in the suggested leadership style for different cultural settings. This section will integrate and discuss more precisely the appropriate leadership style in specific cultural settings. Hofstede's dimensions of cultures will be used to organize this discussion.[liv] Recall that Hofstede's dimensions of culture are uncertainty avoidance, power distance, masculinity femininity, and individualism collectivism. Each dimension of culture will be discussed in order show how students can develop guidelines to deal with leadership in different environments.

Power Distance and Leadership

Hofstede argued that participatory leadership, which has long been encouraged by North American theorists and managers, is not suitable for all cultures.[lv] As noted, employees in high power-distance cultures, such as India for example, expect a manager to act as a strong leader, and become uncomfortable with leaders delegating decisions. In a culture that endorses a more authoritarian style, leader sensitivity might be interpreted as being weak, whereas in cultures endorsing a more nurturing style, the same sensitivity is likely to prove essential for effective leadership. A less negative attitude toward authoritarian leadership will be found in high power-distance societies. In such societies, dominance and ostentatious displays of authority and order-giving might be seen as desirable actions for a leader, such as in South Asia or the Middle East. This contrasts with lower power-distance cultures that prefer their leaders to empower and encourage employee participation in decision making. In more egalitarian societies, such as in Scandinavia or Australia, leaders should emphasize egalitarian leadership when the situation permits (see the Culture box titled Culture and Doing Business in Australia).

Uncertainty Avoidance and Leadership

High uncertainty-avoidance cultures that have an emphasis on rules, procedures, and traditions, may place demands on leaders not expected in low uncertainty-avoidance cultures. In such environments, it can be assumed that leaders are more directive and rely on rules to help guide their decision making. It is important, however, that a leader ensures that members of the organization are clear on the nature of the rules and regulations that are motivating their actions. Environments with high uncertainty avoidance, ensuring that information is well communicated so that there are no surprises, help the members of an organization accept management's actions. One side effect of this approach is that more innovative behaviors may be expected in low uncertainty-avoidance cultures. This can reduce the ability of the leader to respond quickly to decline or strategically threatening situations.

Individualism and Leadership

A high degree of individualism implies that leaders must allow employees to make decisions about their work. This encourages risk-taking, out-of-the-box thinking, and innovation. In a more collective society, a leader may ask for a group consensus before adjudicating the final decision. For example, in Japan, leadership is oriented toward forming and reaching group goals, and leadership also is geared toward preserving group harmony and not publicly questioning leaders. As noted before in discussing Nissan, such consensus-building can be useful to build buy-in, but it can also delay responses when there are critical issues facing the firm.

Masculinity and Leadership

Countries high in masculinity will more commonly place emphasis on male leadership and production along the lines of the 9,1 leader. These countries include Japan and many of the South American countries. In contrast, Sweden is much lower on the masculinity scale, along with the Netherlands and Thailand, and it could be expected to have more female leaders than most countries and place more value on relations and quality of life in the company. Sweden is also a pioneer in creating excellent quality of life within a firm and building workspaces that promote creativity. In spite of cultural proclivities in some countries against women leaders, research suggests that women expatriates coming in from the outside are more readily accepted as leaders than local women are.[lvi] Thailand has a number of women in leadership positions. It should be noted that women are increasingly able to take up leadership positions in even masculine societies. The Philippines, with a strong influence from the Spanish and East Asian masculine societies, has had two strong female presidents in the past twenty years—Corazon Aquino and Gloria Macapagal-Arroyo. Even the high-masculine scoring country

FUJIO MITARAI, CEO OF CANON

Fujio Mitarai of Canon is one of the most respected business leaders in the world. Mitarai has led Canon to becoming the leading producer of cameras and camera equipment in the world. He has been successful by combining traditional Japanese management with Western focus on profit. Mitarai's focus on profit was developed during his leadership of Canon's U.S. subsidiary. He took over the subsidiary in 1961 when it had only seven employees and quickly adapted to the U.S. business environment. Soon after arriving in the U.S. Mitarai put together his first annual report, which showed a profit of $6,000 on sales of $3 million. The low profit rate raised the concerns of the Internal Revenue Service (IRS) who suspected tax fraud. After an audit, it was found that Mitarai had been honest in his profit claims. However, the IRS agents suggested that he close the business and place the money he would have spent on operating the business in a savings account instead, where he'd earn more money. It was at that stage that Mitarai realized that profits, not sales, on which many Japanese firms focus, are what must be made. Over the next 38 years in the U.S., he built Canon into a major force in the production of camera and copy equipment.

In 1995 Mitarai became president of the Canon Corporation, and in 1997 its CEO. Mitarai is far more decisive than many traditional Japanese managers, who look for consensus. For example, he quickly acted in eliminating divisions that sold unsuccessful products, such as personal computers, electric typewriters, and liquid crystal displays. He merged the remaining divisions into four: copiers, printers, cameras, and optical equipment. To increase coordination among the divisions, Mitarai adopted consolidated balance sheets for the units. Mitarai has also kept a strong focus on profit. To encourage employees, he started having daily lunch meetings with senior managers and monthly meetings with middle managers, in which he personally explained his vision and outlined what needed to be done. This communication level is unique in Japan.

However, Mitarai retains many Japanese leadership characteristics, such as maintaining lifetime employment of workers, a traditional Japanese approach to employment that many firms have now dropped. He argues that such commitment to employees will build similar employee commitment to the firm. Thus, Mitarai has combined aspects of traditional Japanese management with aspects from other cultures to produce a unique and highly competitive form of leadership at Canon.

of Germany has elected its first female prime minister, much to the surprise of many German citizens, suggesting that culture is not necessarily destiny.

OVERVIEW OF CULTURE AND LEADERSHIP

In countries with different cultures there may be several appropriate approaches to leadership. No one type of leadership is best, but rather the goal is to match the needs of the local culture with the right style of leadership. It has been noted that making quick or innovative actions can be difficult in countries whose cultures do not support such action. This does not mean that such actions cannot be pursued. Instead, it means that a business person needs to be aware of potential conflict that can arise when actions are not consistent with the culture. In those situations the business person needs a strategy on how to address the potential conflict. The greatest danger is not the potential conflict, but in being caught unaware of that conflict. If that occurs, the individual will spend significant time working to overcome a problem that could have been avoided.

It is also important to remember that in all cultures, a leader needs to build trust with followers. A leader is also, by definition, responsible. Thus, while leaders may approach that responsibility in different ways in different settings, they cannot be afraid to be out in front when necessary. Leaders must also remember that they must have a high degree of integrity, and must be perceived as treating everyone fairly. Finally, a leader in an unfamiliar environment should be willing to admit when he or she does not know something and seek assistance to get the needed answers. There are individuals in all organizations that are willing to help, and employees do not expect a manager to know everything.

SUMMARY

In North America, charisma is often thought of as central to leadership. However, this chapter reminds us that there is much more to leadership than just charisma. Some leadership situations demand strong, charismatic leaders, while there are other situations in which such a person will be quite ineffective. Additionally, although charismatic leaders are effective in many countries and in a variety of situations, there are other leadership styles that can get useful results. Thus, it is critical that business people recognize that culture dictates the leadership approach.

In addition to the trait theories of which charisma is a part are the behavioral theories of leadership. Originally, there were two main behavioral leadership dimensions: task orientation and people orientation. Leaders could be high, moderate, or low on both of those dimensions. It was originally assumed that a leader who was high on task and people orientation would be the most effective leader. Subsequent research on other key conditions, such as employee experience and the favorability or unfavorability of a situation, has given more depth and detail to the behavior model of leadership. Contingency models of leadership, including the Path–Goal and Vroom–Yetton theories have been developed to help differentiate the situations under which a leader should be more directive or democratic in decision making.

Recent empirically grounded work by Daniel Goleman and colleagues has agreed that task orientation and people orientation are inadequate, and has identified six distinct leadership styles ranging from coercive to democratic, depending on organizational goals, the situation, and employee needs. Implicit leadership theories serve to remind us that different cultures are more likely to favor different types of leaders, and this will influence leadership selection. Even cultures that are relatively close to us, such as those in Western and Eastern Europe, place different value on more charismatic, inspirational leadership. Whichever leadership style you choose, be sure that it fits the follower maturity and the demands of the situation. Simply stated, good leadership brings to a situation what the followers lack, be it discipline, vision or just coordination.

MANAGERIAL GUIDELINES

When trying to inspire employees to reach goals and objectives, managers should remember:

1. leadership in different cultures will mean different things.
2. even a concept such as charisma, which has been shown to have a positive impact in a wide variety of settings, can take different forms in different settings.
3. coercive and authoritarian leaders—the more task-oriented leaders—work best under unfavorable situations. Affiliative leaders work well in moderately favorable leadership situations in which they can give employees more freedom.
4. democratic leaders who seek consensus, discussion, and are slow to make decisions are most effective in getting employee buy-in to facilitate employee input and implementation. This is most helpful with long-term planning and major change initiatives across an organization.
5. affiliative leaders who are good at listening to employees and handling employee relations are usually also good at leading employees during stressful circumstances.
6. pacesetting leaders obtain the fastest results from a highly motivated and competent team—project management, R&D, or creative input. Often, a pacesetting leader is a high performer in the field in which he or she is leading.
7. coaching leaders can be effective. Coaching helps an employee improve performance or develop long-term strengths. Novice employees often argue that they prefer this style to help them develop in their jobs.

8. if a firm cannot change leaders to match a situation, then that leader should try to modify his or her behavior to conform to the situation. This is difficult for some people, which is why Professor Morgan McCall recommends carefully taking into account a prospective manager's background or "professional upbringing" when selecting a leader and not his or her "right stuff" traits. For example, if you are trying to get a new overseas office going in your company that requires the general manager to build the business from the ground up, it would be best to look for someone with experience in fast-growing entrepreneurial firms. That person would understand how to get a new business going, particularly in the face of the many constraints faced by new organizations. In contrast, if you needed someone to run an established factory overseas, McCall argues that an "entrepreneurial upbringing" would not be of much help; the manager in that position needs to have experience in budgeting, scheduling, dealing with government officials, unions, and many other challenges that entrepreneurs seldom face. International experience is also important for anyone being given a key international assignment.[lii] That is not to say people cannot learn a much different job—they can, but there will be a learning curve, and many costs to the company as the firm "pays for the education" of the new manager as he or she grows into the job. This may not be an option for a firm that needs a manager to hit the ground running, particularly in a difficult international assignment.

Table 8-1 will be helpful to students and managers as they examine different aspects of leadership.

TABLE 8-1   Leadership Styles and Culture

Leadership Style	Leadership Style and Culture
Coercive	Coercive leadership is necessary in many unfavorable situations where the work has to get done quickly, with little discussion. The challenge for a coercive leader is when to adjust his or her style with the improvement of the situation and the maturity of the followers. Higher power-distance cultures are more accepting of a coercive leadership style, because they are more likely to believe that leaders should act in this way. Still, leaders can have a mini-revolt on their hands if they keep treating followers in a coercive, tyrannical manner if the situation does not call for it and the followers are mature and know their jobs.
Authoritarian (Charismatic)	There is evidence that charisma is positively associated with effective leadership. However, charismatic leaders who cannot put an organization's goals ahead of their own, even at the expense of their own goals and reputation, can be a liability to the organization. Charismatic leaders may be more effective during turnaround situations and other situations requiring radical change. Certain countries with bad experiences with charisma, such as Germany or Italy, may be more hesitant to accept a charismatic leader.
Affiliative	Unlike the coercive and authoritarian styles, an affiliative leader believes that people and relationships are very important to maintain. Proponents of affiliative leadership value individuals and their emotions more than tasks and goals. This style places a premium on communication and flexibility within an organization. Affirmative leadership is more likely to be successful in cultures with lower levels of power distance and more focus on individuality.
Democratic	Will only countries with a democratic tradition accept democratic-style leaders? That is far from certain; democratic, inclusive leadership seems to depend more on the situation and the maturity of the leader and followers. If the followers know a lot about the job, they will expect to be consulted. One problem is that a leader brought up in a high power-distance country where bosses make decisions and followers carry out decisions may find it hard to act in a consultative manner, and followers may find it hard to accept responsibility. But that leader must learn how to encourage discussion and accept decisions from subordinates, particularly in situations where no one is the expert and the leader needs "buy in" from followers.

TABLE 8-1   (Continued)

Leadership Style	Leadership Style and Culture
Pacesetting	A pacesetting leader is obsessive about doing things better and faster, and asks much the same of his or her employees. Pacesetters lead by example and see their role as selecting the right people. Cultures that are very high in masculinity often produce more pacesetting leaders, and these do not work well with the more feminine cultures, in Hofstede's terms. But the pacesetting approach can work well irrespective of culture if all employees are self-motivated, highly competent, and need little direction or coordination, such as with R&D groups, consultants, or legal teams.
Coaching	Coaching is thought to be effective in all cultures, though higher power-distance cultures are less likely to expect coaching. Coaching can help an employee improve performance or develop long term strengths. Coaching takes a lot of time but can be very valuable for employee development and engagement, and often improves an organizational climate significantly. Similarly, the style works well when employees realize how cultivating new abilities can help them advance.

CULTURE AND DOING BUSINESS IN AUSTRALIA

CULTURE

Australia has an egalitarian culture, which is reflected by the low power-distance score in Hofstede's model of cultural values. The familiarity of the culture is reflected in the Mick Dundee character made popular by Australian actor Paul Hogan in the *Crocodile Dundee* films. The concept of "mateship," the leader being "one of the boys," was one of the typically Australian leadership dimensions that reflects the high value placed on egalitarianism and a leader's ability to earn respect through his or her skills, not by the office held. This egalitarianism means that Australian employees will commonly call their boss by his or her first name, or sometimes a nickname. Students in Australia also often address professors by their first name, or the short version of their name (like "GB" for Garry Bruton, or "Dave" for David), and would think it pretentious of professors to want to be addressed by their titles. This is the opposite of how it is in Germany, where professors are often called "professor doctor"—"professor" representing the job title and "doctor" representing the academic degree held. Australian leaders are expected to inspire high levels of performance,

as in most countries, but they are expected to do so without giving the impression of using charisma or of not being anything more than "one of the mates."

Mateship also results in Australians being suspicious of those who offer excessive praise. Instead, their focus is on the facts. The focus on mateship also emphasizes an egalitarian approach to decision making or group decision making on many matters. As a result, decision making in Australia can take longer than in other western countries. Australia has about 21 million citizens and a per capita GDP of roughly $30,000 per year. Australia's economy has been one of the strongest in recent years of all the developed economies. It is difficult to say if this is because of the egalitarian culture, but Australian culture and leadership styles are likely influencing business practices in the Asia Pacific region.

Ashkanasy, N. M. (2007). The Australian Enigma. In Chhokar, J., Brodbeck, F.C., & House, R.J. (Eds.), *Culture and Leadership across the World: The GLOBE Book of In-Depth Studies of 25 Societies*, (299–333). Mahwah, NJ: Lawrence Erlbaum Associates.

ADDITIONAL RESOURCES

Ambrose, S.E. 1992. *Band of Brothers: E Company, 506th Regiment, 101st Airborne from Normandy to Hitler's Eagle's Nest*. New York: Simon & Schuster.

Goleman, D., Boyatzis, R., & McKee, A. 2002. *Primal Leadership: Realizing the Power of Emotional Intelligence*. Cambridge, MA: Harvard Business School Press.

Goodwin, D.K. 2005. *Teams of Rivals: The Political Genius of Abraham Lincoln*. New York: Simon & Schuster.

Maxwell, J.C. 2005. *The 360 Degree Leader: Developing Your Influence from Anywhere in the Organization*. Nashville, TN: Nelson Business.

Useem, M. 1999. *The Leadership Moment: Nine True Stories of Triumph and Disaster and Their Lessons for Us All*. New York: Three Rivers Press.

EXERCISES

Opening Vignette Discussion Questions

1. Why do you think there are differences in the theoretical advice offered to the managers going to China and what actually worked?
2. As you think about the potential for developing a major new market for cereal in China, what might be some other domains that may offer similar major-market opportunities that would be related?

DISCUSSION QUESTIONS

1. Discuss what you think an effective leader would be like if you were in Australia. Contrast that with what an effective leader would be like in India.
2. What would be the potential leadership problems a Chinese manager at Lenovo might encounter as he or she moves into a senior management position at the firm's new New York offices, where he or she will work with former IBM employees?
3. If a South American manager is sent to manage a joint venture in Sweden, what would be the potential problems that he or she could encounter in seeking to lead the organization?

IN-CLASS EXERCISES

1. Give examples of effective leaders, particularly in business. Consider leaders at all levels from CEOs to supervisors to sports coaches.
2. What do effective leaders do?
3. What are the main goals of an effective leader in most organizations?
4. Think of two ways a leader can build trust in his or her ability to lead.
5. Recently in Japan, a train driver for one of the big railroad firms stated that he was compelled to undergo 71 days of re-education, which included cleaning trains and writing essays reflecting on his "mistake." What was this serious error the operator was forced to write about? It was overshooting a train platform by two meters. What type of leadership style is this company employing? Do you think it will be effective in Japan? How about in western countries, such as the U.K. or the United States? See the article below to help you on this exercise.

Faiola, A. (2005, November 30). U.S. baseball manager's softer style throws Japan's social order a curve. *The Wall Street Journal (Asia)*, p. 32.

TAKE-HOME EXERCISES

1. Several management scholars have argued that charisma is not enough for someone to be a leader. Explain why they argue this.
2. How could charisma actually hinder a leader from being effective and under what circumstances?
3. Many people from the West would argue that democratic leadership in which the leader gives followers a say in decisions is the preferred leadership style. When would a democratic leadership style be effective? When would it be ineffective?

4. In Japan, China, and many other Asian countries, a tough, autocratic leader is thought to be necessary to motivate the workforce. Many leaders (including managers, coaches, teachers, and even parents) believe that praise to followers should rarely if ever be given. Why do you think this is the case? Do you agree with this approach to leadership and motivation?

SHORT CASE QUESTIONS

Leadership under Changing Circumstances (p. 246)

1. Studying military history is recommended to learn more about issues such as training, strategy, logistics, management, and leadership. What do you think can be learned from a military setting about these three key concepts? Keep in mind that although the military regularly trains to fight, most armed forces actually spend only a small amount of time actually fighting, and in fact face many of the same strategic and managerial problems that all large organizations face.
2. Why did the invasion of Europe in WWII ("D-Day") require a change in the way Easy Company, as described in *Band of Brothers*, was to be led?
3. Why do you think the "telling and yelling" style of Captain Sobel, the commanding officer of Easy Company, would not have worked well under conditions of combat? Don't most military officers just yell out orders anyway?
4. What type of leadership style would be necessary under combat conditions?
5. Why do you think the regimental commander (Captain Sobel's boss, Colonel Sink) was unaware of Sobel's failings as a leader? What measures was he relying upon to judge Easy's performance? What does this say about how managers should assess the performance of their units and the fitness of the leaders they appoint?

9

DECISION MAKING

Overview

This chapter examines decision making in the international management arena. As has been demonstrated throughout the text, managing a business becomes more complex as the firm internationalizes, not only due to greater physical distance between various parts of the firm, but also because of the cultural distance. Decisions that are relatively easy in firms that are located in a single country may become very difficult in an international setting. This chapter will examine the following topics:

- Models of decision making, including the rational decision-making model and the positive decision-making model
- Current decision-making concerns, including decision heuristics and biases including loss framing and escalating commitment
- Effective decision making in international business
- Group decision making and the problem of groupthink

OCEAN PARK IN HONG KONG

Ocean Park is an amusement park in Hong Kong. With the opening of Disneyland in the Hong Kong market, it was widely assumed that Ocean Park would be driven out of business. Disney is a well known, global theme park operator with deep pockets and an excellent reputation. Ocean Park was an older park with crumbling facilities and it was losing money. Its future was not bright.

The Hong Kong government did something unusual at that point. It asked Allan Zeman, a Canadian-born businessman well known in Hong Kong as the developer of the Lan Kwai Fung entertainment section of Hong Kong, to take over Ocean Park's management even though he had never been there. The Lan Kwai Fung district includes bars and restaurants that are situated in what previously was a red light district. Zeman was able to come in and help to develop the area, which is now the major area of entertainment for young professionals in Hong Kong.

Hong Kong, a city of 7 million people, has proven able to support the two major amusement parks. Disney has largely taken the model for managing their parks in the United States and applied it to its park in Hong Kong. Decision making about how to run the Hong Kong park was often centered in the U.S. and only limited adaptations

were made. For example, the entry to the Hong Kong park is the same U.S. main street that appears in all Disney parks. Some of the adaptations that Disney did implement have not turned out well. A case in point is interpreting the safety consciousness of the people in Hong Kong as a reason to slow down the rides. This only made the rides less thrilling for teenagers and young adults visiting from both mainland China and Hong Kong.

Zeman, despite being born in Canada, has been making decisions for the park in a manner more like a native of Hong Kong. He incorporated more Hong Kong people into decisions to revamp Ocean Park., and the decisions at Ocean Park have fit better with the local people's desires. For example, typical in Chinese culture, Hong Kong is very family oriented. Ocean Park offers grandparents free entry on certain days, based on numbers in their citizen identity cards. The grandparents then bring their grandchildren to the park and spend a lot of money on them. This promotion also fits with the Chinese interest in lucky numbers. Notice the next time you eat a fortune cookie at a Chinese restaurant in the United States—there will likely be lucky numbers on it.

Zeman has also been able to incorporate unique things into Ocean Park that may seem unusual in the U.S. but that fit well in Hong Kong. He has been able to do this not only from his own knowledge of the Hong Kong environment but also by allowing people from Hong Kong to contribute to decision making. For example, Halloween has become a popular holiday in Hong Kong. The city, from its British roots, has celebrated Halloween to some extent for a number of years. But Zeman has incorporated into this Western celebration other things that are unique to Chinese culture, such as images of paper dolls that are believed to travel with the deceased to the next world. Having individuals dressed up as these dolls and walking around in the park is a unique aspect that only comes from decision making that is sensitive to local culture and traditions. As a result of Zeman's effective strategizing and marketing, attendance at Ocean Park over the last four years has increased by over one and a half million, and the park is in a solid financial position once again, in spite of the new competition from Hong Kong Disneyland.

Smooth operator. (2007, October 20). *The Economist*, p. 88.

Individuals make hundreds of decisions every day: when to get up in the morning, what to eat for breakfast, what to wear for the day, and, if it's a workday, how to get to work. Some of these decisions are interdependent; for example, on a workday you will pick clothes appropriate for the workplace, not for the beach. When a person gets to work, the choices increase and become more complex. Decisions regarding who to use for suppliers or how to market a product are complex and often must balance a myriad of consequences and constraints. Many of the decisions managers make will be routine, but others will not. This chapter will focus both on the nature of the decisions themselves and on the process by which they are made. The chapter will also focus on how to avoid decision-making problems. Decision-making problems often can be traced back to a lack of adequate preparation, reflected in the information that is sought (or ignored), how that information is evaluated, and how possible alternatives are assessed. These mistakes tend to be systematic (i.e., they are

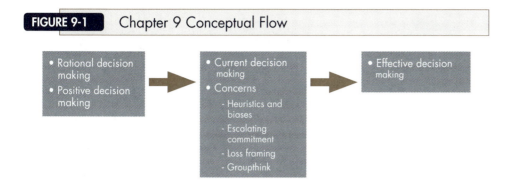

FIGURE 9-1 Chapter 9 Conceptual Flow

consistent and to a certain degree predictable), and because of this they can also be reduced. This is important because decision errors such as wasteful investments or missed opportunities can be very costly.

The higher an individual rises in management, the greater the number of difficult decisions that demand attention, so there is a need to understand the impact of contingencies such as level of responsibility in the organization and its impact on decision making. In international firms particularly, there is also a need to understand any additional complexities and how these complexities impact decision making. This chapter will explore these international dimensions to decision making.

The chapter begins by describing a model broadly known as the rational model of decision making. This model is then examined more critically, by identifying the cognitive limitations that impede such "textbook" approaches to decision making. The latter part of the chapter explores the forms and levels of employee involvement in decision making, including a detailed discussion of self-directed work teams and socio-technical systems. Finally, we discuss the potential benefits and limitations of employee involvement and identify some cultural forces at work. Figure 9-1 summarizes the chapter flow.

RATIONAL MODEL OF DECISION MAKING

The historical foundation for the examination of decision making is what is generally called the rational model of decision making. This model dominated thinking on decision making from the 1800s to the mid-1950s, and is still commonly employed by many individuals. In this model, decision makers determine the appropriate decision criteria, such as price and quality, and then assign weights or levels of importance to them. Different people may place different weights on a criterion because they may value that attribute differently. A manager will then try to rank each decision as to importance and determine the optimal choice, based on these weighted criteria. Decisions under this model are seen as being logically sound, uninfluenced by emotion or other non-rational factors.

The rational decision model has had a major impact on many aspects of business management; most large organizations try to employ numerous decision and operations management tools in their decision making. For example, a central tenet of the rational decision-making model is that there is logical consistency across decisions, regardless of the manner in which available choices are presented. This assumption still lies at the heart of a number of widely used models in finance and economics, such as game theory,[i] which is used to evaluate how

---

FIGURE 9-2   Rational Decision-Making Model

- Define the problem.
- Identify the key decision criteria (based on values).
- Allocate relative weights to the criteria.
- Determine the decision style.
- List solutions and develop any alternatives.
- Evaluate the alternatives.
- Select the choice that maximizes utility based on the weighted criteria of all the feasible alternatives.
- Mobilize resources.

---

different competitors may act and which firms will survive or thrive. In many financial-related businesses, firms employ game theory as the foundation for planning, partly because of the availability of valid and reliable data about the risk and return of assets such as firm stocks or the price of commodities. Thus, the rational decision model provides a useful basis of decision making, not only because it is still used in practice when data are available, but also because it allows us to contrast other decision models with it. We will next discuss each of the component parts of rational decision making in depth. The rational model of decision making is shown in Figure 9-2.

Problem Identification

Problem
Arises when there is a discrepancy between the present situation and the optimal outcome.

Problem identification is the first step in decision making and is arguably the most important. A **problem** arises when there is a discrepancy between the present situation and the optimal outcome. This deviation can be a symptom of more fundamental difficulties within the organization. Therefore, we need to ensure we identify a problem correctly in order to choose the best solution. The decision process is directed toward changing the root causes of difficulties so that the symptoms are reduced or eliminated. This should also lead to the development of decision criteria by which the decision can be weighted.

Appropriate Decision Style

Programmed decision
A decision that follows standard operating procedures. There is no need to explore alternative solutions because the optimal solution has already been identified and documented.

The second step is to determine the most appropriate decision style. A decision maker must choose between a programmed decision or a non-programmed decision. A **programmed decision** follows standard operating procedures, and there is no need to explore alternative solutions because the optimal solution has already been identified and documented. For example, when customers call a General Electric customer service center, operators key the problem into a computer database of 1.5 million issues, and the database provides the best solution. In contrast, new, complex, or abstract problems require non-programmed decisions. In these cases, decision makers must search for alternatives and possibly craft a unique solution. As problems reappear, however, programmed decision routines are formed and knowledge becomes more codified and explicit. In this respect, programmed decisions drive out non-programmed ones. Programmed decisions are faster, more predictable, and routine, and usually do not need an expert to handle them, which lowers costs and enables a firm to serve more customers.[ii]

List of Solutions

The third step in the rational decision model is to develop a list of possible solutions. This usually begins by searching for ready-made, already proven solutions to existing problems. If decision makers cannot find an acceptable ready-made solution, then they would normally try to design a custom-made solution or modify an existing one. All these solutions must first be added to the final list.

Choose Best Alternative

The fourth step in the rational decision-making model involves choosing the best alternative. In a purely rational process, this would involve identifying all the main selection criteria that can help to rate all alternatives. The selection criteria must be ranked by importance and given a weighted rating such as from 1 to 10 or some other scale; then each alternative's total value is calculated from the ratings and criteria weights.

Mobilize Resources

In the fifth step, decision makers must rally employees and prepare sufficient resources to make and implement the decision; a decision that cannot be implemented is just a speculative exercise. Firms must consider the motivation, ability, and role perceptions of employees implementing the solution, as well as situational contingencies to facilitate its implementation. Part of this last step entails evaluating whether the gap has narrowed between "what is" and "what ought to be." Ideally, this information should be based on systematic benchmarks and feedback, so that relevant results and reactions are objective and easily observed.

Problems with Rational Decision Model

Extensive research from cognition, social psychology and behavioral finance has shown that people's decisions are strongly affected by the nature of the data informing a decision and the setting in which that decision is made.[iii] For example, research has shown that it is much easier for a decision maker to cancel a failing project if that person is not the one who approved the project in the first place.[iv] As a result, the rational decision model itself is now recognized as insufficient in describing people's behavior under many conditions. In fact, although organizations want to employ rational, systematic approaches to decision making, particularly with major investments, research suggests that the rational model may be more of an exception than the rule.[v] And when you introduce additional variables such as cross-cultural interaction within an international setting, additional contingencies arise that the rational model cannot address. Thus, while the rational model of decision making is still taught in economics and statistics textbooks as a **normative model** (how things ought to be), it is now recognized that it is not the **positive model** (how people actually behave) of decision making we now commonly recognize in management.

Normative model of decision making
Decision making using a rational model (i.e., how things ought to be).

Positive model of decision making
Actual, day-to-day decision-making model, not idealized.

POSITIVE MODEL OF DECISION MAKING

While we now know that decision making often does not follow the prescribed methods laid out in the rational model, the steps in that model still provide a useful means for understanding how actual practice deviates from the rational model, shedding light on what actually occurs in decision making. In the next

GREATER INTERNATIONALIZATION OF FIRMS AND DECISION MAKING

Chinese firms typically allocate a given percentage of their budget each year to entertainment. This is a throwback to the time when Chinese firms were all state-owned entities and the government ensured that services were provided to employees. Today these funds are typically used both for employees and visiting business people.

One firm that did quite a lot of entertaining was a traditional and well-established Chinese organization. The firm had brought in many foreigners from the West and also had many foreign clients visiting. A high percentage of its entertainment funds were typically spent on these visitors, but some was also spent to offer periodic employee dinners. During a review of how to spend money on employee and visitor activities, the senior managers argued that money should be spent as in the past, that is, on regular lunches, teas, and Chinese-style banquets for both employees and visitors. "That is what the people expect," intoned one senior manager.

But the firm now had young managers from China who had gone to school outside of China as well as a few Western managers. These individuals argued that the younger employees and foreign visitors did not value the regular lunches and banquets; indeed they were complaining that the company had little meeting space, no outside areas to sit in, no coffee room with comfortable seating, and so forth. A local coffee shop had offered to set up a small stand on the company's large premises but this would have required additional outside seating. When the managers reported this to the senior managers they were very surprised, almost shocked. The question they kept asking was, "Why would anyone want to sit outside at lunchtime? How can they have a proper hot meal outside?" One Western manager answered, "They just want to have a sandwich and a coffee and take a break at lunch." The senior manager responded, "Who wants to eat sandwiches everyday? Sandwiches are not a proper lunch. And anyway," he added, "they should be drinking tea and not coffee!"

The company still has not established any break facilities or coffee room, let alone an outside seating area. At this Chinese company, lunch is thought of only in terms of Chinese noodles and dim sum under bright fluorescent lights; anything else, like having a sandwich outside or just a coffee and muffin is not a "proper lunch." The values of the senior executives and their projection made it difficult for them to understand those of the younger employees and foreigners in the organization. Decision making in this setting was difficult because it was hard for the leaders to relate to (much less understand) what the younger and more Westernized employees wanted.

section, we will go back through the steps to look at when and how we now commonly alter the rational model based on our understanding of how decision making actually works.

Problem Identification

Problems, as with opportunities, do not publicly announce themselves. They are recognized and ultimately defined by the decision maker. However, people are neither perfectly efficient nor objective, so problems are often misdiagnosed and opportunities overlooked. One of the key issues in identifying problems is the decision maker's bounded rationality.

Herbert Simon,[vi] in his administrative theory of individual decision making, describes the process that managers (and likely the majority of us) use to make decisions as **bounded rationality**. According to Simon, managers make choices based on simplified and subjective sets of choices. People do not have the ability to process all of the information and analyze all of the possible solutions to a problem. Thus, they employ a means of dealing with this information overload that allows them to narrow problems and possible choices down to something they can process in a reasonable manner. This is why giving a customer or other decision maker too many choices can cause them to freeze up and become unable to make any decision at all. The outcome, however, is that in most cases a manager will make a decision based on limited information and a reduced choice set. A boundedly rational approach to decision making is convenient under some circumstances—how many people have time to evaluate every toothpaste on the

Bounded rationality
According to Herbert Simon, people do not have the ability to process all of the information and solutions that face them. This inability leads them to limit their problems and solutions.

market when they go to the store to buy toothpaste? They make a choice based on very limited information search and evaluation. But for major decisions, particularly ones involving risk and strategizing about the future, boundedly rational decision making can lead to suboptimal decisions because a certain amount of useful information and choices are necessarily ignored. Bounded rationality affects not only the identification of a problem but, ultimately, also the identification of solutions to that problem. Later in the chapter we will see several examples of this.

Appropriate Decision Style

The rational model argues that there are programmed and non-programmed decisions. Programmed decisions are those that largely follow a formula—for example, last month a firm's sales were X, so this month it knows to order X + 1. The impact of bounded rationality is greatest when trying to make non-programmed decisions, and can be viewed along a continuum of rationality. At one end are the programmed types of decisions, and here the rational model is strong and the impact of bounded rationality is limited.

But at the other end of the continuum are non-programmed decisions, where managers must tailor each decision to a particular situation. It is at this end of the continuum that the potential impact of bounded rationality is greatest, because the decision-making procedure here is based on the values, beliefs, attitudes, and behavioral patterns of the decision makers rather than on a strictly rational model. It is important to note, too, that the impact of values, beliefs, and attitudes on decision making is particularly problematic for firms with diverse international settings.

In reality, most firms will have a mixture of both programmed and non-programmed decisions. Some are truly unique and every manager must make a decision based on the reality they perceive. But other decisions may be of a nature where a rational model will work well.

List of Solutions

Upon recognizing that a problem exists, a manager must generate solutions. The key to generating such solutions is gathering relevant information. The psychologist Carl Jung suggested that people have two primary modes of gathering information (i.e., of perceiving): sensing and intuition.[vii] Individuals whose primary mode is sensing use their five senses to gather empirical evidence about a situation. In contrast, individuals who use intuition to assemble (in their minds) the relevant details will depend heavily on their own judgment and less on specific empirical evidence or experience. "Sensors" rely on facts and empirical evidence and are often more inductive, whereas intuitive people rely more heavily on images, emotion and logic and are often more deductive, drawing heavily on certain basic principles from which they prefer not to deviate.

In providing potential solutions, bounded rational decision makers tend to focus on alternatives that are "good enough" rather than on finding the best possible solution. In other words, they engage in **satisficing** (rather than maximizing) by choosing the first "good enough" choice that comes along early in the process. Satisficing occurs because it is difficult to identify all the possible alternatives, and because information about available alternatives is imperfect or ambiguous. It also occurs because decision makers tend to evaluate alternatives sequentially. What constitutes a "good enough" solution depends on the availability of acceptable alternatives. Standards rise when acceptable alternatives are found easily, and they fall when few are available. As in the case of the toothpaste example above, when making smaller purchases (and even some big ones), people will often choose the first pretty good alternative that comes along. They will not make an exhaustive search of all the alternatives. Thus, the satisficing approach may result in people accepting a suboptimal decision in order to save time.

Satisficing
Alternatives that are acceptable or "good enough," rather than the best possible solutions.

PHARMACEUTICAL FIRMS AND IDENTIFYING THE PROBLEM

As stated in Chapter 4, some of the most profitable firms in the world are pharmaceutical firms. These firms must consider current scientific fact while remaining open to new discoveries in approaches to treatment medical conditions.

Physicians treating common peptic ulcers long believed that stress-produced stomach acid was the main cause. Ulcers were thus treated by bland diets, medicines to reduce stomach acid, and if necessary, a difficult and complicated abdominal surgery. Few challenged the status quo, and powerful medical specialists—gastroenterologists and surgeons—controlled the treatment regimen for ulcers.

This paradigm went unchallenged for decades until Dr. Barry Marshall, a family physician in Australia, and a colleague, Dr. Robin Warren, discovered that a bacterial infection was often the cause of peptic ulcers. For years Dr. Marshall argued with the medical establishment and requested funding to study this bacteria, to no avail. He produced data showing the relation between this bacteria and ulcers, but

few physicians took note. Finally, in desperation, Dr. Marshall drank a beaker full of a solution of H. pylori bacteria in front of some colleagues at a medical conference. For a week after he drank the H. pylori, nothing happened. Then, suddenly, Dr. Marshall became sick to his stomach and within a week, he was ill. A colleague performed an endoscopy by inserting a tiny videocamera down Marshall's throat to inspect his stomach. He found the telltale signs of an ulcer: the redness and inflammation of gastritis. Armed with this "discovery," and his finding of H. pylori in nearly all the ulcer patients he had biopsied, Marshall began traveling to conventions of gastroenterologists. After his exuberant speeches announcing that ulcers were caused by bacteria, he was practically laughed off the stage by the specialists. How could bacteria cause ulcers? It took years and years of research in the face of very strong opposition from physicians who would later report that they ignored the data (selective perception), but later found it to be accurate. Their problem was they

simply could not believe that something as common as the H. pylori bacillus caused ulcers, so it had to be something else. The pharmaceutical firms were simply indifferent—more money was to be made in selling antacids and other medicines than a two-week course of antibiotics to kill H. pylori.

Finally, the data did win out, although it was first widely reported in the U.S. tabloid *The National Enquirer*, of all places. In 2005, Drs. Marshall and Warren were awarded the Nobel Prize in medicine for their work on peptic ulcers. Most peptic ulcers would neither have been cured nor the number of surgeries significantly reduced had it not been for these doctors' ability to look beyond standard practice and belief and identify the correct problem. If the medical profession had continued to search for solutions to ulcers only in the area of acid reduction and hormone treatments, the H. pylori bacillus—the real cause of most peptic ulcers—would likely never have been identified.

O'Reilly, B. (1997, June 9). Why doctors aren't curing ulcers. *Fortune*, pp.100–112.

In terms of culture, it is important to remember that different societies vary in how they process information. Recall the discussion of high-context and low-context societies in Chapter 2. Individuals in high-context cultures, such as Arab countries in the Middle East and North Africa, rely much on who is providing the information, their position, and how they present it. Those from low-context societies, such as the United States or Canada, tend to rely more on facts and empirical evidence, though almost anyone can be moved by expert opinion to some extent.[viii] It is relatively easy, then, to imagine how difficult it may be for a firm with operations in both North America and the Middle East to generate potential solutions that both groups agree are useful and to present them in a way that both groups can analyze.

Choose Best Alternative

Evidence-based information search
A process of information search and decision making that does not start with a presumed decision and seeks to evaluate a range of evidence and challenge the emerging solution as it is gradually shaped.

Verdict-based information search
A process of information search and decision making that starts with the presumed answer to the decision and proceeds to only seek out information that confirms the initial verdict or decision.

In choosing the best alternative, an important factor is whether the manager relies on an **evidence-based information search** or a **verdict-based information search** for decision making. Although a manager may be characterized as a "sensing" decision maker, preferring empirical evidence over intuition, these styles of information search are very important in determining what kind of evidence is actually sought out and applied to a decision about the problem. The key difference in the two types of search is the extent to which the decision maker relies on preconceived notions to search for information and frame alternatives. To illustrate the difference between evidence-based and verdict-based approaches, think about the joke where two economists are walking down the street and spot a $20 bill on the sidewalk. The first economist says, "Look, a $20 note. Let's pick it up." The second replies, "It can't possibly be a $20 note, because if it were really a $20 note it would not be lying on the sidewalk. Someone would have picked it up by now." One economist sees the money and wants it. But the other has a preconceived idea that a $20 bill could never be left on the street and so rejects the idea and does not investigate further— using verdict-based information search and decision making, he already knows the bill cannot be real and does not investigate further (losing out on the money in the process).

As another example, consider a decision-making exercise familiar to most of us: a jury used in a court case. Most of the jury may enter the deliberation room "believing" the defendant is guilty and as a result, employ a verdict-based information search where they primarily seek out information (courtroom evidence) that confirms their initial guilty verdict. Such a jury will emphasize evidence that confirms the defendant's guilt; any other evidence that might throw doubt on that guilt is ignored or its source criticized.[2] In contrast, juries that keep an open mind evaluate the evidence as it is made available, and are not afraid to consider evidence that they disagree with or find disconcerting are using an evidence-based approach for their information search and eventual decision making. Juries that use a verdict-based approach able to move more quickly and do not get hung up on technicalities. But they also can overlook important information and are more prone to errors in judgment. People define problems or opportunities based on their perceptions, values, and assumptions. These selective attention mechanisms screen out relevant information, and the quality of the problem definition is lost.

The verdict-based approach to information gathering and decision making creates a *confirming-evidence bias*. This bias leads people to seek out information that supports their existing instincts or points of view while avoiding information that fails to support their beliefs. The confirming-evidence bias not only affects where we go to collect evidence but also how we interpret the evidence we do receive, leading us to give too much weight to supporting information and too little to conflicting information, and even preventing us from searching out information that might challenge our beliefs. It is important to the decision process to seek out a range of information and to avoid premature judgments that will cut short the information search process when useful information for the decision process is still available. That is why it is a good idea to ask people to write down some ideas before coming to a meeting where a key issue is to be discussed and thus avoid being prematurely influenced by those at the meeting.

Moreover, employees, clients, and others with vested interests can influence a decision maker's perceptions and bias them toward a premature decision. Research on strategy has shown how managers with the same type of training and background will often search in one area for a solution and ignore other areas (a problem we will revisit when we discuss the problem of groupthink later in the chapter). For example, the top managers of former Fortune 500 minicomputer maker Digital Equipment Corporation (DEC) all had similar training, had worked as minicomputer engineers for years, and were recognized as leaders in their particular domain. When desktop personal computers started to enter the market, DEC leadership continued to look for minicomputer-related solutions to some of the problems that PCs were starting to be used to solve. DEC's chairman

---

[2]Some students may have seen the classic 1957 film *12 Angry Men*. In that movie, 11 out of 12 jurors are convinced the defendant is guilty of murder and state that verdict out loud to each other, right at the beginning of their deliberations, before even giving their views of the evidence. In fact most of the jurors do not even want to hear about evidence that the defendant is innocent and ridicule the single juror (played by Henry Fonda) who insists on considering all of the available evidence, regardless of its source.

and founder, Ken Olsen, famously stated in 1977, "There is no reason for any individual to have a computer in his home."[ix] As a result, DEC rapidly fell behind microcomputer pioneers such as Apple and IBM, and was unable to participate in the desktop revolution, although it had the engineering talent, resources, and customer relations to be a major player in that business. It was stymied in part by the "verdict" that microcomputers were not that useful, minicomputers were much more powerful, and computing was best done at a central location with computer power piped out to users over wires. In a final irony, DEC was bought out in 1998 by one of the PC companies, Compaq Computer, and much of DEC's technology and product lines were discontinued.

Once a verdict-based decision maker has made up his or her mind, he or she will not examine any evidence that could challenge a conclusion or improve the decision. When confronted with that evidence, they will immediately discount it as unreliable or inapplicable because it came from some particular source with which they seldom agree (though they may never have taken the time to really read or listen to that source), and not because of some concrete concern about its validity.

Too often, verdict-based decision making shows up in organizational settings. Decision makers typically screen out a number of items from consideration to save time. Such screening of evidence is a particular problem internationally, where there is often greater diversity of information. This diversity of information can lead to potentially confounding evidence that the manager will likely ignore or downplay because the bearer of that information is not an insider in the corporation but from one of its distant units.[x] Yet it might be useful inside information about a local market that the headquarters should consider.

Research shows that while evidence-based decision making, which employs a broader information search, is much more likely to lead to better decisions, verdict-based decision making is still very common.[xi] If everyone in a team follows verdict-based decision making and becomes biased in the same direction in this manner, a group-level phenomena called *groupthink* is likely to arise.[xii] Such uncritical consensus thinking is the source of many serious decision errors and suboptimal decision making.[xiii] Groupthink will be considered later in the chapter. The vignette about the Columbia space shuttle accident illustrates the problem of verdict-based information search and decision making.

When diverse opinions are squelched and useful data are ignored when they are presented, important alternatives will go unexamined, and the probability of good decisions is reduced.[xiv] There are several things that firms and individuals can do to help overcome these problems:

- Always check to ensure people are examining a range of evidence with equal rigor.
- Do not lock out otherwise reliable information simply because you do not like its source. Check the information itself for its validity.
- Avoid the tendency to accept confirming evidence without question, particularly when it is from a source that you like.
- Seek evidence that *challenges* your ideas, particularly initial points of view and key assumptions.
- Try to build counterarguments yourself and ask for challenges and comments.
- Give someone in the group charged with making a decision or evaluating a proposal the role of **devil's advocate**,[3] to argue against the decision you are contemplating and challenge its assumptions.

---

[3] The term "devil's advocate" (*advocatus diaboli* in Latin) comes from the Roman Catholic Church. It was a temporary position assigned to someone during the church's process of selecting candidates for sainthood. During the canonization process, the devil's advocate was charged to argue against the sainthood of the candidate. This was to ensure that all the evidence was considered regarding the life of the prospective saint, and that any negatives would be brought to light.

COLUMBIA SPACE SHUTTLE AND DECISION MAKING

Like the earlier Challenger space shuttle, the last Columbia space shuttle mission ended in disaster. During its launch in January 2003, foam insulation debris hit the shuttle, creating a hole in the left wing. Although a couple of NASA engineers suspected the damage to be potentially serious, no one was sure, and thus nothing was done about it, not even figuring out the extent of the wing's damage. When the shuttle's orbiter re-entered Earth's atmosphere, it broke up because of the extreme heat and fire on the wing. Columbia's failure is an interesting and tragic example of verdict-based information search. Post-flight investigations confirmed what the engineers had suspected: the left wing had been damaged by foam insulation that had broken off from the shuttle during take-off and smashed a hole in the wing.

During the two-week period from Columbia's takeoff to its expected re-entry, top managers of the Mission Management Team (MMT) ignored requests from lower-level engineering staff that the Department of Defense be asked to use its spy satellites to photograph potentially damaged areas of the shuttle. The managers could not believe that the foam could have caused any damage, and they refused to consider investigating the problem.

In trying to understand how these disasters came about, consider the following exchange between a Columbia disaster investigator and the MMT chairwoman:

Investigator: "As a manager, how do you seek out dissenting opinions?"
MMT Chairwoman: "Well, when I hear about them..."
Investigator: "By their very nature you may not have heard about them... What techniques do you use to get them? That is, how do you encourage some dissent or questioning of assumptions and plans?"

The chairwoman didn't have an answer.[xv]

When the evidence collected by the Columbia Accident Investigation Board had been sifted through, it became clear that the team had had an opportunity to make a different decision that would have improved the crew's chances of surviving. The team leaders had been asked on different occasions to permit certain members to collect the information they needed to make a reasonable estimate of the shuttle's safety. Team leaders had been advised that the foam might have inflicted enough damage to cause "burn-through"—heat burning through the protective tiles and into the shuttle's fuselage—when the shuttle re-entered the Earth's atmosphere. The possibility was raised that the debris damage might have been severe. And yet the MMT as a whole never came close to making the right decision, or to even seeking out the potentially available evidence. Though many mistakes were made in the decision process, the one that stands out is the verdict-based decision that the breakaway foam probably wouldn't cause any damage, and even if it did, nothing could be done about it, so no further information about the foam strike would be pursued. Unofficially, some of the team's engineers did develop plans to determine how to save the astronauts if there was severe damage to the shuttle's orbiter. Yet the verdict-based information search made by the head of the mission management team stood, and the opportunity to attempt to save Columbia's crew was lost.

BETTER DECISION MAKING

A number of strategies to help managers overcome these problems have been developed within the context of the positive model of decision making. These include creating an early warning system, implementing systems for systematic evaluation, establishing decision support systems, and instituting scenario planning.

Early Warning Systems

A manager can help to avoid the issues discussed above by taking the time to identify in advance any critical issues that could potentially confront the firm. These investigations can be made through discussions with a wide variety of managers within the organization. The firm can then institute an early warning system to identify a problem if it starts to occur. Thus, the manager would not have to be on constant alert to pick out the problem from the constant stream of information. Instead, a system would be in place to help bring the situation to the manager's attention.

To illustrate, it may be difficult given the quantity of data coming into modern organizations to quickly spot a problem in a firm's major product line or to adequately forecast the year-end profit figures. But the firm can use specific warning mechanisms to alert management to potential problems. For example, customer satisfaction ratings falling below a certain threshold or a drop off in repeat business could signal a quality control or service problem, while costs increasing above a predetermined threshold could indicate declining profit margins. Some of these figures are not readily available from typical financial data, or may be difficult to pinpoint, particularly in the case of cost accounting data on allocated costs. Such warning thresholds can be derived from past experience or from pre-set goals for major stakeholders (customers, shareholders, employees, and so forth). The effectiveness of these early warning systems is only as good as their development. However, if carefully planned, alerts can spur an organization to action and prevent conditions from deteriorating further.

Some firms engage in wide data search and data mining to help identify potential issues, using computer programs to search through large databases and organize this information into meaningful trends. Data mining minimizes the perceptual problems that occur when manually looking for trends and patterns in mountains of data.

Systems for Systematic Evaluation

Firms can create processes to ensure systematic evaluation of certain critical information and key forecasts. For example, it is possible for a firm to identify in advance and systematically analyze alternatives for some given problems on a weekly, monthly, or quarterly basis. Typically, such systems are driven by human input (computer-driven systems will be discussed below). To illustrate, when a firm needs to select a job applicant, a systematic evaluation is required that would include (1) identifying the relevant factors against which applicants are judged, (2) measuring applicants on each factor, (3) weighting the importance of each factor, and (4) computing an overall score for each applicant based on the weights and ratings for each factor. (The process for the selection of job candidates will be discussed in detail in Chapter 12, Human Resources Management.)

To illustrate further, Dow Chemical relies on systematic evaluation when deciding which information technology projects to pursue. The company has a cross-functional committee that evaluates each proposal using a point system that factors in the quality of the vendors, the logic of the proposal, and Dow's technical and organizational readiness for change. This process tends to minimize satisficing limitations in the decision process. It also aids information processing because the calculations are systematic rather than based on intuition.

Decision Support Structures

A complementary strategy to systematic evaluation is to create decision support systems to guide the decision-making process. Decision support systems are computer-based programs that guide people through the decision-making process; systems for systematic evaluation are typically human driven instead of computer driven. For example, one firm with which the authors are quite familiar—software developer Cerner Corporation—uses a case-based reasoning process at its help desk. Callers' problems or questions are entered into the system in simple English, and the system replies with questions and eventually solutions to the problems presented. These solutions are organized by topic and made available to all employees online. This decision support system cut in half Cerner's backlog of unresolved client issues and increased customer satisfaction ratings to high levels. Notice that this decision support software turns a seemingly non-programmed decision into a programmed decision. It helps employees identify the problem systematically and search out past solutions that then point to a ready-made solution without the need to evaluate alternatives.

Scenario Planning

Another method that firms use to ensure that they have fully analyzed all potential problems is to employ scenario planning. This method requires a firm to think about what would happen if a significant environmental condition changed, and what the organization should do to anticipate and react to such an outcome. A good question to ask is, "Where are our future revenue and profits coming from, particularly if something important to our firm changes significantly?" Scenario planning explores potential problems and opportunities and asks firms to think about difficult circumstances and competitive challenges. Firms such as the Dutch/British firm Shell Oil and Huawei in China are well known for employing this method to enable them to better think through their assumptions and develop two or three alternative "what if" scenarios associated with major decisions or strategic plans. The advantage of scenario thinking is that the importance of one or two key criteria such as the cost of a raw material or the price of a substitute product can be clearly identified and properly dealt with. See the Ethics Box for ways in which global warming can be thought of in terms of different scenarios with broadly framed costs and benefits of major decisions.

DECISION MAKING ON GLOBAL WARMING

The best science available today on possible global warming scenarios shows that though some causes are natural, various human and industrial activities contribute to global warming. Decision makers who contribute to government policy on this issue must determine the most relevant factors needed to frame the decision making to slow global warming or mitigate its effects. One method being considered is a tax to reduce carbon emissions—thus reducing possible global warming. With this tax, society will sacrifice wealth today, and probably some in the future (called a "welfare loss" by economists) in return for the future benefits of less global warming and fewer associated problems and costs. But to properly make this decision, first it is essential to have a reasonable idea of what the costs would be of global warming if it is left unmanaged, and what the costs would be of stopping it or slowing it down significantly.

The challenge in making assessments about the costs of global warming is that changes in climate set off a complicated set of feedback effects on weather and the environment. Some of these will tend to magnify global warming, yet some will also reduce it. For example, more carbon dioxide should lead to faster plant growth; this pulls CO_2 out of the atmosphere and therefore reduces global warming. But as the atmosphere heats up, polar ice caps melt, causing rising waters and further warming the planet. The list of potential feedback effects is very long, and many effects are interrelated. Because global warming's outcomes are essentially unknown, it is very difficult to assign accurate probabilities, leaving scientists to guess at feedbacks and other long-term outcomes.

These uncertainties are what makes forecasting the climate and determining likely costs of global warming difficult. Estimates of the impact of doubling CO_2 in the atmosphere with no feedback effects is about a 1 degree Celsius increase in temperature—a very manageable increase. But a more likely scenario (with some hypothesized feedbacks included) from the United Nations Intergovernmental Panel on Climate Change (IPCC) argues that a doubling of CO_2 will more likely result in about a 3 degree Celsius increase in temperature over the next

century. The current IPCC consensus forecast is that, under a fairly reasonable decades-long modeling project by the Yale School of Forestry & Environmental Studies and Department of Economics, this amount of warming should result in minor net average global economic costs through the year 2100. Larger negative impacts are predicted in poorer tropical areas, while large northern landmass regions such as Russia, North America, and Northern Europe are projected to benefit. The continental United States and China are projected to experience roughly break-even net impacts. Only if temperatures continued to grow well beyond this level would high costs be incurred. This would lead to potentially costly climate changes that would be felt in the twenty-second and twenty-third centuries, although by a much wealthier and more technologically advanced society. According to the most recent IPCC Summary for Policymakers, a higher end 4 degree Celsius increase in temperatures would cause greater economic losses of 1 to 5 percent of global GDP.

Many advocates of strict global measures to reduce carbon emissions present the issue in terms of the avoidance of costs associated with global warming of about 3 percent of global GDP. This benefit (cost savings) would be realized maybe one hundred or more years later—by future and much wealthier generations. But these rather modest cost savings would justify only very mild abatement of carbon emissions, and there is current thought arguing that this goal can be more productively achieved by innovative firms and entrepreneurs, sometimes in partnership with governments, rather than by large tax increases. That is, the costs of a new tax regime seem higher than the long term benefits, particularly if innovation and incentives to innovate through venture capital and entrepreneurship are downplayed by policymakers and discouraged by much higher taxes. Proponents of more modest efforts to slow global warming also point out that by slowing down economic growth by one percentage point, as the more aggressive carbon taxes would, world economic growth would be greatly reduced in the long run. For example, this reduction would mean the difference between a society that

(Continued)

ETHICS

ETHICS

is four times wealthier than today compared to a society that would otherwise grow sixteen times richer in a 100 years' time. They argue that the much richer society will have many more financial and technological resources to deal with global warming problems.

But costs of global warming are not isolated to small (or even big) future costs associated with managing higher temperatures and sea levels. There is a possibility of more specific climate catastrophes, such as the shutdown of the Gulf Stream or large sea level rises, although accurate probabilities of such events are nearly impossible to assign. Advocates of strict global warming control, who advocate rapid carbon abatement, contend that the downside risks are so catastrophic that we should pay any price to avoid any chance of their occurrence, a concept known as the

Precautionary Principle. It is difficult (some would argue impossible) to determine the probability of events that have never occurred and that have very complex causal mechanisms. If it were possible to determine the probability of such catastrophic events, rational decision analysis could be used to justify the expenditure of large sums to avoid those events.[xvi] For now, policymakers have to weigh the costs of slowing global warming against the significantly reduced economic growth that would ensue given the more aggressive carbon tax and related proposals to determine if the world can live with a slowly warming climate, at least for the time being while technologies are developed to address the problem more fully. Thus, there are rich issues on both sides of this important issue that need to be considered.

CURRENT CONCERNS IN DECISION MAKING

In addition to information search and processing problems, there have arisen a number of more current concerns regarding decision making in organizations. These include heuristics and biases, escalation of commitment, loss framing, and groupthink. Each of these will be examined in turn. See Figure 9-3 for a summary of heuristics and biases.

Heuristics and Biases

In recent years, research has increasingly focused on identifying the cognitive shortcuts individuals use to cope with the complexity inherent in many decisions and their application in the world of business and finance.[xvii] These shortcuts are formally known as **heuristics**. Heuristics simplify the decision making process by providing certain types of mental shortcuts that decision makers can use to make decisions more quickly. As noted earlier, shortcuts serve us well in most situations. Imagine how long it would take to buy toothpaste (or most other products) without relying on expert judgment from a dental association or the recommendations of others for the purchase. As the world has become more complicated, heuristics or decision shortcuts are increasingly helpful in simplifying our lives.

Cognitive psychologist Daniel Kahneman has done a great deal of research on heuristics in decision making, work for which he won the Nobel Prize in 2002. Prior to Kahneman, decision errors were identified with emotion—if a decision maker did not use a textbook rational approach for decision making, then that decision maker was simply being "emotional." In this view, any decision that went awry must have been an "emotional" decision. But later research in psychology,

| **FIGURE 9-3** | Heuristics and Biases |

- **Anchoring.** Anchoring occurs when a person is anchored by an initial impression or relies on one piece of information as the key to decision making.
- **Availability.** The availability heuristic leads to a bias whereby people base their decisions on how easily an example can be brought to mind.
- **Representativeness.** The representativeness heuristic occurs when objects of similar appearance or patterns are assumed to represent something that the data do not warrant.

management, and political science showed that people regularly make decision errors that have nothing to do with any discernible emotional state. Rather, they made consistent mistakes and persistent miscalculations in seeking out information and making decisions. This finding lies at the core of Professor Kahneman and colleagues' research on decision making, which is broadly referred to as **prospect theory**. Prospect theory examines a number of decision-making errors people regularly make stemming from risk assessment, loss aversion, and dependence on a reference (comparison) point. The rational model of decision making assumes that people make decisions based on the optimization of individual self-interest. But people have been shown often to rely instead on heuristics and logical inconsistencies. As a result it seems that mistakes in human decision making are the rule, rather than the exception.

Kahneman and others have shown that although decision heuristics or shortcuts can be helpful to us, they are not always benign. Researchers from psychology, finance, economics, and management have identified a whole range of heuristics people commonly use in making decisions that lead to systematic biases that lead to (highly predictable) decision errors. Even with very simple, one-step decisions, heuristics can push decision makers away from more optimal alternatives. For example, consider a very simple problem: Alternative A offers you a 50-50 chance (like a coin flip) of receiving $1000 or nothing. Alternative B offers you a certain $400. Which option will you take? A quick look at the math tells you that the expected value of alternative A is $500 ($1000 × .50 + $0 × .50), while alternative B is worth $400. Thus, the rational, optimal choice would be alternative A. But if you are like most people, you will not make the optimal choice, but will select the certain $400. Most people hate the feeling of losing something—and if they take the risk and choose the coin flip, they have a 50 percent chance of receiving nothing—so they opt for the certain $400 instead of ending up with no money. This common decision-making bias is known as loss aversion in that people will forgo a superior choice (a potential benefit) to avoid a loss. Even with a simple, one-step, easy-to-calculate decision, the average decision maker can make very big decision errors influenced by heuristics and other common cognitive limitations.

Most people use these shortcuts or heuristics automatically and do not realize they are happening. Heuristics create unperceived biases—traps that increase the possibility of suboptimal decision making. But if an individual can recognize these heuristics and the traps that follow, then that individual can create a process to avoid them rather than accepting information and judgments that are biased and likely incorrect. The heuristics that will be examined include anchoring, availability, and representativeness.

Anchoring Anchoring occurs when a person is unduly influenced by an initial impression or relies on one piece of information as the key to decision making. For example, in one study Kahneman asked individuals to guess the percentage of African nations that are members of the United Nations. People who were asked if the figure was more or less than 45 percent consistently made a lower guess than others who were asked if it was more or less than 65 percent. The only difference was the initial point on which the decision maker (the person answering the question) was "anchored" by the questioner—the higher percentage influenced respondents to make a higher guess. This pattern has held true in many other experiments for a wide variety of guesses on different topics.

Usually once an anchor is set, it biases people toward that value and anchors discussion on that attribute of the product or service. When considering a decision, the mind gives disproportionate weight to the first information it receives. Similar to the verdict-based approach to information search, such initial impressions, estimates, or data anchor subsequent discussion, information search, and

Prospect Theory
Examines risk assessment, loss aversion, and dependence on a reference or starting point. Explains why individuals consistently behave in ways different from what traditional economic and decision theory would predict.

Anchoring
When a manager relies on one piece of information as the key to his or her decision making.

judgments. Recall our discussion of international mergers and acquisitions in Chapter 4, in which we noted that a majority of international mergers and acquisitions fail because managers too often focus solely on rates of return and do not consider key issues like integrating the firms and managing the impact of different cultures on the newly merged firm.

Others have suggested that anchoring affects other kinds of estimates, like perceptions of fair prices and good deals. Anchors take many guises. They can be as simple and seemingly innocuous as a colleague's comment or a statistic from the morning newspaper. Or they can be as insidious as stereotypes about a person's accent, culture, or clothes. In business, one of the most common types of anchors is a past event. As business students you should know that past financial performance is not a guarantee of future performance. Other factors need to be weighed as well. In situations characterized by rapid changes in the marketplace, historical anchors can lead to poor forecasts and, in turn, misguided choices. In addition, because anchors can establish the terms on which a decision will be made, such as the starting price of a negotiation to buy a car or house, the anchors are often exploited as a bargaining tactic by savvy negotiators. Be careful of where you anchor or start out a negotiation, even in a simple bargaining situation at an auto dealer or with your employer; do not anchor yourself in an unfavorable starting place.

Availability
The availability heuristic leads to a bias whereby people base their decisions heavily on an example that can be easily be brought to mind.

Availability A second well-studied and common cognitive shortcut is availability. The availability heuristic leads to a bias whereby people base their decisions heavily on an example that can be easily brought to mind. In these instances, the ease of imagining an example or the vividness and emotional impact of that example becomes more credible than actual statistical probability.

Essentially, the availability heuristic operates on the notion that if you can think of something, it must be important and will become part of your decision. This bias occurs when people place excessive importance on relatively rare, though vivid, events or circumstances. For example, many people believe that "Chinese firms make everything" and have taken over the world's manufacturing and trade. This is because Chinese products are more "available" in cognitive terms: many consumer goods such as clothes and light electronics are made in China, so naturally the "made in China" label seems to be everywhere. The truth is somewhat more complex. China has a much smaller share of world trade than the United States and several other countries.[xviii] And, quite often, Chinese-owned firms are not the ones doing the manufacturing and exporting; it is just that the factory happens to be located in China. Everything is not made in China, but the availability or vividness of consumer goods made in China makes people exaggerate China's importance (or threat) with respect to world trade.[xix]

Media coverage can also help fuel people's availability bias with widespread and extensive coverage of unusual events, such as airline accidents, and less coverage of more routine, less sensational—but perhaps more important—events such as automobile accidents. For example, when asked to rate the probability of a variety of causes of death, people tend to rate more newsworthy events as more likely because they can more readily recall an example from memory. For example, most people believe that having a gun in the house is quite dangerous for children. But few know that children living in homes with a swimming pool are more than 100 times more likely to die in an accident involving the pool compared to children that live in a house with a gun being fatally shot.[xx] Similarly, people often rate the chance of death by plane crash as higher than the chance by car crash. In actuality, death from car accidents is much more common than airline accidents, particularly in many emerging economies with poor roads and little traffic control. People may be afraid to travel to India because of the news of terrorist attacks and sectarian violence, but the probability of encountering such problems in a country the size of India are remote (unless one is seeking out the trouble spots). Yet the likelihood of being in a car accident on one of India's roads is much greater. Additional rare forms of death and injury also seem much more common than they really are because of their inherent drama, such as shark attacks, lightning, and terrorism. The problem lies when people make decisions based on faulty or incomplete information. People are more likely to believe that plane crashes kill more people than car accidents and thus pay relatively little for auto safety, although it would be a relatively simple thing to improve road maintenance and safety to significantly reduce accidents. This can push organizations and governments to invest a great deal of money to prevent very remote events while neglecting safety measures such as improved road safety because safer roads are not vivid or newsworthy.[xxi]

One final cautionary example. When the anthrax scare occurred in 2001 in the United States, the U.S. Postal Service spent $5 billion to acquire equipment to prevent future poisoning of the mail. This was done in spite of a lack of evidence of terrorist involvement (probably a rogue scientist) or evidence that it would continue to be a threat. Five people died from the anthrax attacks, which is most certainly a tragedy, but thoughtful arguments have been made that that amount of public money could have been spent on other safety measures to address much more likely and serious problems. But anthrax was very vivid and dramatic, thus biasing decision making about where to spend money on safety and public health.

In international business, the impact of the availability heuristics can be seen in how Americans view potential markets. For example, today's media representations of Russia are almost universally negative in the United States. Russia is seen as a corrupt, criminal, and dangerous place, almost always hostile to the United States. The result is that most Americans do not recognize that the Russian economy is rapidly growing, its capital markets have done very well in recent years, the rule of law is improving, and tremendous opportunities for American and other foreign firms are emerging.

Representativeness The representativeness heuristic occurs when seeming patterns are assumed to represent something that the data do not warrant. While sometimes useful in everyday life, representativeness can also result from misunderstanding probabilities, seeing patterns where none exist, and neglecting relevant base rates—that is, the underlying relevant population from which that small (pattern) sample is being drawn. For example, people tend to judge an event's probability by finding a "comparable" known event or situation and then assuming that the probabilities will be similar. The vignette about the "hot hand" illustrates this issue.

Humans, as part of making sense of their observations, need to classify things. If something does not fit exactly into a known category or pattern, or have a visible cause, most people will approximate with the nearest similar category available or make a guess as to the cause. This can lead to some significant biases, such as assuming people with certain characteristics will have (or lack) certain skills and knowledge. The representativeness heuristic leads people to believe in spurious causes, such as the mythical "hot hand" in basketball. As noted above, people often incorrectly believe a "hot" player is more likely to perform well at that moment. This all happens because people tend to ignore *base rates* (the relative frequency or likely probability that an event, like making a basket, typically occurs). People also misunderstand that there are always runs (hot streaks) and that over time these tend to even out as performances return back to their averages (i.e., regress toward the mean). This

Representativeness
The representativeness heuristic is when seeming patterns of data are assumed (incorrectly) to represent something that the data do not warrant.

INTERNATIONAL BUSINESS AND THE HOT HAND

Suppose you are the coach of a men's basketball team. Your team is behind by 1 point with only a few seconds left, so a single basket will win the game. Your best player, who has made about 56 percent of his shots in his career, is having a bad night and has made only three of twelve shots. Another player on your team has made his previous six shots, including a couple of long three pointers and has scored 30 points, but his career average over many years is only 46 percent and he's more known for his defense. The defenders guarding those two players are approximately equal in skill, and the other three players are not reliable scorers. Since the game is on the line and you only have time for one more play, which player would you pass the ball to for the game's last shot—your best shooter or the player having the big day? Most people when asked that question would recommend passing the ball to the player who is having the big scoring game, as he has the "hot hand." Yet research on sports and performance confirm what decision-making scholars would argue, that this would be an incorrect decision, and it would be best to ignore the representativeness heuristic and give the ball to the player with the best career average.

Many people, especially sports fans and announcers, would incorrectly recommend giving the ball to the player who has scored 30 points as he is "hot." (Try this question with friends who are basketball fans.) They believe the player with the hot hand is the obvious choice as he has a better chance of making the next shot and the other guy is "cold" anyway. This idea of the hot hand is very common in sports and yet it does not hold up to empirical scrutiny. Basketball players are not more likely to make a shot simply because they have just made several in a row. Players (and anyone else, for that matter) are most likely to perform to their average, or in this case, return to their average—a phenomenon known as regression to the mean. Research has shown that no matter how many shots a player has made or missed in a game, the odds that he will make or miss his next shot do not change and will generally be consistent with his career averages. The idea that someone on a hot streak is more likely to perform better is an example of the representativeness heuristic—people seeing patterns that are not there, or at least that cannot be explained by anything other than natural streaks or base-rate probabilities.[xxii]

The idea of a hot hand can also be applied to international business, particularly in the area of finance. We will discuss this in more detail in Chapter 11.

---

misunderstanding of what (apparent) patterns truly represent (or do not represent) leads gamblers and investors to believe in runs of good and bad luck or streaks of hot and cold. Many streaks and other clusters of similar events are usually little more than the naturally occurring variation that exists with any probabilistic series of events. For example, some people claim to see clusters of cancer incidence near power lines running through certain communities; this was the basis for a large number of lawsuits in North America in the 1990s. When carefully studied, these clusters turned out to be naturally occurring random patterns. No statistical link between power lines and cancer incidence was found, and no study ever showed that brain tumors were caused by low levels of exposure to electric power lines. But tens of millions of dollars had already been spent in lawsuits and bogus awards.[xxiii]

Assumptions about how groups of individuals may act or what they will buy are often based on representativeness assumptions. For example, in the United States, people often assume all Latin Americans will want the same things or act in the same way as Mexicans, only because Mexicans are the Hispanic group that Americans know best. The reality is that many Latin Americans have tastes and behaviors that are very distinct from those of Mexicans, and to simply assume that just because someone speaks Spanish he or she will behave like individuals from Mexico is a mistake. A simple illustration is food: Mexican food is often spicy, but food in Argentina and some other parts of Latin America tends to be relatively bland.

Overcoming Heuristics/Biases No one can avoid the influence of heuristics because they are part of our cognitive makeup, and some mental shortcuts are useful. But managers can reduce the impact of anchors, availability, and representativeness by using the following techniques:

- Always view a problem from different perspectives. Try using alternative starting points and approaches rather than sticking with the first line of thought that occurs to you or that comes up in a meeting.
- Think about the problem on your own before consulting others in order to avoid becoming anchored by their ideas.
- Be open minded. Seek information and opinions from a variety of people to widen your frame of reference and to push your mind in fresh directions. Do not reject ideas out of hand based only on their source. People with a different background or political point of view may have something useful to add to the decision process. Diversity can improve group decision making.
- Be careful when using advisers, consultants, and others. Tell them as little as possible about your own ideas, estimates, and tentative decisions. If you reveal too much, your own preconceptions may simply anchor the discussion prematurely.

Escalation of Commitment

Another more current area of concern is known as **escalation of commitment**, which is the tendency to allocate more resources to a failing course of action. (In poker, this is called "throwing good money after bad.") There are plenty of examples of escalation of commitment in organizational settings. One of the most prominent occurred years ago when the British and French governments continued funding the Concorde supersonic jet long after its lack of commercial viability was apparent. To this day, many refer to escalation of commitment as the "Concorde fallacy." A variety of the escalation of commitment occurs in organizations where significant investment has been made in a project, but the decision makers do not want to go back on that decision and cancel the funding. This specific aspect of escalation of commitment is called the **sunk-cost trap** (see Figure 9-4).

Sunk-Cost Trap What helps to energize the escalation of commitment problem is the sunk-cost trap, which is the deep-seated bias to make present decisions in order to justify past choices. Even when the past choices no longer seem valid, individuals are too often unwilling to give them up. For example, many individuals will refuse to sell a stock or a mutual fund at a loss even though it may be clear that the investment will not turn around. When you do this you are foregoing other, more attractive investments, but doing otherwise would require you to admit that you made a mistake and realize the loss. Firms often put enormous effort into improving the performance of an employee who most individuals recognize should not have been

Escalation of commitment
The tendency to repeat an apparently bad decision or allocate more resources to a failing course of action. (In poker, this is called "throwing good money after bad.")

Sunk-cost trap
Making decisions in order to justify past choices.

| **FIGURE 9-4** | Escalation and Sunk-Cost Fallacy (Sometimes Cognitive, Sometimes Social Psychological) |

- **Escalation of Commitment**. An increased commitment to a previous decision in spite of negative information (chasing sunk costs).
- Are you swayed by arguments that a certain infrastructure project must be finished because "so much has been completed already"?
- If the answer is yes, then you too have been a victim of what psychologists call the "sunk-cost fallacy"—the human tendency to judge options according to the size of previous investments rather than the size of the expected return.
- Truly rational choices would be made only after weighing future costs and benefits. Past costs and benefits are quite irrelevant.

hired in the first place. But firing the person would require acknowledging that past decisions and the associated investments of time or money are now irrecoverable. We know, rationally, that sunk costs should be rendered irrelevant to the present decision, but nevertheless sunk costs still affect people's decisions.

Sometimes a corporate culture reinforces the sunk-cost trap. If the penalties for making a decision that leads to an unfavorable outcome are overly severe, managers will be motivated to let failed projects drag on endlessly in the vain hope that they will somehow be able to transform the projects into successes. Such a culture can also limit risk taking because managers will fear proposing anything remotely risky for fear of failing and being punished. Executives should recognize that in an uncertain world where unforeseeable events are common, good decisions can sometimes lead to bad outcomes. By acknowledging that some good ideas will end in failure, executives will encourage people to cut their losses rather than let them mount.

Causes of Escalating Commitment Researchers have identified several factors that lead to the sunk-cost trap and, in turn, an escalating commitment. These include self-justification, the gambler's fallacy, perceptual blinders, and closing costs.

Escalation of commitment sometimes occurs because people want to present themselves in a positive light, that is, they want to create self-justification for their actions. Individuals who are personally identified with a decision tend to persist because this demonstrates confidence in their own decision-making ability. This persistence is also the decision maker's way of saving face to avoid the embarrassment of admitting past errors. Some cultures (even corporate cultures) have a stronger emphasis on saving face than do others, so escalation of commitment may be more common in those societies where leaders rarely admit mistakes. Thus, in more hierarchical societies, such as in East Asia and Latin America, escalating commitment problems can be particularly widespread.

Many projects result in escalation of commitment because decision makers commit the gambler's fallacy, that is, they underestimate the risk and overestimate their probability of success. They become victims of the gambler's fallacy by having inflated expectations of their ability to control any problems that may arise. In other words, decision makers falsely believe that luck is on their side, so they invest more in a losing course of action.

Escalation of commitment can occur if decision makers do not see the problems soon enough. Through these perceptual blinders, as discussed earlier in this chapter, the decision makers unconsciously screen out or explain away negative information. Serious problems initially look like minor errors. The information necessary to pinpoint and define major problems is downplayed, so the problems are ignored and remain unsolved.

Even when a project's success is in doubt, decision makers will persist because the closing costs of ending the project are high or unknown. Terminating a major project may involve large financial penalties, a bad public image, or personal political costs. This explains in part why BHP's hot briquetted iron (HBI) plant in Western Australia long continued to receive financial support in spite of very high cost overruns. The plant cost about $2 billion to build and was not competitive. Terminating the project proved difficult because of the estimated costs of around $1 billion for doing so and the embarrassment of a number of BHP principals and politicians. The plant was finally closed in 2007 after several years of losses and other problems.[xxiv]

Overcoming Escalating Commitment Problems Managers in particular should be on the lookout for the influence of sunk-cost biases in decisions and recommendations made by their subordinates. Managers can do several things to overcome escalating commitment problems:

- One effective way to minimize escalation of commitment decision problems is to separate decision choosers from decision evaluators. This tends to avoid the problem of escalating investments because a decision maker had to "prove" that he/she was right. For example, banks have been found to be more likely to take action against bad loans after the executive responsible has left. In other words, problem loans were effectively managed when someone else took over the portfolio.
- Publicly establish a preset threshold. If the resulting test falls in the alert region, the decision is to be abandoned or re-evaluated. This is similar to a stop-loss order in the stock market, when stock will be sold if it falls below a certain price.
- Seek to avoid creating a failure-fearing culture that leads employees to perpetuate their mistakes. In East Asian firms, for example, this is thought to be a particular challenge. Such firms are often organized around principles of filial piety, which means loyalty to the father or father figure, such as a boss in the organization. To go against the boss or the decisions they have made would be considered improper and would show poor upbringing and disloyalty.[xxv] Thus, it can be difficult to organize for innovation because employees fear that they will be criticized as disloyal or punished for pointing out errors such as failing projects. A decision or judgment gets evaluated for its loyalty to top management, not its accuracy.
- Recognize that the source of escalation of commitment has deep psychological roots in our desire to protect our egos or prove to others that we were correct. Breaking from the status quo also means taking action, and when we take action, we take responsibility, thus opening ourselves to criticism and to regret. Most individuals will stick with the status quo because it is the safer course, putting us at less psychological risk.
- In rewarding people, look at the quality of their decision making and their decision process, taking into account what was known at the time their decisions were made, not just the quality of the outcomes.

Loss Framing

A third current concern was also identified by Kahneman, who found that most people feel worse about a loss of a given amount than they would feel good about a gain of a similar amount. This loss framing, or loss aversion, means that people tend to focus more on losses (or loss avoidance) than they do on benefits in making decisions. To illustrate, homeowners are more likely to purchase energy-saving insulation when the cost savings are presented in terms of losing money through energy wastage, instead of on any payback or gains provided through lower utility bills.[xxvi] This higher valuing of losses (and thus being more influenced by them) holds for money, opportunities, and other items. People consistently are more influenced by avoiding potential losses than by gains. (See Figure 9-5 for summary of loss framing.)

FIGURE 9-5	Loss Framing

- The loss framing bias means that most people feel worse about a loss of a given amount than they would feel good about a gain of a similar amount. That means people tend to focus on losses (or loss avoidance) in making decisions.
- There is evidence that managers place more importance on information about potential losses than benefits of approximately equal value.
- Items and opportunities are seen to be more valuable as they become less available. This latter propensity is also called the scarcity principle.

That decision makers value losses more than gains of the same amount is reflected in how people value products that are hard to get. Study after study shows that people dislike losses greatly, or missing out on a perceived benefit. Thus, items and opportunities are seen to be more valuable as they become scarcer. (This latter propensity is called the scarcity principle and will be covered in more detail Chapter 10, Influence and Negotiation.) It's important to understand how people value losses. One well-known study showed that potential losses played a far bigger part in managers' decision making than potential gains.[xxvii] Policymakers rate and codify the potential losses associated with every decision. An extreme example is the methodology of "worst-case analysis," which was once popular in the design of numerous organizational systems and is still used in certain engineering and regulatory settings. The idea was to avoid the "worst" worst case scenario, but this may bring higher costs than is necessary.

What can managers do about loss framing? In Chapter 10, we will learn about how loss framing can be used to influence people to buy our products or ideas. A poorly framed problem can undermine even the best-considered decision. But the adverse effects of framing can be limited by taking the following precautions:

- First, do no automatically accept the initial frame, whether it was formulated by you or by someone else. Always try to reframe the problem in various ways. Look for distortions caused by the frames.
- Second, be aware of being overly sensitive to losses, which can also lead to risk aversion. Firms that are afraid to risk anything also miss out on major opportunities.

Groupthink

Groupthink
A mode of thought whereby individuals intentionally and prematurely conform to what they perceive to be the consensus of the group and preference of the leader.

The last major current concern in decision making that will be examined here is groupthink. After the severe blunders at Pearl Harbor and other attacks on the allied forces during World War II, researchers started to examine catastrophic decision failures, especially those originating from groups. In the 1970s, psychologist Irving Janis theorized a group interaction phenomenon he called groupthink, and credited it with being a potentially important influence on group decision making. Although groups generally make better decisions than individuals, **groupthink** is the downside of group decision making, and it must be carefully avoided. Janis defined groupthink as a mode of thinking that people engage in when they are deeply involved in a cohesive in-group, and when the members' striving for agreement override their motivation to realistically appraise alternative courses of action.[xxviii] More generally, groupthink is a problematic manner of decision making that can arise during the group decision process, whereby individuals intentionally conform to what they perceive to be the consensus of the group and preference of the leader. (See Figure 9-6 for details on groupthink.) This emphasis on group harmony and agreement

FIGURE 9-6	Groupthink

- Groupthink is formally defined as "a mode of thinking that people engage in when they are deeply involved in a cohesive in-group, when the members' striving for agreement overrides their motivation to realistically appraise alternative courses of action (or even examine assumptions)."
- Individuals intentionally conform to what they perceive to be the group consensus and the preference of the leader.
- Groupthink may cause the group—typically a committee or organization—to make poorly supported, too-fast decisions which are likely to prove suboptimal or even catastrophic.

FIGURE 9-7   The 8 Symptoms of Groupthink, Divided into 3 Categories

---

Category I: Overconfidence in the Group's Abilities

- Symptom #1 Illusion of Invulnerability—People are more risk-seeking in a group (risky shift—some exceptions)
- Symptom #2 Belief in Inherent Morality of the Group—Related to fundamental attribution error (the other guys are "in it for the money/power, etc.")

Category II: Closed-mindedness of the Group

- Symptom #3 Rationalization—Ignoring contrary evidence and basing decisions only on past (limited) experience (related to verdict-based decision making)
- Symptom #4 (External) Stereotyping of Out-groups

Category III: Group Pressure to Conform

- Symptom #5 (Internal) Self-Censorship—"We don't do that around here," Not Invented Here (NIH) syndrome
- Symptom #6 Direct Pressure—Subtle threats to dissenters
- Symptom #7 Mindguards—Keep dissenting opinions away from leaders; excessive centralization
- Symptom #8 Illusion of Unanimity—Overlook quiet dissent and the leader makes his/her opinion clearly known

---

overrides the ability to consider relevant evidence and the merits of a decision. More specifically, groupthink can cause the decision-making group—typically a committee or large organization—to make poorly supported, hasty, and suboptimal decisions that each member might individually consider to be unwise and would disagree with in private. Team-based decision making provides many benefits—speed, flexibility, and positive team member development. But such teams are also subject to the effects of groupthink, and this can be a major problem because many important decisions about organizational strategy, key threats, or forecasts about the future should be made by decision-making teams or groups.

In his research, Dr. Janis identified eight symptoms that could indicate that groupthink may be occurring. If this is the case, there will be a higher probability of that group making a decision that will be unsuccessful, and possibly even catastrophic. The first two characteristics of groupthink stem from over-confidence in the group's prowess. The next pair reflect the tunnel vision members use to view a problem. The final four are signs of strong conformity pressure within the group. (See Figure 9-7 for a summary of these eight symptoms of groupthink.) These symptoms have shown up in numerous flawed decision processes, for example, the 1986 *Challenger* space shuttle accident, the decisive defeat of French and Allied forces at the start of World War II in 1940, and the failure of the Russian navy to save its ill-fated *Kursk* submarine in 2000.[xxix] These examples will be discussed in greater detail below, along with the eight groupthink symptoms.

1. *Illusion of Invulnerability*. The attack on Pearl Harbor is often cited as a classic example of an illusion of invulnerability. The American naval and army commands never thought that the Japanese naval and armed forces could travel thousands of miles undetected to attack U.S. military bases at Pearl Harbor in Hawaii, and as a result they did not test that very important assumption. This illusion of invulnerability led military authorities to fail to prepare for possible attack, in spite of numerous warnings that war with Japan was imminent, which resulted in perhaps the worst defeat ever inflicted on U.S. military forces.

2. *Belief in Inherent Morality of the Group*. Group members automatically assume the rightness of their cause, and dissenters are judged as unethical or even immoral. At the hearing about the *Challenger* accident in 1986, one engineer noted that NASA managers had shifted the decision rules under which they operated, remarking that the engineers felt they were in the position of having

to prove that the space shuttle was unsafe instead of proving that it might not be safe and that dangers could not be ruled out.

3. *Collective Rationalization.* Despite the launch pad fire that killed three astronauts in 1967 and the close call of Apollo 13, the American space program had never experienced an in-flight fatality. When engineers raised the possibility of catastrophic O-ring blow-by, it was argued that the shuttle had flown successfully about 20 times and there was little reason to think that this would not continue.

4. *Out-group Stereotypes.* Getting critical outside testimony and evidence is important for groups seeking effective decisions. In 1940, French and Allied (British, Dutch, Belgian) forces were defeated in a shocking six weeks by the German *Wehrmacht* with just a little help from their Italian allies.[xxx] The French high command at the start of World War II in Europe failed to learn lessons from the German *blitzkrieg* attacks on Poland. The French generals argued that the Poles were not up to the standard of the French armed forces and Poland was not like France. Thus information about German tank battalions and their coordination with armed troop carriers and *Stuka* dive bombers was mostly ignored.[xxxi]

5. *Self-Censorship.* Returning to the *Challenger* accident, main contractor Morton-Thiokol wanted to postpone the flight. But instead of the engineers clearly stating that they certainly should not launch below 53 degree Fahrenheit (about 11 degree Celsius), they offered equivocating opinions. One engineer suggested that lower temperatures were not in "the direction of goodness" for the O-rings. Managers instructed engineers to make a management decision rather than an engineering one, presumably asking them to ignore some of their data and take a risk—something engineers are loath to do when human life is involved. Engineers were reprimanded by their superiors, so they did not press the issue directly with NASA even when they could have spoken up at the final preflight launch meeting

6. *Illusion of Unanimity.* NASA managers perpetuated the fiction that everyone was fully in accord on the launch recommendation. The managers admitted to the presidential commission that they did not report Thiokol's hesitancy to their superiors. As often happens in such cases, the flight readiness team interpreted silence as agreement.[xxxii]

7. *Direct Pressure on Dissenters.* During the momentous decade of the 1930s in the run-up to World War II, Charles de Gaulle, then a major in the French army, wrote a well-read article and later a book that described the importance of armored vehicles, separate tank battalions, and close ground-air cooperation. He was ignored by the French high command, which temporarily removed him from the promotion list for disagreeing with commanders. The French high command pointed out that they would not tolerate dissent (often termed "disloyalty") such as de Gaulle's. One well-known French staff officer added: "Everyone got the message, and a profound silence reigned until the awakening of 1940 [the German invasion of France in World War II]."[xxxiii]

8. *Self-Appointed Mindguards.* "Mindguards" protect a leader from assault by troublesome ideas. During China's long war with the Japanese during World War II and subsequent fight against Mao Zedong's Communist forces, China's Generalissimo Chiang Kai Shek was well known for not wanting to hear bad news. When asked who his best generals were, he would usually reply that it was those that were the most loyal and did not question his orders. Even when the general was losing all battles he was fighting, Chiang would still be heard to remark "yes, but he is loyal."[xxxiv] In spite of having more resources and troops at his disposal, and assistance at various times from both the Soviet Union and the United States, Chiang

managed to lose most of the battles he fought and was eventually driven out of the Chinese mainland by the victorious Communist armies. A weak grasp of the concepts of total war and grand strategy exacerbated by weak group decision processes that would not give Chiang bad news or suggest the need to change strategy and tactics almost certainly hastened the defeat of Chiang's government forces.[xxxv] Attempting to prove loyalty or to avoid disrupting the harmony of the group by keeping bad news from the group leader or higher management is more likely to lead to groupthink and ill-informed decisions and is most assuredly inadvisable.

As can be seen, groupthink can occur in a variety of settings, including commercial, noncommercial, and professional environments. And groupthink can spoil a decision process to the extent that key assumptions are not tested and alternative strategies (visions) and scenarios are not examined. This is because groups engaged in groupthink tend to lock out outside points of view, employ verdict-based information search (not searching out anything that might disagree with their narrow points of view), suppress internal discussion, fail to challenge key assumptions (and make unwarranted assumptions), fail to consider alternatives, take excessive risk, and do not use the information they have. This creates a poor decision process that can lead to suboptimal and even catastrophic results.

Avoiding Groupthink There are ways that firms can overcome groupthink:

- Take the time to recognize and understand the vastly different ways that people's minds work. Howard Gardner's classic book *Frames of Mind*[xxxvi] explores various different intelligences (linguistic, musical, logical-mathematical, spatial, bodily-kinesthetic, inter- and intra-personal) that, if acknowledged and allowed to interact, can bring a surprising and exciting array of new data into any decision-making process. Ensure that a mixture of different mindsets are present in the group. This diversity can bring different perspectives to problems. But notice that it is diversity of thought and background.
- People also interact and process data in a variety of ways. Each person contains a mix of orientations, from task centered, to learning centered, to people centered. Each of us learn in different "directions," some moving from "the big picture" to the specifics of the particular task or project, and others beginning with details and moving outward to the bigger picture. We also organize data differently, some through step-by-step chronological planning, which is more common in Northern European cultures, and others by starting up something, stopping, and then coming back to it again. Creating space for a variety of cognitive approaches may take time initially, but in the long term, it ensures decision processes that are more creative and effective at problem solving and responding to the unexpected.
- Avoid overly valuing consensus and harmony, especially as a team leader. Remember that harmony is not the ultimate goal: the best decision is. Not everyone has to fully agree; they just have to agree enough to get the job done. Important decisions need to be evaluated on their merits, not because they make boss feel good or contribute to group harmony and agreement. Make sure that differences of opinion are encouraged and appreciated (not just tolerated). Take time to allow every member of the team to express themselves, and work hard to avoid putting pressure on dissenters to conform.
- Create partnerships of people from diverse disciplines, departments, or backgrounds when facing new projects or creative challenges. For example, under the leadership of Jerry Hirshberg, the Nissan Design Center in San Diego, California, hired designers in complementary pairs—people who were as unlike each other as possible—in order to ensure that they would avoid routine thinking and would lead one another into new avenues of creativity.

Different people possess different types of intelligence-linguistic, musical, logical-mathematical, spatial, bodily-kinesthetic, inter- and intra-personal. Bringing many of these ways of thinking and problem-solving together often results in better, more creative, and more thorough solutions to the problems a firm might face.

Flying Colours Ltd/Digital Vision/Getty Images

- Ensure effective processes for aggregating the group's input. Diversity is important, but groups ultimately need to land somewhere; decisions need to be made. It is crucial, therefore, to have effective processes for bringing all the divergent data into a cohesive whole and setting a time limit. It is important to resist the temptation to move into this phase too soon, but when the time is right, the group must be brought together in some way, or chaos, rather than creativity, will result.
- Voting is a method to be used only sparingly, perhaps at the end if no agreement has yet been reached. In some situations more than one alternative can be tried, and the results tested before a final course is chosen.
- In many groups that have taken the time to explore collective wisdom in depth, ongoing debate and dialogue can result in surprising new thinking, shared by the entire group, which opens the doors to the best decision. In this scenario, while consensus is not a goal of the group, it is frequently the result of effective processes. A well-known Native American Indian chief, in explaining how his tribal councils made major decisions, expressed it well in saying that they kept talking until there was nothing left but the obvious truth.[xxxvii]
- Finally, if a group is to be involved in the decision-making process, let it actually make decisions. If the group is treated simply as an advisory structure, or if its findings are dismissed or minimized, group members will simply check out of the process, and the group will experience "death by committee."

In an increasingly globalized and complex world, the collective intelligence of a group or organization is more important than ever. There are now a number of ways for a group's collective wisdom to be developed and utilized, though traditional meetings or via newer technologies. Whether through releasing the potential in relational tools like team building, or drawing on the technological dialogues made available through blogging or other information gathering and discussion, organizations need to work to take advantage of this diversity of thought and experience while avoiding the symptoms of groupthink.

GROUP DECISION MAKING

It is important to note when we discuss groupthink that this is a dysfunctional approach to group decision making. Groupthink and the effective group decision-making process are two very different things. But if a group is functiong well, then group decisions can be very effective.[xxxviii] A group, if it is more organized, is also called a team; a larger, less organized group might be called a "crowd" or a market. It is commonly believed that with a group, you get an average intelligence (and thus an average decision), and that an expert should always be called on to make important, difficult decisions—even unstructured ones where the solution may have a complex series of pathways to the answer.

In fact, group decisions in less structured decision areas like strategizing, making estimates about future price movements, and guessing about capital markets will typically be much better than any one individual's decisions. There are many famous examples of contests where people can win a prize if they guess an object's weight or the number of units in a container. One individual typically gets close, out of the thousands of guesses submitted. But if you average all the guesses together they are almost always exactly on point. To illustrate further, consider the space shuttle crash discussed earlier. Just ten minutes after the *Challenger* exploded over the southern Atlantic Ocean, the stock market pushed down the price of the shares of the four major contractors who were seen as potentially responsible for the crash. By the end of that day, three stocks had recovered to their original price with minor losses. Only the stock of contractor Morton-Thiokol of Utah in the United States, stayed low, indicating that the market was betting that Morton-Thiokol was most responsible for the accident. There is no way the market could have known this: insiders had not dumped the stock, and it would be months before government inquiries uncovered the cause of the accident. But the market came to a "group" decision that ultimately proved correct: it was later determined that the failure of one of Morton-Thiokol's poorly designed O-rings caused the accident.[xxxix]

People often believe that any group is not as smart as the smartest person in the group. Most people also think that one or two experts will be smarter than a group. It is also commonly believed that when using a group (or the market) to make a decision, a simple agreement or consensus will be reached. None of the above is correct or true. The intelligence (wisdom) of a group is not the "average" of the intelligence of each individual in the group. Moreover, the wisdom of groups and markets is not about consensus. Wisdom really emerges from dis-agreement and even conflict. It is what one might call the "collective opinion" of the group (like the price of a stock, or of any product), but it is not an opinion that everyone in the group can agree on specifically. That means you are not likely to find collective wisdom by simple compromise or harmony-maintaining approaches. Some dissent and the giving of opinions are needed. Experts, no matter how smart, only have limited amounts of information. They have cogni-tive biases like everyone else. It is very rare that one person can know more than the sum of a large group of people, and almost never does that same person know more about a whole series of questions, some of which fall outside of his or her expertise. Thus, the current evidence is that group decisions are more effec-tive than individually directed decisions under certain specific, though com-monly occurring circumstances:

1. The decision involves a long-range forecast or prediction, or
2. The situation is strategic (development of a strategic plan).
3. The situation is complex, requiring multiple skills.
4. The situation is such that no one person is an expert on that topic. This could be in a movement out of the organization's traditional area of expertise.

EVALUATING DECISION MAKING IN INTERNATIONAL BUSINESS

Too often, decision makers in international business are not effective or efficient. One concern is that after making a choice, decision makers tend to inflate the quality of the selected alternative and deflate the quality of the discarded alternatives. This perceptual distortion, known as post-hoc justification, results from the need to maintain a positive self-identity. We encountered post-hoc justification with the problem of escalation of commitment also. Post-hoc justification generally gives decision-makers an excessively optimistic evaluation of their decisions, but only until they receive very clear and undeniable information to the contrary. Unfortunately, post-decisional justification also inflates the decision maker's initial evaluation of the decision, so reality often comes as a painful shock when objective feedback is finally received.

ALCATEL-LUCENT

Alcatel is a leading French technology company that acquired Lucent in 2006 for $11 billion. Lucent was formerly known as Western Electric, the manufacturing division of American telecommunications giant AT&T, and home to the legendary Bell Labs where many famous technologies, such as the transistor, were developed. Lucent represented high technology and innovation in the United States, even after being spun off from AT&T in the telecommunication deregulations of the 1980s. With the addition of Lucent, Alcatel hoped to build a world-class global business that could dominate the wireless and hardwired telecommunications industry. Alcatel had strong relationships with European operators, while Lucent had strong ties to North American carriers who had been its customers for many decades. The companies believed that combining their businesses would allow them to address customers across both continents and improve their operational efficiencies to compete in Asia. Alcatel also believed it could generate about $1.7 billion in cost savings over three years based on synergistic economies of scale and scope from the merger.

Prior to the acquisition, Alcatel had shown a strong ability to make good decisions quickly. For example, Alcatel had recently sold many of its unprofitable businesses, such as microelectronics, batteries, cables,

and mobile handsets, choosing to focus on fiber optics and mobile telephony. It also bought into the IP service-router business by snapping up California start-up TiMetra Networks, which now ranks second only to Cisco in this high-growth sector.

However, the acquisition of the much larger Lucent did not generate the expected benefits for Alcatel-Lucent. Part of the difficulties that the firm faced in its decision making related to the organization of the combined firms. To address these issues the firm developed an executive committee of seven senior executives from both companies in 2007 to make crucial decisions about the combined firm's strategy and integration. However, just two of the committee members were former Lucent employees: Cindy Christy, who added Central and Latin America to her existing responsibility for North American sales, and John Meyer, head of services. The merging of North America with Central and Latin America sought to simplify decision making, resulting in just two regions—the Americas and the rest of the world (Sayer, 2007). Alcatel-Lucent at this time also sought to make some changes in the firm's personnel, with the appointment of a new CFO. The outcome of these changes still did not reverse the decline of the firm.

Another key part of the difficulties that faced the combined firms' decision

making was their cultural differences. For example, it has been noted before that the French are very hierarchical with a high power distance. In contrast, Americans tend to prefer very participative decision making and have fairly low power distance. The CEO of the firm came from Lucent while the chairman of the board came from Alcatel. One issue that was difficult to resolve was having headquarters in France while the CEO was in the United States. This physical distance between the CEO and headquarters made decision making slow and collaboration difficult.

The numbers for Alcatel-Lucent do not look good. Since the 2006 merger, the $27.5 billion company has posted six quarterly losses, taken billions of dollars in equipment and asset write downs, and seen its stock price plummet by 50% to less than $10 per share. Not all of this is the sluggish economy after the merger. Telecom investment worldwide is set to rise 2.5% to 5.5% in 2008, while Alcatel-Lucent estimates its sales may decline by low-to-mid single digits.

The outcome was that by 2008 the firm's losses were mounting and dramatic changes were called for. The CEO was fired (from the original Lucent) and the chairman of the board (from the original Alcatel) had to resign. The firm was faced with having to integrate the businesses much

(Continued)

more thoroughly and reduce decision time while increasing decision quality. The firm has had problems in integrating its much different styles. Lucent's decision-style is slow and deliberate, owing to its long association with AT&T in a regulated environment and having many very long-term customers. Alcatel, in contrast, was a much looser confederation of divisions and product lines with a free-wheeling style. As the merger progressed it was estimated that Alcatel was utilizing around 20 different accounting and reporting systems in various parts of the firm. Given the differences in decision style and data reporting, it has proved more difficult than either side anticipated to integrate the two firms and realize the planned cost savings, let alone any synergistic benefits from combining the product line and development efforts. Only time will tell if the new chairperson and CEO can get the Alcatel-Lucent ship back in shape, but a great deal of work in integrating the two firms and aligning the decision systems and data reporting seems to remain.

Sayer, P. (2007). Alcatel-Lucent CFO leaves in management change. Computerworld. http://www.computerworld.com.au/index.php/id;164868684.

Matlack, C. & Schenker, J.L. (2008, June 18). Alcatel-Lucent's troubled marriage. *Business Week*. http://www.businessweek.com/magazine/content/08_26/b4090056678890.htm (accessed July 29, 2008)

Michelson, M. & Wendlandt, A. (2008). Loss-making Alcatel-Lucent dumps CEO and chairman. *Reuters*. http://www.reuters.com/article/newsOne/idUSWEA355220080729.

- The communications, group dynamics, and decision-making processes involved are quite complex in international business. In small groups, diversity of opinion is the single best guarantee that the group will reap benefits from face-to-face discussion. What this means is that diversity—that much-discussed feature of today's work environment—is a very important factor in collective intelligence. While gender, race, age, and cultural diversity all have a role to play, the primary element in effective teams is **cognitive diversity**, the ability of members of the group to *think* differently (not just *be* different in terms of race or gender) and to express their opinions and findings opening in an organizational setting. International companies need to tap the power of cognitive diversity naturally present in their offices and partners around the world.

Cognitive diversity
The ability of members of the group to think differently, and to express their opinions and findings.

DEALING WITH CULTURE AND DECISION MAKING

It has been highlighted throughout this text that culture is an important consideration for those doing business internationally. It is worth discussing specifically some of the cultural factors that can affect decision making. For example, based on differences in a society's orientation to activity—to "getting things done" (see Chapter 1)—some cultures emphasize solving problems, while others focus on accepting situations as they are. In certain cultures, such as the United States, managers perceive most situations as problems to be solved and as opportunities for improvement through change. Other cultures, such as the Indonesian, Malay, and Thai cultures, tend to see no need to change most situations, but rather individuals attempt to accept life as it is and be patient with the situation.

If a "problem-solving" manager receives a notice that a prime supplier will be three months late in delivering needed construction materials, he or she will immediately attempt to speed up delivery or find an alternate supplier. If, by contrast, a "situation-accepting" manager receives a similar notice of delay, he or she might simply accept that the project will be delayed. Situation-accepting managers believe that they neither can nor should alter every situation that confronts them. Problem-solving managers believe that they both can and should change situations to their own benefit. Situation-accepting managers generally believe that fate or God will intervene in the production process (external attribution), whereas problem-solving managers are more likely to believe that they themselves are the prime or only influence on the same process (internal attribution). Consequently, when viewing exactly the same situation, American managers might identify a problem long before their counterparts from the county of Georgia might. Comparative research has demonstrated that managers' perceptions of situations and their definitions of problems vary across cultures.

A key aspect of culture that affects a firm is who makes the firm's decisions. Based on a culture's view of the relationships among people (see Chapters 1 and 2), either individuals or groups will hold primary decision-making responsibility. In North American business, individuals usually make decisions. The popular expression "The buck stops here" reflects the belief that ultimately a single person holds responsibility for a particular decision. In Japan, groups make decisions; most Japanese would find it inconceivable for an individual to make a decision prior to consulting his or her immediate colleagues and gaining their agreement.[xl]

At what level are decisions made? In more hierarchical cultures (see the discussion of Hofstede's power-distance dimension in Chapter 2), only very senior managers make decisions. Lower-level personnel are given responsibility for implementing decisions. Most lower-level Indian employees, for example, would wonder about the competence of a superior who consulted them on routine decisions. The majority of Indian managers prefer a more directive style, and up to 85 percent of their surveyed

---

DECISION MAKING AND VALUES IN THE UNITED STATES AND CHINA

CULTURE

In the classic 1945 film *Valley of Decision*, Gregory Peck stars as Paul Scott, the son of a wealthy industrialist in one of the great U.S. steel centers who has many ideas about newer production practices and better labor relations, which are alien to those of his parents and their business associates. Greer Garson stars as the family's maid, Mary Rafferty, and her father is an employee in one of the plants owned by Scott's father. Scott becomes attracted to the maid's personality and sympathy for the plant workers. In the meantime, labor trouble erupts in the plant—the workers go on strike for higher wages and better working conditions. A group of strike breakers are called in; Scott attempts to persuade his father and his advisers to call off the strike breakers and discuss terms with the labor leaders. But while his father, under pressure from his son, exchanges views with the labor leader, a riot breaks out between the workers and the strike breakers. Scott's father is killed, many men are injured, and the family's home is destroyed. Mary Rafferty's father is killed also. After order is restored, Scott takes over the management of the business and liberalizes its labor policies. As a result, Scott's unsympathetic wife demands a divorce, and Scott and Rafferty are then married.

Chinese-American anthropologist Francis Hsu observed both Chinese and American responses to this film when it was released at the end of World War II. Americans considered the movie to be good drama, because every conflict was resolved in a desirable way. Conflicts with production methods in the workplace were resolved by introducing new views on manufacturing; liberal attitudes toward labor won out; Scott, the progressive son, replaced his conservative father; and true love triumphed in the end.

According to Hsu, Chinese people who saw the film did not agree. Hsu reports that one of his Chinese friends understood the considerable size and extent of American industry and wealth, and he had some understanding of the acrimony in American industrial disputes. He was also aware that Americans are usually ready to experiment with new ideas or to introduce novel methods of production. But they considered both the Peck and Garson characters to be villains. Peck's character, Paul Scott, had no filial piety because he was opposed to his father, and his decision to encourage his father to work more closely with the union undid all that his parents had done. The maid was practically the sole cause of the breakdown of Scott's marriage, his family's ruin, the destruction of Scott's home, and both of their fathers' deaths. When the maid first entered the picture, the family was prosperous, dignified, and intact. If she had not encouraged her young boss in his views, he would not have asked his father to negotiate with the laborers and the father would not have been exposed to their fatal attack. Her own father would not have died in the ensuing battle.

To the Chinese audience, a son in conflict with his father was a bad son, and a maid who would help such a son in his endeavors was bad woman. Through the same Chinese lens, Scott's wife was regarded as an extremely virtuous woman who suffered at malicious hands. The question of the son's unhappiness with his wife as opposed to his possible happiness with the maid should never have been raised. Hsu noted, however, that while the Chinese audience's thoughts about the son's decisions were dominated by concerns about the family and its business, it took almost no account of the workers' difficult situation. The Chinese audience argued that the workers should accept their lot; the hierarchy should remain intact and everyone should know their places—workers, maids, and sons alike.

Hsu, F.L.K. (1981). *Americans and Chinese: Passages to Differences* (3rd ed.). Honolulu, HI: University of Hawaii Press.

subordinates believe they work better under supervision.[xli] By contrast, most lower-level Swedish employees expect to make most of their own decisions about day-to-day operations. Thus, it would not be surprising that Swedes, not Indians, were among the first to experiment with autonomous work groups and platform manufacturing. At Volvo's Kalmar plant, Swedish management gave groups of employees total responsibility for producing cars.[xlii] The group, not senior management, took responsibility for allocating and scheduling tasks as well as for allocating rewards among employees. Senior management could more easliy delegate this amount of discretion to the shop floor in a low power-distance country such as Sweden.

Are decisions made slowly or quickly? American business people pride themselves on being quick decision makers. In the United States, being called "decisive" is a compliment. By contrast, many other cultures downplay time urgency. Some cultures even rate a decision's value proportionally to the length of time spent in making it. In addition, more traditional collective cultures might be concerned that the wishes of the more senior people are respected, whereas in a more Anglo-American context, individual choices are more recognized and expected.

When managers from quick-paced cultures, such as the United States, attempt to conduct business with people from more slow-paced cultures, such as Egypt and Pakistan, the mismatched timing causes problems. Americans, for example, typically become frustrated at Egyptians' slow, deliberate pace and begin to believe that their Middle Eastern counterparts lack the commitment to getting the job done. Egyptians, on the other hand, in observing the Americans' haste to make decisions, typically conclude that Americans' unwillingness to take more time reflects the lack of importance they place on the business relationship and the particular work at hand. The cultural perception of time and other values is a crucial dimension in understanding decision-making behavior cross-culturally.

SUMMARY

Decision making is a challenging task for organizations. Organizations face many important decisions on a regular basis, and decision errors can have serious consequences. First, it is important to remember there are strong psychological forces at work in decision making that affect everyone. These psychological forces or heuristics can be useful because they help us to screen out excess information for trivial and day-to-day decisions, but they can also can create information search and decision biases that push us toward deficient and even irrational decision making. These irrational decisions are not limited to emotional decisions leaped to with little thought, but even seemingly calm and cool decisions can prove to be very suboptimal if cognitive biases are not accounted for. First, decision makers must be sure to conduct earnest information searches for important decisions. It is important to understand that people routinely overestimate their own abilities and knowledge, and tend to assume that their view (or the view of their group or department) is the right one. This causes people to employ verdict-based information search and to search out information that only confirms their initial decision or some other preconceived bias. Research suggests that this is a substandard approach to gathering the information you need to make an informed decision. It is better to practice evidence-based information search, withholding your decision about something until you have sought out adequate evidence, and not just evidence that conforms to a preconceived notion about something. It is the contrary evidence that helps an organization work the kinks out of a difficult decision. Avoid being too dogmatic and didactic ("I'm telling you the way it is," or the more colloquial, "It's my way or the highway").

Money that is already spent is money that no longer should figure in future decisions. The sunk cost fallacy is one of the more common decision-making fallacies, and it results in financial decisions that are incorrectly based on previous investments or expenditures. Such a tendency is problematic for the simple reason that past investments should not affect your future decisions. What matters is how much you need to spend to accomplish what you were trying to do versus the best alternative. Past investment should not count, only what is likely to happen from the present.

In terms of information search and investment, it is hard for people to admit mistakes. That is why it is hard for managers to terminate a failing investment or for people to search for and accept information that goes against their basic beliefs, even if the evidence is sound. People like to try to confirm what they already believe or have decided. This confirmation bias of evidence makes it hard to change patterns of thought and behavior, as well as policies. This is as true for highly rational scientists as it is for business people.

Remember that people tend to weigh certain facts, figures, and events too heavily, putting too much stock in them, which can be explained by a number of decision-making heuristic problems. Anchoring, for example, explains how people fixate on a specific amount or topic and negotiate around that. Similarly, people also tend to place too much emphasis on especially available or vivid information. They also misunderstand probabilities and try to find cause and effect in data that is in fact random.

Another basic principle of decision theory states that it matters how you frame decisions. Since most people tend to be loss averse, if a decision is framed as a loss (or a missed benefit), people are more likely to try to avoid that loss than if the same decision were framed as a benefit. It is important to understand this propensity to loss aversion and how it may cause people to almost irrationally seek to avoid a loss and weight information about losses more heavily than about potential benefits. Also be aware of the groupthink problem, which can harm the otherwise effective group decision process. Allow the group decision process to operate; value diversity of opinion, particularly dissenting views. Encourage innovative thinking, even if it goes against the grain of what your company has practiced for years. Firms grow through the development of new products, new markets, and new businesses, often outside of traditional domains.[xliii]

MANAGERIAL GUIDELINES

What can be done to improve decisions?

- Analyze the situation carefully, and do not rush into major decisions. The "just do it" attitude that the popular culture tends to promote can lead to poorly thought-out decisions, prematurely arrived at.
- Avoid strict dogma. Be open to contrary evidence and publications from a different point of view than your own. Assess the *evidence presented* rather than dismissing it by criticizing the messenger's background, politics, or training, which are not relevant to the *accuracy* and applicability of the evidence itself.
- Be aware of the common heuristics that lead to biases, both for individuals and groups, and try to avoid them. For example, do not be overly influenced by available or vivid information. Just because there were three terrorist bombings in India last year, for example, does not mean that such bombings are "always happening," nor does it mean that traveling to India is particularly unsafe. Try to gather as much data as is feasible to make your decision, and do not let any one piece of data dominate the decision.
- Combine rational analysis with intuition, but understand that "common sense" or intuition is often flawed and affected by the common cognitive biases described in this chapter.
- When possible, treat decisions as part of a series of decisions. That is, do not be too risk averse to avoid a single mistake. Successful decisions cannot occur if you do not make any.
- Use group decision making for unstructured, predictive, ambiguous, or otherwise difficult decisions, particularly where no one is the expert. But beware of groupthink or premature conclusions, which can lead to catastrophic decision errors.

DOING BUSINESS IN THE COUNTRY OF GEORGIA

When many Americans hear Georgia they think of the state in the southern United States. But Georgia is also a country of over 4 million in the Caucasus Mountains around the Black Sea. Georgia was a republic in the USSR until its breakup. From the time of its independence in 1992 until 2004, Georgia was ruled by former Communist Party officials. But in what is now called the Rose Revolution, the population demanded a true democracy. As a result, Georgia has quickly instituted a reformed, market-oriented economy and active democratic institutions. Georgia has even begun conversations to both enter NATO and the European Union.

As part of the political changes in Georgia there has been a strong effort at market liberalization. Georgia is now ranked by the World Bank as number 18 out of approximately 180 countries for ease of doing business. Now investor confidence is strong and the economic growth is approximately 10 percent per year. There are large numbers of Russians and Armenians living in the country. Georgian, the official language, is ancient and very unique, and its written form is unlike any other. Almost all documents must be translated into Georgian if someone wishes to do business there.

Georgia's efforts to enter NATO has angered Russia, which still sees that country as part of its sphere of influence. The result has been that Russia has instituted strong controls on Georgian exports. While this has caused many difficulties for some businesses, it has also forced Georgians to build more connections to Europe and market their products there. Today Germany is one of Georgia's major trade partners. Culturally, Georgians are more conservative than many Europeans. But as Georgia integrates with Europe, it is quickly taking on more typical European attitudes. Family remains a central concern in Georgia and the culture is much more hierarchical than in most European countries.

In 2008 almost all the progress in the Georgian economy was brought to a halt as the country fought a border war with Russia. Although much larger, Russia invaded Georgia and helped two regions whose ethnic origins are Russian declare their independence. These regions are now planning to join Russia as provinces of that nation.

CULTURE

ADDITIONAL RESOURCES

Belsky, G., & Gilovich, T. (2000). *Why Smart People Make Big Money Mistakes and How to Correct Them: Lessons from the New Science of Behavioral Economics* (115–116). New York: Simon & Schuster.

Langewiesche, W. (2003). Columbia's last flight. *The Atlantic Monthly,* 292(4), November, 58–82.

Lomborg, B. (2007). *Cool It: The Skeptical Environmentalist's Guide to Global Warming.* New York: Knopf.

Lomborg, B. (Ed.) (2004). *Global Crises, Global Solutions.* Cambridge: Cambridge University Press.

EXERCISES

Opening Vignette Discussion Questions

1. Recall Chapter 5 in which global and multi-domestic strategies were discussed. Which strategy would Disney represent? How can a firm like Disney still adapt to a local market but also maintain the strong brand image that is so critical to its success around the world?

2. Do you think it's important for executives like Allan Zeman to be familiar with a firm or its products before becoming that firm's leader? Give the pros and cons.

3. Tourists from mainland China are critical of both Ocean Park and Disney in Hong Kong. Do you think the people of Hong Kong would automatically understand customers from China? How should both firms ensure they are able to meet those customers' needs?

DISCUSSION QUESTIONS

1. Think about the eight symptoms of groupthink as discussed in the text. Have you experienced these symptoms in groups that you are a part of or are aware of? How was the decision affected?

2. In this and other classes you have had to conduct projects in teams or groups. Discuss the difficulties in making decisions you have experienced in these groups.

3. Suppose you are a government official of a small but fast growing emerging economy. You have been asked to allow a commonplace recreational product—swimming pools—to be installed in your country for the first time by an American multinational corporation. You have been told that swimming pools directly lead to the death of 600 Americans every year—many of them children—and also cause brain damage in several thousand more children. Should you allow that product into your country? Discuss the pros and cons.

4. Once again, suppose you are a government official of a small but fast growing emerging economy. A company wants to come to your country to start selling a clean fuel that has previously been unavailable there, and it wants to pump the fuel directly into your country's homes. Although it can be burned for heat or energy, the fuel has been known to explode occasionally if improperly handled. It is odorless, colorless, and poisonous; you can not see it escaping from a malfunctioning valve and filling your house. Not surprisingly, this fuel kills about 400 Americans per year. Will you allow companies to sell this potentially dangerous gas in your country? What fuel do you think this is? What decision-making heuristic is implied here that might bias your decision?

5. Think of a time when you conducted an informational search to help you make a major decision, such as to which universities to apply. How did you gather information and finally come to a decision? Did you practice evidence-based or verdict-based decision making?

6. Is there a time you used verdict-based information search that helped to limit your information search but produced a sub-optimal decision? What decision was it and how could that decision have been better made?

IN-CLASS EXERCISES

1. A software developer in Hong Kong is experiencing an increasing number of customer complaints and a general trend toward lower sales. Describe three reasons why senior executives in this organization might be slow to realize that a problem exists or to identify the main cause(s) of these symptoms.

2. A manufacturing company hires a management consultancy to determine the best site for its next production facility. The consultancy has had several meetings with the company's senior executives regarding the factors to consider when making its recommendation. Discuss three decision-making problems that might prevent the consultancy from choosing the best site location.

3. A developer received financial backing for a new business financial center along a derelict section of the waterfront in a large European city, a few miles from the current business district. The idea was to build several high-rise buildings, attract a lot of new tenants to those sites, and have the city extend transportation systems into the newly developed location. The developer believed that over the next decade others would build in the area, thereby attracting regional or national offices of many financial institutions. Interest from potential tenants was much lower than initially predicted and the city did not build transportation systems as quickly as expected. Still, the builder proceeded with the original plans. Only after financial support was curtailed did the developer reconsider the project. Using your knowledge of escalation

of commitment, discuss three possible reasons why the developer was motivated to continue with the project despite its escalating losses.

4. The Ancient Book Company has a problem with new book projects. Even when it is apparent to others that a book is far behind schedule and may not have much public interest, sponsoring editors are reluctant to terminate contracts with authors. The result is that editors invest and therefore waste more time with these projects rather than on more promising projects. As a form of escalation of commitment, describe two methods that The Ancient Book Company can use to minimize this problem.

5. When a large law firm needed to create a task force to make some significant strategic decisions, it put together what it considered a diverse group. The group consisted of three men and three women, all in their late thirties, representing different racial and ethnic backgrounds. The individuals had been active together in a recent political campaign for a certain candidate in that state and would all describe themselves as "progressive." Each person in the group was a lawyer. Though they came from different parts of the United States, they all went to either Harvard or Yale Law School and graduated around the same time. Is this a diverse group? Comment on the pros and cons of this group and the possibility for groupthink.

TAKE-HOME EXERCISES

1. Research both the Cuban Missile Crisis and the Challenger space shuttle crash on the Internet. Develop your own list of advice on how to avoid groupthink.
2. Using your knowledge of culture, research the cultural dimensions of the Arab countries of the Middle East. What aspects of this culture and society do you think would affect your decision making if you were sent there as a manager for a multinational firm?
3. In relation to Take-Home Exercise 2, do you think the decision making in Israel will be different from that in other Middle Eastern countries? Explain why and how. If necessary, select one particular country from the Middle East to discuss this question.

SHORT CASE QUESTIONS

Alcatel-Lucent (p. 290)

1. How could Alcatel-Lucent improve their decision making in the future?
2. Do you think such difficulty is one of the key issues that faces most mergers and acquisitions?
3. Do you think that these decision-making problems would have been present in a Swedish-U.S. merger?

10

INFLUENCE AND NEGOTIATION

Overview

International business people must seek to influence others and negotiate with them in a wide variety of situations. For example, someone in a sales or marketing position must regularly influence customers to buy the firm's products and then must negotiate a price. Managers, especially international managers, will find it difficult simply to order people to do things; instead, it is a process of influence and negotiation that leads to getting things done. This chapter draws on extensive work in psychology, marketing, and negotiation to examine questions of influence and negotiation in international business.

As the text has emphasized, in international settings managers must consciously seek to address the impact of culture on activities such as influence and negotiations. As has been seen throughout the text, culture can affect a wide variety of human interactions in international business, including influence and negotiation. It is important in reading this chapter to remember the problem of projection; that is, do not assume that everyone else will share your values and will play by those rules. What influences you to buy may not influence others, since they may have completely different buying criteria than you. Although principles of influence and negotiation have proven to be fairly uniform across cultures, there are often different conditions present in different cultures, and this creates a variety of ways to implement influence and negotiation principles.

The issues addressed in this chapter include:

- Understanding what persuasion is and its role in the influence process.
- Six primary approaches to influence.
- Negotiations.
- International applications and concerns.

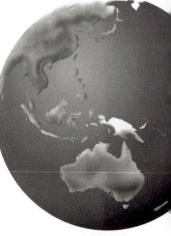

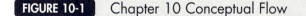

FIGURE 10-1 Chapter 10 Conceptual Flow

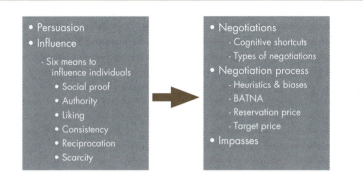

Global managers spend a great deal of time in trying to **influence** people informally and seeking to negotiate with them formally. Think about your day. How often do you ask people to do things? How often can you simply order people to do things? If you are making significant requests, chances are that you almost always have to influence others to do things. Simply ordering them to act in the manner you want is typically not successful. Students may like to think that most managers can simply issue orders, as in the armed services, and then sit back and supervise performance. That is not the case because managers, as opposed to military officers, must regularly influence and negotiate with others to get them to

Influence
Seeking to change people's behaviors.

NEGOTIATIONS FOR UNILEVER IN AFRICA: DOING GOOD WHILE DOING WELL

Unilever, an Anglo-Dutch firm, is one of the world's largest consumer goods companies with sales of over €5 billion. Africa is one of the poorest regions in the world, and more than 40 percent of sub-Saharan Africa lives on less than a $1 a day. Two nations, South Africa and Nigeria, comprise 54 percent of the region's economic output.

Simple sanitary items such as soap are often not used in these impoverished nations and about 140 out of every 1000 children under the age of five die every year. Of these deaths, 17 percent are due to diarrhea and 21 percent to pneumonia—diseases that can be controlled or even prevented by simple hand-washing. This has prompted a unique public–private relationship between Unilever and non-profits, such as Unicef, USAid, London School of Hygiene and Tropical Medicine, and the Gates Foundation, all of whom want to promote more handwashing. Specifically, Unilever hopes to promote its product

Lifebuoy (note that the spelling in the United States of this product is Lifeboy), an antibacterial soap that is ideally suited for these consumers. Unilever is now third in the Ugandan soap market.

The relationship here between the for-profit firm and the non-profits is not typical. There is often much suspicion between these two types of groups, and this agreement took much negotiation between the various parties. In particular the different sides report differences in how they viewed the timing of the program. Unilever was ready once it committed to move forward in an aggressive manner. But the non-profits had extensive bureaucracies and wished to reach a consensus on each issue with all items specified to a great detail. The result was that each side had to come to an understanding of the other. The non-profits needed to begin to trust Unilever, but Unilever knew that the timing of the campaign was vital. In many rural poor nations, individuals may not

have radios. As a result firms and non-profits develop road shows where a truck with a stage takes an entertainment show to remote areas. In this case, the show was to be centered on good health, with speeches on the need for everyone to wash their hands. Unilever with its marketing expertise knew that at certain times of the year like the rainy season or harvesting when people are very busy, the impact of road shows or advertisements is lessened. But this was a new concept to the non-profits.

Unilever and the non-profits together were able to help each other and to help the citizens of Uganda. But it was critical in the negotiation process to reach a better understanding of each other and not allow their biases to interfere with reaching a mutually beneficial agreement.

Russell, A. (2007, November 15). Growth data fuel hopes of new business era in Africa. *Financial Times*, p. 12.

Unilever looks to clean up in Africa (2007, November 15). *Financial Times*, p.18.

Persuasion
Seeking to change people's beliefs or attitudes.

do things. Even military officers cannot always issue orders and expect them to be followed. The U.S. president Abraham Lincoln, who was known for his **persuasion** and influence skills, had to spend a great deal of time trying to convince his subordinates to execute his orders.[i] Even as Commander-in-Chief of the U.S. armed forces, Lincoln had to "sell" his often slow-moving generals on the idea of carrying out needed campaigns to defeat the Confederate rebellion in the U.S. Civil War. President Lincoln even stated that he would hold one general's horse if that general would just go out and win some battles against the Confederacy.[ii] As a testament to the importance and ubiquity of influence skills, Lincoln's generals sometimes came around to his way of thinking, while others regularly refused to heed his orders until finally Lincoln had to replace them.[iii] In this chapter, the focus is on understanding influence and negotiation in cross-cultural settings. The chapter will initially examine these issues as short-term concerns, then examine them as longer-term issues. We will begin by defining and discussing what is meant by persuasion, since persuasion is the foundation for understanding the influence and negotiation process. We will examine six of the main principles of influence identified by well-known social-psychologist Robert Cialdini and other experts in the field that are used in organizations today to influence others in an ethical manner.[iv] We will apply these principles to illustrative situations, including more formal influence and decision-making situations found in negotiations.

PERSUASION

The opening vignette illustrates features of the persuasion that individuals are exposed to literally hundreds of times daily in advertising, promotions, or emails from colleagues and friends.[v] First, it is important to distinguish between persuasion and influence. Persuasion is the effort to change people's beliefs or attitudes, whereas influence is convincing people to actually do something, like purchase a product. Both are important. Many studies on persuasion have focused on attitude adjustment; that is, changing an individual's attitude toward something or some idea.

One very consistent finding in research around the world is that strong attitudes resist change. In fact, when faced with challenges to those strong attitudes, most people will not only seek out sources (people, media, or data) that support their initial beliefs, but they will also ignore any competing views and even lock them out of meetings and discussions. (Recall Chapter 9's discussion about verdict-based information search, the struggle to have the cure for peptic ulcers widely accepted in the medical community, and the problem of groupthink). Even if the data for those alternative views are strong, most individuals will ignore that data, even going so far as criticizing or attacking the messenger rather than arguing against the content of the message. We learned in Chapter 9 that this type of verdict-based information search is more likely to lead to decision errors and can also create the pernicious groupthink problem that is common in all types of organizations today. In this chapter, we look at the problem from the other angle—that is, how one persuades and influences people, especially people with strongly held attitudes that they have always made very public.

Persuasion and Influence

Though the words are often used interchangeably, persuasion and influence are not identical. Persuasion is a change in a private attitude or belief resulting from the receipt of a message. Influence is an action that leads to a change in behavior. The two approaches, persuasion and influence, can work together. For example, you might persuade someone about the importance of a healthy lifestyle and work habits, and then influence them to implement that lifestyle.[vi]

Persuasion is a deeper form of change than influence. To illustrate, if your friend is constantly troubling you about supporting his or her favorite cause, then you might say yes just to stop the incessant banter, while not really being persuaded. If you are really serious about persuading someone to accept a new idea, it is good to recall the words of the Greek philosopher Aristotle who reminded us: "The fool persuades me with his reasons; the wise man persuades me with my own." It is good to remember that just repeating the same things over and over is not likely to be effective if you fail to listen to the other person's comments, problems, objections, or objectives. There are tactics that help you to persuade someone—understanding what they value or what problems they may need to solve is the first place to start, because people will rarely go against their own values.

Early efforts to understand persuasion emphasized the importance of the message itself. Thus, the focus was on issues like the message's clarity, logic, or ease of recall because it was believed that the target person's comprehension and learning of the message's content were crucial to persuasion.[vii] Today, more emphasis is placed on understanding what encourages people to change their attitudes and beliefs. This draws on the **cognitive response model** and focuses on communication and the understanding of individuals' wants, beliefs, and the problems they need to have solved. Individuals' key wants and beliefs are known as the **self-talk of the target audience**.[viii] Persuasion occurs not only in what the communicator says to the target but also in what the target says in response. Thus, it is important for the persuader to listen carefully to the concerns of the target audience. It bears repeating that listening to and understanding the individual you are trying to persuade is quite important, so you must learn to ask questions (or do research) and then listen and summarize.

In particular, it is important to comprehend the most basic reasons why people may respond to a persuasive message. First, many people would like to build a more accurate view of the world and how it works. If a person has a sensing personality and prefers data and evidence, then providing data that is meaningful to that person can be a big first step toward persuading him or her about a new idea or product. Second, people would like to be consistent with their own values. This principle, known as the consistency principle, is important to both persuasion and influence, and will be discussed in the influence section later in this chapter. For now, it is sufficient to say that people would like to be consistent with their values in order to avoid **cognitive dissonance**, which is a negative feeling caused by holding two contradictory ideas simultaneously. Often this means having attitudes, values, or beliefs that do not match one's own behavior.[ix] When this occurs, people will try to remove that dissonance or discrepancy. If you can show how the message helps the listener do that, there is an increased chance that the message will succeed in persuading (or influencing) that person. Third, in addition to caring about what they believe, people also care about what others think. Therefore, a message may work if it helps the target person build social approval and demonstrate the logic and consistency of their new views and behavior (see Figure 10-2).

It is important to remember these three factors because they will make persuasion easier. For potential customers, try to find out what *needs* they have and what *problems* they are trying to solve and then show how your product solves their problem (more on this later in the chapter). Simply repeating your position or

Cognitive response model of persuasion
A model of persuasion that views the most direct cause of persuasion as the self-talk of the target audience, not the persuasion method itself or its deliverer.

Cognitive dissonance
The negative feeling caused by holding two contradictory ideas simultaneously.

| FIGURE 10-2 | Why Do People Yield to a Persuasive Message? |

People may change their minds based on a persuasive message in order to:

- Build a more accurate view of the world and how it works.
- Be consistent with their own values and previous commitments.
- Build social approval and demonstrate the logic and consistency of their new views.

views on a topic (or a standard sales pitch about your product's features) is usually not very persuasive. You also need to *listen to the problems* of the other person in an empathetic manner and then show that person (or target market) how your product or idea solves that problem or fits with that person's values or publicly stated position.[x] This approach to persuasion is similar to the marketing process whereby a firm seeks to find out the *problems and needs of the consumer* and then shows how the product or service can solve those particular problems.[xi]

This process sounds obvious, but think about how most products are designed and sold. How helpful are the frequently asked questions (FAQs) on a manufacturer's website? Do they just state the obvious about the product or tout its features without explaining common uses, tricky features, or potential problems? If your experience is like that of most customers, it is likely that most firms you encounter tend to emphasize their product's features and functions—how many features they have, how fast the product is, how well it works, and so forth—and not how their products can *solve your problems*. For example, at trade shows where firms pitch new consumer electronics technology products such as advanced mobile phones, you will typically hear all about a phone's functions and technological features—its capacity, upload and download speeds, ability to function as a video phone, and so forth. This is all impressive, to be sure, but you will hear very little about the *problems* of the customer and how the phone's features actually can solve those problems. This is also true for advertisements. For example, much has been made about the video function of the 3G and other new phones, but rarely is a problem directly identified that the video phone solves. Do you have a problem that requires you to see who you are speaking to on the phone? Probably not, unless you are a physician or someone else that needs to follow someone's actions or diagnose. Though the video phone has been around since the New York World's Fair of 1964, there has been little demand for it. The technology's sponsors have long failed to show what customer problems are addressed by the video phone, and instead continue to talk about service enhancements and the phone's newest specifications. Customer response has been predictably indifferent, and the proponents of 3G have added another common refrain typical of an improperly positioned and packaged product— upping the features and functions, then complaining that the product is ahead of its time and suggesting that customers just need to be educated about the product. This complaint about uneducated customers is commonly made by firms that have failed to address customer needs or to communicate how their product can help to solve specific customer problems—or even find out customers' problems, for that matter.

This is also quite consistent with what venture capitalists remind entrepreneurs: Do not ask customers to make lifestyle changes in order to adopt a product; that is, do not spend a lot of time educating the customer. It is very hard to make people change their lifestyles; it is far easier to persuade them to change their attitudes toward your product or industry by showing them how your product solves their problems or is very consistent with their current lifestyle and points of view. The failure of Toshiba's HD-DVD format in its battle with Sony's Blu-ray has been attributed to Toshiba's attempts to educate the consumer about HD-DVD's superior technology rather than describing how the format helps users watch and store movies, which is the main problem to be solved for DVD consumers.[xii] See Figure 10-3 for some questions to ask related to this application of the persuasion process in the marketplace.

Given the importance of self-talk and understanding people's problems and situations, it suggests that a manager's criticism of an employee's or position is not likely to help the persuasion attempt; beyond that, the manager needs to seek to connect to the employee's needs.[xiii] Let's consider a company memo intended to

---

FIGURE 10-3 How to Make Your Selling Message More Persuasive

- Does the message about your product help prospective customers understand their situations better?
- Does it solve a particular problem that the customers have? How will it solve that problem? Is that problem solving being communicated clearly to the customers, or are your promotions only mentioning the great features and functions of your product or company?
- Will the innovation help customers do what they are already trying to do more easily and effectively?
- Do you understand their needs and values such that you can identify what they are trying to do? Or are you selling something that does not address any problem or need and is not consistent with their values? If the latter is the case, then you will need to rethink the selling message or the product itself.

---

persuade employees to support a new pay-for-performance plan in a Latin American plant. The plan will be a tough sell in this setting because the Latin American employees typically experience a guaranteed wage with pay standards typically set at the same level throughout the country by negotiations between a union and the employers' association. The union does not prohibit pay-for-performance schemes, so the manager of a foreign-owned plant in that country might think it will be easy to implement such a plan. This would allow the plant to take on a pay structure consistent with those of the company's other factories around the world. But the manager may face far more opposition if he attempts to implement the system without using a more democratic form of leadership and consulting the employees. The manager must think about what the employees would say in response to the letter introducing the plan. The manager will want to find ways to stimulate positive responses in the letter to the employees introducing the plan. In addition to considering features of the intended message (e.g., the strength and logic of the arguments), the manager should take into account an entirely different set of factors that are likely to enhance positive cognitive responses to the message. For instance, the manager may want to lay the groundwork for introducing the pay-for-performance system by sending plant leaders a memo outlining various pay systems and including news stories from the business press about them, including the one that the manger is seeking to implement. The manager will also want to meet with opinion leaders among the employees to ask them to give the plan a try in order to see if more money can be made with the pay-for-performance plan—rather than unilaterally implementing it and "hoping for the best."[xiv] By understanding the employees' situation, the manager can pursue actions that help to prepare workers and their leaders for the changes ahead.

PERSUASION THROUGH PARODY AND ONE INDUSTRY'S RESPONSE

One powerful form of persuasion is parody. Consider the cigarette industry, an industry that has undergone dramatic changes over the last 40 years. These changes ultimately resulted in a ban of all tobacco advertising in 1969. You might think that the tobacco industry argued vigorously against such a ban, but surprisingly, they supported it.[xv] Their support was actually central in creating this ban on TV and radio that has been in place since 1971 in the United States.

What could explain the tobacco industry's support? In the 1960s, the newly passed Fairness Doctrine and public service announcements were granted equal time to explain the health consequences of smoking. This ruling by the U.S. Federal Communication Commission allowed anti-tobacco groups, such as the American Cancer Society, to run ads that parodied the tobacco ads' images of attractiveness and rugged independence (such as the famous Marlboro Man) showing that cigarette smoking led to illness, damaged attractiveness, and addiction. The advertisements were so effective in mocking the tobacco industry's image that cigarette consumption started to decline in the U.S. after the ads started running in the 1960s. But with the tobacco ads prohibited after 1971, anti-tobacco forces were no longer able to receive free air time for their ads. In the first year after the ban on tobacco ads went into effect, cigarette consumption in the U.S. actually rose by three percent, and to top it off, tobacco firms were able to reduce their advertising expenditures by 30 percent.[xvi] The tobacco firms were then able to focus their advertising money on print and outdoor ads and on sponsorship of sporting events, which proved very profitable for them and may have led to an increase in tobacco consumption worldwide.[xvii]

INFLUENCE

Next, we will discuss something that companies in particular are interested in: ethically influencing employees to work effectively for their teams, colleagues, and customers. This is the process of influence, or stated more formally, **social influence**, which is defined as encouraging a change in behavior that was caused by real or imagined external pressure.[xviii] Defining influence in terms of a change in behavior distinguishes it from *persuasion*, which, as discussed earlier, refers to an attempt to change attitudes or beliefs but which may not necessarily lead to immediate behavior change. There are three behavior outcomes deriving from a successful influence attempt: conformity, compliance, and obedience, which will be addressed first.[xix]

Conformity involves changing one's behavior to match the perceived requirements of others—that is, to fit in with those around us. Think of how out of place you would feel if you were not dressed as formally as everyone else at a dinner party. Or maybe everyone was exchanging business cards at a meeting, but you forgot to bring yours along—you probably would not forget them the next time. The key here is that the group or an opinion leader increases your desire to conform by just showing that everyone else is doing things a particular way.

The second and third types of behavioral change are in response to more overt forms of influence. **Compliance** refers to the act of changing one's behavior in response to a direct request. The request may be coming from someone who is not in authority over you, but he or she may be in a position to command some kind of power, such as that possessed by an expert like a physician. Finally, **obedience** is a special type of compliance that involves changing one's behavior in response to an authority's command. For example, a police officer may order a driver to pull over and show his or her license and registration, or a supervisor may require you to work on a new task. Firms around the world normally think it is helpful to seek less overt forms of influence—that is, firms believe it is good to influence employees, customers, and colleagues if the targets of the influence believe the ideas are their own and they do not feel coerced, as with conformity.

Conformity
Changing one's behavior to match the responses or actions of others, to fit in with those in proximity.

Compliance
The act of changing one's behavior in response to a direct request.

Obedience
A special type of compliance that involves changing one's behavior in response to a directive from an authority figure.

Six Universal Principles of Influence

Social psychologist Robert Cialdini has distilled six universal principles of influence from the manifold research on this topic. The principles are universal in that they show up in a range of situations and across cultures.[xx] Figure 10-4 summarizes these principles, and each will now be examined in turn.

FIGURE 10-4   Six Universal Principles of Influence

Research in social psychology has identified six universal principles of influence:

1. **Social proof.** People get their "proof" about a product or idea based on validation from the group.
2. **Authority.** People are influenced by credible authorities. This authority can be the influencer or the testimony of an outside authority.
3. **Liking.** People are more influenced by people they like and have some positive relationship with.
4. **Consistency.** People like to be consistent with their values, and with statements they have made in the past. These values and statements will act to influence them toward making decisions that they feel are consistent with those past actions and statements.
5. **Reciprocation.** People are more likely to say yes to a request from those who have helped them or given them something before.
6. **Scarcity.** The scarcity and uniqueness of a product, service, or activity causes people to more highly value it and want it more.

1. **Social Proof** (also known as the consensus or social validation principle). Research shows that people are more likely to be influenced if they see evidence that many others, especially others they perceive as similar to themselves, are also doing a particular activity or buying a product. It is called "social proof" because the proof comes, not from the product, but from the group of people that is using or recommending the product. Marketers employ this principle in claiming that their products are the fastest growing or largest selling in the market, and by using phrases like, "Do not miss the action and excitement your friends are experiencing."

2. **Authority** (also called the expert principle). As with social proof, people often look for some kind of external validation before they make a decision, and are willing to follow the directions or recommendations of a trusted authority. For example, advertisers often succeed merely by employing believable actors dressed to look like experts (health care professionals, police officers, etc.), who may already be playing those characters on television or in the movies.[xxi]

3. **Liking**. People prefer to listen to individuals who they like or see some connection or similarity with, because they feel that people they like or have some connection with are likely to understand them and have their best interests at heart.[xxii] Research shows that people are more willing to buy insurance from agents who are similar to them in age and political and social preferences, including liking similar brands of beverages and cigarettes.[xxiii]

4. **Consistency**. People are more likely to say yes to a request or agree with something if they see it as consistent with an existing or recently made commitment of their own. The key word here is "precedent." If someone has made a public statement about a subject in the past, that person will be more likely to follow through on that statement, particularly if reminded of it. That is why publicly stated goals are much more motivational than private goals, and good managers will ask their staff to write down their goals for the year. Salespeople understand this influence principle and will ask a prospective buyer (the person they want to influence) questions about their preferences and values and then remind them of how their preferences fit the product. This works because people will rarely go against their own stated values.[xxiv]

5. **Reciprocation**. People are more willing to comply with requests from those who have given them something first. People around the world feel an obligation to reciprocate, so companies provide free samples, home owners put out free drinks to prospective buyers during an open house, and salespeople do favors for customers in hopes that they will purchase something in return.[xxv] Research shows that people are more likely to say yes to something if they perceive that request reciprocation for something that was done for them first.[xxvi] This is true even if the initial gift or favor is much smaller than the subsequent request.[xxvii]

6. **Scarcity**. People want to buy things or do things that they perceive are scarce, unusual, or limited in number. Thus, store promotions warn customers that the most you can buy of an object is six (implying a limited availability), or declare that there is only one day left to make a purchase (implying limited time), or tout a product's differentiated attributes and unique value-add. Scarcity is an effective influencer because people want to avoid any feeling of regret over missing out on something.[xxviii]

Each of these six influence principles will next be examined in greater detail.

Social Proof

There is strong evidence that people like to follow the crowd. That is, people are influenced to act when they think many others are behaving in a certain way or buying a certain product. Because of this, it is helpful to appeal to what the larger

Social proof
A principle of influence that states people are more likely to want to do something if they believe that many others are doing the same thing or buying the same product.

Authority
A principle of influence that states people are more likely to say yes to a request or purchase a product if an authority says it is good to do so.

Liking
A principle of influence that holds that people are more likely to be influenced by those whom they like or with whom they have similarities.

Consistency
A principle of influence that indicates how people are influenced by showing how their previous statements or stated values fit with a recommendation or request.

Reciprocation
A principle of influence that states people are more likely to say yes to a request when the requester has done something for that person in the past.

Scarcity
A principle of influence that argues that people are more likely to buy a product or want to do something that they perceive as scarce, unique, or dwindling in availability.

group is doing. Recall from Chapter 7 on motivation that this appeal to the group is how Lincoln Electric influenced workers at their new plant in Mexico to accept Lincoln's strict pay-for-performance system. Rather than implementing their motivation system by fiat, Lincoln Electric started with social proof. The workers in Mexico were not used to a piece-rate system and were more accustomed to very egalitarian pay rates. Lincoln Electric wisely decided not to force the radically different system on the workers all at once; rather, they selected a couple of volunteer employees to try it out first. When other employees started to see how well the volunteers were doing in terms of pay and bonuses, they started to opt into the system. The whole plant gradually moved to the pay-for-performance system within two years. Productivity went up and worker pay rose. Perhaps most importantly, it was the workers' idea to change, not the company's, so the change was more likely to stick.[xxix]

This use of the influence principle of social proof is but one of several examples of how these principles can be used ethically to influence subordinates, colleagues, customers, and even bosses to accept your ideas or to buy your products, and for them to do so willingly. Using an opinion leader is quite important (and having two is better), particularly in developing countries where competitive market systems are new. Firms should try to find one or two opinion leaders who can be early adopters of the firm's system, of performance-based pay, for example. When opinion leaders accept your system, and say so publicly, others are more likely to follow, as in the Lincoln Electric example, particularly if the opinion leaders can be seen to be doing well under the new system.

People faced with strong group consensus sometimes go along even though they think the others may be incorrect. This occurs even if there is strong evidence that the group is wrong. This phenomenon was investigated in a series of experiments conducted by psychologist Solomon Asch in the 1950s as he sought to understand why so many Germans and Japanese conformed to the destructive and often brutal orders of their leaders in World War II.[xxx] Asch was interested not only in the submission of individuals to group pressure, but also in people's ability to go against those conformity pressures. In one well-known experiment, Asch asked university students in groups of eight to match the lengths of two lines with a comparison line. It was easy to see which of the two lines was the best match. In the control condition, in which there was no group pressure about the choice, 95 percent of the participants got all 12 line matches correct.

But for the subjects in the experimental condition, the results were much different. Five confederates in the room had been instructed by Asch to give wrong answers. Asch's intent was to learn if students could be influenced to go along with the group and select an answer that was obviously wrong. Even though the students saw the right answer, 75 percent went against their own judgment and conformed to the group in giving the wrong answers.

Recently, Dr. Gregory Berns of Emory University conducted a similar experiment and used MRI brain-monitoring devices to learn which parts of the brain were used to process answers to questions. Berns' research confirmed Asch's conclusions that social pressure to conform creates major errors in judgment. As with Asch's study, Berns placed confederates in the group who were instructed to give the wrong answer before asking the lone study participant to answer. The lone participants almost always gave the wrong answers to a shape-matching test, although they had answered correctly when working alone on the same task earlier. People who had been getting near 100 percent of the answers correct when working alone started to get most questions wrong when people before them had answered incorrectly (out loud) first. One participant in the study later said he actually came to believe that the group was correct, and thought he must have been seeing things incorrectly. An MRI of the respondents' brains when they answered revealed that the respondents' visual cortexes were lighting up. The MRI indicated that the people in the experiment were struggling to see if they could believe what their eyes were telling them, particularly when the confederates in the group were telling them to believe something else by giving wrong answers.[xxxi]

It is easy to imagine that in cultures with high group cohesiveness, such as those in East Asia, social validation is extra important. And companies can utilize social proof in a number of other ways. For example, individuals are influenced by knowing that many people are adopting a certain mobile phone and plan, and by the belief that these people are similar to them. If you are a student or business person who travels overseas regularly, you might be looking for a good mobile phone plan that works in foreign countries. You could compare multiple plans, but there is a good chance you would be more influenced by friends who have similar requirements as you do. This is particularly helpful when you are uncertain about what you want. Firms can use this approach on a business-to-business level by pointing out to a prospect that other companies have purchased this product and are doing well with it. They would then put the prospect in touch with some of those similar clients who could explain how they use the company's product. This is particularly helpful in international business because such showcase clients in a foreign location can serve as reference points for other prospective customers there. It also explains why a firm may be willing to sell a new system at a break-even price to a new overseas client just to "get in the door" of that foreign country and showcase the new account to other potential clients there.

Another important point to remember is that if you want to discourage a behavior, it is best *not* to say, "Many people are doing this, but don't you do it." For example, one study looking at "no-shows" in a physician's office (no-shows are people who make an appointment but don't show up for it) noted that after putting up signs saying "No-shows are costly" and "We had 220 no-shows last month," the number of no-shows climbed to about 300 the next month.[xxxii] The fact that so many others were not showing up for their appointments influenced even more patients to miss them. This is also true with public service announcements. Ads that try to discourage behavior such as littering by showing how dirty a place is are essentially telling viewers, "Everyone is doing this, but you should not do it even though everyone else is." This type of message has been shown to *increase* the very behavior that the public service commercial is trying to discourage, so be careful how you use social proof. The lesson is clear: if you want to encourage something, show that many others are doing that same thing, particularly people who are similar to those you are trying to influence. But if you want to discourage behavior, do not say that many others are doing the action you want to discourage. Finally, it should also be noted that when you say, "We have a consensus, so that should convince this particular individual," this is not a correct application of the social proof principle. Social proof means that *many others*, especially others like the person you are trying to influence, are doing something, or buying this product. It is the consensus of the people "out there" that does the influencing.

Authority

People are also influenced by authority and expertise because as with social proof, it gives them a shortcut to an assessment or decision—if the authority says so, it must be ok. The authority principle is helpful to some extent because we do not have time to evaluate every decision we make. The authority principle is a powerful influencer. For instance, would you obey orders from a researcher directing a study (wearing an authoritative-looking white coat) to deliver painful electric shocks to another study participant in response to that study participant's incorrect answer to a quiz question that you just posed? And if so, what would the victim have to say to get you to stop obeying such orders? Or would you stop?

Social psychologist Stanley Milgram sought to answer this very question in a series of famous studies in the 1960s that showed how powerful an authority figure could be in influencing someone to continue with a seemingly harmful experiment.[xxxiii] This hearkened back to the argument given by those accused of war crimes after World War II at the Nuremberg Trials in Germany. The accused individuals repeatedly defended themselves by arguing that they had only been following orders in carrying out mass arrests and executions. In Milgram's experiments, three people took part: the "experimentor," the "learner," and the "teacher." Only the teacher was an actual participant; the experimentor was running the experiment while the learner was a confederate of the experimenter who had specific instructions on how to behave. The teacher was instructed to ask quiz questions of the learner, who was on the other side of a wall. Every time the learner would get a question wrong, the teacher was to give the learner an electric shock as a penalty. The voltage would be increased as they worked through the quiz, to a lethal 450 volts. It should quickly be pointed out that the learners were not really receiving electric shocks, but the person asking the quiz questions did not know this and thought the shocks he or she was administering were real.[1]

Before conducting his experiment, Milgram polled Yale students and professors as to what they thought would be the results, that is, would the teachers in the study continue to ask questions and administer increasingly powerful electric shocks to the learners behind the wall. Generally, the poll respondents believed that very few teachers would inflict a very strong shock, guessing around one percent.[xxxiv] They were in for a shock of their own. Even in the benign setting of a Yale University lab, some two-thirds of the teachers persisted in asking quiz questions all the way to the end of the list and administered supposedly lethal-level shocks of 450 volts, even when the learner answering the questions had fallen silent and was apparently injured or worse. Even when faced with the victims' repeated yelps and subsequent silence, those giving the shocks continued to do so because the authority figure of the lab researcher told them they had to do it—they had agreed and must continue, and that the experimenter would take all responsibility.[xxxv] Although not everyone went all the way up to 450 volts, very few teachers stopped before a possibly lethal 300-volt level.[xxxvi] Subsequent studies had similar results, in a variety of settings.[xxxvii] This study is a strong testimony to the power of authority to influence people to do things and also highlights the need to use authority judiciously and ethically.

As introduced in Chapter 9, the authority or expertise principle provides a helpful decision shortcut because we do not have time to evaluate each and every decision we make. Even in an organizational setting when we make purchases, it is helpful to have some expert opinion on what might be the best product. This could include an objective study or the recommendation of a technical expert who has no financial relationship to the product. Reliance on expert authority, however, can lead us to respond to the trappings (symbols) of authority, such as the style (a manner of speaking or the type of clothing worn), rather than the substance of genuine authority or expertise.[xxxviii] Why else would something as simple as a necktie be called a "power tie"? An expensive tie seems to be worn by people in authority or with high expertise in a certain area.

Indeed, much research suggests that people are more influenced by those who display their credentials and awards as a signal of their authority. Physical therapists who posted their credentials found that they significantly increased the compliance of their patients to the physical therapy regimens.[xxxix] Similarly, firms harness the power of authority by touting their experience, expertise, or scientific recognition (recall the well-known "Four out of five dentists surveyed..." advertisements for Trident sugarless gum). Though it may seem boastful to some people and some cultures, research shows that posting credentials, certificates, and other symbols of expertise is highly influential for employees, clients, colleagues, even patients.[xl] Even in countries such as Japan and China that emphasize the value of

---

[1]No study fooling people into believing they were significantly harming others would be permitted today.

Patrick Kovarik/AP Photo

In China, firms welcome and document visits from high-ranking government officials. Associating with a local authority figure lends legitimacy to their operation.

personal humility, credentialed people are seen as highly credible and are thus influential, and their authority is particularly potent.[xli]

The authority principle is widely seen in international business. For example, in China it is common when a high-ranking government official visits a plant or factory for photos and video to be taken with the official. Those photos will then be widely distributed and hung near the company entrance. This presentation of authority demonstrates that the firm has the right to exist in an environment that can sometimes be hostile to private business as it indicates some level of official support for the firm.[xlii] More recently, firms in China have been basing some of their operations near or on military bases for the same reason—to associate with a local authority figure that lends legitimacy to their operation and can influence local government officials to leave the firm alone and not interfere with its operation. It is important also to note that in influencing someone, you can be an authority and thus wield influence yourself, or you can refer to another authority to do the influencing.

Liking

It can be seen from the preceding discussion that people seek affirmation for their choices from both society ("Everyone is buying this") and from experts ("Expert research shows this is high quality"). They also seek opinions from and are thus influenced by those who they like, are similar to, or feel connected with in some way. Controlled research has identified several factors that reliably increase liking, but two factors stand out as especially compelling: similarity and praise. Similarity increases liking. People who have learned they share social values and political beliefs stand closer together and listen more closely to one another.[xliii] The converse is also true: differences decrease liking and thus influence. If someone disagrees with your political beliefs, you will reduce your influence with that person by rambling on and on about your political views every time you talk to that person. This is especially true if you never bother to listen to other people's views or even try to understand their position. With customers, bosses, colleagues, family, and friends, try to listen more than you talk, particularly if you want to build liking and influence.

Managers can also use similarities to build relations with customers external to the firm and internally. With both groups, informal conversations create ideal opportunities to discover common areas of enjoyment, be it a hobby, a certain sports team, or a type of cuisine. The important thing is to establish connections early, because they create a presumption of similarity and trustworthiness in subsequent interactions. It is much easier to influence people to buy a product, or to build support for a new project internal to the firm, when the people you are trying to influence are already leaning in your direction on other issues.

Praise can also establish liking and increase the probability that someone will say yes to a request. Research has shown that people feel great regard for others who have praised them regularly.[xliv] Although we don't recommend that you give disingenuous flattery, it should be pointed out that even false praise increases liking by those hearing the praise.[xlv] The importance of praise was further confirmed by experimental data showing that positive remarks about another person's traits, attitudes, and performance reliably generates liking for those offering the praise, as well as increasing the subsequent willingness to comply with requests made by the person offering the praise.[xlvi]

As might be expected, while praise can increase someone's liking of you, criticism can have the opposite effect. When a manager criticizes a person's actions and beliefs they are reducing their influence with that person. Certainly, a manager or supervisor must give employees frank assessments (which will be discussed in greater detail in Chapter 12, Human Resource Management). But managers should do so carefully—perhaps starting out with some praise, and an understanding of the employee's situation (note the importance of listening and asking questions again). If the employee did a bad job, take some time to find out what went wrong. Maybe the employee worked late hours but did not focus on the right things. Try to acknowledge the good first, before giving any critique. A person will usually be more open to criticism if they think you care about and are empathic to their situation. Use criticism very carefully, and only when necessary. For example, if you come into someone's office to ask them to do something, it is not a good idea to start with negative comments (like "You know the air conditioning is really too low in here" or "You are having lunch at your desk today? You know that is not good for you"). These criticisms will *reduce* your influence and make it *less* likely that the person will do what you ask. Criticize carefully, prefacing with praise and empathy when possible. Criticism, negative comments, and inflammatory statements reduce your influence. Because words can wound, choose them very carefully, and avoid unnecessary negatives and complaints.[xlvii]

What does a manager do if they have already damaged a relationship by making negative or careless remarks? Able managers can use praise to repair a relationship. Imagine you are the manager and your work necessarily brings you into contact with an employee whom you have come to dislike. No matter how much you help out this employee, it is never enough. Even worse, this employee never seems to believe that you are doing the best you can for him. The department's performance is suffering because of this conflict, and the situation is consistently uncomfortable. Research suggests ways of improving the relationship and your department's performance. Some praise for this employee's work will help to improve the relationship. That praise can be as simple as acknowledging the hard work they are doing or that they are handling a tough job that no one else wanted to do. If you do that, the employee will be more open to subsequent suggestions of how they can improve.

Internationally, there are cultures where negative comments may be even more damaging than in others. For example, in Thailand it is very rare to raise your voice or to offer negative feedback, particularly in the presence of others. The Thai society prizes very positive interactions and careful, face-saving criticism. If a manager from the West imposes a style of feedback characterized by a loud, stern voice in which negative feedback is provided, sometimes with other people present (a style that may be acceptable in the United States and other Western countries), a Thai individual is most likely to completely shut everything out because their response to the negative feedback is so strong. Therefore, in cultures where negative feedback is so damaging, try to give some praise first, do not criticize the employee in front of others, and focus on the person's performance, emphasizing what you would do instead.

Another strategy to build liking (in addition to praise) is to make sure you focus on others' needs instead of frequently talking about what you want.[xlviii] If you find that you are always telling others what you need to get done and what your goals are while failing to ask what the other person may need to get done, then you are focusing only on your situation. Taking the time to listen to someone's specific concerns (as opposed to just asking the superficial, "How are you doing?") will help to build liking (and influence) with that person. Understanding someone else's problems and what they value also helps with the next influence principle—consistency.

Consistency

The fourth universal principle of influence is consistency. Once individuals take a stand or go on record in favor of an idea or product, they typically prefer to stick to that position. A personal commitment ties an individual's identity to a position or course of action, making it more likely that he or she will follow through. This is because most individuals prefer to be consistent with statements and beliefs that they have made public so as to reduce cognitive dissonance, the discrepancy between what someone believes and how they act. Thus, seemingly insignificant commitments can lead to large behavior changes. For example, someone doing fundraising for a charity may be able to improve compliance with a request for money by first getting people to comply with a smaller, related request. In one classic study, researchers in a large city in Israel went to a large local apartment complex, knocked on half of the doors, and asked residents to sign a petition about establishing a recreation center for the handicapped. Because the cause was a good one, almost everyone signed the petition. Residents in the other apartments did not receive a visit and thus served as a control group for the study. Two weeks later, all the residents in the apartment complex were approached and asked to give some money for the recreation center. Among those who had not been asked to sign the petition, the control group, about half agreed to contribute. But nearly all of the people who had signed the petition two weeks earlier, thus making a public commitment in support of the center, donated money.[xlix]

Recall how powerful commitments can be in decision making (Chapter 9). Decision makers in organizations have a tendency to escalate their commitments to investments or decisions that are not working out and should be terminated. Although it is easy to say that a failing investment should be canceled, research shows it can be very difficult for decision makers to do so. Once someone has publicly stated or written something that makes their views explicit, that person's behavior is likely to adhere to that statement. Managers who can obtain a public statement from an employee committing to a goal or action are more likely to see the employee following through on that action. It is particularly effective if you can get it in writing; for example, ask people to send you an email detailing what they will do and when. One senior manager for a major firm in Hong Kong told us that he will send an email asking an employee for a confirmation of some task they will do, but in the email, that manager will deliberately make a small mistake, like writing down the wrong completion date. The employee invariably will come back with an email saying, "No, I agreed to do it by this date." As a result the manager has the employee's commitment in writing—not coerced, but fully voluntary. Indeed, numerous studies have shown how even a small, seemingly trivial commitment can have a powerful effect on future actions. As influence expert Robert Cialdini reminds us, people live up to what they write down.[l] It is important to notice that it is not *your* commitment that will influence people. It is *their* commitment, and your reminding them of that commitment can help to influence them.

Reciprocation

People are more willing to comply with requests from those who have provided something to them first. All societies subscribe to a norm that obligates individuals to repay in kind what they have received (in Portuguese, the word *obrigado* is used for "thank you," but it literally means "I am obligated"). Gifts can increase the numbers of donors and donations.[li] Free samples in supermarkets, free home inspections by pest control companies, and free gifts through the mail from marketers or fundraisers are all highly effective ways to increase compliance with a follow-up request.[lii] The evidence from the United States is that mailing out a simple appeal for donations produces an 18 percent success rate, but adding a small gift such as personalized address labels nearly doubles the donation rate to 35 percent.[liii] And this is with a gift that costs much less than the requested donation, which is consistent with much research into the reciprocation principle: an initial gift can be much lower in value than the subsequent request. Recently, charities in Hong Kong have also started to enclose self-stick personalized address labels with requests for donations.

In the United States, it has been found that purchasing managers who receive a gift are willing to purchase products and services they would have otherwise declined. This raises some discomfort and is why in some firms like Wal-Mart an employee can be fired if he or she has accepted any type of gift from a potential vendor, including a free meal. But in China and many developing countries, gift giving is a legal and established part of the business culture and builds relationships with clients.[liv] In China, it is assumed gift giving will lead to some form of reciprocity, and Chinese managers are known to tell people what they will give in return at the same time they ask for something.[lv] The key for a manager is interpreting the give and take in balancing the reciprocity.[lvi] By contrast, Westerners may deem such a "quid pro quo" scheme (i.e., **balanced reciprocity**, or the asking of something in return right away for a favor done) as inappropriate and too materialistic.[lvii] International managers need to understand reciprocity in the society in which they are working and to ensure that at the same time they are building relationships, they are also responding properly to those who may feel that they have provided something that results in a debt to be repaid.

Balanced reciprocity
Securing a promise of a near-immediate return for a favor done or a gift given; thought to be particularly important in China and in ethnic Chinese communities around the world.

Scarcity

People find objects and opportunities more attractive to the degree that they are scarce, rare, or dwindling in availability. At Florida State University in the 1970s, psychologist Stephen West surveyed students about the campus cafeteria food. He found that food's ratings rose significantly from one particular week to the next, even though there had been no change in the menu, food quality, or preparation. Instead, the improvement in perception of the food seemed to have come from the fact that the cafeteria had partially burned down and cafeteria meals would not be available again for several weeks. FSU students and staff were influenced by the sudden scarcity of the cafeteria and its food, which caused them to rate the desirability of the food much higher than before.[lviii] This illustrates a basic psychological principle called reactance.[lix] Reactance basically states that when we are told that we cannot have or do something, then we want it more. This psychological reaction common to all people helps to explain why scarcity operates as an influence principle. Promotions like "Only two more days to buy" or "You are limited to a maximum of three" encourages people to hurry up by touting scarcity.

Proprietors of nightclubs and restaurant use the scarcity principle by artificially limiting the availability of space. Nightclub owners, for example, commonly restrict the number of people allowed inside even though there is plenty of space, not because of maximum occupancy laws, but because their apparent inaccessibility makes these establishments seem more desirable. Similarly, some restaurant managers use scarcity to limit the number of seats available in order to build up their restaurant's desirability and ratings, particularly among opinion leaders in the community.

Internationally, firms often use the principle of scarcity. For example, the two main supermarket chains in Hong Kong emphasized that unless customers acted quickly, they would miss out on an opportunity to try several new healthy cereal products from the United States. Rather than emphasizing the health benefits of the cereal products the way they were commonly promoted in North America, the Hong Kong supermarkets shrewdly suggested in their ads and promotions that this particular brand was very difficult to get and that customers should take the opportunity to try it during its limited trial run. By emphasizing both the uniqueness of the product and its scarcity (limited availability and limited time), the supermarkets were able to create a buzz for their whole line of cereal products and health foods. Several years later these brands are hard to find in Hong Kong and South China, and when available, they carry a significant price premium.

Scarcity does not just influence consumers but also can be influential inside firms as well. A 1994 study detailed in the journal *Organizational Behavior and Human Decision Processes* showed that potential losses figure more heavily in managers' decision making than potential gains.[lx] This can drive managers to focus on information about threats while ignoring possible opportunities, and can encourage them to be overly risk-averse by trying too hard to minimize losses and avoid making mistakes, as discussed in Ch. 9. It is important to remember that being overly risk-averse and avoiding making mistakes will lead to not trying to do anything. Hockey great Wayne Gretsky once said that he certainly had missed every shot that he did not take. Avoiding mistakes will also increase errors of omission (deciding not to do something that was likely to have worked) and thus potential opportunities will be missed. Managers should be reminded to avoid creating an organizational culture that encourages risk aversion and discourages trial and error in new business opportunities. Scarcity is a powerful influencer, so use it ethically to bring out information about how your product or idea is unique and can bring useful benefits to clients that they do not want to miss out on. Similarly, do not let scarcity and fear of a mistake create too much risk aversion such that you or your organization fail to try anything new or different.

INFLUENCE PRINCIPLES IN FOUR DIFFERENT CULTURES

CULTURE

Do the six universal principles of influence operate the same in different countries and cultures? Are they truly universal? Research suggests positive answers to those questions. Consider the principle of reciprocation. Although some people talk about reciprocation like it only exists in some societies (China in the form of guanxi or connections, for example), research in sociology and social psychology has found that it exists in all societies.[lxi] For example, when Christopher Columbus traveled to the Western hemisphere and discovered the Caribbean Islands, he had no way of communicating with the natives there. How did Columbus signal that his intentions were peaceful? By giving the natives gifts. What

did the natives do in return? They gave gifts. Imagine, two cultures (European and Caribbean Islanders) that had been separated by at least ten thousand years with no common language, being able to communicate. Somehow they knew about reciprocation and knew to give gifts of approximately the same value.[lxii]

People are susceptible to the basic decision shortcuts and cognitive tendencies that characterize all societies. But cultural differences, institutions, and recent history in a country can modify the importance of different influence principles and how they are implemented. Three Stanford University researchers studied worldwide employees of a global bank, examining

(Continued)

four particular societies: the United States, China, Spain, and Germany. They surveyed the bank's branches within each country, asking employees if they would assist a colleague if requested to do so. Specifically, the researchers wanted to know which of the six main principles of influence might be most useful in influencing these employees to offer assistance. As you might guess, it was different for each culture.

The Germans were most compelled by authority; they were more likely to comply with the request in order to follow the organization's rules and regulations. They decided whether to comply by asking if official regulations allowed them to assist others. If the answer was yes, they granted the request.

U.S. employees favored a reciprocation-based approach to the decision to comply. They asked the question, "What has this person done for me recently?" and felt obligated to volunteer if they owed the requester a favor.

Employees in Spain based the decision mostly on friendship and loyalty, regardless of position or status. They asked, "Is this person connected to my friends?" If the answer was yes, they were especially likely to want to comply.

Chinese employees responded primarily to authority, in the form of loyalties to those with high status within their group or organization. When given a request, they asked, "Is this requester connected to someone in my unit, especially my boss or someone high up in the organization?" If the answer was yes, they were more likely to comply.

Although all human societies seem to respond to the same set of influence principles, the weights assigned to the various principles can differ across cultures. Persuasive appeals to audiences in distinct cultures need to take such differences into account.[lxiii]

NEGOTIATIONS

Building on our understanding of persuasion and influence, we next look at another practical application of those topics: negotiations. Just as people regularly try to influence and persuade others, individuals and organizations regularly carry on negotiations. We negotiate with co-workers over a project's schedule and goals, with other organizations over deliverables and dates, with vendors over price, and with family, neighbors, landlords and even the city government. **Negotiating** is the process in which at least two parties with different needs and viewpoints try to reach agreement on matters of mutual interest. There are a number of issues that concern a negotiator, including the familiar cognitive shortcuts that we have seen in this chapter and in Chapter 9—balance of power, rational approaches to negotiations, and types of negotiations. We will examine each in turn.

Negotiating
A process in which at least two partners with different needs and viewpoints try to reach agreement on matters of mutual interest.

Cognitive Shortcuts and Negotiation

We have already discussed cognitive shortcuts and is important to be aware that these same decision heuristics can push people toward suboptimal decisions in negotiations. Even in the careful, studied process of a long negotiation, people's decisions can be affected, perhaps overly so, by availability (vivid examples and stories, particularly emotional ones), loss aversion (not wanting to walk away from a deal that took months to arrange), consistency, and other heuristics that bias decisions. Negotiators need to be aware of these biases because they can and do occur in negotiations.

You will recall from Chapter 9 that it is not necessary to conduct an extensive analysis for most decisions. Similarly, it is not necessary to conduct negotiations in order to influence people: most everyday decisions do not require extensive analysis and negotiation. For a firm, bargaining over an item that is already fairly priced wastes time and money. Many firms today do not competitively bid all products, choosing instead to pay a little more and rely on certain suppliers that they can trust.

You will also recall that a set of decisions may be integrated together in order to make one big decision. For example, durable goods are typically expensive and issues such as delivery and installation must also be negotiated. In China, a negotiator for a state-owned enterprise (SOE) often needs to be able to show his

---

NEGOTIATION AND COMMUNICATION

"What we've got here is a failure to communicate."
—The prison warden to a rebellious prisoner (played by Paul Newman) who he had just knocked to the ground in the 1967 film *Cool Hand Luke*.

Cognitive shortcuts shape people's behavior in many ways. One critical shortcut involves our perceptions of the world. The role of perception is so great that it has given rise to a new philosophy, referred to as *solipsism*, which argues that the whole world is essentially created by an individual and his or her perceptions. It turns out that solipsism has a very practical side known as *plural solipsism*, which basically means to have a common world view. If you hold a plural solipsism of the world, you believe in a planet populated by friendly people who believe in a world like the one portrayed in the old Coca-Cola commercial with everyone singing about wanting to "teach the world to sing in perfect harmony." In this view, after all the cultural rituals are performed and languages translated, people still need to eat, sleep and take care of their families and friends, and so people are all the same. This philosophy underlies the premise

suggested above in the famous film *Cool Hand Luke* and can be detected in a great deal of media and popular culture around the world: We are all the same deep down. Pacific Islanders, Middle Easterners, and business students.

If the whole world is like you and me, then most conflicts must simply be, like the warden said, a result of a failure to communicate. But as we saw in Chapter 2, Culture and International Management, and in this chapter, projecting our own feelings, beliefs, and world views onto others, and assuming others will share our way of thinking and behave as we do can be risky. Studies of cultural values and other differences around the world suggest that people hold some profoundly different world views, and these differences are not simply ones of style, fashion, or language. A contrary view is that culture and context matter a great deal, and in practice, people will have positions that are difficult to reconcile. This confirms the importance of understanding the process of negotiation. Different cultures emphasize different tactics in negotiations and can hold significantly different values.

Nordic and northern European cultures, as well as the U.S., emphasize

fairness in negotiations and are more likely to present a reasonable position. Many other cultures, particularly in the lesser developed economies of the Middle East and parts of East and South Asia, are more likely to start out with a more extreme position to test how far their opponent can be pushed. A Chinese negotiator may start out with a requirement that a partner firm turn over its intellectual property so they can properly produce the product. However, if you are negotiating for your firm, you know this would be impossible. How can the negotiator seriously believe you would do this? Is it just an intimidation tactic? Is it an effort to anchor the discussion around your intellectual property? Is the negotiator really serious? It may be one or all three, and therefore you must be aware of the different processes of negotiation within different cultures along with the differing values and goals they hold.

Hofstede, G., & Hofstede, G. J. (2004). *Cultures and Organizations: Software of the Mind.* New York: McGraw-Hill.

Nisbett, R. (2004). *The Geography of Thought: How Asians and Westerners Think Differently . . . and Why.* New York: Free Press.

---

or her superiors a concession that was obtained from a foreign multinational enterprise, in order to prove the negotiation was handled in an aggressive manner. The MNE can make a number of small concessions that will help the Chinese negotiator look good in front of superiors and show that he or she is not falling prey to the type of unequal treaties that were foisted upon China by the European powers and Japan and in the 19th and early 20th centuries.[lxiv] Smaller concessions might come out of areas such as delivery, installation, and maintenance. It may not seem much to you or your firm, but to the SOE negotiator (or anyone with whom you are negotiating) it might be enough to satisfy the person's supervisors and seal the deal. It is not unlike a gardener agreeing to give greater care to one section of your lawn in exchange for less care over a section you seldom use.

A Rational Approach to Negotiation

In practice, no strategy can solve every negotiation problem. Starting out by asking for a high price in negotiations works in some cultures, such as in China or the Middle East, and in fact may be expected, but in other cultures, such as those in northern Europe, a negotiator who does this might be seen as tricky and dishonest. This increases the likelihood of the deal falling through and bad feelings all around.

Think of a time you had to negotiate something simple, like the price of a watch from a street vendor. Anyone who has traveled to East Asia, Africa, or the Middle East, or even to a number of ethnic neighborhoods in large North American cities, has probably had this experience. How did you feel when the vendor asked $75 for a watch that you knew would probably only sell for about $15 at a retail store, and with no purchase guarantee? Did you take it as just part of the negotiations—part of the fun of bargaining? Or did you think that the vendor was a crook with whom you would certainly never do business? If you thought the former, you are probably from a culture that typically bargains very hard and has a long history of trade, travel, and barter. Such cultures start high and ask for $75 because they expect you to start very low, say at $5, and negotiations proceed from those two extreme positions. By starting high, the seller is trying to anchor the negotiations near that number. Cultures in the Middle East and East Asia, particularly China, will often start negotiations at extremes to test the other party and gauge their commitment to the deal.

But individuals from northern Europe or Anglo-American backgrounds will likely respond negatively to a high initial price. In these cultures, negotiators generally expect each side to bargain fairly and not seek significant advantage. This may be related to the more egalitarian nature of these cultures—the relatively low power distance in the Northern European and Anglo countries—or by the sense of fairness Anglo and northern European cultures try to portray toward strangers.[lxv] If you are the type of person who does not like to start at an extreme price, resist the temptation to call the other side crooks and walk away if they start out the negotiations too high, whether you are buying a watch or negotiating for a long-term lease on a factory in southern China. In international business, it is essential to avoid projecting your own value system onto others, as well as understanding that a person's initial negotiation stance might be part of their culture, or may even reflect what is expected of them by their superiors or the government.[lxvi] Problems in negotiations are often not due only to a failure to communicate.

In this section, we survey some basic principles of negotiation and return to some irrational tendencies discussed earlier that commonly arise in negotiations. When you understand the underlying dynamics of negotiation, you will be able to isolate common biases and mistakes that lead to suboptimal agreements and instead base your decisions on sound business principles. We then discuss specific strategies that strengthen negotiation skills during each of the three stages of a negotiation: preparation, bargaining, and settlement.

Balance of Power

In any negotiation, one side may have more leverage than the other side. Recall from our discussion of Porter's Five Forces model in Chapter 5 that large customers can reduce the profitability of an industry. This is because in negotiations between big and small companies, the large company typically has greater leverage over price. A negotiation's outcome may be of much greater overall importance to the small company, or perhaps even essential to survival, while the large company's threats of walking away may leave the smaller company with no choice but to accept the larger firm's demands.

But it is not always clear which firm has the power in a relationship. An MNE may find that it must tread very carefully in a developing country because its negotiation partner may have the backing of the government. The government may want an MNE to open a factory in their country, but it may also have the choice of several MNEs in that industry and may be able to play each MNE off one another in the negotiation. Negotiating skill is especially critical in such a case because it can help maximize what you receive from the negotiations.

FIGURE 10-5   Two General Types of Negotiations

- **Distributive negotiations**. This type of negotiation assumes a fixed set of resources to bargain over, although this assumption may not be accurate and should be challenged by the other side. It is also known as fixed-pie negotiations.
- **Integrative negotiations**. This type looks aggressively for win-win solutions that also enlarge the resources that both sides might capture in negotiations. It is also known as expanding-pie negotiations.

Types of Negotiations

Negotiations and negotiation issues can be classified into two broad types: distributive (sometimes colloquially known as "fixed-pie") and integrative (also called "expanding-pie") negotiations.

Distributive Negotiations

In all negotiations, the parties seek to divide up available resources. Distributive negotiations are those in which opposing negotiators are concerned only with how the (apparent) fixed pie will be divided. In dividing the pie unevenly, one party's gain would represent the other party's loss; the more one party receives, the less the other party receives. Sometimes negotiations may involve only one issue, such as the cash sale of a watch from a street vendor in Chinatown. In such cases, any gain for one party is at the expense of the other party. The resource they are negotiating for is fixed (the selling price of a good), and the negotiation is purely distributive.

Integrative Negotiations

An integrative negotiation differs from a distributive one in that integrative negotiations have the potential to expand the size of the resources available for the negotiators to divide. Integrative negotiations do this in two ways. First, they expand the range of items of interest in a negotiation and thus make the deal bigger. Second, they try to identify and incorporate issues that the two sides value differently to create additional room for trade-offs and needed concessions. When parties value items differently, they can give some concessions on certain items they value less in exchange for gaining concessions on those they value more, which adds value for both parties.

   Negotiation must involve more than one item to be integrative. Even though negotiating multiple topics simultaneously can complicate the negotiations, including multiple issues can add value for both parties. In practice, an integrative negotiation produces greater winnings for everyone involved. The negotiator with less power in the deal often has more to gain from an integrative negotiation because a purely distributive negotiation awards more of the pie to the stronger side. A negotiator who is in a weaker position should seek an integrative negotiation in which other items are brought into the negotiation. For example, in negotiating a joint venture in a developing country where the government might be involved, an MNE that has less leverage than the local firm may bring other items to the table to help promote the establishment of the joint venture. The Chinese government is typically interested in acquiring technology, both in terms of products and manufacturing processes.[lxvii] Thus, the MNE can use the issue of creating jobs as well as bringing new technology to the region.

CLINICAL TRIALS IN EMERGING ECONOMIES: SOME ETHICAL ISSUES

Many organizations have outsourced a variety of tasks to emerging economies around the world. We have all experienced the overseas call centers for banks, software manufacturers, and hotel reservation lines. In recent years pharmaceutical firms have also started doing some of their clinical trials for drugs in emerging economies.[2] Pharmaceutical firms must extensively research and test their products before public consumption is permitted and governments in emerging economies are very supportive to firms bringing in knowledge industries such as drug and medical device research and development. Basic research is carried out in labs, usually in the firm's home country. Initial tests are done on animals, and later on healthy human volunteers. When a drug is determined to be safe with no apparent side effects the drug is given to humans in clinical trials. In 1997 over 80 percent of these clinical trials occurred in the United States and less than five percent were in countries outside of Western Europe or the U.S. But by 2007 less than 60 percent of clinical drug trials were conducted in the U.S. with approximately 30 percent conducted outside the U.S. and Western Europe. Evidence shows that the number of trials done in China and Southeast Asia will increase rapidly in the coming years.

One reason that many more clinical trials are being done in emerging economies is the diffusion of safety and test standards spurred by globalization. Whereas in the past, the regulations for drug efficacy and safety in the developing world were comparatively lax, today they are becoming much stricter. China, Taiwan, and South Korea, for example, all now require drug trials to be carried out locally before they will approve drugs for their citizens. Other countries such as Singapore and Thailand would like to see more local tests but are likely to approve drugs that are already approved in North America or Europe.

A second reason for the increasing number of clinical trials outside of North America and Europe is medicine's better understanding of regional diseases, both communicable and inherited. For example, there may be as many as 350 million sufferers of Hepatitis B in Asia, compared with around five million in North America. Drug firms have noticed opportunities for developing treatments for populations that suffer from diseases that may be more specific to a particular region. To do so, research protocol suggests that they conduct at least some of this research in the countries that suffer more from the disease. In the case of Hepatitis B, it would be China, where about 15 percent of the population is thought to suffer from that disease. Yet drug firms have been hesitant to conduct the necessary research for a major new drug largely for Asia partly because of the unknowns involved in the research process and working with regulatory agencies. But they will have to set aside these concerns in doing basic research in Asia and following up with clinical trials in several Asian countries to be able to meet this and other difficult diseases such as stomach cancer (also much more common in East Asia) head on.

Clinical trials cost only about half as much in emerging economies. A physician in Thailand will have training comparable to most physicians in the developed world but that costs a lot less. This will facilitate additional research in Asia and help drug companies overcome their resistance to committing basic research there. Nevertheless, drug firms still have concerns about the testing standards in some countries such as China, where some serious patient problems and breaches of testing protocol have occurred with clinical trials; some subjects in clinical trials have died during poorly managed tests. A decrease in the cost and time required in offshore drug testing may lead to drugs being available faster, resulting in the saving of many lives, but many ethical concerns must be taken into consideration as testing and regulatory standards continue to be problematic, even though they are improving. Would you recommend that pharmaceutical firms be more aggressive in researching and testing new drugs in emerging economies? How can they better control the drug testing process in emerging economies where regulations and scientific testing protocol are not well developed? What challenges would you foresee for Western pharmaceutical firms seeking to do more clinical trials in China, particularly with the help of Chinese drug firms and hospitals?

Eaton, M.A. (2004). *Ethics and the Business of Bioscience.* Stanford, CA: Stanford Business Books.

Jack, A. (2008, January 29). New lease on life? The ethics of offshoring clinical trials. *Financial Times*, p. 9.

Troy, D. B. (2006). *Remington: The Science and Practice of Pharmacy* (21st ed.). Philadelphia: Lippincott Williams & Wilkins.

ETHICS

THE NEGOTIATION PROCESS

Sometimes negotiations end with one party dissatisfied. Human error is one reason this occurs. We process information incorrectly or allow our judgments to be swayed by emotions or irrelevant events. In this section we examine those

---

[2]Understand that by doing clinical trials overseas, North American and European pharmaceutical firms are *not* replacing their local clinical trials with those done overseas. To get a drug approved in the United States, for example, a pharmaceutical firm must go through double-blind tests of their drug versus a placebo as well as some other tests (in most cases). The regulations in Europe are slightly less strict, but clinical trials must also be conducted there. Trials done in emerging economies cannot be substituted for locally conducted trials in the U.S. or Europe for the purpose of securing drug approval (Eaton, 2004; Troy, 2006).

things that can affect an international manager's negotiations. We will first return to issues of heuristics, biases, and culture, and introduce some common negotiating terms—Best Alternative to a Negotiated Agreement (BATNA) reservation price, target price, and positioning—as well as the importance of information, trust, impasses, and positive emotion.

Heuristics and Biases Revisited

In Chapter 9, we discussed a number of shortcuts or heuristics that people use in making decisions. Some of decision-making heuristics are quite useful because they reduce the amount of time and effort needed to make a decision, such as leaning on the expert opinion of a pharmacist when buying over-the-counter medicine. But sometimes heuristics can lead to an overemphasis on some information and the complete overlooking of other relevant information. In negotiations the same biases can occur. Some of the most common biases appear at the start of a negotiation, such as unrealistic expectations, improper frames, and anchors. Subsequent problems can occur during the negotiation if previous commitments are over-valued, leading to the escalation of commitment. The heuristics and biases we will examine include the role of unrealistic expectations, anchors, escalation of commitment, over-competitiveness, and framing.

Unrealistic Expectations

Negotiators need to recognize that unrealistic expectations can include those that are too high or too low. An underconfident negotiator who starts out by undervaluing his or her position and bargaining power will make unnecessary concessions or choose a low starting point (anchor). This lack of confidence affects the other members of his bargaining team, and everyone starts to undervalue the team itself. As a result, the team's assets are not well represented. In other cases, negotiators can be overconfident and believe that they know in advance how a negotiation should end, not taking the time to find out what the other side values. This lack of empathy can lead to a confirming-evidence bias that shuts out new sources of information and possible alternatives that may provide value to both sides.

Anchors

Recall that **anchoring** is a cognitive bias that describes the common human tendency to rely too heavily, or anchor, on one piece of information when making decisions. During the decision-making or negotiation process, individuals may anchor on a specific topic or value such as a starting price, and then discussion may proceed around that value or topic. For instance, novice car salespeople often make the mistake of bringing up an item that is not that important to the sales negotiation, such as the price of an option that the customer has not mentioned, and discussion can get sidetracked around that option.

An anchor may be set by a previous transaction price, an industry standard, or a rumored price, as well as an initial offer. In one study on anchoring, a group was asked to write down the last two numbers of their government identity numbers. Right after that, they were asked to submit mock bids on some luxury items. It was found that the half of the audience with higher two-digit ID numbers submitted bids that were consistently higher. Writing down the unrelated first number determined the second number, even though there was no logical connection between them.[lxviii] Because we want signposts and guides to help us with our judgments, the natural tendency is to focus on an anchor, even when that anchor has very little applicability to the current situation or is pushing in an unwanted direction.[lxix] Those bidding first can use anchors to their favor by setting the numbers and topics around which the negotiations will focus. The other side must then try to re-anchor the negotiations in a different area, sometimes by suggesting small concessions or by other means of changing the topic.

Escalation of Commitment

Managers like to succeed and follow through with what they stated they will accomplish. Pressure caused by the threat of failure or not reaching an agreement in a negotiation can be significant. This leads managers to sometimes escalate their commitment during a negotiation until they end up accepting a deal that they should have walked away from. Chinese negotiators are famous for recognizing this characteristic and delaying negotiations until the last minute before their counterparts need to catch a plane, hoping to clinch favorable deals from executives who do not want to leave China empty-handed. Business people should recognize this tactic and be prepared for it. It is also important to avoid escalation of commitment; once a negotiator has committed time and energy to a negotiation, that negotiator must fight against the natural instinct to agree to a deal simply to reach an agreement. Never be afraid to walk away from a deal if it is not what you want, that is, you must know your alternatives, particularly your BATNA and reservation price, which are discussed below.

The Best Alternative to a Negotiated Agreement (BATNA)

BATNA
Best alternative to a negotiated agreement.

Decisions should not be evaluated in isolation, but must be assessed in the context of what other *reasonable alternatives* may be at hand. In particular, negotiators must be fully aware of their **BATNA** or best alternative to a negotiated agreement. This brings one brief historical example to mind. After one particularly large battle between a U.S. (Union) army and a Rebel (Confederate) army during the American Civil War of the mid-nineteenth century, U.S. President Abraham Lincoln was being pushed by his advisors to replace the talented but overly cautious General George McClellan, who was properly blamed for the battle's so-so outcome as well as his failure to follow up and pursue the Rebel army. They urged President Lincoln to replace McClellan with anyone. In the true spirit of a negotiator Lincoln replied, "Anyone may be fine for you, but I must have someone."[lxx] Lincoln understood that McClellan was his best alternative until he could find some suitable (and willing) replacement commanders, which required a lot of trial and error until good leaders such as General Ulysses S. Grant finally emerged.[lxxi]

This example highlights the point that having and identifying alternatives to various key decisions in a negotiation are very important. Decisions should not be evaluated in isolation, but must be assessed in the context of what other reasonable alternatives may be at hand. For example, it is not very helpful to say that a certain decision is bad and that you disagreed with it without proposing *what you would have recommended instead*. In this way, you can make comparisons between your decision and the chosen one and the strengths and weaknesses of both choices. As President Lincoln pointed out, he still had to select *some* general; "anyone" was not a real choice. Practically speaking, this means that negotiators must be fully aware of their alternatives, particularly their BATNA. It is better to quit a lengthy negotiation than to accept a deal at a loss. Do not be afraid to walk away from any negotiation that provides terms that are worse than your best alternative to the negotiated agreement. Remember what the avoidance of escalation of commitment implies here: it is better to quit a lengthy negotiation than to accept a bad deal just to show something for the effort.

The Importance of Information

All of the discussion above about best alternatives, concessions, and positions reminds us once again that having well-organized and relevant information is crucial to effective negotiations. The ancient Chinese philosopher Sun Tzu wrote about the value of information in negotiation and conflict, particularly understanding the other side's strengths, weaknesses, and goals.[lxxii] Many negotiations are multidimensional and offer opportunities for integrative, resource-enlarging solutions. If the negotiating parties do not stay open to mutually beneficial proposals, a negotiation may falter and valuable opportunities may remain unexplored, leaving potential value undiscovered. This is particularly important to enterprises seeking cooperation on development projects and joint ventures. Significant value can be left in the negotiation room if the two sides do not have the tools and information by which agreement can be reached. The more information open to the negotiators, the more likely the "goods on the table" can be identified and made useful to both sides, creating an integrative, win-win negotiation.

It is important to collect as much information as possible because most negotiators will not offer the information up front. Once you and your opponent's underlying interests are known, you can begin to assess relative values. You can trade off concessions on issues that are less important to you in exchange for concessions on issues that are less important to your opponent. Understanding your counterpart's BATNA and reservation price is very valuable, but this is difficult to determine. For example, your negotiation partner might ask, "What's the maximum you will pay?" In effect, he is essentially asking for your **reservation price**, which is something you should never reveal. Sometimes you can answer a different question, or move the discussion toward other topics such as guarantees or delivery dates.

Reservation Price
A reservation price is the absolute bottom price that is acceptable.

ALEX RODRIGUEZ'S NEGOTIATION

The contract negotiations of baseball's Alex Rodriguez in 2000 and again in 2007 are an example of the negotiation process. In 2007, Rodriguez shocked the New York Yankees and Major League Baseball by activating an opt-out clause with three years and $81 million remaining in his contract, and notifying the Yankees in the middle of the 2007 World Series that he wanted a new contract. It was rumored that Rodriguez wanted a new 10-year contract for about $350 million, though he finally did re-sign with the Yankees for less than that. The contract that Rodriguez had opted out of was a 10-year, $252 million, guaranteed contract signed in 2000 with the Texas Rangers—by far the highest contract in sports history, eclipsing the previous record by over 100 percent. (Rodriguez was traded to the New York Yankees in 2004.)

How did Rodriguez's agent, Scott Boras, originally negotiate such a rich contract? In part, Boras reframed the negotiations by distributing a 70-page booklet to interested teams that summarized Rodriguez's statistics and his individual, incremental contribution to team revenues, so teams could see how much he was really worth. The booklet was full of data about how much ticket sales, parking fees, and food concessions went up when Rodriguez was playing. In this way, Boras was able to anchor the negotiations around the total package that Rodriguez brought to his team in terms of extra revenue and profit, and frame discussions away from comparisons with other players in professional baseball and their (much lower) salaries. It certainly made a difference—Rodriguez wanted to sign with his original team in 2000, but ended up with a much more lucrative deal by moving to the Rangers. Finding a more favorable anchor (incremental revenue brought in when Rodriguez is in the game), and reframing away from strict comparison with other players' salaries was key to the quarter of a billion dollar contract. Boras wanted to negotiate a new contract with the Yankees or other teams in 2007 and he convinced his client to exercise the opt-out clause in the original 10 year deal signed in 2000. Rodriguez eventually signed another 10 year contract that basically amounted to an extension of his current one. The Yankees had managed to persuade Rodriguez to drop his $35 million annual salary demand by reframing the negotiations in terms of Rodriguez becoming the greatest third baseman in baseball history and breaking the career homerun record in storied Yankee Stadium.

In order to assess your own strength and set your own BATNA and reservation price, you need to know both your own main or proximate alternatives and those of your counterpart. Your negotiating team's strategic positioning relies on the underlying goals and interests of your opponent and your opponent's stated position. To negotiate most effectively, negotiators need to base their decisions on reliable information. But here, too, individuals are subject to several common biases that influence how information is acquired and processed.

First among these biases is that most people make decisions based on vivid experiences and events. Unfortunately, memory is often selective and subject to the availability heuristic. People make decisions and draw conclusions based on the information and events that they can remember, instead of the necessary facts. We remember vivid, spectacular, or catastrophic events more readily than mundane ones. For example, the Great Depression of the 1930s permanently imprinted the memories of many Americans and Europeans from that era. Experience taught them that neither investments nor jobs could be counted on, and that no amount of savings was enough. Many of those people refused to process information about the safety and profitability of a diversified portfolio of securities and other long-term investments. Instead, they put their money in low-interest, insured accounts and lived more frugally than necessary. Many older Americans still use the expression "play the stock market" like it is a game and not an investment. This problem was not confined to the United States. For decades, some Japanese people kept their savings in accounts with the Japanese Post Office at interest rates hovering around 1 percent. Only in recent years have they learned the value of compound interest and started to demand higher returns on their money.

Second, individuals are often as impressed by the theatricality of a presentation as its substance. Because we more easily recall facts or events that are described to us in vivid terms, negotiators who use picturesque language and concrete examples are more effective in influencing others than negotiators who supply the same information in less vivid terms. Do not be overly influenced by salesmanship and emotion. Cast a skeptical eye on the other side's enthusiasm for their product or capabilities. Beware of statements such as "Our market is huge" or that "Nine times out of ten" something will happen. Instead, seek out hard figures and evaluate them carefully. Negotiators should be sure to provide that data or tell customers where it can be found. It should be noted that it is sometimes said that Chinese negotiators do not like to provide data with their presentations. That preference may be limited to the old state-owned enterprises that were not charged with making a profit but with maximizing production or employment. Newer Chinese organizations today are concerned with profits and data, and that information should be sought out. Negotiators should not settle for broad, unsubstantiated generalizations such as "The market is very big"; rather, they must determine with the help of consulting firms or other knowledgeable people how big the given product market is in specific areas, such as the coastal provinces or major city markets.[lxxiii]

This emphasis on information is also a reminder that a decision *must* be assessed in comparison with other possible decisions. No decision should ever be assessed in isolation. There are always alternatives and opportunity costs; even if the only alternative is doing nothing, it is still an alternative.

Reservation Price

A reservation price is the firm's absolute bottom price that is acceptable. For a firm selling something, the reservation price would be just *above* the BATNA. Reservation prices are most easily defined in single-issue, distributive negotiations and are more difficult to establish in more complex, integrative negotiations. Nonetheless, it is always useful to establish a set of conditions that describes the reservation price. This set of conditions can serve as a benchmark for other offers and help

Micropix/Dreamstime LLC

Visual aids can be very effective when making a presentation because the audience is more likely to understand and recall facts or events that have been described in vivid, picturesque terms.

suggest your position to your opponents without giving away too much information about what you can pay and what you wish to pay.[lxxiv]

Target Price

Negotiators should also set targets for what the price they wish to pay or receive. This is the value that you would like to have—your preferred, or "blue sky," agreement. While reservation price establishes the lowest price you will accept, target price shifts your focus from getting just enough to negotiating what you and the other side want. Focusing on your target during the negotiation gives you a clear vision of what you hope to achieve. The negotiator needs to create doubt in the opponent's mind about the point at which they would prefer to walk away rather than reach an undesirable deal. The negotiating team can create such doubt by emphasizing the target price (not the reservation price) and negotiating terms on other items. If the other side demands concessions, follow the reciprocation principle and ask for concessions in return right away—the other side will be more likely to reciprocate with concessions if you ask right after they asked you for concessions.

Framing

Recall our earlier discussion of loss framing's effect on people's decision making. Research shows that negotiators can react very differently to identical proposals when the perspective, or framing, changes. As anchoring on a specific number can strongly influence negotiations, the way a situation is framed or presented also greatly influences the action taken. If a frame is poorly constructed, a negotiator may unwittingly make a money-losing choice. For example, managers can err by framing an investment solely in terms of gross margins rather than in terms of the strategic value of the decision.

One example from high-end consumer sales shows a very interesting approach to framing. A company offered a range of spas, from the basic outdoor variety for a few thousand dollars to a fancier indoor spa complete with its own room for $15,000, and it was having trouble selling the more expensive spa. Prospects were comparing the expensive interior spa with the cheaper outdoor models and concluding that they were just too expensive. Finally, the firm hit on an idea. Rather than emphasizing the more expensive spa's fancier features and functions (remember the problem of simply pushing features and functions while not listening to and addressing customer needs), they asked prospective customers about something they are all concerned with: the value of their homes. The spa salesperson then asked the customers how much they thought their homes would go up by in value if they added an extra room. Depending on which area of North America they lived in, that answer could be $30,000 or more. The spa salesperson then asked how much it would cost to add a room such as an enclosed porch or a small den to their home, something that could easily top $25,000. The salesperson then pointed out to prospects that buyers of the top-of-the-line spa were able to add value to their homes because the enclosed spa was considered to be an additional room for the house. By adding the spa, customers would meet two of their stated needs: getting the spa they wanted and adding another room to their home. Given the increase in their homes' values, the spa would be an excellent value, in fact it would practically pay for itself. When framed as a comparison with adding a room to the house, instead of in comparison to the cheaper spas, the high-end $15,000 spa became quite desirable and even economical.[lxxv]

Framing is essential to negotiation. For example, instead of focusing on risks in a negotiation, you might want to focus on opportunities. In negotiating your salary, rather than focusing only on the asking salary, you might want to focus on the benefits you can bring in. The type of information brought into a negotiation "sets the table" for the interpretation and understanding of all negotiating that follows.

Finally, remember loss framing and the scarcity principle. People are more influenced by avoiding a loss (or not missing out on some benefit) than by equivalent gains. If you can cast your negotiations in terms of helping the other side not miss out on some benefit, that is usually a more effective frame. In any case, negotiators will want to understand both their own frames and their negotiating partner's, and it may be necessary to test different types of analyses and perspectives to achieve a win-win agreement.[lxxvi]

Fairness and Trust

Most people are very sensitive to fairness issues. Some people will walk away from a good deal just to punish someone on the other side of the negotiation who they perceived as behaving unfairly or being deceptive—even if they would have been better off with that deal. This is illustrated in a well-known experiment often run by economists called the ultimatum game.[lxxvii] There are several versions of the experiment, most of which give two or more participants the chance to split up a sum of money, say $20. If the players can't agree on how to split the money, neither side gets any of it. The players have a limited amount of time to negotiate the distribution of funds. If on the last round, Player 1 seeks to keep, say, $15 for himself and leave just $5 for Player 2, studies show that Player 2 will reject that split, even if by rejecting it he or she is left with nothing as the game ends. Thus, Player 2 will typically punish Player 1 for not being fair, even if it is clear he would be better off by accepting the final $5 offer. After all, his BATNA is zero dollars, and the reservation price would just likely be just a few cents above that. Although people are usually loss-averse, that loss aversion may be overridden by a sense of equity and the desire to punish unfairness. Why else would we make multiple phone calls and write letters about a small sum of cash that we think a company cheated us out of? Most people will say, "It is not the money that is important but the principle of the thing," when explaining an irrational decision to punish unfairness and "get even" at a significant cost to themselves. Interestingly enough, people from poorer countries such as Indonesia will also reject unfair splits in the money—even rejecting final offers equivalent to three days' wages and walking away with nothing—just to get even with those they feel are bargaining unfairly and make sure they also walk away with little or nothing.[lxxviii]

In negotiations, the dynamics can be quite similar. Negotiators often will walk away from an economically rational agreement if they believe they have been unfairly treated or deceived in some way. They will do this even if this agreement is above the reservation price and should be accepted. This problem can be compounded by culture. What is fair for all sides is often difficult to define. A fair outcome for a negotiator from an egalitarian society such as Sweden might be one in which parties share benefits more or less equally. For another society, such as Latin America, a fair distribution would be based on the relative resources and work each person contributed. Someone from yet another culture, as in China or India, might argue that it is fairest to allocate benefits according to need, even if the split in money is very uneven.[lxxix]

Therefore, it is essential that a negotiator be cognizant that fairness is an issue. People who feel they are being treated unfairly become angry and walk away from what still are good deals. Emotions are a part of any negotiation, but negotiators who focus on getting back at the other side because of their unfair tactics may end up hurting themselves as well. Negotiators are much more likely to achieve compromises with opposing parties they like and trust. When we trust someone, we are less likely to suspect ulterior motives, traps, or deception and minimize any perceived unfairness. Most negotiations are not one-shot deals, and we usually expect to maintain an ongoing relationship after an agreement is reached. If you expect to do more deals in the future, trust is essential. Thus, it is valuable to a firm to build trust over time.

Impasses in Negotiations

An **impasse** simply means that you and your partner cannot reach an agreement. The situation may arise that no agreement is improving either side's BATNA. In such cases, a manager needs do some creative, integrative problem solving to create more value, or be willing to walk away from the negotiations. In contrast, a "sweet deal" may exist for both sides but a handshake cannot be reached because the solution is distributive and both sides are holding out for a bigger piece of the negotiation pie and do not want to feel unfairly treated.

Several strategies can help restart stalled negotiations. First, try to focus on underlying interests or values rather than only on positions. Positions may become more matters of pride or fairness rather than substance; in this case, return to what people value and need. Also try to meet your opponent's needs in appearance while fulfilling your team's interests in substance. By focusing on the substance of your interests, you are more likely to uncover new integrative proposals that enlarge the pie for both sides. Second, as the reciprocation principle recommends, make an initial small concession, then suggest one in return. Sometimes people need to be shaken from entrenched positions before they can make significant moves. One arbitrator who works on cases in North America told us that he starts out a negotiation between two parties by offering both of them a concession: he

Impasse
When a manager and his or her negotiating partner cannot reach an agreement.

gives them the first hour of the arbitration at no charge (a substantial gift). He then asks in return that both sides promise to bargain fairly during the negotiation. Research in social psychology over the past 60 years suggests that most people will reciprocate.[lxxx] Third, the arbitrator also suggested that it may be helpful to bring in a third party. A fresh perspective sometimes gets a negotiation back on track.

In some cases, you will not be able to reach agreement. Always terminate a negotiation cordially. Inform the other party that you are sorry no agreement was possible at this time, but that you hope new opportunities will arise in the future. Being genial encourages future agreements and makes it easier to restart negotiations later if circumstances change.

Ultimatum
Requiring someone or a group to do specific thing in a specific way in order for negotiations to continue.

An **ultimatum** is an attempt to break an impasse and force a deal, whereby one party says that the other party must agree to X or the negotiations are terminated. Such an approach is a double-edged sword. It can sometimes get the other side to give in, but it can also prematurely end a negotiation. Managers should always avoid using ultimatums in negotiations unless he or she is willing to carry through with them. If a negotiator makes an ultimatum and then fails to act on it, the negotiator's credibility will suffer. However, it may be possible to keep the door open for resuming negotiations later. If the manager is given an ultimatum by the other party, he or she should realize that sometimes an ultimatum is serious but at other times it may be a bluff. If a manager is faced with an ultimatum from the other party, ignoring it is often the best possible response. It may be possible to pick up the negotiation again and set aside the ultimatum.

Positive Emotion

Anger, pride, overconfidence, and over-competitiveness can all work against you in a negotiation. But emotional reactions can also have positive effects. Negotiators who are in positive moods are more likely to achieve integrative agreements. Amicable, trusting relationships can lead to mutually beneficial exchanges of information and the discovery of opportunities to add value for both parties.[lxxxi]

It is ironic that many aggressive negotiators, who often consider themselves to be the most savvy of business people, fail to understand how much business they may be losing when others perceive them to be unfair or arrogant. People prefer to do business and negotiate with people whom they like and feel to be fair and can develop some relationship with. If a negotiator constantly seeks to squeeze advantages from others, then he or she may only get the one-time business, particularly with Northern European or North American cultures that have expectations of equitable behavior in negotiations.

Moods are also important in negotiations. Studies show that people that are in a sad emotional state are likely to pay about 30 percent more for an item than those in a neutral state. Similarly, they also are likely to sell an item for about 33 percent less than they would otherwise.[lxxxii] Emotions can be very important in negotiation and decision making, and it is important to account for them and not to ignore them. Do not hesitate to replace a negotiator who is not in top form.

Culture in Negotiations

There is a growing literature documenting international negotiating styles.[lxxxiii] Research and descriptions can be found about the negotiating style of Latin Americans such as Brazilians and Mexicans,[lxxxiv] East Asians (including Chinese, Japanese, and Koreans),[lxxxv] people from the Middle East,[lxxxvi] Russians, and others.[lxxxvii] For example, research suggests that Russians are more likely to base their arguments on asserted principles or ideals, somewhat similar to the verdict-based information search discussed earlier. People from China and the Middle East are more likely to start a negotiation at a number that's very favorable to them,

NEGOTIATIONS TRAP

Misunderstanding the culture and negotiation standards of another country can lead to a breakdown in the negotiation process. While politeness and respect may be the way one country negotiates a business proposition, another might use extreme bidding, coercion, and even deception as acceptable ways to negotiate. Countries with similar cultures might be expected to negotiate in similar ways, but this is not always the case, because culture is only one of the many things that determines a country's negotiation style. For example, although China and Taiwan are both Chinese and follow similar tenets of Chinese culture, their negotiations tactics are significantly different.[lxxxviii] Recent history and legal institutions can play a big role in negotiation. A Chinese business person negotiating a deal related to employment head count with a British MNE may refer to aspects of China's socialist system, while a Taiwanese business person would be more likely to appeal to the joint commercial values held by the British and Taiwanese government and industrials systems. This also becomes clear when comparing Austria's negotiation tactics with Germany, a country with which it shares cultural similarities.

Austria

At first glance, Austria would seem to be like Germany. Austria is a central European country that borders Germany, German is the national language, and Austria is culturally very similar to Germany. Yet Austria also has its own identity, rich history, and traditions. Located just south of Germany, Austria is much smaller than her powerful northern neighbor, with a relatively small population of 8.3 million people. Yet Austria has one of the highest economic output per capita with a total GDP of $409 billion, or approximately $49,000 per person. Austria's economy is one of the strongest and best performing in the Euro Zone (the European countries whose currency is the Euro).

History plays a critical role in Austria's identity, and differentiates that country from Germany. For example, the only country the Soviet Union (predecessor to Russia) occupied and then left following World War II was Austria. All other countries the Soviets occupied either were incorporated into the Soviet Union or became puppet states that the Soviet Union controlled through proxy governments. It was for this reason Austria is strongly neutral—they refused to take sides in the Cold War between the forces of the North Atlantic Treaty Organization (NATO) and the Soviet Bloc. Austria still refuses to join NATO. Like Switzerland, Austria has used its neutrality to establish relations with former Soviet Bloc countries and their firms.

These connections to Eastern Europe do not rest on Austria's current position in Europe alone. Further back in history, Austria was the center of the Hapsburg Empire, which existed for several hundred years in central Europe and included Austria, Hungary, Spain, Bulgaria, Romania, and other countries at various times. As a result of these various relationships with surrounding countries, Austrian firms have been able to easily do business with and invest in them as they have liberalized, and have established strong trading and investment relationships.

The two countries' cultures are similar in many ways if one looks just at Hofstede's four cultural dimensions. However, there are other subtle but strong differences between the two countries. For example, Germany has a large and vibrant immigrant community, particularly Turks (immigration into Germany is comparable to immigration into the United States). This immigrant community has integrated in many ways much better than anywhere else in Europe. In contrast, Austria has very few immigrant communities and is also historically xenophobic, which may have limited Austria's access to emerging economies outside of Europe. This can also change the criteria that firms use to negotiate with Austrian counterparts. For example, while Germany might welcome foreign direct investment from Turkey and other countries from West Asia or the Middle East, Austria has been less welcoming in that regard, preferring to focus on developing its Eastern European and Balkan ties. Austria feels that it is a small country and its identity could become overwhelmed by large numbers of immigrants, though they would probably benefit the economy. Germany's population is nearly ten times that of Austria and the country feels more able to encourage foreign direct investment and immigration.

perhaps overly favorable, which can stir resentment in North European negotiating partners. See Figure 10-6 for a summary of regional negotiating styles.

As a negotiation progresses, Russian and Chinese negotiators are known to make fewer concessions than their counterparts and protest about the disrespectful treatment accorded to them. The other side should be ready to have a lot of small points to concede so the Chinese or Russian negotiators can show they are tough bargainers and are making a lot of progress against the foreign firm. Middle Eastern and South Asian negotiators are thought to use more emotional appeals based on subjective feeling. North Americans are more likely to use a factual approach to negotiating, rather than an emotional one, appealing to more objective and provable facts.[lxxxix] South Americans and Arabs may feel unconstrained by

FIGURE 10-6	Regional Negotiating Styles

- Russian negotiators are more likely to use an axiomatic approach to negotiating, appealing to basic principles of fairness and the negotiation process.
- Russian and Chinese negotiators are known to make fewer concessions than their counterparts.
- Middle Easterners, Africans, and South Asian negotiators (e.g., India, Pakistan, Sri Lanka) are thought to use more emotional appeals, whereas European and North American negotiators emphasize data and evidence. Emotional stories and appeals can also be influential to those groups.
- Arab negotiators do not feel limited by time or authority; they frequently approach deadlines casually. This is true with many countries in Latin America as well, although there are exceptions, such as Guatemala and Argentina.
- Chinese negotiators will often use time against Western firms, which feel rushed to complete their "China deals." Savvy Western firms will try to rise above their cultural proclivity to want to "get it done" and take the necessary time to complete the deal favorably.

time limits, and approach deadlines very casually.[xc] In contrast, North Americans generally take deadlines very seriously—even artificial ones—and usually have broad authority to reach an agreement in the time allocated.[xci]

A negotiation becomes cross-cultural when the parties involved belong to different cultures and therefore do not share the same values and behaviors. Many negotiations are cross-cultural as are some domestic negotiations that include multiple ethnic groups. A Singaporean business person negotiating a new e-commerce agreement with a Brazilian, two Malaysian citizens—one an ethnic Chinese and one a Malay—negotiating a large land sale, a U.N. official negotiating with ambassadors from several countries concerning a trade summit's agenda, Mexican executives considering a potential strategic alliance with Norwegians, and Flemish- and French- speaking Belgians determining national language legislation—these are all cross-cultural negotiations. Effective cross-cultural negotiations contain all of the complexity of domestic negotiations with the added dimension of cultural diversity.

It was noted earlier that Chinese negotiators are well known for driving a hard bargain, particularly those connected to the government or state firms.[xcii] But this is not the only tactic that Chinese negotiators use to persuade the other party to reach an agreement favorable to themselves. For example, in formal negotiation sessions Chinese negotiators are also well known for using flattery, identifying the opponent's problems, deception, shaming, and pitting competing foreign companies against one another.[xciii]

International managers facing tough negotiators in China can still be successful, however, if they are firm on what they can offer and what they cannot. They also should seek to build credibility with their Chinese partners by dealing with them fairly. Such credibility can be built not only in formal negotiating sessions but also between sessions. One manager gave the following example:

> Once one of the Chinese negotiators for a client of ours in China insisted that our new machines had some problems and that our technology did not work well. I did not say anything, but when I returned to my hotel, I called the head office and asked an engineer from our home office to check on the problem in the Chinese factory. It turned out that there was no problem, and perhaps something had been set up incorrectly. A couple of days later over the dinner I privately told the Chinese manager that there may have been an error in the set-up as the machine had started working and ran for two days without any problem. I had not said anything at that day's staff meeting so as not to embarrass him in front of his staff and gave him my direct number (at the Hong Kong office) and told him to call me directly with any other problems. After that he became very friendly and even helped us to get that and other orders.

Implied in this story is the recommendation that you do not confront people, particularly more senior people, in meetings about a mistake or a misjudgment he

NEGOTIATION TACTICS ACROSS CULTURES

CULTURE

The use of silence and feigned outrage are two extreme tactics used in negotiation. Japanese often use silence in negotiations, while Americans use it much less and Chinese are somewhere in between.[xciv] Chinese negotiators can alternate between long periods of silence and inaction and blaming and shaming their negotiation partners.[xcv] How do Americans often respond to silence? Past research has shown that American negotiators tend to assume that an offer is not going to be accepted if a Japanese group is silent for an extended period of time. An American negotiator may tend to argue in response to the apparently uncomfortable silence. While the Japanese silently consider the Americans' offer, the Americans interpret the silence as rejection and respond by making concessions (e.g., by lowering the price). Similar dynamics occur when nonnative English speakers negotiate in English. If nonnative English speakers hesitate during a negotiation, usually to make sure they are comprehending what is being said, Americans may also wrongly assume that their offer is being rejected. Silence should never be interpreted as a rejection of a position, and neither should a request for a closer examination of the proposal. A negotiation depends on the information gathered, and the relationships established.

Chinese negotiators may use a different approach. They have learned that repeatedly telling people they made a mistake, it will make them more likely to admit the mistake and perhaps make additional concessions.[xcvi] Chinese negotiators have also been known to regularly remind parties with whom they are negotiating how China was forced into unfair treaties in the nineteenth century and that they will not allow that to happen again. Sometimes the negotiator's country is blamed for concessions given to the European powers or for the Sino-Japanese conflicts of the past 120 years. Research suggests that it is helpful to admit to the problems of the past rather than argue about them. Although the United States never had significant concessions in China, and even donated reparation money granted from a treaty at the end of the Boxer Rebellion to support the founding of Ching Hwa University in Beijing, it may help nevertheless to acknowledge the problems that occurred in those days before moving forward.[xcvii] Research on influence also indicates that it is best to openly acknowledge a past mistake or weakness to get it out of the way and build credibility with the other party. Even making a small concession up front that you may feel is unimportant but that would show good faith to the other side may prove very helpful.

or she might have made when dealing with traditional and high power-distance societies such as in China, Japan, or the Middle East. If a negotiator from the West points out a mistake loudly and publicly, the senior negotiator on the Chinese side will lose face. It is better to take that negotiator aside to mention this, or even speak to his or her subordinate separately, so the problem can be communicated without a loss of face. If possible, the negotiator can try to show concern for the senior negotiator on the other side and acknowledge that they have helped to solve a problem in the negotiation.

SUMMARY

Persuasion and influence are important skills that international managers can learn that will help them in negotiating, selling, and managing on a day-to-day basis. Persuasion is getting someone to change their mind about something, while influence is defined as eliciting a change in behavior or a decision in response to your request. Six universal principles of influence help firms and individuals generate a positive response to a request. These are social proof, authority, liking, consistency, reciprocation, and scarcity. Knowledge of these principles can help managers and organizations empower employees, customers, or clients to make better-informed decisions about, for example, whether to purchase a product or support a particular plan or policy. The six principles are universal in that they apply to different industries and settings around the world, but cultural norms and traditions can affect how a principle may be implemented and which one may be most important.

Some common judgment errors often undermine our abilities to negotiate optimal agreements:

1. Under- or overconfidence. Because of underconfidence, we fail to value our assets adequately. Or because of overconfidence in our own strengths, we fail to consider all relevant information and end up with no deal or one that is below standards. Asking questions, exchanging information, listening carefully to the other party, consulting with others, and taking time to evaluate alternatives thoroughly can all help in assessing issues realistically and rationally.

2. Escalation of commitment. Out of desire to accomplish something or to win, we can escalate our commitments to irrational levels. We control escalation of commitment by evaluating our best alternative to a negotiated agreement (BATNA), establishing a firm reservation price, and walking away from a deal when pressured or not given that reservation price.

3. Over-competitiveness. We can become too competitive and succumb to the myth of the fixed pie. We take "your loss is my gain" positions and fail to explore the full potential of a negotiation. Focusing on underlying interests rather than stated positions is essential for overcoming excessive competitiveness. Remember that both sides can win!

4. Irrelevant anchors. We anchor our bids and offers around historical figures, industry standards, or even first offers that often have little or no relevance to the current negotiation. Information is the key to avoiding getting stuck on irrelevant anchors. Research, ask questions, and listen. Base figures on the most relevant data and reject irrelevant figures.

5. Biased framing. We frame problems too narrowly, take biased perspectives, and fail to consider the most critical issues. Consulting others, calling in third parties, and testing alternative assessment models can help your team gain new perspectives on negotiation issues, as can learning what the other side values and how to frame opportunities in those terms.

6. Unrealistic risk assessment. People often either overestimate or underestimate risks. To improve our risk assessment, list the risks and the rewards and assess the probabilities.

Managers should understand their own goals, evaluate their BATNA, and set their reservation price. They should take their time, ask questions, research information, and exchange information. Search for trade-offs and opportunities to expand and improve your agreement. Then evaluate proposals thoroughly, remaining open to integrative solutions. Never waste time on battling your opponent just for the sake of "winning" the negotiation. Drive home the best possible deal for your team.

MANAGERIAL GUIDELINES

Persuasion and influence are very important skills for managers and business people to have today, particularly those doing business globally. In today's business environment it is difficult to simply order people to do things. They often must be carefully influenced to do things. International business people must work with other departments, alliance and joint-venture partners abroad, government officials, military officers, and a range of customers and stakeholders from around the world, and these people cannot be ordered to do anything. The good news is that persuasion and influence skills can be learned. Effective persuasion to convince others to change an attitude or belief starts with empathy or trying to understand that person's position or underlying values. It is important to remember the old adage, "If you're talking, you ain't learning." And persuasion is all about listening and learning about the other person's problems, concerns, or tasks they need to get done. Only with an understanding of these issues can you identify how your product or service will benefit them *by solving their problems and addressing their concerns*. If you frame things in terms of their problems or stated beliefs, your arguments will be much more persuasive. Be patient and observant. Be a good listener and learn how to ask questions instead of making speeches about your company, your product or your ideas.

The influence principles not only help us to ethically influence people, they also suggest things not to do, such as being quick to criticize someone's work or point of view, constantly bringing up controversial issues unnecessarily, or being negative in your conversation. Doing those things will drive people away from you and *reduce your influence* with them. Unfortunately, these negative behaviors are all too common in day-to-day interactions, but you now know to steer clear of these unhelpful behaviors.

In negotiations, there are some additional precepts apart from the persuasion and influence principles discussed above. In some cases, a deal that is too biased toward your own team may back your opponent into a corner. For example, it may be impossible for them to deliver the goods as promised or to make the payments required. Or if he or she has felt unfairly treated, your opponent's team may not deliver the goods as agreed in the terms of the deal. Expedited service, special treatment in emergencies, and customized production may be essential to a successful partnership, and maintaining a cooperative relationship can be critical. Managers are well served to remember the following in negotiations:

1. Do not insist on too good a deal; remember that some cultures such as North European and North American may see extreme starting positions as a signal of dishonesty. Try to make sure your opponent's position will be viable; that is, look for win-win solutions. Most deals are not one-time-only deals. You also want to build long-term partnerships.

2. Be gracious when you receive concessions. Reassure your opponent that the concession is fair and in the interests of both parties, and helps to meet the other party's needs. After the negotiation is finished, your opponent will be looking for confirmation that they made a good decision. Be sure to give that to them.

3. Be sure that the other party understands the cost of the concessions to your own team, but avoid pouting or bitterness after you have made them. Once you have reached an agreement, you and the other party are now partners and should act accordingly.

4. Avoid misrepresentation. Certain forms of game playing are expected in negotiations, but dishonesty should be minimized under most conditions. You might want to disguise your eagerness to reach an agreement or to frame financial terms in language that is most favorable to you, but direct misrepresentations should be avoided.

5. Distrust will undermine your long-term agreements and block future agreements. Even in one-time business deals, every business person has a responsibility to act ethically. All businesses benefit from a trusting, efficient business environment. Plus, in today's globalized world, word gets around fast if you are always out to squeeze the last dollar out of every deal. Some industries are very clubby and tight, and you and your firm's reputations can precede you. Remember also that reciprocation pays dividends, but to engender reciprocation, you must act first. Be generous when you can and build good will.

DOING BUSINESS IN GUATEMALA

Guatemala is a Central American country of approximately 13 million people and with an annual GDP of approximately $33 billion per year. Guatemala has the second largest economy in Central America and its wealth is heavily concentrated in Guatemala City, the capital, with a population of 2.5 million. Poverty in Guatemala is extensive in rural areas where 60 percent of the population lives. The rural population is over 80 percent indigenous, descendents of the ancient Mayan empire. Approximately 40 percent of Guatemala's population lives on less than $2 a day.

Guatemala shares many of the same cultural characteristics of other Latin American states. There is a strong emphasis on family and a strong desire to have a relationship with an individual before starting business. Thus, business people are well served in seeking to meet and build relationships over time with other business people. This process includes getting to know the family of the person you would like to do business with. There is also a strong emphasis on titles and showing respect to other individuals.

Guatemala has unique differences as well. Guatemalans are typically more prompt than most other Latin Americans. If a time is set for a meeting, they expect that you will be on time. The significant indigenous population raises special concerns. Several Latin American countries, such as Peru and Bolivia, also have large indigenous populations, while others, such as Argentina, have much smaller ones. Indigenous populations have their own languages and cultures. In Guatemala, 23 official indigenous languages are recognized. The business people that you may deal with are likely to be bilingual in Spanish and English due to the strong business connections between the United States and South America. However, if you operate a manufacturing facility or some other factory or plant employing large numbers of people it is likely that many different languages will be spoken in the workplace. The cultural differences in a group like this will vary as well and will present another challenge for management staff.

CULTURE

EXERCISES

1. Do you think that partnerships between non-profit and for-profit entities have the opportunity to be beneficial to all parties as it was in this case?
2. What other societal problems do you think could be solved by for-profit and non-profit entities working together?
3. What are the difficulties that could arise in the negotiations between the parties in those settings?

DISCUSSION QUESTIONS

Opening Vignette Discussion Questions

1. American political consultants now often work for politicians in other countries. Why do you think their persuasion and promotion techniques seem to be transferable to other countries and cultures worldwide?
2. Why might advertising campaigns have to be changed to be effective while campaign methods would not?
3. How must your negotiation style change when dealing with a unionized plant as an active multinational enterprise in a Latin American country versus that in the United States?
4. What differences in cultural biases in making decisions do you think would exist between North American and European managers?
5. Suppose someone says: "I cannot understand why that guy [a mutual friend] did not help me out last week. I mean, we are friends, aren't we?" What influence principle is your friend invoking? What is the downside of depending too much on that principle and what might you recommend to him in dealing with that other guy in the future?

IN-CLASS EXERCISES

- Break into an equal number of teams and then pair up into teams of two. One team will be the seller of a product while the other will be the buyer. Your instructor will give each team some business specifics that the other team is not to know about. Conduct a negotiation to buy a given number of products.
- Influencing someone to do something and motivating someone to do something seem to be about the same. Discuss with your neighbor how these two general actions are different and give one action for each.
- Why is it good to acknowledge a weakness in your argument or position first before proceeding with trying to persuade someone? What does research show about how you will most likely be perceived?
- Break into teams of two. Discuss buying a lathe (a machining tool) and what types of information you might need to have before entering into the negotiation process.

TAKE-HOME EXERCISES

- Research a failed negotiation using an online search engine like Google. Identify what you think was the principal cause of the failed negotiation.
- Research a recent labor or sports figure negotiation. Detail the nature of these negotiations and how they illustrate the concepts discussed in this chapter.
- Based on earlier discussions of mergers and acquisitions, identify an international merger or acquisition using an online search engine. What were the nature of the negotiations that occurred for that M&A? How long did the negotiations take?
- Research negotiations that have attempted to end a standoff in a country or region facing severe political impasses. How do these negotiations differ from those in business?

SHORT CASE QUESTIONS

Negotiations Trap (p. 327)

1. What do you think the differences would be in negotiations in Ireland and Britain? Scotland and Britain?
2. Do you think regional differences in a large country like China also have an impact with different regions having different styles of negotiations?
3. What might be the differences in the negotiations in the same industry, such as venture capital, around the world?

11

EVALUATION AND CONTROL

Overview

This chapter addresses evaluation and control in an international firm. Once management has set its goals and objectives, it needs to evaluate whether the firm is meeting those goals and objectives. The firm also needs to determine if future trends will result in a need for changes in its strategy and goals. If the desired goals will not be met, actions must be taken and adjustments made in the firm's strategy and/or goals. This process is referred to as evaluation and control. The evaluation and control process should be an ongoing effort and not something that occurs only once a year when the business does its strategic planning. Issues related to evaluation and control in international business that will be discussed in this chapter include the following:

- Gap analysis
- Financial, strategic, and cultural controls
- Designing the support structure for evaluation and control processes
- Encouraging best practices, including quality management programs

BARINGS: THE DANGERS OF A WEAK EVALUATION AND CONTROL SYSTEM

Evaluation and control is concerned with determining whether the goals of a firm are being met. If they are not, then the firm either needs a different goal or to take different actions. In some industries the implications of a weak evaluation and control system can be dramatic, such as in the case of Barings bank.

Barings PLC was a London-based merchant bank founded in 1762. The bank had helped to finance the Napoleonic Wars, the Louisiana Purchase by the United States, and the Canadian Pacific Railway. But in February of 1995 Barings was forced into receivership. It was purchased by Dutch bank and insurance company ING for £1 along with assumption of all of Barings liabilities. It was later resold in 2005. Evaluation and control in the firm had collapsed to the point that a single individual in the firm's Singapore office, a trader named Nick Leeson, was able to invest over $1 billion without the firm's knowledge, eventually generating losses of US$1.4 billion, driving the venerable 233-year-old bank into bankruptcy.

Leeson did not have a university education. He had success in working for Barings in Jakarta, Indonesia, and was asked to set up a new office for the firm in Singapore. He hired the Singapore office staff, including his wife, who supervised the paperwork

in the office. Thus, Leeson was both a trader and supervisor of the other traders in Singapore, and had allies in key positions. Barings' system of evaluation and control was weak and its implications were dramatic—a 28-year-old trader was able to invest money in a manner that no one at Barings knew about, and the results of the investments were not known until it was too late.

Barings' evaluation and control system also had no means to truly evaluate the current position of the firm. In large measure this was because of the structure for evaluation—the firm could not tell if it was meeting its financial goals. Barings had acquired Henderson Crosthwaite in 1984 and renamed it Barings Securities Limited. This unit of the firm had been kept as a separate unit until 1993. The merger had consumed the management of the firm, and they argued their attention was diverted when Leeson was active. The merger also resulted in Leeson having no clear immediate supervision. While he needed approval for his high-dollar investments, the individuals who gave that approval, or were responsible to see the resulting performance, was never clearly indentified. Barings had established a matrix form of organization but actual supervision authority was not clearly delineated. (The nature of the matrix structure will be discussed

further in Chapter 13.) Thus, evaluation and control was not able to function.

A key part of the evaluation and control system lies with the board of directors, the CEO, and key management of any firm. However, at Barings these individuals abandoned much of their responsibility. Leeson said of the evaluation and control function at the firm:

> The only good thing about hiding losses from these people [Barings senior management] was that it was so easy. They were always too busy and self important, and were always on the phone. They had the attention span of a gnat. They could not make the time to work through a sheet of numbers and spot that they didn't add up...[i]

As a result of the failure of the evaluation and control system Barings no longer exists as an independent company. Leeson went to jail in Singapore for several years, but wrote a book about his experiences (which made a good profit) and now charges a large sum as a motivational speaker. Hollywood made a film about his exploits called *Rogue Trader* in 1999 starring Ewan McGregor. Needless to say, Leeson did not refund the money he lost.

http://riskglossary.com/articles/barings_debacle.htm

In Chapters 4 and 5, we examined setting company goals and objectives in terms of strategy. Once an international business sets those goals and objectives, it then implements that strategy. The process continues as the firm next determines if it is making progress toward its goals and objectives (**evaluation**), and if not, determines what needs to be changed to move in the desired direction (**control**). The firm also needs to identify any changes in its environment that are likely to affect its ability to meet its goals in the future. Recall the discussion in Chapter 3 concerning political risk. Changes in the government can negate an organization's ability to pursue its goals. For example, a change to an administration that is committed to a program of nationalizing an industry can radically change a firm's prospects in a given country. To illustrate, the rise of a leftist nationalist such as Ollanta Humala in Peru has the potential to radically change the business environment there. Humala argues that international mining companies are

Evaluation
The process of determining a firm's progress toward reaching goals and objectives.

Control
Actions taken to move a firm to better meet its goals after the evaluation of the firm's gap between goals and achievements.

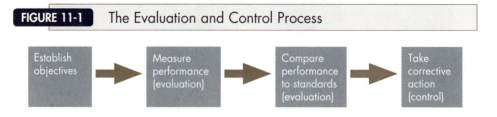

FIGURE 11-1   The Evaluation and Control Process

thieves who have special "sweetheart deals" that are robbing local people of their natural resources. He ran for president in 2006 and came in second, but continues to be a political force in Peru and says he will run for president again. If Humala is elected, he would move Peru from a pro-business to an anti-business profile and the goals and actions of some firms there would have to change accordingly.

As the opening case about Barings illustrates, evaluation and control is crucial to an international firm but can be very difficult to accomplish when a firm has wide geographic diversification. As seen in the opening vignette, a single individual, doing things the firm did not properly monitor, caused the collapse of one the largest and oldest investment houses in Great Britain. While Barings is a particularly glaring example of the constant need to conduct evaluation and control efforts, every firm needs to conduct evaluation and control on an ongoing basis. To illustrate, consider the impact of a relatively simple thing like the exchange rate. Some of the world's leading exporters have historically been firms from Northern Europe. For example, in Finland—a small country of only 5 million people—there are several strong global companies: Nokia is a world leader in telecommunications products; Stora Enso, UPM-Kymmene, and Metsä-liitto's M-Real are world competitors in the domain of wood and paper products (Finland is the world's leader in wood and paper products); and Metso is the world leader in wood-processing equipment. These exports are typically priced in euros. A number of years ago the value of the euro was much lower relative to the U.S. dollar, which made European exports relatively cheaper than their U.S. competitors. However, in recent years these Finnish firms have found their prices to be expensive relative to American products because of the rise of the euro. Finnish and other European firms believed five years earlier—when the Euro was weaker and the dollar stronger—that exports in Asia would be climbing, and they generated business goals to post new employees in the region and build warehousing facilities there. Today, that plan may have no relationship to the economic reality in the region. A firm should not carry out plans without understand the changing economic realities facing a particular region and responding to them as needed. Thus, a firm's effort at evaluation and control is an ongoing process that helps it adapt and change as its environment changes. This chapter will address how an international firm develops such an evaluation and control system. Figure 11-1 summarizes the flow of the material that will be presented in this chapter.

EVALUATON AND CONTROL PROCESS

One of the primary reasons for evaluation and control is that the firm's environment will change over time. As the environment changes, the assumptions upon which a firm's goals are based, and ultimately the goals themselves, can become untenable and dated. These changes may be related to macroeconomics, demographics, the entrance of new competitors into the market, or technological advances. For example, when a competitor develops a new, better way of building a product that results in a competing product that is either cheaper or improved (or both), a firm cannot continue with the goals and actions it had established prior to the change in competitive environment. If the firm continues to promote the more expensive process or inferior product, it will find itself at a competitive disadvantage and could fail.

Business people often like to believe that firms will automatically make changes as their competitive environment changes. However, there are numerous firms and industries that have ignored changes for many years, to their peril. For example, consider that in the last 30 years the music industry has transitioned from selling music on single and long-playing records to 8-track tapes to cassettes to compact disks—and now music downloads. Music firms in both production and distribution have come and gone as those who missed the next trend have either failed or exited the industry, or were bought out and disappeared from view.[ii] The same is true in the disk drive industry: almost no firms were able to successfully create next generation hard disk drives when industry standards shifted to smaller sized disks, as they did several times in the 1970s and 1980s.[iii]

"Evaluation and control processes" is commonly used as a single phrase. This is because the two activities are intertwined processes where the firm asks itself how it is doing and what needs to change. However, in learning about evaluation and control it is helpful to separate the two concepts, examining each separately so that each can be better understood.

Evaluation

The establishment of a firm's goals and objectives, such as firm business strategy, were discussed in Chapter 4 and Chapter 5. The evaluation of how well a firm is meeting these goals is built around three key activities:

1. Evaluating the firm's current status
2. Evaluating forecasts and future direction
3. Evaluating where the firm will end up given changes in the environment, the firm's actions today, and those planned for the future

Figure 11-2 summarizes the evaluation process.

FIGURE 11-2 The Evaluation Process at Three Levels of a Firm's Environment

	External environment	Strategic environment	Internal systems
Evaluate the firm's current status	For example, the decline in the value of the U.S. dollar and the rise in the value of the Euro have affected many exporters.	If a strong international competitor enters the market, the firm needs to respond to the threat.	The firm needs to evaluate its internal systems. The increased availability of information technology means that processes can be benchmarked against the recent past or those of competitors.
Evaluate forecasts and future direction	How will oil prices change in the future?	Can the firm change positioning by moving upmarket?	Does the firm's technological trajectory position it well with the firm's capabilities?
Evaluate various scenarios	How will the firm respond to the doubling of oil prices? What if they go down? This happened to several firms in the 1980s, and they got caught in a bad situation when then President Carter's estimates of future oil prices were 65% too high.	What if the firm moves into higher-end products? How will competitors respond?	Can the firm develop capabilities to meet the future strategic plans?

LITTLE SWAN: KNOWING THE GOALS TO EVALUATE CAN BE A CHALLENGE

To do a thorough gap analysis a firm must have a clear idea of its goals. But determining goals can be challenging. In 1996, a Chinese firm named Little Swan, which is part of Wuxi Little Swan Co. Ltd., controlled 40 percent of the washing machine market in China. Little Swan produced over 2.5 million washing machines in 1999.

Most businesses outside of the United States are part of business groups. These groups go by various names, such as *keiretsu* in Japan and *groupos* in Latin America. In most of the world (outside of Japan) business groups are owned largely by families. Typically, in China these groups are made up of both publicly traded firms and private firms, the government ownership in both types being still prevalent. This dual system of ownership is the dominant organizational structure of almost all business groups in China. (Many people incorrectly assume that "publicly owned" in China means the same thing as in their own countries. In the case of China it clearly does not. In China, the state remains the dominant party in almost all business groups and in the publicly traded firms.)

This dual ownership system made it difficult for firms to determine new goals when profits declined. Is a firm like Little Swan responsible to the shareholders or the government? The government would like to see profits but it also strongly wants individuals to be employed. Investors don't care about individual employment and simply want profits. Little Swan's profits had sagged for several years while it sought to determine which goal it should focus on—profits or employment. In 2002 Little Swan reported a deficit of over 868 million yuan (approximately US$108 million at that time).

This loss convinced the government owners that profits should be the focus or employees would ultimately be out of jobs. As a result, 75 percent of Little Swan was sold to a private investment group. The government stills owns 25 percent but has largely stepped out of the management of the firm. The private investors restructured the firm with a focus on profit as its primary goal and in 2004 reported profits of US$13 million.

http://www.chinadaily.com.cn/english/doc.2005-03/31/content-429786.htm

Chia, X. (2005, March 31). Can Little Swan step out of the mud and fly again? *China Daily*, p. 5.

Gap analysis
Analysis of the gap between what a firm wants to occur and what actually has occurred and is likely to occur.

In answering these questions, evaluation produces what is referred to as **gap analysis**. An organization looks for gaps between what it wants to occur and what actually has occurred or is likely to occur. Each of the steps in gap analysis will be examined in turn.

Evaluation of Current Status

The first step in gap analysis is to evaluate if the firm's strategy is working. This is a determination of how the firm is doing right now in moving from where it is to where it wants to be. The goals and objectives typically include both short-term and long-term time frames. Long-term goals and objectives may take years to attain. However, even for a goal that is five years away there are immediate steps, short-term goals, and objectives that must be met in order to achieve the long-term goals. The firm must judge its current status against both its short-term and long-term goals and objectives if it is to be successful.

To illustrate, if a Chinese appliance maker enters the European market, it will hope to gain significant market share eventually. But if the firm spends millions of dollars expanding its European distribution system, it cannot automatically assume it will be able to gain a foothold there. Instead, the firm's expansion will be a work in progress. In this process, the firm needs to periodically evaluate where it stands relative to its expectations. This analysis would not only include its performance relative to established goals but also whether it is laying the groundwork necessary for future expansion. Thus, an evaluation should include both quantitative and qualitative elements. For the prior example of the Chinese appliance maker, the evaluation should determine things like whether the firm has obtained an understanding of what European consumers want and whether it is meeting those needs. The firm would want to know if its products stack up well against competitors and how it can obtain solid distribution and after-sales service. The appliance maker also would want to know what other segment of the market would be the optimal one to enter in the future and whether it currently is taking steps to enter those segments. In addition to those qualitative items, the firm would also be interested in quantitative items such as the number of products being offered in particular product categories. Many small steps are necessary to be successful over the long term so each of these small steps should be evaluated and controls instituted where necessary to make sure the firm ends up where it desires years later. This is particularly important to emerging-economy firms. For example, it has proved to be a challenge for Chinese firms to directly sell their products abroad. Few Chinese firms have developed the capability to develop products directly for foreign markets and sell the products themselves.[iv] The ability for such firms to establish an evaluation and control process in which the firm learns to change and adapt will be critical to its long-term success.

There are several key evaluations that a firm should conduct during the analysis of its current status.

External Environment As noted in Chapters 2 and 3, the external environment needs to be regularly scanned and evaluated. A firm's competitiveness is directly affected by its external environment. For example, the decline in the value of the U.S. dollar and the rise of the value of the euro in recent years has helped many exporters in the United States, but it has driven up costs for firms needing to import components or raw materials.

Strategic Environment A firm also needs to examine the strategic direction of the industry and its major competitors. A portion of this analysis should be based on Porter's Five Forces Model, which was examined in Chapter 5. To illustrate the need for such analysis, consider the changes that will occur if a very strong international competitor enters your market, as when Microsoft entered the electronic gaming sector. The industry's leaders at the time, Sony and Nintendo, needed to respond to the threat Microsoft posed by emphasizing their own distinctive technologies. Evaluating the strategic environment includes not only analyzing the firm's own actions but also those of the competitors in the industry. One aspect of analyzing industry competitors is to understand the prevailing technological standards and other technological trends. For example, the microprocessor industry has been moving toward low-power chips that are more suitable for mobile phones and IT products. This poses a potentially disruptive challenge to Intel, which has prospered by making better and more powerful microprocessor chips. Those improved chips, though, require more electricity and generate a great deal of heat. Intel's direction was taking the firm away from emerging industry trends that pointed toward increased mobile computing, and Intel had to reevaluate its chip development program and where it puts new research dollars. As result of this internal evaluation and control process Intel developed the Centrino chips, designed to be more useful to new mobile applications such as in notebook computers, phones, PDAs, and iPod-like devices. Thus, Intel overcame a significant challenge posed by the disruptive technological change in its industry that required it to do something much differently. It is important to note that Intel made those changes toward lower-power chips and mobile computing in the face of strong protests from senior engineering people who felt that Intel would lose its laser-like focus on producing higher-powered Pentium chips. This is a very common problem for organizations that are confronted with major disruptive shifts in their industry.[v] First the organizations have to see the problem (and not all firms can do that), and if they do manage to see the problem, responding to it is difficult because many people in the organization will be opposed to a shift away from its traditional focus. Key external stakeholders such as major customers and shareholders are also likely to oppose any radical change in response to the disruption.[vi]

Disruptive technological change is a common source of industry upheaval, as new, upstart firms take on established players or create new niches in the industry, and established firms start to suffer as they struggle to respond to the disruptive change. History shows that most firms are not nearly as successful as Intel was in meeting such disruptive challenges.[vii] Firms need to be attuned to major disruptive changes in their environment and not downplay the changes as coming from some peripheral competitor using seemingly inferior technology. Technologies improve, and competitors on the periphery can become mainstream very quickly in today's environment.[viii]

Internal Systems In addition to evaluating the condition and direction of the external environment, a firm also needs to evaluate the status of its current internal systems. The increased availability of information technology in recent years has given firms quick access to data on the nature of their internal systems and their shortcomings. This is particularly helpful to firms in rapidly acquiring and analyzing key performance measures that were previously difficult to track such as customer satisfaction, market response to a new promotion, and vital cost accounting numbers.

In gathering information about a firm's current status, a key aspect of the evaluation and control processes that should be kept in mind is re-engineering, a concept developed by former MIT professor Michael Hammer.[ix] Hammer argued that too often firms do the same routine over time without bothering to reevaluate whether the process is still relevant or working properly. A process like insurance claims processing may have been efficiently done in the 1980s, but new technology has rendered that process obsolete. For example, today's technology allows certain tasks to be done in parallel, where in the past they had to be done sequentially. Too often firms have not changed their processes as technology or settings change. These firms need to be able to **re-engineer**, or change, their current processes almost on a regular basis, looking for processes that are no longer needed or new ones that are required.

Reengineering
A radical redesign of an organization's processes so that they can be executed in parallel, and the tasks undertaken by nonspecialists. The job's cycle time to completion is reduced in an effective reengineering.

The results for a firm can be significant. For example, Xerox Europe covered 14 countries in Europe and 14,000 employees. The division provided 25 to 30 percent of Xerox's total revenue in 2002. That year Xerox Europe recognized there were shortcomings in its indirect procurements by each country unit. One difficulty was that the system at this stage was not highly automated. Additionally, it was found that the units in each country often purchased goods or services from non-preferred or non-approved suppliers. The impact was that the price was often not competitive, and the tracking of goods, services, and bills owed was hindered. Xerox's system also did not allow managers access to data to review expenses and outcomes in a timely manner.

Thus, Xerox had a shortcoming in its internal systems. In response to the identification of this problem the firm re-engineered its procurement process. Specifically, it introduced a new electronic procurement system that reduced the costs and time associated with procurement. The system also limited the use of non-preferred or non-approved suppliers, and allowed more integrated financials to be produced. The result of this re-engineering was that costs and time spent in procurement and paying of related expenses was significantly reduced.[x]

In conducting its evaluation of current status and direction, a firm needs a richer examination than simply focusing on numbers such as sales forecasts, cash flow, and revenue. Managers should periodically also examine whether the goals are still valid and consistent with business conditions and changes in the marketplace. To illustrate, one European software firm set a financial goal of 5 percent growth per year. However, if the firm underestimated the growth in the market, and the entire market had been growing at 25 percent per year, then meeting the goal of 5 percent growth per year would actually mean the firm is not performing well. Similarly, a business may have a plan to increase

DAEWOO AND INCREASING NEEDS FOR BETTER EVALUATION AND CONTROL

The amount of variation in firm performance that is acceptable may change over time. Korean conglomerate Daewoo spent billions of dollars in the 1990s to build a global auto firm in a number of high-risk emerging markets, such as Poland, Vietnam, and India. By plunging into emerging markets first, Daewoo's goal was to gain the critical mass it needed to emerge as a global automotive leader. Its plan was after it established itself to move from these emerging markets to gain a foothold in the United States, and then move into Western Europe. At first, Daewoo seemed to be making inroads. At the height of the Asian financial crisis in January, 1998, it bulked up even more by acquiring Korea's troubled Ssangyong Motor Co. Daewoo continued to focus on gaining market share rather than profits as it expanded. Thus, in spite of too much overhead and the volatile emerging markets, Daewoo continued to invest in the auto industry—in spite of it being unprofitable—in a bid to become a major player in the auto industry.

But ultimately sales plunged by more than half in South Korea in 1999, and units sold were less than 500 in its important Vietnamese market. Daewoo's debts ran up into the billions of dollars. For one of the first times in Korean business, a major firm was forced by the creditors to restructure, with the chairman losing control of his firm. In 2001, General Motors agreed to buy most of Daewoo Motors to form GM Daewoo. The new company started operation in the fall of 2002, with GM holding a two-thirds stake; the rest belonging to Suzuki and the Shanghai Automotive Industry Corporation. Several old Daewoo plants were spun off as GM determined they would not be profitable. Daewoo was unable to raise money to continue its highly unprofitable auto operations as in years past, largely because of the more globalized financial environment in which financial discipline is enforced by investors and the IMF. Daewoo's evaluation and control system had not kept pace with its increasing international nature.

Daewoo and the Korean government may have been tolerant of the firm's resulting financial position, but there were limits to the amount of debt and nonperforming assets the company could accumulate. The new international creditors let it know quickly that billions of dollars of nonperforming assets were not going to be tolerated for years at a time, and compelled the company to consolidate. By 1999, Daewoo, the second largest conglomerate in South Korea, went bankrupt, with debts of nearly $100 million. Chairman Kim Woo-jung fled to France, and Daewoo factory workers put up "Wanted" posters with his photo. After six years on the run, Kim returned to Korea in June 2005 and was charged with perpetrating one of the largest swindles in history by masterminding an accounting fraud of $43 billion, illegally borrowing about $10 billion and smuggling another $3 billion out of Korea. Kim was finally sentenced to 10 years in jail for the fraud and fined $22 billion. Daewoo was broken up, although it remains in steel and machinery, grain products, and chemical processing, but is out of many of its other businesses including automobiles. The nameplate lives on in a few countries under different management including that of General Motors and India's Tata.

Daewoo founder Kim gets 10-yr term. CNN.com.
http://www.cnn.com/2006/BUSINESS/05/30/skorea.daewoo/index.html (accessed November 18, 2008)

Veale, J., Armstrong, L., Dawley, H., & Muller, J. (1999, August 30). How Daewoo ran itself off the road (int'l edition). *Businessweek Online.*

its market share in a given product-market over the next five years, but that market can also start disappearing within the five years. Consider a firm that set, a number of years ago, a goal to dominate the cassette tape industry. It may have been able to achieve a measure of dominance in cassette tapes, but it would also have seen the industry shifting to compact disks and music downloads. The firm would have been better served by focusing some of its effort on digital media.

An organization must also determine how much variation it is willing to accept in its goals. There may also be variation between the goal set and results achieved. This variation may be small; for example, if sales increased by only 4.9 percent rather than the desired 5 percent for the quarter, does that constitute a material difference? An organization will need to determine not only what variance is acceptable but also whether such variance is acceptable for all goals/objectives. Variance in some goals may not be critical. However, in others, even slight variances can bring very negative results. In conducting gap analysis, managers therefore need to use their judgment, not simply rely on a binary yes or no.

Evaluation of the Firm's Future

The second step in gap analysis is the evaluation of the firm's future direction and its industry. However, such an evaluation cannot be made without predicting what will happen in the same three dimensions identified above:

- External environment
- Strategic environment
- Internal systems

Forecasting the future can be quite difficult for a business. Oftentimes, firms simply extrapolate from the past. However, firms need to be sure that in such extrapolation they are careful to ensure the analysis is relevant and key assumptions are uncovered and tested. In Chapter 9, we discussed the methods of generating information for decision making. Here, we apply some of these methods but focus on generating information on how the future will evolve.

For example, you recall that brainstorming is a method to generate new and novel ideas. In this case, individuals would brainstorm to generate ideas about the firm's present and future revenue drivers and how they might be affected by changes in the general and competitive environment. (See Chapter 3 to review the general environment.) Some firms also use a more formal process of planning called **scenario planning**. Combining well-accepted predictions about future macro and micro trends such as demographics, availability of raw materials, societal change, military alliances, political reform, energy prices, and other information salient to the firm, planners are able to develop various scenarios that are likely to occur. Firms can then craft responses to those scenarios ahead of time, and prepare for some of the changes. For example, Southwest Airlines, a consistently profitable major airline based in Texas in the United States, did some scenario planning early in year 2000 with regard to key cost drivers such as the prices of oil and aircraft (two major cost items for an airline). Its scenario estimated that the price of oil was going up, and Southwest hedged on jet fuel very aggressively. This savvy choice has allowed Southwest the ability to purchase fuel well below market rates while competitors have been faced with major increases in fuel prices. As a result Southwest continues to make a profit while other North American airlines struggle. Scenario planning is discussed more fully in this chapter's section on forecasting.

To illustrate how scenario planning might work, a scenario exercise could include expectations of what will happen in the political or technological domain. If a firm is doing business in the Middle East, what are the expectations for democracy? Democracy may in fact not be favorable for all businesses. The more radical fundamentalist elements may win any democratic elections held in the region, as has occurred in the Palestinian territories and in Egypt. Similarly, new technologies and business systems that may be on the market but have not yet taken a foothold in the firm's market segment or geographic area may create radical change in the future. Consider an industry that may seem impervious to change: marble tombstones. This would appear on the surface to be an industry in which predictions based on population size and past experience should be sufficient to predict the future of the industry in a given country. However, in the last five years the marble tombstone industry in the United States has been affected by Chinese imports. It is now cheaper to mine marble in China, polish it there, and ship it to the United States than it is to mine and polish in the United States. The change has been rapid and dramatic. Thus, simply extrapolating from the past would not necessarily prepare you for change.[xi]

Several methods can be used to build such forecasts of the future. The easiest is simply scanning the environment for changes along the three dimensions (external, strategic, internal). For example, as noted above, Finnish firms are the world's leaders in wood and paper products. These firms cannot just sit at home and predict what the future of its worldwide markets will be. Rather, they need to send

Scenario planning
Forecasting method where participants are given potential scenarios and then asked to build likely responses and outcomes for the business.

managers to professional and industry meetings to gain insights on how the industry will be changing. These firms must also be aggressively seeking insights both from customers and suppliers to gain insight into changes in the market. With the information gained from the interactions at meetings and from customers, they can make better predications about where the firm will be in the future.

Other firms will choose more elaborate methods. For example, some firms will gather top managers together for **brainstorming** sessions. Here a broad topic may be set, but the session is designed to generate as broad a discussion as possible among participants to gain insights into what the future may look like. Some firms even include middle managers in the planning and strategizing process, hoping to acquire insights from the ground-level experience these managers may have with sales, marketing, engineering, or manufacturing. Lever Brothers, the detergent arm of the British firm Unilever, uses brainstorming extensively to generate predictions. Japanese firms have brought middle managers and lower-level employees into the planning process by giving them a role in brainstorming. Many Japanese firms use a bottom-up decision-making process whereby lower-level managers argue out plans and finally present their plans to top management for input and approval. For difficult strategic issues and forecasting future development, it is important to get middle managers and even line employees involved in the planning process in this way, because lower-level employees may be closer to the problem. They can also bring a fresh perspective to the planning and strategizing process.[xii]

As noted above, an important forecasting and planning method is **scenario planning**. Developed first in the halls of government and the military, and improved upon by Royal Dutch Shell some years after World War II, scenario planning has been adopted by a number of firms in recent years. In this method, participants are given potential scenarios and then asked to build likely responses and outcomes for the business. Scenario planning can include firms' competitive environment as summarized by the Five Forces Model and other anticipatory elements that are difficult to formalize, such as subjective interpretations of facts, shifts in values, new regulations, or inventions. These combinations and permutations of fact and related social changes are called *scenarios*. Scenarios usually include plausible but unexpectedly important situations and problems that exist in some form in the present day. For example, one scenario may be that military tension escalates dramatically between India and Pakistan. Managers would then be asked to create a scenario on what might happen to their business, particularly the key threats that they would face and how to respond to them.

At the end of the scenario planning exercise, analysts usually recommend developing an even number of scenarios, such as two or four, that vary from high to low on certain (multiple) key variables or environmental factors. (Scenario planning differs from the more familiar sensitivity analysis, which tends to vary one quantifiable variable while holding others constant to see the likely effect.) An even number is used to avoid the natural tendency of decision makers to select the middle scenario between the two more extreme ones.[xiii]

Finally, the **Delphi method** asks participants to rank different potential outcomes in the future and comment on a written form that they send back to the researchers. Researchers then aggregate and summarize the results, and send those results back to the participants for further comment in an iterative process.[1] The Delphi predictions are refined several times until almost no changes are being made to the predictions, no new information or objections are being raised, and the participants have come to a consensus. Although this method of forecasting is slower than brainstorming sessions, it may help to reduce the problem of group-think (as discussed in Chapter 9), where people are reluctant to speak up for fear of

Brainstorming
A forecasting method in which a broad topic is set out and a discussion among the participants is utilized to gain insights into what the future may look like.

Delphi method
Experts rank different potential future outcomes and through an iterative process these predictions are refined until a prediction of what the future may hold is reached.

[1]This method is named after the Oracle of Delphi in ancient Greece. People would travel great distances to pose questions to the Oracle about the future.

With the Delphi method, Researchers solicit information, questions, and ideas from other participants, then compile and summarize the results. Their report is then returned to the participants for further comment and clarification.

conflict or upsetting the group's balance. In addition, this method is useful because it can occur without all of the group present in the same location. The Delphi method is also good for predicting the changes in a particular industry that will come about from technology. For example, the Danish Technology Foresight Program is an effort by the government and industry in Denmark to predict where certain industries are headed. This effort relies on the Delphi method for its analysis.

Fundamental Evaluation of Firm Direction

While the second step in gap analysis concerned a firm seeking to understand if it met its goals, the third step is a more fundamental periodic evaluation of whether a different strategic direction is needed. Such evaluation does not happen as often as the comparison between current performance and the firm's stated goals and objectives, or the prediction of the firm's future. But the evaluation process needs to identify opportunities or paths that may have emerged recently or that previous evaluations failed to reveal. A firm should not assume it is on the right path simply because it met its current goal for profitability. Periodic introspection by a firm most often confirms its goals and plans; however, it can also open new horizons that have not been previously considered (or even known). This is the current situation in China. China has been economically liberalizing since the late 1970s. However, only in the last few years have many Western firms come to believe that they need to have a "China strategy" in terms of sourcing products, selling to the China, or even locating operations there. A market that was not of interest to many firms only three years ago is now vital to their strategic planning. China had been ignored until strategic evaluation convinced firms that they needed to take a new strategic approach.

One way a fundamental strategic reevaluation occurs is through sessions similar to the brainstorming described above. These sessions commonly involve multiple cross-functional teams of middle managers. In these sessions, the firm's strategy, new products and revenue drivers, and major operational issues are discussed. (Reasons for using cross-functional teams were discussed in Chapter 9.) After the initial discussion, the first step would be to take an entry poll of the participating managers on the need for change. It is likely that the firm would find that there is no groundswell of opinion in favor of change, particularly if the firm is doing well at that time. Managers are likely to approach such a poll with an "If it ain't broke, don't fix it" attitude.

This foundation of what managers perceive then becomes the starting point for a richer discussion. Managers need to understand (and make clear to coworkers) that in many of the most spectacular business failures in the past 100 years, the seeds of failure were sown at the pinnacle of those firms' success. It is when a firm is doing well that it has to give serious examination to its future: what it does well, to what other businesses it could apply its core competencies and core products, and where the real threats are coming from. A good illustration of this is the history of the steel industry. At the end of World War II, the European steel industry had been destroyed and the world's strongest firms were in the United States. At the time, it was unimaginable that many leading firms in the industry would, in a few short decades, emerge from formerly devastated countries like Japan, Korea, and Germany. The Japanese and Korean firms have themselves been hurt by firms from emerging economies like India and China that were not seen as competitors 10 years earlier. A firm's management must be challenged to think beyond where they are now to what can impact the firm. In other words, these managers must be shaken out of their complacency.

Once managers begin to think beyond where their firm is today, the next step is to ask them to figure out where the firm's revenue will be coming from in the next five to seven years and where the biggest threats to the firm lie. It is likely that the managers may not agree on where firm revenue and profit will be coming from in the future, and this debate will help the firm see potential opportunities as well as problems. Firms need to go through evaluation and imagination exercises like this periodically.

To illustrate this process, consider the French firm Cordier, one of the leading French wine producers. Cordier produces very high-end wines, with some bottles costing $3,000 each. France is Europe's largest wine producer, and also the world's leading wine consumer. But annual per capita wine consumption in France has dropped over the last 10 years from 16 gallons per person to 14.5 gallons. As a result, Cordier has decided to start selling wine in small drink packages,[xiv] like the drink boxes commonly used for fruit juice and milk in many countries. Cordier predicted a long-term problem of declining wine consumption and was able to determine that the inconvenience of wine's packaging may have been a key reason behind the decline. Only time will tell if this new innovation will be accepted by the market.

A global firm might conduct a gap analysis on a small scale once annually, and on a larger scale with middle managers meeting from around the world every three to four years. If a firm's environment is rapidly changing, however, it may do it more often. If the firm cannot afford the money or time to fly employees to a central location for such exercises, it can be done using via teleconferencing software coupled with the Delphi technique.

Too often individuals and organizations look at deviations from earlier plans as a negative. When most people encounter a detour sign while driving, they do not see it as an opportunity to explore a different road and more of the countryside. Yet firms should not ignore the major signals the market is sending them. Successful firms are able to obtain a competitive advantage by having the capability to see new opportunities, develop relevant knowledge, and then ensure that knowledge is shared throughout the organization—essentially having an effective knowledge-based management system where ideas are generated and information properly stored so it can be accessed by the firm when needed. The organization's mission, developed by the top management team, gives a general direction. However, it is the capability of the firm's middle managers to see opportunities and implement any needed changes that often determines that firm's success.

Strategy researcher Henry Mintzberg refers to seeing and acting on such opportunities as an **emergent strategy**.[xv] Consider a firm like Apple Inc. Who

Emergent strategy
Managers see opportunities and shift the organization to that new direction.

would have predicted even ten years ago that Apple's most promising and profitable product would be not the MacIntosh, but a handheld music player (iPod), and that Apple would be in the online music business (iTunes), which has contributed mightily to the firm's recent success and return to prominence in the high-technology sector? Top management at Apple had the important ability to recognize an unexpected success and take advantage of this emergent opportunity as they conducted their evaluation of how young people used computers. They realized that young people were using computers heavily to download music and create music compact disks and playlists of songs to carry with them, and moved quickly to create a device and a service that would make these processes easier. Further, with the iTunes online store, Apple combined music storage and playback with the more difficult task of actually locating and downloading digital music. This vertical integration was made easier by Apple's computing and design capability, but it did represent a shift from its traditional business in home computing. If Apple had defined its mission only in terms of micro computers, it would have missed an opportunity to create one of the first hot consumer products of the twenty-first century—one in which they have over 50 percent market share and that, with its sister product the I-Phone, contributes most of Apple's profits. This change in the firm revenues is so dramatic now that Apple recently officially dropped "Computer" from its name and is only known as Apple Inc.

Control

After an organization has evaluated its performance along the three dimensions cited above, it must next address the question of what changes are needed. The decision to actually make changes or not represents the beginning of the control process.

There are four principal mechanisms commonly used to directly exercise control over a firm's daily function:

- Financial control
- Strategic control
- Organizational control
- Personnel control

A firm will use a combination of these various types of control, although usually one will dominate.

Financial controls
Focus on gaps between the desired financial outcomes and the actual outcomes.

Financial Control Financial control focuses on gaps between desired financial outcomes and those actually produced by a firm. Therefore, a firm may have goals such as sales and cash growth, greater gross (profit) margins, increases in operating profit and free cash flow, better inventory turnover, and improved EBITDA (earnings before interest, taxes, depreciation, and amortization). Those goals could be short term, such as the financial performance of the firm this quarter, or they could be long term (two or more years hence). The importance of the goals also can vary with the type of firm: inventory turnover is a very important measure to retailers, while gross profit margins are perhaps most important to high-technology firms that sell high-margin items that do not have a lot of variable and operating costs to allocate. (The iPod has gross margins up to of 50%, which means that Apple sells iPod for twice its cost of goods sold—very good margins for a consumer electronics product.)[2] The goals would then be compared to actual

[2]Companies often use gross margin calculation as a quick way to determine if a product is priced properly based on its cost structure. For high-technology firms that would like to grow quickly, they require gross margins of 67%, which means they must sell a product for three times its cost of goods sold (i.e., gross profits would then be 2/3 the total selling price, hence the 67% margins). Apple sells iPod for twice the product's cost of goods sold, but most of that gross profit goes into marketing and other overhead, particularly R&D, so it can keep the product at the cutting edge of the market.

Ben Margot/AP Photo

Goals regarding financial performance vary depending on the type of firm. For example, reaching a high gross profit margin, such as that associated with the iPod, may be more important to the manufacturer than the retailer of that product.

outcomes for the time period. If a gap is identified, the firm then employs methods to directly improve those financial results. For example, if the firm is not meeting profit goals, then it may make a decision to cut costs.

One difficulty for an international firm was highlighted in Chapter 5: the accounting standards for an international firm can vary. It is critical in evaluating such financial measures that a firm is sure that the financial variables are comparable. However, it should be realized that international firms that have a strict focus on only financial controls risk encouraging a short-term perspective. For example, a firm may push up profits and increase its stock price in the short term with little regard to the long-term position of the firm. One way this is done is by what strategy researchers and consultants C. K. Prahalad and Gary Hamel have derisively called "**denominator management.**"[xvi]

Denominator management occurs when a firm tries to increase its return on investment, or ROI (recall that ROI = return or R divided by invested capital or I) by simply reducing the denominator (I,) while holding or increasing the numerator (R,) constant. A firm can reduce the denominator by selling off assets, closing factories, outsourcing important activities, and reducing investment in amortizable or depreciable assets. These steps may be helpful in a turnaround

Denominator management
A firm tries to increase its return on investment, or ROI, by simply reducing the denominator, that is, reducing the "I" or amount of invested capital in a new project or division of the firm.

situation to conserve or raise cash, but when a firm needs to invest and grow, this so-called denominator management may essentially be financial window dressing to temporarily push up share prices. Choices to reduce investment while pushing up short term stock price can damage a firm's strategic health and long-term prospects.

Alternatively, a firm's ROI, or a sister measurement ROE (return on equity), can decline for several years as the firm exits older businesses, develops new product lines, closes obsolete factories, and opens new ones. All of these can eat up most of a firm's profit, and even reduce revenue and create negative cash flow, but these investments and decisions are critical to a firm's strategic health and long-term success. IBM's sale of its personal computer manufacturing and distribution business to Chinese firm Lenovo is a case in point. IBM has significantly increased value-added services in recent years. The personal computer business had a very low margin and provided little strategic benefit to IBM. PCs were not leading to purchases of the firm's other products such as the higher-end machines from which IBM derives much of its value, IBM got a very good purchase price from Lenovo for its nearly profitless PC division, which IBM has plowed back into its growing information technology service businesses. IBM's actions to improve its strategic position will likely be good for the firm and its stakeholders in the long run, although the initial financial impact in the year preparing for the sale was negative. Thus, the long-term benefit to IBM of selling the PC business was strategically a good decision, but relying strictly on financial measures in a single year would likely have prohibited the sale of the unit.

The quantitative nature of the financial measures makes them easier to evaluate and control, and it also facilitates the pursuit of appropriate corrective measures. Financial controls are often used by firms that have relied on unrelated diversification. Such firms find it difficult to employ strategic and cultural controls (to be discussed later in the chapter), because the firms lack a common strategic direction or culture among employees. It is for this reason that unrelated diversified international firms rely on financial controls. Other international firms whose operations have a very wide diversification are also likely to use financial measures. The ability to compare units and evaluate strategic issues or impose a common corporate culture is difficult. For example, Lakshmi Mittal's LNM Group, the world's largest steel group, relies on such financial measures for its widely diverse and geographically dispersed plants. LNM Group's goal is to be the lowest cost producer in all the markets in which it competes. The widely diverse nature of the steel plants and the focus in each plant on cost control encourage such financial measures.

Strategic controls
Focus on the firm's desired strategic outcomes and the actual outcomes.

Strategic Control Strategic control focuses on ensuring that a firm is meeting its strategic goals. As noted before, a firm's strategic goals can vary widely but often include goals such as becoming the market leader in a given product-market or expanding into a new market. In some cases the measure is easy to quantify, especially if it relates to market share or competitors' positions. For example, in recent years, General Electric asked for its divisions to become number one or number two in their markets; otherwise they would be restructured or sold off. More commonly, however, strategic controls rely on more qualitative measures that are difficult to measure. For example, expanding into the BRIC emerging economies of Brazil, Russia, India, and China is a good long-term move. These markets will ultimately be very attractive. If a business is to be competitive when the markets become lucrative, it needs to already be in those markets, developing distribution channels, relationships, and brand equity. However, relying strictly on financial measures or market position the way GE used to may not result in a firm making the commitment today for long-term success. It should be recognized that expenditures on research and development (R&D) similarly require a qualitative measure of whether the firm is positioning itself where it wishes to be for the long term. R&D is an expense that has a long-term impact and can make the bottom line look worse in the near- to medium-term, but R&D spending is vital to a firm's long-term health.

International firms need strategic controls that ensure appropriate actions are being taken today to help the firm tomorrow, even if the short-term outcomes of these actions are costly. The creation of a future income stream is dependent on the pipeline of innovation that comes from a firm's R&D activities. In using strategic controls, a firm looks for gaps in its strategic goals and outcomes, and then seeks to address them through strategic adjustments and realigning its businesses with its chosen mission and strategy. These adjustments typically involve a substantial commitment of resources and could include actions such as expanding the firm's innovation efforts to develop a new product line or production process, as well as new acquisition and divestment.

Once again, the multinational computer firm IBM provides an excellent example. Since the early 1990s, starting with former chairman Lou Gerstner's tenure as CEO, IBM has increasingly remade itself into a software and information technology services firm, and when IBM sells hardware it tries to bundle more consulting services and support than in the past.[xvii] In keeping with that strategic focus, the new IBM has divested its disk drive, displays, and network processor businesses. IBM has also acquired PricewaterhouseCoopers' consulting services and software companies such as Tivoli, Rational, and Informix. Divesting the PC division is quite consistent with IBM's successful strategy of recent years, and its relationship with Lenovo could give IBM better government relations in China and an inside track to selling more computer services in that major emerging economy. Thus, based on strategic controls IBM is making numerous good decisions even if the immediate financial controls were not supportive.

Organizational Control Another major category of control, and perhaps the most important for an international firm, is organizational control. Organizational control refers to the ability to get individuals to act in the manner desired, consistent with the firm's corporate culture and the relevant national cultures in which it operates. Encouraging such common behaviors and beliefs among employees is critical to a worldwide firm. Wal-Mart is now the largest retailer in the world, and it prides itself on being customer friendly. The greeter who welcomes you at the front door of every Wal-Mart in the world is symbolic of that attitude. However, considering that in many countries there is no retail tradition of being friendly to customers, such behavior may be interpreted to mean that the employee is not working hard or is letting the customers get away with too much. Thus, imagine how difficult it can be for a firm like Wal-Mart to get employees to introduce friendly service that runs counter to the local retailing cultures. The key is building a culture in the foreign location where friendly service-oriented behavior will be the rule rather than the exception. Wal-Mart has a variety of training methods to help employees adopt the expected culture and behavior. Another method Wal-Mart uses to build the culture in environments like China is to have all employees read a book about the company that the firm's founder Sam Walton wrote, so they can understand Wal-Mart's history and traditions.

Wal-Mart currently is opening stores every month in China and expects to increase its 30,000 employees there to 150,000 by 2010. But initially, Wal-Mart expanded very slowly. The company spent its first several years in China identifying and training employees and future managers, who were often hired straight out of university. It then had those individuals work in the firm for a number of years and spent a lot of time training them in Wal-Mart's methods and in providing good customer service. These trained and acculturated individuals have now become the base upon which Wal-Mart is expanding. The new employees

FIGURE 11-3   Control in the International Firm

Financial	Financial controls focus on gaps between the desired financial outcomes and those actually produced by the firm. Therefore, the firm may have goals such as sales growth, expenses, free cash flow, gross profit margins, inventory turnover, and the important EBITA (earnings before interest, taxes, and amortization).
Strategic	Strategic controls focus on the firm's meeting of strategic goals. As noted before, strategic goals could be to become the market leader in a given product market or to expand to a new market. In some cases the measure is easy to quantify, especially if it relates to market share or competitors' positions. For example, General Electric called for their divisions to be number one or number two in a market, otherwise they would be restructured or sold off.
Cultural	The last type of control, cultural control, is perhaps the most important for an international firm that operates in multiple regions of the world. Cultural controls refer to the ability to get individuals to act in the manner desired within the firm consistent with the firm's corporate culture and relevant national cultures in which the firm operates. Symbolic activities seek to discourage those that are not desired.

understand Wal-Mart's low-cost philosophy and commitment to providing excellent value to customers and a good work environment for employees.[3] But Wal-Mart was very clear prior to expanding that it also needed to have local people who understood the local culture before expanding, and thus Wal-Mart's expansion in China has been rather deliberate and controlled.

The strength of organizational control comes from relationships within the firm that encourage individuals to act in a certain way. These relationships act to enforce desired (or discourage undesired) actions and behaviors. Organizational controls can be the most powerful in an organization, but they are also the hardest to change or institute. Organizational controls are typically the least quantifiable types of controls. Managers need to be aware of such controls and employ them to reinforce desirable behaviors and to discourage undesirable ones. Figure 11-3 summarizes the different types of control.

Personnel Controls   The prior three types of control mechanisms occur at the organization level, but there are also controls at the individual level in a firm: personnel performance controls. This type of control involves assessment of how an individual is measured, rewarded, and sanctioned. The criteria that successful firms utilize in their individual-level controls include the following:

1. Top management articulates its vision for the firm, communicates that vision to employees and customers, builds a management team around that vision and related goals, and checks to be sure people are implementing the vision. Those who are not able to make adjustments to implement the vision may be moved to another part of the firm or let go.[xviii]
2. The top management of the firm makes it clear what it is looking for when it selects managers.[xix]
3. Good firms know that training is important and invest in leadership development for higher-level employees as well as job training for lower-level employees.[xx] They measure those results and give rewards based on skills and related outcomes.[xxi]

---

[3]Students in North America should note that while Wal-Mart may be controversial in circles in the United States, in emerging economies the firm is well thought of for providing products that had previously only been found in major cities, or at high prices. Wal-Mart made products available to many lower-income customers for the first time, particularly in emerging economies. The firm also is seen as having revolutionized retailing culture so that customer service has improved dramatically in many emerging economies where they operate, while creating a desirable place to work. Thus, internationally the firm is seen somewhat differently than in North America.

JAPAN VERSUS U.S. EVALUATION AND CONTROL

The evaluation and control systems of Japanese and U.S. multinational firms are quite different in some respects and similar in others. One study that compared human resources practices employed by managers in Japan with those used by American managers in the United States found several key differences. For example, if a Japanese team was successful because of the work of one individual, the Japanese manager tended to give credit to the whole team. This was usually helpful in Japan's more collective culture, but it also sometimes created some challenges. The vaunted Japanese collectivism did not hold when the team had problems. If a manager was able to trace a problem to the action of a certain individual, he or she would hold this employee responsible and make it known publicly.[xxii] In contrast, managers in the United States were willing to assign both credit and blame to individuals.

In addition, while both Japanese and American managers offered greater rewards and more freedom from monitoring to successful individuals on their teams, American managers were more likely to reward high-performing mavericks and encourage more innovation and risk taking. The well-known story of 3M and Post-it Notes illustrates this. 3M gives employees some freedom during the workweek (about 4 hours per week) to "bootleg" or work on unofficial side projects that they feel have some merit for the company, but are not officially funded or sanctioned. If the bootleg project becomes successful, like Post-it Notes did, employee may be given funding and the opportunity to run his or her own product line or division within the company. Individual Americans respect that type of innovative employee.[xxiii] A comparison of these two approaches to personnel evaluation shows that the Japanese tend to use a more social or group orientation, while the Americans are more individualistic. Yet there is evidence to suggest that that collectivism is not in-born, and the Japanese people are becoming more individualistic. Culture is often driven by the group's need to solve common problems, and as those problems change, culture can change with it. The problems faced by Japanese society from the Middle Ages through the twentieth century were best solved by large groups working together, such as farming large rice farms in Japan's cool and rainy climate.[xxiv] With changes in the environment that increasingly reward small project teams, entrepreneurs, or individual inventors (something that has not been well-accepted in Japan), traditional collective tendencies may be giving way to more individualist solutions better suited to modern problems. Only time will tell if Japan and other more collectivist countries will become more individualistic, though preliminary data on culture and cultural change is indicating that this change may be occurring.[xxv]

CULTURE

4. Whenever possible, these companies promote from within, and they communicate this policy to their staff.
5. Many of the best firms see career development as a vital motivational tool.[xxvi]
6. Performance is rewarded through profit sharing, stock options, gainsharing, and professional development prospects. Positive feedback is emphasized.
7. Employees are trusted and the organizational climate is more open when people are not negatively evaluated for making honest mistakes, particularly in attempting innovation.[xxvii]
8. The firms are genuinely interested in what their employees think, and they measure job satisfaction and give feedback on employee satisfaction.[xxviii]
9. Though turnover is low in the best firms, they sometimes do have to fire people, particularly those who are not in accord with the firm's mission or are unable to help the firm meet its goals.[xxix]

Interestingly, changes in the evaluation and control of personnel facilitated the adoption of quality control techniques. An important aspect of quality progress has become a major focus in the modern evaluation and control process of multinational enterprises as well as the personnel evaluation and control systems to implement total quality management (TQM). Statistical quality control has been around as a management discipline for the better part of a century. The concepts, as noted in Chapter 5, were made popular by W. Edwards Deming and Joseph Juran, first in Japan and then in the United States and other parts of the world. Improved quality was not based simply on new technology and statistical technique or individual dedicated suppliers.[xxx] Apart from their philosophies of TQM and statistical process control, Deming and Juran both favored giving line workers more control over the production process, which called for reward, recognition and feedback, and training and empowerment. Employees were given the right to stop the line to fix product problems and even suggest changes in the production process—a revolutionary idea when it was first introduced to traditional command and control production plants.

The outgrowth of this empowerment of workers can be directly seen in the development of **quality circles**. A quality circle is a group of workers that regularly confers on ways to improve both the quality of a product and its production process. Workers in the circles are encouraged to make suggestions and changes to the system. This change in philosophy, first adopted in Japan in the 1950s, helped to make Japanese consumer products among the best in the world. One reason was that Japanese employees were evaluated and rewarded for keeping their workspaces orderly and the machines clean. Japanese firms minimized defects by assigning new employees to flexible and experienced work units that could give them training. Under this system, employees are trained for all jobs on the line and can rotate among jobs as the team requires, which increases flexibility and motivation. Quality targets are set partly in discussion with the team, and it falls on the quality circle or production team to meet those targets.[xxxi]

Although firms in the United States and in most developed countries use flexible and cross-functional work teams to accomplish a variety of tasks, Japanese firms have very effectively honed the use of such teams, particularly for quality control and improving the production process. In Japanese firms, teams are used to encourage incremental learning and to build tacit, hands-on knowledge from trial and error. American employees of Japanese firms are impressed by the Japanese insistence that teams work together to collect data and then communicate internally and with key outsiders to gradually solve problems and improve performance. Small errors are well tolerated, and team members are charged with preventing new managers from making big mistakes that are hard to recover from.[xxxii] Firms worldwide have learned from Japanese multinationals the value of the team for improving quality, the need for the regular training, and the limiting of punishment for small errors.

Institutionalizing Controls

If a gap is identified between goals and performance, then adjustments must be made. There must be support for control mechanisms and for making the necessary changes when gaps exist. Control is a responsibility throughout an organization. Each level of the organization has a different role, and the nature of control is different in each. Each of these levels of control will be reviewed in turn. Note that just as in planning, an effective control process requires that each level be in sync with the levels above and below it. The reporting structure that classically is expected to exist in mature markets is discussed below. How reporting structures vary or what adaptations can be made to them in international settings will also be discussed for each of the stages in the structure.

Boards of Directors The board of directors is a group of individuals appointed by firm shareholders to supervise a firm's activities and top management. These individuals have a fiduciary responsibility to shareholders—a legal responsibility to ensure that the shareholders' best interests are served by the company. This responsibility is both statutory (legal) and normative (based on community-based conventions of behavior). Both legal and normative mechanisms affect board behavior and the ability to govern firms effectively. These mechanisms also vary around the world.[xxxiii]

The board of directors helps to establish control mechanisms and guide how the firm will respond to major changes in its environment. The board should not be involved with the relatively minor variances between expected and actual results. Instead, it focuses on major gaps that may exist and addresses whether a radically different direction for the firm will be needed. Specifically, the board should be involved with the following types of actions that affect control:

1. Understanding the number of ways changes in products and processes of the firm or its competitors can affect firm strategy and its position in the market
2. Monitoring the risks and rewards of major strategic and product initiatives
3. Questioning forecasts and assumptions upon which firm goals and objectives are based
4. Providing a strategic vision and focus[xxxiv]
5. Demanding timely updates on the progress of all major projects
6. Hiring and firing the CEO and other top managers to ensure that the desired actions are in the control process

Boards of directors of many firms are often close allies or family members of the individual who controls the firm. This is particularly true in Asia, where the legal requirements of the board are much weaker than in the Anglo-American system of governance.[xxxv] In addition, in much of Asia, there are no class action lawsuits, which permit large groups of shareholders to sue a firm and its management for breaches of contract and financial shenanigans. One result of this problem is that while firms do not face a principal-agent problem (where employees do not do what is best for the shareholders), they may face a principal-principal problem. The principal-principal problem occurs when majority shareholders take advantage of minority shareholders. This can occur, for example, when owners move valuable assets out of the publicly held firm over to a private firm of their own. If that happened in the United States or the United Kingdom the shareholders could appeal to regulatory bodies such as the Securities and Exchange Commission, or they could pursue a class action lawsuit to reverse the asset sale and seek compensation from the owners and the firms involved. In Asia, these mechanisms are generally not available, and minority shareholders have little recourse against such financial manipulations.[xxxvi]

This problem has been observed by a variety of different studies.[xxxvii] The principal-principal problem represents a significant challenge to government regulators who would like to improve corporate governance in their country and thus improve the investment climate. For example, suppose that you, as a small investor, have purchased a fairly large amount of stock in a manufacturer of artificial Christmas trees in Hong Kong. The firm is a very solid performer, with reasonable growth in its shares and a steadily growing dividend. The net return on your shares, including the dividend, has been running at around 12 percent annually and is poised to go higher because the company has announced plans to increase its dividend again next year. That makes you quite happy with the stock and you buy more of it. Suddenly, with no warning, the firm announces plans to sell most of the Christmas tree business along with excellent real estate assets in southern China to a private holding company, also owned by the firm's founder. He will leave a small and not very profitable business in plastic toys and send some other assets to the (now former) Christmas tree firm as "compensation." You are very angry about this because you thought you were buying a very well-performing Christmas tree company, with excellent plastic molding and spinning technology, and now you own stock in a run-of-the-mill plastic toy firm, one of hundreds in southern China alone. Suddenly your stock starts to fall as most of the company's important assets have been "tunneled" out into the founder's private firm. You study the problem and learn that in Hong Kong there are no class action suits for this kind of case; in fact, you discover that you have no recourse at all. The same is true in other parts of China and also in most other Asian countries where

SARBANES OXLEY AND THE CULTURE

It has been noted before in this text that one of the recent changes to the business environment of U.S. firms is Sarbanes Oxley. This act has many dimensions that affect a board of directors in its evaluation and control functions. A few elements of the law require that the board ensure the firm's auditor not have conflicts in the non-audit work that they do for the firm. The law also requires that that the board take on fiduciary responsibility for items reported in the annual report. The law's intent was to ensure that recipients of financial information get clear and consistent data. The failure of firms such as Enron, a company in which massive fraud occurred and in which the auditing firms were not only providing auditing services but a full range of other products, led to this law.

One unintended consequence of Sarbanes Oxley has been firms moving their IPOs from the United States to the United Kingdom. In fact, many firms such as Electrolux have in fact delisted from the American stock exchanges. The result is that the U.S. leadership in capital formation for world business is now not as clear as it once was.

The negative response to Sarbanes Oxley is in part economic. The cost to meet all of the Sarbanes Oxley requirements is high. The American Enterprise Institute argues that meeting the law's requirements may cost as much as $1.4 trillion. But the response from those outside the United States also represents a cultural component. It is not seen as inappropriate for firms in the United States to reveal almost all information that does not give away strategic secrets. In many cultures, such information sharing is not common. As a result there is a strong negative response to the law and its requirements on what information must be revealed. There is a movement now to reform the law but such changes are not expected to occur soon. The requirements of Sarbanes Oxley may be culturally acceptable to Americans but its impact is not as acceptable to others, which may lead them to list their stock on equity markets outside of the U.S. Sarbanes Oxley is likely having a negative impact on capital formation and the performance of equity markets in the United States.

the firm has some interests. Since the firm's founder has not broken any law, and no civil action is possible, you are stuck. This is the essence of the principal-principal problem, and it happens with frustrating regularity to investors in Asia, particularly those investing in small- and medium-sized companies that they hope will continue to grow and produce significant returns.[xxxviii]

The major solution to this situation in more advanced economies has been a legal requirement that at least part of a firm's board of directors consists of outside directors. This is done in Poland, for example. Alternatively, many firms, as they become more familiar with international competition, see the value of having a board that brings fresh insight and knowledge to the firm. Thus, in countries such as Japan major firms such as Sony and Toyota now prefer boards that include strong, knowledgeable outsiders. However, it should be recognized that in many less economically mature regions the board of directors is still not a major force for control.

It is interesting to note that many U.S. firms have yet to include individuals from outside the United States on their boards. For example, Hewlett Packard, which obtains a very high percentage of its sales from outside the United States, did not have international participation on their board of directors until 2006 when Sari M. Baldauf of Finland was appointed to the board. The same was true with venerable manufacturer Lincoln Electric, which discovered the importance of (not) having top management with international experience as it sought to expand to Europe and Asia.[xxxix]

Top Management From the broad vision set by the board of directors, the top management of an organization will begin to initiate control actions. Top management will address some of the same strategic issues as the board. However, this does not mean that top management should replace the board as the source that sets the strategic direction of the firm. Instead, the top management sets in motion the actions that implement the board's strategic choices. Thus, top management is the principal source of establishing an organization's mission concerning control systems and processes.

To this end, top management must answer a series of questions when determining what projects to undertake. The answers to these questions determine what will be presented to the board, how it is presented to the board, and what recommendations about strategic direction will be made to the board. These questions include the following:

1. Are the firm's activities consistent with the long-term strategy and mission of the firm?[xl]
2. How does what we are doing enhance the value of the firm today? How will it enhance the value in the future?
3. What are the benefits and costs of our activities?
4. What projects or activities should we discontinue?[xli]
5. How does our climate and culture contribute to the firm's mission and key activities?

It is important for international U.S. and European firms that are moving into markets where weak boards of directors dominate to give extra effort to ensure that their own evaluation and control methods are in place. For example, in an alliance with firms with weak boards, the U.S. and European firms should ensure that they maintain strong personal relationships with key top managers. The firm will also require monthly or quarterly financial information, and all financial information should be audited according to international accounting standards by highly respected firms. It is also helpful for the foreign firm to have its own finance person working inside the overseas alliance partner (and a high-level one if the equity investment with the foreign partner is significant) to keep an eye on financial activities. These evaluation and control methods go beyond the classic evaluation and control methods discussed for mature markets. Without these measures, a firm from a mature economy may find that its own evaluation and control methods have not detected problems until it is too late. The weak accounting standards in some countries, the commonly close relationship between business and government regulators, and the presence of a weak board of directors systems in many countries require foreign firms to monitor foreign investments, such as joint ventures, more carefully than they might a local investment. That means putting finance people and (if feasible) some middle management in place to watch the financial and production activities on a day-to-day basis. It may mean requesting additional reports, and getting to know the local bank with which the joint venture does business. It will also mean being familiar with local regulators and how to reach them quickly if there is a problem. All of these steps can help to safeguard a major investment such as a joint venture in fast-growing but relatively chaotic places like Russia, China, and other emerging economies.[xlii]

Divisional Managers and Middle Managers Divisional and middle managers have the responsibility to set in motion the direct implementation of the control mission envisioned by the firm's top management. The divisional managers determine how to enact the mission, and determine what control actions are needed and when, where, and how to implement them in order to successfully complete the control process. These strategies on how the control system will operate then lead to more direct operational actions.

The middle managers, under the guidance of the division leaders, establish further operational details of the control system. These details begin to establish the actions that will take place and include setting the specific goals and objectives that the control system is to achieve (i.e., the specific actions, if any, that are needed).

Middle managers are often charged with implementing changes on the ground and monitoring their results. They will report if the change is not working out, for example if a major new product initiative is proving difficult to manufacture. Sometimes middle managers are called upon to brainstorm strategic change for the firm, particularly if they have regular contact with customers directly or through employees under them.

In international settings, middle managers are critical to the process of evaluation and control. For an international firm that establishes a wholly owned subsidiary or a joint venture overseas, the firm's middle managers are key to helping prevent situations such as what happened at Barings, discussed at the beginning of the chapter. This can be done through methods such as regular meetings in which international divisional managers are brought together to discuss the firm, its strategy, and current and future activities. Such meetings accomplish far more than the items on a given agenda. They help firms to build a common culture and allow for personal evaluation of the actions being undertaken. There should also be a consistent pattern of reports, audited statements, and budgets that have to be met to ensure that individuals are acting in the manner desired. Middle managers must also take time to walk around the plant or the offices to find out what is

---

CITIGROUP IN JAPAN: ENSURING THE RIGHT MANAGERS ARE IN POSITIONS TO IMPLEMENT CONTROL

Citigroup is the largest and oldest foreign bank in Japan. One relatively small piece of the firm's business is private banking. A private bank brings a variety of services, such as banking and investment services, under one roof for very wealthy clients. These clients are typically the target customers of most financial institutions. Citigroup employed 400 individuals in this area of its Japanese business.

Citigroup had warnings that its private banking operations were in trouble in 2000, but the firm did nothing. In 2001, the regulatory agency for Japanese banks flagged Citigroup for infractions of the law including selling securities without a license, a major infraction. The firm attempted to react to these allegations at this stage, but not strongly. The difficulties continued until September 2004 when Citigroup's license for private banking in Japan was revoked by Japanese regulators, a very unusual and highly visible step. Specifically, Citigroup's private banking unit was accused of selling art and real estate for its rich clients, activities it was not licensed to do. It also was found to have misled clients and to have made loans that individuals used to manipulate stocks.

The license revocation had a significant impact on Citigroup in Japan and around the world. A key to the success of private banking is client trust, and the license's withdrawal sent a

message that this trust had been violated. The crisis in Japan was so severe that the Citigroup's CEO, Charles Prince, flew to Japan and in a news conference offered deep bows of apology as is customary in Japan. Such a move is customary for a Japanese CEO, but highly unusual for a U.S. CEO.

In response to its license being withdrawn, Citigroup fired a number of senior managers associated with the problem. Citigroup also created a better evaluation and control system to prevent similar problems in the future. For example, the CEO in Japan is supported by another newly created position—country chief financial officer—and by a legal adviser and compliance officer who are equal in stature to business division heads. In addition, Citigroup set up system-wide compliance officers (those individuals ensuring laws are met in each country) who no longer report to country managers. Instead they report directly to senior managers so problems are identified early. Similarly, the training of key individuals makes clear what the role of evaluation and control is. The expectation is that evaluation and control will be seen as the valuable tool it is and not a necessary evil that the bureaucracy of a large firm requires. In addition, in Japan a midlevel team of employees, dubbed Project K, a play on the Japanese word for "respect," has drafted a tougher set of

internal ethical guidelines. All of that has gone a long way toward placating regulators. However, Citigroup was not allowed to reopen its private banking arm despite these improvements. The firm can reapply for its license but it takes years to obtain. Thus, it was given a year to shut their private equity business. But the bad publicity had other effects on the firm. Its private banking aspects were not as significant as Citigroup's other activities, and it had only 5000 customers and $84 million in profits in 2004. In contrast Citigroup's consumer, corporate, and brokerage arms were larger parts of the firm at that stage. Japan operations earned $769 million in 2004, or 4.5 percent of Citigroup's total. Citigroup's position in Japan suffered as a result of the negative publicity surrounding the private bank elimination. In 2008 Citigroup had to sell its Japanese headquarters to generate cash. The sale of the headquarters to Morgan Stanley was a significant step for Citigroup, which has been in Japan since the early 1900s. In 2008 the firm also had to sell an affiliated investment firm for 15 billion yen ($143 million); the difficulties from the weak evaluation and control system continue to haunt the firm.

Pacelle, M., Fackler, M., & Morse, A. (2004, December 22). Mission control: For Citigroup, scandal in Japan shows dangers of global sprawl. *Wall Street Journal*, 244 (122), pp. A1, A10.

happening on a day-to-day basis. Are empty packages disappearing from the storage area? This could mean that someone is using the firm's packaging for their own products, but selling them as the original. Are extra labels being printed? Someone inside the company could be taking those labels, then putting his or her own product (say beer) inside recycled bottles and slapping the foreign firm's original label on the bottles. (This happened in China to a major foreign brewer, and also to a local one—even the Chinese firm was getting its product pirated inside the country.) This type of fraud is very difficult to stop, unless the foreign firm has its own middle managers on the ground in the foreign location, with at least some of them speaking the local language or dialect.[xliii] If a firm is partnering in some manner with organizations in a country with weak boards of directors and legal standards, having their own finance people and middle management on the ground in the foreign location is a critical means of evaluation and control. The ability to build relationships beyond the top management provides a means of obtaining information on what is actually going on in the alliance or the alliance partner.

Department Managers and Team Leaders The operational details established by managers and team leaders then lead to the actual tactical actions that implement the mission and goals/objectives. Control concerns affect all units in a business, and a particularly helpful unit in this process is the quality control department. This department, in association with other managers and team members, provides the tools for day-to-day evaluation and control mechanisms by department managers and team members.

Many firms establish a quality assurance department. These departments often create quantitative measures of the quality of various product attributes. However, they may also conduct broader quality evaluations concerning whether the firm is making the right decision on a broad range of topics that can affect quality. For example, the quality of a firm's output depends on the quality of its inputs. If inputs are of poor quality, there is little hope that the output, using inferior inputs, will be of acceptable quality no matter how skilled the production people are. Thus, a firm must monitor its total system—inputs, transformations, and outputs—for quality.

A review of the different levels of an organization and their roles demonstrates that the broadest impact on evaluation and control occurs at the board level. From those broad directions, the evaluation and control process becomes more directed and detailed, with each organizational level building on the prior level to become more focused. Figure 11-4 summarizes this relationship.

FIGURE 11-4 Organizational Level and Control

Board of directors	Vision	Broad
Top-level managers	Mission	
Divisional and middle managers	Goals and objectives	
Department managers and team members	Tactics	Narrow

CONTROL AND MISUSE OF PRODUCTS

One critical control factor that faces many firms is what occurs when there is the potential for misuse of the firm's products by purchasers. These purchases may be something that costs very little, such as glue. Many children in Latin America sniff glue to get high. The glue can be as addicting and destructive as any other drug. But does a firm that knows its product is being abused in this manner have a responsibility to control it?

There are other examples that receive more attention. Much technology that is exported can ultimately be used also for military purposes. As a result the U.S. government may seek to limit exports of such goods. For example, a firm like Cray Research needed special permission to sell a super-computer to Russia because of the potential for Russia to use it to design military equipment such as precision guided missiles. Some products may not be directly prohibited from being sold to foreign countries because it's impossible for the government to track everything. The question is if a U.S.

company believes its product may or could be used in a way that could be harmful to the United States does it have an ethical responsibility to deny sales to certain countries?

The issue can affect other items whose relationship to the military is less clear. For example, oil-exploration equipment is not supposed to be sold to Iran by U.S. firms due to security concerns. But often a product may be bought by an intermediary and resold. Does the board of directors and senior management have a responsibility to limit such sales? The difficulty for the board of directors and top management is how to balance these issues with the need to maximize profits. There typically is no direct answer to such concerns but the board and the top management need to consider these issues and establish some guidelines, or only what is prohibited by law will be stopped. As noted in Chapter 2 that is not a sufficient standard for ethical behavior. Other criteria must be used, and cases evaluated one by one.

Implementing Evaluation and Control

A number of issues should be considered by managers in international firms as they implement evaluation and control. As a firm grows in size and international complexity, remaining adaptive and flexible can be difficult. Recall the discussion in Chapter 9 that examined decision making and groups. Each of these abilities becomes particularly critical in the evaluation (and control) activities of an international firm. Other concerns in implementing evaluation and control are discussed below.

Regular Data Gathering & Analysis

A firm should assess its operational environment regularly. This requires that the organization keep watch that no major changes among competitors or changes in external variables loom on the horizon. As noted previously, a firm's strategy is not developed in isolation. The goals and objectives of the organization should be clearly developed in light of potential actions and reactions by competitors. Particularly helpful is tracking and collecting data as recommended by the **Balanced Scorecard**. The Balanced Scorecard, originally developed by Harvard professor Robert Kaplan with consultant David Norton, is a system that summarizes an organization's strategic objectives into four main performance metrics: financial, internal processes, customers, and learning and growth. These metrics can provide feedback on the execution of the strategic plan.[xliv]

Balanced Scorecard
A system that summarizes an organization's strategic objectives into four main performance metrics: financial, internal processes, customers, and learning and growth. These perspectives provide feedback on the execution of the strategic plan.

The Balanced Scorecard is helpful in that not only historical financial measures are used to evaluate firm systems, controls, and performance. Other nonfinancial measures are used to determine if the firm is executing its strategy according to plan.[xlv] Measures such as customer satisfaction and repeat business, and product cycle (production) times are fundamental to understanding how the firm is executing its strategy. A lack of repeat business, for instance, can signal problems in the order fulfillment and post-sales service process, and drive up marketing costs considerably. Firms need to be aware of these measures; something as simple as customer average hold-time on toll-free sales and service lines was not commonly tracked by firms until recently, even though customers report that being kept on hold for a long time while trying to get service is likely to drive them to a competitor.

Validating the Process

Evaluation and control should not be treated as a static process. Instead, it is a process that must change as the environment changes. A change in environment may be due to a competitor's actions, shifting industry trends, or changes in the broad economy. To ensure the evaluation and control effort is looking at the correct issues, a firm needs to ask two questions periodically:

1. Are we measuring what we are interested in? Or are we measuring a variety of things that have little relation to firm performance or organizational climate?
2. How do we make adjustments to better focus on what matters and what the firm does best?[xlvi]

In taking actions to implement these questions, the first priority is to develop a successful system that measures what the organization wants to measure. It helps if the organization has clearly stated goals. With clearly stated goals, the ability to develop relevant measures becomes easier because the organization can focus on those specific items and think creatively rather than having to think too broadly.

However, even with clear goals it is difficult to know if what is being measured is the key to success. For example, two projects may have similar resource requirements with very different potential outcomes. But the resources needed are just one part of the equation. This is related to the problem of seeking short-term ROI through lowering investment and taking on debt to push up share prices temporarily (denominator management).[xlvii] If an organization looks only to see if resources are available, or pushes for short-term profits, then a project with a more positive longer-term potential may be overlooked.

Managers must verify that adjustments need to be made and then determine which adjustments are required. The adjustments needed should emerge from the analysis of metrics and performance gaps, as well as the experience of managers. This requires knowledge development and sharing within the organization.

BIG BOY THAILAND: HARD TO IMPLEMENT CONTROLS

Big Boy is franchised by a U.S. restaurant franchisor called Elias Brothers of Warren, Michigan. These franchises are well known in the United States by the image of a plump boy used as part of its identity. In the late 1990s Big Boy sold its first franchise in Thailand. The initial response was underwhelming. A consultant advised the franchisee to conduct hundreds of interviews to find out why the restaurant was not popular. These interviews were helpful in understanding the issues but changing the business to address them proved difficult.

One issue that became clear was that American food did not translate well to Thailand. The franchisee had to adapt the menu to meet the tastes of the local population by adding noodle dishes, fried rice, and pork omelets. Another issue was the poor quality of food items used to prepare meals. For example, the franchisee had to produce higher-quality hamburger buns—but how do you do this in country that has little idea what a hamburger bun is, let alone how to make a tasty one? McDonald's is able to handle this problem because of the high volume of products it sells. A small four-store operation, like Big Boy, on the other hand, does not have that option. As a result the franchisee had to create its own hamburger mold for the buns, and then find a bakery that could produce the required number of buns needed on a regular basis.

Still another issue was how to operate the business. As noted when examining franchises, typically the franchisor will specify in great detail how the franchise must be operated. Thai culture is very communal and employees typically insist on eating lunch together. This makes it difficult to run a restaurant because customers are always wanting service, making it necessary to have enough staff working at all times. Even though the franchisee identified this as a problem, addressing it effectively was extremely difficult. The owner feared that strict rules against such actions would result in employees quitting in large numbers, hurting service and raising recruitment and training costs. Identifying the problem is sometimes not difficult; developing and implementing solutions can be.

Frank, R. (2000). Big Boy's adventures in Thailand. *Wall Street Journal*, 235(73), p. B1.

Creation of Value

It has been stressed before but merits repeating: the creation of value must be remembered in all activities of the organization, including evaluation and control. The value may not be for the organization alone but also for key stakeholders. For small organizations the concern for value creation is typically clear and commonly stressed because there is an alignment between ownership and control in the firm. However, for large organizations it can be more difficult. There is a need to stress the creation of value for the entire organization in the evaluation and control process at both levels.

Indirect value to other stakeholders is harder to measure and evaluate. Individual firms need to consciously determine how much emphasis they wish to place on such value creation to these other stakeholders and judge their actions accordingly. Some firms put considerable emphasis on indirect value creation. For example, Tony Yeung is a Hong Kong entrepreneur who fled mainland China and the Cultural Revolution in 1972 by swimming 10 hours down the Pearl River from Guangdong Province to reach Hong Kong. Beginning with literally nothing, Yeung was able to save enough to start the Glorious Sun Group in 1977. This company began as a textile company but now has over 1,000 retail stores for jeans in China and Australia under the Jeanswest brand and other names. In addition, Glorious Sun has developed and sold a number of commercial properties. With profits from these activities, Yeung has now created numerous projects to help economic development in China, such as building wells, bridges, and freshwater taps. The foundation affiliated with Yeung's business group has spent over $15 million on such projects over the last five years, greatly benefiting the communities involved. This activity does not contribute directly to efficiency or profits of the business group. However, it has clear indirect benefits, enhancing Glorious Sun's image and building legitimacy with governments in mainland China and other East Asian countries. The indirect value to a firm or shareholders from such effort is hard to measure but is positive.[xlviii]

Best Practices & ISO 9000

Finally, international businesses need to ensure that they are employing best practices. Consistently benchmarking (comparing) the international firm against other leading firms in their industry, or along some specific dimension for firms in other industries, provides valuable insight as to how the firm stacks up against those other firms. The ability to take this information and act on it if a gap is identified is beneficial.

One type of best practices is ISO 9000. ISO is the acronym for the International Organization for Standards, an organization is headquartered in Switzerland that establishes standards for many different domains. One of these domains is quality management standards. These are process standards, not product standards. All types of organizations can have ISO 9000 approval—both for service and manufacturing. The processes on which ISO focuses include items such as management processes, continual process improvement, the involvement of people in the quality process, tracking customer satisfaction, and mutually beneficial supplier relationships. There is actually a portfolio of ISO 900x designations, including ISO 9000, which addresses the fundamentals of the concept and basic vocabulary. ISO 9001 has the requirements for certification and ISO 9004 has the guidelines for performance improvement. Typically, firms refer simply to themselves as "ISO 9000–approved." Another widely used ISO designation is ISO 14001, which concerns operating a facility with strong concerns for pollution control and the environment.

SUMMARY

This chapter has established the fundamentals of evaluation and control in the international firm. As discussed in Chapters 4 and 5, international businesses need to set goal and objectives. The international firm, however, must have systems and procedures in place to evaluate if those goals and objectives are being met. This is the role of evaluation. Once a firm conducts its evaluation, it then needs to determine an appropriate course of action: to do nothing (if it is determined that there is no material problem), change the goal, or change the strategic actions it is taking to achieve that goal. Firms now have a number of new measures at their disposal that come from research in accounting and decision-sciences to help with evaluation and control.[xliv] Generally speaking, a key to the success of the international firm is to ensure it is not making choices mechanically and without thinking. The evaluation and control processes are typically linked to each other. The firm is in a constant process in which it conducts evaluation and then makes changes and follows up with evaluation of these changes. Thus, the two actions—evaluation and control—form a virtuous circle that reinforce each other. The firm must constantly think actively about what it is doing and what the outcomes mean.

MANAGERIAL GUIDELINES

1. Evaluation and control in practice is an ongoing process that happens with the two processes intertwined with each other.
2. Goals and objectives are not set in stone—they should adjust as the environment changes.
3. Managerial actions must also be open to change. The fundamental strategic direction of the firm will typically not radically alter, but as a living entity, the firm should not pursue actions simply because in the past it said it would pursue that path.
4. While the firm is constantly evaluating itself on current actions and future directions, there needs to be an occasional evaluation asking if the firm needs a more fundamental shift in strategic direction. Such a shift should not be taken lightly, but there will be changes in the environment and competitive nature of the industry that merit it.
5. Creativity is important in seeking to predict future challenges to the firm.
6. The critical nature of communication discussed previously in the text is important to keep in mind as details about the evaluation and control process are presented to employees.

Table 11-1 is a helpful summary for students and managers alike as they seek to apply evaluation and control issues in international settings.

TABLE 11-1 Evaluation and Control around the World

Evaluation and Control Issue	International Example
Denominator management	Japanese firms were thought to put a lot of money into new assets and thus did not fall into the trap of denominator management. More recently, it has been learned that for many years, particularly near the end of Japan's boom (late 1980s to early 1990s) Japanese firms had been investing a great deal in assets that were actually giving near zero return on investment. This was symptomatic of many countries in East Asia, particularly in countries such as Japan and Korea where governments or banks would bail out firms that had made poor investments and allow them to continue making those investments in spite of signals from the market and investors that they should stop. A lack of financial controls and safeguards, coupled with massive overinvestment in nonperforming assets (historically the source of many financial panics) led to a financial crisis in Asia in 1997 and 1998.[xlv]

TABLE 11-1 (Continued)

Evaluation and Control Issue	International Example
Developing the capability to market products in foreign countries	Firms in emerging economies have typically produced products for foreign firms that would then sell the products. Building the capability to design and sell products for foreign markets on their own has proved a stubborn challenge for China and other firms in emerging East Asia. Chinese firms have not yet built global capabilities and brands as firms in Japan and Korea did at similar stages in their development. This is something for developed-economy firms to watch when they evaluate Chinese (and other emerging economy) firms' competitive capabilities.
Evaluating threats	There is a well-known adage that "generals prepare to fight the previous war." This often seems true in business as well. Few in the U.S. and U.K. auto business, for example, thought that tough competition would be coming from Japan and Germany—the countries that were defeated and devastated in WWII. Leading firms in consumer electronics were surprised to face very tough competition from Japan and later Korea. Competition often comes from surprising places, particularly from low-end products. If emerging economies learn to sell low-end products outside of their home markets, they could pose a threat to firms in developed economies, much in the way Japanese cars, Korean mobile phones, and now Chinese-made microwave ovens have disrupted numerous established markets.
Brainstorming and strategic change	Japanese firms have illustrated ways to bring middle managers and lower-level employees into the planning process by giving them a role in giving suggestions and brainstorming. As discussed in Chapter 9, for difficult strategic issues and forecasting future development, it is important to get middle managers and line employees involved in the planning process. This is because the lower-level employees may be closer to the problem that needs to be solved. They can also bring a fresh perspective to the planning and strategizing process. This can be particularly challenging for high power-distance cultures and for organizations that have leadership that does not believe lower-level employees or outsiders can bring anything useful into high level strategic discussions.

CULTURE AND DOING BUSINESS IN ISRAEL

CULTURE

Israel is the only active democracy in the Middle East. Israel has a per capita income of over $20,000, higher than Spain, New Zealand, Portugal, and Greece. Following War World II, the British withdrew from their Palestinian mandate, and in 1947 the United Nations confirmed the partition of the former British Mandate of Palestine into two states, one Jewish and one Arab. The Arab countries in the Middle East rejected the division of the land and attacked the fledgling state of Israel in 1948. The Israelis were victorious in that initial war and eventually expanded beyond the original land partition. Most Arab countries are still technically at war with Israel, with no formal peace agreement signed to end the several wars fought since 1948. Interestingly, Israel was founded as a socialist country with much support from the Soviet Union. Israel's economic policies have, however, increasingly emphasized private sector development, capitalism, and high technology entrepreneurship, but it is still estimated that a third of the country is employed by the government, military, or in government-related businesses. The greatest growth areas of Israel's economy are high-technology and venture capital firms.

Today Israel has a diverse ethnic make up. It is estimated that about 80 percent of the population is Jewish with Arabs composing the other 20 percent. The Jewish population comes from widely diverse backgrounds: Israel-born 67.1 percent, Europe/America-born 22 percent, Africa-born 5.9 percent, and Asia-born 4.2 percent. This ethnic makeup affects how business is conducted there. Many business people are internationalized and will conduct business in a manner largely undistinguishable from the United States or the United Kingdom. However, if a man is an Orthodox Jew he may not introduce his wife to a new business partner, and that partner should not inquire about her. There are also sections of many large cities that are predominantly populated by Orthodox Jews. The streets in these sections are closed from Friday at sundown until Saturday at sundown due to the Jewish Sabbath, or day of rest. The typical business week in Israel is Sunday through Thursday, with only five hours of work on Friday from 8:00 a.m. to 1:00 p.m. However, because Israel is a multicultural and multi-religion state, business in effect never stops. The work week is also dependent on other religious groups: Muslims treat Friday as the day of religious observation, while for Christians it is Sunday.

The Israelis are known for being very blunt in their conversation. Thus in business, questions that seem very direct and personal are common. It should also be remembered that Israel is situated amid nations that are still hostile to its existence and all young men and women are required to provide military service. In addition, all men are required to provide one month of military reservist service annually through the age of 50.

https://www.cia.gov/library/publications/the-world-factbook/geos/is/html

ADDITIONAL RESOURCES

Hamel, G. (2002). *Leading the Revolution*. London: Plume.

Charan, R. (2005). *Boards that Deliver: Advancing Corporate Governance from Compliance to Competitive Advantage*. New York: Jossey-Bass.

Christensen, C. M., & Raynor, M. E. (2003). *The Innovator's Solution: Creating and Sustaining Successful Growth*. Boston, MA: Harvard Business School Press.

Clissold, T. (2006). *Mr. China: A Memoir*. New York: Collins.

McGregor, J. (2005). *One Billion Customers: Lessons from the Front Lines of Doing Business in China*. New York: Simon & Schuster.

Niven, P. S. (2006). *Balanced Scorecard Step-by-Step: Maximizing Performance and Maintaining Results* (2nd ed.). Hoboken, NJ: John Wiley & Sons.

Zeng, M. and Williamson, P .J. (2007). *Dragons at Your Door: How Chinese Cost Innovation Is Disrupting Global Competition*. Boston, MA: Harvard Business School Press.

EXERCISES

Opening Vignette Discussion Questions

1. What are some of the ways that an evaluation and control system can prevent problems like those at Barings?
2. What happened to Barings in the end?
3. What do you think of the fact that Leeson is out of jail, has now written a book, and had a movie made about his experience at Barings? Or that he charges thousands of dollars to speak to groups about motivation and proper financial measures and controls?

DISCUSSION QUESTIONS

1. Earlier, we talked about famed strategists C.K. Prahalad and Gary Hamel and their discussion of the concept of "denominator management." List five ways firms can increase short-term return by increasing the "R" portion of ROI. Which of these may be harmful to a firm's long-term strategic position and why?
2. Why do individuals rely so much on financial controls in an international business?
3. One executive from Asia, after having heard the data about the number of meals eaten in and around cars in America is reported to have said, "It's bad that Americans eat one out of three meals (per day) in the car. Our [food] company should urge them not to do that. We should convince them it is better for them to stay home in the morning and eat our instant *jook* [a rice porridge commonly eaten in the morning in Chinese societies]. It would be healthier for them." Respond to that statement. Is trying to change how meals are taken in America a good path to profitability and growth? Why or why not? Shouldn't firms try to educate customers about better ways to live (including the buying of their product)?
4. This chapter covered how the board of directors and CEO play a key role in the evaluation and control processes of an international firm. It was discussed in Chapter 3 that the Sarbanes Oxley Act has had a major impact on how a board and CEO act. What are your thoughts on how this has affected their ability to conduct their evaluation and control activities? How has Sarbanes Oxley affected the likelihood that foreign firms will list their stock in U.S. equity markets?

IN-CLASS EXERCISES

1. A key part of control is knowing what actions to take to correct a situation. Assume you are part of a new management team that has taken over a major fast food company that has fallen on hard times. In trying to implement changes in response to changing demographics over recent years (e.g. an increase in families and children, more meals consumed out of the home, people living further away from work), they determined that the restaurant chain's milkshakes are among the highest margin items on its menu and that they would like to sell more of them. To do that, management commissioned a top consulting firm to conduct some traditional market research (a questionnaire distributed at the restaurants) on who was ordering milkshakes, but the results proved confusing. Sometimes the same customers seemed to be ordering milkshakes in the morning and other times at night. They said they sometimes wanted fruit in the milkshakes, and other times they said they wanted more traditional flavors like vanilla and strawberry (the restaurant currently only sells chocolate). Customers also seemed unsure about what size shakes they liked to order, sometimes favoring a large size, other times a small size. You are charged to make a report to management on these findings. Why do you think the results collected are so confusing? If you were to study the problem yourself, how would you explain why customers are buying milkshakes? And how could your fast food employer benefit from knowing this?

2. After answering the above question, consider how you would increase milkshake sales. What would you change about the product to fit with the current situation? What about the packaging? What about adding new flavors? How about the time of day when milkshakes are sold? Be sure to explain your recommendations.

3. Someday you may work for a global firm from mainland China. How do you feel about that? How different do you expect it would be from working in a firm from your country? (If you are from mainland China, then change the global firm to a U.S. firm to answer the question.) How might the evaluation and control systems differ in the two countries?

4. Divide into teams. Each team is to take on the role of a different part of the world or major country in a region (United States, Europe, United Kingdom, Asia, China, Middle East, Egypt, etc.). Based on what you've learned in this class about different cultures in these regions, what type of evaluation and control system do you think would be needed in that region? Come together as a class and design what your evaluation and control system might look like for a firm like BMW.

TAKE-HOME EXERCISES

1. What is denominator management? How can a firm practice it? Why is this a problem? Find an example of this on the Web. Recognize that the popular press may not use the term denominator management. Instead you will likely have to search on phrases like "underfunding of R&D," "focusing too much on short term profits," etc.

2. Do some research on the problems of control in China, specifically problems with the financial reporting system there. Prepare a summary of the key items that your boss would need to know if he or she were charged with finding a company to acquire in China.

3. One of the major environmental changes in recent years for the food industry is the fact that in the United States nearly one-third of all meals are eaten in the

consumer's automobile, usually breakfast. Assume you are a manager of a breakfast cereal firm. What issues do you face as a result of this sea-change in eating habits? How would you respond to it?

4. Research a country with a reputation for high levels of corruption, such as Nigeria, Russia, or Pakistan. Detail the nature of the corruption that has been reported in the country for your boss in a page or so. Then provide a suggestion for how the firm you both work for may deal with such issues as you begin to do business there. Focus particularly on the evaluation and control system that will be needed to prevent a situation like Barings from occurring.

SHORT CASE QUESTIONS

Citibank in Japan (p. 356)

1. Why do you think the Citigroup CEO went to Japan to bow and apologize since such behavior is not traditionally American?
2. Do you think Europeans may have been more forgiving than the Japanese about the withdrawal of the private banking license? The Canadians?
3. Why do you think the firm did not respond strongly when the problems were first found in early 2000?

12

HUMAN RESOURCES MANAGEMENT

Overview

In operating internationally, one of the most vital assets a firm has is its human resources. The firm needs people both from its home country and the foreign countries in which it operates. If it gets staffing wrong, the added cost to the firm can be inordinately high. Effective management of human resources can be a source of advantage for firms, particularly as they move internationally. Significant problems can also occur if a firm does not manage its human resources effectively. In particular, the ability to place an expatriate employee quickly into an international environment to seize new opportunities or correct problems is important. But if the expatriate is a poor fit and quits the post early, the cost to the firm is very high as the position must be filled again with all the incumbent costs of posting a manager abroad.

Therefore, this chapter will examine how an international firm's decisions regarding hiring, training, employee appraisal and compensation often differ from the firm's home country environment. This chapter will specifically provide insights on the following:

- The role of human resources management in international business
- The major functions of human resources: selection techniques and implementation of selection; training of employees; appraisal, compensation, and rewards; and socialization
- Problems and solutions in international postings—the expatriate dilemma

ASIMCO: EXPATRIATE PITFALLS

An assignment in China can prove to be very challenging for many expatriates—even those who are familiar with the language and culture. After working for a few years in accounting in the United Kingdom, British businessman Tim Clissold went to China to learn Chinese, hoping to work for his firm or another bank there. In the early 1990s, Clissold was hired by Asimco, one of the largest foreign investors in China at the time, to help it secure and oversee its China investments. Started by Jack Perkowski, a successful American banker, and run in China by Clissold, Asimco was able to raise a total of $434 million from private equity firms and private investors. The money was invested in a variety of state and private enterprises in China, such as car-component factories and breweries, with the ambitious goal of creating a large conglomerate of low-cost divisions, chosen from the best of China's state enterprises and other overlooked firms, often in China's interior.

Clissold spoke Chinese well and spent much time and effort courting key government officials to gather support for each venture. But he and his assistants were not able to watch over the farflung ventures that were often located in hard-to-access regions of China's interior. Asimco's best manager, who ran a rubber-parts factory in the mountainous in isolated Anhui Province in eastern China, secretly set up a rival plant nearby that he financed by siphoning money and equipment from the Asimco joint venture. When that manager was eventually found out and fired, he told his workers to package defective products from his own production line in Asimco boxes and send them to customers so they would cancel orders from Asimco. There were battles on the street and around the factory with knives and broken bottles between workers loyal to Asimco and those loyal to the former factory boss. Police and later the army had to be called out to quell the situation.

While that was going on, in southern Zhuhai, near the border with Macau, the director of Asimco's brake-pads factory absconded to the United States with $10 million worth of company letters of credit, assisted by a local bank manager, leaving behind his entire family. Asimco sued the bank for validating the certificates, but ended up liable for the money. An anti-corruption official based in adjacent Guangdong Province promised Clissold he would investigate, but only if he was given a car and money to fund the investigation. Eventually, nearly all of Asimco's $434 million disappeared in such investments around China with investors getting little but some scattered assets in return.

This cautionary tale carries several lessons for doing business in China, but in terms of human resources, it shows how important it is to place the right people in foreign subsidiaries, and to take enough time to find the right middle managers. One or two young, energetic expatriates flying around a country is seldom enough, particularly in a developing economy such as China or India. A factory manager, the head of finance or accounting, and at least one middle manager whose loyalty is to the parent firm are the bare minimum needed to run and monitor a significant operation in China, Russia, or most other developing economies. The expatriates must know the local environment and rely on loyal middle managers and finance managers who can monitor their investments and safeguard company accounts and "chops" (stamps used as proxies for signatures on financial transactions in China), otherwise millions of dollars can be lost.[i]

The human resources management (HRM) function is one the most important for firms in operating internationally. For example, a critical issue facing international firms is staffing of international locations. HRM has an impact on a number of functions in an international firm. These include selection, training, appraisal, and compensation. The flow of the chapter in discussing these issues is summarized in Figure 12-1.

THE IMPORTANCE OF INTERNATIONAL HRM

Finding the right people to fill positions in a division or department of the company that is doing business internationally is difficult, and the wrong person can be very costly. This is especially true if the individual is sent to a foreign location from the firm's home market. These individuals are referred to as **expatriates**. The cost of hiring and placing an expatriate in a foreign location can range from 50 to 200 percent of the expatriate's salary. When hiring an expatriate, costs to the firm include not only finding the right person but also relocation costs

Expatriate
A person from one country who is working and residing in another country.

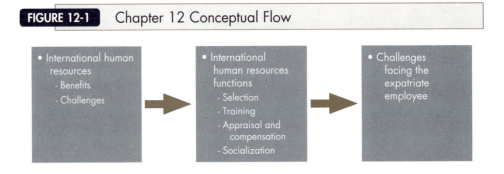

FIGURE 12-1   Chapter 12 Conceptual Flow

- International human resources
  - Benefits
  - Challenges

- International human resources functions
  - Selection
  - Training
  - Appraisal and compensation
  - Socialization

- Challenges facing the expatriate employee

to the foreign locale for the expatriate and his or her family as well as training about the local culture and other preparation costs.

Maintaining an expatriate employee in a foreign location is also expensive, with the expatriate often receiving return flights to the home country for holidays, the firm paying for private school costs for children, and trying to make the expatriate's compensation **tax neutral**. The United States is one of the few countries in the world that charges taxes on the income earned overseas by U.S. citizens.[1] Thus, firms should try to ensure that the employee is tax neutral—that is, the expat should not be paying so much in new taxes that he or she effectively earns less money than back in the home country. In addition, if the expatriate assignment fails, and the person leaves the job and returns home early, there will be lost productivity at the foreign location, new recruiting, training, and travel costs for the next employee, and other expenses commonly associated with employee turnover. With many knowledge-based jobs such as quality assurance, running a research center, or managing engineers, the loss of an expatriate manager may even cause the facility to shut down until a replacement is found. This is very expensive in terms of lost productivity and missed sales opportunities; the firm will also have to search for another person to fill that overseas position, and may have to pay relocation costs and other direct, hard dollar expenses. Thus, the cost estimate of expatriate failure ranges from half a year's salary to two years of salary from the person who left. Since human resources are so important to an international firm, and expatriate failure is very expensive, it is vital that the firm has effective HRM to ensure that the right people with the right skills are available when needed and that turnover is minimized.[ii] Figure 12-2 highlights the extensive nature of this problem for many U.S. firms. Though they have come down somewhat in recent years, expat failures are still a source of concern to management.[iii]

Tax neutral

Firms will try to ensure that an expatriate does not pay more tax by being posted abroad.

HUMAN RESOURCES MANAGEMENT (HRM) FUNCTIONS

In developing human resources to meet the demands illustrated above, there are several major functions to direct. Apart from record keeping and basic administration, often brought to mind by the older term for the HR department, "personnel," HR is sometimes summarized by its basic functions: selection, training and development, appraisal and compensation, and socialization. These functions in an international firm are addressed below, along with examples from firms thought of as exemplary in those areas.

[1]U.S. citizens must pay U.S. taxes on foreign income earned over approximately $80,000 (the first $80,000 earned is exempt), though many of the taxes paid to the foreign locality can be subtracted from the U.S. tax liability.

FIGURE 12-2 Expatriate Recall Rates from Abroad

Recall Rate Percent	Percent of Companies
U.S. multinationals	
20–40%	7%
10–20	69
<10	24
European multinationals	
11–15%	3%
6–10	38
<5	59
Japanese multinationals	
11–19%	14%
6–10	10
<5	76

Source: Tung, R.L. (1982). Selection and Training Procedures of U.S., European, and Japanese multinationals. *California Management Review.* 25(1) 51–71.

LINCOLN ELECTRIC IN EUROPE

Lincoln Electric's experiences in Mexico were discussed in Chapter 7. Its experience in Europe also offers valuable insights on the functions of international HR. In the late 1980s and early 1990s, Lincoln spent almost $325 million expanding beyond its U.S. base to Europe, Japan, and Latin America. None of Lincoln Electric's board of directors had any significant international experience, and no one challenged the significant international expansion plans to multiple foreign countries. The European operations ran into trouble early, losing millions of dollars and causing Lincoln Electric to run a consolidated loss—something they almost never did. The individual European businesses would submit extremely overly optimistic sales-and-profits targets in their budgets, but they invariably missed the targets, often by quite a bit. Even more worrisome, nobody seemed to have a handle on why the targets were being missed or what to do about the gaps apart from just cutting budgets. The European managers had not been brought up under the Lincoln Electric system and seemed content to let the European recession run its course rather than working more aggressively to increase revenue and establish the Lincoln Electric brand in new markets. In the newly acquired German plant, some people were not even working. On one visit that had been announced in advance, three employees were found sleeping on the job. Lincoln Electric decided they had to get out of that plant.

The root cause of the crisis was that Lincoln Electric's leaders had grown overconfident in the company's abilities and systems. They believed that their unique culture and incentive system—along with the dedicated, skilled workforce that the company had built over the decades—were the main source of its competitive advantage, and assumed that the incentive system and culture could be directly transferred abroad. Lincoln Electric employed a polycentric hiring approach, trying to localize its management, but it failed to realize that these managers had not been through the Lincoln Electric system and were not nearly as aggressive in sales and production incentives. Although Lincoln Electric went through a couple of very difficult years, it did finally learn from its mistakes. As former CEO Donald Hastings recalled, "Competing globally requires a lot more time, money, and management resources than we realized. At least five years before we launched our expansion in 1987, we should have started building a management team and a hoard of directors from whom we could have learned how to proceed."[iv] After its initial false start, Lincoln is doing well in its international markets and has successfully implemented its pay for performance system in a number of plants worldwide.[v]

Selection

Effective employee selection can prove to be a major task. A number of challenges surround selection, including the method used and the firm's general approach. In addition to standard selection problems, there are numerous problems with the criteria used to choose expatriates. There are three common methods for selecting new employees: interviews, observation, and various types of written tests. Each will be reviewed in turn with emphasis later in this section given to selecting employees for foreign postings.

Interviews Many firms use interviews to screen people for overseas assignments, agreeing that extensive interviewing of candidates (and their spouses) by senior executives still provide an effective method of selection. The spouse should be interviewed as well because the family plays such a critical role in whether the employee will be able to remain in the international job or will be compelled to return home to keep the family happy. If the family is not happy, it is likely that the expatriate employee will leave, no matter how well the job is going and how successful the employee is.

Professor Rosalie Tung's research on international human resources and expatriates supports the belief on the importance of the family and their involvement in the interview process. For example, in one major study, 52 percent of the U.S. multinational corporations she surveyed reported that they conducted interviews with both the prospective manager and his or her spouse for an international position, and 47 percent conducted interviews with the candidate alone. For technically oriented positions, 40 percent of the firms interviewed both the candidate and the spouse, and 59 percent conducted interviews with the candidate alone.[vi]

Although single individual interviews are a common selection method, research suggests that a single interview by itself is not a very valid predictor of performance.[vii] Instead, multiple individual interviews are more useful. Often, a prospective employee will be sent to speak to multiple people in the group. For example, when Apple was interviewing for new members of the original Macintosh development team, it had someone interview with each member of the team. Only if the whole team liked that prospective employee would the person be hired.[viii] Multiple interviews are also commonly used for higher-level and professional jobs including expatriate positions. Multiple interviews can provide diversity of opinion about the job candidate along with some consensus on whether he or she should be hired.

In China, many multinationals have found that individual interviews are useful in interviewing Chinese job applicants, but there is a need to employ both expatriate and local interviewers. The expatriate ensures that attention is focused on the key selection criteria so that individuals who are offered jobs will indeed have the abilities, skills, and training to do the work. The local person ensures that the prospective hire knows the local culture and customs, and can provide insights regarding the applicant's responses and other behaviors that can be problematic in the international location. Together, the two are able to help identify those candidates most likely to do the best job.

Group interviews
Selection tool in which typically there are multiple candidates and multiple interviewers present at the same time.

Group Interviews Also fairly effective for certain types of jobs—customer service jobs, or factory or facility management—is the group interview. In group interviews typically there are both multiple candidates and multiple interviewers present at the same time. In this case, the expatriate interacts with potential clients (real and role-playing) and potential colleagues. Emphasis is given to how the candidate responds to real situations and how they cooperate with others. Southwest Airlines in the United States has used group interviews very effectively to hire new flight attendants. Prospective flight attendants are evaluated by current flight attendants, the Human Resources (HR) department (called the "People Department" at Southwest), and customers (airline passengers). Similarly, Southwest Airlines will have mechanics interview mechanics, and pilots interview pilots. Southwest's belief is that the employees in the field doing the job will know best the kinds of people needed.

Cathay Pacific Airlines in Hong Kong also uses group interviews to evaluate prospective flight attendants' personalities and how they interact with various groups and each other. The goal of this Asia-based airline is similar to Southwest's in that they hire service personnel with engaging personalities who can work well with others and have an even temperament. Group interviews are often employed for filling midlevel and lower-level positions. Group interviews also facilitate another type of selection method, the observation method, because the way interviewees interact with customers and potential colleagues is one good indication of how they might fit in and perform.

Observation Method The hiring decision can also be accomplished through observation of the prospective employee interacting with colleagues, giving a presentation, or actually performing a job. This method is more common for certain jobs—research, engineering, professional organizations, governments, and universities. To illustrate, it is typical for a job candidate applying for a faculty position in a university to present his or her research to a group of professors and to a class of students to see how he or she interacts with individuals in each situation. Firms do similar things. As mentioned above, Southwest Airlines includes observation in some of its selection processes. The firm wishes to see how the individual will act in the actual setting. Southwest's former chairmen Herb Kelleher told the story of how he liked to place an individual who was actually already a Southwest Airlines pilot among a group of pilot applicants. The Southwest pilot would observe the applicants when they thought no one from the firm was present. Southwest also watches applicants in other settings, such as when they go to the cafeteria for lunch. The firm wants to see how they relate to people while there, particularly when the applicants do not know they are being observed.[ix]

The observation method is particularly helpful in selecting individuals for overseas assignments. For example, a prospective employee may be asked to give a presentation to a group that does not speak the same first language as the potential expatriate, such as a group of Chinese retail managers currently visiting the home office in the United States for training. The firm wants to see if the applicant is able to modify his or her speaking style in response to the demands of the setting. For example, does the prospective expatriate use a lot of slang and uncommon terms in his or her daily speech that will present problems when dealing with local employees and clients in non-English-speaking countries? Many North American idioms such as calling an idea "cutting edge" (or even worse, "bleeding edge"), often are confusing to others outside North America. A "punt" in North American football means to kick away the ball and is used to mean to dispose of an unwanted situation or responsibility. Yet in Britain and other parts of the current and former British Commonwealth (Australia, New Zealand, Jamaica, Hong Kong, Singapore, and so forth), a punt is a wager, and a "punter" is not a kicker but a gambler. Baseball metaphors such as "out in left field" or "that was a home run" should be avoided, as they will not be understood by most non-native English speakers. It is important for the expatriate to make efforts to rid his or her speech of slang, impenetrable idioms, and references to very local issues so as to improve his or her understandability.

Similarly, does the prospective expatriate speak at the same speed with individuals who are non-native speakers? Ideally you should speak a little more slowly and pronounce words more carefully in speaking to non-native speakers who do not have a lot of experience with your language. Additionally, the firm will want to observe if the applicant expresses a condescending or impatient attitude toward foreign listeners who fail to understand what the expatriate said the first time. The firm needs to know whether the applicant can adapt and change as the setting requires, and the observation method of selection is well suited to identify likely troubles before the firm expends extensive resources placing someone into an international setting.

To illustrate, one HR professional with whom the authors are acquainted told a story about observational interviewing for an important job in Taiwan. He recalled:

> I had been interviewing for a Taiwan posting and had settled on two roughly equal job candidates. At a lunch in a Chinese restaurant, I saw that one of the candidates was uncomfortable with the food—he was scooping through the food with his spoon, apparently looking for something. I asked him what was wrong. He said that he was looking for "weird seafood" in his bowl. After that lunch I decided that he might have trouble acculturating to Taiwan, particularly given that food is such a center of business and social activity for most Chinese people, especially business people. If the person is only comfortable eating at McDonalds or Burger King, why go abroad?

Written tests Another method used in hiring is written tests. One such test is the Structured Questionnaire Method. Arco, a large oil and energy company, has used this method effectively to test for management and marketing savvy, as well as temperament (happiness, anger, or patience). Other written tests used, typically together, include intelligence (IQ) tests and integrity tests. Another written test that may be used when hiring individuals to place in international assignments is one that measures the candidate's **cultural toughness**. This test assesses whether the candidate appears able to work in a specific country.[x] A similar test is the **cultural intelligence test (CQ)**. The higher an individual's score on the CQ test, the more likely that person can succeed in a cross-cultural setting such as an expatriate assignment.[xi]

It should be recognized, however, that written tests also have their limitations. To illustrate, in China selection tests have been found to have limited value. For example, one large U.S. consumer goods firm has reported that the analytical problem-solving tests that it uses in screening applicants will eliminate half of the applicants from North America and Europe, but only 12 percent of Chinese applicants. This is a result of the outstanding analytical training that these individuals receive at prestigious Chinese universities.[xii] So the company needed to find other tests for identifying the very best applicants, as analytical ability is only one of several skills needed in managerial positions. Similarly, the use of psychological testing or Western-style assessment center exercises does not have a good reputation in China. For one thing, the Chinese education system generally does not train students to analyze open-ended hypothetical situations whereby they

Cultural toughness
Selection test that assesses whether a candidate appears able to work in a specific country.

Cultural intelligence test (CQ)
Selection test that evaluates a person's ability in a cross-cultural setting.

CHINESE FIRMS EXPAND TO EUROPE AND NORTH AMERICA

As the Chinese economy continues to grow, Chinese firms are increasingly going global themselves, many for the first time. Chinese companies have had both successful and unsuccessful experiences on their road to globalization. They have taken over parts of venerable western firms with long histories such as IBM, Thomson, and RCA. Chinese managers have found it is more difficult than they thought to communicate with European employees. They have also reported difficulty in keeping employees happy. The employees assume that Chinese management knows very little about modern management system and process. For example, Mr. Li, a manager at China's TCL subsidiary in France (taken over from French appliance firm Thomson) complained that his French colleagues turn off their mobile phones on the weekend and this hurts their work. Other local employees have complained about the late hours the Chinese parent insists on. Chinese firms in the United States have also experienced problems with the workforce. American employees in one major Chinese firm reported that they like to know what management is planning, but in the Chinese firm they feel they are on a purely need-to-know basis. Thus they are told about their immediate job and little else. Employees in both firms reported that the Chinese management did not take their suggestions seriously. This has led to difficulties in recruiting talent and a lot of turnover at these firms with the resulting costs. It takes much longer for a company to build the capabilities to operate and manage global businesses, as evidenced by the fact that Japanese, Korean, and Taiwanese companies typically spend over 10 years to build their global capabilities and suffer a lot of turnover and problems with local staff. These capabilities can by no means be developed in a short time.

Zhang, J. (2005, June). Global misadventures. *China International Business*, pp. 20–22.

must build an argument and supply evidence for a certain position. Nor does it teach lateral thinking (thinking beyond the literal answer to the actual problem at hand) particularly well. As a result, expatriate evaluators find it hard to draw conclusions about the suitability of the Chinese candidates based on their performance in problem-solving exercises alone.

Overview of Selection Methods

It should be recognized that whether a firm uses interviews, observation, or written tests, the most useful test for a given firm will also take local culture into account. For example, in Anglo-Saxon cultures, what is generally tested is how much the individual can contribute to the tasks of the organization. In these cultures, assessment center exercises, intelligence tests, and measurements of competencies are the norm. In Germanic cultures, the emphasis is more on the quality of education geared toward a particular (job) function. The recruitment process in Far Eastern cultures is very often characterized by ascertaining how well a person fits in with the larger group. This is judged in part by the elitism of higher educational institutes attended, such as the University of Tokyo in Japan. Latin cultures will tend to emphasize personality, communication, and social skills more than intelligence or job function.[xiii] The acceptance of selection devices vary around the world. For example, Hong Kong and Taiwan are averse to questionnaires.[xiv] Written references are less common in France than other European and Anglo countries as French people are reluctant to give written references. Situational and scenario tests are used more in the United Kingdom, Holland, and Germany than in France and Belgium. In contrast, multiple choice tests are more common in France and Belgium than in the Northern European and Anglo countries.[xv] Whichever selection tests are employed, they should be used judiciously, employing local versions of the tests when possible.

Implementing Expatriate Selection In making their selection firms may employ some or all the methods above. However, in implementing these selection methods a firm should focus on learning specific things about the potential job candidate. Particularly, for those positions which require that the individual be stationed abroad there are some key factors to focus on, including adaptability to different cultural settings, self-reliance, health, a balance of age and experience, motivation for international job, and family.

Adaptability to Cultural Change While it was noted above that people with international postings must have a certain level of cultural intelligence, they must also be able to adapt to different and changing circumstances. No matter how well they think they know a culture, they will have some degree of culture shock at the start, and will continue to encounter frustrations in their new environment, even after becoming accustomed to that environment. In fact, it is expected that many of the most effective international managers suffer this cultural shock, because it shows that the expatriate manager is becoming involved in the new culture and not just isolating him or herself from the environment. To illustrate the culture shock that can occur, one North American assigned to Japan described this experience to the authors in the following way:

> On my first week in Japan, living in an isolated area in the foothills of Mount Fuji, I was getting tired of the monotony of the salty Japanese cafeteria food of fish and pickled vegetables, so I walked down to the local Mom and Pop store to buy something more familiar to eat. As yet unable to read Japanese, I decided to pick up what looked like a jar of peanut butter. I was not sure that's what it was, but it looked like peanut butter, and there was a picture of what looked like a peanut on the package. I bought the jar and some bread and eagerly went back to the

company dorm to have a peanut butter sandwich. To my dismay, when I opened the jar and started to spread the paste on the bread it didn't smell like peanut butter. Turns out, it was some kind of raw soybean paste. It had almost the same color and texture of peanut butter but certainly did not taste like peanut butter. And it had the same salty taste that almost all of the cafeteria food had. I later found I had to walk about seven miles downhill to a larger store to buy peanut butter and other more familiar foods, and then seven miles uphill back to my living quarters. This was all a surprise to me to live like that in "modern Japan."

While many expatriates are typically very happy at the start of their overseas assignments, after a few months there is often a downturn in contentment with the job and the foreign location, which can lead to a significant drop in mood. But if the expatriate understands that this downturn in mood after a few months is very common and is to be expected, he or she will be better able to weather this period and adjust. In fact, after the first two years, most people become more satisfied with their overseas assignment than when they first arrived. So if you feel very discontented after working in a new country for a few months, do not worry, this downtown in mood is very common and should pass in time.

Organizations examine a number of characteristics in determining whether an individual is adaptable. Examples include experiences with cultures other than one's own, previous overseas travel, a knowledge of foreign languages (fluency generally is not necessary, however), and recent immigration background or heritage. Others include (1) the ability to integrate with different people, cultures, and types of business organizations; (2) the ability to sense developments in the host country and accurately assess them; (3) the ability to solve problems within different frameworks and from different perspectives; (4) sensitivity to differences and nuances in culture, politics, religion, and ethics; and (5) flexibility in managing operations on a continuous basis despite a lack of assistance and gaps in information.

When are expatriates better able to adjust? In research conducted among expatriates in China, Professor Jan Selmer found that those who were best able to deal with their new situation had developed coping strategies characterized by sociocultural and psychological adjustments, including (1) having experience in adjusting to new situations, (2) learning how to interact well with host-country nationals outside of work, and (3) feeling reasonably happy and being able to enjoy day-to-day activities. In addition, if the expatriate possesses the personality trait of openness to new experience, this also helps with cross-cultural adjustment. Sociability was also correlated with effective adjustment, as the expat can get to know people in the foreign office better.[xvi]

Independence and Self-Reliance In many overseas assignments, expatriates have more responsibility than they had at the home office. They also have fewer people to call on for assistance and guidance. At company headquarters, a large staff of advisors may have been available to provide assistance and guidance, but in foreign assignments, expats must be more self-reliant. Some of the indicators of independence and self-reliance that employers are looking for include prior experience working with customers in the field, special project or task force experience, a hobby that requires a high degree of self-reliance, and a record of extracurricular activities or athletics in school. Most organizations also require that their expatriate managers be in good physical and emotional health, because developing countries often do not have the all of the medical resources available in more developed countries.

A firm is not only interested in an employee's physical health but also their psychological health. For example, it is important that an individual have the ability to withstand culture shock. Key parts of this evaluation would include the person's marital status and family setting. If a person is in a troubled marriage, the person's psychological stress will grow worse when he or she moves overseas. A prospective expat who has a child with a special need will often find moving

CULTURAL SENSITIVITY: HOW MUCH IS TOO MUCH?

Firms often seek to adapt to the culture of different key customers, such as the Chinese high-rollers in Las Vegas casinos. The casinos refer to Chinese people who are willing to spend $50,000 on a single hand of cards or a million dollars in a weekend as whales. It is estimated that 80 percent of whales are from Asia, because gambling is a key part of Chinese culture.

Las Vegas casinos have also sought to adjust their product mix and presentation to attract these customers. For example, many casinos offer Asian-themed baccarat salons and noodle bars. Asians on the whole prefer card games rather than roulette or craps because they feel they have some control over baccarat and their skill can allow them to be successful. Other casinos have built their facilities to make the Chinese feel comfortable. For example, Harrah's opened a gambling and dining area inspired by architectural elements of the Ming and Song Dynasties at their Showboat Casino in Atlantic City. Hong Kong and Taiwan singers regularly perform to majority Chinese audiences in Las Vegas showrooms.

But firms can go too far in seeking to be multicultural. Coca-Cola is often thought of as the prototypical culturally sensitive global firm. Robert Goizetta, Coke's longtime chairman who oversaw Coke's rapid growth in the 1980s and 1990s, was originally from Cuba. Doug Daft was one of Goizetta's successors and hailed from Australia, though Daft worked all around the world. But some have argued that Daft carried cultural sensitivity too far. When he was appointed CEO in 1999, Daft wanted to internationalize Coke's traditional U.S. headquarters in Atlanta, Georgia. As part of this effort he brought in a Feng Shui master, a person who specializes in the Eastern philosophy of arranging interior facilities to keep them in harmony with nature.

Feng Shui is drawn from Taoism and sees energy throughout the world. Its goal is to ensure that all things are in harmony with their surroundings by balancing the energies of any given space to assure the health and good fortune for people. There is an effort to place objects in a manner so as to improve *chi* or energy. Gentle wind and smooth water have positive connotations, while harsh winds and stagnant water are linked with negative elements. Feng Shui consultants try to promote the flow of positive energy, prevent the leakage of nourishing energy, and curb the development of negative energy.

The Feng Shui master hired by Coke reorganized the firm's Atlanta lobby and some executive offices according to Feng Shui principles. Desks were turned in various ways so they were "properly" facing doors to allow good energy to flow in. Many mirrors and objects with points on them were removed because of the bad luck they could project. These changes happened in spite of the desk owners who protested that the move was inconvenient for them. The Feng Shui master also had several statues, including a large green dragon, placed in Coca-Cola's lobby, presumably to scare away evil spirits. For a number of employees, that was the last straw. They complained to management about the inconvenient desk arrangements, uncomfortable furniture, loss of space, and ugly gargoyle-like statues placed where fine art had been. Being a culturally sensitive company is one thing, but ignoring local tastes, in this case those of Americans, is not a good thing for any company to do. And besides, the American employees argued that Coca-Cola was not being sensitive to their culture.[xvii]

Firms have to be careful how they choose to internationalize their settings. It can work well in some situations, but the Coke example shows how firms can push their employees to the point that they do not feel comfortable.

Hays, C. (2004). *Pop: Truth and Power at the Coca-Cola Company.* London: Hutchinson.

Rivlin, G. (2007, June 13). Las Vegas caters to Asia's high rollers. *The New York Times*, p. B1.

abroad more difficult because the special services on which they may depend are not as readily available. As a result, many firms have very specific characteristics that they look for in an employee. For example, one U.S. oil company operating in the Middle East considers middle-aged men with grown children to be the best able to cope with cultural shock, and for some locations in the desert, people from Texas or southern California can adjust better than those from New England.

Education, Age, and Experience. Education is important in selecting individuals for international assignments, and almost all firms will build on formal education through their own training and development efforts. For example, Germany's Siemens corporation gives its international management team specific training designed to help them deal more effectively with the types of problems they will face on the job. Most firms placing an employee in an expatriate position will also strive for a balance between age and experience. There is evidence that younger managers are more eager for international assignments and have more openness to new experiences and new cultures—important traits for succeeding as an expat.

HIERARCHY AND PROTOCOL: AN AMERICAN EXECUTIVE IN LONDON

An American executive moved to London to manage his company's British headquarters. Although the initial few weeks passed relatively uneventfully, it bothered the executive that visitors were never sent directly to his office. A visitor first had to speak with the receptionist, then the secretary, and then the office manager. Finally, the office manager would escort the visitor to see him. The American became annoyed with this practice, which he considered a total waste of time. When the manager finally spoke with his British employees and urged them to be less formal and to send visitors directly to him, they seemed upset.

After a number of delicate conversations, the American executive began to understand the greater emphasis on formality and hierarchy in many British firms, particularly in well-established, traditional organizations like banks and trading firms. He slowly learned to be more patient when his colleagues greeted guests using their more formal, multi-step approach. Visitors to the British headquarters continued to see the receptionist, secretary, and office manager before meeting the American executive. The executive was better able to get things done after understanding British protocol and not fighting it, frustrating as it seemed to him at the beginning.[xviii]

But by the same token, young people often are the least developed in terms of management experience and technical skills.

To gain the desired balance, many firms send both young and seasoned personnel to the same overseas post. A team should be selected for both its youth and its experience, taking into consideration reporting relationships, specific responsibilities, authority, necessary connections, and professional judgment as to how much experience is best suited to a specific job. Many companies consider an academic degree, preferably a graduate degree, to be important to an international executive, as well as some international exposure, which helps to reduce the expatriate's learning curve in the new country.[xix]

Language Training In implementing the selection process, language ability is very important. English is the primary language of international business, and most expatriates from all countries can converse in English. However, those who can speak only English are at a disadvantage when doing business in non-English-speaking countries. Language is an effective method of learning about a country and the customs of its people. Traditionally, U.S. managers have done rather poorly in learning foreign languages and tend to downplay their importance. Executives in Japan, Western Europe, and South America, however, placed a high priority on speaking more than one language, which is often compulsory in their countries from an early age. Prospective expats should show some commitment to foreign language learning if they are to be posted to a non-English speaking country for an extended period of time. Previous study is particularly helpful.

Motivation for a Foreign Posting When evaluating candidates for overseas assignments, a firm also should consider the employee's reasons for wanting to work abroad. Just wanting to work overseas is not sufficient motivation. Individuals must be engaged at work and believe in the significance of the job. Applicants who are unhappy with their current situation and want to get away are less likely to become effective expatriates. Successful expats often will also exhibit openness and a pioneering spirit. Other motivators include the desire to increase one's chances for promotion and the desire to establish the firm in a foreign location. Several large European and U.S. multinationals treat international experience and an understanding of the overseas environment as being critical for promotion to the upper ranks. Even firms with limited international activity have realized that having middle and top managers with international experience on staff is important in case the firm wants to expand its international activities.[xx]

Many expats are also encouraged by extrinsic motivators such as a supplemental wage and benefit package. For example, Lockheed Martin provides expats with housing while in the foreign country, compensation for their children's schooling, trips home each year for the family, as well as a food and expense allowance. As a result, many expatriates are able to save a great deal of money while working for the firm abroad.

Utilizing Expatriates for Foreign Assignments

A key question in the selection process is when to use an expatriate and when to rely on a local employee. The discussion above suggests that expatriates can be relatively expensive in comparison with local employees, especially in emerging economies. But there can be reasons to use a local employee beyond just cost savings (we discuss the pros and cons of hiring local employees later in the chapter). First, however, we examine the benefits and drawbacks of using expatriates.[xxi]

Advantages to Using Expatriates There are distinct advantages to using an expatriate as opposed to a host-country local for a foreign assignment. These include their knowledge of the firm, their loyalty to the firm, and the symbolism for the business.

First, because they have worked for the company in the home country, expatriates are familiar with the company's resources, processes, and values.[xxii] They also have knowledge of the firm's management processes and culture. Expatriates also have a detailed knowledge of company policies, procedures, and corporate culture and how to transfer them to new local hires. Second, using expatriates enables companies to maintain a "foreign image" in the host country which may enhance its legitimacy.[xxiii] This can improve marketing and open doors for the firm. In China, for example, an expatriate may be thought of as having extra expertise, and certainly having a different background and experience than locals. This can come in handy to international firms in knowledge industries such as consulting.[xxiv] The placement of the expatriates also demonstrates the firm's commitment to the international aspects of the business.

Third, allegiance to the firm is another advantage in filling a foreign posting with an expat. The expatriate often is highly loyal to the firm and has many connections within it, in contrast to someone from the local country who may

An expatriate can help establish a firm's commitment to the international aspects of the business, while simultaneously bringing knowledge and experience to the firm's host-country location.

Michael Newman/PhotoEdit

not have worked for the company very long at a high-level position. (This issue is addressed further below.) Thus, using an expatriate enables international firms to select people with proven loyalty to the company (recall the Asimco in China story above). This helps provide credibility at headquarters when the expatriate conveys information, especially information concerning the adaptations the company must make to succeed in the foreign market.[xxv]

Disadvantages of Using Expatriates There are, however, some disadvantages to using expatriates in an international setting. These include the expenses involved, the person's unfamiliarity with local needs, and the inability to adapt.

First, expatriates are expensive. A full expatriate compensation package in an important position that includes salary, benefits and relocation expenses and vacation passage home for the whole family can cost from $300,000 to $1 million annually.[xxvi] This may be one of the biggest HR expenditures a firm has to make, apart from CEO compensation. Adding to the expenses is the fact that the expatriate posting is often unsuccessful, creating additional expenses for the firm in finding a replacement. Research has shown that 10 percent to 20 percent of all U.S. managers sent abroad returned early because of difficulties in adjusting to the foreign country or related job satisfaction. Moreover, many of those who stayed for the duration of the posting did not perform up to their firms' expectations, and many also quit to join a competitor.[xxvii]

These expenses and potential problems mean that training is also important in preparing expatriates before they start their foreign assignment. This is not as much of a problem for large international business enterprises as it is for small and medium-size enterprises (SMEs) that compete in the global arena, because smaller firms often do not have the financial means to establish such programs. Smaller firms can send their expatriate candidates for private training, particularly language training, but this is also costly. Yet without such training, expatriates are more likely to make costly mistakes in conducting business abroad.[xxviii]

Second, the expatriate and/or his or her family may not be particularly motivated to learn about the new culture and may not adapt to it well. This could result in expatriate failure—bringing the expatriate back to the home country early, which as we have seen can end up costing the firm about the equivalent of two years' salary.[xxix] Even when an expatriate is able to adapt, there is still a significant learning curve. Initially, even after going through the training program, the expatriate is still not completely familiar with the subtleties of the local culture, language, laws, and legal processes. People can be taught the formal systems, but informal, tacit knowledge has to be gained through field experience. Lack of such knowledge can hurt performance. Where to buy certain things, whom to call, which government agency needs to be consulted, where the best deals are for products and spare parts, and many other day-to-day details of business can be difficult for expatriates.

Communication problems may amplify some of these problems, and miscommunication is very common. For people in societies that ranked high on performance orientation, such as those in North America, presenting objective information in a direct and explicit way is an important and expected manner of communication, whereas in China, Russia, or other lower-context countries, this type of direct, factual communication may be misunderstood, at least initially. Russia, for example, ranked low on performance orientation, and hard facts and figures are not readily available or taken seriously there. In those cases, a more indirect approach may be better. For instance, if someone in China has made a mistake, an expat from North America may want to use a direct approach and point that mistake out, even in front of other staff. A less direct, more diplomatic approach would be to take that person aside and ask what he or she thought about the problem and how it could have been avoided. While some would find this approach frustratingly slow and sometimes confusing, people from countries ranking lower on Hofstede's production orientation scale prefer such discourse and place a premium on relationships.

Given the 20 percent failure rate in expatriate assignments, firms need to work harder to ensure that those individuals are successful. For example, HRM should establish the selection criteria for the expatriate. Management's involvement ensures that the selection will be based not only on technical know-how but also on acculturation skills. Others outside human resources typically focus on technical skills because the failure of the home-country national on the job is most often directly linked to technical shortcomings.[xxx] But the human resources manager knows that issues such as family can also affect the success of a foreign posting.[xxxi] Thus, it is important to have the human resources manager ensure that a rich set of concerns are incorporated into the selection process.

The firm can help to ease the family's transition into the new environment. The evidence is that most international firms do not take the family into consideration when making assignments. It has been found that prospective expats who were interviewed with their spouses for a job are more likely to succeed than those who were interviewed alone. Previous studies have shown that 70 percent of international firms did not have comprehensive pre-assimilation or preparation training programs.[xxxii] Only short briefings were done, and this has not improved much in recent years.[xxxiii] But such assimilation programs have been shown to be important to the success of the expatriate.

Utilizing Host-Country Employees for Foreign Assigments

Just as with expatriates, there are both benefits and drawbacks to hiring local host-country employees as managers, particularly senior managers. A firm must balance these advantages and disadvantages against those of the expatriate when choosing which to employ in a given country.

Advantages of Using Host-Country Employees Hiring a number of locals, particularly in management positions, can enhance a company's image in the host country and even give it additional bargaining power with the local government. Such locals also know the language and customs and have extensive tacit knowledge about how things are done in that country and region.

First, host-country locals are already familiar with the local language, culture, and customs, so they do not require expensive training in language proficiency or acculturation. The locals also know their way around. They know the government, the financial people, where to buy things, whom to call, and how to get things done. In addition, locals may be productive right away. Unlike expatriates, local employees do not need time to adapt to the local environment and can be productive from the beginning of the assignment if they know their job and the company system. Yet a firm may also need to train them directly. For example, Wal-Mart in China felt that local managers needed time to work with managers from the United States who knew the Wal-Mart system. This is consistent with what professor Morgan McCall has called "selection stressing experience and professional upbringing."[xxxiv] The professional upbringing of the manager suggests where the manager should be placed in the organization and what type of job he or she can best cover.

Another advantage to filling management positions locally in a foreign country is the locals' tacit knowledge. Host-country nationals have important tacit knowledge about idiosyncratic local commercial practices. Host-country nationals understand the subtleties of the local business situation, information that can help establish and maintain a good relationship with customers, clients, government agencies, employees, and the general public. Also, employing host-country nationals is often less expensive than employing home-country or third-country nationals (such as a Malaysian posted to China from an American firm), especially in lower-wage countries. In China, for example, managers are paid salaries and other benefit packages that are only 10 percent to 15 percent of expatriates' or third-country nationals, and no expensive repatriation programs are needed.

Third, having host-country nationals in management positions, especially at higher levels, may enhance the company's reputation in a foreign country that has strong nationalistic or populist movements. It may also enhance host-country employees' morale because these employees may appreciate working for a boss of the same nationality rather than for a foreigner, and they may also appreciate the opportunity for advancement within an organization that employs many local managers and supervisors. Frequently, international firms recruit students from universities located in the region of their foreign plant. For example, Gillette uses the AIESEC student exchange program, and Emerson Electric recruits host country locals right out of local universities in the foreign location. General Electric and Wal-Mart also recruit new management trainees from foreign universities in the country in which they intend to hire. The selector needs to be thoroughly educated about the specific educational institution, its language, and the culture-based courses that it offers to the students who are being selected. The intent is to hire people directly into the firm's system. When it moved into China, Wal-Mart found that local retailers and their employees had a much different view of what retail sales and service meant. Wal-Mart felt that the local retail workforce had learned a number of bad work habits, possibly from years of working in Chinese state-owned enterprises. It decided early on to hire new employees right out of China's universities and inculcate them with Wal-Mart's low-cost and service culture and work ethic. Wal-Mart had some unexpected difficulty early with employee behavior that they did not expect: there was significant employee pilferage and employees regularly took naps during office hours. The latter behavior is not uncommon in state enterprises in mainland China. Wal-Mart dealt quickly to eliminate undesirable behaviors, particularly insisting on no employee naps, even on break times. Wal-Mart has become a preferred place for China's graduates who are interested in retail or service business in general as a result of its training and development programs and excellent reputation in China. In the process of such training, the firm has also developed very good connections with local governments in China.[xxxv] Many Wal-Mart employees have returned to their home towns, bringing back their excellent training in retail to start specialty retail chains. China's retail industry has been transformed in just two decades from a Soviet Union style system of products being locked inside glass cases to a system that looks just like a modern, advanced retail system in Hong Kong, Japan, or the West.

Disadvantages of Using Host-Country Locals There are also some disadvantages to host-country locals, including difficulty finding qualified people, possible mixed loyalties, and lack of understanding of the company's culture and processes.

First, it may be difficult to find qualified people at the local level with the right skills for the assignment, especially in less-developed countries. Currently in China there is much talk of the war for talent among larger firms. There are significant shortages of middle managers in particular.[xxxvi] And it also may be difficult to assess local people's ability. Sometimes a degree or training program in the local country may not be equivalent to what is earned at an internationally recognized institution.

To illustrate, in China some 33 percent of the university students study engineering, compared with 20 percent in Germany and just 4 percent in India. But an engineering program in China can often mean little more than a technical-school training program. Moreover, relative to engineering graduates in Europe and North America, Chinese students get little practical experience in projects or teamwork. The result is that China's pool of young engineers considered suitable for work in multinationals is thought to be just 160,000—much fewer than in America and no larger than that of the United Kingdom.[xxxvii] Shortages of trained personal are now being reported in China, hindering its entrance into information technology and outsourcing service businesses. This is a concern for foreign firms making a new investment in China or any foreign market—the labor market has to be investigated with a local consultant before settling on a suitable location.

Second, the host-country employee's loyalty to his or her country or community may interfere with company policies.[xxxviii] Thus, in settings such as Bolivia or Venezuela, where political leaders are charismatic, nationalistic, and seek to limit the profits of international firms operating in their countries, local managers can prove difficult to manage. Their friends and family are often pressuring them to cooperate with the political leaders, but if they do their actions will hurt their international employers.

To illustrate the issue of loyalty, consider that in China, as in many developing countries, laws and institutions are somewhat underdeveloped, making personal connections especially important for getting things done, particularly in transactions with other organizations and the government. Connections, or *guanxi*, are very important, and foreign firms going to China are tempted to hire those with good *guanxi*. That is generally a good practice, but it must be considered carefully. Sometimes loyalty to an individual goes far beyond company loyalty. One major multinational snack food company hired a senior local sales manager to run its sales efforts in China. That manager had excellent training with another multinational firm, knew many local and regional distributors, and could speak English quite well, which made it easy for him to work with the firm's top management back at the home office. The manager then proceeded to build up the sales staff directly with his own network of contacts, many from his previous firm. In a short time, he had built up this sales force with people who were directly loyal to him, not to the company. The snack foods firm was initially pleased with the swiftness with which the manager built up the sales force and energized sales. Later, however, it came to the firm's attention that he was making personal side deals with distributors he knew to get kickbacks. After being confronted, the sales manager left, and shortly thereafter, so did a majority of the firm's sales force. In the end, the company was left with a huge disruption in sales and a lot of angry distributors, because the sales manager had made all kinds of promises and obligations that the company simply could not honor.[xxxix] As always, hiring must be conducted judiciously.

A third disadvantage is that host-country nationals may not understand the international company's culture and ways of doing things. They may not have sufficient knowledge of the firm's policies and culture, particularly the informal decision-making network back at headquarters, which may differ considerably from the official organizational chart. The attitude towards minorities, women, ethics and the environment, or may be very important to the international firm and its stakeholders, but such values may differ significantly in the host country. Attitudes toward bribery and paying taxes may be more lax in the foreign location. A local manager's talk may be consistent with the international firm's culture but their walk (actions) may often reflect their local cultural orientation or training.

TRAINING

A second major HR function is training. Expatriates must be prepared to assimilate into many different cultures and move globally. Foreign language training is important, but the ability to live and work in another country (and culture) requires a cultural flexibility that comes from studying other countries and cultures and understanding that the way you do things at home may not be the way people do things abroad. A corporation-run training program for the expatriate manager pool is important in preparing expatriate executives for a specific region and to help the expat build that cultural flexibility. Teaching about the region's language, recent history, culture, technical shortcomings in the region are all essential. For top managers, foreign-educated lawyers can explain the laws of the specific region and other subtleties not covered in standard expat training.

ETHICS AND BUSINESS REALITIES

ETHICS

A key part of a firm's culture is its ethics. Firms have taken strong ethical stands in recent years on many issues, including the environment. One such firm is General Electric, which has moved to reduce emissions of greenhouse gases in order to reduce global warming. The $163-billion firm seeks to develop new products that help others reduce carbon dioxide emissions. These products include simple things, such as new lightbulbs, and more complex items, such as new emission equipment for coal-fired utilities. GE has also sought to reduce its own energy usage, and has saved over a $100 million a year in reduced energy costs.

Most controversially, GE has received push-back from customers as it has sought to educate them on carbon emissions or encourage them to change the manner in which they do business. Customers have often responded that they simply want to buy the products, not be lectured to, and GE has had high-profile confrontations with individuals in the energy industry. GE also continues to invest in coal-fired utilities even though they are some of the country's major producers of carbon dioxide.

Despite its high profile in promoting the reduction of greenhouse gases and its leadership in seeking to limit global warming, GE also has its own investment needs. The firm spends considerable efforts seeking to balance these two issues, a problem faced by many similar businesses. Having strong environmental values is good, but ultimately the business needs to make a profit. This balancing of interests can be particularly hard for an international firm as it seeks to employ individuals from a host country. The choices faced are typically not profit or environment related. Instead, it is a nuanced balance that is not easily reached by someone who does not have an understanding of the host country's culture and institutions.[xl]

The results of a major study by international HR scholar Professor Rosalie Tung indicated that nearly 60 percent of the international Japanese firms surveyed sponsored formal training programs for their expatriates. The programs, in general, consist of the following components: language training, general training, field training, graduate programs in a foreign country, in-house training programs, and use of external agents to help the expat. Tung also found that American firms doing business internationally did not invest as much as Japanese firms in such programs, because for American firms employment tends to be short-term—if they invest in an employee's development and he or she leaves, the company will not recapture the costs.[xli] Some firms such as Proctor & Gamble have addressed this problem by establishing a mentor program to help the expatriate manage his or her career progression.

This problem of preparation may have improved in recent years, partly because of the attitudes and (self) preparation of expats themselves. For example, in a recent study, Tung noted that many expatriates (including a large number of Americans) were quite successful in navigating their international postings and returning back to their home country with intact career paths. She hypothesized that this stemmed from a more cosmopolitan outlook of the new expatriate class in America and other Western countries. Many had learned one or two additional languages through their own study, and had worked or studied overseas, sometimes multiple times and for extended periods of time. An implication of the research is that including regular language study and exchange programs or extended trips overseas when possible can help you to be better prepared to live and work abroad.[xlii]

APPRAISAL AND COMPENSATION

The third important facet of HR is the appraisal and compensation process. One aspect of compensation was covered in Chapter 7 on motivation. More detail is addressed in this section.

Appraisal

Performance appraisal can be defined as a systematic and periodic review of employee performance, normally on an annual basis. The basic purpose of employee evaluations is to build better-performing organizations and to aid in the professional development of employees. Proper appraisal is an important step to properly motivating and compensating an employee while maintaining a degree of pay equity within the organization. There are several types of performance appraisal. The more common approaches to performance appraisal are summarized below.

The Written Essay This method of employee evaluation involves a manager writing an essay about what he or she considers to be an overall assessment of an employee's performance. It is important to note that nothing obligates the manager to justify anything within the assessment. A second variation has the manager rating an employee using a list of terms such as "above average," "fair," or "poor" on key performance criteria that the firm wants to encourage. This approach is useful because managers subjectively choose evaluation criteria that they think can describe their performance fairly; a certain evaluation criterion can highlight one key aspect of an employee's performance that would have been missed by most other criteria. But this method's subjectivity can deny the firm reliable feedback about employee performance. Evaluations that include further explanation and commentary on performance can help employees to eliminate mistakes and improve their performance.

A second approach is the **trait rating** appraisal. With this method, a list of personality traits and job attitudes important to the job is created and the supervisor must assign a numerical or descriptive rating of the employee's performance. Traits may include items such as cooperation, motivation, flexibility, and attitudes. This approach assumes that one can define and rate traits objectively, and it is often used in conjunction with written feedback or, if available, direct productivity measures. For example, Lincoln Electric has a letter grading system (A, B, C, etc.) of employee traits, behaviors, and attitudes such as teamwork to help form the basis for that employee's annual bonus. A number of banks in East Asia use this approach, including HSBC and Hang Seng Bank in Hong Kong. This system has been successfully implemented in several countries—even those countries thought of as more collective or less production oriented such as Mexico. Some critics argue, however, that, in practice, traits are too broadly defined, as are the criteria for evaluating each trait, or the system is too open to favoritism—perhaps the boss has a favorite trait in mind such as an extraverted or exuberant personality. An introverted person might get a lower evaluation (and raise) at the end of the year based in part on that one trait. One way to combat this problem of fairness is to use **360 degree evaluations**, that is, evaluations by the supervisor, coworkers, subordinates, and even customers or clients outside the immediate work area. This adds a reliability check to see if the manager is treating his or her subordinates well or is pushing them too hard to achieve a performance bonus. If the traits necessary to succeed are well understood in a job, the trait rating approach can work well.

360-degree evaluations
Evaluations of an employee conducted by the supervisor, subordinates, peers, and sometimes customers.

A third approach to appraisal is the **critical incident approach**, which focuses the evaluator's attention on those tasks and behaviors that are key in making the difference between executing a job effectively and executing it ineffectively. The critical incident approach was first popularized in the U.S. and German militaries around World War II with after-action reports describing leaders' and units' behavior under different situations, the successes and failure that occurred, and how problems could be fixed going forward.[xliii] This method was initially used both to transmit knowledge to the rest of the military about what went right and what did not and how an officer in question performed. Critical incidents are important to the military because these are very important to understanding an action's outcome as well as to the overall organizational learning and memory as incidents are recorded and codified into record for future use. For example, salespeople can find out what worked (and what did not) for other salespeople in the past. Marketers can learn about past promotions in an emerging economy such as China and therefore what might be expected to work well in India or Russia, for example.

The critical incident approach to appraisal has since filtered down from the military to organizations in government and the private sector, both large and small.[xliv] A supervisor using this approach will document the employee's on-the-job behaviors in important situations, designating each behavior or incident as either unsatisfactory or satisfactory and then comparing the frequency of satisfactory incidents to unsatisfactory ones. The degree of objectivity can vary depending on the appraiser and what different appraisers view as critical incidents. Managers need to ensure they have sufficient quantity and quality of employee observational opportunities. This can work well with jobs that are otherwise difficult to quantify, and when the supervisor doing the appraising has worked in that particular job and understands what it takes to do well. It is also helpful in that critical incidents are well codified and employee actions debriefed and analyzed.

A fourth approach is called the **behaviorally anchored rating scales (BARS)**. The BARS approach uses the constituents of critical incidents along with graphic rating scales. BARS uses careful job analysis to determine the behaviors required for a particular job. BARS measures behavioral performance factors rather than personality or attitudinal factors on a scale, for example from one to five or from best to worst. For any particular job, BARS involves identifying the complete range of relevant job behaviors and designing appropriate performance dimensions for that job. Southwest Airlines developed a BARS system for its employees based on the most successful and least successful employees in different jobs with the airline. Southwest hires and trains based on these scales and also carries out evaluations guided in part by employee performance on these behaviors. Firms often ask an experienced HR professional to help identify the best performers and worst performers in various jobs in the company, as well as the key behaviors that they are evaluated on. BARS can work well when a job's tasks are well understood and performance can be measured in quantitative terms.

A fifth approach to employee performance appraisal is **managing by objective**, or **MBO**. First popularized by longtime management scholar Peter Drucker, MBO is a process that involves management and employees agreeing to key goals and ways in which they can be reached. MBO was devised as a method of incorporating performance planning into performance appraisal. The manager, or manager and employee together, decides which goals must be achieved by the employee. Consistent with goal-setting theory, goals are connected to a time schedule, are specific and measurable, and become the measure of the employee's performance. Typically, the goals are established at the beginning of an appraisal period and measured at the end of it. Objectives can be set in all domains of activities (production, services, sales, R&D, customer satisfaction, peer review, finance, information systems, and so forth). Objectives can be collective for a whole department or the whole company, or individualized. A system of MBO appraisal can also incorporate other rating systems. MBO employs the principle from goal-setting theory that employees are more likely to accomplish goals that they set themselves or to which they jointly agree. It is argued that MBO-style management and appraisal can trigger employees' unethical behavior by encouraging them to meet goals in any manner possible, such as distorting financial figures to achieve their agreed-upon targets. MBO is also thought to encourage short-term, overly narrow bottom-line mindsets, neglecting innovation and longer-term thinking.[xlv] It is important to remember that, as we saw in Chapter 7, goals work best when they are negotiated with the employee and made public.

Additional Organizational Applications

One of the more novel, though controversial, approaches to appraisal that has appeared in recent years is a variation of the written essay evaluation system. This system of **employee differentiation** was popularized by Jack Welch, the former CEO of General Electric, and it "force ranks" employees into three categories based on what is generically called a vitality curve. In the GE system, there is the top 20 percent, the middle (or "vital") 70 percent, and the bottom 10 percent. This system of appraisal, in which a supervisor typically provides a written evaluation with a ranking, has generated a great deal of debate. Proponents of the forced ranking claim that it is more effective than most qualitative systems for employee appraisal in which employees do not receive honest and specific appraisals because managers are not willing to give them, nor are they incentivized to provide such feedback. They point out that in the most common evaluation systems, managers give most employees a good rating; even low performers receive an "okay." [xlvi] The GE system forces managers to write frank appraisals that can help employees who are not performing well. This system may even reduce lawsuits because the poorly performing employees are fired or transferred after multiple performance warnings. Too often, forced rank proponents argue, poor employees receive acceptable ratings until some critical instance occurs and they are fired without a proper trail of poor evaluations to support such an action.

Opponents of the GE system claim that it hurts teamwork and innovation. They add that it is possible to build teamwork and innovation ratings into performance evaluations to make sure employees are not just stressing personal, individual performance. Others add that such an individual achievement-oriented system would not work well in egalitarian countries such as Sweden or collective societies such as Japan.[xlvii] Welch responds that the differentiation or forced rank system works because mediocre-performing employees improve their performance. Or they move to a different part of the firm and find tasks they can do better and may prefer—something that is very consistent with advice from career scholars as well, that is, try to find work that you enjoy and are good at.[xlviii]

What does the empirical research say about GE's system of employee differentiation or forced ranking? The limited research on forced ranking systems suggests that they produce a short-term improvement in overall division and group performance that fairly quickly levels off, perhaps because the worst performers are removed in a timely fashion. Although former GE boss Welch swears by forced ranking and contends that it has helped GE and other companies considerably in overall performance and management development, others complain about the harmful competition it creates among employees. Some add that forced ranking injects fear into the workplace. When Southwest Airlines began to experiment in ways to develop more accurate metrics for individual employee performance, it found

There are many methods available for evaluating an employee's performance.

Dynamic Graphics/Creatas/Jupiter Images

the forced ranking system emphasized blame for mistakes for the bottom 10 percent and produced more nonproductive competition. Perhaps while such a model initially may be accurate—10 percent of employees are probably underperforming and need to be replaced or assigned other tasks—after each iteration the average quality of employees will increase, at which point the forced ranking system will start to kick out good performers. These adequately performing managers will be fired or moved to other jobs, and the department or company will lose good employees.

Motorola, Microsoft, and many consulting firms, accounting firms, and law firms use a variation of the force ranking system to eliminate the worst performers. Welch has commented that one of the most asked questions he gets in his talks around the world is about GE's forced rating system. The usual argument is that the forced rating system would not work in a society that is low on individuality (like China), or high on the relational scale (like in Latin America), or even more egalitarian (like Sweden). Welch usually answers by suggesting that the questioner try the method out in part of his or her firm, much like Lincoln Electric's application of their reward system in Mexico (discussed in Chapter 7). Experimenting with the system in a limited way will allow a firm to see how it works without exposing the whole company to major change.

A key question a firm must ask is what is the objective of the review itself. Is it to identify and transfer out poor performers? Is the firm seeking to recognize the best managers and employees? Does the firm want to provide the basis for compensation decisions or promotion? Alternatively, is it a tool to plan for personal development? Perhaps the firm wants some aspect of all of these goals. Too often it is unclear what a firm wants in changing to employee differentiation. But for the system to be effective, the objective needs to be specified by the organization and communicated to employees. As with the old adage "What gets measured is what gets done," it is essential for an organization to give managers direction about the purpose of the performance appraisal, whether or not it's a forced ranking system or a basic verbal feedback.

How often should reviews be conducted? W. Edwards Deming, the famed quality guru introduced earlier in the book, argued that reviews should be held regularly, not just once a year but more often, with feedback provided either in written or verbal form, and that there should be no surprises. Imagine if a football coach waited six months before giving the players feedback! When a player makes a mistake, coaches talk to that player about it right away and explain why it was a mistake. In the same way, for short-term reviews verbal feedback is usually sufficient. For longer-term reviews, written feedback and grading schemes are helpful. Employees can be graded on their production, but also on quality control, checks and balances like teamwork, attention to quality, coaching of other employees, and so forth. Firms can base regular pay on productivity, measuring individual work or team work, but bonuses and other rewards often come from the grading schemes. At Cleveland-based manufacturer Lincoln Electric, straight-A performers in several graded categories of performance (such as teamwork and attendance) can receive sizeable bonuses, often amounting to tens of thousands of dollars. Employees report that the annual bonus is the best and most motivating part of their jobs. Lincoln's incentive and HRM system has led to a history of industry-leading productivity and employee compensation innovations, which have helped to keep Lincoln Electric a worldwide leader in the production of welding equipment and among American leaders in manufacturing productivity.

Compensation

Working hand in hand with the appraisal system is the key human resource function of compensation. We discussed compensation at a general level in Chapter 7 on motivation and go into additional detail here. A central part of the compensation decision an international firm must make is whether to establish an overall policy for all employees or to distinguish among home-country nationals (expatriates), host-country locals, and third-country nationals. It is common for international business to distinguish between expatriates and locals. Thus, an expatriate petroleum engineer may be doing a similar function to the local petroleum engineer in Indonesia, for example, but the expatriate would be paid much more for the work. It is quite common for most firms to also distinguish between types of expatriates. For example, different policies may be set on the basis of length of assignment or on the type of function to be carried out.[xlix] In all cases, the policy should be based on the idea that the expatriate must not suffer a loss because of his or her transfer. Furthermore, the approach selected should not demoralize the foreign subsidiary's staff; for instance, significant and overly visible pay inequity between the expatriate and his or her local peers can create bad feelings and undermine morale, so firms should be careful to consider equity issues carefully.[l]

This does not mean that everyone should be paid the same. Even egalitarian countries expect some pay inequity, and research shows that an optimal amount of pay inequity is when the top earner in a division earns about fifty times the lowest (regular) employee pay.[li] As discussed in Chapter 7, it has sometimes been argued that an aggressive pay-for-performance scheme will be rejected out of hand for cultural reasons by countries with a lower production orientation, such as Mexico or by highly collective cultures, such as China. Years ago a number of books and articles on international business warned business people against introducing such "American systems" into foreign cultures. After nearly 30 years of evidence on appraisal schemes in Mexico, China, and other countries, it has turned out that pay-for-performance appraisal schemes with a heavy variable component were in fact not failures but were well received if implemented carefully, even if they were for individual-based incentive schemes.[lii] One of the most radical piecework systems, developed by manufacturer Lincoln Electric, was never expected to be accepted in Mexico, as noted in Chapter 7. Variations have since been accepted in China and other countries. You will recall that Lincoln did not initially introduce the scheme, instead at first appraising and paying employees with a traditional salary structure. But Lincoln slowly introduced the scheme, giving workers the choice of being included in it. Lincoln's Mexican workers gradually saw that those who got into the piecework scheme were earning more money, and more clamored to join. After only about two years, Lincoln's compensation scheme had been fully implemented in their Mexican plant. The social proof of the successful piecework system, as noted in Chapter 10, had a more powerful impact in influencing Lincoln's Mexican employees than did any cultural propensity toward an egalitarian and relational workplace. The Mexican employees watched a few of their colleagues do the work and make extra money, and they decided they could do the same, opting for pay for performance also. Similarly in China, individual piecework schemes have been widely and successfully implemented in spite of warnings from some culture writers and anthropologists to give only group incentives in this collective culture. Fortunately, theorizing has given way to solid empirical evidence, and firms are introducing individual incentives in jobs where they make the most sense, such as light manufacturing, sales, and marketing. For jobs for which group incentives make more sense, such as an airline crew working together to get a plane off safely and on time, group incentives are often more convenient and effective.[liii] This suggests that the nature of the job is more important in formulating the compensation system than the local culture. It also suggests that people respond to incentives and positive feedback in much the same way all around the world, although the implementation of a compensation system may necessarily be different (and more deliberate) in countries less accustomed to pay for performance and individual rewards.

Compensation policies seek to satisfy numerous objectives.[liv] In the case of expatriates, for example, the compensation policy should be consistent and fair in its treatment of all categories of expatriate employees. The policy must work to attract and retain expatriates in the areas where the corporation has the greatest need. It should also be consistent with the organization's overall strategy and structure, and should serve to motivate employees and provide incentives where needed.

It has been estimated that, on average, expatriates cost employers two to five times as much as corresponding home-country employees, and even more in some lower-wage countries.[lv] There are a number of key aspects to developing the compensation of an expatriate if the firm chooses to place such employees in a foreign environment. These include benefits, base salary, allowances, and tax treatment.

Ineffective expatriate compensation plays a big role in the failure of expatriate assignments. Therefore, international firms need to establish policies for careful and effective management of expatriate compensation. To do so requires that the firm have knowledge of the foreign country's laws, customs, environment, and employment practices, as well as an understanding of the effects of currency exchange fluctuations and inflation on compensation. Within the context of changing political, economic, and social conditions, establishing policy also requires an understanding of why certain allowances are necessary. Recall (from Chapter 7) that pay equity is also a concern. For example, in most of Europe executive pay will be much lower than in the United States. So in asking a U.S. executive to move to a European subsidiary, the executive's pay package will likely be higher than that of their European colleagues. To avoid equity concerns with the European staff, sometimes a portion of the U.S. executive's pay can be in the form of benefits, such as payments for children's schooling, housing benefits, home travel, travel for families, and so forth, which seems to be acceptable to local staff. These sorts of expatriate benefits can be better justified or framed in terms of the expatriate having to work in a foreign country and facing higher expenses, and inequities based on benefits sometimes sit better with the local staff.[lvi]

An assignment in a difficult environment, such as much of Africa, would require greater compensation than an assignment to a more developed environment like Western Europe. A 25 percent hardship allowance is common for more difficult postings. Companies will pay, but only upon completion of the assignment. If the expatriate wants to come home earlier or be transferred, he or she will forfeit the allowance. Figure 12-3 lists the highest and lowest ranking hardship locations for expats.

Base Salary   International firms tend to use the home-country national's home salary as a base to determine expatriate compensation. **Base salary** is the amount of money that an expatriate normally receives in the home country. In the United States, this has been around $175,000 for upper-level middle managers in recent years, and this

Base salary
Amount of money that an expatriate normally receives in the home country.

FIGURE 12-3   Hardship Rankings of Cities for Expatriates*

5 Highest in Hardship, Requiring Greater Employee Compensation	5 Lowest in Hardship
1) Moscow, Russia 2) Almaty, Kazakhstan 3) Kinshasa, Zaire 4) Beijing and Shanghai, China 5) New Delhi and Mumbai, India	1) Buenos Aires, Argentina 2) Hong Kong, China 3) Budapest, Hungary 4) Dubai, United Arab Emirates 5) Sao Paulo/Rio de Janeiro, Brazil
	◆ All North American cities tied for sixth.

*Criteria: security, sociopolitical tension, housing, and climate.

Sources: ExpansionManagement.com. (1998). Warning: Living in the U.S. may cause culture shock. http://www.expansionmanagement.com/cmd/articledetail/articleid/l4811/default.asp (website accessed December 4, 2008); Bensimon, H. F. (1998). Is it safe to work abroad? *Training & Development* 52(8), 20–24.

rate is similar to that paid to managers in both Japan and Germany. Exchange rates, of course, also affect the real wages. Therefore, a German manager working for a U.S. firm but assigned to Spain would have a base salary that reflects the salary structure in Germany. Expatriates from the United States have salaries tied to U.S. pay levels. Salaries usually are paid in home currency, local currency, or a combination of the two. Base pay also serves as the benchmark against which bonuses and benefits are calculated. Expats posted to countries with volatile currencies should ask the company about getting paid at least partially in the home currency. Firms should be sensitive to the possibility of currency fluctuation and maintaining their expatriate employees' compensation levels in terms of the home currency.

Conditions that force compensation policies to differ from those used for home-country expatriates include inflation and cost of living, housing, security, school costs, and taxation. Furthermore, home-country expatriates often require a salary premium as an inducement to accept the foreign assignment or to endure the hardships of a foreign transfer. In the United States, when an international business enterprise has determined the type of hardship, it can refer to the U.S. State Department's *Hardship Post Differentials Guidelines* to ascertain the appropriate level of premium compensation.

The practice of international businesses paying a higher salary to expatriate managers than to host-country managers (or even managers from a third country) can discourage local managers, especially when they have an equal level of responsibility and workload. International firms must determine how to deal effectively with such inequities, as discussed in Chapter 7. Some believe that international firms should have a standard global policy relating to compensation; that is, regardless of the varying costs of living, all of the corporation's managers in all countries should be compensated on the basis of a standard global salary range based on the level of authority and responsibility. This policy, of course, is debatable and difficult to implement. Most companies will pay based on what the local market will bear, and what managers and professionals expect to be paid.

Allowances and Benefits As noted earlier in this chapter, international businesses generally pay expatriates certain allowances. These include cost-of-living, housing, education, and relocation allowances. Cost-of-living allowances pay the expatriate for differences in expenses between the home and foreign country. Housing allowances help the expatriate maintain his or her home-country living standards. Education allowances ensure that the expatriate's children will receive at least as good an education as they would receive in the home country. Relocation allowances usually pay for moving, shipping, and storage expenses, temporary living expenses, and other related expenses.[1]

Another important part of an employee's compensation package is the benefits provided. Approximately one-third of compensation for regular employees in the United States consists of benefits. These benefits make up a similar, or even larger, portion of expatriate compensation. Additionally, most international firms provide expatriates with extra vacation and special leaves. The international firm typically will pay the airfare for expatriates and their families to make an annual visit home, for emergency leave, and for expenses when a relative in the home country is sick.

Taxation For the expatriate, a foreign assignment can mean being double-taxed, by the home-country and the foreign-country governments. This problem is mitigated in the United States by an income exclusion of about $80,000, and by the United States having a reciprocal agreement with some countries whereby an expatriate would pay taxes only in the United States and not the host country. International firms are subject to varying tax rates around the globe. Rates are different from country to country, and they change within countries from time to time. For example, the

TRANSNATIONAL CORPORATIONS AND HRM

The nature of transnational corporations raises many interesting human resource management problems. For example, when a worldwide organization is heavily integrated it can be expected to have managers who will travel extensively. The advent of communications technologies, such as email, has helped firms easily keep in touch, but there is still a critical need to be on location. Conversations between people have a richness that cannot occur through email. Similarly, when there are problems or special projects, people are needed on site.

Transnational corporations are facing increasing problems with monitoring employee tax liability as employees are asked to spend more time abroad. You normally pays taxes in your home country; simply visiting another country for business or pleasure does not create any new tax liability. Most countries, however, now have length-of-stay laws that require expats to pay local taxes if they spend most of your working time within their borders. For example, Britain requires expats to pay taxes if they spend three months or more working there. Transnational corporations with active businesses or a regional headquarters in Britain often have employees who have spent enough time in Britain to be liable for British taxes.

Increasingly, transnational corporations must actively track the countries where their employees are working and how much time they are spending in any given country because it is easy to become liable for taxation. A firm has a duty to help the government obtain the taxes it is owed through withholdings. If a country can prove that a firm or its employees avoided paying taxes required by length-of-stay laws, the firm (and the employee) can be in for some penalties and legal difficulties.[lvii]

current maximum marginal tax rate for those working in Hong Kong is about 16 percent, versus about 35 percent in the United States. In practice this means an American expat in Hong Kong will pay about 16 percent in taxes on about the first $80,000 of income, and then at the higher, U.S. rate above that. A firm's compensation packages must consider how specific compensation practices can be adjusted in each country to provide, within the context of the corporation's overall policy, the most tax-effective, appropriate rewards for expatriate, host-country, and third-country managers.

SOCIALIZATION

The last of the main human resource functions is socialization. This function contains two parts. First is the need to socialize local hires into the company culture. This occurs with careful selection and training. For example, as mentioned earlier, Wal-Mart has emphasized hiring new employees right out of university, before they have the opportunity to learn any other ways of doing business, thereby inculcating their service and cost-control culture in employees who may have never shopped in a Wal-Mart.

The second type of socialization is essentially an acculturation of the expatriate to the local environment. As we have seen before, this can be a difficult process. In recent years, the vast majority (86 percent) of Japanese multinational firms recalled 5 percent or less of their expatriates. In contrast, only a quarter of U.S. international firms recalled expatriates at that same low rate, while another quarter of firms had to recall expats at a much higher rate.[lviii] The Japanese home-country headquarters provides more comprehensive training and employee support than many U.S. firms provide for their expatriates, as well as better guidance from Japanese expatriates who are established in the region already.[lix] U.S. nationals have traditionally been less successful than the nationals of Japanese firms in expatriate assignments, although there is evidence that this is changing as U.S. nationals get more international exposure and American firms gain more experience and benefit from the services of very experienced organizations such as the U.S. State Department.[lx]

ADDITIONAL CHALLENGES FACING EXPATRIATES IN INTERNATIONAL POSTINGS

Some disadvantages of using expatriates were discussed above. In addition, expatriates face many challenges for which they must be prepared. Firms can help, at minimum, by providing some briefing on these problems and by providing training when possible. These include the foreign country's physical and social environments, varying technical sophistication, conflicting objectives and policies between the country and the firm, pitfalls in the human resource planning function, and inadequate repatriation programs.

Physical Environment

Expatriates often encounter adaptation problems caused by both the physical and the sociocultural environments, especially when these environments differ significantly from the expatriate's home environment. For example, geographical distance may result in a type of separation anxiety for expatriates and family members.[lxi] Sometimes the food and weather are much different than in the home country. For example, for someone from southern Europe coming to a Midwestern U.S. state like Michigan or Minnesota, it is important that their preparation include instruction on how to deal with the snow. Otherwise, the first eight-inch snowfall with subfreezing temperatures will be a rude introduction to their new home. Japanese people accustomed to living in very safe cities must be briefed on which neighborhoods of North American cities to stay out of. The first expatriates to China during its early reform period were similarly surprised and ill-prepared by China's lack of basic services, even in the capital of Beijing. For example, accounting people from American Motors's home office could not understand why their expatriate staff in Beijing were spending so much on hotel laundry services, and asked the expatriate staff why they didn't take their clothes to a laundromat. The China expatriates replied that there were no laundromats anywhere in Beijing, and hardly any small professional service businesses of any kind, for that matter.[lxii] The accountants had assumed since there were numerous Chinese-owned laundries in North America, China itself must also have a large number of them, which was not the case.

Social Environment

The social environment can present another major problem for expatriates and their families. The problem can start with language. If an expatriate and his or her family are not capable of communicating in the local language, it can create difficulties. Work difficulties will be most apparent because the expatriate must do everything through interpreters. This makes it harder to build rapport with employees, and translation problems are rife. The expatriate manager may also need to have his or her own interpreter (as opposed to the locally hired one) to be sure that things are being translated accurately. This becomes more challenging if the local language is difficult to read and learn. For example, China and Japan both use a pictograph language that originated in an early Chinese dynasty over 3,000 years ago, although Japan also employs phonetic scripts along with Chinese characters.[lxiii] There are tens of thousands of different Chinese characters, which makes learning these languages rather difficult for most expatriates. These language problems will affect expatriates' ability to deal with individuals and business groups outside the organization, including local partners, bankers, unions, suppliers, and customers, which in turn can hamper the expatriates' effectiveness.[lxiv] Given that the language of international business is now overwhelmingly English, most expatriates do not need to be fluent in the language of the host country. Nevertheless, it is helpful to learn some of the local language, even a difficult language such as Chinese or Thai, and to have translation readily available, especially from translators loyal to the company.[lxv]

Lack of Adequate Training for Foreign Assignments

Many large firms in North America spend little time preparing employees for foreign assignments. Most of the firms that sponsor training programs use environmental briefing programs only. This type of briefing that gives background on the country, its climate, culture, and other basic information, is helpful, but it should be accompanied by contact with individuals familiar with the local environment in the foreign country, preferably other expatriates who have lived there. The adoption of more rigorous training programs could significantly improve the expatriate's performance in an overseas environment, thus minimizing the incidence of failure.[lxvi]

However, changing the behavior of experienced managers could pose a challenging task for a company's training system. First, expatriates without a background in business or psychology, such as more technical staff, generally may not believe in such training. Those conducting the training must bear in mind that the relevance of the training and preparation must be shown to the trainees through specific cases and scenarios; that is, they must not only tell people about the culture but also show how understanding it can help them. If potential expatriates fail to grasp this, the resulting lack of cultural savvy is likely to cause a lot of trouble down the road.[lxvii]

Second, many expatriates believe that the way things are done in their home country is the way to do it and that the HR people and the overseas staff do not know how to handle things properly. If such an expatriate has been highly successful in the past, it may be hard for that person to listen to advice about ways to behave, and the trainer may expect defensive behavior when explaining what to do and how the expatriate may need to change. For instance, consider an executive from the United States who insists on giving his prospective mainland Chinese partners a hug upon greeting them, something that generally makes Chinese people uncomfortable. Or one who calls on the Chinese partners by name during a presentation and insists they answer a question even though they clearly look uncomfortable and do not look able to give an answer. It is important to understand that executives from China and much of Asia typically do not like physical contact, and that gestures such as finger-pointing or singling people out in meetings can be seen overly aggressive or even rude. Expatriates and foreign employees alike should be briefed on cultural differences such as these before the assignment, even if they are initially reluctant and skeptical of such training.

Third, their workload in the midst of preparation for their transfer may not leave expatriates sufficient time for an intensive training program. Even something as basic as language training and communication skills may get neglected. Even if the expatriate does not have time for any language training, the problems of translation must be made clear—mistranslations and miscommunication with locals in foreign assignments are all too common.

Communication Challenges Communication and speaking style is something that firms can coach expatriates on (or any employees dealing extensively with the firm's foreign employees), and it is enormously important to do so. Consider communication problems that have nothing to do with language fluency but concern the use of terms, topics, and expressions. For example, many Americans regularly refer to local events that are familiar and of interest to Americans but are unfamiliar and uninteresting to the rest of the world. Many people in the world have little interest in American politics and do not find repeated references to U.S. politicians, issues, and elections particularly meaningful or interesting. And regardless of what country you may be from, the excessive use of slang and local-interest items in speaking to foreigners can be a problem—a problem that you should try to prevent if you would like to work internationally.

To address this, start with a simple exercise: try listening carefully to the conversations of your friends. Do they use a lot of slang terms? Do they give explanations in terms of local references and stories that would be unfamiliar to foreigners? For example, an American referring to "late in the fourth quarter" (an expression from North American football or basketball meaning near the end of the game) would elicit blank stares from many people from outside of North America. We once heard a Canadian speaker in Hong Kong talk about not arguing with "the ump." He was talking about the umpire in baseball (equivalent to the referee in basketball), but hardly anyone in the room understood what "ump" meant and the point was lost. Try to be aware of those sorts of expressions and remove them from your daily speech when talking to foreigners, unless you have time to explain them as you go along (which means you need to be aware of them in the first place). Removing such expressions from your speech takes a lot of time and effort, and it is helpful to practice doing so before interviewing for an international assignment because firms will be watching for this, especially if your job requires much speaking, presenting, or training in the foreign country. Of course, using home-country references is less of a concern if you speak the local language well, but it is important to remember that many expatriate assignments entail meeting people from many different foreign countries. If you are in a meeting and talking to people from Japan, China, Pakistan, and Malaysia, you will be speaking English, and all the above rules about slang and avoiding overly local (to you) content and references apply.[lxviii] And remember to be patient. If a person from another country does not seem to understand what you are saying the first time, *do not just say the same thing again more loudly.* Explain it or ask your question in a different way. Do not give up too easily; getting your points across clearly and appropriately to foreigners is a key part of the skill set you develop as an expatriate. Figure 12-4 gives some examples of basic communications problems to avoid.

A formal training exercise entails having the expatriate being trained speak to a trainer (or a colleague) who identifies all the slang and potentially unclear expressions being used. It is surprising once you hear yourself speak how much slang and otherwise unclear or ambiguous phrases emerge from your speech. In preparing for an international assignment, practice using more common words

---

FIGURE 12-4   Common Communication Problems to Avoid

1. Use more common words and phrases (i.e., say "Go by bus," not "Take the bus" or "Develop in a different market" not "Incubate in a remote market").
2. If people do not understand the first time, do not just say the same thing again, more loudly. *Explain it a different way.*
3. Use props and common frames of reference when possible (stories the listeners will be aware of), use time words—tenses present a problem in many languages.
4. Try to avoid slang. Do you know what "Do not throw my airplane" means? Probably not, unless you are from Hong Kong. It means "Do not stand me up," but if you are not from North America, you probably do not recognize that expression either, hence the problem with using slang. Both expressions mean the same thing: "Do not miss our meeting (or date) and leave me waiting somewhere." If you use those expressions around people unfamiliar with them, your idea will be missed completely.
5. Avoid sports-related terms and other local references that only people from your country or region would understand.
6. Learn local conversational rituals such as what people say when they greet each other. North Americans commonly say, "How are you?" Chinese will ask, "Have you eaten yet?" These are both simply ways of saying hello.

and phrases. For example, it is probably better to say "go by plane" and not "take the plane" (which sounds to some non-English speakers like you want to carry the plane somewhere), or "develop in a different market" as opposed to "incubate in a remote market." Slang like "to the tune of" or "Does this ring a bell?" or "It's not over till the fat lady sings" are also difficult to understand for foreigners not familiar with English slang. (Think about those expressions and what they mean literally.)

In training for an expatriate assignment or simply in dealing with people who are not fluent speakers of English, it is important to practice critical listening skills: pay attention to the actual words you and others are using and make sure they are appropriate and easily understandable. Expats should be sure to learn local conversational rituals such as what people say when they greet each other. North Americans commonly ask, "How are you?" This is simply a way of saying hello; they are not asking for a medical report. Chinese will ask, "Have you eaten yet?" Sometimes westerners misunderstand that this is a simple greeting, taking it to mean that the Chinese person is asking them to go to lunch or dinner. But like "How are you," it is simply a greeting. Many people from the Philippines will ask, "Where are you going?" To many people this question seems intrusive. But once again, it is just a way of saying hello, and is not to be taken literally. Expats should pay attention to other common conversation rituals such as how to ask for favors, or how to thank people for help, because these rituals help smooth conversations and allow work to get done.[lxix] Though it takes persistence and time to become accustomed to using plain words and terminology, most people can modify their speech simply by paying attention to what they are saying and avoiding certain words or phrases that are likely to be understood. Be patient and make note of the words and expressions that people do not typically understand in the country you are working in, and remove them from your speech.

Technical Sophistication

Expatriates often encounter differences in technical sophistication in the foreign country, a problem that conflicts with their expectations. A key problem for expatriates occurs when they attempt to apply successful home-country managerial and organizational principles in the foreign country. The expatriate may experience considerable frustration because differences in the local culture may make implementation of a new technology or technique more difficult. For example, some countries' firms have shown much reluctance to spend money on indigenizing technology, which occurs after a machine is purchased, when the firm spends additional money on training, maintenance, complementary technologies to make the original one work better, and any modifications to the technology.[lxx] This can prove a source of frustration to an expatriate who may be accustomed to high technology, but it is to be expected when working in developing economies.

Parent Objectives and Policies

Expatriate managers also encounter difficulties because they are responsible for implementing objectives and policies formulated by the home office. Problems can occur when these objectives and policies conflict with the managerial situation experienced by the expatriate manager and with the mandates imposed on him or her by the central government or local officials.[lxxi] That is, the expatriate manager must conduct the foreign operations within constraints imposed by the home office, local laws, and government officials. In many countries there is a great deal of corruption, and officials expect payments to expedite transactions. Much like the Chinese anti-corruption official mentioned in the opening case example, they may expect payments to do their jobs or to speed them up. Most countries, including the United States, now allow for companies to make facilitation payments to speed up a process for which a government official is already legitimately responsible. As noted in Chapter 2 on ethics and corruption, it is important for expatriates to learn what their firm policy and home country laws allow them to do in this regard.[lxxii]

A key problem can occur when a firm centralizes decision making and gives little decision power to the foreign subsidiary. If the expatriate manager's authority is visibly constrained, his or her opportunity to establish and maintain an effective relationship with locals may be reduced. This is especially true in foreign locales where there is high power distance such as in India. If the expatriate manager lacks authority and does not take charge, his or her standing with the host country employees can be harmed.

Family

Another challenge for expatriates is keeping the family happy.[lxxiii] The inability of the expatriate's family to adapt to living and working in the foreign country is a major cause of expatriate failure. Spouses, for example, may not be able to work and can feel isolated, particularly when language and customs are very different. This creates stress for the expatriate's family members, who then create problems for the expatriate, which in turn can result in on-the-job failure. The spouse is the one who has to stay at home and deal with managing the home and dealing with delivery people and repairmen, who in most foreign countries are unlikely to speak much English.

Professor Tung found that the majority of the respondents in a survey of personnel administrators indicated that they recognized the importance of family to successful performance in a foreign assignment, yet few U.S. MNCs actually took it into consideration in the selection decision, and that this problem has persisted over the years.[lxxiv] The U.S. multinationals that interviewed both candidates and spouses to determine suitability for foreign assignments experienced significantly lower incidents of expensive expatriate failure than those that did not. Companies need to be sensitive to these problems and provide some support to help expatriates with the transition. A spouse who does not like the country and demands to leave is a very common reason for the failure of expatriate assignments.

Other Sociocultural Issues in Human Resources Management

Several other sociocultural issues may be present that managers and expatriates must be aware of. These include the societies' power distance, the position of women, and general climate. As we saw in the Chapter 2 discussion on culture, power distance can create a problem for Western expatriates working in high power-distance countries such as East Asia, India, and the Middle East. People are usually addressed more formally in these countries, and titles are important, as is one's position in the organizational hierarchy. To communicate with a colleague high in an organization in a high power-distance society, an expatriate may have to speak through an intermediary, such as that colleague's assistant or secretary, something that might make North Americans or Australians uncomfortable. Another problem is cultural resistance to expatriate female managers. Such cultural bias may show up, particularly in countries with high masculinity scores on Hofstede's cultural values dimension, including Korea, Japan, Latin America, and much of the Middle East. Some locals may worry that a female expatriate will have less influence over decisions at headquarters.[lxxv] It is important that the female expatriate has authority to make decisions, and the firm should make this clear to local employees and other organizational partners. But there is recent evidence to

PANDESIC: HIRING TOP MANAGERS WITH THE RIGHT EXPERIENCE

Pandesic, the high-profile joint venture between Intel and SAP, was launched in 1997 to create a low-end disruption selling enterprise resource planning (ERP) software to small businesses that could not afford the full-blown ERP system. Intel and SAP hand-picked some of their most successful, tried-and-true executives to lead the venture.

Pandesic grew to one hundred employees in eight months, and quickly established offices in Europe and Asia. Within a year it had announced forty strategic partnerships with companies such as Compaq, Hewlett-Packard, and Citibank. Pandesic executives boldly announced its first product in advance of launch to warn would-be competitors to stay away from the small business market space. The company signed distribution and implementation agreements with the same IT consulting firms that had served as such capable channel partners for SAP's large-company systems. The product, initially intended to be simple ERP software delivered to small businesses via the Internet, evolved into a completely automated end-to-end solution. Pandesic was a dramatic failure. It sold very few systems and closed its doors in February 2001 after having burned through more than $100 million.

The executives who ran the firm were all experienced senior managers and salespeople. However, they had always run large organizations with a lot of resources and support staff. When it came to running a small entrepreneurial organization, these executives were unprepared. The big organization executives made the product too complicated, staffing was too expensive, and the organization scaled up too fast before gaining enough new clients. It is important to remember that in addition to having international capabilities, international managers still have to be able to operate the businesses they are expected to manage, and previous experience with a similar situation is vital if the executives and their teams are to hit the ground running.[lxxvii]

show that even in the masculine countries, foreign women are accepted into authority positions, possibly because the local culture is not threatened because it is not the local women that are leaving their homes to work.[lxxvi] Still, some Middle East countries present a more difficult problem because the rights of women, such as the right to drive, are restricted. Certain other countries in parts of Latin America or Africa may present real safety problems for foreign women executives, and firms must take care to check on local security issues.

Strict Islamic countries may similarly present a problem for expatriates who have trouble acculturating to an environment with little familiar entertainment. Many products and entertainment options from home are less likely to be available. TV programming, sports, and even news magazines such as *The Economist* may be censored and difficult to get. Web sites may be blocked, and even emails and email attachments may be interfered with by local security forces. Alcohol may be difficult to purchase or be very expensive. Such a posting could be particularly uncomfortable for women, as their rights would be limited by local law and customs. Expatriates need to be aware of such issues and prepare for the very different social environment.

Repatriation

Repatriation of the expatriate to his or her home country is often overlooked by the company and the expatriate. Offhand, you might not think of expatriates returning to their home countries as being a problem. But interestingly, this can create a host of problems for the expatriate worker and family. The expatriate may end up returning to the same job at home with no promotion and may thus feel the time on the foreign assignment meant little to his or her career. Sometimes an expatriate will return home only to find that a former colleague got a good promotion, or a former subordinate may now be the expatriate's boss. The returned expatriate is no longer in a central position at work, after having gotten used to giving orders and having quite a bit of help getting things done at work—or even at home. For example, in India, the family may have been able to employ domestic help and the employee provided with a driver. (In China, most international firms will not permit their employees to drive because of security issues on the road.)

Similarly the family may feel out of place back at home, particularly if children spent several formative years in the foreign country. The expatriate's spouse may also miss some of the conveniences that were given to executive expatriates. Another job change may be imminent, because the experience that expatriates acquire in foreign assignments often makes them more marketable outside the home corporation.[lxxvii] As a result, after a lengthy assignment, a home-country national needs up to eighteen months to settle back into a U.S. job.[lxxviii] In part, this is why U.S. firms are typically shortening overseas assignments. Headquarters should have a staff ready to assist any returning expatriate in reestablishing a living situation. The firm should give the returning expat help in reestablishing residence back in the home country. Counseling for the expatriate and his family may be required due to semi-culture-shock.

How do firms prepare expatriates to handle overseas assignments and generally manage their human resources more effectively in foreign locations? They must think strategically about human resources and implement tactics that can reduce expatriate failure and other HR problems in the host country, as in the opening Asimco case example. In particular, because Japanese firms have much experience in managing far-flung subsidiaries and are good at preparing expatriates, they provide some good examples of preparing and managing human resources in the foreign subsidiary.

SUMMARY

This chapter has described the HR function, how it may differ in international firms that have to staff international offices, the questions facing expatriate employees, and when to use expatriates versus host country local employees. International firms have three options for selecting management staff for their foreign operations: send someone from the home country, hire someone in the host country, or hire someone from a third country. The chapter discussed the relative advantages and disadvantages of hiring expatriates and locals, and presented the factors HR managers must consider when deciding whether to use a home-country national, a host-country national, or a third-country national. This chapter also discussed several reasons expatriates fail, including the foreign country's physical and social environments, the expatriate's openness to culture, and communication issues. Other important factors in the expatriate experience were also addressed, such as differences between the home office and the foreign subsidiary, gender and family issues, and the importance of repatriation programs. Also presented were frameworks for selecting and developing effective expatriates, for administrating expatriate programs, and for administering expatriate compensation.

MANAGERIAL GUIDELINES

Managers should remember the following guidelines as they go forward in different environments and seek to move employees to accomplish particular goals and objectives:

1. Strong human resources management leads to greater workforce productivity, improved organizational climate, better employee engagement with the firm and its activities, and other significant benefits. The human resources

department should not be neglected or shunted off to a corner office. Good empirical evidence from both the management and economics fields now strongly shows that excellence in HRM leads to excellent employee and firm performance and superior returns to investors.

2. Given its importance, the human resources function needs to be given support from the firm's top management. Selecting, developing, and rewarding talent is quite important and needs to be seen as part of firm strategy.

3. HR should be explicitly linked with overall strategic planning and should deliver the quality and quantity of leaders the company will need in the future to achieve its goals.

4. Selection is quite important. For firms that need to staff international locations, it is helpful to find employees who have some international experience, preferably experience in living abroad. Multiple interviews and tests for cultural intelligence are helpful in determining a prospective employee's international capabilities. Similar interviews and tests need to be given to foreign employees working for the firm's overseas office.

5. Training is also important for employees going overseas. At a minimum, it is necessary to give briefings on culture and language. Even simple things like when to shake hands, what to say upon on introduction, and what basic language rituals are used each day should be learned.

6. Training is also important in hiring foreign nationals to work in the overseas office. It sometimes takes several months or longer to inculcate the firm's culture, ethics, and values in a foreign national. This is especially important in emerging and transition economies that have much different cultural and commercial traditions, and very little experience with doing business outside of their own regions.

7. There are many appraisal methods, all of which have benefits and drawbacks. It is important for the firm to understand what behaviors and objectives it would like to encourage. It is helpful to try to appraise and reward the behaviors that it thinks will lead to the desired outputs. Remember that what gets measured and rewarded is more likely to get done.

8. Monetary rewards are valued by most employees, but it is important not to neglect non-monetary rewards such as added control over one's job, added tasks that the employee finds interesting, and clear feedback and praise the employee can use to improve at the job and learn more skills.

9. Even if the expatriate is carefully selected and given training, foreign assignments are challenging. Firms can help by giving the expatriate help in settling in, and giving aid to the expat's family with the move and getting settled. Expatriate failure is costly, and a main reason for this is the family's dissatisfaction.

10. Human resources can be used to help the firm achieve its objectives. Top management needs to understand the type of workforce it seeks to build; this is particularly important when going to a new country where the slate is clean and the firm can inculcate its values among new hires.

11. Remember the importance of experience when selecting managers, particularly for a foreign assignment. What type of organization did the candidate work in before? What type of international experience does he or she have, including experiences during school? The work of Professor Morgan McCall on "high fliers" and developing global executives (see Additional Resources section below) provides an excellent guide to the selection and development process for top managers and expatriates.

DOING BUSINESS IN COSTA RICA

Costa Rica is known as the Switzerland of Latin America. It has had a long period of democracy with an active democratic process. The population is principally of European extraction, in contrast to many Latin American countries, such as Guatemala, with populations that have very high percentages of indigenous natives.

Costa Rica differs in many ways from other Latin American countries. For example, Costa Ricans are considered by many to be the most punctual of all Latin Americans. Therefore, it is vital that individuals be on time for appointments. Costa Rica is also different from most Latin American countries in that the power distance is low.[lxxix] Thus, there is less hierarchical organization in business with employees having a far greater desire to have an input into the running of an organization. There is also a greater emphasis on collectivism than is seen in many Latin American countries,[lxxx] so the group and group cohesion is very important.

Costa Rica does, however, have some similarities with its Latin American neighbors. For example, the role of the family is greater in all Latin American countries than in North America.[lxxxi] There is a strong focus on children and spending time with the family, unlike North Americans who tend to focus more on workplace issues. Costa Rica is also strongly Catholic, like most Latin American countries.

In doing business in Costa Rica it should be recognized that most Hispanic people have two surnames: one from their father, which is listed first, followed by one from their mother. Only the father's surname is used when addressing someone. (This can vary around Latin America, so be sure to ask how people are addressed when traveling to those countries.) Using titles is very important, therefore, when conducting business in Costa Rica. Your title should be shown on your business card and you should acknowledge other people's titles when addressing them. Lunch is typically the largest meal of the day and it's not uncommon for it to last a full afternoon, particularly if business is involved.

CULTURE

ADDITIONAL RESOURCES

Axtell, R. E. (Ed.). (1993) *Do's and Taboos Around the World* (3rd ed.). New York: John Wiley & Sons.

Hess, M. B., & Linderman, P. (2002). *Expert Expatriate: Your Guide to Successful Relocation Abroad—Moving, Living, Thriving.* London: Nicholas Brealey Publishing.

Kaplan, R. S., & Norton, D. P. (1996). *The Balanced Scorecard: Translating Strategy into Action.* Boston, MA: Harvard Business School Press.

Lewis, R. D. (2005). *When Cultures Collide: Leading Across Cultures.* London: Nicholas Brealey Publishing.

McCall, M. W. (1997). *High Flyers: Developing the Next Generation of Leaders.* Boston, MA: Harvard Business School Press.

McCall, M. W., & Hollenbeck, G. P. (2002). *Developing Global Executives.* Boston: Harvard Business School Press.

Morrison, T., & Conaway, W. A. (2007). *Kiss, Bow, or Shake Hands* (2nd ed.). Avon, MA: Adams Media.

Peterson, B. (2004). *Cultural Intelligence: A Guide to Working with People from Other Cultures.* Yarmouth, ME: Intercultural Press.

Smith, S., & Maz, R. (2004). *The HR Answer Book: An Indispensable Guide for Managers and Human Resources Professionals.* New York: AMACOM Books.

EXERCISES

Opening Vignette Discussion Questions

1. Could Asimco have done any preparation in terms of human resources to avoid the problems they faced?
2. Do you think this problem is unique to China?

DISCUSSION QUESTIONS

1. How does the international HRM function differ from the domestic HRM function?
2. What selection criteria are most important in choosing people for an overseas assignment? Identify and describe the four that you judge to be of most universal importance, and defend your choices.
3. Building on your answer to Question 2, discuss the theoretical dimensions that may affect anticipatory and in-country adjustment of expatriates. How can these be turned into selection criteria?
4. Why are individuals motivated to accept international assignments? Which of these motivations would you rank as positive reasons? Which would you regard as negative reasons?
5. Discuss the host-country characteristics that might influence the staffing method.

IN-CLASS EXERCISES

1. You are the manager of the international HRM function for a firm whose top management is assigning an executive from the home office to head one of the firm's foreign subsidiaries. Relative to the cultural adaptation phases, what would you advise the top management?
2. Regarding Exercise 1, what questions would you ask the top management in order to be sure that the right expatriate has been selected?
3. What are the international HR implications that can be drawn from the Japanese, European, and U.S. international-expatriate practices? What could U.S. firms do better to prepare someone for an expatriate assignment to mainland China?
4. How could information technologies assist in managing global human resources?
5. Complete the Cultural Intelligence questionnaire below to identify your own cultural intelligence or CQ. The statements reflect different facets of cultural intelligence. For each set, add up your scores and divide by four to produce an average. Our work with large groups of managers shows that for purposes of your own development, it is most useful to think about your scores in comparison to one another. Generally, an average of less than 3 would indicate an area calling for improvement, while an average of greater than 4.5 reflects a true CQ strength.

Cultural Intelligence (CQ)[lxxxii]
Rate the extent to which you agree with each statement, using the scale:
1 = Strongly disagree, 2 = Disagree, 3 = Neutral, 4 = Agree, 5 = Strongly agree.

_____ Before I interact with people from a new culture, I ask myself what I hope to achieve.

_____ If I encounter something unexpected while working in a new culture, I use this experience to figure out new ways to approach other cultures in the future.

_____ I plan how I'm going to relate to people from a different culture before I meet them.

_____ When I come into a new cultural situation, I can immediately sense whether something is going well or something is wrong.

TOTAL _____ ÷ 4 = _____ **Cognitive CQ**

_____ It is easy for me to change my body language (for example, eye contact or posture) to suit people from a different culture.

_____ I can alter my expression when a cultural encounter requires it.

_____ I modify my speech style (for example, accent or tone) to suit people from a different culture.

_____ I easily change the way I act when a cross-cultural encounter seems to require it.

TOTAL _____ ÷ 4 = _____ **Physical CQ**

_____ I have confidence that I can deal well with people from a different culture.

_____ I am certain that I can befriend people whose cultural backgrounds are different from mine.

_____ I can adapt to the lifestyle of a different culture with relative ease.

_____ I am confident that I can deal with a cultural situation that's unfamiliar.

TOTAL _____ ÷ 4 = _____ **Emotional / motivational CQ**

TAKE-HOME EXERCISES

1. Expatriates spending extended periods of time in foreign countries are often trained in dinner table etiquette, such as what to eat and drink, and what to talk about during a meal. They are also schooled in proper dress code and in proper protocol for interacting with hosts. The International Business Center Web site (http://www.international-business-center.com) offers information on business etiquette for a variety of countries. Look for information on protocol for an international assignment in South Africa (click on Africa at the left of the webpage). Write down a list of things you should keep in mind as you go abroad to South Africa that may be different from what you are used to.

2. Imagine you are going to work in the Philippines as an HR manager for a North American firm with offices there. After being there for a short time another expatriate from Canada comes to speak to you. Laura tells you that the locals have been quite rude to her. You ask her to describe why she feels this way. She tells you about several minor incidents. For instance while waiting for an elevator at the end of the day a lady she barely knew asked, "Where are you going?" Laura said she just smiled but felt that question was a bit funny, especially since the day before she had been asked by another colleague, "Have you eaten yet?" Write down something you would tell Laura about her Filipino colleagues' communication rituals for basic, polite greetings. (To answer this question look up Professor Deborah Tannen and colleagues, and their work on communication rituals in different countries).

SHORT CASE QUESTIONS

Cultural Sensitivity: How Much Is Too Much? (p. 375)

1. Why do you think Feng Shui works for casinos but did not work well for the Coca-Cola company at its headquarters in Atlanta?
2. Do you think Coke could have done something to make the application of Feng Shui work?
3. Where else would Feng Shui work well for a firm?

13

THE STRUCTURE OF THE INTERNATIONAL FIRM

Overview

A key implementation issue for international firms is organizational structure. When a firm's structure, goals, and capabilities are aligned appropriately, the firm's chances for success are enhanced. When a firm's structure is not consistent with the firm's goals and capabilities, the firm's chances for success are hurt. The choice of structure is important to an international business because organizational structure is the glue that ensures the organization remains connected and functions across the geographic and cultural distances over which it operates. Thus, the ability to maximize firm effectiveness is heavily affected by structure, and its importance increases as the distance between units and the level of cultural variation increases.

This chapter examines the key issues associated with organizational structure:

- The variety of structures a firm can employ and their benefits and drawbacks
  - Simple
  - Functional
  - Multidivisional
  - Strategic business unit
  - Matrix
- How to pick the structure that is right for your organization
- Issues surrounding restructuring firms, including firm turnaround and reengineering

HONDA STRUCTURE

Developing a means or structure for meeting strategic goals is a requirement for a firm's success. A firm cannot simply say it hopes to accomplish a specific goal without having developed a structure for attaining that goal. The structural changes that occur in a firm sometimes involve the entire organization. However, it is more likely that the firm identifies an area of need, determines what strategic and tactical changes need to be made in that area, develops a structure that is consistent with those changes, and then implements the plan for that given area, not the entire firm.

Honda Motor Company is a major competitor in the global auto manufacturing industry. Honda's home market is Japan—a major source of their revenues. Japanese auto sellers are dominated by a series of large dealerships that are typically owned by one of the large Japanese business groups. Often the large dealerships are owned by companies other than Honda although the large dealerships are still part of a business group. (Recall that business groups are the vertically and horizontally integrated groupings of businesses that dominate outside of North America.) At the same time, many small- and medium-sized auto dealers are owned by individuals. The Japanese auto industry is highly competitive and independent dealers, while smaller than those owned by large business groups, are critical to Honda's overall profitability.

Many consumers and the dealers themselves complain that the small- and medium-sized auto dealers were not being served well by Honda. Honda was also concerned that these auto dealerships sometimes were not being run efficiently and revenues were not as high as they should be. To address these problems, Honda developed a new structure in which it transferred 120 employees from corporate offices to the small- and medium-sized dealerships. It was expected that this change in structure would lead to these dealerships getting better service and, in turn, help them increase revenues. Honda also committed to provide more and better training programs to help ensure more effective management of the small and medium dealerships. The new structure is seen below.

Typically an auto manufacturer makes money not only by selling autos but also by supplying parts to auto dealers. The dealers, in fact, may make as much money from the servicing of autos as they do in selling the cars. Historically, Honda had operated its automobile sales and auto parts suppliers as two separate businesses, which meant that delivery and service to the dealers came from two sources. However, Honda's dealers did not see these two activities as separate businesses. The auto dealers needed autos and parts and wanted a single source for both.

In 2005 Honda announced it was changing from a strategic business unit structure where auto sales and auto service were separate units to a functional structure in Japan by recombining sales and service under one roof (one for both main regions of Japan). The firm combined auto sales and auto parts sales into a single division, with two such functional divisions operating in Japan—one division would serve in eastern Japan and the other western Japan. Each of these divisions would be able to supply the auto dealers' needs for either automobiles or auto parts. Improved customer service was the ultimate goal for the new structure. The old and new structures are seen below.

Honda's strategic goals and its organizational structures could not be separated because they were critical to each other in the overall success of the company.

Source: Honda to fortify Japanese domestic automobile and power products sales operations. Honda Corporate Press Release, May 23, 2005.

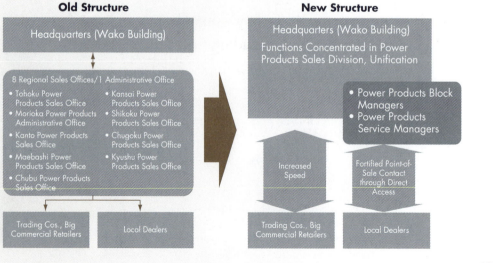

Old Structure

Headquarters (Wako Building)

8 Regional Sales Offices/1 Administrative Office
- Tohoku Power Products Sales Office
- Morioka Power Products Administrative Office
- Kanto Power Products Sales Office
- Maebashi Power Products Sales Office
- Chubu Power Products Sales Office
- Kansai Power Products Sales Office
- Shikoku Power Products Sales Office
- Chugoku Power Products Sales Office
- Kyushu Power Products Sales Office

Trading Cos., Big Commercial Retailers

Local Dealers

New Structure

Headquarters (Wako Building)
Functions Concentrated in Power Products Sales Division, Unification

- Power Products Block Managers
- Power Products Service Managers

Increased Speed

Fortified Point-of-Sale Contact through Direct Access

Trading Cos., Big Commercial Retailers

Local Dealers

(Continued)

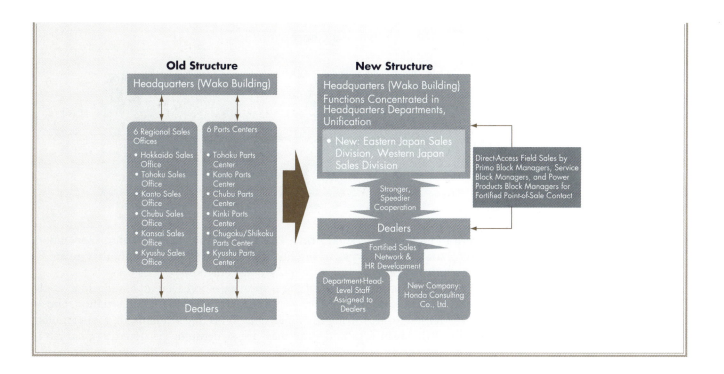

A key implementation issue for an international firm is the **organizational structure** that it will employ. A firm's structure is the official manner in which the various tasks and parts of the business are to interact, coordinate, and report with each other, and at what levels decisions are made. As firms select strategies that take them to foreign markets, they often find that more complicated organizational structures are needed to manage their far-flung global operations. Harvard business historian Alfred Chandler found that a firm's structure is determined by its strategy, and that as firms pursue aggressive growth to attain scale economies with multiple locations, firm structure changes to support the expansion strategies.[i] Since this pioneering work, management writers and consultants have focused considerable energy on organization structure, its antecedents, and its impact on firm performance.[ii] Today, it is widely recognized that firm structure needs to fit with the firm's strategy and its degree of internationalization to be successful.

In Chapters 4 and 5, we discussed how a firm's strategy should direct what it does. Chandler found that strategy was central to choosing the appropriate organizational structure for a firm. If a firm wanted to achieve certain strategic goals but did not put in place a structure that was consistent with the chosen strategy, the firm would find it difficult to implement that strategy or benefit fully from it. In short, a business may have a great strategy, but unless it has the right structure it will find it hard to achieve its organizational goals.

The strategy–structure relationship is not, however, a one-way street. As much as strategy drives structure, structure can also affect a firm's strategy. To illustrate, music company Universal Music Group (UMG) wanted a decentralized structure that maximized local responsiveness in order to meet the demand for different music and local artists in its many foreign locations. Once the structure was selected, UMG went about developing a multi-domestic strategy that fit with the desired structure and maximized local responsiveness by setting up a division in each country in which it has major operations. Getting in step with the local music scene would be difficult for a music company that did not have a physical presence in that market to evaluate local talent and understand local tastes, though it is a more expensive structure to undertake compared with centralizing firm activities in one location. Organizational structure is a similar critical

Organizational structure
The official manner in which the various parts of a business are to report and coordinate with each other, and at what levels decisions are made.

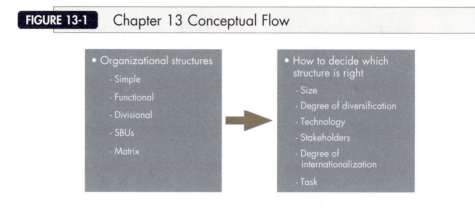

FIGURE 13-1   Chapter 13 Conceptual Flow

- Organizational structures
  - Simple
  - Functional
  - Divisional
  - SBUs
  - Matrix

- How to decide which structure is right
  - Size
  - Degree of diversification
  - Technology
  - Stakeholders
  - Degree of internationalization
  - Task

concern to most international firms. This chapter lays the foundation for understanding the different types of organizational structures and how they relate to the implementation issue for an international business.

We first discuss structure as if the firm in question were operating in a single country. We then discuss that firm's structure in the context of international business. The reason for this sequence of presentation is that students are more familiar with domestic businesses and how they are structured. As noted in Chapter 1, while international business is increasing, many firms still operate primarily within their home countries. Only about 20 percent of the world's GDP comes from industries that can be called global, though that is increasing steadily. Once this terminology is clarified, we go on to examine how firm structure changes as a firm expands internationally. We examine how organizations should pick an organizational structure for the firm. This leads to a discussion of how structure can be changed if necessary. Finally, informal structures are discussed. The flow of the chapter is seen in Figure 13-1.

DIFFERENT ORGANIZATIONAL STRUCTURES

The need for different types of organizational structure is consistent with a firm's growth and evolution. As an enterprise becomes more complex there is a need for its organizational structure to change, as the enterprise has more people and a greater need to achieve coordination between its various units. One of the trade-offs that both private and public enterprises face is that as an organization introduces more complex structures to increase coordination between various groups and departments, it invariably introduces more bureaucracy, more formally described as a greater **administrative component**.[iii] The administrative component is the proportion of support staff to line workers. C. N. Parkinson, a professor at the University of Malaya (now National University of Singapore), formulated what is called **Parkinson's Law**, which argues that work expands to fill the time available. A similar proposition applies to adding administrators; Parkinson noticed that in the British Colonial Office and in the British Admiralty during the twentieth century, the administrative component rose steadily, irrespective of any real change in the amount of work to be done.[iv]

Increasing the administrative component can produce better planning, coordination, and training because of the greater staff available to the organization. But increasing the administrative component also increases the time needed to make decisions, impedes communication among departments, and reduces commitment to the organization as a whole. It is important to understand this trade-off between efficiency and effectiveness as we examine structure in this chapter. That is, as you increase effectiveness in a firm, you are likely sacrificing some degree of efficiency, so a firm must make some choices as it develops its structure. The organization will also want to ensure the structure is consistent with its overall business

Administrative component
The ratio of support staff (e.g., secretaries and supervisors) to line staff directly engaged in the production and distribution of an organization's products and services.

Parkinson's Law
Parkinson's Law states that work expands to fill the time available for its completion. Several corollaries are possible, such as an organization's administrative component grows wtih time.

FOSTER'S: STRUCTURE CHANGE FOLLOWING AN ACQUISITION

As noted above, change in structure can be hard. In Chapter 4 we saw that a firm can alter its portfolio of businesses by making an acquisition. When an acquisition is made the resulting organization will typically need to change its organizational structure. Foster's is a well-known beer that is sold in over 150 countries. The Foster's Group owns other beer brands as well, such as Victoria Bitter, Shanghai Beer, and Carlton Draught, with brewing operations and different brands in 10 different countries. The Foster's Group is also one of the major wine producers in the world with wineries in 25 different countries. The firm's major wine brands are Wolf Blass and Beringer, although the firm has a wide range of other boutique and specialty labels as well.

In May 2005, Foster's Group bought one of the largest wine producers in Australia, Southcorp. Its major brands included Penfolds, Lindemann's, and Rosemount Estate. The Foster's Group became the number one company in terms of market share in the United States, the United Kingdom, and Australia as a result of this acquisition.

Most of the resulting internal restructuring took place in Australia because the Foster's Group and Southcorp are both headquartered there. Changes in the vineyards were limited because there were few economies of scale to be obtained; the danger Foster's sought to avoid was creating combinations that would destroy the uniqueness of each brand of wine. The marketing and sales teams were combined because significant economies of scale can be obtained in those areas. The Foster's Group combined the Carlton and United Beverages divisions of Foster and the Australian division of Beringer to create an integrated sales and marketing team that covered all 12 sales channels. Foster's used a single division to cover all of its wine sales in Australia in order to avoid cannibalizing itself—a challenge that is difficult to overcome but essential for becoming the most successful and largest wine producer and retailer in the country. The Foster's Group was able to clearly identify the need to change its internal structure in order to meet strategic business goals and successfully did so.

Gettler, L. (2005, May 27). Foster's bottles up Southcorp prey. *The Age.*

http://theage.com.au/articles/2005/05/26/1116950821447.html

strategy. For example, if a firm has staked out a low cost position, then it needs to ensure that that efficiency is the principal focus of its structure. However, in a differentiation strategy the focus is more on effectiveness and less on cost as it builds the firm's structure.

The structures examined here are those most commonly used, and include the simple, functional, divisional, strategic business unit (SBU), and matrix structures. The students should note as they examine these structures that each one is successively more complex. In this chapter, we will look at classic examples of these structures, but in reality many firms use variations of these structures, mixing the various organizational forms and developing a structure that matches their specific needs. The basic building blocks for all of these structures are the ones examined here although they may take parts from each structure for their specific needs.

Simple Structures

A simple organizational structure is typical of new ventures. Figure 13-2 summarizes this structure. As you can see in the figure, the firm's founder/CEO is the center of the business and everything essentially is coordinated through that founder. To illustrate, consider that a new business may have only one or two employees. The business is small, so those employees can check almost all key issues with the founder/CEO before acting, which may be as simple as asking a question from across the room. This business form can continue for a considerable time even as a firm grows. For example, a firm with several hundred employees may still maintain a simple organizational structure, particularly in slower-moving or less complex product market where activities are standardized and can be contracted out, such as property development. This structure is often associated with family-owned businesses, where the founder is the family patriarch and the

---

HARBIN PHARMACEUTICAL: COMPLEXITY IN ORGANIZATIONAL STRUCTURE

As discussed in this chapter, a firm's structure is not always clearly defined or easily understood. Many international firms have quite complex internal structures that may be difficult for people from mature western countries to follow. For example, Harbin Pharmaceutical in the Northeast of China, near Korea, is the leading producer of medicines in China. The pharmaceutical industry in China is much more fragmented than that of the United States or Europe. In 2005, there were an estimated 3,500 pharmaceutical companies in China. (This is actually 25 percent less than a year earlier and 50 percent less than in 2002, as the government has been actively encouraging industry consolidation.) Contrast this with the United States, where there are fewer than 100 pharmaceutical firms.

The pharmaceutical industry in China is getting ready to take off as the income of Chinese citizens continues its steady climb. The only truly national pharmaceutical firm in this fragmented market today is Harbin, which is owned principally by the Harbin city government at 45 percent ownership; the remaining ownership is fragmented. Harbin has two listed divisions and a total of 24 subsidiaries. Some of these subsidiaries are pharmacies that distribute the firm's drugs. It is not uncommon in China for pharmaceutical firms to distribute their own drugs and to deliver them to hospitals and patients. Harbin's structure includes segments that are publicly traded, those that are not traded, and businesses that would normally not be considered to be part of a similar business in the West. Investors and others need to be clear about the structure of the firm as they either compete or cooperate with such an entity.

Pharmaceutical group begins reorganization. (2005, May 28). *China Economic Net,* http://en.ce.cn/Industries/Medicine/ 200412/22/t20041222_2638755.shtml.

Zamiska, N. (2005, May 6). Chinese drug firms consolidate. *Wall Street Journal Europe,* p. A14.

---

founder's children and other relatives hold key positions. However, the simple structure can often hinder growth because the founder is limited in his or her ability to address numerous firm details, as well as a host of other growth-related problems.

The classic problem for an entrepreneur is when and how to move away from this simple form to a more complex structure. A key reason that entrepreneurial firms are so successful is that they are typically small enough that the founder/ CEO is not an isolated entity but someone the employees know intimately. You would expect, in fact, for the founder/CEO to know all of the employees relatively well in a new entrepreneurial firm, which makes the employees feel they are part of a team. In turn, the founder/CEO knows the business's details well enough that he or she can closely monitor all expenses and actions to ensure that the business achieves all of its goals.

However, as the business grows and gains more customers and employees, a simple structure can result in the founder/CEO being overwhelmed with details and being unable to focus on all of the key elements. While better coordination of

---

FIGURE 13-2   Simple Structure

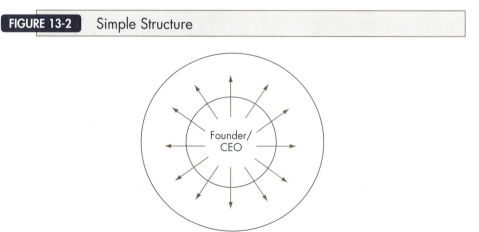

the organization may result when a growing firm moves away from the simple structure, there are also costs. The more elaborate structure results in a greater distance between employees and the founder/CEO since there is now a layer of management that reports to the founder/CEO. Most employees will now report to those managers, not the founder/CEO directly. Additionally, the close monitoring of items such as expenses may no longer occur.

Recall the discussion of agency theory in Chapter 5. Agency theory was developed principally by researchers in economics and finance to highlight the fact that individual employees will often act in their own self-interest rather than in the interest of their employer. Thus, someone who is part owner in a firm will use firm resources more carefully than will an employee. As an agent of the firm, a manager is charged with acting just like an owner toward firm resources, but in reality this often does not occur. If it were the manager's own money being wasted (as it would be in the case of a part owner), the manager would be more diligent about eliminating waste. But when it is other people's money, agency theory predicts that the manager will be less diligent. This implies that as owners remove themselves from managerial issues, different patterns of behavior will start to develop. As a founder/CEO creates a more elaborate organizational structure to avoid being swamped by details, he or she loses a degree of interaction with employees and is unable to monitor employees and expenditures as closely as before.

Earlier chapters mentioned the important Overseas Chinese diaspora, the approximately 50 million ethnic Chinese living outside of mainland China. (Hong Kong and Taiwan are included because of their cultural and institutional differences from mainland China.)[v] As noted previously, this group has a combined economic impact comparable to all of mainland China.[vi]

The typical organizational form of businesses owned by Overseas Chinese is a variation of the simple structure. The head of the organization is typically the family patriarch who sits at the center of the organization, with all major decisions being approved by him and with information going up to him before being disseminated throughout the firm.[vii] Some organizations owned by Overseas Chinese are quite large, in contrast to the entrepreneurial organizations discussed earlier. The reason that such large organizations can employ this variation of the simple structure is that typically these businesses are concentrated in more regulated, low-technology and slower-growth areas where there is limited or predictable change occurring. Many of these firms do not focus on building brand image and instead function as **original equipment manufacturers (OEM)** for U.S. and European firms such as Dell and Philips.[viii] Additionally, there are family members throughout the organization who support the firm founder and sometimes run firm subsidiaries. Finally, recall from Ch. 2 that the culture of Overseas Chinese is heavily based on Confucian teachings and as a result is very hierarchical. Thus, individuals in the organization typically look for direction from the organization's head and will follow the direction more closely than might occur in an organization with a Western culture, what Hofstede referred to as a high power-distance setting. (See the discussion on power distance in Ch. 2.) The simple structure works well for Overseas Chinese businesses even when they are quite large due to the nature of the decisions that are required, the culture of the individuals involved, and the types of businesses run, which are usually in slower-growth industries such as real estate, trading, and light manufacturing.[ix]

OEM
Original equipment manufacturers.

Functional Structures

As a firm grows it may find that it needs greater coordination; under these conditions, a firm often will move to a functional organizational structure. In this structure, the firm organizes itself around the organization's major functions. These functional areas correspond to majors that students can take in business

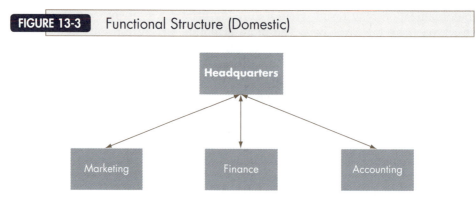

FIGURE 13-3   Functional Structure (Domestic)

schools. For example, students can major in marketing, accounting, finance, and production—and these areas are the key functional areas of a firm. The benefits of a functional structure include the fact that the firm can avoid duplicating activities and may benefit from scale economies in activities such as marketing and finance (i.e., there is only one marketing department for the whole firm). However, the risks are that employees begin to focus more on their functional areas and become less engaged with the firm as a whole. Figure 13-3 presents this structure.

Some major corporations and other organizations are able to maintain a functional organizational structure. For example, the national bank of Spain is the Banco de España, which performs many of the same duties as the U.S. Federal Reserve, that is, monitoring and promoting the economic health of the country. The functional structure of the bank includes the following departments:

- Directorate General Operations, Markets and Payment Systems
- Directorate General Banking Regulation
- Directorate General Economics, Statistics, and Research
- Directorate General Banking Supervision
- General Secretariat
- Associate Directorate General Internal Affairs
- Internal Audit Department

For the Banco de España, the functional concerns are not marketing, accounting, and so on, that may be expected in other organizations. Instead, as a government linked firm, its main activities consist of the major functions of bank regulation: statistics, bank supervision, internal affairs, and auditing. This difference highlights one insight about analyzing functional structures—the structure should be relevant to the business at hand. If production is not a key area for the business's success, then it will not be a major functional department in the organization. The functions around which a firm organizes should be those that are keys to its success.

As noted in Chapter 6, as firms internationalize they typically prefer to export goods initially rather than spending the money to open in a foreign location. In this case, the firm's functional organization appears similar to Figure 13-3, but with one exception—there is one department dedicated to exports. This structure variation is seen in Figure 13-4. As a firm begins to develop operations in different countries, it is expected to keep that structure. Typically, however, the functional structure is not used by international firms that have operations in large numbers of countries. Instead, those firms will have a matrix organizational form. Briefly, a matrix organizational structure might be organized along functional areas, but it also organizes things along national or regional dimensions. Thus, not only are the firm's accountants organized as accountants, but all of the accountants in Europe

FIGURE 13-4   Functional Structure (International)

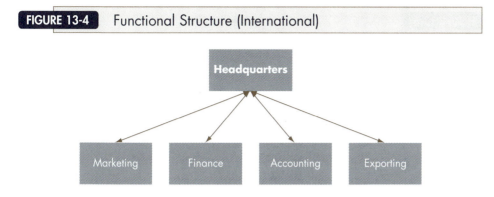

are also connected. Therefore, keep the basic functional structure in mind when the more complex matrix structure is introduced.

Divisional Structures

As a firm grows it may find that the various parts of the business are too large to effectively coordinate with a simple functional structure. In this case, the firm develops what is called a multidivisional, or M-division, structure. In an M-division structure, the firm is divided into different divisions, sometimes along product lines, each of which has its own internal set of functional areas. Thus, as seen in Figure 13-5, each division will have its own functions such as accounting, finance, marketing, and production.

The early M-division firms first emerged in the late 1800s, primarily in the United States and Germany, and they proved to be very competitive. Using their size, they were able to cut costs and drastically lower the price of their products such as oil, chemicals, and clothing dyes, making these products more available to smaller firms and individual consumers.[x] The M-division structure is closely associated with Alfred Sloan, the individual after whom the Massachusetts Institute of Technology (MIT) Sloan Business School is named. Sloan was CEO of General Motors (GM) in the 1920s. When Sloan arrived at a relatively young GM, he found eight brands of automobiles in this single organization, largely because of acquisitions. The brands included familiar names like Chevrolet, Oldsmobile, Buick, Pontiac, and Cadillac as well as less familiar names such as Oakland, Scripps-Booth, and Sheridan. All of the brands were competing in the middle of the market. Their average selling price in 1921 was about $1,200 (about $14,000 in 2009 dollars. Figure 13-6 summarizes GM's automobile prices when Sloan arrived.

FIGURE 13-5   Division Structure (Domestic)

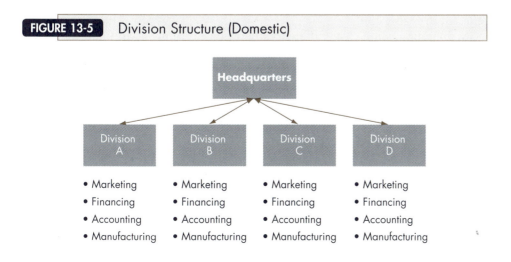

FIGURE 13-6   GM's 1921 Price Scheme when Alfred Sloan Arrived

Chevrolet:	$795–$2,075
Oakland:	$1,395–$2,065
Oldsmobile:	$1,445–$3,300
Scripps-Booth:	$1,545–$2,295
Sheridan:	$1,685
Buick:	$1,795–$3,295
Cadillac:	$3,790–$5,690

Note the overlap between the brands and the potential for significant competition among the divisions and confusion for the customer. The similarity in pricing made it difficult for customers differentiate between an Oldsmobile and a Buick, or an Oakland and a Scripps-Booth. Sloan recognized this problem and reorganized the corporation to eliminate the Oakland, Scripps-Booth, and Sheridan brands. He then repositioned the remaining brands along different price points and tried to remove overt competition between divisions.[xi] The new pricing scheme was developed along with the full separation of the divisions to allow them to operate relatively autonomously. Figure 13-7 summarizes the reorganized GM following Sloan's reorganization.[xii]

The divisional structure proved beneficial to GM—and many other companies that follow it—because it allowed each division to operate more efficiently in a given business area, and to develop expertise specific to its technology and markets. In addition, the cost structures of the divisions were such that the cars could be priced differently without confusing consumers. GM was far ahead of its competitors and most other types of firms in this regard, and this facilitated GM's growth into the largest auto firm in the world. It also decentralized decision making by allowing those closer to the customers more decision power. The drawbacks of a divisional structure is that it duplicates many functional skills and can have a lack of coordination between divisions and problems with sharing resources and capabilities. This has to be managed carefully, something that GM did well in the early days of its restructuring by maintaining careful price separations between its brands.

In recent years, however, GM has drifted away from this careful positioning domestically, allowing considerable overlap between its brands and low levels of cross-divisional cooperation. As of the 1990s, GM's brands once again showed considerable overlap, resulting in confusion for customers and less-than-helpful competition among its car divisions.[xiii] The range of GM's prices in the 1990s is reflected in Figure 13-8.

Maintaining some clear differences between divisions is an important component of proper multidivisional structure. GM overcomes such overlap internationally by having regional divisions for different sections of the world that

---

FIGURE 13-7   GM's Divisional Repositioning in the 1920s under Alfred Sloan

Chevrolet:	$450–$600
Pontiac:	$600–$900
Oldsmobile:	$900–$1,200
Buick:	$1,200–$1,700
Cadillac:	$1,700–$2,500

| FIGURE 13-8 | GM Positioning in 1995 as Demonstrated by Divisional Price Ranges |

Saturn:	$9,995–$12,895
Chevrolet:	$7,295–$67,543 (Corvette)
Pontiac:	$9,904–$26,479
Oldsmobile:	$13,510–$31,370 (Aurora)
Buick:	$13,734–$31,864 (Riviera)
Cadillac:	$32,990–$45,330

Source: Adapted from Trout, J. (1995). *The New Positioning* (pp. 52–53). New York: McGraw-Hill.

combine the products in those regions under one organizational structure. Thus, GM mixes product-focused divisions with geographically based international divisions. The Asia-Pacific division covers the geographic region of Australia, China, India, Indonesia, Japan, Korea, Malaysia, the Philippines, Russia, Singapore, and Thailand. With this structure GM has been able to avoid the overlap in products that occurs domestically since they do not offer all the same products that GM offers in North America. These divisions also have products that do not appear in the United States. For example, in China GM markets Cadillac as its upscale nameplate, the popular Buick Excelle in the mid range, the Chevrolet Spark as an economy car aimed at office workers, and the Wuling minivan in rural areas. The Wuling is produced through a joint venture, with GM holding a 34 percent stake, Shanghai Automotive Industry Corporation Group holding 50.1 percent, and Wuling Automotive holding 15.9 percent. This minivan is a special product for the China market that can haul large amounts of material during the week and can easily be cleaned to transport family and friends on the weekend. Thus, the international GM has much clearer focus on its product lines in markets such as China. It is interesting to note that GM's international sales, particularly in emerging economies like China, have been a bright spot at a time when its financial returns in the United States have been lackluster.

The GM example, however, also demonstrates a difficulty that can arise with international divisions. At one time the international divisions acted largely as independent firms. As a result, GM would often not achieve economies of scale and scope between its international units. For example, even in the case of a simple thing like a car radio, GM uses a total of 270 different models, which reduces the economies that might be available if the number of models were reduced. As result, GM has moved in recent years to make the international divisions less independent. Today, GM still has international divisions, but it is seeking to centralize key decisions on design and manufacturing.

In making decisions about divisions, one thing that firms like GM have to keep in mind is whether they want to pursue multi-domestic or global strategies. If the firm has a multi-domestic structure, then it will be likely that each division will be operated independently. However, if a firm wishes to obtain economies of scale and scope, it will need an organizational structure that more closely links its divisions so that it can employ a global strategy more effectively. Part of GM's difficulty is that it has often been unclear as to whether it would rather pursue a multi-domestic or global strategy, and this confusion has been reflected in its organizational structure.

There are different means to organize divisions. For example, one way to organize divisions for firms that have many products is to place the various products that are connected in some manner together in a single division. For example, the British advanced materials firm Johnson Matthey has divisions for catalysts and chemicals, precious metals, colors and coatings, and electronic

GATX CORPORATION

Corporations can choose to change their structure from large independent companies to interconnected divisions within a single company that purposely coordinate all business activities. GATX Corporation is a specialized leasing company involved in four businesses, each of which is now a separate division. GATX Railroad, which leases railroad cars in North America, Europe, and South America, has interests in 168,000 railroad cars around the world. This division also leases railroad engines. GATX Air specializes in aircraft leasing with involvement in the leasing of over 300 commercial aircraft worldwide. GATX Specialty Finance finances a broad range of asset-based financial services. And American Steamship Company provides shipping of dry-bulk commodities on the Great Lakes of the United States and Canada. In 2004, GATX had sales of over $900 million.

In 2001, GATX had two major operating units. There was concern that the two units were not coordinated in their actions; as a result, the firm combined the two units into one, which now holds all four divisions. Now there is greater coordination in the various aspects of the business.

The figure below summarizes their organizational structure.

Source: 2001 GATX news release and web page.

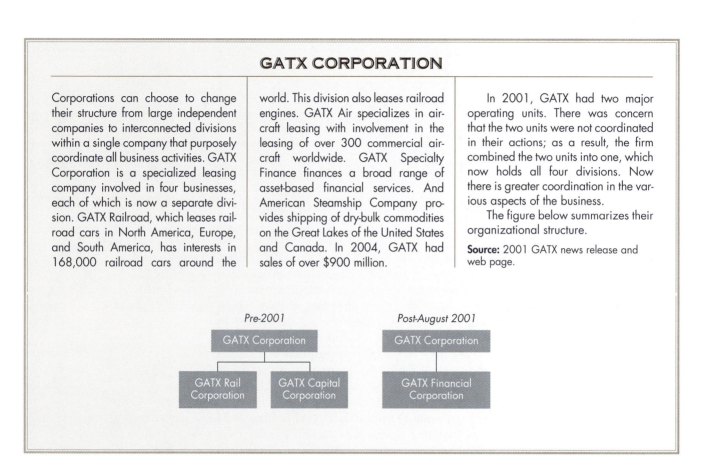

materials. Each division has a variety of different businesses, each business being connected in some manner. To illustrate, the colors and coatings division focuses on being an integrated supplier of decorative products and associated raw materials for ceramics and glass. The division is structured into four businesses: glass, pigments and dispersions, structural ceramics, and tableware.

The addition of an international division to a firm's domestic M-divisional structure is illustrated in Figure 13-9. The division is not so much to sell new

FIGURE 13-9 Division Structure (International)

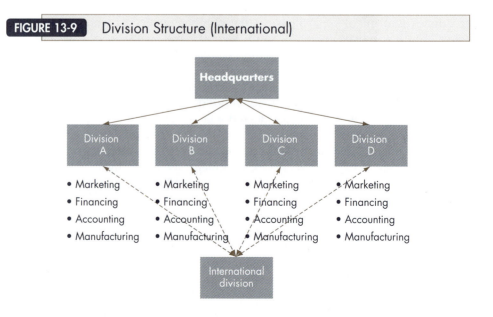

FAMILY BUSINESS IN EAST ASIA AND LATIN AMERICA

We know that Yum! is active in East Asia and Latin America. As it competes in this region Yum! faces competition from a unique type of business model that also has a different structure. These firms are typically family-owned-and-run businesses with simple internal structures, and are typically major property developers, banks, and agricultural concerns. Even though some of them can grow to over a billion dollars in annual revenue, they manage to maintain a simple internal structure, one that is centralized and hierarchical, funneling nearly all major decisions through the founder and family members. This differs somewhat from firms in an Anglo-American setting, which, as they grow, commonly decentralize their operations with the founder giving up some control to professional managers and outside investors.

Although institutional investors, such as the major mutual fund companies and the big banks and accounting firms, have encouraged the family-run firms from these developing economies to adopt a separation of ownership and control to keep family from dominating the firms' strategy and operations, they have been slow to do so. What is the reason for this? In the case of East Asia, some have argued that the culture of the Overseas Chinese views business ownership as an asset, so the families are reluctant to share control with people outside of an inner circle of family and close associates.[xxix] Latin American business may also emphasize simple structures in slower growth industries that the founding family can more closely control. Second generation owners are thought to behave in a similar way, although it has been argued that subsequent generations may be more inclined to seek investors and outside management to grow their businesses and become more globally competitive. A trend toward less family ownership and the pursuit of revenue growth seems to be emerging in Asia. Time will tell how widespread this trend will become.

Ahlstrom, D., Young, M. N., Chan, E. S., & Bruton, G. D. (2004). Facing constraints to growth? Overseas Chinese entrepreneurs and traditional business practices in East Asia. *Asia Pacific Journal of Management*, 21(3), 263–285.

CULTURE

products (although the products sold internationally may vary from those sold domestically) or to offer a service not offered in the domestic market. Instead, it is a means to take products sold in the domestic market and package them for global markets.

An example of an international division can be seen in the American fast-food company Yum! Brands (previously known as Tricon Global Restaurants). The firm was formed as a **spin-off** from Pepsico; that is, Pepsico created a separate company of a prior division that had held its three restaurant businesses. The name "Tricon" represented the three restaurant chains that were the foundation of the firm, Kentucky Fried Chicken (KFC), Pizza Hut, and Taco Bell. Tricon later purchased Yorkshire Global Restaurants, owner of the Long John Silver's and A&W chains, and as a result the company changed its name to the broader Yum! In the United States Yum! Brands maintains a division for Pizza Hut, a second division for KFC, and a third division for Taco Bell. However, all three brands are housed in one international division for doing business outside the United States. As noted earlier, this international division has been a particularly good performer for Yum!. For example, KFC has done very well in China, and Pizza Hut is quite popular—and a somewhat upscale brand—in many Latin American countries.

Spin off
To make a separate company of a prior division, for example when Pepsico spun off its restaurant division to form YUM!

Strategic Business Unit

As firms grow larger they may find that they have so many distinct and different businesses that another layer of management must be created to handle the complexity. For example, a firm like GE has hundreds of different business areas in which it is involved. If GE's CEO Jeffrey Immelt were to try to meet regularly with the head of each one of those businesses, it would take all of his time. As a result, some large firms put comparable divisions together into single units called **strategic business units**, or SBUs. An SBU is operated essentially like a separate business within the corporation; all businesses related to a given domain are centered in that SBU. The benefits of an SBU include greater ease and speed in decision making and prompt responsiveness to customers. However, an SBU with

Strategic business unit (SBU)
A business division within a larger firm that is charged with managing a particular category of product or service.

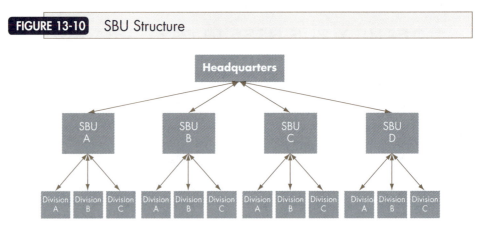

FIGURE 13-10   SBU Structure

its extra layer of management causes some divisions to work at cross purposes, as in the GM example above. Figure 13-10 summarizes this structure.

One example of the SBU structure is the French luxury products firm LVMH, which produces over 50 different brands. LVMH organizes its diverse businesses into five different SBUs:[xiv]

1. The *LVMH Fashion and Leather Goods* SBU includes Louis Vuitton, Loewe, Celine, Berluti, Kenzo, Givenchy, Christian Lacroix, Marc Jacobs, Fendi, StefanoBi, Emilio Pucci, and Thomas Pink.
2. The *wine and spirits* SBU offers Moët & Chandon, Dom Pérignon, Veuve Clicquot, Krug, Pommery, Mercier, Ruinart, Canard Duchêne, Château d'Yquem, Chandon Estates, Cloudy Bay, Cape Mentelle, Hennessy, Hine, Newton, and MountAdam.
3. The *perfumes and cosmetics* SBU sells Parfums Christian Dior, Guerlain, Parfums Givenchy, Parfums Kenzo, Bliss, Hard Candy, BeneFit Cosmetics, Urban Decay, Fresh, and Make Up For Ever.
4. The *watches and jewelry* SBU concerns TAG Heuer, Ebel, Zenith, Benedom, Fred, Chaumet, and Omas.
5. The *selective retailing* SBU involves retailers Duty Free Shops, Miami Cruiseline, Sephora Europe, Sephora AAP, Le Bon Marché, La Samaritaine, and Solstice.

A review of the LVMH SBUs shows that there is commonality to the different businesses under each SBU. The CEO of the firm can then deal directly with each SBU's head, not the heads of the 50 different businesses. Thus, this organizational form allows the head of LVMH to better manage the organization's time and focus. This organizational form also allows each SBU to develop the special skills necessary for its businesses and for the relevant managers to better understand how to address their business's problems and concerns. For example, the head of the wine and spirits SBU understands issues that the perfume-related businesses would never face.

Matrix

A matrix organizational structure is a hybrid structure, combining different organizational forms. The matrix is the most complicated of all the structures examined. As noted in the discussion of the functional structure earlier in this chapter, it may be difficult to effectively maintain a functional structure when your firm has operations in numerous countries. Instead, a firm may employ a matrix that employs a functional structure in which the firm's accountants, marketing team, and so on, report to their country managers as well as to the heads of their functional areas. Effectively, this results in employees reporting to two individuals.

FIGURE 13-11 Matrix

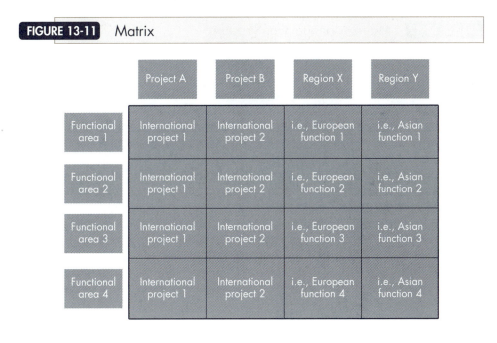

A matrix can also be generated for major projects the firm may have to manage. For example, in an aircraft-manufacturing firm like Airbus it is common for engineers to be in a large engineering department. However, if Airbus has a major project to build a new jet, some engineers will also be assigned to that project. In this case, the engineers will have two bosses: the project manager and their functional boss (e.g., the engineering manager).

A matrix structure is beneficial because it allows fast decision making by tying different aspects of the business together, but it also results in an employee having two bosses, which can lead to conflict. Typically, the organization designates one of the managers as the main reporting manager to overcome such difficulties. Figure 13-11 summarizes this organizational form. It shows what the matrix structure would look like if employees from several functional areas (such as engineering or accounting) were assigned to a particular project or to a geographic region.

To illustrate a matrix in action, consider again GM's handling of its information technology (IT) needs. By the mid-1990s, GM had outsourced all of its IT work to its computer service subsidiary EDS (Electronic Data Systems), which GM had acquired in 1984. However, because EDS was divested by GM in 1996, it was necessary for GM to redevelop this key skill quickly. To do this, GM's chief information officer (CIO) named five IT officers who were to be responsible for different areas of the firm. Those IT units were not the same as the firm's divisions. For example, for IT purposes one individual was in charge of North America while each of the major brands in North America also has its own IT department. Finance also has its own information technology officer, while elsewhere in GM, IT is a functional area within each geographic division overseas. The resulting five units for IT were therefore North America, Europe, Asia-Pacific, Latin America, Africa and the Middle East, and finance. The CIO also hired five process information officers to work horizontally in different specialties across all divisions around the world. These process officers were concerned with product development, supply chain management, production, customer experience, and business services. The process officers and the information officers had different views of what was important to the firm. There were also different reporting relationships; the process information officers reported to the corporate CIO alone, but the information officers were in a matrix structure,

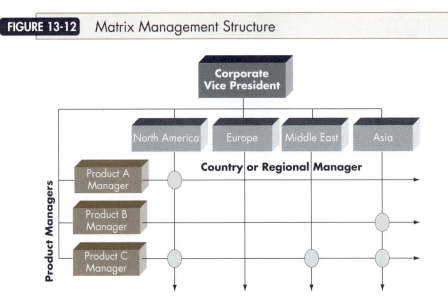

FIGURE 13-12 Matrix Management Structure

reporting to both the CIO of the firm and to their division heads. It is estimated that this approach has allowed GM to lower its IT budget by $1 billion (25 percent) in recent years. Where previously GM used 7,000 different information systems in its numerous plants and offices, today there are now fewer than 3,500.[xv] Figure 13-12 presents the matrix structure at GM in the technology domain.

Overall, the matrix format is one of the most difficult to manage. Reporting to two managers violates some of the basic managerial guidelines you likely learned in your introductory management classes on unity of command. Who has not experienced the frustration of having two bosses give conflicting orders? But such a structure can work particularly well in settings where there are highly trained and highly skilled workers. These workers are able to work with each other as colleagues, and the direct and immediate supervision for given tasks is less critical.

JAPAN, KEIRETSU, AND CULTURE

One type of organization related broadly to a matrix is a *keiretsu*, as introduced in Ch. 11. Ch. 2 and 4 introduced the concept of business groups in cultures outside of the United States. You will recall that business groups are entities that are typically vertically and horizontally integrated and connect a large number of businesses. These businesses may be connected through relationships, as in China, or through ownership, as in Japan. The period after World War II saw the rapid rise in the power of business groups in Japan. Japan's collective orientation resulted in a strong united effort to rebuild the nation, and Japan sought little foreign direct investment to generate this rebuilding. (This is in contrast to China, which relies heavily on FDI for its economic growth today.) Instead, the government and business groups became closely aligned in an effort to rebuild the nation.

Japan's government today is less closely aligned with business groups but their importance remains significant. Six major business groups still exist in Japan today. These groups are only 0.007 percent of the registered companies in Japan but represent approximately 20 percent of capital and 18 percent of sales by business in the nation.[xxx] The structure of these groups can be quite complex. For example, the figure below illustrates the degree of difficulty in creating a structure for Matsushita. Matsushita had sales of $71 billion in 2004 and was comprised not only of the well-known brand Panasonic, but also home appliance, semiconductor, lighting, healthcare, and automotive system companies. This wide dispersion of businesses and the relatively low performance led to a restructuring effort, including creating a unified research, development, and design effort.

(Continued)

CULTURE

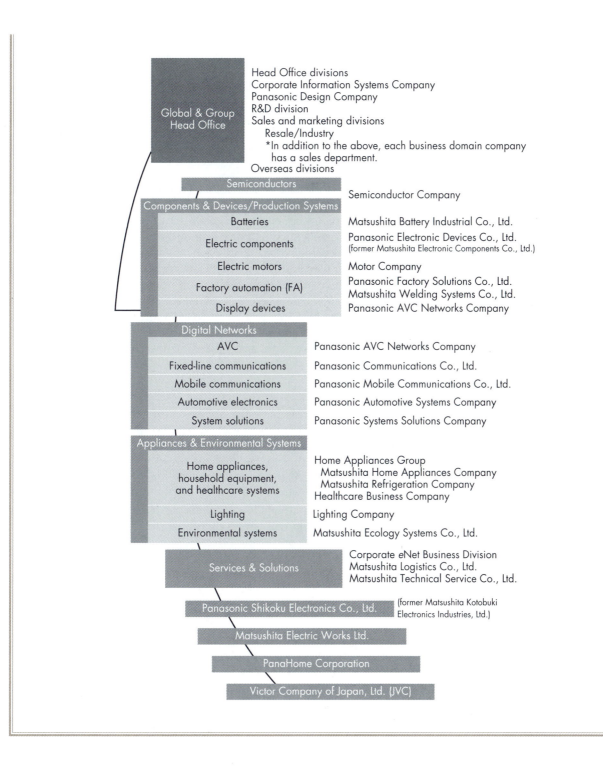

HOW TO DECIDE WHICH STRUCTURE IS RIGHT

How does a firm decide which structure is right, and when? The discussion up to this point has focused on the structures changing as the firm grows. This is correct, but the structure decision should be based on more than just growth. Management theorist Frederick Taylor, famous for his scientific management approach, argued that there was one best way to organize work and implied that this included organizational forms. However, it is generally agreed that there can be multiple forms that can work, depending on firm size, technology, strategy and degree of internationalization.[xvi] Organizations need to adopt the structure that fits their situational factors because this leads to higher organizational performance, and the organization needs to look at a variety of factors to choose which may be the best structure.[xvii] The issues to consider include the size of the firm, the diversification in the firm's portfolio of businesses, the technology used in the business, the nature of stakeholders, the level of internationalization, and the task pursued.

Size

Economies of scale
Average unit costs decline as production quantity increases over a limited period of time.

As a firm grows in size, it may be able to secure **economies of scale**, which exist when the average unit costs of a good or service decline as the quantity produced increases. However, there are limits to such cost savings because firms may have to invest more in fixed assets such as plant size and additional machinery, and large organizations can become both difficult to manage and costly, as Parkinson's Law predicts. Otherwise it would be most efficient to have one big organization doing everything. But there are limits to the size of an organization. The result is that as an organization grows, new layers of management are introduced to allow the various entities in the business to be controlled more effectively. However, these new layers of management create their own operational costs in slowed decision making, reduced innovation, and the turf battles that result.

Degree of Diversification

Recall from Chapter 4 that firms have the ability to pursue related or unrelated diversification. That is, a business can consist of activities that are consistent with each other or it can comprise separate businesses that work independently of each other. A large organization with activities that are strongly related to each other is expected to have a functional structure or perhaps a divisional structure based either on customers or geography. However, if a firm utilizes unrelated diversification, then it needs to have a structure that allows the businesses to operate effectively on an independent basis, so it likely will have a divisional structure based on product. Alternatively, if a firm is large and using related diversification, then it could be expected to pursue an SBU form of organization in which sets of businesses are connected but the businesses in the SBU are independent of other business areas.

Technology

The nature of the technology used by a firm makes a significant difference in how the business is operated and should be structured. For example, think of a business domain that is focused on low-technology areas such as the production of steel, or coal mining. The nature of the product and technology in these areas does not lend itself to an attempt to connect the various businesses together in the same way that a restaurant chain would need to do. For example, if a firm had steel manufacturing plants in Poland, China, and South Korea, there is little reason to expect a benefit for making them work together. The technology used in the steel business is such that there is no easy way to secure **economies of scope** from the businesses being closely connected to each other and sharing assets and technology to reduce cost or create other synergies—they will tend to function in a stand-alone capacity. Instead, the steel making firm might consider the geographic nature of the business when considering a potential organizational structure. In contrast, a high-technology business such as software development would be closely connected. Consider Microsoft's effort to integrate its research and development center in China or India with its efforts in Washington state in the United States. The structure has to be much tighter and better integrated because the products developed are typically not created solely in one location but with inputs from across the firm.

Economies of scope
Cost savings that result from performing two activities jointly, such as manufacturing one type of car in a plant during the day, and at night, producing a different car that was previously produced somewhere else.

Stakeholders

In choosing a structure, a firm needs to be aware of the stakeholders who have a significant impact on the organization. The firm needs to ensure that the form of the organization is such that these parties' interests are satisfied. For example, the telecommunications industry is normally one that has extensive governmental oversight, and firms in this industry need to ensure that their structures meet the needs for regulatory oversight. If different branches of the government regulate different aspects of a business, such as fixed-line versus mobile service, it then makes sense to have different units address these areas to simplify the interaction with government regulators.

Degree of Internationalization

As indicated throughout this chapter, the degree of internationalization plays a key part in the choice of organizational structure. It was noted in Chapter 4 that a firm can choose a multi-domestic or global strategy. A multi-domestic strategy allows the businesses in each nation to operate separately. In contrast, a global firm has a single strategy around the world. A firm can employ most of the structures discussed here with either strategy. However, the nature of the structure likely will vary with each strategy chosen. For example, a firm with a multi-domestic strategy may have a divisional structure, but those divisions would be organized around the business in the countries in which it operates. Alternatively, a firm with a global strategy will organize around product divisions that cut across national borders, so that efficiencies and economies of scale around those products can be more easily obtained.

Geographic Scope

An issue related to degree of internationalization is the nature of the countries in which the firm operates. If a firm is involved in a set of countries that can also be subdivided into distinct cultures, then it may be best to have a divisional structure to address each one. For example, if the firm has operations in Quebec, France, Belgium, and Switzerland that address the French-speaking market and another set of operations in China and Singapore, it may be best to create two separate divisions: one with principally French-speaking personnel and another with strong Chinese language capacity. Alternatively, if a firm's international operations are in the United States and a nearby (in both distance and culture) country such as Canada, then a functional structure may work best because setting up separate international divisions for these areas would not be warranted. Therefore, a firm needs to consider which countries it is involved in as it establishes its structure.

Task

A firm must also evaluate the benefit trade-off between mechanistic and organic structures. **Mechanistic structures** are those that emphasize stability and hierarchical decision making. Such structures are appropriate in low-technology domains where decisions are made in a hierarchical fashion; major decisions (and some minor ones) come from the top and work their way down through the organization. In a business with a low cost strategy, such a mechanistic structure is desirable, because most parts of these businesses focus on keeping costs as low as possible. Minimal variation in product and innovative processes are things that consume the firm's financial resources. Thus, in this situation, it is desirable to have a mechanistic structure.

Mechanistic structures
Structures that are highly inflexible and static, typically in low-technology domains.

However, firms working in high-speed production often also employ a mechanistic structure, with their human resources and other functions given narrow ranges of flexibility. For example, Texas Instruments employs a mechanistic structure in order to be able to have a fast and highly efficient mass production cycle for its businesses, as does Matsushita in Japan. Many mass producers maintain a mechanistic structure with a fairly strict hierarchy in the interest of carefully controlling costs. While Wal-Mart is often thought of as the quintessential cost-cutter, Matsushita is also well known in Japan for worrying about costs to the penny and investing a great deal to take cost out of the manufacturing process. As we have seen in Chapter 5, firms such as Wal-Mart and Matsushita are innovators on the production-process side, but they often use a predictable and lower-cost mechanistic structure to implement a low-cost strategic positioning.

Organic structure
A flexible structure, often decentralized.

Alternatively, a firm may choose to have an **organic structure**, one that is more flexible, innovative, and able to adapt to its environment. In environments where change is rapid, an organizational structure needs to able to adapt and respond as quickly as the environment. An outcome of this need to adapt is the flat organization, one frequently discussed type of organic structure that has few layers of management. For example, Koch Industries is one of the largest privately held firms in the United States. There are different job titles within the firm, but it seeks to keep those different layers of management to a minimum. Koch Industries also makes a point to cross-train all employees. The result is that this oil refining firm, generally not a highly profitable industry in the United States, has been able to quickly adapt and change as new opportunities arise. Koch Industries has become one of the dominant producers of tennis courts in the United States, and it has a number of loosely related businesses, including oil-trading, industrial gases and liquids, asphalt, fibers and intermediates, minerals, fertilizers, chemical technology equipment, pulp and paper, and ranching. Most of this diversified set of activities relates to petroleum, but it is the firm's ability to respond quickly and creatively that is critical to its success. Today, Koch operates in approximately 50 countries and employs approximately 30,000 people.

Organic structures need highly skilled and motivated employees, which leads to a particular type of organic structure that has come to be called the learning organization. The learning organization concept is closely associated with Peter Senge, MIT professor and founder of the Center for Organizational Learning at MIT's Sloan School of Business. In his well-known 1990 book *The Fifth Discipline*, Senge defines learning organizations as

> organizations where people continually expand their capacity to create the results they truly desire, where new and expansive patterns of thinking are nurtured, where collective aspiration is set free, and where people are continually learning to see the whole together.[xviii]

Senge's main thesis is that for an organization to become a learning organization it must embrace five disciplines. First, it must build shared vision in order to achieve a common commitment to long-term results and achievement. Second, the organization must foster the understanding and examination of people's mental models as important to strategic planning and change. People typically resist change and do not like modifying what they do and think they know. Because a person's existing mental model of a particular situation often resists new information, such as what is understood about the company's capabilities and mission, it can be a major obstacle to creating and supporting needed change. Techniques to encourage critical thinking that can be used to encourage creativity and foster readiness and openness to change were discussed in Chapter 9.

Third, team learning is needed so that the learning is passed on from the individuals to teams (i.e., the organization as a whole). Teams can often make better decisions than individuals in complex or ambiguous settings. Teams are also

Jon Feingersh/Blend Images/Getty Images

Among the many benefits to working in teams are knowledge sharing, cooperation, and realistic problem solving.

useful for making forecasts of the future, particularly in situations where no one is an expert. This also increases buy-in because the more people who are involved with the decision and who make a public commitment to it, the more likely that the change or plan will be implemented. Fourth, personal mastery is the individual's motivation to learn and become better (hence the term *mastery*). And finally, the fifth discipline is that of systems thinking, which allows individuals to see a holistic, systemic view of the organization as a function of its environment.

Honda's decisions concerning its entry into the U.S. motorcycle market is an illustration of the competitive advantage of having a learning organization. Honda entered the market in the late 1950s during the fall season, not understanding that spring is the season for new motorcycle purchases. This was not an auspicious start. Honda was unable to secure proper distribution for their motorcycles, and the motorcycles that were fine on Japan's system of small roads were not powerful enough for California's freeways and they suffered repeated breakdowns and engine problems. Additionally, Honda did not secure proper parts and repair facilities, so it spent a good deal of money repairing the first-generation motorcycles they had brought to the United States, which was was money that it could ill afford to spend. A consulting firm might have advised Honda to quit, go home, and come back later when it was a bigger, financially stronger firm. But Honda noticed that a small motorbike they were not focusing on selling was getting a lot of attention when one of the Honda managers took it out for a ride on the weekends in the California hills. Deciding there might be a market for smaller, offroad motorbikes, Honda decided to introduce the small motorcycle—named the Supercub—into the U.S. market. The Supercub filled or perhaps created a key niche: the recreational and racing "dirt bike." By the early 1960s, Honda had not only recovered from its early mistakes, but was able to secure about two-thirds of the U.S. market for motorcycles of all sizes. Honda's organic structure in the United States gave it room to experiment and find a product that proved highly suited to the U.S. market while only later using what it learned in moving upmarket.[xix] Thus, from Senge's perspective, success comes from an organic organization that fully engages individuals and permits experimentation.

IMPLEMENTING CHANGE IN AN ORGANIZATIONAL STRUCTURE

Organizational change is a very difficult process for a firm, regardless of whether it is the structure or a business activity that is changing. This difficulty expands as the firm becomes more international. The dispersion of different cultures, people, and distance all act to make changing organizational structure difficult.

There are a few fundamental rules that should underlie any efforts to change a firm's structure if the business ultimately determines it needs a different organizational structure. These rules apply whether the structural change affects a small part of the firm or its entire organization.

First, participation and communication are important to this process. Rather than saying to employees that the structure has changed and they now report to someone new, employees need to be told why the change is necessary. Michael Hammer, who created the concept of reengineering, referred to this as "building a burning bridge."[xx] Reengineering rests on the assumption that over time

---

TELIA: RESTRUCTURING IN SWEDEN

One of the largest firms in Sweden is Telia, a telecommunications firm that is comprised of over 50 different businesses with over 34,000 employees in 100 countries. Telia began a restructuring program in 1995. Three major unions represent the workers of the firm.

In 1992, Telia pursued restructuring, but the effort was widely seen as a failure because of widespread demonstrations and employee hostility following the restructuring. A subsequent restructuring effort in 1995 was pursued in a different manner. The head of personnel determined to work with the unions to design a program that minimized worker dislocation but still allowed the firm to achieve its goal of becoming more competitive. Part of this change was an education process on Telia's part. For example, the personnel department prepared statistics on the requirements of the restructuring and the implications if these restructurings were not pursued. Specifically, the personnel department prepared a worst-case scenario of replacing employees based on the typical rule of last-in, first-out (that is, the more recent hires are the first ones released by the firm). The unions, convinced of the need to restructure, were determined to work with the firm. One method they used was to

agree to set aside the law that covered layoffs (the Employment of Security Act). The law allowed for such cooperative arrangements but they were rare at the time in Sweden.

Telia and the unions were in negotiations for an entire year but ultimately came up with a solution that was good for all parties. Telia initially identified those areas they wanted to restructure. Then it developed a consultation team for each division. This team was composed of all three unions and management. The team initially determined the skills necessary to fill the jobs that would result from the restructuring. Then the firm placed 20,000 of its employees who were affected by the restructuring in a new division. These employees would have to apply for the new jobs. A consultation committee in each area determined if the employees had the skills required to fill the new positions. Approximately 6,400 people were not competent for the new jobs, and these individuals were given the choice of changing occupations in the firm where their skills were a better fit (i.e., a lower skilled job), or receiving training for a year for the new jobs. If neither choice was suitable the individuals could leave the

firm or take early retirement. Natural attrition resulted in only 200 employees having to be let go. However, the firm was able to restructure itself significantly and thus become more competitive.

This approach to restructuring is very consistent with Swedish culture, which places a high priority on the collective good. While Telia was able to move its strategic orientation in the early 1990s, by early 2000 it realized that it needed to make other changes. Specifically, the firm sought to reorganize its: the five business units: Telia Mobile, Telia International Carrier, Telia Networks, Telia Internet Services, and Telia Equity. Each business area is responsible, within its product area, for the group's total earnings across all markets in Sweden and throughout the world. This new structure gives greater independence to each business group.

Pacts for employment and competitiveness: Case studies. Telia. European Foundation for the Improvement of Living and Working Conditions.

Telia: Comparable Financial Figures 1999–2000 in the New Group Structure. (2001, April 19), http://findarticles.com/p/articles/mi_m0EIN/is_2001_April_19/ai_73399134.

businesses create and build up processes that no longer establish value for the firm and may even hinder its business. Therefore, there is a need to periodically reevaluate what customers actually value and how a firm can deliver value, and not load up the product or service with a lot of features the customers do not value. However, firms and individuals are reluctant to make changes without clearly recognizing the need for change.

The goal is to have employees think of the solution or at least feel like they helped to generate the solution. Participation can come through facilitated discussions with employees. One means to help ensure that employees are supportive of a change is to think of ways to connect the compensation system to changes in structure. For example, there may be bonus pools for those who adapt more quickly and use the new structure in some meaningful way.[xxi] Such participative techniques may not work in highly hierarchical political environments in which there are limits on many types of change, but evidence shows that building such support is even more critical in these types of environments. Even in countries where unions are strong and the protection of workers extensive, workers and their unions have come to recognize that only profitable companies are able to pay wages and fund pensions.[xxii] In these settings, if workers and their unions are educated about the problems of the firm, then they will be more willing to change and adapt in order to protect their jobs in the future. It is for this reason, in part, that there are more restructuring efforts using reengineering, and its employee-involvement processes, in Europe than in the United States.[xxiii]

It is vital that top management and affected units also support a structure change. If a manager is seen as fighting a change, the people who work for that person may also resist the change, and this resistance can result in failure of the change effort. As a result, those in leadership positions must be supportive or accept a change in the terms of their employment. The manager may be fired, but a more likely approach for a large multinational is transferring the individual to a part of the firm away from the domains that are undergoing the structural change.[xxiv]

Implementing structural change can be difficult. However, firms are usually well served in creating a plan regarding how and when the change is to occur. This plan then forms the backbone of the effort to ensure that those plans are followed. This aspect of change management was discussed in detail in Chapter 11. The various other issues highlighted here were explored in detail earlier in chapters on motivation (Chapter 7) and influence and negotiation (Chapter 10).

INFORMAL ORGANIZATIONS

Most of this chapter has concerned formal organizational structure. However, as the discussion of flat and learning organizations hint, there are also strong impacts on the firm from informal organizations, which were briefly discussed in Chapter 2. Informal organizations are the unofficial connections that exist among individuals in a business. These networks of connected individuals and departments within and across firms reveal important patterns of connectivity outside formal structures—who really has the decision power in an organization and sometimes how work actually gets done. This was discussed in greater detail in the context of decision making in Chapter 9, so we do not dwell on it here. However, note that such informal structures and groups in a business can be stronger than the formal organizational structure, and they are important to understand. This understanding can confer an advantage for those doing

---

FORMAL AND INFORMAL CODES OF ETHICS

ETHICS

Organizations usually have a large informal component that is not codified in charts and rules. United Technologies' (UTC) Code of Ethics is an extensive statement of its Corporate Principles and Standards of Conduct. The code addresses the firm's relations with suppliers, customers, employees, shareholders, and various communities worldwide. It also addresses competitor relations and its employees' responsibilities to both internal and external stakeholders. Each of these main categories is, in turn, divided into specific topics. Under Conduct toward Employees, the code lists sub-topics of adherence to equal opportunity, workplace environment, drug and alcohol abuse at work, the privacy of employees, communications policies (including use of email), training, and compensation and benefits. In total, there are 35 subsections in the UTC Code of Ethics. Additionally, the company has created a network of Business Practices/Compliance Officers to explain elements of the Code and to advise employees who may have a specific question (United Technologies). Obviously, UTC takes its formal Code very seriously.

But there is also an informal aspect to the UTC code. Where the formal code may address unambiguous moral circumstances, there are always situations that require an interpretation of rules and may rely more on personal ethics than those formally discussed at the corporate policy level.

How do individuals learn how to respond to those "gray" areas of organizational behavior? What does an employee do if the Code does not address a particular circumstance? Perhaps the answer lies in the staff's stories about solutions to ethical conundrums or morally bounded situations that have occurred within the organization and which, when taken as a whole, eventually frame the ethical limits of employee responses in the future. In other words, codes of conduct represent what the firm espouses individuals should do normatively, while stories transmit to others what individuals in the firm actually did do—successfully or not. These stories function a little like a judicial ruling in common law: they interpret and apply existing laws and form the basis for future behavior in the organization (in effect, "This is how we handled this situation before, and it turned out okay").

Brown, J. S. (2005). Narrative as a knowledge medium in organizations. In Brown, J. S., Denning, S., Groh, K., & Prusak, L. (Eds.). *Storytelling in Organizations: Why Storytelling Is Transforming 21st Century Organizations and Management* (Chapter 5, pp. 53–96). Burlington, MA: Elsevier Butterworth-Heinemann.

Buchholz, R. A., & Rosenthal, S. B. (1998). *Business Ethics: The Pragmatic Process Beyond Principles to Process.* Upper Saddle River, NJ: Prentice Hall.

United Technologies Corporation Code of Ethics. (2005). Hartford, CT: Corporate Practices Office.

---

business with that firm. Managers are well served to understand these structures and to use them to their benefit.[xxv]

SUMMARY

Organizational structure is a critical element to a firm's success. However, there is no dogmatic answer about which structure is best. As an organization grows, there is a need for greater coordination between the various parts of the business, but that coordination comes at the cost of increased bureaucracy. The key is for the organization to match its structure with its given situation and strategy, and the decision must be based on the judgment of the organization and its members as to what works best.

International business increases the cultural and geographic distance between the various units of the business, which makes the choices of structure that much more difficult. However, regardless of the particular structure chosen—whether it be simple, functional, divisional, SBU, or matrix—the structure is the critical glue that helps the international organization hold together and act as an effective entity.

MANAGERIAL GUIDELINES

1. Structure and strategy are intertwined and important to each other. The firm cannot prosper if the two are not aligned.
2. Well-known business historian Alfred Chandler argued that organization structure followed a firm's chosen strategy; but structure can also facilitate the choice of strategy, particularly as the firm acquires or enters new businesses.

3. The alignment of structure and strategy needs to consider a varied set of issues, such as diversification (both level of product and internationalization), size, and stakeholders.

4. The structure should allow a firm's strategy to be implemented correctly. Thus, the structure should support those types of actions that are needed by the strategy. For example, a flexible, flat structure allows individuals to be creative and may more effectively support a differentiation strategy. However, a flexible, flat structure does not align well with a strategy of overall cost control.

5. The firm's national culture also helps to determine which organizational structure may be more appropriate. Cultures that emphasize high power distance typically use more mechanistic structures that emphasize hierarchy, irrespective of strategy. If a firm is going to structure differently from what its strategy suggests, it will be necessary to educate employees about the reasons for the differing structure. High-technology firms in the more hierarchical societies of East Asia and Latin America struggle with the structural imperative to have a looser, more organic structure versus the typical preferences of the founding family for a more mechanistic and formal structure placing power within the family's inner circle.

6. The structure can be different from that which the culture may have indicated was optimal, but employee involvement becomes even more important in these settings so that there will not be conflict.

7. In mature organizations, the ability to create learning organizations can provide a competitive advantage as the firm's employees learn to adapt and change.

Table 13-1 is helpful to students or managers as they analyze the type of structure they can expect in different international settings.

TABLE 13-1 Firm Structure around the World

Region	Question about Commonly Held Beliefs	Reality
North America	Are all firms flatter and less centralized in the United States and Canada?	While firms in North America, particularly Silicon Valley in California, are thought to have pioneered the flat, egalitarian organizational structure, not all North American firms have adopted this structure. For example, firms that pursue low cost strategies that leave little room for innovation from the prescribed production system will be quite hierarchical, almost military-like in their structure. Chandler's adage that firm strategy should generally dictate structure is usually observed. But business academics and consultants do teach the value of flat organizations and self-leadership, and the trend may be toward more egalitarian, organic structures.
East Asia—Overseas Chinese	Are firms very hierarchical in Overseas Chinese firms?	Overseas Chinese firms around the Pacific Rim, much like Italian and Latin American firms, are usually family-owned and operated businesses. This structure is quite hierarchical, with the many decisions funneled up to the firm chairperson and managing director (equivalent in the United States to the CEO), who is often the same individual. Middle managers and lower-level employees, particularly those outside of the family, are given little say over major firm policy. Some firms have tried to change this. Hong Kong–based telephone maker VTech takes pains to state that it is not run like a traditional Chinese family firm. Firms seeking faster growth believe that they need to shed some of the hierarchical practices associated with family firms, and this may be slowly happening.[xxvi] In mainland China, the newly created family firms seem to be following the example of their Overseas Chinese cousins by creating hierarchical, mechanistic structures.

TABLE 13-1   (Continued)

Region	Question about Commonly Held Beliefs	Reality
Europe	Do European multinationals often use matrix structures?	Some would argue that European firms such as ABB in Switzerland formalized and popularized the matrix structure. After many years, ABB finally abandoned the matrix structure, leaving authority largely with the product divisions. Other European firms have followed this restructuring, opting for more simplified division structures.
Japan	Are Japanese firms somehow different from those in other developed markets?	The elite Japanese firms (e.g., Toyota, Honda, Canon, and Matsushita) have given the world of international business several management innovations such as the Just-in-Time manufacturing system and the concept of core competencies.[xxvii] To better implement the sharing of core competencies and the resulting core products, these firms were also pioneers in implementing the transnational strategy that emphasized organizational learning and allowed for firms to better share skills and personnel. Managers from outside of Japan have tried to understand how to structure large firms as innovative, learning organizations with the help of academics such as Peter Senge, Gary Hamel, and others.[xxviii]
Latin America	Are Latin American firms typically functional and hierarchical?	Family firms are often dominated by a patriarch-founder, with information and decision power centralized around this figure. Key information is kept inside the family. This is consistent with the high power distance found in Latin America, as well as the family structure of businesses. Outsiders may have difficulty getting promoted in such firms, unless the firm has made a commitment to permit more outsiders into the top management team. Firms in Latin America seem to be shifting away from the family structure even more slowly than in East Asia.

CULTURE AND DOING BUSINESS IN JAPAN

Japan has the second-most technologically advanced economy in the world behind the United States. Japan has over half of the world's operating robots and produces 25 percent of the world's high-tech products, and is the third largest in purchasing power, behind the United States and China. The nation has an aging population and relatively high levels of government debt. However, recently Japan's economy has been in a recovery and is growing stronger after a number of years of weak performance.

Japan has a strong and distinct culture. In conducting business in Japan, several cultural customs should be considered, such as hierarchy. Negotiations between organizations are conducted by business people of equal rank and status, and age is given deference equivalent to status within a company. Status is important because it is what gets you connected with business contacts—either your own status or that status of a colleague who acts as an intermediary in meeting others in the business world. The status and relationships of individuals will further affect a wide variety of issues, such as how to sit in a meeting or at dinner. In Japan, the highest-ranking official always sits at the head of the dinner table and the rank of others attending the dinner will determine how close they are allowed to sit to him. Visitors are shown where to sit by the host.

Similar to Chinese culture, Japanese culture views "face" as important. Therefore, showing anger is typically viewed negatively because it results in directly confronting someone. Instead, individuals find a way to say no without directly confronting someone with a negative answer. Careful attention must be given to what is said and how it is said when interacting with others in Japan. Recall from the discussion in Chapter 2 of high-context versus low-context societies and how this cultural predisposition shapes communication. The Japanese typify a high-context society; so there must be great sensitivity to the context in which statements are made. If someone from Japan tells you, "That will be difficult," that probably means no.

The Japanese are also a society with high collectivism, and though they are becoming more individualistic, group cohesion remains very important. This is frequently seen in decision making where numerous individuals are consulted. Sometimes this creates a much slower decision-making process than many Westerners are accustomed to.

ADDITIONAL RESOURCES

Bryan, L. L., Fraser, J., Oppenheim, J., & Rail, W. 1999. *Race for the World: Strategies to Build a Great Global Firm.* Boston: Harvard Business School Press.
Galbraith, J. (2000). *Designing the Global Corporation.* New York: John Wiley & Sons.
Yip, G. (2002). *Total Global Strategy II* (2nd ed.). New York: Prentice Hall.

EXERCISES

Opening Vignette Discussion Questions

1. Do you think Japan's cohesive culture helped Honda make the structure changes discussed?
2. We previously looked at the work of Dr. Deming and the quality movement. Japan has a strong interest in the concepts of quality. How do you think those concepts would have affected the structural changes identified here?

DISCUSSION QUESTIONS

1. Why do you think strategy and structure are so interconnected?
2. We discussed the Overseas Chinese extensively in this chapter. Many religious and ethnic minorities around the world, many of whom are recent immigrants, are more economically successful than the dominant population. For example, the Protestants in France, the Greeks in the United States (who have the highest education level on average of any ethnic minority), and the Germans and Italians in Latin America have all excelled in their adopted communities. Why do you think such ethnic or religious minorities have been able to develop greater achievements in certain fields than others?
3. Name key advantages and disadvantages of three different organizational structures.
4. Are there specific industries in which you would expect a matrix structure to do particularly well?

IN-CLASS EXERCISES

1. Most U.S. students are familiar with Wal-Mart. (For students outside the United States, treat this as a take-home exercise and read about Wal-Mart before answering.) Wal-Mart owns a company called Sam's Club, a low-cost retail warehouse unit, that sells products in bulk and that has many international operations. Break into teams and design what you might think would be a good organizational structure for the firm. Present your ideas to the class. Your instructor will present Wal-Mart's actual organizational structure after you have discussed your ideas with the class.
2. The defense industry has something that is referred to as set-asides. In a set-aside, a foreign government, such as Poland, agrees to buy U.S. military equipment. A certain percentage of the equipment must be purchased within Poland. Break into teams and design what you believe would be a matrix structure for an international defense industry firm like Lockheed Martin.
3. Assume you and a team of other students from your school form a new firm that quickly grows to 100 employees. The firm is an Internet company that designs marketing programs for major international clients that are in the

business of selling oil-industry equipment. What should your structure look like at this point in time? Present your ideas to the class.

4. In an earlier chapter we learned about the case involving the failure of Barings, the British investment firm that fell into ruin when a single employee in Singapore invested large sums of money without the firm's knowledge or approval. How could such a situation have been avoided by changes in structure?

TAKE-HOME EXERCISES

1. Research the organizational structure of a Fortune 500 company. Present your findings to the class, and be prepared to discuss the reasons why you believe the firm pursues this given structure.
2. Research a large multinational firm in a country other than your own. Can you find any substantive differences in the organizational structure that may be due to culture?
3. Research and contrast the organizational structure of McDonald's and YUM! Brands. Why do they have such different structures?
4. Research a large Korean firm like Samsung and its chief European rival Philips. Why do their structures differ so much?

SHORT CASE QUESTIONS

Telia: Restructuring in Sweden (p. 424)

1. Why do you think Telia had to restructure employee hierarchies in addition to the overall organization of the business?
2. Why do you think there was such a lapse in time between the two restructurings within Telia?
3. Would a U.S. firm be able to restructure its employees in the same manner as Telia?

14

THE FUTURE OF INTERNATIONAL MANAGEMENT

Overview

This chapter summarizes this text on international management and focuses on what can be expected in the future for international managers and their organizations. The future is always difficult to predict, but there are a few key issues on which many people would agree. These issues include the continuing spread of globalization and the importance of international management, the growing importance of entrepreneurship and entrepreneurial enterprises in the world economy, greater concern about the environment, and increasing attention given to the poorest populations and regions of the world. These issues and how they impact international management, as well as potentially important opportunities for firms and entrepreneurs, will be examined in turn. In addition, financial panics and their implications for international firms will be examined. The specific questions that will be addressed include the following:

- Summary of the importance of international management and the opportunities it offers to firms and individuals.
- What are entrepreneurial firms and who are entrepreneurs?
  - What is their role in the world economy?
  - What are born-global firms?
- What role might the natural environment play in the future of international business?
- Who are "the bottom billion"?
  - What has been occurring in the poorer parts of the world?
  - What is their outlook for the future and what role does international management have to play in improving their lives and economic opportunities?
- What is the future of globalization and international management?

SAFARICOM: PROFIT AND THE LOWEST INCOME POPULATION

Kenya is a poor country with a gross national income per capita of $530 a year and close to half of its 36 million citizens living on less than one dollar a day. But this poverty has not prohibited mobile phone operator Safaricom from making a very good profit. It is estimated that Safaricom's profits in 2007 were $270 million on sales of $705 million. Total profits for the firm were up 41 percent from the previous year.

Safaricom purposely targets low-income individuals by introducing services and payment plans that are affordable. For example, Safaricom provides its mobile phone services on a "pay as you go" manner. Similar payment plans exist in mature markets such as the United States where SIM cards are purchased in minimum values of $10, but in Kenya SIM cards are offered for as little as 50 Kenyan schillings (or about 75 cents). Safaricom has also noticed the trend for a single family or extended family to purchase a single phone, with each member of the family using minutes purchased individually.

This purchasing pattern by individuals in Kenya helped Safaricom recognize that its competition may not be like that faced in mature markets. In mature markets mobile phone operators see other similar operators as their major competition. Safaricom does face other mobile phone operators in Kenya. But Safaricom sees its major competitor as being other non-essential consumer expenditures such as whether the person chooses to buy a beer, a cigarette, or air time for their phone. The firm must provide high service and ensure that it has characteristics that consumers desire.

The ability of the lowest income individuals to obtain mobile phone service has brought significant changes. There are obvious examples of people who are now able to keep in touch with family members, which previously was not possible. But there are also very substantive economic changes. For example, day laborers can now locate where there is a need for work, allowing them to more easily make a living. Also, the market for farmers' goods can vary widely in Kenya, and Safaricom offers a service in which farmers can quickly find the market price of goods before they sell. Thus, a farmer can identify the market willing to pay the highest price and decide for themselves perhaps to hold a product rather than sell on any given day. Many individuals in Kenya do not have bank accounts, but they may need to send money to someone. Safaricom now offers a service that allows individuals to do this through their phones for 5 percent of the amount sent. The firm also allows individuals to deposit money in this manner with over 650 representatives around Kenya.

Safaricom's major shareholder is Vodaphone. Although not publicly listed yet, this is one of Safaricom's ultimate goals. It is now estimated that one in four individuals in Kenya has a mobile phone. Safaricom hopes to continue to expand its sales until it reaches a similar number of customers in mature markets. While the average revenue per phone user may be lower than in mature markets the profit per user is much higher. While Kenya may seem poor relative to a country with a more mature economy, Safaricom has been able to both be profitable and change people's lives for the better.

Jopson, B. (2007, October 9). How Safaricom gives voice to Africa. *Financial Times*, p. 14.

Bottom billion
The world's poorest billion people who have largely missed the economic progress that has come from globalization over the last 25 years.

International management is a domain that experiences frequent change. It has been stressed in the text that international competition will increase as more economies mature and their firms become global. However, there are several issues that will affect international managers and their global businesses increasingly in the future that merit extra discussion. These issues are entrepreneurship, the environment, and the **bottom billion**—the world's poorest billion people—many of whom have missed the economic progress that has come from globalization over the last 25 years. Because some of these issues are still quite new in terms of international management, over the long term these issues will grow in importance to business. Figure 14-1 summarizes the flow that will occur in the chapter.

INCREASED IMPORTANCE OF INTERNATIONAL MANAGEMENT

Business people and policymakers alike generally agree on the increasing importance of international business and the positive change and economic growth it can bring to a country. Because of the support of this cross-border trade and

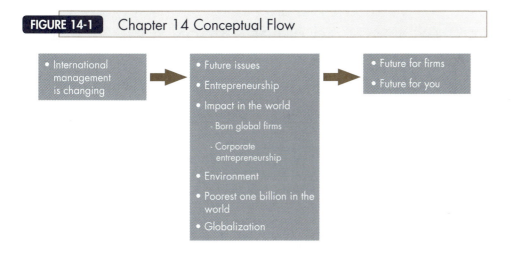

FIGURE 14-1 Chapter 14 Conceptual Flow

investment, many students today will likely find themselves working in multinational enterprises, whether at home or abroad. This has been the trend since World War II ended in 1945, and it has accelerated in recent years with the establishment of the WTO and its free trade policies. The post-World War II years saw a major expansion of world trade. From 1948 through 1972, world exports grew from $51 billion to $415 billion, representing a sevenfold increase in monetary terms and a fourfold increase in volume.[i] Yet today's world trade dwarfs all prior statistics. With falling trade barriers in the past 20 years, world exports continued their growth, rising from roughly $4 trillion in 1990 to about $7 trillion in 1999. By 2006, total world exports had doubled again to nearly $14 trillion.[ii]

Trade between corporations or individuals takes place when both sides are made better off by the exchange. Since both sides are made better off to some degree, economists would argue (and can show in mathematical and empirical terms) that wealth is created from trade on both sides. More tumultuous economic upheaval is also expected with freer trade and competition as was discussed in Chapter 1, although the increase in oil and commodity prices and turmoil in numerous asset markets is not linked to poverty but to increasing demand and prosperity, particularly in emerging economies. By exponentially expanding international trade since the end of World War II the world has become much wealthier.

This growth in trade is also illustrated by the international success of large firms such as Coca-Cola. By the early 1990s, Coca-Cola earned higher profits selling soda to the Japanese than to Americans.[iii] Now Mexico has a higher per capita consumption of Coca-Cola than any other country, and a very respectable GDP of around $10,000 per person. Similarly, General Motors (GM) now makes much more profit in Europe and China than in the United States. In China, Buick is considered one of the most desirable automobile brands to own. Mexican cement maker Cemex derives more than four-fifths of its revenue from outside of its Mexican market.[iv] The *21st Century Report* states two-thirds of the world's CEOs expect to generate employment and revenues increasingly from outside their firm's home country.[v] Many CEOs view foreign competition and markets as key factors in their firm's business success, particularly the management of human resources.[vi] Do you expect to work for Buick in Shanghai? Or for Cemex's plants in Europe? Or even one of the big Mexican food companies, Gruma? Not planning to move to Mexico? That is okay, because Gruma has a large corporate office in suburban Dallas. Chinese computer firm Lenovo has extensive facilities in North Carolina, and the chairman has even moved with his family there from Beijing. You can expect the presence of multinational enterprises of all kinds and the importance of international management to become even more significant to all of us in the future.

GENERATION X AND Y GO INTERNATIONAL

CULTURE

With trade barriers falling and foreign direct investment increasing substantially, many firms have been sending large numbers of employees overseas. Many universities now provide opportunities for their students to go on international exchanges, and once students have gone abroad, they are more likely to look for the opportunity to work there. International experience helps to differentiate you from thousands of new graduates. Firms look for young employees to work overseas because they are often more flexible and may have fewer family concerns. Additionally, advances in travel and communications make it easier to check on international operations.

Historically, employees sent abroad were in their 40s and even 50s, sometimes senior managers with spouses and children. Now they are often twenty-somethings and single. For younger employees, the challenges differ from those for older employees. Firms need to help ensure that young professionals are able to build a solid professional experience, along with a reasonable career path. It's particularly important to make sure a young expatriate does not feel he or she does not have a future with the corporation.

Another major challenge for young employees abroad and their firms is the acculturation process. Much has been discussed about understanding the culture of the country where you are working. Part of that is being introspective, and understanding the challenges that you will face in a new environment, particularly a much different one. A more seasoned manager can understand how to adapt internationally from their experience but a young person may have had no experience with various cultures. In parts of Asia, it is difficult to get a cold drink with a meal. Even on the hottest day of the year in Hong Kong when the temperature is 95 degrees (35 Celsius), many restaurants will bring you hot water to drink with your meal. Requests for cold water will bring puzzled stares from the service staff. In Australia, and many European countries, stores close early. On a beautiful weekday afternoon in Perth, Western Australia, most stores may be closed. In parts of Europe such as Italy, people go to lunch for two hours and many banks and government offices are closed at lunch and into the late afternoon. It's difficult to get things done until you successfully adjust to these types of inconveniences.

You may also be surprised to find out that people outside of your organization who do not know you or are not your subordinate may not be helpful, and even view you with distrust. This often surprises people from less hierarchical societies, such as Northern Europe or North America, where people are taught to be helpful to others, regardless if they are a stranger or an important person. In many other cultures, usually those that are more hierarchical in nature, it is less common to do things for those who have no connection to you, or are not above you in some way. It is frustrating for expats to try to get things done in a culture where they almost certainly have to pay to get a basic task completed and cannot get help from those they do not know well. It takes time to come to terms with the loss of familiarity and ability to get things done, along with the loss of freedom to move about in the new place (particularly if you do not speak the local language), and having to adjust to cultural norms—some of which you may not like and may never really come to appreciate, even after a long period of living in that culture.

Morrison, T., Conaway, W. A., & Borden, G. A. (2006). *Kiss, Bow, or Shake Hands: How to Do Business in Sixty Countries.* Avon, MA: Adams Media.

ENTREPRENEURSHIP AND INTERNATIONAL MANAGEMENT

The attention devoted to entrepreneurship and innovation has increased greatly in recent years as economists, government policymakers and the general public has learned how closely economic and job growth is tied to innovation and firm formation.[vii] Researchers have recognized the importance of understanding the entrepreneurial process,[viii] leading to the creation of worldwide studies on entrepreneurship such as the Global Entrepreneurship Monitor (GEM), a not-for-profit research consortium cosponsored by businesses, governments, and universities around the world to study entrepreneurship in dozens of countries.[ix]

Management scholars conceptualize entrepreneurship a little more broadly than do most pundits or economists. In management, **entrepreneurship** is defined as value-creation activities by individuals, either in creating a new enterprise or building a new business or product line within an existing organization.[x] This activity shows up in varying degrees in the world's economies, depending on their level of development and related institutional support for entrepreneurship. Developmental economists, for example, distinguish three major stages of development (beyond basic subsistence farming and hunter-gatherer societies) that

Entrepreneurship
Value-creation activities to create new enterprises or build a new business or product line within an existing organization.

business people need to be aware of as they seek to do business overseas.[xi] In the first stage, an economy specializes in the production of agricultural products and small-scale service and manufacturing. This typically represents an agrarian economy in an early stage of development dominated by family-run farms and household businesses and is marked by high rates of non-agricultural self-employment. Sole proprietorships (the self-employed) probably account for most farms and small manufacturing and service firms in this stage.

In the second stage, the economy shifts from small-scale household production toward manufacturing. Businesses tend to move from family-based entrepreneurial capitalism to more Big Unit and managerial capitalism in which larger firms exist and are encouraged by government policy, and individuals work for others managing firms or as workers in a firm.[xii] In this stage in some economies, family business can remain quite important,[xiii] but this stage is marked by decreasing rates of entrepreneurship, and self-employment actually declines. There are several reasons for this decrease in entrepreneurial activity during this early economic development. As an economy becomes wealthier, the average firm size should increase because professional managers run those companies and they become more successful. Many people in the workforce find they can earn more money by working for somebody else. Increases in the capital stock either through private enterprise, direct foreign investment, or government ownership will increase the returns to wage earners compared to most small business entrepreneurial activity. Thus, entrepreneurial activity can temporarily decline as an economy moves from basic agricultural subsistence toward increased manufacturing. This in part explains why, in economies in East Asia such as Singapore and Malaysia, it has been found that young people are not very interested in entrepreneurship as the economies have moved away from proprietorships and farming. Instead, the young people want to take advantage of the opportunities available in the myriad of multinational firms with locations in Southeast Asia.

In the third stage of development, with increasing wealth the economy shifts away from manufacturing toward services. This stage is marked by a return to increasing entrepreneurial activity. Empirical evidence suggests that the distribution of firms in developed countries has begun to shift away from larger corporations (with some exceptions such as in Japan and Korea, where large conglomerates and business groups dominate), toward entrepreneurial activity. During this stage there is also an increasing number of start-up firms plus greater employment associated with small- and medium-sized companies, which contribute greatly to an economy's steady growth. One notable exception to this general pattern occurred during the 1970s in the United States, United Kingdom and other developed countries when entrepreneurial activity was being discouraged by high taxes on income and investment, along with high levels of government ownership in many sectors of the economy.[xiv] Reforms that commenced in the late 1970s in the United States and United Kingdom as well as China and parts of Latin America started to increase entrepreneurship and contributed substantially to economic and employment growth in those regions.[xv]

These stages imply that a U-shaped relationship exists between entrepreneurial activity and economic development in the global economy. This is why countries like Uganda, Peru, Ecuador, and several lesser-developed African countries all have high levels of entrepreneurial activity—"necessity entrepreneurship," as it is often called—along with very low levels of per capita income, while countries with a high level of development also show high levels of entrepreneurship. International managers should be aware that a low level of entrepreneurship in a country does not necessarily mean the country does not have potentially innovative employees, or has employees who will resist innovation and empowerment, as is sometimes suggested. As we have seen with the case of Lincoln Electric in Chapter 10, careful introduction of a flexible pay-for-performance system is possible even in countries with a very hierarchical and risk averse workforce, if done carefully using opinion leaders and peer examples to influence the workforce.[xvi]

Entrepreneurs

The role of entrepreneurs is critical not only to the prosperity of the global economy but also, increasingly, for the creation of needed innovations. Some people have the mistaken perception that entrepreneurs are confined to niches in domestic economies, with the real economic impact coming from large multinational companies that produce a majority of the world's wealth and products (recall our discussion of transnational firms). The reality is much more complicated in that multinational enterprises produce a little more than half of the world's output. That leaves room for family business and entrepreneurial firms to generate substantial economic value. Moreover, evidence suggests that entrepreneurial firms excel at creating new jobs.[xvii] For example, firms such as Microsoft and Federal Express were started approximately three decades ago and are still headed by some of their founders, so while they are MNEs, they are also entrepreneurial firms. Both firms are directly responsible for creating large numbers of jobs, and helping to improve other firms' productivity and ability to create many more jobs of their own.

Thus, entrepreneurs have demonstrated their importance creating important new goods and services that have aided in the global economy's development. Interestingly, though, most classical economics does not concern itself with entrepreneurs. Many economists see entrepreneurs as a nonessential issue to business. In this view, entrepreneurs and entrepreneurial firms will develop if the economy and its institutions are strong enough; entrepreneurship happens naturally as a result of institutions and is not an economic factor to focus on. Even twentieth-century economist Joseph Schumpeter, famous for his concept of creative destruction and his work on the importance of entrepreneurial firms, saw entrepreneurs largely as the bearers (not creators) of economic change and growth.[xviii] In this view, entrepreneurs help to bring new inventions and innovations to the market, but are often not the prime movers behind many innovations, at least not in any systematic (and teachable) way.

Some economists now argue that this traditional view of entrepreneurship is incomplete,[xix] stating that entrepreneurs (and therefore entrepreneurship) are observable and valuable, and can be encouraged by society's institutions.[xx] Recall that entrepreneurship is more broadly conceptualized by management scholars as value-creation activities and the seizing of economic opportunities and efficiencies. As opposed to the occupational definition of entrepreneurship that refers to business owners only, this is called the behavioral notion of entrepreneurship. Entrepreneurs in this behavioral sense do not necessarily need to be business owners—they can create significant value within a large organization, including government agencies and nonprofits. A new focus has arisen at the crossroads of behavioral entrepreneurship and the dynamic perspective of occupational entrepreneurship, one that considers venture creation and innovation to be the hallmark of entrepreneurship.[xxi] The entrepreneur, therefore, is someone who specializes in making judgmental decisions about the coordination and deployment of scarce resources. The term emphasizes that the entrepreneur is an individual and that entrepreneurial decisions are not simply a routine application of standard rules and production functions. Entrepreneurship's importance to the growth of firms and economies is well expressed in recent work on this topic.[xxii]

Impact of Entrepreneurship around the World

As noted above, many analyses of economic development tend to focus on large corporations and neglect the innovations and competition that small start-ups contribute to the overall economy. For large corporations, the ability to affect national economic growth is influenced by general business conditions, specific to each country. In this view, large firms influence economic growth through the construction of new plants, which, in turn, creates job opportunities. Additional growth arises out of productivity gains through scale economies from organizational growth and corporate venturing.[xxiii] For potential entrepreneurs, the decision about starting a business is influenced by additional characteristics within the existing business environment.[xxiv] These are referred to as entrepreneurial framework conditions, which are closely related to the country factor conditions discussed with Porter's Diamond model of national competitiveness in Chapter 3. These conditions comprise a country's capacity to encourage start-ups, along with the skills and motivations of those who wish to go into business for themselves. When successfully combined, these conditions will lead to new businesses, which in turn will increase innovation and competition within the marketplace. The result is a positive influence on a region's economic growth.

In spite of the debates surrounding the nature of entrepreneurs and entrepreneurial firms, entrepreneurship's positive effect on economic growth is being increasingly recognized by countries as they try to build indigenous entrepreneurship and attract venture capital and MNEs to foreign direct investment. For example, the Organization for Economic Cooperation and Development highlights the critical role of entrepreneurs as agents who accelerate the generation, application, and spread of innovative ideas and economic growth.[xxv]

A Lack of Entrepreneurship

What happens to a developed economy that has low levels of entrepreneurship? Can its economy survive with big organizations alone? What are international business people to think about investing into such an economy? Is it unrealistic to expect creativity from the people in that country? Questions such as these have surrounded Japan for many years. But Japan is not alone in this regard; many of the fast-growth economies of Southeast Asia such as Korea and Taiwan now also face this question because their costs have risen and as a result their large firms are outsourcing jobs.[xxvi] Although Japan has innovative large firms, the level of entrepreneurship in Japan has been lower than that of many other comparable countries.[xxvii] The Japanese economy, for example, from the early 1960s through 1989, was one of the fastest growing (and most studied) in modern times. From automobiles to watches to a vast array of consumer electronics, Japanese firms cut a swath through the paths of their European and North American competitors. Western scholars and pundits praised Japan's (apparently) careful economic planning and the focus of Japan's interlocked networks of business groupings such as Mitsui, Mitsubishi, Matsushita, and Sumitomo and their allied banks.[xxviii] Japan was characterized by extraordinarily high savings rates, which, in turn, promoted a low cost of capital.[xxix] At the micro level, scholars attributed Japan's economic momentum to the dedication of its workforce to improving productivity and quality at low costs. Scholars cited the absence of similar factors in Europe and the United States, meanwhile, to explain the stagnation affecting those countries.[xxx]

The flaw in the arguments that were promoting the Japanese institutional system—such as close connections between banks and firms, industry groupings, cross holdings, and close government and firm cooperation—is that the system tended to neglect entrepreneurship. Indeed many of the innovations that drove Japan's stunning economic growth in the 1960s, 1970s, and 1980s were made by (then) medium-sized enterprises that were disrupting the dominant North American and European manufacturers. Firms such as Sony and Honda introduced multiple lower-end products that created new industries and eventually drew significant business from larger firms that were unable to adapt. Japanese firms were able to enter markets at the low end and compete effectively with their less flexible Western competitors. Japanese firms excelled at creating smaller, less

| FIGURE 14-2 | Relatively Constant Position of U.S. Economy to Other Major Economies of the World |

Ratio of PPP adjusted per capita GDP in selected countries and regions to U.S. per capita GDP					
	United States (GDP per capita, constant 2000 dollars)	All EU countries	France, Germany, and UK	Japan	China
1975	$19,830	0.74	0.76	0.72	0.03
1989	$28,090	0.72	0.75	0.80	0.06
1995	$30,165	0.74	0.77	0.83	0.09
2001	$33,983	0.75	0.77	0.77	0.12
2003	$35,373	0.73	0.75	0.74	0.14

Source: Bhidé, A. (2006). *Venturesome consumption, Innovation and Globalization*, p. 38.

expensive, more reliable, mass market goods. They then gradually moved upmarket, and Western firms found they were unable to respond to Japan's disruptive threats at the lower end.[xxxi]

Yet much has changed for many Japanese firms since Japan's decades of heady economic growth. The United States has experienced a largely uninterrupted economic expansion from the 1980s until recently. Other countries such as the United Kingdom have also achieved levels of prosperity that few could have imagined a couple of decades ago. Several Western economies that were traditional laggards such as Australia, New Zealand, and Canada have experienced similar runs of solid growth. Japan, in contrast, experienced extended economic stagnation for all of the 1990s that only recently appears to have abated. Figure 14-2 summarizes Japan's relative position in the world economy since the 1970s in terms of per capita GDP in comparison with the United States, the European Union (EU), and China. The relative GDPs of the world's major economies in comparison to the U.S. economy have not changed much since the 1970s. The exception is China, which went from 3 percent of the U.S. economy in per capita GDP terms in 1975 to 14 percent in 2003.

The slowing of Japan's growth since the late 1980s is partly due to its lack of entrepreneurship. The rapid growth created by entrepreneurial firms such as Sony as they introduced numerous disruptive products slowed as they grew into larger firms that no longer excelled at creating new markets. Sony, for example, created numerous disruptive new-market innovations up through the early 1980s, but after the Walkman, they largely stopped creating new markets. Instead, Sony has been growing through established product innovation such as the Vaio notebook PC. Similar stories can be told about other Japanese firms that achieved size and success.[xxxii] The positions of the larger firms were reinforced by Japanese government policy that discouraged venture financing and restricted labor market mobility.[xxxiii] The government has tried to take steps to improve competition (see the "Directing Entrepreneurship in Japan" vignette). While previous Japanese government policies might indeed have reduced "confusion in the marketplace" (a common euphemism in Asia for competition), Japan would like to encourage innovations that would once again create new markets and industries. But Japan still lags in the development of such ventures and the resources they require. For example, the *Asia Private Equity Review* reports that the money available for private equity

DIRECTING ENTREPRENEURSHIP IN JAPAN

How did the Japanese government help to encourage entrepreneurship during its economic takeoff period some four decades ago, and what is the effect today on its industries? Japan's Ministry of International Trade and Industry (formerly MITI, but now called Ministry of Economy, Trade, and Industry [METI]) became famous for its ability to coordinate multiple companies' investments toward targeted industries and economic growth objectives in the 1970s and 1980s, which was discussed in several well-read academic works at that time.[xxxiv] But as with many government developmental programs, the Japanese government learned that catching up was a lot easier than leading. It continued to maintain a sharp focus on incremental improvements to products and processes. These government-sponsored product and process improvements were very valuable in beating competitors on cost, particularly in consumer electronics and machine tools. But it was hard to extend this model of government–industry cooperation in developing disruptive innovation and creating new industries. For example, this focus on incremental change led to expensive programs in cutting-edge technologies, such as the Fifth Generation Computer Systems project that proved to be a circuitous technological path that eventually failed. This diverted resources away from the early-stage, disruptive innovations that entrepreneurs typically excel at. Japan has had very little private equity and start-up financing available to the entrepreneurs that help to create these industries, and government policy did not help in this area either.[xxxv]

Japanese policymakers have been trying to reform the country's financial system and industrial structure. Some of these reforms seem to have helped the country's financial stability; for example, the merger of Fuji Bank, Dai-Ichi Kangyo Bank, and the Industrial Bank of Japan were across *keiretsu* (rival business groups). But these moves are also likely to weaken these institutions' abilities to foster new disruptive businesses. For instance, Japan recently passed a law that gave communities the right to ban large-scale retail enterprises that might introduce too much competition into the local retail environment. But such laws work against entrepreneurship in Japan and prevent some Japanese industries such as retail, from becoming globally competitive. Japan still has many of the world's most innovative large companies such as Toyota and Sony. But government policies that worked well during Japan's economic takeoff period may be hindering entrepreneurs from creating the Sonys of the 21st century.[xxxvi]

investment in Japan grew from $17.8 billion in 1995 to only $25 billion in 1999—just a fraction of what was added to America's private equity coffers during this period.

It should be noted that this problem of an absence of entrepreneurship is not limited to Japan; similar problems with entrepreneurship have been reported in a number of East Asian economies that they are heavily dependent on property development, banking, and basic export processing with little global branding or new technology development.[xxxvii] Although they have experienced steady economic growth, officials in these countries are concerned about encouraging more entrepreneurship and indigenous technology development.[xxxviii]

Entrepreneurship is very important for economic development. Economic development variables positively related to opportunity entrepreneurship include exports as a percentage of GDP, research and development expenditures, and education spending.[xxxix] As a greater proportion of a population becomes involved in opportunity entrepreneurship, and as more people leave necessity entrepreneurship (self-employment), the more levels of economic development and income will rise.

Born Global Entrepreneurial Firms

As we saw in Chapter 5, businesses that are not diversified will only have to make choices about a business-level strategy because they are in only one business. This is the situation that most entrepreneurial firms find themselves in. The model of internationalization seen in Chapter 6 argues that firms start out with a domestic-only focus, but as they grow larger they seek out either new markets or cheaper inputs to their products. Because of this, international business is not typically an issue for an entrepreneurial firm.

However, it is increasingly recognized that entrepreneurial firms are participating in the world's increased globalization. The growth of these entrepreneurial

Born globals
Entrepreneurial firms that are started as international firms.

global ventures is facilitated by the removal of trade barriers, advances in manufacturing, and big drops in logistics and communications costs, as well as advances in process manufacturing.[xl] These entrepreneurial firms have been called "**born globals**" because the firms are born as international firms. International entrepreneurial ventures bring new products, services, technologies, and work processes to consumers and populations all around the world.[xli] This recognition of young global firms is a relatively recent development.[xlii] It has been found that in areas such as advanced technology domains, entrepreneurial firms need to compete internationally almost from day one of their existence because their products can be copied relatively quickly, and the firms will not obtain the full benefit of their innovations if they fail to sell quickly in markets around the world.

Similarly, the need for internationalization is particularly acute for entrepreneurial firms from small product or small geographic markets. If there is a large potential customer base for a product in a single country such as the United Kingdom or a geographical region such as North America, there may be no need to internationalize. However, in small markets, whether there are fewer customers for the product worldwide or fewer customers in the given country in which the firm originates, the need for greater sales from other regions of the world encourage internationalization from the firm's inception.

To illustrate such a global start-up, consider a firm that served stock trading clubs in the United States. These clubs typically gather once a week or once a month to discuss stocks, and a fee for membership is typically required. Club members then vote after several meetings and invest the club fees in a stock. Over time, the club builds a portfolio of stocks that it continues to buy and sell. However, it takes reasonably complex software to track the value of the portfolio and the money invested by each club member, including what they are entitled to when they leave the club. The firm that develops this type of software has a Las Vegas mailing address but is, in fact, run by a Russian, an Australian, and a Turkish national. It has several employees, but the flow of information and decision making goes through the founders. Thus, rather than a single founder, there are multiple founders in different locations. As a result discussion among top management occurs through email and conference calls. However, it is clear that if this firm grows much larger, a different organizational structure will be needed to allow better coordination between the various parties.

The control of resources in different countries allows a global entrepreneur to overcome the inherent disadvantage of engaging in international business activities when competing with incumbent competitors in the host countries. The use of the word "control" is intentional here to avoid the unnecessary implication of ownership. Global entrepreneurs can effectively control certain sets of resources without actually owning them. For example, a transnational entrepreneur may obtain particular information or knowledge about a potential market opportunity through personal contacts or other means. This intangible and tacit knowledge cannot be clearly defined and is not accompanied by particular ownership. The network factor becomes very important here because strong social and business networks can serve as the institutional foundations for transnational entrepreneurship. Social and political institutions significantly shape the attitudes and behavior of transnational entrepreneurs. These networks and institutions provide the necessary strategic infrastructure to enable the success of these transnational entrepreneurs.

Resources and Strategy of Entrepreneurial Firms

Entrepreneurial firms have special needs compared to more mature firms, which focus on firm assets. You will recall from Chapter 4 that a firm's assets can be classified as either tangible or intangible. Tangible assets are those things that can be touched by the entrepreneur, such as equipment and money. Intangible assets

The successful entrepreneur requires tangible assets, such as financing, as well as intangible assets, such as industry expertise and a network of valuable contacts.

are those things that the entrepreneur cannot touch or count because they do not, per se, have a physical basis. Entrepreneurial firms often do not have the financial resources to succeed, and it is commonly believed that the absence of the tangible asset of money is the greatest reason for the failure of a new business. However, for the entrepreneurial venture that needs to compete internationally, it is equally critical that they have intangible assets in the form of contacts around the world.

To illustrate, large established firms like SAP of Germany or Carrefour of France can go almost anywhere in the world and be recognized. Such large established firms will have any number of local firms and government officials willing to help them accomplish their goals. However, it is much more difficult for an entrepreneur to get the same attention. Consider that if an entrepreneur is active in an area like the oil industry and develops a new technology, then the entrepreneur will need to sell that product in countries as diverse as Norway in the European Union, China, the various countries in the Middle East, plus Mexico and Venezuela in Latin America. How can such a start-up instantaneously develop a network of individuals to call on to help sell the product? Thus, it is particularly difficult for entrepreneurial firms to compete internationally even if they must do so to be successful, due to the constraints of tangible assets that almost all start-ups deal with, as well as the need for intangible assets such as relationships.

One outcome of the special challenges faced by international entrepreneurship is that particular domains appear to be able to support international entrepreneurship efforts better than others. For example, California's Silicon Valley is a major center of high-technology entrepreneurship, with many engineers who are immigrants to the United States. These immigrants have come from many areas, but numerically large numbers come from Taiwan and India. One result of these connections to original homelands is that these engineers have been able to encourage international entrepreneurial ventures.

To illustrate, Taiwanese engineers are one of the largest groups in Silicon Valley. Following the establishment of diplomatic relations between the People's Republic of China and the United States in 1972, there was great nervousness in

Taiwan about the long-term prospects of their economy. As a response, many Taiwanese began to send their children to the best schools in the United States. Particularly drawn to engineering, these individuals went to some of the leading schools such as Stanford and Berkeley, and many remained in the United States after graduation, particularly in Silicon Valley. The result has been that as these individuals over time become entrepreneurs, they often develop businesses in which the product is researched in the United States, designed and tested in Taiwan, and produced in China.

For Indian entrepreneurs, the pattern is somewhat different. The big growth in outsourcing to India began in the late 1990s due to the massive fear of the "millennium bug," a computer problem based on the inability of many software programs to handle dates past 1999. There were not enough programmers in the United States to fix this problem, but many Indian programmers in the United States still had contacts back in India with software engineering and support skills. The result was the rise of entrepreneurial firms that offered outsourcing to do programming and other activities for U.S. customers. The American firms were so happy with the outcomes of the subcontracting, including the cost savings, that they chose to outsource other activities to India. This has led to the rapid growth of numerous international entrepreneurial ventures that handle outsourcing in India, as well as innovative firms springing up in India to develop a variety of new services.[xliii] In both the case of Taiwanese and Indians, individuals' ability to maintain a network of relationships in other countries created successful opportunities for their entrepreneurial ventures.

Typically, an entrepreneurial firm that is international from its beginning will pursue a focus-differentiation business strategy (recall the classifications in Chapter 5 of business-level strategies). In doing so, it will build a full set of assets, both tangible and intangible, that will be critical to its success. E-business has increased the entrepreneur's ability to compete internationally because they can now be located anywhere and deal with individuals in any given country relatively cheaply. As a result, the future will bring more born global entrepreneurial firms. New competition is emerging from developing countries such as India and China.[xliv] As Western firms learned from Japanese and Korean competitors as these economies matured, tough competition can also come from emerging-economy firms, some of which are born global. It is important for firms to pay attention to particularly low-end, potentially disruptive competition coming from abroad.

Corporate Entrepreneurship

The focus of the discussion up to this point has been on entrepreneurship by small or start-up businesses. There is a related concept that has drawn considerable attention: corporate entrepreneurship. Many mature firms can become stagnant and so bureaucratic that they fail to innovate, but these firms can try to regain their competitiveness by pursuing internal **corporate entrepreneurship**. That is, the mature firms begin to act more like small start-up firms, taking greater risks and reducing their bureaucracy. Sometimes firms will use different terms to describe their actions, such as corporate rejuvenation, but the concepts are the same.

Corporate entrepreneurship is a concept that has been widely supported, but implementing the concept is commonly the most difficult. Just as in a classroom where students will normally sit in the same seat each semester even if they are not required to do so, making changes inside a firm is very difficult. Typically the steps that a firm needs to accomplish such a change are as follows:

Corporate entrepreneurship
Mature firms that act more like small start-up firms by taking greater risks and reducing bureaucracy.

- **Build a sense of urgency for the change.** Employees often may not understand the severe difficulties the firm faces and therefore need to be educated about the firm's setting so that they will be more willing to make any changes necessary. Without such an understanding, the changes the firm is able to make may be limited.

- **Conduct a full examination of the firm—its opportunities and threats.**
- **Have a thorough understanding of its activities**. There may be many activities the firm is currently doing that do not create value and that need to be abandoned. However, there may be other opportunities the firm has not yet addressed.
- **Benchmark the firm against what competitors are doing.** Benchmarking involves comparing a firm's activities against the best in the industry. The knowledge built up in benchmarking can also be useful in building a sense of urgency among employees.
- **Focus on the customer.** The firm has to have a rich understanding of the customer and their problems. (Recall the discussion in chapter 10 about understanding customers' problems when trying to influence them.) As noted in Chapters 4 and 5, the firm must have a competitive advantage in whatever it does. Thus, the firm must ensure that it understands fully what the customer today desires so it can ensure that its product or service excels at meeting that need.
- **Implement needed changes in a rational and timely manner.** Change is difficult for organizations. Too often, firms begin a change process that has more in common with the metaphorical "death by one thousand cuts." No firm can live in a constant state of turmoil, because individuals will become less risk-seeking due to uncertainty about their own and the firm's future. The firm needs to develop a clear and rational set of choices, communicate those choices, and then motivate employees to implement them. The firm then should be allowed to see if those changes generate the desired effect.
- **Focus on key employees.** All organizations have key employees who are internal opinion leaders that influence others. These employees are usually veterans of the firm and are particularly important in knowledge-based organizations. These individuals need to be the focus of the corporate entrepreneurial effort because they likely have multiple career opportunities and may leave the company if they become discouraged or fearful for their jobs. A key fact for all organizations is that the most marketable people have the greatest opportunities. Thus, ensuring that these key individuals understand the corporate entrepreneurship effort and its goals is critical.

IMI AND MANUFACTURING PROSPERING TODAY IN ENGLAND

It sometimes seems that all manufacturing will eventually exit developed markets such as those of the United States and Europe. It is true that many firms have moved their manufacturing to countries with cheaper emerging markets, and manufacturing's share of many developed economies has declined. For example, in the United States in 1980 manufacturing's share of GDP was over 20 percent, but by 2003 it had dropped to only 14 percent. The decline in manufacturing has been even more severe in Britain, a country that was once known as the workshop of the world because the large amount of manufacturing that took place there. Even in 1980 over 25 percent of Britain's GDP came from manufacturing, but by 2003 that number had slipped to 14 percent. This does not mean that manufacturing has disappeared completely. In fact, today Britain is experiencing a small manufacturing renaissance.

This renaissance is seen in firms like IMI, one of the largest engineering companies in Britain. Starting in 2001 IMI sold off many of its 18 business units as it sought to eliminate all businesses that did not offer high value-added products that competed on something other than price. For example, product units like copper cables were sold. Instead, today IMI focuses on high valued-added domains like valve systems for power plants. Such products have high levels of engineering and the product's quality is critical to the purchaser.

IMI has also increased the technical information and service support they offer. For example, maintaining power plant valves provides 30 percent of the IMI's cash flow in this division. Manufacturing firms like IMI have also sought to become more efficient in their manufacturing process, which has required the firms to be flexible and adaptable.

These changes have resulted in an improvement in the profitability of manufacturing firms and their presence being a key part of the British economy. Increasing competition from emerging economies has forced manufacturers like IMI to improve and innovate.

Willman, J., & MacNamara, W. (2007, September 7). An uplifting experience: How British industry is once more finding ways to make a profit. *Financial Times*, p. 7.

Corporate entrepreneurship has particular importance for many economies that are in transition from being centrally planned to being market-oriented. In such economies there are many firms in which a corporate entrepreneurship transformation is critical since the old state firms must move to being competitive in the new market economy. To date in Eastern/Central Europe or the newly independent states of the former Soviet Union, few firms have been able to generate this corporate entrepreneurship themselves in domains other than raw materials. Instead, the manufacturing firms that have been successful at corporate entrepreneurship have typically been bought by an international firm that brought in its own systems. In China, the transition to market economy has been more deliberate. However, China's state-owned enterprises (SOEs) have not reformed in step with many other parts of the economy, and SOEs still employ a large percentage of China's workforce. While there is great discussion about China as an exporting powerhouse, almost all high-value manufacturing exports from China are by Western, Taiwanese, or Japanese firms that do the manufacturing in China and then export the products from China. Thus, China gets credit for the exports, but many of them do not originate from indigenous Chinese firms.[xlv] For example, in high-technology exports roughly 80 percent of Chinese exports come from foreign firms.[xlvi] Domestic Chinese firms dominate in domains such as textiles and garments but have not been successful in transitioning on the whole to global competitors in high-value goods. There remains a strong need for corporate entrepreneurship in China, particularly in upstream innovation from R&D, and downstream innovation such as brand building and distribution.

Entrepreneurship and Innovation: Upstream and Downstream

In spite of various debates over the role of individual entrepreneurs versus corporate entrepreneurship, there is little dispute about the importance of entrepreneurship overall to national prosperity. But firms need to recognize that their prosperity is part of a global system. Particularly, firms in mature economies need to be aware of the critical role that basic research, component research, and manufacturing have on their ultimate success. A country's scientists, engineers, and educational institutions as well as its manufacturers and service providers play a critical role in success.[xlvii] Recall from Chapter 3 (Porter's Diamond of national competitiveness) that a society's ability to innovate is the result of researchers publishing more papers, securing more patents, and launching and successfully manufacturing (and thus exporting) more products. The well-known economist Richard Nelson has brought this argument into focus, arguing for the importance of **upstream innovation** for maintaining competitiveness.[xlviii]

But it is important to remember that upstream innovation—research and development, basic science, and university-company partnerships—is not the only important component of innovation and a prosperous society.[xlix] Upstream components rely on other innovation that must be present for a firm to be successful, so downstream innovation—removed in the value chain from the basic research on the product—is also very important. Downstream innovation is a firm's ability to use research and basic product components and package them together to create a new, salable product or service. It is also the indigenization of other technologies into a firm's production and development systems to facilitate the product's creation and delivery. Basically, there are three broad components of downstream innovation that are important to competitiveness: **technology indigenization**, turnkey innovation, and innovation in marketing and distribution.[l] Technology indigenization represents resources allocated for training workers and engineers to use equipment, for linking that equipment more effectively into the firm's systems, for diffusing that knowledge throughout the firm, and for the study of the science and engineering embodied in a new piece of equipment and how to best fit it into

Upstream innovation
Scientific research, basic product research and development, and university–company partnerships on developing new products.

Technology indigenization
Integrating technologies into a firm's production and development systems (sometimes modifying them in the process) to facilitate the creation and delivery of a product to customers or service to employees.

the firm's processes. Indigenization spending typically accounts for about one-third of technology import spending.[li] Technology indigenization is important to the proper application of new technology and for deriving benefit from it. Even if firms do not create their own technology, they still need to try to adapt it to their own needs and understand it if they are to be competitive. In contrast to many countries, Chinese firms have not invested much in indigenizing technology since the market reforms started in that country in 1978.[lii]

Another component of downstream innovation is turnkey innovation. That is, many successful entrepreneurial firms do not develop their own technology; rather, they combine and distribute inventions and innovations generated by others upstream. Thus, a turnkey firm would buy other firms' technology, such as computers, communication devices, sensors, and operating systems, and use this technology to put together its own products. For such firms, the value-added comes from creating integrated systems out of technology's various components.[l] Thus, the ability of individuals and firms to acquire and use new products and technologies may be as important as the development of such products and technologies.

Innovation in marketing and distribution represents a third component of downstream innovation. Firms that are innovative in packaging products, building brands, and developing new markets are generating upstream innovation. Alliance partners and customers are willing to work with a new firm and take a chance on its products and services and sometimes combine the services as important leading-edge customers.[liii] These also play a role in the innovativeness of an economy.

Entrepreneurship Summary

Entrepreneurship will likely be increasingly important in the world whether it is of the domestic-only, born global, or corporate variety. The world's economic growth is tied to increasing levels of entrepreneurship and various types of innovation. While in the past entrepreneurship was largely seen as irrelevant or hard to predict, today it is known to be crucial for economic development.

ENVIRONMENTALISM AND THE FUTURE

There is an increased focus today on the business and the natural environment, with many major corporations now employing an expert in corporate sustainability. This individual's job is to help the firm lower its energy consumption and minimize its negative impact on the environment. But these environmental efforts typically are designed to not only help our environment but also to ensure there is a market-oriented foundation to the actions. Thus, while there is a great concern for the environment, there is a similar recognition that these changes can be made to pay for themselves and not be just charity by the firm.

To illustrate, FedEx has over 70,000 trucks and 670 airplanes that deliver its daily packages. As a result, the world's largest shipper puts into the environment over 250,000 tons of greenhouse gases a year. FedEx has a commitment to reduce that environmental impact, and is shifting from medium-duty diesel trucks to hybrid gasoline/electric trucks. The hybrids cost approximately $75,000, or 75 percent more than diesel trucks, but over the ten-year life of the truck, they pay for themselves in lower fuel costs.

Much of the environmental movement focusing on sustainable market solutions can be traced to the nonprofit Rocky Mountain Institute in Colorado, founded in 1982 by Armory Lovins.[1] This institute seeks to educate firms on how environmental concern and innovation can pay for themselves. It builds on Lovins' well-known book *Natural Capitalism*, which argues that by rethinking their processes and choosing materials wisely, firms could produce less pollution, earn more money, and minimize the need for recycling. Today, the Institute's influence is far greater than its $10 million budget would indicate.

It should be recognized that there is also controversy regarding how some firms have approached their environmental responsibility. Production of energy from renewable sources not only generates the energy itself, which ultimately consumers use, but for each 1,000 kilowatts of energy generated there is also **one renewable energy certificate** (RECs) generated. These certificates can be sold or bought. The firm that buys them is helping to subsidize the production of energy by renewable means, and can argue that each REC purchased offsets 1,000 kilowatts of energy they use from traditional energy production methods such burning coal, which is a heavy greenhouse gas producer.

Today Johnson and Johnson (J&J) says it has reduced its contribution to greenhouse gases by 17 percent. This effort led the U.S. Environmental Protection Administration to give J&J its Green Power Leadership Award in 2006, and the firm has been praised by the World Wildlife Federation. But in fact almost all of Johnson & Johnson's 17 percent reduction is due to purchased RECs. The firm's energy consumption has remained relatively constant.[liv] J&J has helped to strongly promote the creation of the alternative energy industry in the United States, but it is questionable whether its REC purchases make J&J as environmentally conscious as it would like to appear.

Renewable energy certificate (REC)
Certificate for each 1,000 kilowatts of renewable energy that can be bought or sold. Governments create such certificates for tax purposes and to encourage alternative energy. The production of energy from renewable sources not only generates the energy itself which ultimately consumers use, but for each 1,000 kilowatts of energy generated there is also one REC that can be sold or bought.

WALKERS CRISPS AND LABELING THEIR ENVIRONMENTAL FOOTPRINT

ETHICS

One of the key ethical issues that will face business in the future is the environment—in particular greenhouse gases and global warming. Al Gore, former vice president and U.S. senator, lost the 2000 presidential election by the narrowest of margins to George W. Bush. Gore went on to become an influential and celebrated spokesman on global warming and the natural environment, and wrote a bestselling book and an award-winning film by the same name, *An Inconvenient Truth*. By 2007, Gore had won a Noble Peace Prize, an Oscar for best documentary (for *An Inconvenient Truth*), and several other awards for his work. Partly as a result of his efforts, the existence of global warming has become widely accepted, and the discussion has shifted to how best to deal with it.

This broad societal concern for global warming has in turn led firms to seek to position their businesses as part of the solution, not the problem. But the ethical issue that dominates is how to contribute to significant change, not just public relations hype. Some firms, such as Walkers Crisps, one of Britain's leading makers of salty snacks,

have committed to labeling their product packages with messages revealing the amount of carbon used to produce the product (i.e., transportation of ingredients to the plant, energy used to make the product, transportation to retailers). Walkers is not alone in agreeing to provide such information. In the future, Dairy Milk Chocolate Bars (a Cadbury Schweppes subsidiary) and a number of other firms will provide the same information.

One of the great difficulties is that there is disagreement on how to measure this type of information. Profit and non-profit groups are currently striving to develop an acceptable means to determine this carbon-use information. In the future it can be expected that divulging carbon use will increase sales. The belief is that the customers will be able to make a decision to purchase a product based on price and environmental impact. Do you think this is a good ethical approach to such environmental issues?

Harvey, F. (2007, October 12). Food footprinting coming soon to a label near you. *Financial Times*, p. 4.

---

[1]See https://www.rmi.org/sitepages/pid23.php for information on the Rocky Mountain Institute.

THE BOTTOM BILLION AND INTERNATIONAL BUSINESS

While the world's economy has grown dramatically in recent years, approximately one-sixth of the world's population has benefited little from this growth. In fact, some countries have moved backward in their development. An indicator of this decline is the fact many African countries have seen life expectancy decline dramatically. For example, life expectancy in Botswana has decreased 20 years since the 1970s, to just 36 years today, despite the fact that Botswana's economy has performed fairly well in recent years. Figure 14-3 summarizes that fall in sub-Saharan Africa, where the decline in life expectancy has been the most dramatic. According to the United Nations, in 1960 the richest 20 percent of people in the world accounted for about 70 percent of total income. In 2000, that figure reached 85 percent. Over the same period, the income accruing to the poorest 20 percent of people in the world fell by over half to about 1 percent, though rising in absolute terms.

This extreme inequity of wealth distribution suggests to some that the poor cannot participate in the global market economy, even though they constitute a large part of the world's population. This problem has not escaped the attention of various groups, the most visible being the United Nations, which established a millennium goal in 2000 of eliminating extreme poverty by 2015. As a part of this goal the United Nations wants to ensure the following:

1. Direct assistance to local entrepreneurs to grow their businesses and create jobs
2. Deworming school children and the control of other childhood diseases in affected areas
3. Eliminating school fees
4. Ending user fees for basic health care in poor countries
5. Providing free school meals for schoolchildren
6. Providing mosquito nets to those affected by mosquito transmitted diseases
7. Guaranteeing access to electricity, clean water and sanitation

Economists Craig Burnside and David Dollar of the World Bank maintain that developing countries that follow good fiscal, monetary, and trade policies can

---

FIGURE 14-3 Changing Life Expectancy

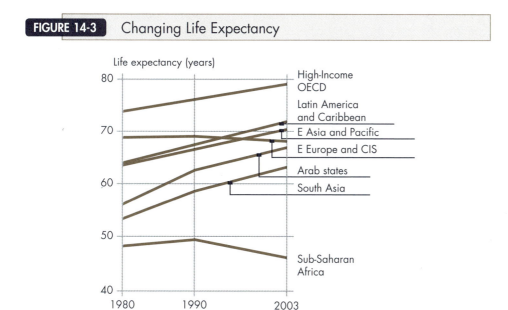

Source: United Nations

| FIGURE 14-4 | Ten Most- and Least-Livable Countries* |

Most Livable	Least Livable
• Norway	• Niger
• Iceland	• Sierra Leone
• Australia	• Burkina Faso
• Canada	• Mali
• Luxembourg	• Chad
• Sweden	• Guinea-Bissau
• Switzerland	• Central African Republic
• Ireland	• Ethiopia
• Belgium	• Burundi
• United States	• Mozambique

* Based on the Human Development Index, Human Development Report 2006, United Nations Development Programme, http://www.nationmaster.com/graph/eco_hum_dev_ind-economy-human-development-index (website accessed November 21, 2008).

benefit from foreign aid. But the World Bank data have not been independently corroborated. William Easterly, Ross Levine, and David Rodman of the National Bureau of Economic Research updated the World Bank data and found no positive correlation between foreign aid and economic growth, calling into question current models of foreign aid.[lv]

Instead of stimulating economic growth, Easterly and colleagues argue that foreign aid has done little to alleviate poverty and may have even facilitated the bane of developing countries: corruption. This is especially true in Africa, the world's poorest region. Today, the EU demands that even the poorest among new EU members contribute to the European foreign aid agency, EuropeAid. But a growing body of evidence suggests that far from helping the poor countries, foreign aid slows economic reform and development, and thus retards growth.

Africa, for example, has been the largest recipient of foreign aid. But Africa has experienced decades of economic stagnation, and some countries have declined economically since their early days of independence over four decades ago. In sub-Saharan Africa, where much foreign aid has been directed in recent decades, per capita gross domestic product is now *11 percent lower* than in 1974. Ghana, for example, had inflation-adjusted per capita income of $800 in 1967, but by 1997, that figure had fallen to $370. As a result, Africa today accounts for a greater percentage of the world's poor than ever before. In 1970, only 10 percent of the world's poor people lived in Africa. Today that number is up to 50 percent, even though former poor regions such as East Asia and the Indian subcontinent have experienced sustained economic growth. Figure 14-4 cites which of the world's countries are the least desirable in which to live. Most of these have suffered from a declining standard of living.

As Easterly and colleagues have pointed out, regions that received less foreign aid per capita fared better, such as countries in East and South Asia. Increasing levels of globalization have also been overwhelmingly positive in terms of alleviating poverty.[lvi] China and India were both among the lowest-income countries in the 1970s. Today, however, these countries and their citizens have made dramatic progress as they have taken part in the world's globalization and are steadily bringing some two-fifths of the world's population out of poverty. In the future, one of the key issues will be whether these same benefits of economic growth can be extended to the bottom one-sixth of the world's population.

In fact, given their vast size, the poor regions of the world represent a multitrillion-dollar market. According to World Bank projections, the bottom-income population could increase to more than 6 billion people over the next 40 years because the bulk of the world's population growth occurs there. The perception that this "bottom of the pyramid" is not a viable market fails to take into account the growing importance of the informal economy among the poorest of the poor, which by some estimates accounts for 40 to 60 percent of all economic activity in developing countries.

Though the population is quite high and there is significant collective buying power in the poorest regions of the world, the people are hard to reach via conventional distribution methods, credit, and communications. The quality and quantity of products and services available in this population is generally low. Therefore, much like an iceberg with only its tip in plain view, this massive segment of the global population—along with its massive market opportunities—has remained largely invisible to the corporate sector.

Multinational enterprises must recognize that this market poses a major new challenge: how to combine low cost, good quality, sustainability, and profitability. Multinational enterprises cannot exploit these new opportunities without radically rethinking how they go to market. For example, Hindustan Unilever Limited (HUL), a subsidiary of Great Britain's Unilever PLC that is considered to be a well-managed company in India, has been a pioneer among MNEs exploring markets at the bottom of the pyramid. For more than 50 years, HUL has served India's small elite who could afford to buy their products.

In the 1990s, a local firm, Nirma Ltd., began offering clothes detergent products for poor consumers, mostly in India's rural areas. In response to Nirma's competition, HUL created a new detergent, called Wheel, which was formulated to substantially reduce the ratio of oil to water in the product, responding to the fact that the poor often wash their clothes in rivers and other public water systems. HUL decentralized the production, marketing, and distribution of the detergent to leverage the abundant labor pool in rural India, quickly creating sales channels through the thousands of small outlets where people at the bottom of the pyramid shop. HUL also changed the cost structure of its detergent business so it could introduce Wheel at a very low price point for these poor rural consumers. The result has been very positive for the firm.

Contrary to popular assumptions, the poor can constitute a very profitable market—especially if multinational enterprises change their business models. There are billions of people in this group, and although they are a very low-income population, collectively they represent substantial buying power. For example, the poor can buy collectively, such as a whole village buying several mobile phones or other electronics. The bottom of the pyramid is not a market that allows for the traditional pursuit of high margins; instead, profits are driven by volume and capital efficiency. Margins will be low, but unit sales can be extremely high, and repeat business and inventory turnover can be very high also. Higher inventory turnover allows the retailer and manufacturer to sell with lower margins. Products such as electronics used for education and communication, basic health care products, and other goods can significantly improve the lives of the poor and help them start businesses. In addition, many emerging economies are growing steadily, and hundreds of millions of people have been lifted out of abject poverty, particularly in those countries transitioning from statist systems such as China and India. International business has a big opportunity to improve the lives of the very poor, and firms that focus only on gross margins and bigger-income markets will miss opportunities at the bottom of the economic pyramid.

UNDERSTANDING FINANCIAL PANICS

What caused the recent financial panic, how uncommon are such events, and how do these upheavals play out? In addition, how can firms respond to financial upheavals to protect themselves and maintain some stability in turbulent change?

Is This Financial Panic Unprecedented?

Financial panic

Financial panics include a variety of situations in which some banks and financial assets suddenly lose a large part of their value and bad debts multiply quickly.

Although there had been signs of problems in the months before, the **financial panic** of 2008 became manifest in earnest with the failure, merger, and bail out of several large U.S. and European financial institutions. Yet the 2008 panic, though perhaps intensified by the globalization of financial markets, is by no means a unique event. There have been many financial panics in the past, such that historians have calculated that the probability of a significant financial panic occuring in any given year is about one chance in thirty.[lvii] This implies that there is roughly a one in three chance that a financial panic should occur in any decade—something for which international firms need to be prepared.

There have been many asset run-ups in the past, followed by financial upheaval and sometimes panic.[lviii] Many students will have heard of the dot-com asset bubble of the late 1990s where the NASDAQ Composite Index was at 1,140 in March 1996, rose to 5,048 in March 2000, and returned to 1,140 in October of 2002. Real estate booms have not been confined to the United States. At one point in the 1980s the land on which Tokyo's Imperial Palace stands was priced higher than all of the land in California. Although the high real estate prices were not sustainable, analysts were still citing improving household balance sheets as a reason to believe the mortgage borrowing binge was sustainable.

How Do Financial Panics Play Out?

Efficient market theory is often used to explain the value of stock, land, and financial markets. The key message of the efficient market hypothesis is that asset prices are always at the correct price. That is to say, today's market prices, no matter what they are, correctly reflect assets' true values, based on both current economic conditions and investors' best estimate of how those conditions will affect the price in the future. According to the efficient market theory, price changes observed in financial markets are the result of markets responding to a constant stream of new information. The efficient market theory argues that the market correctly reflected share price value during the dot-com bubble of the late 1990s. But every day, financial markets move in ways that simply cannot be explained by that theory.

As Benoit Mandelbrot, a pioneer in fractal geometry and a longtime critic of mainstream finance theory wrote in 1999, the problem is that established modeling techniques presume that all price changes are statistically independent—that is, today's fluctuations have nothing to do with tomorrow's—and that price movements are normally distributed. But if stock prices are related and price movements do not fit a normal distribution, then radically large market shifts including asset bubbles and financial panics are much more likely to occur than capital market theory predicts. And we know from Chapters 9 and 10 that people can sometimes behave very irrationally and then follow each other in a mob-like behavior.

In summary, what do we know about financial panics and recoveries and how should international managers be prepared? There are several facts that finance scholars and economic historians have discerned from studying financial manias and panics that are valuable to investors and business people alike:

1. Irrational behavior does occur from time to time in financial markets. Sometimes it comes in the form of irrational exuberance and market run-ups as with the dot-com financial mania of the late 1990s, or the Japanese and Hong Kong real estate markets in the 1980s and 1990s, respectively. Other times it comes in the form of irrational underexuberance as markets run down and probably overreact, as in the financial crisis of 2007–8, or Japan's decade-long downturn in the 1990s. Major financial panics that extend across country borders have occurred over the past couple centuries at the rough rate of one every 30 years, and minor ones more frequently.[lix] That means unless government policy-makers can find a way to engineer a safer financial system, business people need to have contingency plans in place for significant downturns in their sales volume and even potential liquidity crises.

2. There is a general and discernable pattern to how financial panics play out. Usually there is a positive economic euphoria that takes the form of over-trading and overborrowing, then economic distress and significant drops (30 to 80 percent) in asset prices that were sky high before, followed by a liquidity crunch and numerous business failures.[lx]

3. The economic system needs a lender of last resort such as a central bank or a government to step in—and in the right way—to restore confidence and liquidity and prevent major failures in the financial system.[lxi]

4. International firms can expect to be buffeted by the winds of financial crises at regular intervals. For example, the Asian Financial Crisis of 1997–8 did not affect North America and Europe directly, but many firms were still hurt as currencies and stock markets plummeted, markets dried up, and their customers and alliance partners around Southeast Asia suffered through significant downturns. Firms must use scenario planning to generate action plans in case their markets, suppliers, or financiers are hit by a financial tsunami. Currency hedging, careful diversification of portfolios, flexible work rules, and variable compensation plans can all help firms remain flexible enough to ride out financial panics. And it is important to remember that financial panics do end eventually, and firms that were able to invest on downturns will be well positioned to enjoy the ensuing recovery.

FUTURE OF INTERNATIONAL MANAGEMENT AND YOU

As the textbook draws to a close, it is hoped you have seen that while many of the basic management concepts you learn in business schools today apply around the world, there is a serious need to adapt those concepts as you internationalize. The world will only become more internationally oriented. A strictly North American focus will become a rarer and rarer activity for business. But as firms internationalize, they will need to take the basic concepts they know from Anglo-American business research and adapt those concepts internationally.

Many readers will find that they will live and work outside of their home countries for extended periods of time. You will find that it is important to be familiar with the country in which you will work, particularly its culture and business practices. The concepts presented in these chapters, ranging from culture and institutions to the external environment and firm strategy, from human resources to influence and negotiation, all contain invaluable facts and skills that you should not neglect as you do business internationally.

As internationalization continues, new issues will undoubtedly arise, issues that are not even considered today. In the last few years sovereign wealth funds have come to the forefront. These are funds set up by governments to invest in private firms. These funds have been around for a number of years, but they were not widely considered when their leading generator was Singapore. But today, countries like Russia, China, and Saudi Arabia dominate sovereign wealth funds, and it is not always clear where those countries' financial interests end and political and business intelligence begin.

Someday in the not-too-distant future, you may find yourself working for a foreign company—maybe in your own country. Even in major continental economies such as the United States, Russia, and Brazil, many MNEs have set up shop and hire large numbers of local employees. How do you deal with a boss from a foreign country that may not share your norms and values? For example, because Russia and China both have little protection for intellectual property; you may find that computer programs you created or magazine articles you wrote will suddenly appear in China with someone else's name attached to them. American workers have found that Japanese firms have a much different way of doing things and that it takes some adjustment to adapt to the new setting. Firms from China, Russia, Brazil, India, and other countries may be coming to your hometown, not only with their products but also with their jobs and differing cultures. See how many of the top Chinese firms you have heard of (see Figure 14-5). The future for you will increasingly be one of great opportunity but also great challenge. The

FIGURE 14-5   Ranking by Average ROA of China's Top Non-State Firms, 2001–2005

Ranking	Company Name	Average ROA	Industry
1	Huawei	22.2	Telecommunication
2	ZTE	16.27	Telecommunication
3	Lenovo	15.3	IT and electronic
4	SAIC	12.08	Auto
5	Geely	11.6	Auto
6	Haier	8.6	Household appliance
7	Wanxiang	8.27	Auto
8	Midea	6.73	Household appliance
9	Panda	6.16	Household appliance
10	TCL	5.16	Household appliance
11	Bird	4.72	IT and electronic
12	Skyworth	4.2	Household appliance
13	BOE	3.03	Telecommunication
14	Hisense	1.36	Household appliance
15	Konka	−0.53	Household appliance
16	Changhong	−3	Household appliance
17	Brilliance	−6.66	Auto

Source: Adopted from Hang, 2007.

more you become aware of your opportunities and challenges, the more successful you will be in the long run.

CONCLUSION

There is little doubt that the world's developing economies are creating excellent opportunities—opportunities that cannot be ignored. China represents a major opportunity for firms, not only for its large and growing numbers of consumers, but also for its excellent manufacturing base. The same might be said of India, although India may ultimately become a greater service platform than manufacturing platform. There are well over a billion consumers in each country, and, as we have seen, there are good customers for properly packaged and priced products even among their poorest citizens.

Some people have played up the potential threats of internationalization, rather than its opportunities. They argue that with increasing access to advanced technology, jobs will shift from workers in rich countries to cheap, educated labor in economically developing countries. They claim that free trade with developing economies is a recipe for mass unemployment, huge wage inequalities, and a massive migration of firms to low-wage countries. In a reversal of roles, economically developing countries that historically were considered victims of multinational exploitation would now be viewed as villains, stealing capital and jobs and, ironically, creating inequities by destroying the wealth of developed economies.

On the surface, this pessimistic scenario appears true, especially when comparing the hourly wages of production workers. In the late 1990s, it cost $28 an hour to employ a production worker in Germany, $19 an hour in Japan, and $18 an hour in the United States, but only $5 in Hong Kong, $1.75 in Mexico, and 50 cents in Sri Lanka.[lxii] Many believe it will soon be possible for countries to have high productivity, advanced technology, and low wages—the "world is flat" model.[lxiii] Many electronics firms, for example, already employ more production workers and as many skilled workers in East Asia as in the home country. The Italian sportswear maker Fila produces only a small percentage of its sportswear in Italy. The same is true for many garment manufacturers around the world.[lxiv]

But as we have seen, some churning of jobs and reorienting of production toward countries with comparative advantage in particular areas is inevitable, and from an economic welfare point of view, quite desirable. This negative viewpoint of international business and globalization downplays the positives that manufacturing in a foreign location can bring to a firm and to employees in the firm's home country. There will almost certainly be a need for a firm to employ people in accounting, finance, and marketing, even if the firm moves some of its production offshore.[lxv] And, as we have seen, simply manufacturing a product in a country does not give a company (or that host country) control over the product, as is implied by globalization's critics. While the host country certainly benefits from outsourcing, the foreign firm still controls the most important parts of the process both upstream and downstream. Upstream innovative investment includes a product's design and production process, while the downstream innovation process includes marketing, promotion, and contact with leading-edge customers and distributors. This is proving very difficult for firms in most developing countries and further underscores the importance of international managers in building the necessary capabilities for both upstream and downstream innovation, and then determining the best places to produce and sell the products.[lxvi] Economies in East Asia that were once thought to be following Japan and South Korea in building competitive brands and competing with Western multinationals are failing to produce globally competitive products by their indigenous firms. This is not to say that these economies are not benefiting from globalization—research on a large range of dimensions shows they are benefiting greatly—but rather underscores the difficulty of global competition and the importance of international management to prosperity.

Developed economies, far from losing out to the growing prosperity of the developing countries, can benefit from that prosperity. Efficient economics and trade is not a zero-sum game. Billions of new consumers in the developing world will markedly increase demand for exports from the developed countries as their economies continue to improve. In just the past decade, for example, exports from high-income to low- and middle-income countries have already more than doubled. Singapore's exports have increased 150 times since 1960; Malaysia's exports have increased 118 times and now exceed that country's GDP (something made possible because exports figures do not subtract the value of components that may come from elsewhere).[lxvii] And these countries have also become significant consumers of goods and services from North America and Japan.

In addition, optimists contend that both advanced and developing economies benefit from increased competition. Greater economies of scale and better allocation of resources resulting from increased competition and financial diversification are improving expected rates of return for all players. The inflows of foreign direct investment into economically developing countries are impressive, increasing sevenfold from $19 billion to $148 billion in the 1990s.[lxviii] Over the same period, foreign direct investment into developing countries increased from 12 percent to nearly 50 percent, with China taking up a large share, and India's share gradually increasing considerably.[lxix] But foreign direct investment continued to flow into the developed economies, with the United States, the United Kingdom, and Holland near the top in inbound FDI.

Examples of new global operations and alliances abound. Global companies such as Asea Brown Bovari, Honda, IBM, Lenovo, British Petroleum, Sony, and Motorola each do business in more than 50 countries. Business today is international and the individual businesses, films, industries, and societies that clearly understand the new rules of doing business in a global economy will prosper. Those that do not will falter. It is no longer business as usual. Global competition with all of its perks and pitfalls is here to stay. Managers of businesses everywhere will have to think in terms of international business and its many opportunities.

MANAGERIAL GUIDELINES

1. Entrepreneurship and value creation are getting more attention around the world. Managers can find ways to empower employees to innovate and help create value, even in traditional production-based firms.
2. Competition is also coming from firms in emerging economies, some of which are born global. It is important for firms to pay particular attention to low-end, potentially disruptive competition coming from abroad.
3. Firms must be more willing to send young professionals abroad. Expatriates are no longer only senior executives. Firms should provide training for those younger professionals they may send abroad.
4. One key challenge for young workers posted abroad and their firms is the acculturation process. Though firms should assist in preparing for the international assignment, individuals should also make their own preparations, particularly in terms of learning about the language and culture of the new country assignment.

DOING BUSINESS IN MALI

Mali is a country of 14 million in West Africa and is one of the poorest countries in the world with an annual per capita income of $440—not much more than one dollar a day. One of Mali's official languages is French, based on its colonial past. In Mali, French firms have a competitive advantage over firms from English-speaking countries such as the United States and the United Kingdom This historical relationship with France has created a civil law system as opposed to the U.S. or British-style common law tradition. In addition, all documents and product specifications must be available in French so as to be accessible to the entire population.

Eighty percent of Mali's population engages in farming, livestock production, or fishing. Cotton is Mali's biggest export. It can be difficult for entrepreneurs to establish a business in Mali because it came in at 158 out of the 178 world economies that the World Bank ranked for ease of doing business. The costs to build a warehouse, including obtaining necessary licenses and permits, completing required notifications and inspections, and obtaining utility connections, are an estimated 1300% of the annual per capita income. An entrepreneur must pay 58 different taxes when starting a business; this compares to 15 in the mature economies of the OECD.

The majority of people in Mali are Muslim, so the business culture is very conservative. Pork, shellfish, and alcohol are typically not served at meals. As in many sub-Saharan countries in Africa, business arrangements should include a relatively high level of protocol in which respect is paid to the party you are meeting, ensuring that adequate attention to their rank and role in society is given. In addition, developing a relationship with the person you are doing business with is key, so try not to rush if doing business in West Africa.

CULTURE

5. It is crucial for firms to provide clear career paths for younger professionals going overseas. Expatriates must not feel that an overseas posting means they are "out of the way and forgotten."

6. Although younger expats may not have families to bring abroad with them, they will still face acculturation challenges. It is important to learn about the pitfalls in doing business in another country. In international business, little things can mean a lot; small mistakes overseas can make headlines and even turn into international incidents. International business is sometimes akin to a diplomatic posting in the foreign service or State Department.

7. Expats must be careful not to project their own values onto their new colleagues and clients abroad, because they may not be the same, particularly in culturally different regions of the world.

ADDITIONAL RESOURCES

Executive Planet website:
http://www.executiveplanet.com/index.php?title=Main_Page

International Business Etiquette and Manners:
http://www.cyborlink.com/

Professor Geert Hofstede's country cultures:
http://www.geert-hofstede.com/

U.S. Central Intelligence Agency Worldfactbook:
https://www.cia.gov/library/publications/the-world-factbook/index.html

World Bank website:
www.worldbank.org.

Glossary

Acquisition. The outright purchase of a firm or some part of that firm.

Administrative Component. The ratio of support staff (e.g., secretaries and supervisors) to line staff directly engaged in the production and distribution of an organization's products and services.

Agency theory. The recognition that those who own firms and manage them are now separated. Thus, the agents may act in their own best interest rather than that of the firm.

Alderfer's ERG needs hierarchy. A hierarchy-of-needs model comprised of three main needs—existence, relatedness, and growth (ERG).

Anchoring. When a manager relies on one piece of information as the key to his or her decision making.

Attribution error. Occurs when people try to determine cause and effect in their lives and make assumptions about what actions led to this situation.

Authority principle. An influence principle that states people are often influenced by recommendations or requests of an authority or expert.

Availability. The availability heuristic leads to a bias whereby people base their decisions heavily on an example can be easily be brought to mind.

Backward integration. A form of vertical integration that involves the purchase of suppliers of a firm's product.

Balanced reciprocity. Securing a promise of a near-immediate return for a favor done or a gift given; thought to be particularly important in China and in ethnic Chinese communities around the world.

Balanced Scorecard. A system that summarizes an organization's strategic objectives into four main performance metrics: financial, internal processes, customers, and learning and growth. These perspectives provide feedback on the execution of the strategic plan.

Base salary. Amount of money that an expatriate normally receives in the home country.

BATNA. Best alternative to a negotiated agreement.

Behavioral theories. Leadership theories that argue that specific, learned behaviors can differentiate leaders from non-leaders (or successful leaders from unsuccessful leaders), and are behaviors that can be learned.

Big Unit capitalism. A Big Unit economy will be dominated by Big Business, Big Government, and Big Labor. The Big Unit economy generally produced efficient but rigid, pyramidal organizations and government departments that were full of soft niches that relaxed standards and did not demand (and reward) excellence and accountability in work and educational quality.

Born globals. Entrepreneurial firms that are started as international firms.

Bottom billion. The world's poorest billion people who have largely missed the economic progress that has come from globalization over the last 25 years.

Bounded rationality. According to Herbert Simon, people do not have the ability to process all of the information and solutions that face them. This inability leads them to limit their problems and solutions.

Brainstorming. A forecasting method in which a broad topic is set out and a discussion among the participants is utilized to gain insights into what the future may look like.

Bretton Woods system. The Bretton Woods system was a negotiated monetary order after World War II to govern monetary relations and currency exchange rates among independent states.

Business strategy. How the firm will compete in a specific product-market.

Business-level strategy. How a specific business will operate in order to succeed in that specific marketplace.

CAFTA. Central America Free Trade Agreement, a free trade agreement (not a treaty) among the U.S. and several Central American countries and the Dominican Republic. CAFTA is also seen as a stepping stone toward the Free Trade Area of the Americas (FTAA), another, more ambitious free trade agreement, which encompass South American and Caribbean countries. Canada is negotiating a similar trade agreement.

Capabilities. Functional skills that a firm develops and which are the foundation on which a firm builds its strategy.

Charisma. Ability to inspire or influence other individuals.

Civil law. Originated in Ancient Rome and is used on the European continent and to a lesser extent, in China today. This approach to the law uses statutes and comprehensive codes as the primary building blocks, relying heavily on legal scholars to formulate and interpret the laws.

Cognitive dissonance. The negative feeling caused by holding two contradictory ideas simultaneously.

Cognitive diversity. The ability of members of the group to think differently, and to express their opinions and findings.

Cognitive response model of persuasion. A model of persuasion that views the most direct cause of persuasion as the self-talk of the target audience, not the persuasion method itself or its deliverer.

Commercial paper. Bonds that corporations issue directly to the public in order to raise capital.

Common law. Legal systems primarily built on legal precedent established by judges as they resolve individual cases; those case opinions have the force of law and strongly influence future decisions. Common law originated in medieval England and is used in the United Kingdom, the British Commonwealth, and in Britain's former colonies, such as the United States, Singapore, Hong Kong, and India.

Communism. A political system that relies on a dictatorship to govern.

Competitive advantage. Something that a firm does better than any of its nearest competitors, which allows the firm to have an advantage with customers over those competitors.

Competitive scope. The breadth of products a firm will offer, such as the range of customers and/or distributors sold to, and the geographic region the firm will cover.

Compliance. The act of changing one's behavior in response to a direct request.

Conformity. Changing one's behavior to match the responses or actions of others, to fit in with those in proximity.

Confucius. Chinese philosopher who lived from 551 to 479 BCE. He was from eastern China and was a well-known and well-traveled teacher and philosopher.

Consistency. A principle of influence that indicates how people are influenced by showing how their previous statements or stated values fit with a recommendation or request.

Consortia. Where several organizations join together to share expertise and funding for developing, gathering, and distributing new knowledge.

Contingency theory. Theory in which the type of leadership needed is based on the situation being faced.

Control. Actions taken to move a firm to better meet its goals after the evaluation of the firm's gap between goals and achievements.

Copyright. The exclusive right to control reproduction or adaptation of creative works, such as books, movies, music, paintings, photographs, and software. Typically, the copyright holder has the exclusive right to control the product for between 10 and 30 years, depending on jurisdiction.

Core competence. A capability that is most critical to the firm's success.

Corporate entrepreneurship. Mature firms that act more like small startup firms by taking greater risks and reducing bureaucracy.

Corporation strategy. Establishes how diversified the firm is to become and in what domains that diversification will occur.

Cultural intelligence test (CQ). Selection test that evaluates a person's ability in a cross-cultural setting.

Cultural sensitivity. Heightened awareness for the values and frames-of-reference of the host culture.

Cultural-toughness. Selection test that assesses whether a candidate appears able to work in a specific country.

Culture. Acquired knowledge people use to interpret experience and actions. This knowledge then influences values, attitudes, and behaviors.

Delphi method. Experts rank different potential future outcomes and through an iterative process these predictions are refined until a prediction of what the future may hold is reached.

Denominator management. A firm tries to increase its return on investment, or ROI, by simply reducing the denominator, that is, reducing the "I" or amount of invested capital in a new project or division of the firm.

Devil's advocate. Someone who argues against the decision being contemplated, allowing the rationale for the decision to be checked.

Differentiation strategy. Seeks to provide some aspect of a product or service that differs from that of competitors, such as higher quality, to increase the likelihood of customers paying a premium for the product.

Disruptive innovation. A new technological innovation, product, service or business model that overturns the existing dominant innovation or technological standard in the marketplace.

Disruptive technology. Also known as a disruptive innovation, it is a new technology that unexpectedly displaces an established technology, often from the lower end of the market, such as the personal computer's defeat of more powerful minicomputers.

Distributive justice. Asserts that inequality is acceptable if employees have fair access to resources and opportunities such that they recognize any inequality to be the result of their own effort and not because of favoritism by management.

Downstream innovation. The ability to use research and basic product components and to package them together to create a new, salable (sometimes branded) product or service. It is also the indigenization of other technologies into a firm's production and development systems to facilitate creation and delivery of a product.

Economic rent. Profits above what should be the norm of the industry, given its level of risk.

Economies of scale. Average unit costs decline as production quantity increases over a limited period of time.

Economies of scope. Cost savings that result from performing two activities jointly, such as manufacturing one type of car in a plant during the day, and at night, producing a different car that was previously produced somewhere else.

Emergent strategy. Managers see opportunities and shift the organization to that new direction.

Entrepreneurship. Value-creation activities to create new enterprises or build a new business or product line within an existing organization.

Escalation of commitment. The tendency to repeat an apparently bad decision or allocate more resources to a failing course of action. (In poker, this is called "throwing good money after bad.")

Ethnocentrism. The ethnocentric view of culture holds that an individual or a firm will believe that their own way of doing things is the best, and will not seek to adapt to local cultural practices.

European Union (EU). Twenty-seven European countries bound by specific treaty and standard legal and commercial agreements in a large number of areas.

Evaluation. The process of determining a firm's progress toward reaching goals and objectives.

360-degree evaluations. Evaluations of an employee conducted by the supervisor, subordinates, peers, and sometimes customers.

Evidence-based information search. A process of information search and decision-making that does not start with a presumed decision and seeks to evaluate a range of evidence and challenge the emerging solution as it is gradually shaped.

Exit barriers. Barriers that keep firms in an industry and thus can exert downward pressure on industry profits.

Expatriate. A person from one country who is working and residing in another country.

Export. The shipping of a good from the home market to markets outside the home country.

Expropriation. When a government seizes the ownership of a private asset or assets.

Extrinsic motivation. Refers to motivation based on external motivating factors, such as payments, rewards, working conditions, praise or punishment.

Face. Respect of a person's peers; avoiding embarrassment.

Financial controls. Focus on gaps between the desired financial outcomes and the actual outcomes.

Financial panic. Financial panics include a variety of situations in which some banks and financial assets suddenly lose a large part of their value and bad debts multiply quickly.

First mover. The first firm into an area, whether a product or national market. Sometimes multiple firms can enter a product market within the same year and are usually considered multiple first movers.

Foreign Direct Investment (FDI). Investment by foreigners in a nation typically in plant and equipment.

Forward integration. A form of vertical integration whereby a firm's activities are expanded to include the direct distribution of its products and services.

Franchising. A type of alliance where a contract is established between the parent (franchisor) and the individual who actually buys the business unit (franchisee) to sell a given product or conduct business under its trademark.

Functional strategies. Those strategies that direct what occurs in individual functional areas, such as marketing, finance, and accounting.

Gap analysis. Analysis of the gap between what a firm wants to occur and what actually has occurred and is likely to occur.

Giri. Japanese word, which loosely translated means the right way to behave, though in practical terms it refers directly to Japan's complex system of gift-giving and exchange relations in society.

Global strategy. When a firm chooses to compete in the same manner in all countries.

Globalization. Globalization is a modern term used to describe the changes in societies and the world economy that result from dramatically increased international trade, foreign direct investment, and cultural exchange.

Greenfield venture. A firm may choose to establish itself in a given country without the aid of a partner.

Group interviews. Selection tool in which typically there are multiple candidates and multiple interviewers present at the same time.

Groupthink. A mode of thought whereby individuals intentionally conform to what they perceive to be the consensus of the group and preference of the leader.

Hadiths. Several volumes compiled well after the Koran. A major source of Islamic law and moral teachings. Early Muslims used oral traditions regarding the early history and prehistory of Islam and the practice of Muhammad and his first followers, and wrote them down so that they might be preserved.

Harmonization. Efforts between nations to have the same code of standards for products and how they are treated in regards to tariffs.

Horizontal merger and acquisition. Occurs when the acquired and acquiring firms are in the same industry.

Hygiene factors. According to Herzberg's theory, these are factors such as working conditions, salary, and job security that influence a job.

Impasse. When a manager and his or her negotiating partner cannot reach an agreement.

Implicit leadership. Recognizes the process by which persons are perceived as leaders and follows the same basic social-cognitive processes that occur in other contexts of perceptions of persons.

Import substitution. A trade and economic term based on the premise that developing countries should attempt to locally build products that they currently import. Import substitution concomitantly requires high protective tariffs and monetary policy to create an overvalued domestic currency.

Indirect import. Goods may have most of the value added in one country but due to trade barriers the product is shipped to another country where final production on the good occurs, with the good then being listed as an export from that country.

Industrial organization (IO) economics. A branch of economics that focuses on market efficiency and inefficiency.

Influence. Seeking to change people's behaviors.

Intangible assets. Non-monetary, non-physical assets that cannot be physically measured. Intangible assets include copyrights, patents, trademarks, know-how, and collaboration activities.

Internal locus of control. Whether people feel that they can control things themselves or whether forces outside them control their future.

Intrinsic motivation. Motivation based on internal motivating factors. Such intrinsic rewards are internal to the person, such as the satisfaction of meeting a goal or learning a new skill.

Iron Rice Bowl. In China, the concept of the state meeting all worker's needs: not only food, but schools for kids, hospitals, and even vacation locations for workers. These benefits were typically organized around the large state enterprises they served.

Keiretsu. Vertically and horizontally integrated business groups that dominate the Japanese economy.

Key success factors. Things that are important to customers and help determine a business' success in a given industry.

Late entrants. Firms that enter a market after others are clearly there.

Leaders. Individuals who significantly affect the thoughts and behaviors of others, often through persuasion.

Learned needs theory. Proposed by Harvard psychologist David McClelland, this theory suggested there were three basic learned needs: power, affiliation, and achievement.

Licensing agreement. In such an agreement, a firm agrees to pay a firm for the right to either manufacture or sell a product. The firm selling the right to this product typically loses the right to control various aspects of the product when manufactured or sold by the licensee.

Licensing arrangement. One firm agrees to pay another firm for the right to either manufacture or sell a product.

Liking. A principle of influence that holds that people are more likely to be influenced by those who they like or with whom they have similarities.

Low-cost strategy. Where a business seeks to sell a product at or near the lowest possible price in the firm's chosen market segment.

Market for corporate control. The ability to take over a poorly performing firm and turn it around to profitability.

Market power. Occurs when a firm has enough market-share to shape that market's actions. It can be a strategic motivation for a merger or acquisition.

Market-based economic system. Relies on individuals in the society to determine the price of any good.

Maslow's hierarchy of needs. Maslow's theory contends that as people meet basic needs, they seek to satisfy successively higher needs that occupy a set hierarchy.

Mechanistic structures. Structures that are highly inflexible and static, typically in low-technology domains.

Merger. Occurs when two firms combine as relative equals.

Mission. A simple statement of the basic purpose or reason for the business to exist and its activities.

Motivation. The driving force behind an individual's actions that energizes and directs goal-oriented behavior.

Motivators. In Herzberg's motivation-hygiene theory, these are positive influencers, such as job involvement, that are intrinsic to a job and that can push employees to higher levels of performance.

Multi-domestic strategy. A parent company allows each market to adapt to local conditions and pursue the strategy they choose best in that local market.

Multinational enterprise. Large firm that operates in a large number of countries.

NAFTA. The North American Free Trade Agreement, known usually as NAFTA, links Canada, the United States, and Mexico in a free trade sphere. NAFTA went into effect on January 1, 1994.

National champions. A firm that is the only firm producing a certain good in its country, and is protected by high tariffs and favorable monetary policy. Although usually a product of import-substitution policies to reduce imports, most countries intend their national champion firms to become competitive exporters, though few are. (Airbus is one notable exception.)

Nationalize. When a government decides a good or factory will be owned by the national government.

Needs. Represent things or conditions that people would like to have.

Negotiating. A process in which at least two partners with different needs and viewpoints try to reach agreement on matters of mutual interest.

Non-tariff trade barriers. A barrier to free trade that takes a form other than a tariff, for instance quotas or inspection requirements for imported products such as VCRs, automobiles and dairy products.

Normative model of decision making. Decision making using a rational model (i.e., how things ought to be).

Obedience. A special type of compliance that involves changing one's behavior in response to a directive from an authority figure.

OEM. Original equipment manufacturers.

Organic structure. A flexible structure, often decentralized.

Organizational structure. The official manner in which the various parts of a business are to report and coordinate with each other, and at what levels decisions are made.

Outsourcing. Outsourcing (or contracting out) is often defined as the delegation of non-core operations or jobs from internal production to an external entity (such as a subcontractor) that specializes in that operation.

Parkinson's Law. Parkinson's Law states that work expands to fill the time available for its completion. Several corollaries are possible, such as an organization's administrative component grows with time.

Parochialism. Belief that there is no other way of doing things except what is done in one's own culture.

Patent. Granted to a new, useful, and non-obvious invention. It gives the patent holder a right to prevent others from copying the invention without a license for 20 years from the filing date of a patent application.

Persuasion. Seeking to change people's beliefs or attitudes.

Piecework. A type of work in which a worker is paid a fixed "piece rate" for each unit produced or action performed.

Polycentric. The polycentric view of culture holds that multinational enterprises (MNE) should treat each international subsidiary largely as a separate national entity. This means that the subsidiary should do things in a local manner; and MNE subsidiaries may come to differ from each other.

Positions. Bids, offers, and stated objectives for settlement terms.

Positive model of decision making. Actual, day-to-day decision-making model, not idealized.

Price. The exchange ratio for goods and services between what the seller is willing to sell the good for and what the buyer is willing to pay.

Privatize. When government-owned businesses are sold to private individuals or groups.

Problem. Arises when there is a discrepancy between the present situation and the optimal outcome.

Product platform. A package of products that complement each other.

Programmed decision. A decision that follows standard operating procedures. There is no need to explore alternative solutions because the optimal solution has already been identified and documented.

Projection. An unconscious assumption that others share the same or similar beliefs, values, attitudes, or positions on any given subject.

Prospect Theory. Examines risk assessment, loss aversion, and dependence on a reference or starting point. Explains why individuals consistently behave in ways different from what traditional economic and decision theory would predict.

Protocol. Rules for how individuals in a business setting are to interact with each other.

Quality circles. A group of workers who meet on a regular basis to discuss ways of improving the quality of work.

Reactance. When people are told that they cannot have or do something, they tend to want it more.

Reciprocation. A principle of influence that states people are more likely to say yes to a request when the requester has done something for that person in the past.

Red hats. Businesses that the government owns, but which they allow professional managers run.

Reengineering. A radical redesign of an organization's processes so that they can be executed in parallel, and the tasks undertaken by nonspecialists. The job's cycle time to completion is reduced in an effective reengineering.

Renewable energy certificate (REC). Certificate for each 1,000 kilowatts of renewable energy that can be bought or sold. Governments create such certificates for tax purposes and to encourage alternative energy. The production of energy from renewable sources not only generates the energy itself which ultimately consumers use, but for each 1,000 kilowatts of energy generated there is also one REC that can be sold or bought.

Repatriation of profits. The ability of a firm to take the profits it makes in a country out of that country.

Representativeness. The representativeness heuristic is when seeming patterns of data are assumed (incorrectly) to represent something that the data do not warrant.

Reservation Price. A reservation price is the absolute bottom price that is acceptable.

Resources. Tangible and intangible assets that firms possess.

Return on investment (ROI). Return measured by dividing profit by assets or invested capital.

Satisficing. Alternatives that are acceptable or "good enough," rather than the best possible solutions.

Scarcity. A principle of influence that argues that people are more likely to buy a product or want to do something that they perceive as scarce, unique, or dwindling in availability.

Scenario planning. Forecasting method where participants are given potential scenarios and then asked to build likely responses and outcomes for the business.

Second movers. Those that follow the first movers into a market.

Sensitivity analysis. Asks planners to make changes in usually one variable only, to see the likely effect.

Shari'a law. The law system inspired by the Koran, the Sunna, the Hadiths, older Arabic law systems, parallel traditions, and the work of Muslim scholars over the two first centuries of Islam.

Shrinkage. Loss of goods due to stealing or breakage, often in a retail store.

Social proof. A principle of influence that states people are more likely to want to do something if they believe that many others are doing the same thing or buying the same product.

Socialism. An economic policy that can take several forms, in which in its purest form, the state owns all assets of the society. The belief is that if the assets are held by all then all individuals will benefit.

Spin off. To make a separate company of a prior division, for example when Pepsico spun off its restaurant division to form YUM!

Strategic alliance. A partnership of two or more corporations or business units to achieve strategically significant objectives that are mutually beneficial.

Strategic business unit (SBU). A business division within a larger firm that is charged with managing a particular category of product or service.

Strategic controls. Focus on the firm's desired strategic outcomes and the actual outcomes.

Strategic tactics. Strategic actions that help to implement a strategy, such as a new promotion program that would implement a focus on differentiation business strategy.

Strategy. A coordinated set of actions that fulfills the firm's objectives, purposes, and goals.

Stuck in the middle. Where a firm has neither a clear low-cost nor a clear differentiation strategy.

Sustainable competitive advantage. The ability to have a competitive advantage over a period of time.

Tangible assets. Those things that can be touched by an entrepreneur, such as equipment and money.

Tariffs. Taxes on imported (not exported) goods.

Tax neutral. Firms will try to ensure that an expatriate does not pay more tax by being posted abroad.

Technology indigenization. Integrating technologies into a firm's production and development systems (sometimes modifying them in the process) to facilitate the creation and delivery of a product to customers or service to employees.

Township and village enterprises. Unique types of businesses in China that grew out of worker brigades organized by Chairman Mao, the chairman of the Communist Party at the founding of the People's Republic of China.

Trade deficit. A negative balance of trade when a country is importing more than it exports. Usually defined and reported in material trade terms, excluding services and investment.

Trademark. A distinctive symbol used to distinguish the products or services of different businesses.

Trait theory. Argues that people have underlying traits or characteristics that lead to either superior leader or follower performance.

Transfer pricing. Pricing of goods and services within a multi-divisional organization that are supplied to other division or foreign subsidiaries.

Transformational leadership. A combination of learned skills and the ability to transform an organization in new, substantive ways.

Transnational firm. In this type of firm the business assets are highly specialized, but interdependent with the other assets of the firm. The contribution of each nation is integrated with the worldwide network of businesses to provide to the whole the benefits of that nation. Knowledge developed in any unit is shared worldwide within the business.

Transnational strategy. Strategy that combines aspects of multi-domestic and global strategy.

Turnkey operation. One part of the company is responsible for setting up the plant and equipment while another operates the plant.

Turnkey. When a firm can enter the market immediately with a ready-made application that allows the firm to start doing business immediately

Ultimatum. Requiring someone or a group to do specific thing in a specific way in order for negotiations to continue.

Upstream innovation. Scientific research, basic product research and development, and university-company partnerships on developing new products.

USSR. The Union of Soviet Socialist Republics, the communist federation of states headed by Russia.

Valence. The anticipated satisfaction or dissatisfaction that an individual feels about an outcome.

Value chain analysis. Breaks the firm's activities into primary activities and support activities.

Verdict-based information search. A process of information search and decision-making that starts with the presumed answer to the decision and proceeds to only seek out information that confirms the initial verdict or decision.

Vertical integration. When a firm expands its business into areas that are at different points along its production path for a given product.

Vertical merger or acquisition. One where one firm is a supplier to the other or vice versa.

White goods. Goods, such as washer, dryers, and refrigerators.

Wholly owned subsidiary. An organization form where the parent owns the local firm completely; typically the organization would focus only on the country in which it had entered.

World Trade Organization (WTO). An international organization that oversees a large number of agreements defining the rules of trade between its member states.

Bibliography

Chapter 1

i Gilboy, G. F. (2004). The myth behind China's miracle. *Foreign Affairs*, 83(4), 33–48.

ii The *Far Eastern Economic Review* (Sept. 2, 1999).

iii Drezner, D. W. (2004). The outsourcing bogeyman. *Foreign Affairs*, May/June.

iv Drezner, 2004.

v Drezner, 2004.

vi Smith, A. (1776). *The Wealth of Nations*; Bhagwati, J. (2004). *In Defense of Globalization*. Oxford: Oxford University Press.

vii Perhaps the best explanation of the value of globalization is from Jagdish Bhagwati (2004) *In Defense of Globalization*. A single chapter treatment of globalization can be found in World Bank economist Tim Harford's (2006) book *The Undercover Economist: Exposing Why the Rich Are Rich, the Poor Are Poor—and Why You Can Never Buy a Decent Used Car!* (Chapter 9). New York: Oxford University Press.

viii Wessell, D., & Davis, B. (2007, March 28). Pain from free trade spurs second thoughts. *Wall Street Journal*, Col. CCXLIX(72), pp. A1, A14.

ix Hammer, M. (1994). *Understanding Reengineering*. Cambridge, MA: Hammer Videos.

x Landes, D. (1998). *The Wealth and Poverty of Nations: Why Some Are So Rich and Some So Poor*. New York: W.W. Norton.

xi This analogy is drawn from John Kotter's *The New Rules* (1995). New York: Free Press.

xii Bhagwati, J., & Wolf, M. (2004). *Why Globalization Works*. New Haven, CT: Yale University Press.

xiii Central Intelligence Agency. *The World Factbook*. https://www.cia.gov/library/publications/the-world-factbook/index.html (accessed June 24, 2008).

xiv Europa Key figures. http://europa.eu.int/abc/keyfigures/index_en.htm

xv Information from the Office of United States Trade Representative. http://www.ustr.gov/Document_Library/Fact_Sheets/2004/NAFTA_A_Decade_of_Success.html

xvi http://www.cia.gov/cia/publications/factbook/geos/ch.html

xvii Nair, A., Ahlstrom, D., & Filer, L. (2007). Localized advantage in a global economy: The case of Bangalore. *Thunderbird International Business Review*, 49(5), 591–618.

xviii Nair, Ahlstrom, & Filer, 2007.

xix Peng, M. W. (2001). How entrepreneurs create wealth in transaction economies. *Academy of Management Executive*, 15(1), 95–110.

xx ABB case, http://icmrindia.org/casestudies/catalogue/Business%20Ethics/BECG052.htm

xxi Kidder, R. M. (1996). *How Good People Make Tough Choices: Resolving the Dilemmas of Ethical Living*. New York: Harper Paperbacks.

xxii Kidder, 1996.

xxiii A very interesting account of four different subcultures in the United States can be found in Walter Russell Mead's classic article in *The National Interest*, "The Jacksonian Tradition and American Foreign Policy." Winter (1999/2000), pp. 5–29. For a book-length treatment see Mead, W. R. (2001). *Special Providence*. New York: Knopf.

xxiv Halliday, F. (2005). *The Middle East in International Relations*. Cambridge: Cambridge University Press.

Chapter 2

i Readers from large, diverse countries, such as Russia, India, or even the United States will question the proposition that culture is fairly homogeneous in their countries, though other important factors, such as laws or societal institutions that are influenced by national culture, will be fairly uniform.

ii Barone, M. (2005, Winter). *Hard America, Soft America: Competition vs. Coddling and the Battle for the Nation's Future*. New York: Three Rivers Press; Mead, W. R. (1999/2000). The Jacksonian tradition and American foreign policy. *The National Interest*, 56, 5–29.

iii Halliday, F. (2005). *The Middle East in International Relations: Power, Politics and Ideology*. Cambridge: Cambridge University Press; Hofstede, G., & Hofstede, G. J. (2004). *Cultures and Organizations: Software of the Mind*. New York: McGraw-Hill.

iv Hobsbawm, E., & Ranger, T. (Eds.) (1992). *The Invention of Tradition*. Cambridge: Cambridge University Press.

v Hobsbawm & Ranger, 1992; Hofstede & Hofstede, 2004.

vi Harris, M. (1979). *Cultural Materialism: The Struggle for a Science of Culture.* New York: Random House; Halliday, 2005; Hobsbawm & Ranger, 1992.

vii Levine, R. (2003). *The Power of Persuasion: How We're Bought and Sold.* New York: John Wiley & Sons.

viii Levine, 2003.

ix Hofstede & Hofstede, 2004.

x Beech, H. (2005, August 22). The wasted asset. *Time.* http://www.time.com/time/asia/covers/501050829/story.html.

xi Kiegler, P. J. (2003, December). The China puzzle. *Workforce Management,* pp. 28–33; Mahbubani, K. (2001). *Can Asians Think?* Hanover, NH: Steerforth Press; Nisbett, R. (2003). *The Geography of Thought: How Asians and Westerners Think Differently . . . and Why.* New York: Free Press.

xii Kiegler, 2003.

xiii Nisbett, 2003.

xiv Hall, E. T. (1976). *Beyond Culture.* New York: Anchor Press.

xv Ambler, T., & Witzel, M. (2004). *Doing Business in China* (2nd ed.). London: Routledge Curzon.

xvi Hall, E. T., & Hall, M. R. (1960). The silent language of overseas business. *Harvard Business Review,* May–June; Hall, E. T. (1976). *Beyond Culture.* New York: Anchor Press.

xvii Tannen, D. (1995). The power of talk: Who gets heard and why. *Harvard Business Review,* September–October, 138–148.

xviii Perlmutter, H. V. (1969). The tortuous evolution of the multinational corporation. *Columbia Journal of World Business,* IV, January–February, 9–18.

xix Landes, D. S. (1998). *The Wealth and Poverty of Nations: Why Some Are So Rich and Some So Poor.* New York: W.W. Norton; Sowell, T. (1996). *Migrations and Cultures: A World View.* New York: Basic Books.

xx Kluckhohn, F. R., & Strodtbeck. F. L. (1961). *Variations in Value Orientations.* Evanston, IL: Row & Peterson.

xxi Putnam, R. (2000). *Bowling Alone: The Collapse and Revival of American Community.* New York: Simon & Schuster.

xxii Hofstede & Hofstede, 2004.

xxiii Nisbett, 2003.

xxiv Smith, T. C. (1959). *The Agrarian Origins of Modern Japan.* Stanford, CA: Stanford University Press.

xxv Ahlstrom, D., Nair, A., Young, M. N., & Wang, L. C. (2006). China: Competitive myths and realities. *SAM Advanced Management Journal.* 71(3), 4–10; Gilboy, G. (2004). The myth behind China's miracle. *Foreign Affairs,* 83(4), 33–48.

Chapter 3

i Baumol, W. J. (2004). *The Free-Market Innovation Machine: Analyzing the Growth Miracle of Capitalism.* Princeton, NJ: Princeton University Press; Baumol, W. J., Litan, R. E., & Schramm, C. J. (2007). *Good Capitalism, Bad Capitalism.* New Haven, CT: Yale University Press; Friedman, T. L. (2000). *The Lexus and the Olive Tree: Understanding Globalization* (Revised Edition). New York: Farrar, Straus and Giroux; Landes, D. S. (1998). *The Wealth and Poverty of Nations: Why Some Are So Rich and Some So Poor.* New York: W.W. Norton; Sachs, J. D. (2005). *The End of Poverty: Economic Possibilities for Our Time.* New York: Penguin Press.

ii Lott, J. R. (2007). *Freedomnomics: Why the Free Market Works and Other Half-Baked Theories Don't.* Washington, DC: Regnery Publishing; Wolf, M. (2004). *Why Globalization Works.* New Haven, CT: Yale University Press.

iii Bennhold, K. (2006, April 8). Economics, French-style. *International Herald Tribune.*

iv Peng, M. W. (2000). *Business Strategy in Transition Economies.* Thousand Oaks, CA: Sage Publications.

v Bhagwati, J. (2004). *In Defense of Globalization.* Oxford: Oxford University Press.

vi Friedman, 2000.

vii Sachs, 2005, p. 211.

viii James, H. (2003). *Europe Reborn: A History, 1914–2000.* Harlow, UK: Pearson/Longman.

ix Finn's speed fine is a bit rich. (2004, February 10). *BBC News.* http://news.bbc.co.uk/1/hi/business/3477285.stm.

x Gilboy, G. J. (2004). The myth behind China's miracle. *Foreign Affairs,* July–August, 83(4), 33–48.

xi Volkov, V. (2002). *Violent Entrepreneurs: The Use of Force in the Making of Russian Capitalism.* Ithaca, NY: Cornell University Press; Hoffman, D. E. (2002). *The Oligarchs: Wealth and Power in the New Russia.* New York: Public Affairs Books.

xii Heilbroner, R. L. (1999). *The Worldly Philosophers: The Lives, Times and Ideas of the Great Economic Thinkers* (7th ed.). New York: Touchstone.

xiii Case, K. E., & Fair, R. C. (1999). *Principles of Economics* (5th ed.) (p. 822). New York: Prentice Hall.

xiv Braudel, F. (1972). *The Mediterranean and the Mediterranean World in the Age of Philip II, Vol. 1.* (1st U.S. ed.). New York: Harper & Row; Sowell, T. (1994). *Race and Culture: A World View.* New York: Basic Books.

xv Diamond, J. M. (1998). *Guns, Germs, and Steel: The Fates of Human Societies.* New York: W.W. Norton & Co.

xvi Harris, M. (1979). *Cultural Materialism: The Struggle for a Science of Culture.* New York: Random House.

xvii Landes, 1998.

xviii Baumol, W. J., Litan, R. E., & Schramm, C. J. (2007). *Good Capitalism, Bad Capitalism.* New Haven, CT: Yale University Press; Prahalad, C. K. (2004). *The Fortune at the Bottom of the Pyramid: Eradicating Poverty Through Profits.* Philadelphia: Wharton School Publishing.

xix Gwartney, J. D., & Lawson, R. A. (2004). Economic Freedom of the World, 2004 Annual Report. *Frazer Institute Canada Report Economic Freedom.*

xx Solow, R. M. (1956). A contribution to the theory of economic growth. *Quarterly Journal of Economics*, 70, 65–94.

xxi Sachs, J. D. (2001). Tropical underdevelopment. NBER Working Paper W8119 (Feb.). New York: National Bureau of Economic Research.

xxii Olson, M. (1984). *The Rise and Decline of Nations: Economic Growth, Stagflation, and Social Rigidities.* New Haven, CT: Yale University Press; North, D. C. (2005). *Understanding the Process of Economic Change.* Princeton, NJ: Princeton University Press.

xxiii Boisot, M., & Child, J. (1988). The iron law of fiefs: Bureaucratic failure and the problem of governance in the Chinese economic reforms. *Administrative Science Quarterly*, 33, 507–527.

xxiv Harrison, L. E., & Huntington, S. P. (Eds.). (2001). *Culture Matters.* New York: Basic Books.

xxv North, 2005.

xxvi Schumpeter, J. A. (1950). *Capitalism, Socialism and Democracy.* New York: Harper Perennial.

xxvii Porter, M. E. (1990). *The Competitive Advantage of Nations.* New York: Free Press.

xxviii Heckscher, E. F., & Ohlin, (1991). In B., Flam, H., & Flanders, M. J. (Eds.). *Heckscher-Ohlin Trade Theory.* Cambridge, MA: MIT Press.

xxix Johnson, C. (1984). *MITI and the Japanese Miracle: The Growth of Industrial Policy, 1925–1975.* Stanford, CA: Stanford University Press.

xxx Porter, 1990.

xxxi Taylor, A. (2007, August 13). Asian economies near demographic cliff. *Financial Times*, p. 4.

xxxii Pfeffer, J. (1998). *The Human Equation: Building Profits by Putting People First.* Boston: Harvard Business School Press.

xxxiii Hubbard, G. (2006). The productivity riddle. *Strategy+Business*, 45, 1–6.

xxxiv La Porta, R., Lopez-de-Silanes, F., Shleifer, A., & Vishny, R. W. 1998. Law and finance. *The Journal of Political Economy*, 106(6), 1113–1156; La Porta, R., Lopez-de-Silanes, F., Shleifer, A., & Vishny, R. W. (2000). Investor protection and corporate governance. *Journal of Financial Economics*, 58(1,2), 3–27.

xxxv Lubman, S. (1999). *Bird in a Cage: Legal Reform in China after Mao.* Stanford, CA: Stanford University Press.

xxxvi Ahlstrom, D., Bruton, G.D., & Lui, S.Y. (2000). Navigating China's changing economy: Strategies for private firms. *Business Horizons*, 45(6), 49–59.

xxxvii Ahlstrom, D., Young, M. N., & Nair, A. (2002). Deceptive managerial practices in China: Strategies for foreign firms. *Business Horizons*, 43(1), 5–15.

xxxviii Shaw, M. N. (2003). *International Law* (5th ed.). Cambridge: Cambridge University Press.

xxxix Shah, A. (2007). Poverty around the world. *Global Issues.* http://www.globalissues.org/TradeRelated/PovertyAroundTheWorld.asp.

xl Youngers, C. (1999, March 9). U.S. Policy in Latin American and the Caribbean. *Foreign Policy in Focus*, Vol. 3. http://www.fpif.org/progresp/volume3/v3n07_body.html.

xli Ferguson, N. (2008). *The Ascent of Money: A Financial History of the World.* New York: Penguin Press HC.

xlii Transparency International http://www.transparency.org/cpi/2003/cpi2003.en.html.

Chapter 4

i Collis, D. J., & Montgomery, C. A. (1995). Competing on resources: Strategy in the 1990s. *Harvard Business Review*, 118–128.

ii Prahalad, C. K., & Hamel, G. (1990). The core competence of the corporation. *Harvard Business Review*, 66 (May–June), 79–90.

iii Prahalad & Hamel, 1990.

iv Café de Coral Group is the largest Chinese restaurant group selling Chinese fast food. Café de Coral has 120 restaurants worldwide, compared with 150 McDonalds in Hong Kong.

v Porter, M. (1998). *Competitive Advantage: Creating and Sustaining Superior Performance.* New York: Free Press.

vi Holmstrom, B., & Kaplan, S. N. (2001). Corporate governance and merger activity in the U.S.: Making sense of the 1980s and 1990s U.S. *The Journal of Economic Perspectives*, 15(2) (Spring), 121–44; Peng, M. W. (2005). *Global Strategy* (p. 457). Eagan, MN: Thomson South-Western.

vii Dolbeck, A. (2004, July 12). Good news for the M&A market. *Weekly Corporate Growth Report.* http://www.findarticles.com/p/articles/mi_qa3755/is_200407/ai_n9435310.

viii Ip, G., & King, N. Jr. (2006). Engine of globalization runs into big roadblocks. *Asia Wall Street Journal.*

ix Henry, D., & Jesperson, F. (2002, October 14). Why most big deals don't pay off. *BusinessWeek*, 60–70; Sirower, M. L. (1997). *The Synergy Trap.* New York: Free Press.

x Rappaport, A., & Sirower, M. L. 1999. Stock or cash? *Harvard Business Review*, 77(6), 147–158.

xi Walsh, F. (2005, February 9). Booming Reckitt plays it cool on takeover front. *Knight Ridder Tribune Business News*, p. 1.

xii Ledgard, J. (2005). Skoda leaps to market. *Strategy+Business*, Fall, 58–69.

xiii Wright, P., Kroll, M., & Elenkov, D. (2002). Acquisition returns, increase in firm size, and chief executive officer compensation: The moderating role of monitoring. *Academy of Management Journal*, 45(3), 599–608.

xiv Jensen, M. C., & Meckling, W. H. (1976). Theory of the firm: Managerial behavior, agency costs and ownership structure. *Journal of Financial Economics*, 3, 305–360.

xv Wong, G., McGregor, H., Mak, V., & Ng, P. (2002). Social Capital at Work in PCCW's Acquisition of Cable & Wireless HKT. Centre for Asian Business Cases, School of Business, The University of Hong Kong.

xvi Hitt, M.A., Harrison, J. S., & Ireland, R. D. (2001). *Mergers and Acquisitions: A Guide to Creating Value for Shareholders*. New York: Oxford University Press.

xvii http://www.nutraingredients.com/news/ng.asp?id=35419-vertical-integration-the.

xviii Vodaphone posts strong profits. (2000, November 17). *BBC News*. http://news.bbc.co.uk/1/hi/business/1022674.stm.

xix Finkelstein, S. (2003). *Why Smart Executives Fail: And What You Can Learn from Their Mistakes*. New York: Portfolio.

xx Finkelstein, 2003, p. 298.

xxi Kogut, B. (1988). Joint ventures: Theoretical and empirical perspectives. *Strategic Management Journal*, 9, 319–332.

xxii Hitt et al., 2001.

Chapter 5

i Nalebuff, B., & Brandenburger, A. (1997). Co-opetition: Competitive and cooperative business strategies for the digital economy. *Strategy & Leadership*, 25(6), 28–33.

ii Chandler, A. (1994). *Scale and Scope: The Dynamics of Industrial Capitalism* (reprint ed.). Cambridge, MA: Belknap Press.

iii Porter, M. E. (1980). *Competitive Strategy: Techniques for Analyzing Industries and Competitors*. New York: Free Press.

iv Wright, P., Kroll, M., & Tu, H. (1991). Generic strategies and business performance: An empirical study of the screw machine products industry. *British Journal of Management*, 2, 57–66.

v Christensen, C. M. (1997). Making strategy by doing. *Harvard Business Review*, 75(6), 141–156.

vi Ries, A., & Trout, J. (1994). *The 22 Immutable Laws of Marketing*. New York: HarperBusiness.

vii Hamel, G., & Prahalad, C. K. (1994). *Competing for the Future*. Cambridge, MA: Harvard Business School Press.

viii Evans, P., & Wurster, T. S. (1999). *Blown to Bits: How the New Economics of Information Transforms Strategy*. Cambridge, MA: Harvard Business School Press.

ix Kim, E., Nam, D., & Stimpert, J. L. (2004). The applicability of Porter's generic strategies in the digital age: Assumptions, conjectures, and suggestions. *Journal of Management*, 30, 569–589.

x Farris, P. W., & Moore, M. J. (2004). *The Profit Impact of Marketing Strategy Project: Retrospect and Prospects*. Cambridge: Cambridge University Press; also see Tellis & Golder (1996) for a critique of PIMS. Tellis, G., & Golder, P. (1996). First to market, first to fail? The real causes of enduring market leadership. *Sloan Management Review*, 32(2), 65–75.

xi Roth, K. (1992). Implementing international strategy at the business unit level: The role of managerial decision-making characteristics. *Journal of Management*, 18, 769–789.

xii Procter & Gamble making big inroads in Russia. U.K. White Goods. http://www.ukwhitegoods.co.uk/modules.php?name=News&file=print&sid=239

xiii Oyelere, P. B., & Emmanuel, C. R. (1998). International transfer pricing and income shifting: Evidence from the UK. *European Accounting Review*, 7, 623-635.

xiv Pagell, M., & Krausse, D. R. (2002). Strategic consensus in the internal supply chain: Exploring the manufacturing—purchasing link. *International Journal of Production Research*, 40, 3075–3092.

xv Deming, W. E. (1982). *Out of the Crisis*. Cambridge, MA: The MIT Press International.

xvi Peters, T. J., & Waterman, R. H. (1982). *In Search of Excellence: Lessons from America's Best-Run Companies*. New York: Harper & Row.

Chapter 6

i http://www.detnews.com/2005/autosinsider/0504/23/1auto-159177.htm.

ii Tannen, D. (1995). The power of talk: Who gets heard and why. *Harvard Business Review*, September–October, 138–148.

iii Chambers, E.G., Foulon, M., Handfield-Jones, H., Hankin, S.M., & Michaels III, E.G. (1998). The war for talent. *McKinsey Quarterly*, 3, 44–57.

iv Foreign Direct Investment Rose by 34% in 2006. United Nations Conference on Trade and Development (UNCTAD). 2007. http://www.unctad.org/templates/webflyer.asp?docid=7993&intItemID=1528&lang=1 (accessed on October 2, 2007).

v Foreign Direct Investment Rose By 34% in 2006. 2006. UNCTAD press release. http://www.unctad.org/Templates/webflyer.asp?docid=7993&intItemID=1528&lang=1 (accessed October 5, 2008).

vi Viramani, A. (2005, October 2). Bringing down tariffs without hurting. *NewsInsight.* http://www.indiareacts.com/archivespecialreports/nat2.asp?recno=29&ctg=.

vii Nair, A., Ahlstrom, D., & Filer, L. (2007). Localized advantage in a global economy: The case of Bangalore. *Thunderbird International Business Review,* 49(5), 591–618.

viii Yan, A., & Luo, Y. (2001). *International Joint Ventures: Theory and Practice.* Armonk, NY: M.E. Sharpe.

ix Weidenbaum, M., & Hughes, S. (1996). *The Bamboo Network: How Expatriate Chinese Entrepreneurs Are Creating a New Economic Superpower in Asia.* New York: Free Press.

x Purcell, V. (1965). *The Chinese in Southeast Asia* (2nd ed.). London: Oxford University Press.

xi Ahlstrom, D., Young, M. N., Chan, E. S., & Bruton, G. D. (2004). Facing constraints to growth? Overseas Chinese entrepreneurs and traditional business practices in East Asia. *Asia Pacific Journal of Management,* 21(3), 263–285; Seagrave, S. (1995). *Lords of the Rim: The Invisible Empire of the Overseas Chinese.* New York: G.P. Putnam Group.

xii DeFrancis, J. (1986). *The Chinese Language: Fact and Fantasy.* Honolulu: University of Hawaii Press.

xiii Tan, T. W. (Ed.) (1990). *Chinese Dialect Groups: Traits and Trades.* Singapore: Opinion Books.

xiv Seagrave, 1995.

xv Tan, 1990.

xvi Hamel, G., & Prahalad, C. K. (1994). *Competing for the Future.* Boston: Harvard Business School Press.

xvii Yan & Luo, 2001.

xviii Mann, J. (1997). *Beijing Jeep: A Case Study of Western Business in China.* Boulder, CO: Westview Press.

xix Mann, 1997.

xx For a very recent, instructive, and cautionary tale about western firms' odyssey in China, see Tim Clissold's 2006 book *Mr. China: A Memoir.* New York: Collins.

xxi Boulding, W., & Christen, M. (2001). First mover disadvantage. *Harvard Business Review,* October, 20–21.

xxii Levinson, M. (2006). *The Box: How the Shipping Container Made the World Smaller and the World Economy Bigger.* Princeton, NJ: Princeton University Press.

Chapter 7

i Keillor, G. (1985). *Lake Wobegon Days.* New York: Viking Press.

ii Butler, T., & Waldroop, J. (1999). Job sculpting: The art of retaining your best people. *Harvard Business Review,* September–October, 144–152.

iii Trompenaars, F. (1993). *Riding the Waves of Culture.* London: The Economist Books.

iv Trompenaars, 1993, p. 86.

v Semlar, R. (1989). Managing without managers. *Harvard Business Review,* September–October, 2–10.

vi Alderfer, C. P. (1972). *Existence, Relatedness, and Growth: Human Needs in Organizational Settings.* New York: Free Press.

vii Hofstede, G., & Hofstede, G. J. (2005). *Cultures and Organizations: Software of the Mind.* New York: McGraw-Hill; Trompenaars, 1993.

viii Alderfer, 1972.

ix Hofstede & Hofstede, 1993.

x Kovach, K. A. (1987). What motivates employees? Workers and supervisors give different answers. *Business Horizons,* 58–65; Morse, G. (2002). Why we misread motives. *Harvard Business Review,* 81, 1–18.

xi Herzberg, F. (1968). One more time: How do you motivate employees? *Harvard Business Review,* January–February, 54–62.

xii Adler, N. J. (2002). *International Dimensions of Organizational Behavior* (4th ed.) (p. 175). Cincinnati, OH: South-Western College Publishing.

xiii McClelland, D. C., Atkinson, J. W., Clark, R. A., & Lowell, E. L. (1953). *The Achievement Motive.* New York: Appleton-Century-Crofts.

xiv McClelland, D. C. (1961). *The Achieving Society.* Princeton, NJ: Van Nostrand.

xv McCall, M. (1998). *High Fliers.* Boston: Harvard Business School Press.

xvi Bradburn, N. M., & Berlew, D. G. (1961). Need for achievement and English economic growth. *Economic Development and Cultural Change,* 10, 8–20.

xvii DeCharms, R., & Moeller, G. H. (1962). Values expressed in American children's readers: 1800–1950. *Journal of Abnormal and Social Psychology,* 64, 136–142; McClelland, D. C. (1961). *The Achieving Society.* New York: Van Nostrand Reinhold.

xviii Barone, M. (2004). *Hard America, Soft America: Competition vs. Coddling and the Battle for the Nation's Future.* New York: Crown Forum.

xix Kerr, S. (1975). On the folly of rewarding A, while hoping for B. *Academy of Management Journal,* 18, 769–783.

xx McCall, 1998; Butler, T., & Waldroop, J. (1997). *Discovering Your Career in Business.* New York: Perseus Books Group.

xxi Sagie, A., Elizur, D., & Yamauchi, H. (1996). The structure and strength of achievement motivation: A cross-cultural comparison. *Journal of Organizational Behavior,* 17(5), 431–444.

xxii Hundal, P. S. (1971). A study of entrepreneurial motivation: Comparison of fast- and slow-progressing small scale industrial entrepreneurs in Punjab, India. *Journal of Applied Psychology,* 55(4), 317–323.

xxiii Hines, G. H. (1973). Achievement, motivation, occupations and labor turnover in New Zealand. *Journal of Applied Psychology,* 58(3), 313–317.

xxiv Aronoff, J., & Litwin, G. H. (1971). Achievement motivation training and executive advancement. *Journal of Applied Behavioral Science,* 7(2), 215–229; Miron, D., & McClelland, D. C. (1979). The impact of achievement motivation training on small businesses. *California Management Review,* 21(4), 13–28.

xxv Adler, N. J., & Boyacigiller, N. (1995). Global organizational behavior: Going beyond tradition, *Journal of International Management,* 1(3), 73–86; Hofstede, G., & Hofstede, G. R. (2005). *Cultures and Organizations: Software of the Mind.* New York: McGraw-Hill.

xxvi Jaeger, A. M., & Kanungo, R. N. (Eds.). (1990). *Management in Developing Countries.* London: Routledge.

xxvii Kovach, 1987; Kovach, K. A. (1995). Employee motivation: Addressing a crucial factor in your organization's performance. *Employment Relations Today,* Summer, 93–107.

xxviii Vroom, V. H. (1964). *Work and Motivation.* New York: Wiley.

xxix Butler & Waldroop, 1997.

xxx Jaeger & Kanungo, 1990.

xxxi Adams, J. S. (1963). Toward an understanding of inequity. *Journal of Abnormal and Social Psychology,* 67, 422–436.

xxxii Adler, N. J. (2002). *International Dimensions of Organizational Behavior.* Cincinnati, OH: South-Western College Publishing.

xxxiii Akerlof, G. A. (1984). Gift exchange and efficiency—wage theory: Four views. *American Economic Review,* 74, 79–83.

xxxiv Dawson, S. (2000, May 16). Unhappy employees pose greater risk than hackers. *Straits Times* (Singapore), p. 43.

xxxv Friedman, T. L. (2005). *The World Is Flat: A Brief History of the Twentyfirst Century.* New York: Farrar, Straus and Giroux.

xxxvi For discussions on China's industrial organization and management in early republican China, see Fenby, J.

(2004). *Chiang Kai-shek: China's Generalissimo and the Nation He Lost.* New York: Carroll & Graf; Zanasi, M. (2006). *Saving the Nation: Economic Modernity in Republican China.* Chicago: University of Chicago Press.

xxxvii Buck, P. S. (1931). *The Good Earth.* Shanghai: Far Eastern Books.

xxxviii Fok, L. Y., Hartman, S. J., Villere, M. F., & Freibert, R. C. III. (1996). A study of the impact of cross cultural differences on the perceptions of equity and organizational citizenship behavior. *International Journal of Management,* 13, 3–14.

xxxix Pfeffer, J., & Sutton, R. I. (2006). *Hard Facts, Dangerous Half-Truths and Total Nonsense: Profiting From Evidence-Based Management.* Boston: Harvard Business School Press.

xl Ahlstrom, D., Si, S. X., & Kennelly, J. (1999). Free agent performance in major league baseball: Do teams get what they expect. *Journal of Sport Management,* 13(3), 181–196.

xli Locke, E. A., & Latham, G. P. (1990). *A Theory of Goal Setting and Task Performance.* Upper Saddle River, NJ: Prentice Hall; Collins, J. (2005). *Good to Great and the Social Sector*s. Boulder, CO: Jim Collins.

xlii Collins, 2005.

xliii Butler & Waldroop, 1997, 1999.

xliv Kovach, 1987.

Chapter 8

i For a scholarly treatment of Mao's rule in China, particularly during the Cultural Revolution, see MacFarquhar, R., & Schoenhals, M. (2006). *Mao's Last Revolution.* Cambridge, MA: The Belknap Press of Harvard University Press.

ii Yukl, G. (2006). *Leadership in Organizations* (6th ed.) (p. 432). Upper Saddle River, NJ: Pearson Education, Inc.

iii Hofstede, G. (1993). Cultural constraints in management theories. *Academy of Management Executive,* 7(1), 81–94.

iv House, R. J. (1995). Leadership in the 21st century: A speculative enquiry. In A. Howard (Ed.), *The Changing Nature of Work.* San Francisco: Jossey Bass.

v Adler, N. J. (2002). *International Dimensions of Organizational Behavior* (4th ed.). Cincinnati, OH: South-Western.

vi Bass, B. M., & Stogdill, R. M. (1989). *The Handbook of Leadership* (3rd ed.). New York: Free Press.

vii Dorfman, P. W. (1996). International and cross-cultural leadership research. In B. J. Punnett, & O. Shenkar (Eds.), *Handbook for International Management Research* (pp. 267–349). Oxford: Blackwell.

viii MacFarquhar & Schoenhals, 2006.

ix Conger, J. A. (1989). *The Charismatic Leader: Behind the Mystique of Exceptional Leadership.* San Francisco: Jossey-Bass; Howell, J. M. (1988). Two faces of charisma: Socialized and personalized leadership in organizations. In J. A. Conger, & R. N. Kanungo (Eds.), *Charismatic Leadership: The Elusive Factor in Organizational Effectiveness* (pp. 213–236). San Francisco: Jossey-Bass; Khurana, R. (2002). The curse of the superstar CEO. *Harvard Business Review,* September; Collins, J. (2001). *Good to Great.* New York: HarperBusiness.

x Tichy, N. M. & Devanna, M. A. (1986). *The Transformational Leader.* New York: John Wiley & Sons; Bass, B. M. (1985). *Leadership and Performance beyond Expectations.* New York: Free Press.

xi Bass, 1985; Den Hartog, D. N., Van Muijen, J. J., & Koopman, P. L. (1997). Transactional versus transformational leadership: An analysis of the MLQ. *Journal of Occupational and Organizational Psychology,* 70(1), 19–34.

xii Tichy & Devanna, 1986.

xiii Bass, 1985.

xiv Fiol, C. M., Harris, D., & House, R. J. (1999). Charismatic leadership: Strategies for effecting social change. *Leadership Quarterly,* 10(3), 449–482.

xv Lowe, K. B., Kroek, K. G., & Sivasubramanian, N. (1996). Effectiveness correlates of transformational and transactional leadership: A meta-analytic review. *Leadership Quarterly,* 7, 385–425.

xvi Howell, J. M., & Higgins, C. A. (1990). Leadership behaviors, influence tactics, and career experiences of champions of technological innovation. *Leadership Quarterly,* 1, 249–264; Shamir, B., Zakay, E., Breinin, E., & Popper, M. (1998). Correlates of charismatic leader behavior in military units—subordinates attitudes, unit characteristics, and superiors' appraisals of leader performance. *Academy of Management Journal,* 41(4), 387–409; Roberts, N. C. (1985). Transforming leadership: A process of collective action. *Human Relations,* 38, 1023–1046; House, R. J., Spangler, W. D., & Woyke, J. (1991). Personality and charisma in the U.S. presidency: A psychological theory of leadership effectiveness. *Administrative Science Quarterly,* 36, 364–396.

xvii House, R. J., Hanges, P. J., Javidan, M., Dorfman, P. W., & Gupta, V. (Eds.) (2004). *Culture, Leadership, and Organizations: The GLOBE Study of 62 Societies.* Thousand Oaks, CA: Sage Publications.

xviii Dorfman, 1996, p. 271.

xix Graurnan, C. F., & Moscovici, S. (1986). *Changing Conceptions of Leadership* (pp. 241–242). New York: Springer-Verlag.

xx Conger, 1989; Howell, 1988.

xxi Bass, B. M. (1990). *Bass and Stogdill's Handbook of Leadership: Theory, Research and Managerial Applications* (3rd ed.) (p. 196). New York: Free Press.

xxii Bass, B. M. (1997). Does the transactional-transformational paradigm transcend organizational and national boundaries? *American Psychologist,* 52(2), 130–139; Singer, M. S., & Singer, A. E. (1990). Situational constraints on transformational versus transactional leadership behavior, subordinates' leadership preference, and satisfaction. *Journal of Social Psychology,* 130(3), 385–396.

xxiii Dorfman, P. W., Howell, J. P., Hibino, S., Lee, J. K., Tate, U., & Bautista, A. (1997). Leadership in western and Asian countries: Commonalities and differences in effective leadership processes across cultures. *Leadership Quarterly,* 8(3), 233–274.

xxiv Goleman, D., Boyatzis, R., & McKee, A. (2002). *Primal Leadership.* Boston, MA: Harvard Business School Press.

xxv Burns, 1978.

xxvi Bass, 1985.

xxvii Marcoulides, G. A., Yavas, B. F., Bilgin, Z., & Gibson, C. B. (1998). Reconciling culturalist and rationalist approaches: Leadership in the United States and Turkey. *Thunderbird International Business Review,* 40, 563–583.

xxviii Faiola, A. (2005, November 30). U.S. baseball manager's softer style throws Japan's social order a curve. *The Wall Street Journal (Asia),* p. 32.

xxix Thierry et al., 1999.

xxx Collins, J. (2001). *Good to Great.* New York: HarperBusiness.

xxxi Tung, R. L. (2001). *Learning from World Class Companies.* Florence, KY: Cengage Learning Business Press.

xxxii Jim Collins interview with Charlie Rose. The Charlie Rose Show. Aired June 2002.

xxxiii Frederick, J. (2002, December 9). Going nowhere fast. *Time,* 160(22), 36–41.

xxxiv Goleman et al., 2002.

xxxv Goleman et al., 2002.

xxxvi Fiedler, F. E. (1967). *A Theory of Leadership Effectiveness.* New York: McGraw-Hill.

xxxvii Hersey, P., & Blanchard, K. H. (1993). *Management of Organizational Behavior.* Upper Saddle River, NJ: Prentice Hall.

xxxviii Evans, M. G. (1974). Extensions of a path-goal theory of motivation. *Journal of Applied Psychology,* 59, 172–178; House, R. J. (1971). A path-goal theory of leadership effectiveness. *Administrative Science Quarterly,* 16, 321–338.

xxxix Kagan, R. (2008). *The Return of History and the End of Dreams.* New York: Knopf.

xl Kelner, S. P. Jr., Rivers, C. A., & O'Connell, K. H. (1996). *Managerial Style as a Behavioral Predictor of Organizational Climate.* Boston: McBer & Company; Goleman et al., 2002.

xli Ahlstrom, D., Young, M. N., Chan, E. S., & Bruton, G. D. (2004). Facing constraints to growth? Overseas Chinese entrepreneurs and traditional business practices in East Asia. *Asia Pacific Journal of Management*, 21, 263–285.

xlii Goleman et al., 2002.

xliii Goleman et al., 2002; Sasser, W. E., Schlesinger, L. A., & Heskett, J. L. (1997). *The Service Profit Chain*. New York: Free Press.

xliv Goleman et al., 2002.

xlv Maney, K. (2004, April 21). SAS workers won when greed lost. *USA TODAY*. http://www.usatoday.com/money/industries/technology/2004-04-21-sas-culture_x.htm.

xlvi Goleman et al., 2002.

xlvii Cringley, R. X. (1996). *Accidental Empires* (reprint ed.). New York: Collins Books; Scully, J., & Byrne, J. A. (1987). *Odyssey: Pepsi to Apple... A Journey of Adventure, Ideas, and the Future*. New York: HarperCollins.

xlviii Goleman et al., 2002.

xlix Konrad, E. (2000). Implicit leadership theories in Eastern and Western Europe. *Social Science Information*, 39(2), 335–347; Lord, G. R., & Maher, J. K. (1991). *Leadership and Information Processing: Linking Perceptions and Performance*. Boston, MA: Unwin Hyman.

l Lord & Maher, 1991.

li Garten, J. E. (2001). *The Mind of the CEO*. New York: Basic Books.

lii Bass, 1990; Hofstede, G. (1993). Cultural constraints in management theories. *Academy of Management Executive*, 7(1), 81–94.

liii Konrad, 2000; Shama, A. (1993). Management under fire: The transformation of managers in the Soviet Union and Eastern Europe. *Academy of Management Executive*, 7(1), 22–35.

liv Hofstede, G., & Hofstede, G. J. (2005). *Cultures and Organizations: Software of the Mind*. New York: McGraw-Hill.

lv Hofstede, 1993.

lvi Adler, 2002.

Chapter 9

i Von Neumann, J., & Morgenstern, O. (1944). *Theory of Games and Economic Behavior*. Princeton, NJ: Princeton University Press; Dixit, A. K., & Nalebuff, B. J. (1993). *Thinking Strategically: The Competitive Edge in Business, Politics, and Everyday Life*. New York: W.W. Norton & Company.

ii Ayres, I. (2007). *Super Crunchers: Why Thinking-By-Numbers Is the New Way to Be Smart*. Bantam, New York.

iii Cialdini, R. (2008). *Influence: Science and Practice* (8th ed.). New York: Allyn & Bacon; Belsky, G., & Gilovich, T. (2000). *Why Smart People Make Big Money Mistakes and How to Correct Them: Lessons from the New Science of Behavioral Economics*. New York: Simon & Schuster; Tversky, A., & Kahneman, D. (1979). Prospect theory: An analysis of decision under risk. *Econometrica*, 47(2), 263–292.

iv Staw, B. M., & Ross, J. (1987). Understanding escalation situations: Antecedents, prototypes, and solutions. In B. M. Staw, & L. L. Cummings (Eds.), *Research in Organizational Behavior*, Vol. 9 (pp. 39–78). Greenwich, CT: JAI Press.

v Kahneman and Tversky originally described this deviation from rational decision making, which they termed the framing effect. See Kahneman, D. & Tversky, A. (2000). *Choices, Values, and Frames*. Cambridge: Cambridge University Press; Belsky & Gilovich, 2000.

vi Simon, H. (1957). *Administrative Behavior: A Study of Decision-making Processes in Administrative Organization*. New York: Free Press.

vii Jung, C. G. (1971). *Psychological Types*. Princeton, NJ: Princeton University Press.

viii Cialdini, 2008.

ix BBC News, September 7, 2007. http://news.bbc.co.uk/1/hi/technology/6981704.stm (accessed October 23, 2007).

x Frey, D. (1982). Different levels of cognitive dissonance, information seeking, and information avoidance. *Journal of Personality and Social Psychology*, 43, 1175–83.

xi Sunstein, C. (2003). *Why Societies Need Dissent*. Boston: Harvard University Press.

xii Janis, I. (1977). *Victims of Groupthink*. Boston: Houghton Mifflin.

xiii Janis, 1977.

xiv Janis, 1977; Surowiecki, J. (2004). *The Wisdom of Crowds*. New York: Anchor Books.

xv Langewiesche, W. (2003). Columbia's last flight. *The Atlantic Monthly*, 292(4), 58–82.

xvi Lomborg, B. (2007). *Cool It: The Skeptical Environmentalist's Guide to Global Warming*. New York: Knopf; Lomborg, B. (Ed.). (2004). *Global Crises, Global Solutions*. Cambridge: Cambridge University Press.

xvii Belsky & Gilovich. 2000; Tversky & Kahneman, 2000; Thaler, R. H. (1994). *The Winner's Curse*. Princeton, NJ: Princeton University Press.

xviii Ahlstrom, D., Nair, A., Young, M. N., & Wang, L. C. (2006). China: Competitive myths and realities. *SAM Advanced Management Journal*, 71, 4–10.

xix Gilboy, G. (2004). The myth behind China's miracle. *Foreign Affairs*, 83(4), 33–48.

xx Levitt, S. D., & Dubner, S. J. (2006). *Freakonomics* [revised and expanded]: *A Rogue Economist Explores the Hidden Side of Everything* (pp. 135–136). New York: William Morrow.

Handbook of Chinese Psychology (pp. 309–321). Oxford: Oxford University Press; Xin & Pearce, 1996.

lvii Sahlins, M. (1972). *Stone Age Economics*. New York: Aldine de Gruyter; Befu, H. (1977). Social exchange. *Annual Review of Anthropology*, 6, 255–281.

lviii Kenrick, D. T., Neuberg, S. L., & Cialdini, R. B. (2007). *Social Psychology: Goals in Interaction* (4th ed.). New York: Allyn & Bacon.

lix Brehm, S. S., & Brehm, J. W. (1981). *Psychological Reactance: A Theory of Freedom and Control*. Oxford: Academic Press.

lx Shelley, M. K. (1994). Individual differences in lottery evaluation models. *Organizational Behavior and Human Decision Processes*, 60(2), 206–226.

lxi Gouldner, A. (1960). The norm of reciprocity: A preliminary statement. *American Sociological Review*, 25(2), 161–178; Fisher, J. D., Nadler, A., & DePaulo, B. M. (Eds.). (1983). *New Directions in Helping. Vol. I, Recipient Reactions to Aid*. New York: Academic Press.

lxii Levine, R. V. (2003). *The Power of Persuasion: How We're Bought and Sold*. New York: John Wiley & Sons.

lxiii Morris, M., Podolny, J., & Ariel, S. (2001). Culture, norms, and obligations: Cross-national differences in patterns of interpersonal norms and felt obligations toward coworkers. In W. Wosinka, R. B. Cialdini, D. W. Barrett, & J. Reykowski (Eds.). (2001). *The Practice of Social Influence in Multiple Cultures*. Mahwah, NJ: Lawrence Erlbaum Associates; Levine, 2003.

lxiv Lee, 2003.

lxv Fukuyama, F. (1995). *Trust*. New York: Free Press.

lxvi See Acuff, F. (2008). *How to Negotiate Anything with Anyone Anywhere Around the World* (3rd ed.). New York: AMACOM.

lxvii Lee, 2003.

lxviii Hammond, J. S., Keeney, R. L., & Raiffa, H. (1998). The hidden traps in decision making. *Harvard Business Review*, 76(5), 47–54.

lxix Teach, E. (2004, June 2). Avoiding decision traps. CFO.com. http://www.cfo.com/printable/article.cfm/3014027?f=options (accessed November 8, 2008).

lxx Donald, D. H. (1995). *Lincoln*. New York: Simon & Schuster.

lxxi Williams, 1993.

lxxii Michaelson, G. A. (2001). *Sun Tzu: The Art of War for Managers; 50 Strategic Rules*. New York: Adams Media.

lxxiii Lee, 2003; Zeng, M., & Williamson, P. J. (2007). *Dragons at Your Door: How Chinese Cost Innovation Is Disrupting Global Competition*. Boston: Harvard Business School Press.

lxxiv Fisher, R., & Ury, W. L. (1992). *Getting to Yes: Negotiating Agreement Without Giving In*. New York: Penguin.

lxxv Goldsten, Martin, & Cialdini, 2007.

lxxvi Fisher & Ury, 1992; Cialdini, 2009.

lxxvii Henrich, J., Boyd, R., Bowles, S., Camerer, C., Fehr, E., & Gintis, H. (2004). *Foundations of Human Sociality: Economic Experiments and Ethnographic Evidence from Fifteen Small-Scale Societies*. Oxford: Oxford University Press.

lxxviii Henrich et al., 2004.

lxxix Lee, 2003.

lxxx Cialdini, 2009; Fisher et al., 1983.

lxxxi Lerner, J. S., Small, D. A., & Lowenstein, G. (2004). Heart strings and purse strings: Carryover effects of emotions on economic decisions. *Psychological Science*, 15, 337–341.

lxxxii Lerner et al., 2004.

lxxxiii Acuff, 2008; Tinsley, C. R., & Weiss, S. E. (1999). Examining international business negotiations and directions for the future. *International Negotiation*, 4(1), 95–97; Weiss, S. E. (1996). International negotiations: Bricks, mortar, and prospects. In B. J. Punnett, & O. Shenkar (Eds.), *Handbook for International Management Research* (pp. 209–265). Cambridge, MA: Blackwell.

lxxxiv Weiss, S. E. (1994). Negotiating with 'Romans'— Part 1. *Sloan Management Review*, Winter, 51–62; Weiss, S. E. (1994). Negotiating with 'Romans'—Part 2. *Sloan Management Review*, Spring, 85–100.

lxxxv Tung, R. L. (1982). U.S.–China trade negotiations: Practices, procedures and outcomes. *Journal of International Business Studies*, 13, 25–38; Tinsley, C. H. (1998). Models of conflict resolution in Japanese, German and American cultures. *Journal of Applied Psychology*, 83, 316–323; Tung, R. L. (1984). How to negotiate with the Japanese. *California Management Review*, 26(4), 62–77.

lxxxvi Wright, P. (1981). Doing business in Islamic markets. *Harvard Business Review*, 59(1), 34–41.

lxxxvii Acuff, F. (2008). *How to Negotiate Anything with Anyone Anywhere Around the World*. (3rd ed.). New York: AMACOM; Tinsley, 1998.

lxxxviii Acuff, 2008.

lxxxix Glenn, E. S., Witmeyer, D., & Stevenson, K. A. (1977). Cultural styles of persuasion, *International Journal of Intercultural Relations*, 1(3), 52–66.

xc Hofstede, G, & Hofstede, G. J. (2005). *Cultures and Organizations: Software of the Mind*. New York: McGraw-Hill.

xci Hofstede & Hofstede, 2005.

xcii Lee, 2003.

xciii Chan, J. L. (2003). *China Streetsmart: What You MUST Know to Be Effective and Profitable in China*. Singapore: Pearson Education Asia Pte Ltd.; Lee, 2003.

xciv Graham, J. (1985). The influence of culture on the negotiation process. *Journal of International Business Studies*,

16(1), 81–96; Pye, L. W., & Pye, M. W. (2006). *Asian Power and Politics: The Cultural Dimension of Authority.* Cambridge, MA: Belknap Press.

xcv Kassin, S., & Kiechel, K. (1996). The social psychology of false confessions: Compliance, internalization, and confabulation. *Psychological Science*, 16(6), 481–486; Pye, L. (1982). *Chinese Commercial Negotiating Style.* Cambridge, MA: Oelgeschlager, Gunn and Hain.

xcvi Lee, 2003.

xcvii Pye, 1982.

Chapter 11

i Leeson, N., & Whitley, E. (1996). *Rogue Trader: How I Brought Down Baring's Bank and Shook the Financial World* (p. 141). New York: Little Brown and Company.

ii Hamel, G., & Prahalad, C. K. (1994). *Competing for the Future.* Boston, MA: Harvard Business School Publishing.

iii Christensen, C. M. (1997). *The Innovator's Dilemma.* Boston, MA: Harvard Business School Publishing.

iv Gilboy, G. J. (2004). The myth behind China's miracle. *Foreign Affairs*, 83(4), 33–48; Ahlstrom, D., Nair, A., Young, M. N., & Wang, L. C. (2006). China: Competitive myths and realities. *SAM Advanced Management Journal*, 71, 4–10.

v Christensen, 1997.

vi Christensen, C. M., & Raynor, M. E. 2003. *The Innovator's Solution.* Boston, MA: Harvard Business School Publishing.

vii Christensen, 1997.

viii For more detail on how to identify disruptive innovation and respond to it, see Christensen, C. M., Johnson, M. W., & Rigby, D. K. (2002). Foundations for growth: How to identify and build disruptive new businesses. *MIT Sloan Management Review,* Spring, 22–31; Zeng, M., & Williamson, P. J. (2007). *Dragons at Your Door: How Chinese Cost Innovation Is Disrupting Global Competition.* Boston, MA: Harvard Business School Publishing.

ix Hammer, M., & Champy, J. (1993). *Reengineering the Corporation: A Manifesto for Business Revolution.* New York: HarperBusiness.

x mySAP™ Supplier Relationship Management At Xerox Europe, www.sap.com/solutions/business-suite/srm/pdf/CCS_Xerox.pdf

xi Hamel & Prahalad, 1994.

xii Hamel, G. (2002). *Leading the Revolution: How to Thrive in Turbulent Times by Making Innovation a Way of Life* (revised ed.). Boston, MA: Harvard Business School Publishing.

xiii Fahey, L., & Randall, R. M. (1998). *Learning from the Future.* New York: John Wiley & Sons.

xiv Colchester, M. (2007, August 24). Can wine in a sippy box lure back French drinkers? *Wall Street Journal.*, http://online.wsj.com/article/SB118791573049507305.html?mod=dist_smartbrief

xv Mintzberg, H., Quinn, J. B., & Ghoshal, S. (1998). *The Strategy Process.* New York: Prentice Hall.

xvi Hamel & Prahalad, 1994.

xvii Gerstner, L. (2002). *Who Says Elephants Can't Dance? Inside IBM's Historic Turnaround.* New York: HarperCollins.

xviii Key to success: People, people, people. (1997, October 27). *Fortune*, p. 232; Collins, J. (2001). *Good to Great: Why Some Companies Make the Leap—and Others Don't.* New York: HarperBusiness; Pfeffer, J. (1998). *The Human Equation: Building Profits by Putting People First.* Boston, MA: Harvard Business School Publishing.

xix McCall, M. (1998). *High Fliers.* Boston, MA: Harvard Business School Publishing.

xx Pfeffer, 1998.

xxi Welsh, J., & Welsh, S. (2007). *Winning.* New York: HarperBusiness.

xxii Sullivan, J. J., Suzuki, T., & Kondo, Y. (1983). Managerial theories and the performance control process in Japanese and American work groups. *Academy of Management Proceedings*, 98–102.

xxiii Adler, N. J. (2004). *International Dimensions of Organizational Behavior.* Cincinnati, OH: South-Western/Thomson Learning; Sullivan et al., 1985.

xxiv Smith, T. C. (1959). *The Agrarian Origins of Modern Japan.* Stanford, CA: Stanford University Press.

xxv McShane, S. L., & Travaglione, T. (2006). *Organizational Behavior on the Pacific Rim* (Chapter 1). Singapore: McGraw-Hill.

xxvi Pfeffer, 1998.

xxvii Hamel, 2002.

xxviii O'Reilly, C. 2000; Heskett, J. L., Sasser, W. E., & Schlesinger, L. A. (1997). *The Service Profit Chain.* New York: Free Press.

xxix Collins, J. 2001; Pfeffer, 1998.

xxx Garvin, D. (1984). Japanese quality management. *Columbia Journal of World Business*, Fall, 3–12.

xxxi Garvin, 1984.

xxxii Sullivan, J. J. (1992). Japanese management philosophies: From the vacuous to the brilliant. *California Management Review*, Winter, 34(2), 66–87.

xxxiii Young, M. N., Ahlstrom, D., & Bruton, G. D. (2004). The globalization of corporate governance in East Asia: The transnational solution. *Management International Review*, 44(2), 31–50.

xxxiv Young, M. N., Buchholtz, A. K., & Ahlstrom, D. (2003). How can board members be empowered if they are spread too thin? *SAM Advanced Management Journal*, 68(4), 4–11.

xxxv Young et al., 2004.

xxxvi Young, M. N., Peng, M. W., Ahlstrom, D., Bruton, G. D., & Jiang, Y. (2008). Corporate governance in emerging economies: A review of the principal–principal perspective. *Journal of Management Studies*, 45(1), 196–220.

xxxvii Young, Peng, Ahlstrom, Bruton & Jiang, 2008.

xxxviii Young, Peng, Ahlstrom, Bruton & Jiang, 2008.

xxxix Hastings, D. (1999). Lincoln Electric's harsh lessons from international expansion. *Harvard Business Review*. May/June, 162–178.

xl Collins, 2001.

xli See Collins, 2001, especially Chapter 4, "Confront the Brutal Facts (Yet Never Lose Faith)".

xlii For a cautionary tale about investing in China see Clissold, T. (2006). *Mr. China: A Memoir*. New York: Collins. Also see McGregor, J. (2005). *One Billion Customers: Lessons from the Front Lines of Doing Business in China*. New York: Simon & Schuster.

xliii Ahlstrom, D., Young, M. N., & Nair, A. (2002). Deceptive managerial practices in China: Strategies for foreign firms. *Business Horizons*, 45(6), 49–59; Ahlstrom, D., Young, M. N., & Nair, A. (2003). Navigating China's feudal governance structures: Guidelines for foreign enterprises. *SAM Advanced Management Journal*, 68(1), 4–14.

xliv Kaplan, R. S., & Norton, D. P. (1996). *The Balanced Scorecard: Translating Strategy into Action*. Boston, MA: Harvard Business School Publishing.

xlv Kaplan, R. S., & Norton, D. P. (2008). *The Execution Premium*. Boston, MA: Harvard Business School Publishing.

xlvi For an excellent discussion on firm mission and focus, see Collins, J., & Porras, J. I. (1994). *Built to Last: Successful Habits of Visionary Companies*. New York: HarperBusiness.

xlvii Hamel & Prahalad, 1994.

xlviii Ahlstrom, D., Bruton, G. D., & Yeh, K. S. (2008). Private firms in China: Building legitimacy in an emerging economy. *Journal of World Business*, 43, 385–399.

xlix For more information on additional firm performance measures, see Kaplan & Norton, 1996, 2008, and Niven, P. S. (2006). *Balanced Scorecard Step-by-Step: Maximizing Performance and Maintaining Results* (2nd ed.). Hoboken, NJ: John Wiley & Sons.

l Kindleberger, C., & Aliber, R. (2005). *Manias, Panics, and Crashes: A History of Financial Crises* (5th ed.). Hoboken, NJ: John Wiley & Sons; Krugman, P. R. (1994). The myth of Asia's miracle. *Foreign Affairs*, 73 (6), 62–78; Porter, M. E., Takeuchi, H., & Sakakibara, M. (2000). *Can Japan Compete?* New York: Basic Books; Radelet, S., & Sachs, J. (1998). The East-Asian financial crisis: Diagnosis, remedies, prospects. *Brookings Papers on Economic Activity*, 1, 1–90.

Chapter 12

i Clissold, T. (2004). *Mr. China*. London: Robinson; Chan, J. L. (2003). *China Streetsmart: What You MUST Know to Be Effective and Profitable in China*. Singapore: Pearson Education Asia.

ii Hastings, D. F. (1999). Lincoln Electric's harsh lessons from international expansion. *Harvard Business Review*, 77(3), 162–178.

iii Harzing, A. K. (1995). The persistent myth of high expatriate failure rate. *The International Journal of Human Resources Management*, 6(2), 457–474.

iv Hastings, D. F. (1999). Lincoln Electric's harsh lessons from international expansion. *Harvard Business Review*, 77(3), 162–178.

vi Tung, R. L. (1982). Selection and training procedures of U.S., European, and Japanese multinationals. *California Management Review*, 25(1), 57–71.

vii Robbins, S. P. (2003). *The Truth About Managing People ... And Nothing But the Truth*. London: FT Press.

viii Carlton, J. (1998). *Apple: The Inside Story of Intrigue, Egomania, and Business Blunders*. New York: Times Business/Random House.

ix Cohen, A., Watkinson J., & Boone, J. (2005). Southwest Airlines CEO grounded in real world by professor. Babson Insight, special to SearchCIO.com. Accessed March 25, 2006. http://searchcio.techtarget.com/originalContent/0,289142,sid19_gci1071837,00.html

x Mendenhall, M., & Oddou, G. (1985). The dimensions of expatriate acculturation: A review. *Academy of Management Review*, 10(1), 39–47.

xi Early, C., & Mosakowski, E. (2005). Cultural intelligence. *Harvard Business Review*, 82(10), 139–146.

xii Bjorkman, I., & Lu, Y. (1999). A corporate perspective on the management of human resources in China. *Journal of World Business*, 34(1), 16–25.

xiii Hoecklin, L. (1994). *Managing Cultural Differences* (p. 124). Wokingham, UK: Addison-Wesley.

xiv Ryan, A. M., McFarland, L., Baron, H., & Page, R. (1999). An international look at selection practices: Nation and culture as explanations for variability in practice. *Personnel Psychology*, 52(2), 359–391.

xv Levy-Leboyer, C. (1994). Selection and assessment in Europe. In H. C. Triandis, M. D. Dunnette, & L. M. Hough (Eds.), *Handbook of Industrial and Organizational Psychology*, Vol. 4 (pp. 173–190). Palo Alto, CA: Consulting Psychologists Press.

xvi Selmer, J. (1997). Effects of coping strategies on sociocultural and psychological adjustment of Western expatriate managers in the PRC. *Journal of World Business*, 34(1), 41–51.

xvii Hays, C. (2004). *Pop: Truth and Power at the Coca-Cola Company*. London: Hutchison.

xviii Hofstede, G., & Hofstede, G. J. (2005). *Cultures and Organizations: Software of the Mind*. New York: McGraw-Hill.

xix Hastings, 1999.

xx Hastings, 1999.

xxi For more problems expatriates face, see Thornton, R. L., & Thornton, M. K. (1995). Personnel problems in "carry the flag" missions in foreign assignments. *Business Horizons*, January/February, 59–65.

xxii Christensen, C. M., Roth, E. A., & Anthony, S. D. (2004). *Seeing What's Next: Using Theories of Innovation to Predict Industry Change*. Boston, MA: Harvard Business School Press.

xxiii Ahlstrom, D., Bruton, G. D., & Yeh, K. (2008). Private firms in China: Building legitimacy in an emerging economy. *Journal of World Business*, 43(4), 385–399.

xxiv Miller E. L., & Cheng J. L. (1978). A closer look at the decision to accept an overseas position. *Management International Review*, 18(1), 25–27.

xxv Prahalad, C. K., & Lieberthal K. (1998). The end of corporate imperialism. *Harvard Business Review*, 76(4), 68–79.

xxvi Butler, C. (1999). A world of trouble. *Sales and Marketing Management*, 151(9), 44–50.

xxvii Black J. S., & Gregersen, H. B. (1999). The right way to manage expatriates. *Harvard Business Review*, 77(2), 52–63.

xxviii Butler, 1999.

xxix Butler, 1999.

xxx Miller, E. L. (1972). The selection decision for an international assignment: A study of decision makers' behavior. *Journal of International Business Studies*, 3(2), 49–65.

xxxi Tung, R. L. (1981). Selection and training of personnel. *Columbia Journal of World Business*, 16(1), 68–78; McCall, M. W. (1998). *High Fliers: Developing the Next Generation of Leaders*. Boston, MA: Harvard Business School Press.

xxxii Tung, 1982.

xxxiii Black & Gregersen, 1999.

xxxiv McCall, 1998.

xxxv Troy, M. (2004). Overseas reputation diligently guarded to avoid repeating domestic disputes. *DSN Retailing Today*, 43(23), 33.

xxxvi Farrel, D., & Grant, A. J. (2005). China's looming talent shortage. *McKinsey Quarterly*, 4, 70–79.

xxxvii Farrel & Grant, 2005.

xxxviii Prasad, S. B., & Shetty, Y. K. (1976). *Introduction to Multinational Management*. New York: Prentice Hall.

xxxix Chan, J. L. (2003). *China Streetsmart: What You MUST Know to Be Effective and Profitable in China*. Singapore: Pearson Education Asia.

xl Kranhold, K. (2007, September 14). GE's environmental push hits business realities. *Wall Street Journal*, CCL(88), pp. A1, A10.

xli Tung, 1982.

xlii Tung, R. (1998). American expatriates abroad: From neophytes to cosmopolitans. *Journal of World Business*, 33(2), 125–144.

xliii Murray, W. (1986). Clausewitz: Some thoughts on what the Germans got right. *Journal of Strategic Studies*, 9(2–3), 267–286.

xliv Sullivan, G., & Harper, M. V. (1997). *Hope is Not a Method*. New York: Broadway.

xlv Castellano, J. F., Rosenzweig, K., & Roehm, H. A. (2004). How corporate culture impacts unethical distortion of financial numbers. *Management Accounting Quarterly*, 5(4), 37–41.

xlvi Welsh, J., & Welsh, S. (2005). *Winning*. New York: HarperBusiness.

xlvii Welsh, J., & Welsh, S. (2006). *Winning: The Answers*. New Delhi: HarperCollins.

xlviii Butler, T., & Waldroop, J. (1996). *Discovering Your Career in Business*. New York: Basic Books; Welsh & Welsh, 2006.

xlix Tung, 1982.

l Frazee, V. (1998, September 9). Is the balance sheet right for your expatriates? *Workforce*, 77(9), 19.

li Pfeffer, J. & Sutton, R. I. (2006). *Hard Facts, Dangerous Half-truths, and Total Nonsense: Profiting from Evidence-based Management*. Boston, MA: Harvard Business School Press.

lii E.g. see Hastings, 1999.

liii Bethune, G., & Huler, S. (1999). *From Worst to First: Behind the Scenes of Continental's Remarkable Comeback*. New York: John Wiley & Sons.

liv Dowling, P., Schuler, R. S., & Welch, D. E. (1993). *International Dimensions of Human Resource Management* (p. 117). Cincinnati, OH: Thomson South-Western.

lv Reynolds, C. (1997). Expatriate compensation in historical perspective. *Journal of World Business*, 32(2), 118–132.

lvi Fryer, B., Milkovich, G. T., Thinnes, J. A., Yaffe, J., & Kokott, D. (2003). In a world of pay. *Harvard Business Review*, (81)11, 31–40.

lvii In search of stealth: Expatriate workers (The rise of the stealth expat). (2005, April 23). *The Economist*, pp. 62–64.

lviii Tung, 1982.

lix Baker, J. C., Ryans, K., & Howard, G. (1988). *International Business Classics* (pp. 283–295). Lexington, MA: D.C. Heath and Co.

lx Reynolds, 1997; Tung, R. L. (1988). *The New Expatriates: Managing Human Resources Abroad*. Cambridge, MA: Ballinger; Tung, 1998.

lxi Heenan, D. A. (1970). The corporate expatriate: Assignment to ambiguity. *Columbia Journal of World Business*, 5(3), 49–54.

lxii Mann, J. (1997). *Beijing Jeep: A Case Study of Western Business in China*. Boulder, CO: Westview Press.

lxiii Ostler, N. (2005). *Empires of the Word: A Language History of the World*. New York: HarperCollins.

lxiv Rahim, A. (1983, April). A model for developing key expatriate executives. *Personnel Journal*, pp. 312–317.

lxv Skapinker, M. (2007, November 9). Whose language? *Financial Times*, p. 9.

lxvi Tung, 1982.

lxvii See the excellent article by former National University of Singapore Business School Dean Christopher Early and colleague in *Harvard Business Review* on cultural intelligence (Early & Mosakowski, 2005).

lxviii Lewis, R. D. (2005). *When Cultures Collide: Leading Across Cultures*. London: Nicholas Brealey Publishing.

lxix Tannen, D. (1996). *Talking from 9 to 5: Women and Men at Work*. Lancaster Place, U.K.: Virago Press.

lxx Gilboy, G. (2004). The myth behind China's miracle. *Foreign Affairs*, 83(4), 33–48.

lxxi Bruton, G. D., Ahlstrom, D., & Chan, E. S. (2001). Foreign firms in China: Facing human resources challenges in a transitional economy. *SAM Advanced Management Journal*, 65(4), Autumn, 4–11.

lxxii Rahim, 1983.

lxxiii Butler, 1999.

lxxiv Adler, N. J. (2004). *International Dimensions of Organizational Behavior* (5th ed.). Cincinnati, OH: South-Western/Thomson Learning; Tung, 1982, 1988.

lxxv Israeli, D. N., Banai, M., & Zeira, Y. (1980). Women executives in MNC subsidiaries. *California Management Review*, 23(1), 53–63.

lxxvi McCall, M. W. (1998). *High Fliers: Developing the Next Generation of Leaders*. Boston, MA: Harvard Business School Press.

lxxvii Adler, 2004.

lxxviii Hofstede & Hofstede, 2005.

lxxix Hofstede & Hofstede, 2005.

lxxx Fukuyama, F. (1995). *Trust: The Social Virtues and the Creation of Prosperity*. New York: Free Press.

lxxxi Clague, L., & Krupp, N. B. (1978). International personnel: The repatriation problem, *The Personnel Administrator*, April, p. 32.

lxxxii Butler, 1999.

Chapter 13

i Chandler, A. D. (1969). *Strategy and Structure: Chapters in the History of American Industrial Enterprise* (paperback ed.). Cambridge, MA: MIT Press; Chandler, A. D. (1990). *Scale and Scope*. Cambridge, MA: Belknap Press.

ii Scott, W. R. (2003). *Organizations: Rational, Natural, and Open Systems*. Upper Saddle River, NJ: Prentice Hall; Donaldson, L. (1995). *American Anti-Management Theories of Organization: A Critique of Paradigm Proliferation*. Cambridge: Cambridge University Press.

iii Parkinson, C. N. (1993). *Parkinson's Law*. Cutchogue, NY: Buccaneer Books.

iv Parkinson, 1993.

v Kemenade, W. V. (1998). *China, Hong Kong, Taiwan, Inc.: The Dynamics of a New Empire*. New York: Vintage Books.

vi Backman, M. (1995). *Overseas Chinese Business Networks in Asia*. Canberra: Australian Government.

vii Ahlstrom, D., Young, M. N., Chan, E. S., & Bruton, G. D. (2004). Facing constraints to growth? Overseas Chinese entrepreneurs and traditional business practices in East Asia. *Asia Pacific Journal of Management*, 21, 263–285.

viii Ahlstrom et al., 2004.

ix Weidenbaum, M., & Hughes, M. (1996). *Bamboo Network: How Expatriate Chinese Entrepreneurs Are Creating a New Economic Superpower in Asia*. New York: Free Press.

x Chandler, A. D. (1990). The enduring logic of industrial success. *Harvard Business Review*, 68(2), 130–140.

xi Trout, Jack. (1995). *The New Positioning*. New York: McGraw-Hill.

xii Trout, 1995, pp. 52–53.

xiii Trout, 1995, pp. 52–53.

xiv Rugman, A. M., & Girod, S. (2003). Retail multinationals & globalization: The evidence is regional. *European Management Journal*, 21(1), 24–45.

xv Prewitt, E. (2003, September 1). GM's matrix reloaded. *CIO Magazine*. http://www.cio.com/archive/090103/hs_reload.html

xvi Donaldson, 1995.

xvii Donaldson, 1995.

xviii Senge, P. M. (1990). *The Fifth Discipline: The Art and Practice of the Learning Organization* (p. 3). New York: Doubleday/Currency.

xix Christensen, C. M., & Raynor, M. E. (2003). *The Innovator's Solution: Creating and Sustaining Successful Growth*. Boston: Harvard Business School Press.

xx Hammer, M. (1990, July/August) Reengineering work: Don't automate, obliterate. *Harvard Business Review*, pp. 70–91.

xxi Heathfield, S. M. (2005). Consequences and employee involvement during change. http://humanresources.about.com/od/changemanagement/a/change_wisdom.htm.

xxii Friedman, T. L. (2000). *The Lexus and the Olive Tree: Understanding Globalization.* New York: Anchor Books.

xxiii Enterprise modeling and simulation in reengineering. (1994, December). *Hewlett Packard Journal.* http://www.hpl.hp.com/hpjournal/94dec/dec94a10b.pdf

xxiv Heathfield, S. M. (2005). Executive support and leadership for change management. http://humanresources.about.com/od/changemanagement/a/change_lessons_2.htm

xxv Stephenson, K. (2006). *The Quantum Theory of Trust: The Secret of Mapping and Managing Human Relationships.* Upper Saddle River, NJ: Prentice Hall.

xxvi Ahlstrom, Young, Chan, & Bruton, 2004.

xxvii Prahalad, C. K., & Hamel, G. (1990). The core competence of the corporation. *Harvard Business Review,* 65(3), 79–90; Lieberthal, K., & Lieberthal, G. (2003). The great transition. *Harvard Business Review,* 81(10), 70–79.

xxviii Senge, 1990; Hamel, G. (2002). *Leading the Revolution: How to Thrive in Turbulent Times by Making Innovation a Way of Life* (revised ed.). Boston: Harvard Business School Press.

Chapter 14

i Damels, J. D., Ogram, E. W., & Radebaugh, L. H. (1982). *International Business Environments and Operations* (3rd ed.). Reading, MA: Addison-Wesley.

ii The CIA World Factbook. List of Countries by Exports. http://en.wikipedia.org/wiki/List_of_countries_by_exports, accessed November 11, 2008; WTO reports. 2007. WTO: 2007 PRESS RELEASES. http://www.wto.org/english/news_e/pres07_e/pr472_e.htm (accessed January 17, 2008).

iii Shapiro, A. C. (1992). *Multicultural Financial Management* (4th ed.) (p. 5). Needham Heights, MA: Allyn & Bacon.

iv The challengers. (2007). *The Economist,* 386(8562), 61–63.

v Hambrick, D. C., Korn, L. B., Frederickson, J. W., & Feny, R.M. (1989). *21st Century Report: Reinventing the CEO* (pp. 1–94). New York: Korn-Feny and Columbia University's Graduate School of Business.

vi Hambrick, Korn, Frederickson, & Feny, 1989.

vii Baumol, W. J. (2004). *The Free-Market Innovation Machine: Analyzing the Growth Miracle of Capitalism.* Princeton, NJ: Princeton University Press; Christensen, C. M., Roth, E. A., & Anthony, S. D. (2004). *Seeing What's Next: Using Theories of Innovation to Predict Industry Change.* Boston: Harvard Business School Press.

viii Bhide, A. V. (2000). *The Origin and Evolution of New Businesses.* New York: Oxford University Press; Baumol, 2004.

ix Acs, Z. (2006). How is entrepreneurship good for economic growth? *Innovations,* Winter, 97–107.

x Timmons, J. A., & Spinelli, S. (2008). *New Venture Creation: Entrepreneurship for the 21st Century* (8th ed.). Boston: McGraw-Hill/Irwin.

xi Acs, 2006.

xii Barone, M. (2005). *Hard America, Soft America: Competition vs. Coddling and the Battle for the Nation's Future.* New York: Three Rivers Press.

xiii James, H. (2006). *Family Capitalism: Wendels, Haniels, Falcks, and the Continental European Model.* Cambridge, MA: Belknap Press.

xiv Barone, 2005.

xv Yergin, D., & Stanislaw, J. (2002). *The Commanding Heights: The Battle for the World Economy* (revised updated 2nd ed.). New York: Free Press.

xvi Hastings, D. F. (1999). Lincoln Electric's harsh lessons from international expansion. *Harvard Business Review,* May/June, 3–11.

xvii Christensen, C. M., Craig, T., & Hart, S. (2001). The great disruption. *Foreign Affairs,* March/April, 80–95; Timmons & Spinelli, 2008.

xviii Schumpeter, J. (2008). *Capitalism, Socialism and Democracy.* New York: Harper Perennial Modern Classics.

xix Baumol, W. J., Litan, R. E., & Schramm, C. J. (2007). *Good Capitalism, Bad Capitalism, and the Economics of Growth and Prosperity.* New Haven, CT: Yale University Press; Timmons & Spinelli, 2008.

xx Baumol, 2004.

xxi Timmons & Spinelli, 2008.

xxii Christensen, Craig, & Hart, 2001; Christensen & Raynor, 2003.

xxiii Porter, M. E. (1980). *Competitive Strategy: Techniques for Analyzing Industries and Competitors.* New York: Free Press; Johnson, C. A. (1983). *MITI and the Japanese Miracle: The Growth of Industrial Policy 1925–1975.* Stanford, CA: Stanford University Press.

xxiv Porter, M. E. (1990). *The Competitive Advantage of Nations.* New York: Free Press.

xxv Acs, 2006.

xxvi Christensen, C., & Hart, 2001; Studwell, J. (2007). *Asian Godfathers: Money and Power in Hong Kong and Southeast Asia.* New York: Atlantic Monthly Press.

xxvii Christensen et al., 2001; Porter et al., 2000.

xxviii Fallows, J. (1995). *Looking at the Sun: The Rise of the New East Asian Economic and Political System.* New York: Vintage; Johnson, 1983.

xxix Vogel, E. F. (1979). *Japan as Number One: Lessons for America.* Cambridge: Harvard University Press.

xxx Johnson, 1983; Vogel, 1979.

xxxi Christensen, Craig, & Hart, 2001.

xxxii Christensen, Craig, & Hart, 2001.

xxxiii Christensen, Craig, & Hart, 2001; Porter, M. E., Takeuchi, H., & Sakakibara, M. (2000). *Can Japan Compete?* Basingstoke, UK: Macmillan.

xxxiv Johnson, C. A. (1983). *MITI and the Japanese Miracle: The Growth of Industrial Policy 1925–1975.* Stanford, CA: Stanford University Press; Vogel, E. F. (1979). *Japan as Number One: Lessons for America.* Cambridge, MA: Harvard University Press.

xxxv Porter, M. E., Takeuchi, H., & Sakakibara, M. (2000). *Can Japan Compete?* Basingstoke, UK: Macmillan.

xxxvi Christensen, C. M., Craig, T., & Hart, S. (1002). The great disruption. *Foreign Affairs,* March/April, 80–95; Porter, M. E. (1990). *The Competitive Advantage of Nations.* New York: The Free Press.

xxxvii Studwell, 2007.

xxxviii Baumol et al., 2007.

xxxix Acs, 2006.

xl McDougall, P. P., & Oviatt, B. M. (1996). New venture internationalization, strategic change, and performance: A follow-up study. *Journal of Business Venturing,* 11(1), 23–40.

xli McDougall & Oviatt, 1996.

xlii McDougall & Oviatt, 1996.

xliii Khanna, T. (2008). *Billions of Entrepreneurs: How China and India Are Reshaping Their Futures—and Yours.* Boston: Harvard Business School Press.

xliv Khanna, 2008; Zeng, M., & Williamson, P. J. (2007). *Dragons at Your Door: How Chinese Cost Innovation Is Disrupting Global Competition.* Boston: Harvard Business School Press.

xlv Ahlstrom, D., Young, M. N., Nair, A., & Wang, L. C. (2006). China: Competitive myths and realities. *SAM Advanced Management Journal,* 71(4), 4–10; Gilboy, G. J. (2004). The myth behind China's miracle. *Foreign Affairs,* 83(4), 33–48.

xlvi Gilboy, 2004.

xlvii Porter, 1990.

xlviii Nelson, R. R. (1993). *National Innovation Systems: A Comparative Analysis.* New York: Oxford University Press; Nelson, R. R., & Wright, G. (1992). The rise and fall of American technological leadership: The postwar era in historical perspective. *Journal of Economic Literature,* 30 (December), 1931–1964.

xlix Porter, 1990.

l Bhidé, A. (2006). *Venturesome consumption, innovation and globalization.* Paper presented at the Joint Conference of CESifo and the Center on Capitalism and Society—Perspectives on the Performance of the Continent's Economies. Venice, July 21–22; Gilboy, 2004.

li Gilboy, 2004.

lii Gilboy, 2004.

liii Bhidé, 2006.

liv Von Hippel, E. (2006). *Democratizing Innovation.* Cambridge, MA: The MIT Press.

lv Elgin, B. (2007, October 29). Little green lies. *BusinessWeek,* 45–52.

lvi Easterly, W. (2006). *The White Man's Burden: Why the West's Efforts to Aid the Rest Have Done So Much Ill and So Little Good.* New York: Penguin Press HC.

lvii Ferguson, N. (2008). *The Ascent of Money.* New York: Penguin Press.

lviii Kindleberger, C. P., & Aliber, R. (2005). *Manias, Panics, and Crashes: A History of Financial Crises* (5th ed.). New York: John Wiley & Sons.

lix Ferguson, 2008.

lx Ferguson, 2008; Kindleberger & Aliber, 2005.

lxi Kindleberger & Aliber, 2005.

lxii Bhagwati, J. (2004). *In Defense of Globalization.* Oxford: Oxford University Press.

lxiii U.S. Department of Labor. (1998). *Hourly Compensation Costs in U.S. Dollars. Table 1.* (September). Washington, DC: U.S. Department of Labor, Bureau of Labor Statistics.

lxiv Friedman, T. L. (2007). *The World Is Flat 3.0: A Brief History of the Twenty-first Century.* New York: Picador.

lxv Wolf, M. (2004). *Why Globalization Works.* New Haven: Yale University Press.

lxvi Bhagwati, 2004; Wolf, 2004.

lxvii Bhidé, 2007.

lxviii Studwell, J. (2007). *Asian Godfathers.* London: Profile Books.

lxix *Economic Outlook* 1998. International Monetary Fund (October). Washington, DC.

Name Index

Subject Index